The Luftwaffe War Diaries

THE
LUFTWAFFE
WAR
DIARIES
THE GERMAN AIR FORCE
IN WORLD WAR II

CAJUS BEKKER

Translated and edited by Frank Ziegler

DA CAPO PRESS • NEW YORK

Library of Congress Cataloging in Publication Data

Bekker, Cajus, 1924—
    [Angriffshöhe 4000. English]
    The Luftwaffe war diaries: the German air force in World War II / Cajus
Bekker; translated and edited by Frank Ziegler.—1st Da Capo Press ed.
        p.   cm.
    Originally published: Garden City, N.Y.: Doubleday, 1968.
    Includes bibliographical references.
    ISBN 0-306-80604-5
    1. Germany. Luftwaffe—History—World War, 1939–1945. 2. World War,
1939–1945—Aerial operations, German. I. Title.
    D787.B3513   1994   94-11183
    940.54′4943—dc20   CIP

*First published in the German language in 1964
under the title* ANGRIFFSHÖHE 4000 by
Gerhard Stalling Verlag, Hamburg 11, Michaelisstrasse 4

First Da Capo Press edition 1994

This Da Capo Press paperback edition of *The Luftwaffe War Diaries* is an
unabridged republication of the edition originally published in New York
in 1968. It is reprinted by arrangement with Doubleday & Company.

Published by Da Capo Press, Inc.
A Subsidiary of Plenum Publishing Corporation
233 Spring Street, New York, N.Y. 10013

FOREWORD

By former Luftwaffe General Paul Deichmann

I am writing this introduction at the author's request, and do so gladly. From the German point of view his book represents a memorial to the fallen, a tribute to the survivors, and a warning to generations to come. Apart from that, it is the first account of the air war of 1939–1945 to come from a German source.

There are still very few people in Germany who know what really happened in that war. Though its operations were almost world-wide, wartime security, plus both German and Allied propaganda, have shrouded them in a veil of secrecy which even today has not been penetrated. Believe it or not, there are many German airmen who still do not know the context of the operations in which they were themselves engaged.

I myself have been the recipient of many complaints. As a general staff officer and field commander since before the war, and for ten years afterwards occupied with Luftwaffe history, I have been asked repeatedly: "Why is there no comprehensive history of the air war from the German point of view?"

This hiatus has become all the more glaring since the formation of a new German Luftwaffe as a constituent of N.A.T.O. Our sons and grandsons who fill its ranks keep asking: "What really happened in that war of yours?" Unsatisfied with accounts of individual experience, they demand to know the why and the wherefore. And the answers they get are mostly unsatisfactory.

In all countries it used to be, and in most still is, the practice after the conclusion of a war—even when the wartime government is no longer in power—to issue for the benefit of the public and the armed forces an official or officially sponsored account of what happened. After all, anyone who has taken part in such a serious undertaking as war has a right to be told about it, and then to make his own judgments.

In Germany alone no official account of the air war has appeared, nor is likely to do so for some time. Because of this I congratulate the present author on his courage in starting a very difficult task. Obviously, written for the general public as it is, his book makes no pretension to being a substitute for a comprehensive military history. Within the compass of some five hundred pages that would not be possible. I can however say, from my own war experience, that by his evaluation of a mass of German documentary material,

5

his study of the official war histories of other countries, and his interrogation of numerous wartime Luftwaffe leaders, he has succeeded in presenting a story which is accurate in both detail and context. As such, his book goes a long way to filling the existing vacuum, and no doubt will find its place in the archives of military literature.

I might add that the previous serialisation of considerable portions of the work in a widely read German illustrated periodical has had a beneficial effect on the publication in book form. The interest this serialisation aroused in ex-Luftwaffe circles enabled the author both to elucidate and amplify many details.

Having co-operated for many years with the war records departments of former enemy powers, I also know very well that a work such as this one has been long awaited in other countries. Consequently the German publishers have had little difficulty in arranging for it to appear abroad in several languages. I only hope that its publication there will have the effect of mitigating some of the existing prejudices against the German wartime Luftwaffe.

Soon after the war I was commissioned to investigate the history of the German Luftwaffe on behalf of a leading western power. One day, while talking to the high-ranking officer in charge of this investigation, I asked him why a powerful country like his, which after all had won the air war against Germany, showed so much interest in our Luftwaffe. To my surprise he answered, in effect, that they wanted to find out how, with its "handful of weapons and aircraft", it was able to hold out for so long against the air forces of the world. Surely this tribute to German courage speaks for itself?

In this book's descriptions of battle, danger and death there is, however, no exaltation of war. How could there be, when the airmen of our country paid the biggest price of all? Men who know what war is like, who have stared death in the face more than once, are war's most bitter and resolute opponents, and the champions of peace. Yet they also know that in the age of the atom bomb, as throughout history, the freedom and even the life of their country depend on the readiness of its citizens to give their lives in its defence. May they in consequence feel it their bounden duty to prevent the spectre of war ever rising over their country again.

[Amongst the appointments held by General Deichmann before and during the war were: Director of Operations on the Luftwaffe General Staff; Chief of General Staff of II Air Corps, *Luftflotte* 2, and to Commander-in-Chief South (Kesselring); Commander of 1 Air Division; G.O.C. I Air Corps and "4th Luftwaffe Command" (previously *Luftflotte* 4). After the war he directed for many years a research group concerned with air war history, later known as *Studiengruppe Luftwaffe*. In acknowledgement of his work in this field he became, on December 31, 1963, the first foreigner to receive from the U.S. Air Force its Air University Award, previously only conferred on six high-ranking American officers.]

PREFACE

To present the history of the wartime German Air Force in a single volume is no easy task. That may be one reason why up to the present no official work on the subject has yet been published. Because of its absence it seemed to me important to write something that would expose certain false conceptions that arose during the war and have continued since.

What I had in mind was to produce an accurate and objective account of the main events that took place in the major theatres of the war: in the West, in Russia, in the Mediterranean, and in Germany itself. Owing to the multiplicity of events, however, such an account cannot hope to be anything like complete. Thus if I have described certain operations in detail, it is only because they were typical of a host of others. Important developments in the air aspect of the war have been condensed in my *Summary and Conclusions* at the end of each chapter.

Needless to say, I could not have written this book had not a great many people volunteered their help. Though my grateful thanks are due to them all, to name them individually would be invidious owing to the large number who must remain anonymous. I must, however, mention the various institutions, groups and associations which put their comprehensive documentary material at my disposal, and whose members confided their personal experiences. Of these I may perhaps single out the *Studiengruppe Luftwaffe* in Hamburg-Blankenese, the *Arbeitskreis für Wehrforschung* (Defence Research Association) in Stuttgart, the *Luftwaffenring* in Bremen and its affiliations, and above all the German Paratroop, Bomber and Fighter associations.

I further wish to thank my German publishers, as well as my publishers and translators in France, Great Britain, Italy, Japan, Spain and the United States, who have enabled my book to appear in their respective countries, and not least the production and editorial departments of the German magazine *Kristall*, whose initial part-serialisation first attracted the interest of readers both in Germany and the outside world. This, by putting me in touch with hundreds of participants in the events described, enabled me to supplement the material already to hand with their personal impressions, and to make use of letters from thousands more.

It is inevitable that a book like this, which lies mid-way between history and eye-witness reporting, will be viewed by some as over-critical, by others as not critical enough. Further, many German readers will probably object to the fact that the space available has allowed no mention of many events in which they may have taken part. I am fully aware of the limitations of the contents, and only claim to have begun a task that calls to be completed.

Perhaps I should also explain why the history of the Luftwaffe in the last year of the war has only been summarised. The reason is that in its fight against hopeless odds, both on the eastern and western fronts, the Luftwaffe had little influence, as from mid-1944, on the eventual outcome of the war. Though the desperate situation, with the increasing awareness of imminent collapse, involved both the command and the fighting forces in many dramatic scenes, I have refrained from an attempt to portray these last months in comparable detail for lack of reliable documentary material. I should have had to rely purely on the personal recollections of the participants, many of them conflicting. This I preferred not to do. In any case the period has been covered by the accounts of a number of airmen such as Adolf Galland, in his outstanding book *The First and the Last.*

If, therefore, the last phase of the air war has not been given such detailed treatment, it is not because of any intention to laud the Luftwaffe's victories, while suppressing its defeat. The seeds of this defeat were sown in its over-hasty creation, its unpreparedness for a war of long duration, and its lack of aircraft types for certain important roles. The first chapter makes this clear. None the less, I believe that I have succeeded in steering clear of any "if-only-this-and-that" speculations. Facts after all, and not theories, speak for themselves.

This book only claims to be a report of the war in the air as it took place, without any attempt to give judgment on the morality of the whole thing. War generates emotions, and wartime propaganda exaggerates heroism. In defeated Germany peacetime propaganda has done nothing but pour scorn on all military virtues. The main victim of both is truth.

Thus my main preoccupation has been to disentangle the facts. Only then can anyone form an independent opinion. War is not glorious, as all those nations who took part in it know from the sufferings it entailed. I even dare to hope that my book will contribute to the realisation that, whatever their differences, they must learn to live together in peace.

CAJUS BEKKER,
Hamburg

TRANSLATOR'S NOTE

It will help the reader of this book if he has some understanding of the structure of the wartime operational Luftwaffe, and of the terms used to denote the different levels in the chain of command. Though the pattern varied with the size and nature of the campaign, this chain of command was roughly as follows:

Formation	Rank of Commander
Oberbefehlshaber der Luftwaffe (Supreme Commander)	*Reichsmarschall*
Chef des Generalstabes der Luftwaffe (Chief of Air Staff)	*General der Flieger* (Air General) *Generaloberst* (Colonel-General)
Luftflotte 1 (First Air Force)	*General der Flieger* (Air General) *Generalfeldmarschall* (Field Marshal)
I Fliegerkorps (I Air Corps)	*Generalleutnant* (Lieutenant-General) *General der Flieger* (Air General)
1 Fliegerdivision (1 Air Division)	*Generalmajor* (Major-General) *Generalleutnant* (Lieutenant-General) *General der Flieger* (Air General)
Geschwader (= Group, c. 100–120 a/c)	*Major/Oberstleutnant* (Major/Lieutenant-Colonel) *Oberst/General Major* (Colonel/Major-General)
Gruppe (= Wing, c. 30–36 a/c)	*Major* (Major) *Hauptmann* (Captain) *Oberstleutnant* (Lieutenant-Colonel)
Staffel (= Squadron, c. 9–12 a/c)	*Oberleutnant* (First-Lieutenant) *Hauptmann* (Captain)
Schwarm (fighters only) or *Kette* (sections of 4 or 3 a/c)	*Unteroffizier* (Corporal) *Leutnant* (Lieutenant) *Oberleutnant* (First-Lieutenant)

N.B.—Each *Gruppe* also had a *Stabskette* ("staff section"), and each *Geschwader* a *Stabsstaffel* ("staff squadron").

9

Though in the above table I have inserted an approximate English term after each formation, in the text I have considered it less misleading to adhere in some cases to the German terms. This applies particularly to the most frequently mentioned formations: *Geschwader* and *Gruppe*. To translate the former as "Group" and the latter as "Wing" (the nearest R.A.F. equivalents) would not be a happy solution to the problem, especially as they are usually referred to by quite untranslatable abbreviations. Only *Fliegerkorps* ("Air Corps"), *Fliegerdivision* ("Air Division"), *Staffel* ("Squadron") and *Schwarm* or *Kette* ("Section") have been anglicised in the text.

The basic operational unit was not the *Staffel* or Squadron (as in the R.A.F.), but the *Gruppe*, which, though it nominally formed part of a particular *Geschwader*, often operated independently of it. Normally there were three *Gruppen* to a *Geschwader*, but this varied as did the number of first-line aircraft in any *Gruppe* (in theory 30–36, but often a good deal fewer).

Within a higher command echelon such as a *Luftflotte* or an Air Corps were to be found the types of *Geschwader* suited to a particular campaign—such as *Kampfgeschwader* (bombers), *Stukageschwader* (dive-bombers) or *Jagdgeschwader* (single-engined fighters). The term *Zerstörer* (literally "destroyer") was used to represent the heavy twin-engined fighter, the Messerschmitt 110. Somewhat misleading, too, is the term *Lehrgeschwader* (abbreviation LG), which might be equipped with any kind of aircraft. Only two in number, they were originally formed for the purpose of training *leaders*, but after the war began proudly kept their designation as élite units.

The abbreviations, retained in the translation, indicate both the type and size of a particular formation. Thus KG 1—*Kampfgeschwader* 1 (bombers), JG 54—*Jagdgeschwader* 54 (single-engined fighters), etc. The *Gruppen* are represented by Roman numerals which precede the type and number of the *Geschwader*: e.g. II/StG 1 stands for the second *Gruppe* of *Stukageschwader* 1, I/ZG 2 for the first *Gruppe* of *Zerstörergeschwader* 2. A preceding Arabic numeral indicates a *Staffel* also according to its membership of a *Geschwader* (not a *Gruppe*)—e.g. 1/JG 3.

Coastal and special units had somewhat different designations, but these hardly require elaboration.

It will be seen from the table above that the personal rank of officers commanding at the same level varied considerably. Instead of being given an acting rank, as in the R.A.F., they bore the title of their command. Thus young, successful pilots became promoted to commands without gaining personal rank, so that we often find a *Major* (major) as *Kommodore* of a *Geschwader*, and a *Hauptmann* (captain) as *Kommandeur* of a *Gruppe*, and so on.

Finally, it is important to remember that in Germany both Anti-aircraft (Flak) and Paratroop units (as opposed to air-landed troops) were under Luftwaffe, and not Army, command.

F.Z.

CONTENTS

LIST OF PLATES

LIST OF MAPS AND DIAGRAMS

ILLUSTRATION ACKNOWLEDGMENTS

Maps and diagrams: Werner Schmidt. Drawing of the fortress of Eben Emael: August Eigener. Photographs: Bayer (1), Bibliothek für Zeitgeschichte (1), Datan (2), Dillschneider (2), French Navy (1), Heinkel (4), Henrich (1), Heumann (1), Imperial War Museum (2), Messerschmitt (4), Schaller (4), Schödl (1), Sturm (1), Süddeutscher Verlag (6), Ullstein (21), U.S. Air Force (2), Wundshammer (6). The remaining photographs were lent from private and military collections.

1

BLITZKRIEG ON POLAND

1. Codeword "Ostmarkflug"

It was August 25, 1939. An oppressively hot day was drawing to its close. At Schönwald Castle in Silesia the tops of the ancient trees were still bathed in sunlight, but beneath their branches it was already dusk. No peaceful evening, however, was in store. In front of the castle there was a constant coming and going. Dispatch riders rattled up and down the sandy drive. Luftwaffe orderlies ascended and descended the stairways. A command car, with the unit markings of a reconnaissance squadron on its fender, sped away in a cloud of dust.

The dust veiled everything, imparting an air of unreality to the scene. It swallowed up the sound of bustle, constricted people's throats and drowned their voices. Or was it perhaps not only the dust but thoughts of the morrow? For tomorrow the war was to start.

At 18.30 hours the Luftwaffe's commander-in-chief, Hermann Goering, had flashed the crucial codeword from Wildpark Werder near Potsdam—the codeword for which the two eastern *Luftflotten*, and all their units and formations, had for days been waiting with mounting restlessness; the codeword which spelt "the solution of the Polish question by violence". And now it had been given: " '*Ostmarkflug*' August 26, 04.30 hours."

Schönwald lies just east of the Silesian county town of Rosenberg, on the road to the Polish frontier crossing of Grunsruh, six miles away. It was there that the air commander, Lieutenant-General Freiherr von Richthofen, had set up his battle headquarters. But this mercurial little general did not like being so far behind the front.

"We must get properly tied up with the spearhead of the infantry," he said.

In other words there must be good communications. If they failed to function, no commander could lead his men; and it had been one of the Luftwaffe's most bitter experiences in Spain that usually they did not function.

At the end of the Spanish civil war Richthofen had been in command of the Condor Legion, and since those days his present staff had been with him almost to a man. This gave him a special advantage: his was the only operations staff in the Luftwaffe concentration against Poland with quite recent campaign experience—experience which should prove effective, if not decisive, when it came to providing air support for the army.

And that, in a nutshell, was Richthofen's job. His close support formations
—four *Stuka Gruppen*, one ground-attack and one long-range fighter *Gruppe*
—were billed to breach the Polish frontier fortifications to let in the 10th
Army from Silesia, and after the break-through to help an armoured wedge
push on straight to Warsaw.

No wonder that Richthofen wanted to be in close touch with the battle
front; he aimed to set up his staff headquarters the next day on ground
already cleared by the dawn's fighting. But that meant his communications
would have to be working, and about these he remained very sceptical. They
were a job for the administrative command, and at the moment no one knew
what was happening.

"Listen, Seidemann," said Richthofen to his chief of staff, "should there
be any change in tomorrow morning's plan, I doubt very much whether we
shall hear about it."

The time was a few minutes to eight. Little did Richthofen know how
quickly the evening's events would confirm his fears.

Below on the frontier road leading to Grunsruh stood the commander-in-
chief of the 10th Army, Artillery General von Reichenau, with his aide-de-
camp, Major Wietersheim. For half an hour the motorised columns had been
rolling past them to the east.

Schönwald lay in the middle of the XVIth Army Corps' concentration area; and this Corps, under Major-General Hoepner, was the 10th
Army's spearhead. Its two armoured divisions, the 1st and 4th, were due to
break over the Polish border on a front of only a few kilometres at 04.30
hours. Exploiting the surprise and confusion of the enemy, they were to
press on without turning to right or left. Out-flanking both the Polish concrete emplacements at Lublinitz to the south and the Wielun defences to the
north, as well as the industrial area of Tschenstochau, their drive was
directed straight to the Warte crossing at Radamsko. (See sketch on page
44.)

The air leader had thus given thought to his choice of a frontal location.
He had gone further and asked the 10th Army chief to share his quarters with
him. Reichenau had gladly accepted, for the castle had been most tastefully
appointed by its owners, the von Studnitz family. Under the same roof, and in
neighbouring rooms, army and air force generals could not have been in
closer touch for the morrow's attack by the former's *Panzers* and their
support by the latter's *Stukas*.

Shortly after eight o'clock both were standing at the castle gates, watching
the endless column of vehicles, when Lieutenant-Colonel Hans Seidemann
dashed up to them, out of breath.

"Excuse me, General, but Operation '*Ostmarkflug*' is off!"

As Richthofen gazed at him speechlessly, he went on: "The message has
just come through from 2 Air Division. At the Führer's command
hostilities will not be opened on August 26th. Troop concentrations will
continue."

Richthofen snorted. "What a lovely mess! All right, Seidemann, get out
the cancellation orders . . . by 'phone, radio, dispatch rider, every means you
can. And get every unit to acknowledge receipt. Not a soul must take off
tomorrow, not a single machine. Otherwise we shall be blamed for having
started the war!"

Excusing himself from Reichenau, Richthofen rushed off. The radio van and signals tents adjoining the castle had become hives of activity as orders were encoded and telephone operators tried to get connected. Outside the dispatch riders raced off.

Richthofen's *Gruppen* and squadrons had only been sent forward to their operational bases that afternoon. From some no word had yet been received, and he had no idea where they had got to. The bases lay, of course, much too far apart and too far behind the front. No one at home had learnt a thing from the reports he had sent from Spain.

Colonel Günter Schwarzkopff's *Stuka Geschwader* 77 with its two *Gruppen* had landed up at Neudorf, west of Oppeln, and the two *Stuka Gruppen* of *Lehrgeschwader* 2 under Colonel Baier in Nieder-Ellguth on the Steinberg. Major Werner Spielvogel's ground-attack *Gruppe*, II/LG 2, lay miles away from its prospective target at Altsiedel. It was equipped with the Henschel Hs 123 biplane, whose fuel capacity was good for a radius of little more than eighty miles.

"If Spielvogel ever reaches the front, he will have used practically half his fuel already," growled Richthofen, and immediately ordered an air strip to be got ready for this unit at Alt-Rosenberg, close behind the frontier.

Finally there was *Gruppe* I of the long-range fighter *Geschwader*, ZG 2 under Captain Genzen at Gross Stein, south of Oppeln. Would the cancellation orders reach them all in time?

Around 20.30 hours von Reichenau put his head through the door. "Well, my dear friend," he said good humouredly, "it looks as though we shall have to go to war without the Luftwaffe." Answering Richthofen's quizzical stare, he added: "For me no cancellation order has come. I am marching!"

For hours the 10th Army commander had been completely out of touch with his chief of staff, Lieutenant-General Paulus, located in the woods north-east of Oppeln. On the road below the troop movement still proceeded blithely to the east. Without personal orders Reichenau declined to do anything to stop it.

To resolve the confusion Richthofen offered the 10th Army commander to get through to Berlin on the Luftwaffe radio network and put the question directly. Reichenau agreed, and shortly afterwards—it was nearly nine—the following unusual radio message crackled through:

"Air commander requests information for army commander: Do cancellation orders also apply to 10th Army?"

On went the message through the "usual channels": from Richthofen's H.Q. to 2 Air Division; from there to *Luftflotte* 4; and finally to the Commander-in-Chief Luftwaffe. As they decoded it, the signals officers hardly believed their eyes.

Time passed. 21.30, and still the tanks rattled eastwards past the castle.

22.00: now the infantry columns were marching past to the nearby frontier.

22.30: the air commander breathed again as the last of his units signalled receipt of the cancellation orders. But still the infantry seemed to have no clue.

Finally, one hour short of midnight, came an answering radio message from

Berlin. The Commander-in-Chief Luftwaffe, on behalf of the High Command, Armed Forces, wished to make known to General von Reichenau that the cancellation order also applied to the 10th Army. And shortly after midnight the regiments started to roll back.

Now it became clear why the army chief had not previously been notified. His Army had in fact received the counter-order from Army Group South in the early evening. But Reichenau had already driven forward to his advanced H.Q., and for the whole evening communications between the staff at Turawa and the commander at Schönwald had remained interrupted. Even dispatch riders did not get through.

Lieutenant-General Paulus, in Turawa, had his hands full getting the counter-orders through to the Army Corps, from them to the Divisions, and from the Divisions to the Régiments; not to mention to the detachments, battalions and companies right on the frontier, and above all to the special-duty shock troops whose job was to sneak behind the enemy lines from midnight on, four hours before the general assault. He could assume that his commander-in-chief would scarcely go to war by himself if the Army made a massive about-face. He therefore informed the field elements first. 'All the same it would have been a miracle if, in the few hours left, every man forward on the frontier had got to know that the attack was off.

In fact, this was almost achieved. In the 10th Army's whole area only one assault detachment failed to get the news. This lay in front of the 46th Infantry Division's sector, opposite the Polish emplacements at Lublinitz. During the night, as ordered, it crept forward into hostile territory, and at 04.30 its thirty men opened fire on the Poles. At any moment the German battalions should sweep forward from the frontier and envelop the foe in a pincers movement. But on the frontier all remained quiet. The detachment was shot to pieces.

There was one other case. On the right wing of Army Group South, in the area of the 14th Army under Colonel-General List in Slovakia, a railway tunnel was seized in a surprise raid: a vital supply artery once the German attack got going. In this case the storm detachment had to be recalled and the tunnel yielded. The Poles had hardly regained it when they blew it up and made it impassable.

These two mishaps robbed the attack, when it came, of all surprise, and dispelled any lingering doubts the Poles still had as to whether the Germans were in earnest. In the next few days air reconnaissance established that reinforcements were pouring into their frontier provinces on every road and railway: a direct result of the last-minute halt by the German armies. Now each day the enemy must be counted stronger.

Reichenau and Paulus had to change the 10th Army's whole plan of attack. Armour and motorised units were brought back into the second line, and the spearhead was now the infantry. The job was to crack open the frontier and force gaps through which the armour could thrust forward in depth. What previously could have been accomplished by surprise could now only be achieved by bitter fighting.

The other German armies had similarly to remuster their forces at top speed. However, such tactical displacements did not affect the basic operational objective. This was, in the words of the ground forces' Commander-in-Chief, "to anticipate an orderly mobilisation and concentration of the Polish

Army, and to destroy the main bulk of it west of the Vistula-Narev line by concentric attacks from Silesia and Pomerania and East Prussia".

Everything depended on whether the mighty arms of the pincers could be closed in time: in time to prevent the main bulk from escaping over the Vistula into the wide regions of east Poland. If the plan succeeded, the Poles would be caught in a giant trap, and the whole campaign could be decided west of the river.

But the plan also implied that the German Luftwaffe would first achieve air sovereignty over Poland, and further that German bombers could disrupt the roads and railways in the hinterland. Not only that, but the Luftwaffe was also expected to play a leading part in the battle itself: bombers and dive-bombers, long-range and short-range fighters, were to harass the ground troops continuously to hammer home the idea that capitulation was the only way out.

It was the first time in history that an air force had been called upon to play such a decisive role in a battle. It was, indeed, also the first time that an independent, self-sufficient air arm had ever taken part in a war. How would it fulfil the expectations that the High Command reposed in it? Was it really strong enough for all these jobs: air to air, air to ground, at the front and beyond it?

How strong in fact was the Luftwaffe? At the end of the Polish campaign the legend went around the world of an air force of irresistible strength and crushing power—a legend that a wily German propaganda did its best to maintain. It did it indeed so successfully that the legend not only outlasted the war and the collapse of Germany, but has actually continued right up to the present day.

Here are two examples taken at random. In *The War in Poland*—a study of war history published in 1945 by the American military academy of West Point—it was stated: "In the summer of 1939 Germany had achieved her objective of possessing the strongest air force in the world. Civilian and military training had produced a reserve of nearly 100,000 pilots. Production was estimated at around 2,000 aircraft per month. At Germany's disposal was an air strength of 7,000 first-line machines, divided into four air forces." The authoritative, multi-volume war history, *The Royal Air Force 1939–45* gives the Luftwaffe's strength on September 3, 1939—the day Britain declared war—as exactly 4,161 first-line aircraft.

What were the actual figures? The one reliable and relevant German document—the daily strength report of operational aircraft, produced by the Quartermaster-General for the C.-in-C. Luftwaffe—tells a very different story. During the Polish campaign the operative Luftwaffe comprised *Luftflotte* 1 "East" under Air Force General Albert Kesselring, and *Luftflotte* 4 "South-East" under Air Force General Alexander Löhr. On September 1, 1939 they together had at their disposal not more than 1,302 first-line aircraft.

In addition there were in the east 133 machines which came under the direct command of the C.-in-C. (Goering). Apart from two bomber squadrons for special missions they comprised only reconnaissance, weather reconnaissance and transport machines. Thirty-one reconnaissance and communications squadrons totalling 288 aircraft had been handed over to the army.

Finally one may count the fighters whose role was the air defence of eastern Germany, though only a few of these became involved in the air battle over Poland, and that on its periphery. In administrative areas I (Königsberg), III (Berlin), IV (Dresden) and VIII (Breslau) they comprised twenty-four squadrons with a total of 216 machines.

Thus at a generous estimate the total number of aircraft that the Luftwaffe could call up against Poland was 1,929. Of these only 897 were "bomb-carriers"—i.e., bombers, dive-bombers and ground-attack machines—adapted to the actual air offensive.

Goering had thrown two-thirds of his entire strength into the east. The remaining third, which held watch in the west, comprised 2,775 front-line machines of all types. Of them only 1,182, or about forty per cent, were "bomb-carriers".

These humble figures imply three things: at the outset of the war the Luftwaffe was substantially weaker than generally supposed; it was by no means a purely offensive weapon; at this early stage of its build-up, when Hitler chose to go to war, it was fit only for a short blitzkrieg on *one* front.

However, the value or superiority of an air force cannot be measured only by numbers. And technical modernity is never final. In May 1939, still three months before the outbreak of hostilities, the Luftwaffe's chief of staff, Hans Jeschonnek, said in warning: "Do not let us deceive ourselves, gentlemen. Each country wants to outstrip the other in air armament. But we are all roughly at the same stage. In the long run a technical lead cannot be maintained."

In Germany in 1939 these were words of heresy. He uttered them before a group of high officers of all services who, under the code name "*Generalstabsreise Schlesien*", had been summoned to a meeting in dreamy Bad Salzbrunn, west of Oppeln in Silesia.

In his warnings about over-optimism concerning the Luftwaffe's numerical and technical superiority Jeschonnek had a clear purpose: "There is another thing, and that is tactics. In this field everything is new and undeveloped. By concentrating our thoughts in this direction we could win a real superiority over the enemy."

So it was that Luftwaffe tactics became the dominant theme at Bad Salzbrunn for the ensuing study groups, command discussions and map exercises. They were given their last polishing-up before the war that loomed ahead. Above all the simple question, "What shall we do with our 800 *Stukas* and bombers?" multiplied into a host of minor problems. What, for instance, should be the timing of a joint attack by a bomber and a dive-bomber group on target number 1,076—Warsaw-Okecie airfield? Clearly, owing to their different modes of attack, they could not strike simultaneously. But which should go in first? The *Stukas*, in order to have maximum vision for their precision attacks? Or the horizontal bombers, so as to draw off the enemy air defence and so give the *Stukas* an easier task? Could long-range fighters deal with the enemy flak? How were they to protect the *Stukas* without impeding the latter's attack?

These were just a few problems out of a multitude. "Tactics are so new and undeveloped." The only experience was that of the Condor Legion in Spain, and time was pressing. Hitler had already announced to the chiefs of the three services his intention "to attack Poland at the first suitable opportunity".[1] But still no one believed that this could be so soon.

"Our weaknesses in training, equipment and operational readiness were only too well known," wrote General Speidel, then chief of staff of *Luftflotte* 1, "and were again and again dutifully reported to higher authority." But on August 22nd Speidel was present at Obersalzberg when Hitler informed his service chiefs of his resolve to march against Poland forthwith. "Like many other officers," Speidel confided in his diary, "I left the Führer's meeting in unmistakable dismay." That very same afternoon the Luftwaffe operations staff took up its battle quarters in the labour camp of Wildpark Werder near Potsdam.

In the afternoon of August 24th Goering flashed the codeword "*Unterstellungsverhältnis Weiss*", and the organisation plan for the Polish operation was put into execution. By August 25th every *Gruppe* and *Geschwader* had left its peace-time base and reached its operational one.

The afternoon and evening of the 25th saw the dramatic prelude already described. The fateful signal "*Ostmarkflug*" was given for the following morning, and a few hours later cancelled.

Six days of waiting ensued. Six days of torment, which raised the highest hopes . . . hopes of a peaceful settlement of the conflict. Speidel wrote: "We still believe that a continuance of negotiations would help to bring the Führer to reason."

On August 25th Britain's prime minister announced the conclusion of a further mutual-aid pact between his country and Poland, and even Hitler could no longer count on Britain's weakness to keep her quiet. But now nothing would deter him from carrying out the assault. In the preceding years too many improbable successes had been achieved, and now he would not yield an inch.

At 12.40 hours on August 31st the six days of waiting were ended by the issue of "War Directive No. 1". The torment was over and hope expired. The war began at 04.45 hours on September 1st.

First-Lieutenant Bruno Dilley, commanding 3 Squadron of *Stuka Geschwader* 1, peered with strained eyes from the cockpit of his Ju 87B, trying yet again to get his bearings. Patches of fog blocked his vision in all directions.

His sortie was like a nightmare. Only the feel of the control stick in his hand and the droning of the Junkers engine forward smacked of reality. Behind him, back to back, sat his radio operator, Master-Sergeant Kather, trying not to lose sight of the other two planes of the section.

Yesterday Dilley would have thought only a madman could send him on such a hedge-hopping sortie in fog. Now he had been picked to make the first air attack of the war and drop the first bomb on an enemy target.

The German operations plan envisaged the rapid linking up of East Prussia with the Reich. Supplies for the 3rd Army were to start coming up by rail as soon as possible. But there was one particularly vulnerable bottleneck: the Vistula crossing at Dirschau. On no account must this bridge be

[1] Taken from the shorthand report of Hitler's statement in front of the commanders-in-chief of the three services, their chiefs of general staff and eight other officers on May 23, 1939, in the Berlin Chancellery, and testified to by the signature of Lieutenant-Colonel Schmundt. All quotations in this book from declarations, orders, etc., stem from authentic records, even though their sources, in a popular work such as this, are not all given *seriatim*.

blown. An army task force under Colonel Medem was to push forward from Marienburg by armoured train, take the bridge by surprise and secure it, while the Luftwaffe pinned the Poles down by repeated attack, and stopped them blowing the bridge before Medem arrived.

It was this on which Dilley was engaged. His target was not the bridge but the ready-prepared detonation points close to the station. A microscopic target; just a dot on the town plan. For days his squadron had been rehearsing this attack against a dummy target near its base at Insterburg. Further, they had several times boarded the Berlin-Königsberg express, and, crossing the Dirschau bridge, established that the detonating leads ran along the southern slope of the railway embankment between the station and the bridge. On this they built their plan: they would attack at low level and let fly with their bombs at closest possible range.

For this special mission they had yesterday been sent forward from Insterburg to Elbing. And now this accursed fog. It hung over the airfield at scarcely 150 feet, trailing patches right down to the ground.

All the same Dilley was willing to risk it. From Elbing to Dirschau is but a stone's throw: eight minutes' flight. He would go in first, followed by Lieutenant Schiller and then an experienced N.C.O. Taking off in the half-light at 04.26 they turned south and raced close over the tree-tops through the fog patches.

At 04.30—exactly a quarter of a hour before the official outbreak of hostilities—they caught a brief glimpse of the dark ribbon of the Vistula ahead, and Dilley turned north to follow its course. Now he knew that he could not miss the bridge. His fears were groundless: there it was already in the distance. The great steel construction was unmistakable.

04.34: on all sides the country seemed wrapped in peace. But three *Stukas* raced over the ground at thirty feet towards the embankment left of the Dirschau bridge . . . three *Stukas*, each with a 500-lb. bomb under the fuselage and four 100-lb. bombs under the wings.

Just short of the embankment Dilley pressed his release button, jerked back the stick, and had already cleared the railway with a mighty leap as his bombs exploded behind him. Following in echelon to port and starboard the other two pilots also hit the target.

It was the first *Stuka* attack of World War II, and took place fifteen minutes before "X-hour".

One hour later a squadron of III/KG 3 took off into the unknown from Heiligenbeil, flying horizontal Do 17 Z bombers. They, too, had ground visibility over Dirschau, and dropping their bombs from some height reported fires in the town.

But meanwhile Colonel Medem's armoured train had come to a halt. In feverish haste the Poles succeeded in patching up the mangled leads, and at 06.30, long before the Germans arrived, one of the twin bridges sagged under the explosion and crashed into the Vistula. The Luftwaffe's first attack, though successful in itself, had not achieved its purpose.

And here another legend must be exploded: that the Polish campaign—and with it World War II—opened early on September 1, 1939, with a crushing offensive blow by the Luftwaffe.

It is true that its air formations lay all ready at their operational bases—serviced, fuelled and bombed up. Not indeed 7,000 aircraft, not even 4,000,

1. In the first years of the war a number of bomber *Geschwader* were equipped with the light Dornier Do 17, originally designed as a "fast bomber."

2. Leader of the Luftwaffe close-support forces during the "blitz" campaigns, Major-General von Richthofen in his Fieseler Storch.

3. The Henschel Hs 123, with which the Luftwaffe furnished tactical support to the Army during the ground battles.

4. Polish fighters of the type PZL 11c, which despite their marked inferiority engaged the Luftwaffe over Warsaw.

5. German bomber attacks on Polish airfields destroyed many antiquated aircraft—as well as the hangars, which shortly afterwards the Germans could well have used themselves.

6. During the Polish campaign the heavy long-range fighter, Messerschmitt Bf 110 (in foreground) —here escorting Ju 87s—still proved an effective weapon. Over Britain it proved highly vulnerable.

7. Flak units (which were under Luftwaffe command) first established their reputation as excellent ground artillery in the Polish campaign. Later the flat-trajectory fire of their 88-mm guns proved specially effective against Russian tanks.

but still 897 "bomb-carriers", and about the same number of long and short-range fighters and reconnaissance machines.

It is also true that the crews were well acquainted with their targets, of which they carried remarkably detailed maps. But the great blow was never launched—not, at least, at the appointed hour early in the morning of September 1st. It was stifled by fog.

In it one could see the pattern the war was to follow. For months the great operation had been planned ahead. Hundreds of general staff officers had studiously worked out all the details, and thousands of men now stood by to put the finished plan into execution . . . only to have the weather put paid to the whole thing. From the whole of *Luftflotte* 1 only four bomber *Gruppen* managed to get off the ground by six o'clock, and in the course of the morning only two more. And these were happy if they found any target at all.

Even Goering felt obliged to call off operations. As early as 05.50 he sent out the radio message: "Operation 'Seaside' will not take place today." "Seaside" was to have been a concentrated attack by every *Geschwader* on the Polish capital. But over Warsaw the cloud ceiling was only 600 feet, and below it visibility was less than half a mile.

The 4th Air Force in the south[1] enjoyed better conditions, even if they were by no means ideal. It was still dark as Lieut.-General von Richthofen set off from Schloss Schönwald to cover the few miles to the frontier. The time was a few minutes after 04.30. In less than a quarter of an hour the frontier would become the front.

With dimmed headlights the air commander's staff car drove past the endless columns of infantry, then came to a halt at a labour camp. From here it was a half-mile walk to his command post just south of the frontier crossing of Grunsruh. His orderly officer, First-Lieutenant Beckhaus, accompanied him.

Half way there, there was a crackle of rifle fire. Further to the north artillery rumbled.

"Exactly 04.45, General!" commented Beckhaus.

Richthofen nodded. He stood still and listened.

"The firing of these first shots made a stark impression on me," he later wrote in his private diary. "Now the war was surely in earnest. Thought till now it would only be political or confined to a show of force. Am thinking about France and England, and believe no longer in the possibility of a political settlement after what is being done now. The quarter of an hour's walk to my command post made me very worried about the future. But when Seidemann reported to me on my arrival, I had overcome my feelings. From now on it was the practical business of making war, as ordered."

Day dawned slowly in a damp mist. The ground lay curtained in fog.

"Shocking weather for flying," said his chief of staff, Lieutenant-Colonel Seidemann. "When the sun starts shining on this mist, the *Stukas* won't be able to see the ground."

The first take-off reports came through. Richthofen went outside. There everything was strangely quiet—no sound of battle, only isolated shots.

[1] For the order of battle of the operational Luftwaffe against Poland on September 1, 1939, see Appendix 1.

Hardly the thunder of war. But then, just before sunrise, came the "battle-planes".

Quite suddenly they were there. It was Major Spielvogel's *Gruppe*, II/LG 2, which had taken off from Altsiedel, as ordered. Soon they were circling the frontier stream, buzzing angrily like a stirred-up hornet's nest. They looked oddly antiquated, these Henschel biplanes with their fat round radial engines, and the pilots sitting up "naked and unashamed" in their open cockpits. No front armour-plating or glazed cabins here. In a "battle-plane", as these ground-attack aircraft were called, the pilot sat as in the old days face to face with the enemy.

Across the frontier Captain Otto Weiss, leader of 1 Squadron, identified his target: the village of Panki (or Pryzstain), where the Poles had entrenched themselves. Raising his hand in signal to his colleagues, he pressed the stick forward to attack.

Thus fell the first bombs on the southern front, just ahead of the 10th Army. They were light "Flambos" (as they were called) with percussion fuses, exploding on contact with a hollow sound. They set anything they hit on fire, wrapping it in smoke and flames.

The attack could be watched quite clearly from the general's command post, and was repeated by the second "battle-plane" squadron under First-Lieutenant Adolf Galland—later to become famous as a fighter leader. Other planes burst over the tree-tops in sections to rake the Poles with machine-guns.

Meanwhile light flak opened up as the enemy manned his defences, and infantry weapons joined it. The firing reached a climax, and continued long after the Henschels had left.

This dawn attack on the village of Panki, on September 1st, was the first instance in World War II of direct support by the Luftwaffe of an attack by ground troops. That evening the report of the Armed Forces High Command, reviewing the Luftwaffe's contribution to the day's events, stated: " . . . In addition, the Army's advance was effectively supported by several *Geschwader* of battle-planes."

"Several *Geschwader*!" . . . The phrase implied several hundred aircraft, inasmuch as at the war's outset a normal *Geschwader* of three *Gruppen* was composed of ninety to a hundred machines. In fact it was just one *Gruppe* that attacked the enemy—the thirty-six biplanes of Major Spielvogel's II/LG 2!

These certainly did their stuff. For ten days they shadowed the XVIth Army Corps as it advanced towards Warsaw and the Vistula, attacking each time the tanks and motorised infantry met stiff resistance. Finally, in the great clinching battles at Radom and on the Bzura, they flew up to ten sorties a day.

But for the close support of the Army on September 1st Richthofen could muster only this single *Gruppe* of Henschels, and two of his four *Stuka Gruppen*. What had happened to the other two? Angrily the general read again yesterday's order which, on the eve of the opening attack, deprived him of half his already inadequate dive-bomber force. With other bomber units of the 2nd Air Division they were to be launched against Cracow and other airfields behind the enemy lines. It seemed to him a great mistake. Could there be any higher priority than supporting the Army by hammering a breach in the enemy's frontier fortifications?

For weeks German propaganda had been boasting of the irresistible strength and hitting power of the Luftwaffe. But the latter's chief of general staff, Lieutenant-General Jeschonnek, had the actual figures before him. They gave him something of a headache. So many units had been shoved to and fro on paper, that unless the western front was to be bled entirely white, the total number of "bomb-carriers" he could muster for the Polish operation amounted to scarcely 900, or more likely 800, for one must always deduct ten per cent for aircraft which for some reason or another would be unserviceable.

Jeschonnek knew well that if victory could not be gained by force of numbers, only planning and tactics could make up the deficiency. In other words the available strength should not be scattered, with a *Gruppe* here and a squadron there (which was precisely what was happening at the moment). The Luftwaffe's main point of effort must be defined and its strength concentrated, if not against a single target, then against a definite group of similar targets.

After much discussion the command staff had drawn up an order of precedence for Luftwaffe operations. First, and most urgent, was the destruction of the enemy air force.

According to the latest intelligence reports the Poles possessed a good 900 first-line operational aircraft—including some 150 bombers, 315 fighters, 325 reconnaissance machines, plus fifty naval and a hundred other communications aircraft. In numbers, and also technically, their air force was of course inferior to the German one. If, however, it were disregarded, it could cause serious damage. It could hamper air attacks, bomb the German army, perhaps even drop bombs on German soil.

"A decision in the air must precede a decision on the ground"—so the Italian, Douhet[1], had proclaimed in his study of air warfare. And the German Luftwaffe subscribed to his doctrine. Complete air sovereignty over Poland must be its prime objective.

Second in order of precedence was "co-operation with Army and Navy", whenever and so long as these were engaged in decisive operations. In this case indirect support in the shape of air attacks on troops and lines of communication behind the enemy front had priority over direct participation in the ground operations, such as the Henschels were engaged in.

During a pause in operations more significance was attached to "attacks on the sources of enemy strength", i.e., the centres of war industry in the interior.

With only slight deviations the Luftwaffe retained this order of precedence right through the war. During the thirty-day Polish campaign its importance, thanks to the superiority of German weapons, was not perhaps very marked. But later its application—or non-application—was to hold the balance between victory and defeat.

So it was that the leader of the close-support force, Richthofen, came to be deprived by *Luftflotte* 4 of so many *Stukas*. If the Army wanted massive close air support, it would have to wait till the afternoon of the opening day, at least.

That morning the Luftwaffe had more important work to do. Its bombers

---

[1] General Giulio Douhet (1869–1930) had as early as 1921, in his book *Air Power*, propounded the controversial theorem of subjugating a foe mainly by attack from the air.

and dive-bombers launched a protracted attack on the enemy's airfields—on hangars and runways, aircraft dispersal areas and peripheral aviation works. They struck at the Polish air force at every vulnerable point. The main blow fell on Cracow—a target that was never intended. But farther north the formations either failed to find their targets, or because of the bad weather were redirected south before take-off.

Over Cracow the weather had cleared, and early reconnaissance had shown the airfield to be occupied. Sixty Heinkel 111s, comprising *Gruppen* I and III of KG 4, took off from their base at Langenau in Silesia. KG 4 was in fact the only *Geschwader* of *Luftflotte* 4 that was equipped with these standard medium-range bombers. The others had Do 17Es or Do 17Zs.

First Lieutenant Evers, commander of III *Gruppe*, had ordered his pilots to fly in close formation for better self-protection against enemy fighters. But up at 12,000 feet there were no Poles to be seen, and the escorting twin-engined fighters of I/ZG 76 had nothing to do. After a flight of barely forty-five minutes the bombers were over the target. Though Cracow lay in light mist, it was easy to recognize and a few seconds later down came the bombs ... forty-eight tons of them, and all plumb on target.

There followed a dive-bombing attack by the *Stukas* of I/StG 2 under Major Oskar Dinort on hangars and runways, after which the two bomber *Gruppen* of KG 77 could not fail to spot the target, marked as it was by fires and columns of smoke. These, however, prevented clarity of vision, so when it was III *Gruppe's* turn to go in, its leader, Col. Wolfgang von Stutterheim, ordered it to do so at low level. Racing over the airfield at barely 150 feet, the Dornier "Flying Pencils" laid a line of 100-lb. bombs down the length of the runway, and seconds later they burst against the concrete.

When KG 77 landed back at Brieg, a great many of their planes were seen to be damaged—not by enemy flak, let alone fighters, but by their own bomb splinters flying up at them.

Apart from Cracow, there were *Stuka* attacks on the airfields of Katowitz and Wadowice, while II/KG 77 attacked Krosno and Moderowka. Later, as the weather cleared, KG 76 was sent against Radom, Lodz, Skierniewice, Tomaszow, Kielce and Tschenstochau. The He 111Ps of Lieutenant-Colonel Erdmann's II/KG 4 flew a distance of 300 miles, right through a bad-weather zone over Slovakia, all the way to Lemberg, where they dropped twenty-two tons of bombs on the runways and hangars.

Everywhere the German bombers strove to strike a knock-out blow against their main enemy—the Polish air force. But did the blow really register? Certainly the runways had become pocked with bomb craters. Hangars had been split open by the force of high explosive; stores had gone up in flames; and everywhere, singly or in groups, stood the burnt-out skeletons of aircraft destroyed on the ground.

Despite all this there remained an uncomfortable feeling, which grew stronger as the hours passed. What, it was asked, had happened to the Polish air force? Its non-appearance was quite unexpected. Granted the Germans had had the advantage of surprise, granted the enemy's ground organisation had been severely stricken. But surely the Poles could have attempted *some* defence in the air, could have sent up *some* fighters against the German bombers? It was hoped they would, so that German superiority could be exerted, and a decision reached.

As it was, the Armed Forces Command's report read: "The Luftwaffe today achieved air sovereignty over the entire Polish combat zone . . ."

It was just not true. Only here and there had a few Polish fighters attacked the German bombers and been repelled. Otherwise the Polish air force had not offered battle, but avoided it. The question was: Why? Was it weaker than supposed? Or had it withdrawn to specially camouflaged airfields to prepare a counter-attack? It will be seen later how seriously the Luftwaffe top command in Berlin viewed the danger.

At Richthofen's command post close behind the front the morning hours of September 1st passed slowly by. He and his staff waited patiently for the fog to disperse so as to launch the *Stukas*. They also awaited reports from the front, and requests for air support of the XVIth Army Corps' advance. They expected urgent signals reporting enemy resistance which needed to be broken by precision air attacks. Nothing of the sort happened. The Army seemed to have forgotten the Luftwaffe's existence. Or was the higher command not yet in the picture?

With his experience in Spain behind him, Richthofen knew just what to do. He would send his own liaison officers equipped with signal vans, or at least portable radio sets, right up into the front line. Requests for air support would then be flashed directly to him, instead of over the time-wasting network of Army Division to Army Corps, and back from *Luftflotte* 4 to the appropriate Air Division.

There was another big advantage in this system inherited from Spain. The ground troops, whenever they encountered opposition, would need either artillery support or air support, and the young Luftwaffe officers with them could best decide whether the latter would be effective. Was ground visibility sufficient? Could the enemy be pin-pointed from the air? What type of aircraft was best suited for the attack: bombers, dive-bombers or "battle-planes"? Such were the questions they could decide.

But on the morning of September 1st this system was not yet in operation. The "battle-planes'" targets were picked at random. *Stukas* of I/StG 76 under Captain Walther Sigel went off early to attack the Wielun defences; a *Gruppe* of StG 77 was sent by 2nd Air Division against the line of emplacemènts at Lublinitz 23. That was all.

Finally Richthofen had had enough, and at 11.00 he sent for his Fieseler Storch. Climbing in, he took off from the potato patch next to his command post, equipped only with a map and field radio, to have a look at the front for himself. What he saw was the Germans attacking with rifles from the village of Panki, while the Poles answered with machine-guns. He saw German soldiers lying about wounded. Flying over the battlefield, he took in the whole scene.

Unintentionally he flew right over the Polish lines and came under accurate fire. Bullets slammed into the fuselage and lacerated the tail unit. The tank was riddled by machine-gun fire and petrol sprayed out as from a watering can. Happily the aircraft didn't catch fire, and, crippled though it was, he managed to lift it out of the infantry's effective range. Then he flew back to the frontier in a wide curve and landed just in time, with a coughing engine and an empty tank.

The C.-in-C. of the German air-support force had been all but shot down on the first day of the war. He had been guilty of doing just what he had forbidden his pilots to do: to make senseless low-level sorties over the enemy lines.

It was the vulnerability of a slow, low-flying aircraft to enemy flak that had caused Richthofen years before, as chief of aircraft development at the Luftwaffe Technical Bureau, to come out flatly against the whole dive-bomber idea. He held that, in a war, any dive below 6,000 feet would be suicide. But history had played a prank on him. Now the once despised dive-bomber was his strongest weapon.

However, his own experience over the Polish lines, plus the reports that came in from the units, all telling of losses and damage caused by intensity of ground fire, made him issue a new order: "No low flying will take place except strictly in the course of duty!"

The lesson of the first day of hostilities was clear: the Polish ground defences were not to be trifled with.

At noon came the results of air reconnaissance—itself hindered by poor visibility and ground mist. Strong concentrations of Polish cavalry were reported at Wielun, opposite the left wing of the XVIth Army Corps. More had been seen at Dzialoszyn on the Warte, north of Tschenstochau, and in the same area troop transporters on the railway from Zdunska. The *Stukas* were going to be needed.

I/StG 2 had its headquarters on the Steinberg near Oppeln, whence there was a splendid view over the plains. But today no one looked at it. Since this *Gruppe* had returned from its morning operation against Polish airfields the atmosphere had been one of carefully concealed tension.

Suddenly the telephone rang. The C.O., Major Oskar Dinort, in peacetime a well-known competition pilot, found the *Geschwader* commander, Colonel Baier, on the line.

"They've come, Dinort!" said the latter. "New ops orders. Get over here right away."

On Nieder-Ellguth airfield, at the foot of the Steinberg, the *Stukas* were towed from under cover and the engines started. The briefing at *Geschwader* H.Q. was short. 30 Ju 87 Bs, with their characteristic kinked-up wings and rigid, stilt-like undercarriages, stood waiting for the word go. At 12.50 they took off and headed eastwards.

Small hamlets and isolated farmsteads slipped past below them. Then something larger appeared indistinctly through the mist. According to the course they were on, it could only be Wielun. Major Dinort put aside the map and looked down, searching for details. Plumes of black smoke rose from the landscape, and in the town adjoining the main road a few houses were burning. That was it, the road! On it, near the entrance to the town, minute but unmistakable, like a jerkily wriggling worm, was the enemy column.

Dinort put his plane in a turn to port. A quick glance back to confirm that his squadrons were assuming the appointed attack formation, then he concentrated solely on the target. As he did so, his hands automatically went through the so often practised drill:

> Close radiator flap
> Turn off supercharger
> Tip over to port

8   9

Some outstanding dive-bomber pilots. **8.** Colonel Schwarzkopff, the *"Stuka* father," killed at Sedan on May 14, 1940. **9.** Major Dinort, famous as a peace-time aviator, and later commander of StG 2. **10.** First-Lieutenant Dilley, who carried out the first *Stuka* operation of the war. **11.** Captain Sigel, commander of I/StG 76, which suffered a severe reverse just before the opening of hostilities.

10   11

12. A Ju 87B *Gruppe* makes its approach. Dive-bombing was an obsession of the Luftwaffe high command, but the axiom that "all bombers must dive" proved to be a calamitous error.

13. A *Stuka* "scramble." Pilot and gunner climb aboard their Ju 87, with its characteristic reverse gull wings fixed undercarriage.

14. Another *Stuka* "scramble." In this picture, the engine has just been started.

Set angle of dive to 70 degrees
Accelerate: 220, . . . 250 . . . 300 m.p.h.
Apply air brakes—making a nerve-racking screech.

With every second the target swelled. Suddenly it was no longer an impersonal worm creeping over a map, but a living column of vehicles, men and horses. Yes, horses, and Polish riders. *Stukas* against cavalry . . . like a battle between opposing centuries. Such was war.

On the road everything was thrown into wild confusion. The horsemen tried to break away into the fields. Dinort concentrated on the road, aiming with the whole machine. At 3,500 feet he pressed the release button on the control column. As the bomb went, a shudder ran through the plane. He broke away in a climbing turn, taking avoiding action against enemy flak. Finally he looked down. The bomb had landed just beside the road. Wooden particles flew through the air, and there was a gush of black smoke. The other *Stukas* were diving on their targets.

It happened thirty times. After planting their bombs the pilots pulled sharply up, weaving between the coral strings of red-hot flak that were thrown up at them. Then they formed up over the town for a new attack. This second target was at Wielun's northern exit. Dinort spotted a large farmstead, which seemed to be serving as an H.Q. Soldiers swarmed all round it. Troopers had collected in a large courtyard.

This time the staff section's planes attacked together. From only 3,500 feet up they tipped over, screamed down to 2,500, and let go their bombs. In a few seconds smoke and flames masked the tragic consequences of inequality of weapons.

Nor was this the end of the anguish. The same targets were attacked again by *Gruppe* I of StG 77—the *Geschwader* of Colonel Schwarzkopff, known as "the *Stuka* father". And when further troop movements in the Wielun area were reported, a bomber *Gruppe*—I/KG 77 under Major Balk—was ordered to continue the work of annihilation.

In the course of a few hours ninety dive-bombers and bombers launched their bombs against the concentrated target of this Polish cavalry brigade. After that it no longer existed as a fighting force. The remnants fled eastwards in disorder. That evening they came together in isolated knots far from the scene of the attack. And the same evening, a keypoint of the Polish frontier defences fell into German hands.

By this action the Luftwaffe had clearly played a decisive part in the ground battle. Astonishingly, it had done so on the first day of hostilities—at a moment when its prime task was to subdue the Polish air force. But that air force had never appeared. So a number of units could turn already to the second task: support of the Army and Navy.

Air General Kesselring, C.-in-C. of *Luftflotte* 1 up in the north, had already infringed the rules of precedence the evening before. Placing two extra dive-bomber *Gruppen* at the disposal of Colonel Ulrich Kessler, leader of KG 1 at Kolberg, he had ordered this reinforced "Kessler *Geschwader*" next day against Polish harbour installations, warships and coastal batteries in the region of Danzig Bay, Gdingen, Oxhöft and the Hela peninsula.

At the start the dense fog on the morning of September 1st prevented any attack in force, and only I/KG 1 managed to get off at 06.00 and raid the Polish naval air base at Putzig-Rahmel.

By noon the fog over Pomerania and East Prussia had somewhat dispersed, and by the afternoon the whole twenty *Gruppen* of bombers and twin-engined fighters of *Luftflotte* 1 were airborne, as if to make up for the delay. I/KG 152 bombed flak defences and petrol dumps at the airfield of Thorn. II/KG 26 scored direct hits on buildings and rail installations in Posen-Luwica. I/KG 53 attacked the runway and hangars at Gnesen, while II/KG 3 —one of the few *Gruppen* to get off the ground in the morning—hit an ammunition dump south of Graudenz.

In the late afternoon I/KG 1 flew another sortie against Thorn, and KG 2 went against Plozk, Lida and Biala-Podlaska. As for the 120-odd *Stukas* of 1 Air Division—two *Gruppen* of StG 2, IV/LG 1 and the naval *Stuka* squadron 4/186 (destined for the aircraft carrier *Graf Zeppelin*)—to these fell the special mission of a series attack on the naval bases along the Danzig Bay.

Despite these operations ranging over the whole of northern Poland, it was not forgotten that the main target of *Luftflotte* 1 was Warsaw itself. At Goering's wish the capital was billed for a mass attack by the whole bomber strength of both *Luftflotten* during the afternoon of the first day— Operation "Seaside". He had already had to cancel it early in the morning owing to the bad weather.

Warsaw, indeed, was not only the political and military heart of Poland, and its centre of communications. With numerous air-frame and aero-engine factories, it was also the centre of aircraft production. If a mortal blow against the Polish air force was to be struck, it was surely here.

As a prelude, Heinkel 111s of II/LG 1 took off from their base at Powunden in East Prussia for a morning attack on Warsaw-Okecie airfield. Though ground visibility was miserable, a number of bombs hit the hangars of the state-owned PZL works, where bombers and fighters were produced.

A long pause ensued, waiting for better weather. An operation by KG 27 was postponed from hour to hour. Finally at 13.25 Berlin gave the word. The *Geschwader*, still based at its home airfields of Delmenhorst, Wunstorf and Hanover-Langenhagen in North Germany, had a long way to fly—470 miles to the target! Only after the attack would it transfer from *Luftflotte* 2 "North" to *Luftflotte* 1 "East".

At 17.30 the three Heinkel 111P *Gruppen* reached Warsaw. Now the capital was given little breathing space. A few minutes previously LG 1 from East Prussia had again bombed Warsaw-Okecie and the two other airfields, Goclaw and Mokotow, while the radio stations of Babice and Lacy, which sent out coded orders, were under precision attack by a dive-bombing *Gruppe*—I/StG 1 under Captain Werner Hozzel.

At this point the long-expected happened. The Polish air force at last rose to the defence. Over the centre of Warsaw took place the first air-to-air combats of World War II. Two squadrons composing some thirty fighters of type PZL 11c—known as their leader Group-Captain S. Pawlikowski's "pursuit-plane formation"—became engaged with the twin-engined Me 110s of I/LG 1, which formed the escort to the German bombers. The *Gruppe* was led by Captain Schleif, for its C.O., Major Grabmann, had that morning been wounded in an exchange of fire with a single Polish fighter.

Schleif spotted the enemy far below as they climbed up to do battle, and went after them in a shallow dive. But the Poles weaved away skilfully. The victim of surprise seemed, rather, to have been a Messerschmitt. It slunk away, apparently crippled, and immediately there was a Polish fighter on its tail. But the seemingly certain prey was only decoying the fox to the hounds. At eighty yards Schleif had the enemy full in his sights, fired a burst from all guns, and the PZL was brought down.

The Messerschmitts repeated the trick four times. While one played the role of wounded duck, the others awaited their chance to ambush. Result: five victories in just a few minutes. After that the Poles withdrew, and it was also high time for the Me 110s to set course for home.

Two days later, on September 3rd, there was a second air battle over Warsaw. Again some thirty PZL 11cs came in to attack; and again I/LG 1 scored five victories for the loss of only one of their own aircraft. Afterwards, with twenty-eight confirmed, it became the top-scoring *Gruppe* of the Polish campaign.

By 18.00 hours on September 1st fog had again set in so thick over *Luftflotte 1* zone of operations that further efforts were impossible. At his headquarters at Henningsholm near Stettin, General Kesselring and his staff drew up the balance sheet.

Despite the delays caused by the weather, on the first day of hostilities thirty sorties at *Gruppe* strength had been flown. Of these, seventeen had been against the enemy air force's ground installations such as airfields, hangars and factories, eight in support of the Army, and five against naval targets. Some thirty enemy aircraft had been destroyed on the ground, and altogether nine in the air. Against this, fourteen German planes had been lost, mostly owing to the remarkably accurate Polish flak. On the other hand no real air battle had taken place. The Poles had avoided it. Kesselring wrote in his terminal report:

"*Luftflotte 1* enjoys superiority throughout its combat zone"—but also: "To a large extent the enemy air force remained unseen."

The latter statement tallied well with the experience of *Luftflotte* 4 in the south. The headache the reports caused to the Luftwaffe command staff in Berlin is reflected in the orders issued for September 2nd. The words were repetitive and sometimes sharp:

"*Luftflotten* 1 and 4 will on 2.9 continue to pursue hostilities against the enemy air force. . . . Special watch will be resumed on air bases contiguous to Warsaw, Deblin and Posen. . . . The C.-in-C. orders that the whereabouts of Polish bombers shall be located, and that for this purpose adequate reconnaissance patrols shall be flown from first light onwards. . . . Pending location of the enemy bomber force, our own bomber units will remain on ground in readiness for immediate attack."

The German Luftwaffe was to wait on its opponents. Would the Polish bombers come? Would the second day of war see them hit back?

The *Geschwader* was cruising high in the sky over southern Poland, course east in tight formation. Within the larger wedges of the *Gruppen* flew the smaller ones of the squadrons—all so precisely ordered that they might be flying on parade. 12,000 feet below, windows gently rattled to the drone of the eighty-eight bombers. At the tip of the formation flew Colonel Martin Fiebig with a section of the staff squadron. On this morning of September

2nd he was leading his *Geschwader* himself. It was KG 4, known as the "General Wever" *Geschwader* after the Luftwaffe's first chief of general staff, who had crashed to death in 1936.

As the eighty-eight Heinkels flew unresisted and irresistibly onward, their crews scanned the skies vainly for an opponent. All they saw were the escorting Me 110s occasionally glinting in the sun. There was just one squadron of them—all that 2 Air Division deemed necessary.

KG 4's group of targets, Nos. 1015/1018, lay around the traffic junction of Deblin, on the Vistula fifty-five miles south of Warsaw. It possessed no fewer than three airfields, all of them left intact the day before.

Shortly after 10.00 hours they saw the shining ribbon of the river, and the *Gruppen* split up. All at once there was a storm of flak. It was dense, but too low, the shells exploding 1,000 feet or so beneath the bombers.

The Heinkels began their attack. As yesterday over Cracow, Katowice, Kielce, Radom and Lodz, the bombs exploded in lines along the runway throwing up fountains of debris, and mushrooms of orange flame where they hit the hangars.

Shortly after this attack a flight of four Me 110s went down in a steep glide. On the edge of the airfield they had spotted several aircraft which the bombers had spared.

Lieutenant Helmut Lent—years later one of Germany's most successful night-fighter pilots—pressed home his attack on one of the larger machines. With its robust fuselage and elongated cockpit, it resembled a German *Stuka*. At a hundred yards he fired a burst from his four machine-guns, and in a few seconds the Polish aircraft was blazing like a torch. Pulling out, Lent turned and dived on his next victim. When after a few minutes the 110s climbed away to catch up the rest of the formation, they left the wrecks of eleven Polish aircraft burning on the ground.

During the morning of September 2nd the Deblin airfields suffered the same fate as dozens of others had suffered already. And the attacks continued. Blow after blow fell on the Polish air force—against its ground installations, failing its appearance in the air. Throughout the day reconnaissance patrols kept every airfield under observation as far as eastern Poland. And wherever aircraft were identified on the ground, the bombers were sent in to destroy them.

As the morning wore on tension at headquarters increased. Staff and operations officers at Major-General Loerzer's 2 Air Division and Air General Löhr's *Luftflotte* 4 H.Q. waited hourly for reports of the enemy, while single- and twin-engined fighters sat at cockpit readiness to intercept any attack. They waited in vain, for the Poles never appeared.

A few reports came in of scattered attacks on German bombers by sections of at most two or three fighters. A solitary observation plane had sneaked over the frontier and dropped a few bombs—all duds—at Peiskretscham, north of Gleiwitz. Round noon it was reported that the Poles were flying reconnaissance patrols over their own country: airborne outposts which radioed back the approach of German bombers.

Just a few fighter and reconnaissance planes—no bombers! The squadrons of the Polish bomber brigade, with their modern twin-engined PZL 37 "Elks", seemed to have been swallowed up into the ground.

The tension subsided. The view began to prevail—and was soon proclaimed officially abroad—that the Polish air force had been knocked out on the ground by the first hammer blows against its bases. In the words of the Armed Forces report for September 2, 1939:

"All aircraft existing in hangars or in the open were set on fire. From this it can be assumed that the Polish air force has received a mortal blow. The German Luftwaffe has won undisputed mastery over the whole of Poland."

A quite different conclusion was reached by the Polish major, F. Kalinowski, at this time a pilot with Colonel W. Heller's bomber brigade, and later a wing-commander in the Royal Air Force.

"The German Luftwaffe," he has reported, "did exactly what we expected. It attacked our airfields and tried to wipe out our aircraft on the ground. In retrospect it seems quite naïve of the Germans to have believed that during the preceding days of high political tension, and with their own obviously aggressive intentions, we would leave our units sitting at their peace-time bases. The fact of the matter is that, by August 31st, not a single serviceable plane remained on them. In the previous forty-eight hours all of us had been transferred to emergency air-strips. As a result, the Germans' opening air blast completely failed in its purpose. . . . ."

Kalinowski added that all the Polish aircraft destroyed by German bombs and guns in hangars or in the open were either obsolete or otherwise unbattleworthy; whereas the 400 aircraft with real "teeth"—160 fighters, eighty-six bombers, 150 reconnaissance and army-co-op planes—made in the first week of the campaign a brave showing against great air superiority.[1]

What are the facts? In the afternoon of September 2nd the 1st and 2nd squadrons of ZG 76 clashed with Polish fighters while cruising over Lodz. In the violent dog-fight which ensued two PZL 11cs were shot down by Lieutenant Lent and First-Lieutenant Nagel, but their own side lost three Me 110s.

Next day the "Army of Lodz" squadrons had another success in shooting down a number of German army observation planes. But on September 4th they found their masters. A squadron of I/ZG 2, under First Lieutenant von Roon, again offered battle over Lodz. For this *Gruppe's* Me 109Ds the obsolescent, high-winged PZLs were no match. Eleven Polish fighters crashed in flames or had to make forced landings, severely damaged. The Messerschmitts also destroyed one of the modern "Elk" bombers in the air and three further PZL 37s on the ground.

But now, having overcome its first bewilderment, the Polish bomber brigade also made itself felt. Taking the defences unawares, its squadrons launched a number of attacks on the spearhead of the German armoured forces. Late in the afternoon of September 2nd the XXI Army Corps, marching from East Prussia against Graudenz, urgently requested bombardment of an airfield at Strasburg (Poland). From it bombers and ground-attack planes were making repeated sorties against the German infantry.

The following day the 1st and 4th *Panzer* Divisions, pushing ahead of the 10th Army, suffered heavy losses from the air on reaching Radomsko, and likewise called for help from the Luftwaffe. After that, however, Polish air activity diminished daily. The German advance had been too swift and deep, and the Luftwaffe's blows against communication lines and supply bases too devastating.

"The turning point was September 8th," Kalinowski reports. "The supply

[1] For the strength of the Polish Air Force, see Appendix 3.

situation had become hopeless. More and more of our aircraft became unusable. There were no spare parts. Just a few bombers continued operating up till the 16th. . . . On the 17th the remaining serviceable planes received orders to withdraw to Rumania."

So ended the efforts of the Polish air force to defend its country. By the start of the second week it had virtually ceased to exist.

In his contribution to a multi-volume work produced by the General Sikorski Institute in London, and dealing with the causes of Poland's downfall, Colonel Litynski wrote that the worst consequence of the initial German attack on airfields, roads, and railways was the complete dislocation of communications: "Already by the second day the telephone and teleprinter systems had broken down. Reports and orders became hopelessly confused. If they reached their recipients at all, they came through in the wrong order, and the text was often completely distorted. As a result there was virtually no effective military command from the start."

This was what the first German air attacks had achieved. The "destruction of hangars and runways," contributed nothing. This the Luftwaffe very soon realised. When, after a few days, the troops reached the first airfields that had been bombarded, the claims of the intelligence commission were remarkably modest. Bombs on hangars, its report stated, had been completely wasted. All the aircraft destroyed on the ground were old training machines, and all the bomb craters could be filled in almost immediately. As for the attacks on the aircraft industry, they had done more harm than good, for now the Germans could not use it themselves.

This report, of course, remained top secret. The public was kept in complete ignorance. They were told only of the non-stop bombing raids, the peerless power of the Luftwaffe, and above all the morale-shattering effect of the dive-bomber.

2. The Birth of the Stuka

Without his *Panzers* on the ground and his *Stukas* in the air, Hitler's "blitz" campaigns at the beginning of World War II would have been unthinkable. Again and again it was the Ju 87B dive-bomber that struck the mortal blow.

On the morning of September 3rd eleven of these machines braved the heavy flak and dived on the Polish naval base of Hela. They were intended for the carrier-borne 4/186 squadron, and as their target they chose Poland's most modern warship, the minelayer *Gryf*. After a hit on the quarter-deck and several near misses against the hull, the ship was wrenched from the quay. But it still floated.

In the afternoon they came again, and with their howling sirens (called "Trumpets of Jericho") dived down into an inferno of flak. One Ju 87 was shot down; the two N.C.O.s Czuprna and Meinhardt crashed to their death. But their colleagues bombed accurately. First-Lieutenant Rummel and Lieutenant Lion both scored direct hits, forward and amidships, on the 1,540-ton destroyer *Wichr*, which promptly sank. Aboard the *Gryf* the forecastle was pulverised and magazines went up in flames. It was finally finished off in a low-level raid by the general-purpose coastal squadron 3/706 under Captain Stein. Burning and listing heavily, it sank in shallow water.

Above all, it was the *Stuka* that cleared the way for the German armour and infantry, and made rapid victory possible. How then, it may be asked, did it happen to be there?

The origin and development of the German dive-bomber is inseparably linked with the name of one man: Ernst Udet. The same Udet who, with sixty-two victories, had been the most successful German fighter pilot of World War I, apart from Manfred von Richthofen. The man whom the Allies, despite their complete ban on German flying, had failed to keep on the ground; who had rigged himself a flying machine and in deepest secrecy gone on flying. The man who had become the "patron saint" of stunt flyers; whose breath-taking aerobatics almost on the "deck" had thrilled spectators in thousands. A man with a charmed life, survivor of a dozen crashes. A man with an obsession.

On September 27, 1933, at the factory airfield of Curtiss-Wright in Buffalo, U.S.A., Udet was trying out the then sensational airplane, the Curtiss Hawk. It was not new to him. Two years previously he had already used this robust biplane to demonstrate his hair-raising stunts before an applauding crowd at a flying display held at Cleveland, Ohio. He let the machine fall like a stone, pulled out a few hundred feet from the ground, and climbed at once back into the sky.

From the first moment he was thrilled with the plane. If only he possessed one, what a difference it would make to his flying displays back home!

Now he was trying out two of them. Not only that, but they were his for the asking—he could buy them! He could not yet believe it. At the last moment, surely the U.S. authorities would refuse an export permit. After all, these machines, with their diving performance, had a military potential. One could, for example, use one to dive from high altitude on a warship, and sink it with a single bomb. It did not occur to Udet that the American defence ministry thought just nothing of such ideas, and that that was the only reason he got his permit.

But there was, also, the question of finance. The two planes together cost a small fortune—over $30,000. And though Udet had made a lot of money, he had thrown it away again with both hands. Where was he to raise the sum?

The answer was: from the political revolution in Germany. The National Socialists had just come to power, and Herman Goering, himself a fighter pilot of World War I, had been appointed Reich Commissioner of Aviation by Hitler.

Goering planned to build up a new Luftwaffe, secretly. Many former pilots, casting aside their hard-won civilian jobs, joined him. But not Udet. For the moment Goering could offer only office jobs, and Udet wanted to fly.

Goering did not give up. As soon as he heard about Udet's fanciful dive-bombing ideas, he saw the chance of holding the popular flying idol in this direction. He signalled:

"Udet, buy a couple of those Curtiss-Hawks on your own account. We will defray the cost."

He had said "we". Udet still did not believe it. Confronted by Curtiss-Wright's sales director, he hesitated.

"But Mr. Udet, the money has already been lodged with our bank!"

Goering made one condition. Before the two planes became Udet's absolute property, they were to be submitted to a thorough examination by the Rechlin test centre, branch of the new Luftwaffe's Technical Office.

Scarcely had Rechlin unpacked and put them together before a commission from Berlin arrived, in December 1933. Udet himself demonstrated the aircraft's diving power. Four times he climbed into the sky, dropped like a stone, pulled out laboriously, and repeated the performance. When it was over, he was in no state to climb out of the cockpit. The repeated dives, and still more the levellings-out, had sapped all his strength.

Erhard Milch, Goering's secretary of state, eyed the hero's sudden pallor quizzically. If Udet himself was not happy in the machine, who would be? What was the idea anyway? This diving business was nonsense. No material would stand up to it for long, let alone human beings! The Hawks were pronounced to be quite unsuitable as the basis of a German air force.

So Udet got them back more quickly than he had anticipated. Now they were really his, and he flew them again and again. The human constitution can adapt itself to almost anything. By the summer of 1934 he had achieved such mastery in the vertical dive that for the first time he was ready to feature it in his aerobatic displays. Then, on one of his last practice flights at Tempelhof, disaster overtook him, during the always crucial pull-out. Under pressure from the stick the Hawk reared up. The tail unit failed to take the strain, and after fluttering wildly fell off. But Udet survived. His parachute opened just before his heavy body hit the ground. Once more he had enjoyed amazing luck.

But the dive-bombing idea had caught on. Officers and engineers of the Technical Office developed it further—at that time right against the declared wishes of their immediate superiors.

They calculated just what sort of blueprint would be required if a contract for a dive-bomber were eventually placed with the arms industry. To withstand the tensile strain of repeated diving such a machine must, above all, be exceptionally robust. It must be able to attack in an all-but vertical position, yet its speed must be restricted by air brakes to below 375 m.p.h.—the limit, it was then considered, for both material and men.

The greatest headache was the engine. In 1935 the best output of an aeroengine was around 600 horse-power, and no more powerful one was in sight. So equipped, an aircraft would be slow and vulnerable during both the approach and breakaway. Hence the need to provide space for a second crew-man armed with a machine-gun to defend the rear—the direction from which enemy fighters would attack.

While the technical details of the future *Stuka* thus took shape, it was still officially banned, but its tactical merits were coming to be recognised by the new Luftwaffe's first chief of staff, Lieutenant-General Walther Wever.

Horizontal bombers at high altitude could use their bombs only against area targets. Reliable bomb-sights did not yet exist. A dive-bomber, however, would aim with the whole aircraft, and its accuracy would be much greater. A few *Stukas* with just a few bombs could, it was believed, achieve better results than a whole *Geschwader* of high-flying horizontal bombers. This consideration tipped the scales. For with raw materials in short supply, economy was the first consideration.

One of the most resolute opponents of the *Stuka* was, oddly, the chief of the Technical Office's development section, Major (as he then was) Wolfram Freiherr von Richthofen, cousin of the famous fighter ace. At Berlin's

15. The man largely responsible for Luftwaffe equipment—in his capacity as head of the Technical Office, and later as chief of air supply—was Ernst Udet, here seen talking to Professor Willy Messerschmitt. It was he who introduced the idea of the dive-bomber after his experience with the Curtiss Hawk, which he brought from the U.S.A., and later decided on the manufacture of the Ju 87.

16. The Curtiss Hawk, which Ernst Udet brought back from the U.S. **17.** A Ju 87, releasing its bombs in a dive.

18. The gunner, with his single 7.90mm MG 15, guards the *Stuka's* rear. The Ju 87 was a slow aircraft, particularly vulnerable after pulling out of a dive.

Technical High School he had taken a degree of doctor of engineering, and the terms of his present appointment were the promotion of new ideas. But the *Stuka* roused in him the deepest mistrust. His reasons: it would be much too slow and unwieldy; accuracy of aim would only be possible in a dive below 3,000 feet—and that would be the end. At that level they would be shot down like a row of sparrows by flak, not to mention enemy fighters!

It says much for the Technical Office that the development contract was nevertheless placed with industry as early as January 1935, with Richthofen still in office. There was even to be a competition, in which Arado, Blöhm & Voss, Heinkel and Junkers would all take part. In this the firm of Junkers had a clear advantage. What the Luftwaffe wanted had already been projected on the drawing-board by its chief engineer, Pohlmann, in 1933. It was in fact the Ju 87, which embraced all the present military-cum-technical requirements. The first prototype could be built at once.

Junkers also had the benefit of many years of recent experience. Already before 1930 the firm had a branch at Malmö in Sweden, where the K 47—a two-seater fighter with dive potential—was built. This was now used as a "test bed" for the air brakes prescribed by the Luftwaffe. It was even equipped with an automatic pull-out device coupled to the altimeter.

So only a few weeks after the air ministry had delivered its blue print, the first prototype, known as the Ju 87 V1, was already in the air. Its bulky frame with low-set inverted gull wings, elongated glazed cockpit, and rigid under-carriage with fairings like trousers, was hardly a thing of beauty. But solid and robust it was.

Although air brakes had still to be mounted, the steepness of dive attained during test flights constantly increased—till one day in autumn 1935 the unknown limits were exceeded. During the dive the tail unit was ripped off and the machine hurtled into the ground. Patiently the tests were pursued with the next two prototypes, the V2 and V3.

In January 1936 Udet at last yielded to the pressure of his old war comrades and joined the new Luftwaffe as a colonel. His first position was that of Inspector of Fighters. But his chief interest, now as before, remained the work on the embryo dive-bomber. In his little Siebel touring plane, he flew restlessly from factory to factory, urging the people concerned to greater efforts. Arado's dive-bomber was an all-metal biplane, the Ar 81; Blöhm & Voss of Hamburg's was the Ha 137, which failed to follow the blueprint inasmuch it was only a single-seater, and more suitable as a "battle-plane" than as a dive-bomber.

In the end it was touch and go between Heinkel and Junkers. Heinkel had built a very racy-looking plane, the He 118, but its dive stability had still to be shown. In this respect Junkers with their Ju 87, were far ahead of their competitors.

At this stage of affairs June 1936 was to be a decisive month for the Luftwaffe. On June 3rd its chief of Staff, Wever, suffered his fatal crash while at the controls of a Heinkel "Blitz" over Dresden. On the 9th Richthofen, from his office at the Technical Bureau, issued his last fulmination against the *Stuka*. In secret directive LC 2 No. 4017/36 he ordered: "Further development of the Ju 87 shall be discontinued. . . ."

A day later, on June 10th, Ernst Udet took over the Technical Office in succession to General Wimmer. Goering had offered him this post before, but he had hung back, hating the idea of sitting at a desk. He only accepted now because as head of the Bureau he could help the *Stuka* to stage its final break-through.

Richthofen joined the Spanish Civil War as chief of staff to the Condor Legion. The *Stuka* idea had triumphed.

The question as to whether Heinkel or Junkers should get the production contract was shelved pending comparison trials of their two aircraft in the autumn. The Ju 87 could dive steeply and pull out safely. The He 118 was considerably faster and more manoeuvrable, but its test pilot had only been diving obliquely. It was believed that was the limit of its tolerance.

A few months later Udet decided to see for himself. Casting all caution to the winds, he stood the He 118 on its head—and promptly crashed. As so often before, he escaped at the last moment by parachute.

The die was cast. The birth-pangs of the Ju 87 *Stuka* were over.

On August 15, 1939, at the air base of Cottbus, *Stukas* were lined up in formation with running engines. They belonged to I/StG 76, known as the "Graz" *Gruppe*, because their peace-time station was in Styria, Austria. Now, as part of the war preparations against Poland, they had been moved up to Silesia and placed under the orders of Lieutenant-General von Richthofen. But today, under the eyes of the Luftwaffe's top brass, they were to make an attack in close formation on the military training ground at Neuhammer, with cement smoke bombs.

The C.O., Captain Walter Sigel, had briefed his pilots to approach the target in attack formation and go down in quick succession. Then the weather reconnaissance planes landed and reported 7/10 cloud cover over the target area between 6,000 and 2,500 feet, but good ground visibility below. The mode of attack was correspondingly adjusted. They were to approach at 12,000 feet, dive through the clouds, and get the target in their sights during the last 900 –1,200 feet before pulling out.

"Any questions? Then Tally-Ho!"[1] Sigel concluded, and minutes later the *Stukas* taxied to the start, took off in sections, and formed up into a wedge over the airfield.

Like all *Stuka* units just before the war, I/StG 76 was equipped with the latest-pattern Ju 87B. Its chief advantage over the A—of which just a few had operated in Spain—was its much more powerful Jumo 211 Da engine, whose output of 1,150 h.p. was nearly double that of its predecessor. It could carry a bomb load of 1,000 lb., had a cruising speed of some 200 m.p.h., and a radius of action of approximately 125 miles. This was still not enough for long-range operations, but was adequate for army support. And that was what the *Stukas* were mainly there for.

At 06.00, as high above the clouds I/StG 76 approached its target, Captain Sigel gave the word to assume attack formation. He would go in first with his adjutant, First-Lieutenant Eppen, on his left, and his technical officer, First-Lieutenant Müller, on his right. Squadrons 2 and 3 were to follow, and finally 1 Squadron, which as the wedge dissolved now took up its position at the rear.

The leader of this squadron, First-Lieutenant Dieter Peltz, was later in the

---

[1] In German : "*Hals- und Beinbruch !*"—the traditional farewell to pilots about to take off. Literal translation : "Break your neck and legs!"—*Translator's Note.*

war to become General-Officer Commanding bomber forces. At this moment neither he nor any of his men dreamt that their present tactical position was to save their lives.

As on a hundred practices the C.O. tipped over and began his dive. Section after section followed, screaming down towards the cloud.

Ten seconds . . . fifteen seconds . . . they should be through the milk-white fog. But how long is fifteen seconds? Who can calculate time during a dive? No good looking at the altimeter; the needle had gone haywire. Each pilot just thought to himself: "Any moment the cloud will end, and you must line up like lightning on the target. . . ."

Captain Sigel wiped the sweat from his brow as he plunged deeper and deeper through the murk. At any instant now the ground must come into view. Suddenly the white curtain ahead darkened. In a split second he took things in: that dark patch just ahead was the *ground*! With at most 300 feet to go he was diving to destruction—and with the whole *Gruppe* after him! Wrenching the stick towards him he shouted into the microphone:

"PULL OUT! PULL OUT! IT'S GROUND FOG!"

The forest rushed up at him. Just ahead was a ride cut through it. The Junkers sailed into it, reared up and just came under control. He had missed the ground by literally six feet, and made his getaway along the ride between the trees.

Climbing carefully up, Sigel looked around. To the left Eppen had crashed through the trees and remained hanging in the branches. To the right Müller's plane burst into flames. He was spared witnessing the rest.

Every one of 2 Squadron's nine aircraft went full tilt into the ground. Most of 3 Squadron got clear. The rest pulled out too convulsively, began a loop and fell stern first into the forest.

Lieutenant Hans Stepp, section leader in the last squadron to go down (No. 1), had just started his dive when the desperate voice of his C.O. reached him on the radio. At once he pulled back the stick and shot up through the cloud again. As he circled above it with his squadron, brown smoke gushed through and rose up towards the heavens.

At one blow the Luftwaffe had lost thirteen dive-bombers and twenty-six young air crew. Witness of the catastrophe was Wolfram von Richthofen, the man who had consistently opposed the *Stukas*, but who was now about to lead them in war. When Hitler heard the news, he stared speechlessly out of the window for ten minutes. But however superstitious he may have been, there is no evidence that he was in the least deterred from his warlike designs.

A court of enquiry was summoned the same day, under the presidency of General Hugo Sperrle. But no charge could be preferred. The ground fog must have materialised in the bare hour between weather reconnaissance and operational take-off. The C.O., immediately he grasped the danger, had done his utmost to warn his men.

His unit, I/StG 76, was at once brought up to strength by stripping the other *Stuka* formations. From the first day of the Polish campaign it was sent against fortifications, cross-roads, bridges, railway stations and trains. In the resulting destruction the tragedy of Neuhammer was soon forgotten.

On the morning of September 2nd Generals Reichenau and Richthofen reached an agreement that priority *Stuka* support should be given to

Lieutenant-General Schmidt's 1st *Panzer* Division. Far ahead of the XVIth
Army Corps, it was now thrusting north past the heavy Tschenstochau
defences towards the crossing of the river Warte. The Luftwaffe's main task
was to frustrate every enemy counter-movement; its secondary one to cover
the division's exposed southern flank.

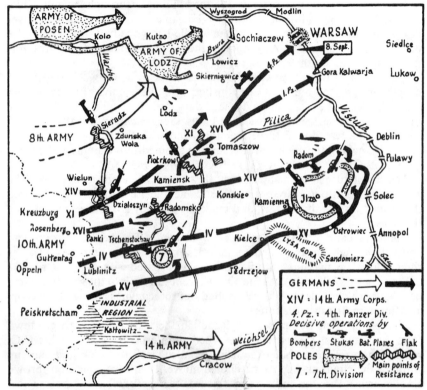

The Battle of Poland. By the eighth day of the Polish campaign advanced elements of the
German armour were already in Warsaw, and the Polish army, on the point of disintegrating, was everywhere falling back on the Vistula. To this success the Luftwaffe had
greatly contributed. Its concentrated bomber, dive-bomber and low-level attacks ahead of
the German front broke the Polish resistance. The map shows the sector of the 10th Army
as it pushed forward from Silesia, supported by formations of *Luftflotte* 4. Raids by the
latter also paralysed the enemy's traffic and communications networks.

With remarkable precision forty *Stukas* of I/StG 2 and I/StG 76 managed
to destroy the railway station of Piotrkow at the very moment when Polish
troops were detraining. Colonel Schwarzkopff's StG 77 launched repeated
attacks on enemy columns near Radomsko; and the XIth and XIVth Army
Corps radioed for air support against stiff Polish resistance encountered in
their advance on the Warte at Dzialoszyn.

Richthofen had ordered his reconnaissance squadron, 1 (F)/124, to keep a
standing patrol of one Do 17 over the great Warte bridge south of Radomsko.
The "Flying Pencil" crews were not only to report on Polish movements,
but prevent any preparations to blow up the bridge by making low-level
attacks with machine-gun fire and fragmentation bombs. For it was towards
this important crossing that the 1st *Panzer* Division was pushing.

Next morning, September 3rd, the 1st and 4th *Panzer* Divisions, having surprised and taken their bridges the night before, were north of the Warte and pushing on far ahead of the rest of the front past Radomsko towards Kamiensk and Piotrkow.

Further west along the Warte both *Stukagruppen* of Colonel Baier's LG 2 dive-bombed Dzialoszyn in support of the XIth Army Corps, which then took the city without loss, in face of a foe who was seemingly paralysed.

Scarcely had the *Stukas* and "battle-planes" completed these tasks ahead of the 10th Army's left wing, when in the afternoon they were sent south to help its right. This had encountered a strong enemy concentration southeast of Tschenstochau. Here, under pressure of air attack, there took place on September 4th the first, mass surrender; that of the 7th Polish Division.

So it went on—hour after hour, day after day—all along the van of the 10th Army's front. For the first time in history a powerful air force was taking a direct part in ground operations. Its telling effect surprised both friend and foe. Yet to the Army the concept of air support was so new and strange that frequently, however critical the situation, it was neither called for nor even considered. The Luftwaffe had often to "force" its help upon the ground troops uninvited.

But the new principle of warfare had its growing pains. As the impetuous advance proceeded, it often became difficult for aircrews to locate the front, or to distinguish between the last units of the enemy and the first of their own. If Richthofen had not had his own liaison officers right up in the van, confusion would have been complete.

Even so, there were unfortunate incidents. German bombs were dropped on German lines. Panels laid out by the troops to mark the front were usually not clear enough. On September 8th, in their efforts to close the enemy's line of retreat, the *Stukas* smashed the Vistula bridges at Gora Kalwarja at the very moment when advance elements of the 1st *Panzer* Division were arriving on the western bank. This effectively prevented the division from forming a bridgehead on the other side and continuing its advance.

Such mishaps were, however, exceptional. They did not detract from the important role played by the "flying artillery" in the swift advance of the ground forces. This included, besides direct assault on centres of enemy resistance at the front, the even more effective disruption of his supporting lines in the rear. In this *Stukas*, bombers and long-range fighters all took part. Bridges, roads, railways, and above all communications, were all blasted into irreparable disorder, with the result that the enemy could no longer organise his resistance nor develop a plan of operations. From day to day the whole troop-movement system behind the front became more and more chaotic.

At war's outset the Poles presented a united and only gradually yielding front. But from the fourth day onwards the Germans began to break through and outflank their opponents. The Polish retreat was outpaced by the German advance.

As this pushed on along the roads, the Poles would melt into the woods on either side, and lie hidden from the eyes of the Luftwaffe. Then, when night came, they would resume their retreat cross-country towards the Vistula. Though this was no organised movement, the Poles knew well that only beyond the Vistula lay salvation, that only there could a new front be established.

Equally, the Germans knew that only on the river's western bank could a swift decision be obtained. Only there could the enemy be outflanked, encircled and forced to surrender. At all costs his escape over the river must be prevented. Their own troops must get there first.

Thus, along the whole front, there began a race for the Vistula.

3. "The Night of Ilza"

On September 7th air reconnaissance located strong enemy forces opposite the right flank of the 10th Army. They were concentrated north-east of Lysa Gora in an area of wooded hills and south of Radom, and their centre was thought to be in the extensive forest bordering the town of Ilza. Their movement was clearly eastward, towards the Vistula crossings.

General von Reichenau issued orders for an encirclement operation, as follows: The XIVth Army Corps was to push forward past Radom towards the Vistula at Deblin to cut off the north. The IVth, following more slowly in its wake, was to act as a rearguard stop, closing the trap from the west; while the XVth, racing forward on the right, was to complete the encirclement, interposing itself between the enemy and the river.

Early next morning Lieutenant-General Kuntzen, commanding the 3rd "Light" Division, sent out from Ostrowiec the "Ditfurth" Combat Group to reconnoitre Ilza and Radom. This Group, which took its name from Colonel von Ditfurth, commander of the 9th "Mounted" Rifle Regiment, consisted besides his own regiment of No. 2 Company of the 67th *Panzer* Battalion, No. 1 Battalion of the 80th Artillery Regiment, and lastly No. 1 Battalion of the 22nd Flak Regiment with four batteries.

Flak as a field weapon. On September 8th the Luftwaffe's I/*Flakregiment* 22, during the attack on Ilza, provided direct covering fire for the infantry. The following night, positioned in the very front line, it repulsed all counter-attacks, thus at a decisive moment preventing a Polish break-through to the Vistula. It was the birth of a reputation that later became legendary.

The last, which belonged to the Luftwaffe, had advanced with the forefront of the Army to provide on-the-spot protection against any attacking Polish aircraft. But while none of these had been seen, the last few days' advance had been so breathless that the range-finding and communication sections had got held up in the traffic, and only the batteries themselves had come through.

Thus for anti-aircraft purposes these were now of little use. They could, however, justify their presence by taking part in the ground battle. Both infantry and artillery knew what penetrative power the flak shells, with their flat trajectory, possessed—especially when directed against visible ground targets.

Round noon the Group's advance elements reached Pilatka, the last village before Ilza, two and a half miles on. They could go no further, for suddenly the "cavalrymen" had to take cover under a heavy concentration of fire from the hilly terrain round Ilza's old fort, "*Alte Schanze*". At the same time clouds of dust rising from the roads entering the town from north and south marked the approach of enemy columns. Further troop movements were seen to the north-east. The woods to the south-west, though quiet at the moment, must also be full of Poles.

The enemy artillery fired ferociously. From Hill 241, two miles west of Ilza, it commanded the whole field of operations. A troop, 2/Kav.Sch.Rgt. 8, was sent against it, but could only proceed a few hundred yards.

As his other units reached Pilatka from the east, Colonel von Ditfurth put them into positions west of the village, and the rifle sections slowly worked their way through the rolling country towards Ilza. But half a mile from the "*Alte Schanze*" they came under heavy fire and could go no further.

At 13.20 Major Weisser, commanding I/Flakregiment 22, reached Pilatka ahead of his batteries, and had to dodge rifle and machine-gun fire to get to Ditfurth's command post. There he was ordered to bring up his batteries through the village, position them south of it, and give the hard-pressed riflemen direct covering fire.

First to join battle were six 20-mm guns of 5 Battery under Lieutenant Seidenath. These were followed by three others, while IV Platoon was held back as battalion reserve. Seidenath pointed all nine guns to the south, since it was in that direction that an attempt to encircle the town would have to be made, the frontal attack having been repulsed.

Meanwhile the flak battalion's 2 and 3 Batteries, with their heavy 88-mm guns, took up position somewhat further east, adjoining the regular artillery's 105-mm field howitzers. Conditions for the former were by no means favourable. They stood in a depression, screened by the rise and fall of the ground from view of the enemy—ideal for the howitzers, with their curved trajectory directed by forward observers, but not for the flak, which required direct sighting on the target. Here this was impossible. One gun had only to be located on a rise for its crew to be mown down before they could fire a shot.

So for the moment the flak guns had to be content with more distant targets. Once their shells slammed into a Polish troop column on a stretch of road north of Ilza which happened to be in their visual field. But in the infantry battle raging little over a mile from their own positions the 88-mms could take no part.

There, right in the front line, were the 20-mm guns of 5 Battery. But while these fired south, they were themselves exposed to machine-gun fire from the "*Alte Schanze*" on their western flank. The slightest movement of the crews brought a hail of bullets.

In the end their situation became untenable. The battery commander, Captain Röhler, ordered III Platoon at least to be dragged out of the line of fire of the Polish mortars and anti-tank guns. This was successfully accomplished, and the three guns took up a new, staggered position which later, during the night battle, proved most advantageous.

At the same time, namely 18.00, the German infantry and flak guns had to meet the first Polish counter-attack from the south, supported by artillery, tanks and flame-throwers. If the Poles felt strong enough to attack in daylight, one wondered what they would be up to after dark.

Right amongst the Germans' most advanced positions, just 800 yards from the *"Alte Schanze"*, was Hill 246. On it crouched the German artillery spotters. During the afternoon they had spotted a whole string of enemy machine-gun and anti-tank posts which could not be brought under their own artillery fire, and were equally impossible targets for the Luftwaffe's 20-mm flak guns in their present positions. The cry went up:

"Put a flak gun on Hill 246!"

Obediently the crew of 5 Battery's no. 3 gun, led by Section Leader Maurischat, man-handled their weapon on to a knoll just behind the vital hill. But from here its field of fire was still limited, so the bombardiers, rushing their 16-cwt. charge down its slope, tried to get its momentum to carry it up the slope of Hill 246 opposite. Half-way up it stuck.

Down ran the observation officers and, putting their weight behind it, forced the gun up to just short of the summit. With everything ready and the magazines loaded, gunner Kniehase lined up his target with the observers' telescope and took his seat. Then, choosing the moment when the Poles were reloading their nearest machine-gun, officers and men pushed the gun to the pinnacle and it opened up. Forty shots were fired, straight into the target.

Almost at once Kniehase and his gun were behind the hill again. Not a moment too soon, for seconds later the summit was lashed with fire.

The performance was repeated eight times. And each time one enemy machine-gun or anti-tank gun post was reduced to silence, to the cheers of the troopers, who for hours had been pinned down in the undulating scrubland unable to inch forward or back.

Finally Kniehase lined up his weapon on a tall watch-tower rising above the *"Alte Schanze"*, from which several heavy machine-guns commanded a huge area. In four bursts he fired eighty high-explosive shells at the loopholes and platform.

The machine-guns were silenced, but the tower stood: the missiles could only scratch it. Soon it would be manned afresh.

It was after seven o'clock, and daylight was starting to fade, when suddenly officers and men turned in surprise at the sound of a continuous low buzzing. Oblivious to the enemy fire, a heavy German prime-mover was towing an 88-mm gun up the eastern flank of Hill 246. Major Weisser had sent one of 3 Battery's weapons to support the lonely 20-mm with its much greater fire power.

But the summit was too small. As soon as the gun was unlimbered it wobbled about. Setting frenziedly to with spades, observation officers and crews worked to enlarge the platform and secure the gun. Finally, in the twilight, the first shot was fired. A miss, and once more the gun fell askew. More levelling and another shot: a direct hit on the tower. The third shell broke away the masonry on one side, and after a series of further hits the tower disintegrated in dust and rubble. It was high time, for night had fallen.

Hill 246 was evacuated and the two flak guns returned to their batteries. Though all his units were in the front line and he had no reserves, Colonel von Ditfurth still believed he could hold his positions, even at night.

But shortly after eight o'clock the Poles launched their first mass attack and the German front was thrown back. Enemy armour thrust along the way to Pilatka, and Ditfurth himself was mown down by machine-gun fire while defending his command post, gun in hand.

As the German infantry fell back before the enemy's hour-long barrage, men streamed through the flak positions, singly and in groups. But the young Luftwaffe officers succeeded in rounding up a lot of them, and formed them into a new defence line between the guns. The Poles, however, were hot on their heels. Suddenly they were standing there, right in the middle of 5 Battery's site. Brandishing his revolver, Lieutenant Seidenath forced the enemy soldiers to join his gunners in pushing the guns around to face this new line of attack from the west.

No sooner was this done, than the 20-mm flak roared forth from every barrel against the oncoming enemy. This direct barrage was too much for the Poles, and their attack was broken.

For the moment the flak had held its positions. But could it go on defending itself in the dark against the further attacks that were bound to follow?

At 19.30 hours Captain Röhler had already sent 5 Battery's searchlight squadron forward from the train of vehicles. Unfortunately its advance coincided with the Polish attack down the Ilza-Pilatka road. Two searchlights were damaged and caught up in the general whirl of retreat. But the other two were unscathed, and fighting their way against the tide managed to reach 5 Battery's position after the enemy had already outflanked it.

To Seidenath the two 60-cm searchlights came as a godsend. Carefully he arranged them so that they could illuminate the battery's foreground from either side.

The night was pitch-black. Around 23.30 hours Polish words of command were heard just in front of the German positions. The message to get ready to fire was passed in a whisper from one crew to the next. Then the right-hand searchlight was switched on. As the enemy ducked under its glare, the flak hammered forth. After three seconds the light went out, to be replaced by the left one. So they alternated, changing their positions during the moments of extinction. Before the Poles could aim the machine-guns at the shining orbs they had always gone out.

In this way, after a quarter of an hour's battle, this attack too was beaten off. Two further ones were likewise unsuccessful. Towards 05.30 hours 5 Battery at last received orders carefully to break contact and try to join up with the main German defence line which had formed five miles to the rear.

Meanwhile both the 88-mm batteries, Nos. 2 and 3/Flak 22, had also been overtaken by events. Since 03.00 hours they had encountered overwhelming Polish forces pouring out of the woods to the south in an all-out attempt, under cover of darkness, to break through to the north-east: to the Vistula.

The heaviest attack came at 04.10. In dense formations the Poles came storming over the intervening hillocks. Hand-to-hand, with bayonets fixed, the crews fought to defend their guns. The German losses in officers and men were grievous. Amongst those who fell were the C.O., Major Weisser, and 3 Battery's commander, Captain Jablonski.

Finally the 20-mm guns of 5 Battery's III Platoon opened fire into the Polish flank, and this attack also came to a bloody halt. As the enemy faltered the bombardiers sprang from cover and, joining in personally, drove them back up to 800 yards in the direction they had come from.

But the "charge of the Luftwaffe" did not eliminate the danger. Increasing machine-gun fire lashed into the flak positions, and the Poles advanced yet again. First-Lieutenant Rückwardt, now the senior surviving officer of the whole 1st Battalion, had already twice sent his adjutant, Lieutenant Haccius, back to Divisional H.Q. to request support.

As the battle continued, the Germans were anxiously counting their remaining ammunition, when over the hillocks rolled four German tanks. Guns blazing, they had joined in the fight, and once again the enemy was put to flight.

They had arrived in the nick of time. Under their protection the flak force withdrew, leaving behind three 88-mm guns of 3 Battery whose prime-movers had been destroyed, but not before their firing mechanisms had been dismantled.

It was already daylight as the batteries drove eastwards at full speed along the road from Pilatka. For the road was now being used by the enemy too. As they proceeded they came under rifle fire from its ditches. Twice Rückwardt had to order the leading 88-mm to be unlimbered to provide covering fire as the rest dashed on. And after five miles they reached the German defence line.

The night of September 8th–9th—"The Night of Ilza"—had ended. This battle, in which soldiers of the Luftwaffe prevented parts of the 16th Polish Division from reaching the Vistula, was the foundation of the legendary reputation that the Luftwaffe's flak contingents later achieved as a field force.

With daylight, the Poles had to retire to the cover of their woods. For by now the German encirclement had been completed. After 09.00 a new armoured attack by the 3rd ("Light") Division cleaned up the Ilza area. And after that the airborne Luftwaffe went in for the clinching battle. Richthofen's whole force, bar the Henschels, dived down upon the half-dozen Polish divisions now surrrounded south of Radom. Flying low over the battlefield, they sought out their targets on roads, tracks, and in villages.

"With their white crosses on their backs, the tanks showed us the way," a squadron commander of Colonel Schwarzkopff's StG 77 reported. "Wherever they went, we came across throngs of Polish troops, against which our 100-lb. fragmentation bombs were deadly. After that we went almost down to the deck firing our machine-guns. The confusion was indescribable."

On this September 9th Richthofen sent more than 150 *Stukas*, together with single- and twin-engined fighters, again and again against the surrounded Polish divisions. And on the ground the pincers went on tightening remorsely. On September 13th the last Polish units in the Ilza woods laid down their arms.

All the same, the Radom encirclement was of secondary significance. The focus of the war had shifted to the approaches to the Polish capital. On September 7th the XVIth Army Corps' two *Panzer* divisions had broken through the enemy's last defence positions on either side of Piotrkow. Next day the 1st reached the Vistula at Gora Kalwarja, and the 4th a main road north-east of Tomaszow with a sign reading:

"To Warsaw—125 kilometres."

Now the Luftwaffe's wholesale bombing of railways, stations and trains paid its dividend. The Poles could bring up no new reinforcements against the German armoured spearhead. In one great movement in the afternoon of September 8th, supported by the Henschel squadrons of II/LG 2, the 4th *Panzer* Division reached the periphery of Warsaw. At five o'clock General von Reichenau ordered this "open city" to be taken by a *coup de main*.

Next morning the bombers and dive-bombers of the 4th Air Force were to open their attack on the city's military keypoints—*if* it was defended. The Luftwaffe was ready. But the question remained: Would the Poles turn their beautiful capital into a battlefield?

4. Warsaw—an "Open City"?

Adjoining the Polish stud farm of Wolborz, near Tomaszow, a piece of tolerably level ground now served as II/LG 2's operational airfield. Like other close-combat aircraft, such as the *Stukas* and fighters, the Henschels had moved forward after a few days to emergency bases in Poland to keep up their "flying artillery" support of the swiftly advancing ground forces.

The Wolborz strip had been chosen by a well-tried method. If a car could be driven over a piece of ground at 30 m.p.h. without too many bumps, then it would also do for the Henschel "one-two-threes". Two hundred yards was all they needed.

But early in the morning of September 9th just one aircraft—a Fieseler Storch—took off and headed for Warsaw. This was the C.O., Major Spielvogel, who for some days had made it his practice to go and investigate the front line situation for himself. After that his squadrons could join battle with clear instructions. Today, with the tanks about to push into Warsaw itself, his reconnaissance seemed all the more necessary.

Flying low along the main road, the Storch reached the city, Corporal Szigorra sitting at the controls to let Spielvogel concentrate on his observations. First into view came a sea of houses, amongst which stretched a wide field of bomb craters and ruined hangars: Okecie airfield, scene of so many attacks by bombers and dive-bombers at the campaign's outset. Already beyond this, heading for the districts of Mokotow and Okhota, Spielvogel spotted the vanguard of the German armour. Directing Szigorra to fly on ahead of it, he began looking for prospective targets such as camouflaged gun positions, pockets of resistance or barricades.

Suddenly he located a battery of light flak protected by the embankment of the Warsaw-Radom railway. In the same moment it opened fire on his Storch. Shell splinters and bullets smacked into the fuselage and cockpit, Szigorra slumped down, hit in the stomach.

Spielvogel reached for the control column. But there was no hope of making a getaway. All he could do was try a forced landing on the street below—right in the middle of the Polish defences and perhaps 600–700 yards ahead of the German vanguard.

Despite continuous fire he managed to do it without crashing. Leaping out, he ran to the other side and pulled out his wounded pilot just before the machine burst into flames. Then he too sank to the ground, hit in the head.

Shortly afterwards the advancing troops found both airmen close beside the burnt-out wreck of their plane. Spielvogel—a reserve officer universally loved for his paternal nature—was dead. In his place, as leader of the *Gruppe*, Richthofen appointed the C.O. of 4 Squadron, Captain Otto Weiss.

Meanwhile 4 *Panzer* Division, in accordance with orders, had pushed deep into the built-up area. With his very limited force Lieutenant-General Reinhardt straddled three roads from the south and south-west leading to the suburbs of Mokotow, Okhota and Wola. As on the previous evening the Germans met bitter defensive fire. It came from dugouts and other prepared positions which the Poles had reinforced and barricaded during the night. Clearly they had no thought of yielding their capital without a struggle.

But still the attack gained ground, the tanks in the van, the shock troops in their wake. Then all at once there came a whine of shells, which exploded on all sides of the approach roads.

There could be no doubt, the Poles were firing from the east bank of the Vistula, from batteries in the suburb of Praga. To break up the German attack their shells were deliberately aimed at the western part of their own capital. They clearly intended to defend it at all costs—even the cost of their own dwelling houses. There could be no more talk of an "open city".

It was the signal Richthofen's close-combat formations had been waiting for. At their forward bases of Tschenstochau and Kruszyna the *Stukas* taxied to the runway. Colonel Schwarzkopff's StG 77 had just been reinforced by a new *Gruppe*, III/StG 51, so that Richthofen now had five *Gruppen* totalling some 140 *Stukas* at his disposal. And it was 140 *Stukas*, type Ju 87 B, that with perfect ground visibility took off for Warsaw.

Since the early attacks on Warsaw's airfields, aircraft factories and transmitting stations by Kesselring's *Luftflotte* 1 from East Prussia and Pomerania, only small formations had operated against the capital. These had bombed shunting stations and the Vistula bridges—without notable success.

The raid of September 8th was on a larger scale. Half-rolling into their dives over the shining ribbon of the Vistula, the *Stukas* dived with screaming sirens on their targets.

The bridges swelled at an uncomfortable rate in the bomb-sights. They were not the targets, but served as orientation posts divided up between the different units. The real targets were on the eastern bank: the heavy batteries that were shelling the western city. In a hail of flak the *Stukas* released their bombs, pulled out and zoomed up again.

Other formations bombarded the roads and railways leading from Prague to the east, to block, or at least interrupt, the frenzied enemy troop movements.

In the western city the ground resistance grew stiffer. The "battle-planes" were sent in, and many a street barricade had to be stormed by the infantry. By ten o'clock advance elements of the 35th *Panzer* Regiment and the 12th Rifle Regiment had reached Warsaw's main railway station. But here they ground to a halt. Their flanks, presented to a maze of streets on either side, were completely unprotected for miles back. The enemy had only to make a determined counter-attack for the two regiments to become entirely cut off. Realising the danger, General Reinhardt ordered a temporary cease-fire, and the regiments were pulled back to the outer suburbs. Reinhardt's report to the XVIth Army Corps read:

"After heavy losses my attack on the city has had to be discontinued. Unexpectedly sharp resistance by the enemy with all weapons has rendered a single armoured division supported by only four infantry battalions a quite insufficient force to obtain a decisive outcome. . . ."

But there was something else. Far in the rear of the over-extended XVIth Army Corps a development had occurred that no one had reckoned with—serious enough for the Luftwaffe, much against Goering's will, to suspend all operations against the city. It had to fly to the help of the 8th Army, dangerously threatened far to the west.

What had happened was this: the furious advance of von Reichenau's 10th Army to Warsaw and the middle Vistula had made it extremely hard for its northern neighbour, Blaskowitz's 8th Army, to keep up. Advancing via Lodz, the latter's task was to maintain contact on the north and plug all the holes the 10th Army had left in its rear, and do so with the utmost celerity. But the 8th Army consisted at the outset of only four infantry divisions. And the more it stepped up the rate of its advance, the less it was able to protect its own northern flank.

The danger was all the greater inasmuch as just to the north of it was a Polish force of equal strength proceeding in the same direction. Both were headed east, to Warsaw and across the Vistula. It was a collision course.

The kernel of this Polish force was the "Army of Posen". Till now it had scarcely been in action, the German lines of advance having by-passed it to the north and south. Its four divisions and two cavalry brigades were thus still up to full strength. Furthermore it was reinforced by parts of the "Pomerellen Army", which had withdrawn southwards before the German 4th Army's assault on Bromberg.

The Polish field commander, General Kutrzeba, had seen his chance as early as September 3rd: to make an attack southwards on the weak northern flank of the German 8th Army. But the Polish high command had withheld its permission. Kutrzeba was ordered to withdraw his divisions eastwards intact.

The Poles marched by night, and by day lay up in the forests. All that the German army reconnaissance planes spotted was an occasional troop column. They had no idea that here was a whole army in a splendid position to take their own troops in the rear.

On September 8th and 9th the Poles reached the region of Kutno, with the Vistula to the north of them and its tributary, the Bzura, to the south.

On the southern bank of the Bzura the 8th Army's 30th Infantry Division under Major-General von Briesen was formed up as a staggered rearguard, facing left and back. It was nothing but a slender screen.

General Kutrzeba did not let his chance slip twice. During the night of September 9th–10th he attacked southwards across the Bzura, piercing the German line in a number of places at the first attempt. The 30th Infantry Division streamed back in retreat.

It was the first and only large-scale offensive operation by the Poles during the whole campaign, and it forced the Germans to take drastic remedial action. General Blaskowitz's whole 8th Army had abruptly to stop its dash towards Warsaw and the Vistula, and turn right round to repair the enemy breaches in its rear. Not only that, but the 10th Army units inside Warsaw's periphery had to quit the capital and march back to front against the Bzura. This chess move by the 10th Army's chief of staff, Lieutenant-General Friedrich Paulus—later to command the Army of Stalingrad—contained the germ of his plan to turn the German reverse into a battle of encirclement in which the Poles would be annihilated.

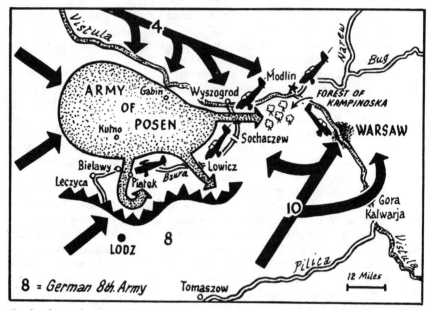

Battle of encirclement on the Bzura. While the German 8th and 10th Armies pushed forward to Warsaw and the Vistula, the Polish "Army of Posen", still fully intact, produced a threatening situation in their rear. The danger was overcome thanks to non-stop operations by the Luftwaffe, which led to the enemy becoming surrounded on the Bzura. After a nine-day battle 170,000 Poles gave themselves up.

Meanwhile the situation was so serious that on September 11th the German Army Group South, for the first time since the war's outbreak, called urgently for the commitment of maximum air strength against the region of Kutno. Any further attack on Warsaw, by either ground or air forces, had suddenly become quite out of the question.

All the more singular, therefore, was the scene enacted that same morning on the advanced landing field of Konskie, when a Ju 52 touched down bringing Hitler and his staff for a tour of the front. Up marched General von Reichenau, who solemnly boasted to the Führer that his army had already entered Warsaw on the tenth day of the campaign.

Richthofen, who was also present, could hardly believe his ears. Nothing about the army's withdrawal! Nothing about the perilous situation on the Bzura! He made haste to get back to his command post as soon as he could. The role of his close-support units was now more important than ever before.

On their landing field adjoining the Wolborz stud farm the Hs 123s of II/LG 2 stood ready for take-off. Captain Weiss, the new C.O., had briefed his squadron commanders on the new strategic set-up. The mission: low-level attacks on enemy columns near Piatek and Bielawy south of the Bzura. The Polish advance must at all costs be halted. For the "biplane battlers" the target, this time, would hardly be difficult to find. It was a whole army storming to the south.

With ten days' war experience behind them, the Henschel pilots had discovered what their main weapon was. It was not the brace of 100-lb. bombs they carried below the wings. Nor was it the two machine-guns atop the engine. It was something much more subtle: the psychological effect of the frightful noise made by the airscrew at certain revs. Optimum r.p.m. for this were 1,800. A glance at the instruments and they could be achieved. The planes then went down emitting a sound like heavy machine-gun fire.

So attuned, the Henschels now dived down to thirty feet above the enemy, spreading panic and terror in their train. Men and horses broke their ranks. Vehicles crashed together into inextricable knots. Hardly a column escaped being dispersed.

The strange thing was that the "battle planes" could not risk firing a shot. Their machine-guns were designed to fire through the airscrews, but at these high revs. they would shatter them in pieces.

All the same, these obsolescent, open-cockpit biplanes achieved results that, measured by the number of bombs they dropped, were astonishing. Not that II/LG 2 carried the flag alone. From their new air-strips round Radom several *Stuka* formations delivered precision attacks throughout the Kutno area. They wrecked the Bzura bridges, tore up the roads, and wreaked havoc on the advancing columns of armour and vehicles.

Even the long-range bombers, which in the previous few days had been chiefly engaged in attacking rail and industrial targets far to the east of the Vistula, were brought into the battle. Mainly concerned was 1 Air Division under Major-General Grauert. At the outset of the campaign this had operated from Pomerania with the *Luftflotte* 1, but at the end of the Tucheler Heath fighting it had been transferred to the 4th Air Force in Silesia. KG 1 (Lieutenant-General Kessler), KG 26 (Colonel Siburg), and KG 4 (Colonel Fiebig) now bombed the enemy in waves.

Such an air assault could not be withstood for long. After two days the Polish advance south of the Bzura had been broken, and the crisis of the German 8th Army was over.

Incidentally, the Army contributed to a breach of Luftwaffe "security". At the express request of Army Group South a regiment of airborne troops, belonging to the High Command Reserve, was transported in Ju 52s and thrown into the battle north of Lodz. They belonged to a force which the Luftwaffe had built up under the strictest secrecy. Known as 7 Air Division, they comprised both airborne troops and paratroops, under the command of Lieutenant-General Kurt Student.

At its base in the Liegnitz region 7 Air Division lay at instant readiness to carry out a number of operations behind the enemy lines that were successively planned for it: the first at Dirschau, the second to take the Vistula bridge at Pulawy, the third to create a bridgehead on the San at Jaroslaw. But each time the orders were cancelled at the last moment, on the second occasion when the parachutists were already embarked and about to take off.

It seemed that the High Command was not yet ready to disclose its possession of this "secret weapon". All the more incomprehensible, therefore, was the committal to the Bzura front now of the division's only air-landing troop, the IR 16 under Colonel Kreysing. Student dubbed the order "the start of 7 Air Division's sell-out". The paratroops themselves were kept back. All they did instead was to garrison airfields and head-quarters in the Polish communications zone. As Student said: "We might as well have spared ourselves the effort of training them."

During the night of September 12th–13th General Kutrzeba, the Polish commander, had to withdraw his divisions back across the Bzura, and this regrouping became the new centre for attack. The German encirclement was not yet complete, and during the next few days the Poles tried to break through it eastwards towards Warsaw and Modlin.

As the battle flared up in different places, the Luftwaffe again kept up a constant succession of attacks with hundreds of planes, culminating in the uninterrupted low-level attacks of September 16th and 17th. This time even a long-range fighter *Gruppe* from East Prussia took part.

This was Major Grabmann's I/LG 1, whᴖse twin-engined Me 110s had fought the majority of the air-to-air battles over Warsaw at the start of the campaign. Now it was allocated a narrow strip of front from the Bzura-Vistula confluence to Gabin. Grabmann limited each squadron to just ten minutes over the target area: five minutes for approach, five for withdrawal. But during their brief appearance his men were ordered to use up their entire ammunition, machine-guns and 20-mm cannon alike.

They did not have to look for a target. It was everything that moved; on roads, tracks, fields and clearings—wherever the remnants of the Polish army tried to force their way through.

Back home at their East Prussian base the squadron commanders gave their reports to the C.O. Grabmann looked silently into their faces, then voiced the general opinion: "Oh, for a fair and decent dog-fight!"

General Kutrzeba reported on the repeated *Stuka* and Henschel attacks on troop concentrations both sides of the Bzura, and on the fords and field bridges across it, as follows:

"Towards ten o'clock a furious air assault was made on the river crossings near Witkovice—which for the number of aircraft engaged, the violence of their attack, and the acrobatic daring of their pilots, must have been un-precedented. Every movement, every troop concentration, every line of advance came under pulverising bombardment from the air. It was just hell on earth. The bridges were destroyed, the fords blocked, the waiting columns of men decimated. . . ."

At another point he wrote:

"Three of us—my chief of staff, another officer and myself—found some sort of cover in a grove of birch trees outside the village of Myszory. There we remained, unable to stir, till about noon when the air raids stopped. We knew it was only for a moment, but had we stayed there the chances of any of us surviving would have been slight."

On September 18th and 19th the Polish resistance collapsed. A few divisions and a few groups of stragglers, by keeping close to the Vistula through the Kampinoska forests, managed to get through to Modlin. But the mass of the Polish army, numbering 170,000, was captured. For the first time the part played by the Luftwaffe in ground operations had been decisive.

While the Battle of the Bzura was raging, the Luftwaffe's C.-in-C. in Berlin had implemented two important decisions about its future application:

1. From September 12th onwards, but mostly a week later, large numbers of bombers, dive-bombers, long- and short-range fighters were withdrawn from Poland and posted back home.

2. The provisions of "Operation Seaside"—the mass attack on Warsaw—appeared again in Luftwaffe orders.

On September 13th the operations' air commander, Richthofen, was ordered on the telephone to pit his forces against the north-western district of the city—not only *Stukas*, but horizontal bombers as well.

Richthofen's after-comments on the inadequate preparations were as follows:

"Only 183 aircraft engaged the enemy. . . . Chaos over the target was indescribable. Not a single unit attacked at its appointed time, and aircraft nearly collided in the act of bombing. Below there was just a sea of flame and smoke, so that accurate assessment of results was impossible."

And this was called the first "terror" raid of World War II! The documentary evidence available suggests the contrary. Daily orders of the Luftwaffe high command included the reiterated precept: "Military targets only." Even these were "to be spared if situated in heavily populated city areas." (Directive for September 2nd.)

For the large-scale attack on Warsaw ordered for September 17th the orders, signed by Goering himself, read:

"Priority of attack shall be given to public utilities (water, gas and power sources), barracks and ammunition dumps, the *Woywod* building, citadel, ministry of war, inspectorate general, traffic centres and known battery positions. See Warsaw sketch-map."

This sketch-map, on which military installations were prominently marked, formed part of the very complete target material carried by every bomber crew.

Did the Luftwaffe adhere to its orders? Amongst much other evidence about this is the report of the French air attaché in Warsaw, General Armengaud. On September 14th he informed his government in Paris:

"I must emphasise that operations by the German air force have been in conformity with the rules of warfare. Only military targets have been attacked. If civilians have been killed and wounded, it was only because they remained in proximity to such targets. It is important that this becomes known in France and England, lest reprisals be taken for which there is no cause, and so that we ourselves do not unleash total war in the air."

From the end of the Battle of the Bzura onwards the German siege ring squeezed ever more tightly on the adjacent strongholds of Warsaw and Modlin, but it was not until September 24th that the German armies had really closed in for the attack. Attempts to persuade the Poles to give in without a struggle—"to save useless bloodshed and the destruction of the city"—had started eight days previously. And when the German emissary returned without result, a dozen He 111s of I/KG 4 set off in the afternoon of September 16th to fly over the capital. Acoustically supported by a heavy thunderstorm they dropped a million leaflets. These bade the population quit the city within twelve hours by the eastern exits, should the military commander fail to accept the ultimatum to yield it peacefully.

Next morning the Poles announced the dispatch of their own emissary to negotiate the evacuation of the civil population and the diplomatic corps. As a result the mass attack billed for the 17th by both German *Luftflotten* was cancelled. But the Polish negotiator never appeared.

On the very same day the Russian army irrupted into eastern Poland. It made Hitler press for speed. The Russians wanted to reach the previously agreed demarcation line—which included the Vistula at Warsaw[1]—by October 3rd. By then the Polish capital must be in German hands.

The leaflet raids were repeated four times, on September 18th, 19th, 22nd and 24th. Four times the Polish leaders were again notified that continued resistance was senseless, and that responsibility for the consequent losses inside the city would be theirs alone. But the Poles did not respond. Instead they set up fresh defences, lined the streets with trenches and turned dwelling houses into fortresses. Well over 100,000 troops barricaded themselves for the coming street battle.

But first came the Luftwaffe's blow. From 08.00 hours on September 25th, a grotesque scene was enacted over Warsaw. Besides the bombers and dive-bombers, ceaselessly unloading their deadly cargoes on the western city, there also droned over the houses thirty Ju 52 transporters laden with incendiary bombs, which two soldiers shovelled out from the sides in batches.

Richthofen, to whom Goering had entrusted the conduct of the air operation, had available on that day no fewer than eight *Gruppen* of dive-bombers totalling some 240 Ju 87B's. But none of them could deliver incendiary bombs, and instead of the expected He 111 *Geschwader* he was given only this single *Gruppe* of transport machines. The lumbering gait of the old Ju 52s made them easy targets for the Polish flak, and two of them crashed in flames. Furthermore, "bombing with coal-shovels" was hardly a perfect method. Helped by a strong east wind, it led to a number of incendiaries landing amongst the crews' own infantry.

At this the staff of the 8th Army, forming the western sector of the siege circle, flew into such a passion that they demanded the instant cessation of all bombing. Despite the fact that only a few days previously the Luftwaffe had rescued this same Army from its critical position on the Bzura, the latter now wanted no help from it. The bombing—so argued General Blaskowitz —merely produced fires and smoke which masked the targets his own artillery wanted to shoot at.

At ten o'clock there was a dramatic scene when Richthofen flew over to 8th Army H.Q. to try to straighten things out. Neither Blaskowitz nor von Brauchitsch, the C.-in-C. of the ground forces, paid the slightest attention to his evidence. Presently Hitler himself strode in. Without moving a muscle he listened to the arguments of the generals, then turned to Richthofen and said just two words:

"Carry on!"

By the late morning the great smoke cloud over Warsaw had risen to 10,000 feet and begun to drift slowly up the Vistula. Each hour the bombers and dive-bombers found it more difficult to locate their allotted targets. But

---

[1] A secret clause of the German-Soviet non-aggression pact, signed in Moscow on August 23, 1939, established this line of demarcation along the rivers Narew, Vistula and San. By the frontier treaty of September 28th between the two powers it was moved further east to the River Bug.

the assault went on—an assault not on an open city but on a beleaguered fortress; not on the dwellings of civilians but on a deeply staggered defence system manned by 100,000 soldiers.

Since the event it has been repeatedly asserted that the Luftwaffe smashed Warsaw with 800 bombers. In fact, the total of bombers, dive-bombers and ground-attack aircraft that Richthofen could muster on September 25th came to little over 400. The rest had long since been recalled by Goering to the west. By making three or four sorties each these 400 aircraft dropped 500 tons of high-explosive bombs and seventy-two tons of incendiaries on Warsaw. As night fell, the red glare of the burning capital on the banks of the Vistula could be seen for miles around.

Warsaw bled from a thousand wounds. Yet the Germans had made an honest attempt to spare both men and city. This fact cannot be disregarded by any objective review of the events.

Next day Warsaw offered its surrender, and early on September 27th its capitulation was officially signed.

On both these last two days the *Stukas* attacked Modlin, the last bomb falling at midnight on September 27th. Then here, too, the enemy could resist no more.

Blitzkrieg on Poland—Summary and Conclusions

1. *The "lightning campaign" against Poland was no easy undertaking. The Poles put up a stubborn resistance, and although the campaign lasted only four weeks in all, the Luftwaffe lost during this time no less than 743 men and 285 aircraft, including 109 bombers and* Stukas (*a detailed analysis of the losses is given in Appendix 2).*

2. *Despite all assertions to the contrary, the Polish air force was not destroyed on the ground in the first two days of fighting. The bomber brigade in particular continued to make determined attacks on the German forces up to September 16th. However the Polish aircraft, inferior both in numbers and in design, could hardly contest the supremacy of the Luftwaffe in the air.*

3. *It was above all by its support of the ground forces, both direct and indirect, that the Luftwaffe contributed to the speedy conclusion of the campaign. Its opponents suffered more from the disruption of their communications than from the bomb-attacks on airfields and factories, the effectiveness of which was greatly over-estimated.*

4. *Far from being an "open city", Warsaw proved to be strongly fortified and bitterly defended. Repeated demands for surrender were in vain, and on September 25th, 1939, a single heavy air raid brought about the capitulation of the Polish capital.*

5. *Co-operation between the Luftwaffe and the Army in the Polish campaign laid the pattern for future "blitz" operations. However, the campaign also showed that the Luftwaffe was strong enough only for a war which was limited in length and conducted on a single front.*

2

NORTH SEA TRIANGLE

1. Mutual Target: The Fleets

On the afternoon of September 4th, 1939, the sky over Heligoland Bight was heavily overcast. A stiff nor'wester drove the rain clouds low over the North Sea against the German coastline. Sometimes they were down to only 300 feet above the waves. Within this confined space a group of heavy twin-engined aircraft were droning eastwards. Five of them, followed at some distance by another five. In this weather the markings on their wings and fuselages were all but indistinguishable.

They were not, however, German machines, but British: ten Bristol Blenheims, the fastest bombers of the Royal Air Force. On the day following their country's declaration of war they had come to make the first attack. "The weather in the Heligoland Bight was bloody," writes Squadron-Leader K. C. Doran, who led the way with the first five aircraft from 110 Squadron. "A solid wall of cloud seemed to extend from sea-level to about 17,000 feet. We obviously had to keep below it to stand any chance of finding our target. So we went down to sea-level. . . ." [1]

It was a worth-while target. In the morning a reconnaissance plane had spotted a number of German warships in the Schillig Roads outside Wilhelmshaven and off Brunsbüttel in the Elbe estuary. But the radio message that reached England was very distorted, and it was decided to wait, however impatiently, for the reconnaissance pilot's return.

At last, towards noon, he touched down at Wyton airfield. The photographs he brought back confirmed his report. The battle cruisers *Gneisenau* and *Scharnhorst* were in the Elbe, and the "pocket battleship" *Admiral Scheer*, with cruisers and destroyers, in the Schillig Roads. Bomber Command decided to strike at once. But it could not be done that quickly.

Owing to the weather the only possible attack was a low-level one. But the Blenheims were loaded with "semi armour-piercing" bombs, and these would only penetrate if dropped from a height. Doran adds: "So off came the

[1] *Royal Air Force 1939–45* (H.M.S.O., 1962), Vol. I, p. 38.

500-lb. S.A.P. and on went 500-lb. G.P. with eleven seconds delay fuse. . . .
The war was only twenty-four hours old, but already the bomb-load had been
changed four times."

At last the machines were ready. Only the best pilots were allowed to fly.
Five Blenheims of 110 Squadron and five of 107 left Wattisham for this leap
in the dark. Another five took off from Wyton, but these lost their way, and
after flying around for some hours returned with their mission unaccom-
plished.

Doran meanwhile flew on eastwards at the head of his five Blenheims,
doggedly changing course when the time calculated to reach the predeter-
mined turning-point had elapsed.

Visibility was virtually nil as the Blenheims now pushed south towards the
German coast. Once outpost patrol-boats appeared like phantoms through
the murk, and at once were lost to sight again. And then, suddenly, the coast
loomed ahead.

Doran studied his map and made comparisons. To starboard the islands,
with the mainland behind, and somewhat to port a deep inlet. It was the
mouth of the Jade. They were exactly on course to Wilhelmshaven, right on
target!

"An incredible combination of luck and judgment," was his assessment.
"Within a few mintutes cloud base lifted to 500 feet and we saw a large merchant ship; no—it was the *Admiral Scheer*."

At once the formation broke up. The first three Blenheims formed into
line ahead, and with short intervals between them flew straight for the German
battleship. The fourth and fifth machines broke away to port and starboard
and climbed briefly into cloud. They were to attack the ship from either side
and disperse the enemy defensive fire. The German flak was to be given no
time to consider which of the five aircraft to engage first.

So, at least, was the plan the British had worked out. A lightning attack
on their victim from all sides, by five Blenheims, and at mast height, and all
within eleven seconds. For after eleven seconds their bombs were timed to go
off, and if by then the last Blenheim was not clear it might be hit by the bomb
explosions of the first.

On paper the plan was good. In practice it was of course subject to a few
small, but decisive, changes.

The *Admiral Scheer* lay at anchor in Schillig Roads. On board the crew
went about their normal duties. High above, on the foremast platform, stood
the flak operations officer. Together with a Luftwaffe officer he had just been
going through the aircraft recognition tables. All at once a loud-speaker came
to life: "Message from port watch to quarter-deck flak MG, Herr Captain-
Lieutenant: three aircraft at six o'clock."

The lieutenant looked astern through his binoculars. Three dark dots were
rapidly approaching the ship.

It was against orders. The lieutenant shook his head angrily. How often
must one tell these Luftwaffe fellows to keep their distance from all warships!
If not, the flak crews would get nervous and shoot another of them down.

Suddenly the Luftwaffe officer beside him explained: "They aren't ours!
They are Bristol Blenheims!"

Within seconds the air raid alarm bells jangled through the ship. Doran
writes: "We saw the matelots' washing hanging out around the stern and the

crew idly standing about on deck. However, when they realised our intention was hostile they started running about like mad."

Before a shot could be fired the first bomber was on them. Just missing the mast, it screamed diagonally over the after-deck. Two heavy bombs crashed onto the ship. One dug itself in and came to rest; the other bounced along the deck, then rolled overboard into the water. No explosion! Then at last the flak began firing angrily at the retreating Blenheim.

Almost at once the second was upon them with the same results as the first. One bomb plummeted into the sea with a great fountain of water just a few yards from the gunwale—an especially dangerous spot for a delayed-action bomb, for it could work like a mine and hole the ship deep below the water-line.

But now at Schillig Roads all hell had broken loose. Over a wide area lines of tracer laced the air, as over a hundred flak barrels—from the ships and from the numerous batteries ashore—concentrated their fire on each aircraft as it dived out of cloud.

The third Blenheim did not reach the *Scheer*, but broke sharply away some hundred yards short because, according to Doran, it could not be on target within the prescribed eleven seconds. Its bombs splashed harmlessly into the water. The same applied to the fourth and fifth—except that one of them, riddled by flak, burst into flames and crashed into the sea close to the bird-sanctuary island of Mellum.

The five Blenheims of 107 Squadron fared worse. Attacking somewhat later than Doran's 110 Squadron, they bore the whole brunt of the now fully alerted defences. Only one of them returned; the others were all shot down. As one Blenheim fell it crashed sideways into the bows of the cruiser *Emden*, tearing a large hole and causing the war's first casualties in the German Navy.

That, for the British, was the only positive result of this surprise, and cer-tainly most courageous, attack. What about the strikes on the *Admiral Scheer* with the eleven-second bombs? The "vest-pocket battleship"—as the English called the *Scheer* class—was lucky. None of the bombs exploded. Three hits: three duds.

A simultaneous attack by fourteen Vickers Wellington bombers on the two largest warships lying off Brunsbüttel—the *Gneisenau* and the *Scharnhorst*—also miscarried. The ships' iron ring of anti-aircraft fire was virtually im-penetrable. One Wellington crashed in flames, another fell to a German fighter. For though the weather could scarcely have been less favourable for fighter operations, a fighter *Gruppe*—Major Harry von Bülow's II/JG 77—none the less took off from Nordholz. Sergeant Alfred Held's Me 109 took the Wellington by surprise before its pilot could reach cloud cover. It was the first German fighter victory over a British bomber in World War II. Soon afterwards Sergeant Troitsch of the same *Gruppe* brought down a Blenheim.

For British Bomber Command the result of this September 4th operation was a grave disappointment. Its hopes of striking a heavy blow at the German fleet at the very outset of the war had been frustrated. Virtually nothing had been achieved—at heavy cost. Of the twenty-four bombers that set out seven failed to return, and many of the rest suffered various degrees of damage.

"The Royal Air Force", wrote the official British Admiralty historian, Captain Roskill, "was anxious to put its theories about the deadly effect of bombing attacks on warships to the test. . . . The failure of these raids was a sharp rejoinder to those who had so confidently predicted that air-power had made large surface warships obsolete."

On the German side things were much the same. During these first weeks and months of the war there were between R.A.F. and Luftwaffe a lot of parallels. Both were under orders to wage war, as it were, with velvet gloves, with the following specific negatives:

No bombs to be dropped on enemy territory; no enemy civilians to be harmed; no merchant ships to be attacked; no flying over neutral countries.

Thus for both air forces the only legitimate targets left were enemy warships on the open sea or in the roadstead. As soon as they were in harbour, docked, or moored against a pier, they too must be left unmolested.

Apart from the fact that neither side wanted to take the blame for starting indiscriminate bombing, the Germans had another plausible reason for hanging back. Hitler believed that Britain would soon "see reason" and be ready for peace—a mood that would surely be changed by German air raids. Furthermore, the Luftwaffe must first have done with the Polish campaign before it could gather its strength for an offensive against the West.[1]

The British government of the time has often been charged with failing, in September 1939, to exploit the two-way front that Germany then faced. Concentrated air attacks on strongpoints in north-west Germany would certainly have compelled Goering to withdraw a large proportion of the Luftwaffe from Poland, thus appreciably alleviating that country's military position.

"The inertia and weakness of our politicians were a godsend to the Luftwaffe," was the verdict of the British air-war expert, Derek Wood, in a work published in 1961.

But the War Cabinet under Chamberlain stuck to its resolve: no bombs on Germany unless the Germans started dropping them on England.

The official history, *Royal Air Force 1939–1945*, has a quite simple and sober explanation. At the end of September 1939 Bomber Command's frontline strength was only thirty-three squadrons totalling 480 aircraft. Since the British credited their opponents with three times this number, "all-out action was obviously against our interests until a more satisfactory balance of forces could be achieved. With expediency reinforcing the dictates of humanitarianism . . . the measures open to Bomber Command were accordingly those which could be carried out under the policy of conserving and expanding the bomber force until we were at liberty . . . to 'take the gloves off'."

In Germany, in September 1939, there was a man whose hands were similarly tied. This was Lieutenant-General Hans Ferdinand Geisler, who with his staff had taken over the Hamburg air administrative command, situated at Blankenese in Manteuffel Strasse. Geisler was in charge of the

---

[1] During the first three weeks of the war *Luftflotten* 2 and 3 in the west disposed of twenty-eight fighter squadrons totalling 336 aircraft, five twin-engined fighter *Gruppen* with 180 aircraft, and nine bomber *Gruppen* totalling 280 medium bombers. The emphasis at this time was thus on air defence.

newly formed 10 Air Division, whose main task was to wage war on Britain's seaborne forces.

Even if Goering's strict instructions had not forbidden Geisler to start any action against Britain itself, it was quite impossible for him to do so, for at the moment he hardly possessed a single bomber. His only *Geschwader*, KG 26, still in the process of formation, had been transferred to Poland.

Though by mid-September the so-called "Lion" *Geschwader* was back at its operational bases on Heligoland Bight, it consisted at first of only two *Gruppen*, comprising some sixty He 111s. Most of its pilots and squadron commanders, like the C.O. himself, Colonel Hans Siburg, had previously belonged to the Navy.

The German Navy's C.-in-C., Admiral Erich Raeder, had agreed to recommend the transfer of his airmen to the Luftwaffe with a heavy heart. For years the two services had disputed as to which should have the conduct of air operations over the sea, and finally Goering's maxim, "Everything that flies belongs to me," had won the day. All that the fleet air arm was left with were a few coastal formations equipped with reconnaissance and shipboard planes.

In pursuance of his resolve that the air-sea war should be conducted by the Luftwaffe, Goering promised in November 1938 that he would have thirteen bomber *Geschwader* ready for this role by 1942 (any earlier war with Britain, Hitler had positively assured him, could be ruled out). This would stop any drain on the rest of the bomber force.

Compared with this splendid assertion, the actual force available at the outset of hostilities—just the two *Gruppen* of KG 26—was modest indeed.

To be sure, *Luftflotte* 2 ("North") under Air General Hellmuth Felmy did get one other bomber unit early in September. It was then called "Experimental Gruppe 88", and was the first to be equipped with a plane which the Luftwaffe hoped would achieve a decisive technical break-through: the Junkers Ju 88 "wonder bomber".

However, neither Felmy nor his chief of staff, Colonel Josef Kammhuber, fancied throwing a unit that was still under training, with mechanically unproven aircraft, straight into war operations. Though the unit had meanwhile been renamed I/KG 30, they posted it away again from Jever to the airfields of Hagenow-Land and Greifswald in Mecklenburg and Pomerania.

Its C.O., Captain Helmut Pohle, reported:

"Just one section, under Lieutenant Walter Storp[1], remained on stand-to at Westerland on the island of Sylt. General Felmy told us that it would be employed at the next appearance of the British fleet. My suggestion that he should forthwith use the whole *Gruppe* for this purpose was declined."

Luftflotte 2 then extended its warning to the high command in Berlin. The new Ju 88 should not be put into operation in "dribs and drabs", but only when it could make itself felt. Let the first attack be by at least a complete *Geschwader*, at least a hundred aircraft.

Goering and his chief of staff, Jeschonnek, turned deaf ears. This business of the Ju 88, and its readiness or non-readiness, had been going on for far too long. Two years before, in 1937, it had been heralded as an unarmed bomber, fast enough to elude any fighter aircraft. Then, after all, it had been equipped with a defensive armament. And after that had come the demand

---

[1] Later, in 1944, to become Major-General and "General of Bombers."

for a dive-potential like that of the *Stuka*: always new requests, resulting in new problems and fresh delays in production.

The aircraft had been supposedly ready for series production on September 3, 1938. On that date the Junkers firm was given its contract. Its director-general, Dr. Heinrich Koppenberg, received from Goering a comprehensive mandate which concluded: "I want a powerful force of Ju 88 bombers in the shortest time possible!"

Since then a year had elapsed and the war had started. But the Ju 88s in the hands of the Luftwaffe still numbered fewer than fifty. The supreme commander decided that the machine had been doctored enough. It was high time it proved itself. The "wonder bomber" must achieve a success to establish its prestige.

Late in the afternoon of September 26th the telephone rang in the office of Captain Pohle, I/KG 30's commander at Greifswald. Jeschonnek himself was on the line: "Congratulations, Pohle! Your section at Westerland has sunk the *Ark Royal*!"

Pohle knew the chief of general staff too well, after a long period of working with him, not to recognise the ironic undertone.

"I don't believe it," he said.

"I don't either," answered Jeschonnek. "But the Iron One [Goering] does. Fly to Westerland right away and find out what's true and what isn't."

Who had reported the sinking? Was it 10 Air Division, who had directed the operation against the flotilla? What had really happened?

On the morning of September 26th Naval Group West had sent out its long-range reconnaissance planes over the North Sea prior to a destroyer operation on the following day. They were Do 18 flying boats of the coastal squadron 2/106, based on Nordeney. Towards 10.45 one of these was north of the Great Fisher Bank.

Its observer suddenly started. Through a gap in the clouds he had just sighted a warship. No, it wasn't one, it was a whole fleet!

Again and again the Do 18 circled the solitary cloud-gap, while pilot and observer feverishly counted up the great naval units: four battleships, an aircraft carrier, plus cruisers and destroyers. Down below them sailed the British Home Fleet!

The precise wording of the Do 18's radio signal electrified the German coastal staffs. Here at last was the long awaited chance to attack—practically the only chance, within the scope of the existing orders, to hit the enemy at all.

Shortly after 11.00 the telephones were already jangling at the bomber base on Sylt. "Operation order. Map square 4022. Long-range reconnaissance in contact with enemy. Attack with 1,000-lb bombs."

The British flotilla did in fact consist of the battleships *Nelson* and *Rodney*, the battle-cruisers *Hood* and *Renown*, the aircraft-carrier *Ark Royal* and three cruisers. Not far off lay the 2nd Cruiser Squadron with four further cruisers and six destroyers.

The force that was sent to attack this armada was modest indeed. At 12.50 nine He 111s, of the "Lion" *Geschwader*—i.e., No. 1 Squadron of KG 26—took off under Captain Vetter. Ten minutes later these were followed by the readiness section of the "Eagle" *Geschwader*—the four Ju 88s under Lieutenant Storp—which now had the chance of proving its worth.

That was all that 10 Air Division could, or would, muster. There, far away from its bases and shadowed by German reconnaissance planes, stood the bulk of the British Home Fleet at sea, and the Luftwaffe "exploited" its opportunity with a mere thirteen bombers!

Low down below the clouds the four Ju 88s chased each other north-westwards. This, they hoped, would be the quickest way to find the enemy once they had reached his given position. Pilot of the third machine was a Corporal Carl Francke, known to his comrades as "Beaver" Francke because of his well-kept beard. By next morning his name was to be on everybody's lips.

Francke was in fact a certified engineer and aircraft technician. He knew the Ju 88 well, having been in charge of its technical trials at Rechlin. But apart from that he was a dedicated flyer. In 1937, at an air concourse at Zurich where world experts held their breath at the incredible speed of the German aircraft, he had already joined Udet in demonstrating a Me 109 tuned for maximum performance.

Just before the war he had volunteered as a pilot in his friend Pohle's test team, rather than be stuck for ever at Rechlin. So it happened that, as a mere corporal, he was now flying one of the first four Ju 88s ever to take part in an offensive action.

After a flight of a bare two hours the ships came into view ahead. Francke pulled through cloud up to 9,000 feet. Cloud density was about eight-tenths, affording only an occasional glimpse of the sea below. Then suddenly, through a gap, a great ship appeared: the aircraft-carrier!

Without hesitation Francke flicked over and dived steeply down on the target.

Not a gun opened fire. He must have taken the ship completely by surprise.

Then a cloud bank masked his vision, and when he was through it the carrier was no longer in his bomb-sight. Impossible to correct the dive: he knew the plane too well, and what its diving limits were. He was aiming too much to the side. There was only one thing to do: pull out and start again.

But now the ship's anti-aircraft defences were at last letting fly. If only he had aimed right the first time, he could have pressed home his attack virtually without opposition.

Francke waited eight minutes, then dived again—this time into a hail of flak. But now he was properly lined up. The carrier was fixed in his bomb-sight like a spider in its web.

A press on the button, and the bombs fell. Immediately the automatic pull-out operated, and he was back in a climb.

While Francke concentrated on avoiding action to get out of the flak, his radio-operator and tail-gunner kept their eyes glued on the carrier below. Suddenly Sergeant Bewermeyer shouted: "Water fountain hard beside the ship!"

Even Francke risked a glance downwards. There was a big spout of water close to the gunwale. And then came a flash on the bows.

Was this a hit, or just the flash of a heavy flak gun? If the latter, what had happened to the second bomb, automatically released just after the first?

The ship was now too far away to observe any further details. Anyway that was not their job. They were thankful to have got away from the flak with whole skins.

The crew's radio report sounded guardedly optimistic: "Dive-attack with two SC 500 bombs on aircraft-carrier; first a near miss by ship's side, second a possible hit on bows. Effect not observed."

Hardly had Francke landed back at Westerland when the cheering started. Only the "Lion" *Geschwader's* commander, Colonel Siburg, was sceptical.

"Did you actually see her sink?"

"No, Colonel."

"In that case, my dear fellow," Siburg grinned, "you didn't hit her either!"

As a former naval officer Siburg knew from experience that a flash or even drifts of smoke from an enemy ship were by no means conclusive evidence of a strike by one's own guns. But of course the Luftwaffe were not to know this. Meanwhile the wires at 10 Division H.Q. were burning. Full of impatience, the C.-in-C. Luftwaffe in Berlin wanted to know why no report had been sent of the sinking of the British aircraft-carrier.

"Because nothing about such a sinking is known here," signalled the divisional operations officer, Major Martin Harlinghausen. Truly, all he had in his possession was Francke's carefully worded report, which he at once passed on to Berlin.

But once started, the mischief continued. A reconnaissance patrol was sent out to discover what had happened to the *Ark Royal*. Finally, towards 17.00, came the first report: "Enemy flotilla in square X; two battleships and covering vessels; full speed, course west."

The aircraft-carrier had disappeared!

In Berlin no one hit on the obvious explanation that the formation had split up, and that the *Ark Royal* was now proceeding with the section which the patrol had not sighted. A new order was dispatched over the radio: "Look out for oil patches!"

Shortly afterwards even a suitable oil patch was found—overlooking the fact that the North Sea is studded with them. Was this not enough proof that the *Ark Royal* and its sixty aircraft now lay on the bed of the ocean?

Goering, Milch and Jeschonnek debated whether, after all, it might be advisable to await for the British to make some announcement. But German propaganda had already got its teeth into the affair. "German Luftwaffe sinks Britain's latest aircraft-carrier! And with a single bomb!" It was a windfall.

When Captain Pohle, in obedience to Jeschonnek's order, landed at Westerland late in the evening, Corporal Francke forgot all about military discipline. "Pohle, old boy!" he cried excitedly to his commanding officer, "There's not a word of truth in it. For God's sake help me get out of this frightful mess!"

But Pohle was too late to arrest the momentum. Next day the German High Command published its report of the attack on the British fleet. It read: "Apart from the destruction of an aircraft-carrier, a number of hits were scored on a battleship.[1] All our aircraft returned safely."

Even Goering now added his official seal. He sent his personal congratulations to Francke, promoted the corporal to lieutenant with immediate effect, and decorated him with the Iron Cross, grades I and II.

---

[1] One bomb from the remaining three Ju 88s of I/KG 30 did hit the *Hood*, but was a dud and bounced off. I/KG 26 attacked the cruiser squadron, but all their bombs missed their targets.

The British Admiralty countered. It announced drily that the aircraft-carrier *Ark Royal*, which the Germans reported to have sunk, had returned undamaged to her base. It even issued to the press a picture of her entering the same.

This according to German propaganda was a trick, a vain attempt by the British to hide the severity of their loss. On September 28th even the high command took issue with the "tendentious" British announcement, confirming that a 1,000-lb bomb had *hit* the carrier. Its new report, however, no longer contained the words "destroyed", "sunk" or "annihilated". But the German Press still persisted with the full story.

The fact of the matter is that at the beginning of October the *Ark Royal* steamed to the south Atlantic, there to take part in the month-long hunt for the German raider, *Admiral Graf Spee*. Only after the British aircraft-carrier was finally torpedoed and sunk in the Mediterranean on November 14, 1941, by the U-boat *U 81*, were German reports about its previous "sinking" quietly altered.

The Luftwaffe chiefs in Berlin did not have to wait so long for the truth. It dawned on the general staff next day.

So it was that both Luftwaffe and R.A.F. were greatly disappointed by their first efforts to assail each other's fleets. Something had gone wrong. On both sides disillusionment set in.

Months later, when Goering met Francke again at the Luftwaffe test centre at Rechlin, he said lugubriously: "You still owe me an aircraft-carrier."

On October 9, 1939, I/KG 30 were at last all together at Westerland on the island of Sylt. The C.O., Captain Pohle, climbed out of his Ju 88 in a bad temper. Once again his unit had made a sortie against the British fleet, and again nothing had been achieved.

He was called to the telephone. Goering wanted a personal report. Pohle answered bitterly: "We were just sent to an area where there was no enemy!"

This time it had been a joint action with the Navy. A task force consisting of the battle-cruiser *Gneisenau*, the cruiser *Köln* and nine destroyers, had gone out with the objective of luring the British Home Fleet from its bases into the North Sea. That done, the Luftwaffe was to "have a go" at it.

This time, moreover, Lieutenant-General Geisler's staff officers—his division had just been raised to the status of a corps—had made proper preparations. Instead of an attack by a few isolated aircraft, it was to be by I/KG 30 and the whole of KG 26, reinforced by two *Gruppen* of LG 1. KG 1 (known as "Hindenburg") stood in reserve "to deliver the *coup de grace* to a disabled enemy". Altogether Geisler and his chief of staff, Major Harlinghausen, had committed 127 He 111s plus twenty-one Ju 88s.

Yet once more the operation ended as a flop. Most squadrons, after searching vainly for the enemy, returned to base with the last of their fuel. Others—notably I/KG 30's 4 Squadron—claimed ten bomb strikes on British cruisers, not one of which could be confirmed.

Next morning there was a big conference at the Reich Air Ministry in Berlin. These failures had to stop. Goering was angry: "I have another word to say to you, gentlemen. There was this matter of the *Ark Royal*. . . ."

He looked challengingly around at his closest colleagues: at Milch, secretary of state; Jeschonnek, chief of general staff; Beppo Schmid, chief of air intelligence; Udet, quartermaster-general; Coeler, chief of the "fleet air arm", and many others. None of them had anything to say. But Captain Pohle had also been summoned to the meeting—as commander of the only available Ju 88 unit. Now Goering turned directly to him.

"Pohle," he said, "we've got to score a success! There are only a few British ships that stand in our way: the *Repulse*, the *Renown*, perhaps, too, the *Hood*. And, of course, the aircraft-carriers. Once they are gone, the *Scharnhorst* and the *Gneisenau* can rule the waves. . . ."

He went on to promise the earth: "I tell you now, every man who helps get rid of these ships will be awarded a house of his own and all the medals that are going."

He concluded with some obscure "tactical advice": "Do as we did in World War I against the enemy's aeroplanes. Am I right, Udet?"

Udet smiled. He had scored sixty-two victories, Goering twenty-two. Once again "the Iron One" was giving way to arrogance.

Pohle remarked: "*Herr Generalfeldmarschall*, it is the ambition of every air-crew to destroy as many aircraft on a carrier as General Udet did in World War I."

It made Goering happy; Pohle was dismissed from the meeting with smiles. From now on his *Gruppe* was to stand at Westerland at constant readiness to deliver the knock-out blow to the British fleet.

But it was, in fact, the U-boats which scored the first real successes. Already on September 17th the *U 29* under Lieutenant Schuhart had sunk the British aircraft-carrier *Courageous* west of Ireland. During the night of October 13th–14th Lieutenant Prien's *U 47* crept through the heavy defences and entered the great naval base of Scapa Flow—a daring escapade that deserved even more than it achieved. Contrary to belief the British Home Fleet was at sea, and all he found was the battleship *Royal Oak*. This he sank with two salvoes of three torpedoes.

However, this attack led indirectly, two days later, to an operation by Ju 88 dive-bombers. For now ship movements off the east coast of Scotland were under constant watch by German air reconnaissance. On October 15th a battle-cruiser was sighted, presumed to be the *Hood*. Early next day it was further reported to have entered the Firth of Forth.

At 09.30 Jeschonnek gave his operations order on the telephone to Pohle in Westerland. He added: "I also have to convey to you a personal order from the Führer. It runs as follows: Should the *Hood* already be in dock when KG 30 reaches the Firth of Forth, no attack is to be made."

Pohle said he understood, but Jeschonnek continued urgently: "I make you personally responsible for acquainting every crew with this order. The Führer won't have a single civilian killed."

There it was again—the concern to keep the war within bounds. Neither the Germans nor the British wanted to drop the first bombs on the other's homeland. So warships were the only legitimate targets, and then only so long as they were at sea. Once tied up, they were forbidden fruit, and military opportunity must give way to political considerations. For in Berlin it was still hoped that the conflict with Britain could soon be settled.

At 11.00 on October 16th, I/KG 30's bomber squadrons took off. By 12.15 they had reached the outer estuary of the Forth and started to push inland.

"We flew in loose section formation," Pohle reported, "for Department 5 (of the Luftwaffe general staff) had informed us that no Spitfires were stationed in Scotland."

Unfortunately for Pohle this information was incorrect. British Fighter Command had based two Spitfire squadrons, Nos 602 and 603, at Turnhouse, near Edinburgh. Furthermore that very morning a Hurricane squadron, No. 607, had alighted at Drem, on the Firth's south bank.

In the event of German bombers approaching, the fighters were to intercept them well out at sea, guided by the local radar station. As luck would have it, at lunchtime on this very day the station suffered a power failure, and the Hurricanes and Spitfires only got the alarm when the drone of the Ju 88s was heard 12,000 feet above their bases. Valuable minutes had thus been lost, giving time for the bomber squadrons to seek out their targets in peace.

As Pohle flew at the head of his scattered formation, Edinburgh came into view below. For the first time since the war began a German bomber unit was flying over the United Kingdom. There was the great bridge separating the outer and inner Firth of Forth, and immediately beyond it, on the north bank, the docks at Rosyth naval base.

At once Pohle spotted the ship that he had come to sink, distinguished by its length and much greater width from the smaller ships around. It could only be the *Hood*. But she was no longer at sea, but in dock—or rather, in the sluice gate leading to it. She must have just arrived.

"She was a sitting target," Pohle reported, "but orders robbed us of our prize. . . ."

In spite of this he put his machine into a dive. A number of cruisers and destroyers lay in Rosyth roadstead, and he picked out one of the largest, the cruiser *Southampton*. The ack-ack opened up in a frenzy of fire. Though his machine was shaken by explosions, Pohle imperturbably pressed home his attack, diving at an angle of nearly eighty degrees.

Then it happened: first a short, sharp bang, followed by a cracking and tearing sound. Then an icy blast hit the crew's faces. The cabin roof had blown off—at a speed of some 400 m.p.h.!

Pohle could not tell whether it was the result of a flak hit or whether the dive had exceeded the plane's limit of tolerance. The same fault had appeared during the Ju 88's flight tests at Rechlin—further evidence that the machine had been thrown into operations before its teething troubles were over. But he still kept control, and dived on down with the *Southampton* plumb in his bomb-sight. Some 3,000 feet up he released his 1,000-lb. bomb. It came clear away.

It was later confirmed that the bomb struck the 9,100-ton cruiser amidships in the starboard superstructure. But it never went off. After penetrating three decks obliquely, it emerged again at the side of the ship and finally sank an admiralty launch that was tied up against it.

But the bomber crew had neither time nor opportunity to study the effect of their missile. For hardly had Pohle pulled out before his radio-operator called out: "Three Spitfires are attacking!"

"It was too late to take avoiding action," Pohle reported. "Our port engine was hit at once and started smoking. I turned seawards, hoping to reach the German fishing cutter *Hörnum*, which the Navy had proposed to station at a given point off the Scottish coast during our attack."

But the Spitfires came at him again. Against them the Ju 88, the "wonder bomber", with its single backwards-aiming MG 15, was a sitting duck. Machine-gun bullets slammed into the cabin, and both radio-operator, and rear-gunner were hit. Reaching Port Seton in East Lothian, Pohle pushed the machine right down to the water. But the Spitfires were still after him. At their third attack the observer was also badly wounded. And now the starboard engine failed as well.

"We were finished," said Pohle, describing these last dramatic moments. "I spied a trawler steaming north, and thought perhaps I could still reach it. After that I lost consciousness."

It was a British fishing boat, and in a few minutes its men were on the spot with their dinghy. Pohle was the only one of his crew still alive, and they pulled him out before the aircraft sank. Later the still unconscious German captain was transferred to a British destroyer. Only after five days did he regain consciousness in Port Edwards Hospital on the Firth of Forth's north bank.

A second Ju 88 was also lost by I/KG 30. Net result of the attack: the cruisers *Southampton* and *Edinburgh*, plus the destroyer *Mohawk*, suffered slight damage.

The next morning, October 17th, four machines of the same unit, under its new commander, Captain Doench, took off again. This time the target lay even farther away: Scapa Flow.

In face of massive anti-aircraft fire the four Ju 88s pushed right on to where the Royal Navy should be at anchor. But apart from the aged training-cum-depot ship *Iron Duke*, whose side was torn out by near-misses, they found that the birds had flown.

The British Admiralty had ordered its Home Fleet to withdraw to the Clyde, the approach to Glasgow on the west coast of Scotland. There its capital ships were well out of range—though they still needed only one extra day's cruising to reach either the North Sea or the northern Atlantic approaches.

The Royal Air Force attributed this withdrawal of the battle fleet to German attacks. Its official historian writes: "By two or three boldly executed strokes, and at a total cost of four aircraft, the German Air Force and the U-boat service between them scored a resounding strategic success."

What about the R.A.F.'s own bombers? After trailing their coats at Wilhelmshaven on September 4th, would they now return to the assault?

2. The Battle of Heligoland Bight

Monday, December 18, 1939, was a cold but sunny day. The German North Sea coast and the East Friesian islands were lightly veiled in mist. Above about 3,000 feet, however, the sky was clear as a bell, with visibility extending to the ultimate horizons.

"Splendid weather for fighters," announced Lieutenant-Colonel Carl Schumacher, commanding officer of JG 1, stationed since a few weeks at Jever in East Friesland.

"The Tommies are not such fools—they won't come today," his adjutant, First Lieutenant Miller-Trimbusch, dutifully replied.

Four days ago it had been different. The weather had been filthy: snow and rain, with cloud-pockets right down on the sea. But suddenly the cruiser *Nürnberg* and a number of destroyers had been assailed in the Jade estuary by a dozen Wellington bombers.

On the day previous to that both the *Nürnberg* and the *Leipzig* had been torpedoed at sea by the British submarine *Salmon*—but both had got back under their own steam. It was then up to the R.A.F. to finish them off. But things had not worked out. First the fury of the flak had prevented any accuracy in the bombing, and immediately afterwards von Bülow's Me 109s took over. Despite the protective cloud-curtain five Wellingtons were shot down into the sea.

"Most of von Bülow's fighter pilots were ex-naval men," explained Schumacher, the *Geschwader's* chief. "In that weather any normal unit would have made a mess of it, and come home empty-handed."

Later, the British admitted that a sixth bomber had been lost on the way home.

But all that had been four days ago. Today not only was the weather better, but Schumacher had at last got the reinforcements he had asked for. Yesterday the long-range fighter *Gruppe*, I/ZG 76, with its distinguished record in Poland, had been posted from Bonninghardt to Jever and put under JG 1's command. Schumacher's fighter force now consisted of the following units:

II/JG 77 under Major von Bülow, at Wangerooge;
III/JG 77 under Captain Seliger, at Nordholz near Cuxhaven;
I/ZG 76 under Captain Reinecke, at Jever;
Fighter *Gruppe* 101 (renamed II/ZG 1) under Major Reichardt, with one
   squadron at Westerland/Sylt and two at Neumünster;
The night-fighter squadron 10/JG 26 under First-Lieutenant Steinhoff,
   at Jever.

All in all, counting first-line aircraft only, Schumacher had a force of eighty to one hundred single- and twin-engined fighters which he could put into the air within minutes of an alarm. The question was, did the British reckon with such a high-powered defence force? Certainly they would be mad if they came today, with a sky like blue satin providing such perfect conditions for the defence.

Since the first days of the war British Bomber Command had had to revise its plan of attack. Its earlier system, by which the bombers only took off after reconnaissance sightings of enemy warships, had proved too time-wasting. By the time they arrived the ships had usually disappeared or had run into harbour, where it was not permitted to attack them.

The new system, very soon adopted, consisted of "armed reconnaissance" flights by formations of at least nine, and usually twelve, twin-engined bombers of the types Blenheim, Wellington, Hampden and Whitley. Suitably bombed-up, these patrolled over Heligoland Bight looking for worthwhile targets.

But even this system had failed to obtain results. On September 29th five Hampdens had been shot down while attacking off Heligoland, and both October and November had gone by without a single success. Once, during the afternoon of November 17th, an R.A.F. reconnaissance plane again reported warships homeward bound in the Bight, but this time Bomber

19. The Battle of Heligoland Bight. The theory that by flying in close formation, these Wellingtons could break through the German defense turned out to be false, and many were shot down.

20. A downed Wellington after the Battle of Heligoland Bight.

21. A contemporary news picture featuring some of the British crews who returned safely from the Battle of Heligoland Bight.

22. Lieutenant-Colonel Schumacher, who commanded the Me 110s in the Battle of Heligoland Bight.

23. At the outset of the war the single-seater Me 109 was more than a match for any opponent.

24. The twin-engined Me 110 won a notable defensive victory against the British Wellington bombers on December 18, 1939 in the Battle of Heligoland Bight.

Command declined to send out its planes on the pretext that by the time they reached the spot it would be dark.

Such "tepid indecision" put the First Lord of the Admiralty, Winston Churchill, into a rage. British shipping, he said, was suffering mounting losses from German mines and U-boats, and the German Luftwaffe even attacked the strongly defended naval bases of Rosyth and Scapa Flow. Why, he demanded angrily, did the R.A.F. not venture to Wilhelmshaven?

Upon this Bomber Command received new instructions to attack enemy ships even if they were inside the air-defence zone between Heligoland and Wilhelsmhaven. Declared objective: The destruction of an enemy battle-cruiser or pocket battleship. It was reminiscent of Goering's challenge of October 10th in Berlin: "We've got to score a success!"

Now, five weeks afterwards, in London, Churchill was calling for the same thing. For in the German warships the British saw the biggest threat to their vital ocean supply arteries.

The first British attack under the new directive took place against Heligo-land on December 3, 1939. A few bombs fell on the island, but the warships in the roads remained unscathed. The operation, however, did bring Bomber Command a ray of hope. All the twenty-four Wellingtons that took part returned intact. They had received strict orders not to break formation, and to drop their bombs from a height of 8,000 feet. The few German fighters which were on the spot scored no victories. Could it be that against tight bomber formations the Me 109s were powerless?

Curiously enough the British had not even credited the German fighters with a success on December 14th in the battle of the Jade estuary already referred to. They attributed their loss of six bombers to other causes: bad weather, ships' flak, and loss of fuel from holed petrol tanks. So it came about that the chances for the next attack were viewed in England with undue optimism. Towards noon on December 18th bomber squadrons 9, 37 and 149 assembled over King's Lynn for an offensive operation—in spite of cloudless skies over Heligoland Bight, so perfect for fighters. "Shoulder to shoulder, like Cromwell's Ironsides", as an R.A.F. tactical analysis put it, the tightly packed formation presented a spectacle of imperturbable morale and fighting power.

At 13.50 hours two German radar stations picked up the approaching bombers. They were the naval radar station on Heligoland and the Luft-waffe experimental station under Signals Lieutenant Hermann Diehl, situated on the Wangerooge sand-dunes. Both had *"Freya"*-type installations.

Diehl calculated the bombers' distance from the coast at 113 kilometers, or twenty minutes' flying time. Enough time, one would think, to get the fighter units into the air to intercept the enemy while he was still over the sea.

In the event it took exactly twenty minutes for the radar report to reach the *Geschwader* commander—or rather, before his staff believed it.

Part of the blame can be attributed to the very indifferent communications system between Navy and Luftwaffe. At the war's outset this had been practically non-existent. Though Schumacher, in the few weeks since assuming his command, had striven to get "wired in" to the Navy's early-warning network, far too much time was still lost before a report from Heligoland passed through the Wilhelmshaven naval exchange and reached H.Q. Fighters at Jever.

Against this Lieutenant Diehl had a direct line to Jever, and at once got on the telephone. But his announcement received no credence. Tommies approaching in weather like this? Instead of producing a "scramble", all he received was the sceptical reply: "You're plotting seagulls or there's interference on your set."

The signals officer hesitated. Finally he put through a call direct to the adjacent fighter unit at Wangerooge, II/JG 77. But its C.O., Major von Bülow, was just then at *Geschwader* H.Q. in Jever.

Meanwhile, the British bombers had made their accustomed turn off Heligoland, while leaving the island at a respectful distance, and were pushing on south towards the Jade. By R.A.F. accounts they had comprised, at the start, twenty-four Wellingtons, of which two had returned with engine trouble. They flew in four tightly packed formations.

Naval observers on Heligoland counted just double: forty-four. And that in broad daylight, perfect visibility, and not a cloud on the sky! The contradiction has never been explained.

The first German fighters finally to become airborne comprised a flight of six Me 109s of the *night*-fighter squadron 10/JG 26, with First-Lieutenant Steinhoff at their head. They alone were in a position to attack the Wellingtons before they reached Wilhelmshaven.

But "Cromwell's Ironsides" were not to be routed—not yet at least. Wing-tip to wing-tip, in tight formation, they droned their way above the Jade and over the Schillig Roads. Then, as if on parade, they flew over Wilhelmshaven at 12,000 feet. But no bombs fell from them. Heavy flak swelled to a hurricane. The Englishmen ignored it, and flew again over the great naval base. Then, still without dropping a bomb, they set course to the north and north-west. Only now, on the way back, did the Battle of Heligoland Bight develop. The bombers were set upon by flight after flight of single- and twin-engined fighters, and pursued till they were far out over the open sea.

Probably the first victory was that of Corporal Heilmayr in a Me 109, at 14.30 hours. It was followed immediately by that of Steinhoff. Diving down from the beam for the second time he hit his target with a full blast of cannon and machine guns, and the Wellington turned over and spun into the sea in flames.

And still the squadrons were being scrambled. The twin-engined *Gruppe's* staff flight had just returned to Jever from an observation patrol along the coast, and scarcely had time to refuel. From Jever the bombers could clearly be seen from the ground as they headed first for Wilhelmshaven and then turned north-west for home.

Lieutenant Hellmut Lent, whom we have met before, fussed impatiently with the controls as his radio-operator, Corporal Kubisch, jumped in behind and Paul Mahle, 1/ZG 76's armoury flight-sergeant, crouched on the wing changing a drum of 20-mm ammunition. Determined not to miss his chance, Lent opened the throttle and taxied off, leaving Mahle to slide off the wing and hurl himself to the side to avoid being struck by the tail unit.

Swiftly the Me 110 gained height. With the unrestricted visibility Lent could follow the air battle from far away. The British main formation was now north of Wangerooge, with German fighters buzzing around it. That would be Bülow's crowd, thought Lent. Then he spotted two Wellingtons sneaking off westwards over the sand-banks. In a few minutes he had reached their altitude and attacked.

The Vickers Wellington bomber was equipped at the extreme rear of its fuselage with an unpleasant gun-turret armed with twin-machine-guns. In formation flight these bombers thus possessed considerable fire power astern. They were much more vulnerable from above and from the beam, for there they presented a blind spot unprotected by any of their six machine-guns. It was at this spot that Lent delivered his first attack, firing with all his guns. It seemed to have no effect, so throwing caution to the winds he placed himself directly astern and at the same altitude, and with a well-directed burst silenced the tail-gunner.

The Wellington was now "easy meat". After a further burst it gushed thick black smoke. The English pilot pushed the stick forward and actually managed to make a forced landing on the island of Borkum. A few seconds later the machine burst into flames, and only Flying-Officer P. S. Wimberley got out alive. Time 14.35.

Lent, however, resumed the chase, pursuing the second Wellington out to sea. It was flying ten feet above the waves. He fired a burst, this time at once from astern, and later wrote in his combat report: "Both the enemy's engines began burning brightly. As the plane hit the water the impact broke it apart, and it sank." Time: 14.40. Five minutes later, by the same method Lent brought down a third Wellington which had already been shot up. This plunged into the sea fifteen miles north-west of Borkum. Other Me 110s also had successes over the same piece of sea. First-Lieutenant Gresens, his No. 2, Corporal Kalinowski, and Lieutenant Graeff—all of 2 Squadron, ZG 76—each claimed a victory around 15.00 hours.

Lieutenant Uellenbeck flew his Me 110 far out to sea, hot on the heels of two Wellingtons, which he caught up thirty miles north of the Dutch island of Ameland. He shot down the one on the left, but was himself hit by the rear-gunner of the other. One bullet wounded Uellenbeck in the neck and his radio-operator, Corporal Dombrowski, in the arm. After requesting a bearing they succeeded, however, in bringing their plane safely to Jever.

That the British bombers knew how to defend themselves was also brought home to the same squadron's commander, Captain Wolfgang Falck. He and his No. 2, Sergeant Fresia, ran into a close formation of returning Wellingtons twelve miles south-west of Heligoland at 11,000 feet. The ensuing battle lasted from 14.35 till 14.45. Fresia scored two victories right away, and Falck's opponent likewise dived into the sea in flames. But the rear-gunner of the adjacent Wellington aimed well and truly. "My starboard engine," Falck reported, "jerked to a standstill. Petrol streamed out from the wing, and it was a miracle the plane didn't catch fire. As it was, Sergeant Waltz and I were hard put to it to prevent our ammo. going up. The whole cabin was full of smoke." He steered due south for base, hoping to reach Jever without further mishap. But then the second engine cut out, and there was only one hope left: to stretch his glide as far as Wangerooge and attempt a dead-stick landing.

The remaining ammunition was shot away and the fuel tanks drained, leaving nothing to catch fire or explode on impact. Finally Falck used the compressed-air pump to lower the under-carriage.

The ground rose up with alarming speed. There was a violent jolt—which the plane withstood—and they were coasting down the runway, coming to rest just short of the control tower. They were home.

A similar adventure befell First-Lieutenant Dietrich Robitzsch. His and one other Me 109 were the only ones of his squadron (from Jagdgruppe 101 at Neumünster) to join the air battle in time. After shooting down his target he too was hit by another Wellington in the engine cowling. Glycol spurted all over his windscreen, robbing him of vision. With difficulty he approached base, but shortly before getting there his overheated engine seized up. He had to land at once, but was forced to choose an impossible spot: right amongst the trenches and dugouts of a troop-training ground. The right tyre burst, the machine spun right round, but finally came to rest. Robitsch climbed out unscathed.

The whole battle was over in half an hour. By 15.00 the rest of the hard-hit British bombers were out of fighter range.

First to land at Jever was the *Geschwader* commander, Schumacher himself. For days to come the wreck of the Wellington he had dispatched remained sticking out of the mud-flats off Spiekeroog. One after the other, reports of successful combats came in. It seemed no squadron had returned empty-handed. Suddenly, however, Schumacher realised that there was no report at all from III/JG 77. His adjutant confessed the truth. In the general excitement of the alarm the headquarters staff had clean forgotten to notify Captain Seliger and his *Gruppe* at Nordholz. When someone thought of them after eight minutes, it was already too late. In the report to the international press next day in Berlin Schumacher was quoted as saying that he had even been able to keep squadrons "in reserve". That, of course, sounded much better—and could also apply to the feeble efforts of Major Reichardt's Jagdgruppe 101.

But the most astonishing report came from Borkum. There Lieutenant-General Wolff, of XI Air Administrative Region, happened to have witnessed the crash-landing of the first Wellington shot down by Lent. Shortly afterwards he appeared at Jever and took the *Geschwader* commander aside.

"We examined the wreck minutely," he said. "Believe you me, Schumacher, there wasn't a single bomb on board!"

This detail about the biggest air battle so far in war history remains wrapped in mystery to this day. It is on record that not one bomb was dropped, either at the Schillig Roads or Wilhelmshaven itself. The British explanation was that every vessel was in dock or harbour where the fall of bombs would endanger the lives of German civilians.

But surely the Wellington that crash-landed on Borkum either would have jettisoned its bombs before doing so, or else was not carrying any. According to the statements of its pilot, Flying-Officer Wimberley, and another prisoner, Flight-Sergeant Russe, no attack was intended—only a "navigation flight" over Heligoland Bight! Instead of bombs, they asserted, the bombers carried reinforced crews—to initiate new pilots and observers.

Should that version be true, then the British losses on December 18th were even graver. Aircraft could be replaced, but aircrews shot down over the enemy zone were lost for ever.

What were the true losses on both sides on this crucial date? Those of Schumacher's fighter outfit numbered just two Me 109s. One was that of First-Lieutenant Fuhrmann. After three fruitless attacks from the beam he forgot all discretion and rules and attacked afresh from astern, precisely in the field of fire of the rear-gunner and his twin machine-guns. And since the Wellington was not alone, but flew on the left of a flight of four, Fuhrmann received the "full treatment".

His Messerschmitt was riddled with bullets, his engine belched black smoke, and he himself must have been severely wounded. His plane plunged towards the sea, but at the last moment he managed to pull out and ditch it perfectly with a broad white trail of foam, some 200 yards off the island of Spiekeroog. Watchers on the shore saw him struggle from the cockpit and get clear before the machine sank.

With his last strength the pilot swam towards the island. But his heavy flying suit soaked up the icy water and dragged him down. Before the coast-guards could alert a boat the sea had won and he sank, scarcely a hundred yards from safety. The other Me 109, flown by a young Austrian from Graz, was seen to dive straight into the sea. The British told a different story. That night their Air Ministry declared that a formation of R.A.F. bombers had carried out an armed reconnaissance off Heligoland Bight with the object of attacking any enemy warships encountered at sea. They were met by strong forces of fighter aircraft and in the course of violent combats had destroyed twelve Messerschmitts. Seven bombers had not returned.

Evidently even the British were sometimes encouraged to view events through the rose-tinted spectacles of propaganda.

According to the British Press six of the dozen German aircraft allegedly destroyed were of the twin-engined Me 110 type, of which Hitler and Goering had such high hopes. The fact is, that of the only unit with these aircraft to be engaged—I/ZG 76—not a single machine was missing, even though some returned considerably damaged.

In his combat survey for JG 1, Schumacher attributed this damage to the "tight formation and excellent rear-gunners of the Wellington bombers". On the other hand: "Their maintenance of formation and rigid adherence to course made them easy targets to find."

The conclusions of I/ZG 76's commander, Captain Reinecke, in his own report were:

"The Me 110 is easily capable of catching and overtaking this English type (Vickers Wellington) even with the latter at full boost. This provides scope for multiple attacks from any quarter, including frontal beam. This attack," he added, "can be very effective if the enemy aircraft is allowed to fly into the cone of fire. The Wellington is very inflammable and burns readily."

This last view was confirmed by Air Vice-Marshal Baldwin, A.O.C. 3 Group, Bomber Command, which had mounted the operation. In a critical analysis he wrote: "Many of our aircraft were observed during and after the combat to have petrol pouring out of their tanks. . . . The vital necessity of fitting self-sealing tanks to all bombers cannot be over-emphasized."[1]

Baldwin also admitted that previously no one had considered the possibility of fighter attack from the beam, and that the Wellingtons had been unable to defend themselves against such tactics.

Such official criticism naturally remained secret. For the benefit of the public the R.A.F. persisted with its propaganda version that Bomber Command

[1] *Royal Air Force 1939–45*, Vol. I, p. 46.

had scored a significant victory over the German fighter force, and that only seven of their own aircraft had failed to return.

But initial German claims were also too high to stand the test of subsequent examination. For I/ZG 76 alone Reinecke had claimed fifteen victories, and for II/JG 77 von Bülow—who himself had to return shortly after taking off with engine trouble—claimed another fourteen. After adding the score of the night-fighter squadron, 10/JG 26, Schumacher arrived at a grand total of thirty-two, while XI Air Admin. Region in Hamburg made it thirty-four. The latter figure was forwarded to Berlin.

Here it should be emphasized that German fighter pilots were not allowed to make claims at will. Before any claim was finalised it had to go through many "bureaucratic" channels. At the outset they had to answer a whole list of standard questions: time, position and altitude of combat; nationality and type of aircraft claimed. The combat report then had to give a description of how victory was achieved, and finally exact data as to whether it could be confirmed by observers on land or sea. As if that were not enough, a colleague had to testify in writing that he had witnessed the combat and seen the enemy aircraft crash. The following is an example.

At 14.45, at the height of the battle, an Me 110 north of Langeoog had attacked the rear left Wellington in a formation of seven. Pilot was Gordon Gollob, later to become the world's leading fighter "ace", with 150 accredited victories. He made his attack from left astern.

"My fire was accurate," ran his combat report. "After the attack I climbed to port and saw the Wellington, pouring out smoke from its stern, curve off to the left and disappear downwards. . . ."

In view of the strict British orders not to break formation, it certainly seemed the Wellington had been downed, and Gollob turned his attention to the next opponent. About the crash of the first he later wrote: "Not observed— for an aircraft on fire over the sea is bound to crash into it, and there were moreover many others to be shot down. . . ."

This little taunt against the bureaucratic reporting procedure was duly punished. Five months later Berlin returned his combat report and its claim endorsed "Not accepted". Altogether seven of the thirty-four victories claimed by JG 1 on December 18, 1939, were subsequently rejected by the Reich Air Ministry in Berlin, "because they cannot be established with complete certainty."

In the light of subsequent experience it can now be taken as certain that, with the battle breaking up into numerous individual engagements, many a victory was in all good faith reported twice. This view is also subscribed to by the German Fighter Pilots' Association in a publication of April 1963.

The figures issued by the British after the war confirm that of the twenty-two Wellingtons that reached Heligoland Bight on an armed reconnaissance, twelve were shot down and three more were so badly damaged that they had to make forced landings on the English coast and broke up. Surviving German fighter pilots who took part still view these figures sceptically. Above all, the disclosure that many of the Wellingtons carried no bombs raises the suspicion that there may have been a second formation about which the British sources are silent. Be that as it may, a loss of over two-thirds of the operating force verged on the catastrophic. It was the death knell of the widely held opinion: "The bomber will always get through!"

From now on it was evident that either the bombers must confine themselves to operations by night, or else they must be provided with strong fighter escort. This verdict was to have a decisive influence on the future conduct of the war.

3. The Invasion of Scandinavia

On April 6, 1940, Hamburg's Hotel Esplanade was throbbing with activity. Military vehicles blocked the approaches, and a constant flow of Luftwaffe officers disappeared into the interior. A few weeks previously this hotel had been taken over as HQ of X Air Corps, which controlled all Luftwaffe units for the coming Operation "*Weserübung*"—the occupation of Denmark and Norway by German forces.

Originally this operation formed no part of German strategy, which—in the event of the conflict failing to terminate with the end of the Polish campaign—was directed entirely at an attack on the West. On September 2, 1939, Germany had declared the inviolability of Norway, so long as this was not infringed by a third power. But by September 19th the British were already planning to stifle the German shipments of Swedish iron ore which were routed from Narvik through Norwegian territorial waters.

On January 6, 1940, the British foreign minister, Lord Halifax, in notes to Oslo and Stockholm[1], declared that His Majesty's government proposed to take suitable measures to prevent the use of Norwegian territorial waters by German merchantmen. In pursuance of these measures it might become necessary from time to time for the Royal Navy to enter these waters and conduct operations therein.

Despite the protest of the Scandinavian countries—on January 8th the Norwegian foreign minister Koht informed Halifax that never had Norwegian neutrality been so outspokenly threatened—the Supreme Allied War Council resolved on February 5th to land four divisions at Narvik and occupy the Swedish iron mines of Gällivare.

Under the threat of these developments the German high command appointed a special staff with the code-name "*Weserübung*" to plan countermeasures. This took up office on February 3rd. On March 28th the Allies finally gave orders for the mining of Norwegian waters on April 5th, to be followed by landings at Narvik, Trondheim, Bergen and Stavanger. In the event the Germans only just anticipated them.

So now on April 6th Lieutenant-General Hans Ferdinand Geisler had called his subordinate commanders to Hamburg to be put in the picture.

[1] Churchill, in *The Second World War*, makes no mention of these notes. Though the author has cited to the publisher official Swedish and Norwegian documents for both their text and the Scandinavian protest, a comparison with Churchill's account, and with that of Captain MacIntyre, R.N., in his book *Narvik*, suggests that this whole introduction does less than justice to the Allies. Three points may be mentioned. First, though a scheme for an Allied landing at Narvik and three other points was approved on February 5th (to take place in mid-March), this was primarily to aid the Finns, and when the latter surrendered to Russia the British Cabinet at once withdrew its approval. Second, Norwegian territorial waters were in the event not mined till April 8th (not 5th)—i.e. just one day before the German landings. Third, the *Altmark* episode had already shown that the Norwegians could not or would not protect their neutrality against German infringement. As for the view that the German invasion was only to anticipate Allied threats, Raeder has stated that Hitler ordered his Supreme Command to prepare for a Norwegian operation as early as December 14th (after he had met Quisling), and on February 20th he appointed Falkenhorst to command it. On April 1st (a week before the British mining) he signed the order for the operation to take place on the 9th.—*Translator's Note.*

From Major Christian of the general staff they received their detailed operational orders for "Weser Day".

By this time numerous naval transport convoys were already on the way, with the invasion ports some days ahead of them. Warship flotillas too had been embarked with troops and awaited their sailing orders, timed to bring them in a surprise appearance off the Norwegian coast at "Weser" zero hour, early on April 9th. The whole operation depended for its success on the Luftwaffe and the Navy solving the transport problem. Only if the crucial harbours and airfields were taken at one blow could the necessary reinforcements follow.

The command briefing at the Hotel Esplanade was very thorough. Specially appointed for Operation "*Weserübung*" was an air-transport chief, Lieutenant-Colonel Freiherr von Gablenz, who now expounded the time-table to which it was essential his units should adhere if disaster at the landing airfields was to be avoided. Consisting as it did of eleven *Gruppen* totalling some 500 transport aircraft, it was no mean force. Most of them were triple-engined Ju 52s, though one *Gruppe* was equipped with four-engined Ju 90 and Focke-Wulf Fw 200 super-heavies. For the whole force the landing airfields in Denmark and Norway numbered just four:

1. and 2. Aalborg-East and Aalborg-West in northern Jutland, to provide staging posts for operations against Norway.
3. Oslo-Fornebu, as a base for the occupation of the Norwegian capital.
4. Stavanger-Sola on the south-west coast of Norway, as a defensive air base against attacks by the British fleet.

For the first time in history it was planned to drop paratroops on these four airfields. The timing was precise: e.g., for Oslo-Fornebu it was to be at zero hour plus 185 minutes.

After that the parachutists were given just twenty minutes to capture the airfield and secure it for the landings that were due to follow at zero hour plus 205 minutes, bringing in a normal infantry battalion. Other Ju 52 squadrons would then land in succession an advance party of Luftwaffe administrative staff, an airfield servicing company, a further infantry battalion, the command staff of General von Falkenhorst, signals and engineer units—and, between-times, such initial supplies as fuel, pumps and hoses.

The actual paratroops, for Fornebu, consisted of only two companies: 1 and 2/FJR 1 under their battalion commander Captain Erich Walther. As air cover there were to be just four long-range fighters—later raised to eight—from 1/ZG 76 under First-Lieutenant Hansen. When these reached Fornebu they would have fuel for only another twenty minutes' flying, and so without more ado would have to land there themselves.

On April 7th, only thirty-six hours before zero hour, the plans of X Air Corps had in one respect to be drastically altered. The paratroops billed for the Aalborg drop became urgently wanted elsewhere.

Captain Walter Gericke, company commander of 4/FJR 1, was drinking coffee at his base in Stendal, when a special messenger arrived to fly him to G.H.Q. in Hamburg. At the Hotel Esplanade the chief of staff, Major Harlinghausen, led him to a giant wall-map.

"See this bridge?" he said, tapping with his finger a red line between the Danish islands of Falster and Seeland. "It's three kilometres long and the only land link connecting the Gedser ferry terminal in the south with Copenhagen." Gericke watched his finger. "We've got to capture this bridge intact," Harlinghausen added ominously. "If you were dropped with a couple of platoons, do you think you could hold it till the infantry arrive from Gedser?"

Gericke was confident. It was just the sort of job he and his paratroops had trained for. Soon afterwards he was on the return flight to Stendal, listing the things he had to get: a tolerably reliable map, a plan of the adjacent town of Vordingborg, and a picture postcard of the small island of Masnedö between Falster and Seeland, showing the bridge in the background. On April 8th Gericke's company moved to its forward base at Uetersee. The other two companies of the parachute regiment's first battalion already lay at Schleswig (for Oslo) and at Stade (for Stavanger), complete with their transport planes.

At last the air-transport fleet received the code-message for the following day: "Weser North and South 9 Metre High Tide."

At the appointed time of 05.30 the twelve Ju 52s of 8 Squadron/KG zbV 1[1] took off for Denmark, with Gericke's men aboard. The weather there was tolerable, whereas the departure of the other units was delayed indefinitely by heavy fog belts over the Skagerrak. Shortly after 07.00 hours a platoon of Gericke's company was parachuted down over Aalborg. That was all that could now be spared for the capture of the two important airfields. However, the Danes put up no resistance.

No. 8 Squadron's remaining Ju 52s crossed the western arm of the Baltic and steered straight for their target. Shining in the rays of the rising sun the far-stretching bridge came into view ahead. At 06.15 Gericke gave the signal to jump, and within seconds the transports had emptied themselves. White parachutes oscillated down upon the little isle of Masnedö. No shots were fired, no sirens wailed in alarm. The country still seemed wrapped in sleep.

Captain Gericke landed close to the embankment leading to the bridge. His first action was to set up machine guns upon it. From there he could rake the Danish coastal fort to provide covering fire for his men, many of whom had dropped from the sky scarcely a hundred yards from its concrete cupolas. But the fort held its fire. The paratroops rushed towards it. Without even taking time to find their arms-containers, they stormed it with only their pistols. The sentries put up their hands in alarm, and the Germans burst into the billets. Within minutes the whole garrison was disarmed.

Another detachment, seizing bicycles, pedalled furiously for the bridge. There, too, the guard gave itself up without a shot. But what was the surprise of the paratroops when a column of German infantry was seen marching towards them. It was an advance troop of III Battalion, Infantry Regiment 305, which according to plan had crossed by ferry from Warnemünde to Gedser, and finding no opposition had pushed on to the north.

Machine-gunners and paratroops now jointly penetrated Vordingborg and occupied the bridge connecting Masnedö with Seeland. Within an hour the mission had been completed. Thus the first parachute operation in war history was also the most bloodless. But the secret of this new military weapon had now been exposed. The trump card of surprise, better saved for a more vital occasion, would seem to have been wasted.

[1] Transport *Geschwader* carried the designation: *Kampfgeschwader zur besonderen Verwendung*—i.e., "Bomber *Geschwader* for special duties."

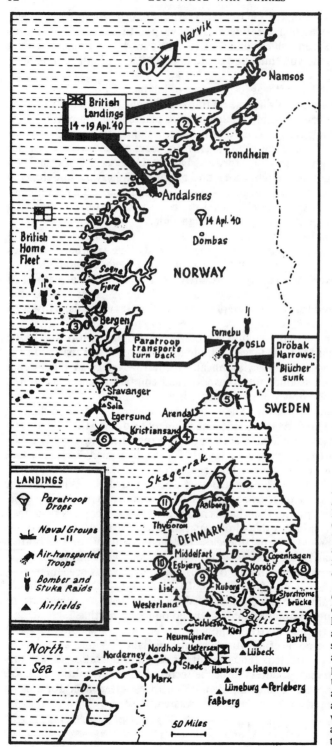

Invasion of Scandinavia. Known as Operation *"Weserübung"*, the assault on Denmark and Norway, opened on April 9, 1940, with the German occupation of harbours and airfields. The map shows the operations areas of warships, paratroops and air-transported troops, also the German airfields from which the bombers and transports took off.

While the occupation of Denmark was proceeding so peacefully, a fiasco was brewing for the Luftwaffe transport units headed for Norway. As the morning of April 9th went by, the met. men offered no hope of even passable visibility over Oslo and Stavanger. Over the Skagerrak, which both formations had to cross, the fog reached almost from sea-level to 2,000 feet, with further cloud-layers above.

Low-level flight was thus out of the question, and if they flew above cloud, how would they know when to descend? And what if, at the critical moment, they found themselves with no ground visibility at all, right amongst the rocky cliffs of the Norwegian fiords?

At the head of the first wave—II/KG zbV 1—flew First-Lieutenant Drewes, bound for Oslo-Fornebu. Aboard his twenty-nine Ju 52s crouched Captain Erich Walcher's paratroops, all ready to jump. But the nearer Drewes approached Oslo Fiord, the worse the weather became. Vision was reduced to a bare twenty yards, so that even the neighbouring aircraft of his own section were sometimes swallowed up in fog.

Drewes gritted his teeth and flew on, well aware of the vital importance of his mission for the success of the whole enterprise. Suddenly one of the section leaders astern reported over the V.H.F.: "Calling C.O.: I have two aircraft missing."

Both had vanished without trace in a bank of fog. It was the deciding factor. If they flew on, Drewes could no longer be responsible. He gave orders to set a reciprocal course, and at 08.20 Hamburg received the signal: "Turning back owing to bad weather. Am proceeding to Aalborg."

At the Hotel Esplanade the signal confirmed the worst fears. For there it was already known that the Norwegians were not giving up without a struggle. The sequence of events was as follows:

For three hours a German warship flotilla in Oslo Fiord had been locked in battle with the batteries of Fort Oskarsborg, which controlled the Drobak Narrows. Its flagship, the heavy cruiser *Blücher*, had been sunk at 07.23 by shells and torpedoes; and when and whether the remaining cruisers could break through and land their cargoes of troops at Oslo was doubtful.

It was all the more vital, therefore, that Fornebu should be taken, so that at least the airborne landings could proceed according to plan. But now the paratroops were returning, with the second wave of transports due in twenty minutes to land an infantry battalion—II/IR 324—at an airfield that had not been captured.

Lieutenant-General Geisler had received strict orders from Goering that, in the event of the paratroops failing to make their drop, the succeeding waves of transports were to be recalled forthwith. In exasperation their commander, Freiherr von Gablenz, tried to dissuade the G.O.C.: "I refuse, *Herr General*, to order my units to return! They can force a landing even though the air-field has *not* been secured."

"Then the Norwegians will shoot them to pieces!"

"The first troops to be landed will soon cope with the defences," von Gablenz persisted obstinately. "At least give the first unit that gets there the chance of deciding whether to land or not." He reasoned on: "Aalborg is now saturated. If we land the Oslo lot there as well, there will be a disaster."

He failed to make his point. Geisler sent out a radio signal ordering the whole force to turn back. Authority: X Air Corps. But now something most unusual happened; something that defied the accepted axiom that a good soldier is one who blindly executes orders.

In charge of the transport *Gruppe* following the paratroops—i.e., *Kampfgruppe* zbV 103—was a Captain Wagner. Though he received the orders to return, he decided to disobey them. The reason was that he got them just as he was approaching Fornebu, and they seemed so stupid that he took them for a trick of the enemy. Above all, the authority, "X Air Corps", aroused his suspicions. Was his unit not under the command of "Transport Chief Land", von Gablenz? Surely only that source could issue such a drastic order?

So Captain Wagner flew on. The pilots, after all, were experienced blind-flying men. The densest fog belt had lain in front of the coast. Now, just before Oslo, the weather was clearing, and one was beginning to see. There seemed no reason for not landing at Fornebu. The command section was already over it. Wagner flew a circuit and looked down. The airfield was quite small. At one end of the two asphalt runways the ground rose sharply, at the other it fell away into an arm of the sea. Not exactly ideal, but no great problem for "old Aunt Ju".

On it, however, stood the flaming wrecks of two aircraft. The battle, it seemed, had already begun. Sure enough, there, banked in flight, were German long-range fighters. Relieved, Wagner signalled his pilot to land. The Ju 52 banked steeply, then swept down to the runway.

Suddenly the fuselage was splintered by heavy machine-gun fire. First casualty was Wagner himself. There was a groaning of wounded men. The pilot re-opened the throttle and pulled the machine up again. What now? Disconcerted, the squadron commander of 1/ZG 76, First-Lieutenant Hansen, watched the scene from his Me 110.

For half an hour he and his squadron had battled with the enemy. First, at 08.38, they had been attacked out of the sun by nine Norwegian single-seater fighters—Gloster Gladiators. None the less at 08.45, as ordered, he had started circling the airfield to provide covering fire for the paratroops. After the short, sharp air battle two of his own planes were missing.

The remaining six reconnoitred the airfield, letting fly at the anti-aircraft defences, and setting on fire two Gladiators on the runway. Then they waited and waited. But the paratroops never arrived. Three red warning lights stared at Hansen from his instrument panel. At any moment the fourth would go on, and that would mean his tanks were empty. It had been calculated they would have fuel for twenty minutes' flying over Fornebu. During that period the paratroops were to capture the airfield. And now the time was up.

Then at last, at 09.05, the first section of Ju 52s was seen approaching. The Me 110s circled on the flanks to pin down the machine-gun posts at the vital moment, and waited for the parachutes to mushroom. . . . How were they to know the planes were already those of the second wave, and that there were no paratroops in them?

Hence Hansen was taken completely by surprise when the leading Ju 52 first came in to land, then under heavy fire flew off again.

Things had gone far enough. Three of his six Me 110s were flying with just one engine. And they were all on their last drops of petrol. They must land at once. And if no one else felt competent to capture Oslo-Fornebu, the fighter crews of 1/ZG 76 would do it themselves!

Hansen called on the radio: "Lieutenant Lent, go in and land! We'll give covering fire, then follow you."

Obediently Lent banked left and went in to land, black smoke issuing from his starboard engine. In view of the shortness of the runway he had to put the plane down right on the edge of the airfield to have enough run; with only one engine the problem was magnified. The champion of Heligoland Bight lowered his undercarriage and flaps. A few minutes previously he had scored his fifth victory of the war against the Gloster Gladiator of the Norwegian Sergeant Per Schye. Now for him and his radio operator, Corporal Kubisch, a good landing meant the difference between life or death.

A hundred yards before the airfield boundary his aircraft sagged too low to clear it. He applied full boost to the port engine and the aircraft slewed violently to starboard. He righted it with difficulty, and saw the runway beneath him. But the speed was now excessive, the landing stall too late . . . the run would be too long.

Hansen and the other four Messerschmitts kept their eyes glued upon their comrade. Belting across his approach they aimed at the machine-guns firing from concrete emplacements. None the less bullets spurted behind and beside the landing aircraft.

Suddenly Hansen saw a second plane landing simultaneously: a Ju 52. It was —as was established later—the signals aircraft of the missing paratroop unit, which was to prove very useful. But at the moment disaster threatened. The 52 was landing on the second asphalt runway. If the two machines collided at their point of intersection, the whole airfield would be completely blocked for any further landings.

Furiously Hansen surveyed the scene from aloft. All this time they had waited for the transports, and at the very last moment, when they themselves could remain airborne no longer, the Ju 52s had to come barging in across their line. Lent could thank his stars that the landing speed of his Me 110 exceeded that of the Ju 52: he had passed the runway intersection before the latter got there. But his speed was *too* great. There was no hope of stopping in time. Fleetingly Hansen hoped he would manage to take off again. But at the end of its run Lent's plane dived head-first down the boundary slope.

That was the last Hansen saw, for now he had to concentrate on his own landing. His starboard engine too had been hit. White steam hissed menacingly from the overflow-pipe, and the oil temperature was racing upwards. If the engine lasted one more minute, he would make it. Crossing the boundary almost on the deck, he throttled back and pulled the stick gently towards him. The plane settled. Closely missing the two burning Gladiators he ran on towards the Norwegian machine-gun posts. They were quiet. Then he saw that another Me 110 had landed ahead of him, and was getting out of his way. "Also alive!" was his surprised reaction.

Carefully he applied the brakes, and ten yards short of the boundary slope his machine came to rest. His radio-operator had his thumb on the firing button, but the airfield guns, active a minute before, were now silent. Had the Norwegians stopped resisting?

In fact, the commander of the Gladiator squadron, Captain Erling Munthe Dahl, watching the Me 110s dive on the airfield, had said over the radio: "Calling all Gladiators! Land anywhere, but not, repeat not, Fornebu. It is under attack by the Germans."

Two of his fighters had already landed there: one with engine trouble, the other, piloted by Sergeant Waalar, badly damaged from combat with the 110s. Both had promptly been set on fire by Hansen and his men, and Dahl wanted to save the others from a similar fate.

Five Gladiators therefore landed after the battle on frozen lakes north and west of Oslo. Four of them broke through the ice, or else had to be abandoned as a result of combat damage or petrol shortage. Thus in the end there was only one survivor. As the first German aircraft came in to land, Captain Dahl and his ground personnel withdrew to Fort Akershus. Flak and machine-guns, after firing on the first two planes, gave up, and the Norwegian defence of Fornebu, though no one knew it, had ended.

Jumping from his machine, Hansen guided in the remaining Me 110s. Then he drew up the five of them on the north-westerly boundary, giving the radio-operators a clear field of fire towards a wood. Even Lent appeared, on foot. He had left his Messerschmitt with sheared undercarriage, virtually a write-off, a few yards from a house beyond the airfield boundary. By a miracle both he and Kubisch had come out unscathed. The latter had even dismantled the rear machine-gun, and with ammunition drum in place now brought it up to reinforce his squadron colleagues—the handful of men who had just captured a defended air-field from the air!

At 09.17 a new section of Ju 52s came in to land. The ground-run of the heavy machines carried them close up to the rocks that housed the Norwegian flak posts. Barely a quarter of an hour earlier these had claimed the commander of KG zbV 103, Captain Wagner, as he made his daring touch-down.

Now not a shot rang out. Out climbed the grey-uniformed infantrymen and stretched their legs. Finding everything peaceful, they lit cigarettes. Hansen's hair stood on end. Rushing over to them, he hurriedly pointed out the locations of the Norwegian flak and machine-gun posts. Then at last they took cover and sent out shock detachments, which presently returned with prisoners. The Norwegians had thrown in the sponge.

Meanwhile one Ju 52 landed and taxied straight up to the fighter planes, where it was greeted with loud rejoicing. It was the squadron's own trans-porter! Captain Flakowski, 1/ZG 76's blind-flying instructor, had brought it safely through the bad-weather front over the Skagerrak. Aboard were welcome reinforcements in the shape of the squadron's six key maintenance men, plus a full load of ammunition.

Over Oslo Fiord Flakowski had several times met sections of Ju 52s which had turned back, and which by approaching and rocking their wings indicated that he should do the same. His response had been to open the door of the control cabin and call back to his men: "Get your pistols out! There's fighting at Oslo."

Now they had arrived. The armourer artificer, Paul Mahle, at once went off with his colleagues to repair the damaged planes, and Captain Flakowski, calling together a bunch of soldiers, started a thorough reconnaissance. Finally he directed the Norwegian prisoners to clear the smouldering wrecks of the two Gladiators from the runway.

Then First-Lieutenant Hansen thought he was dreaming. A large, light-blue American car drew up, and out stepped a German officer in full formal uniform. It was Captain Spiller, Luftwaffe attaché in Oslo. Hansen reported with his air-crews.

"What's happened to the paratroops?" asked Spiller. "And the battalion of infantry?"

Hansen said he did not know. It seemed that the whole *coup* against Oslo depended for its success on the air-landing at Fornebu, since the warships bringing sea-borne infantry were still held up in the Dröbak Narrows.

"You must report at once back to Germany that the airfield is taken," Spiller ordered. "Otherwise we shall go on waiting for the transport *Gruppen* until it is too late."

Thereupon a message was proudly tapped out from the signals Ju 52: "Fornebu in our hands, 1 Squadron/ZG 76." The signal was picked up at Aalborg and re-transmitted to X Air Corps H.Q. in Hamburg. There the eight Me 110s had been considered written off. And now came not only a sign of life, but a report, scarcely to be credited, that Fornebu was ready for landings!

Meanwhile the ordered flight sequence of the transport *Gruppen* had lapsed into chaos. 5 and 6 Squadrons/KG zbV 1, with the paratroops on board, had as described been compelled by the heavy fog to turn back before reaching Oslo Fiord. Two or three of their Ju 52s, which had lost contact owing to the conditions, did in fact land at Fornebu half an hour behind schedule.

KG zbV 103, due to arrive twenty minutes behind the paratroop formation, had been ordered by X Air Corps to return, but went on. Most of the transports did, however, turn back after their commander, Captain Wagner, had fallen a victim to anti-aircraft fire in the act of landing. Only his deputy commander, Captain Ingenhoven, with a handful of other transports, managed to get down on to the airfield. These were the planes that landed almost simultaneously with 1/ZG 76's fighters.

The end result was that, on the morning of April 9, 1940, Oslo-Fornebu was held by a motley handful of men from Infantry Regiment 324, a few paratroops, and the crews of the aircraft that brought them. Led by one or two resolute officers, particularly Captains Flakowski and Ingenhoven, this little band disarmed and secured the airfield.

"About three hours afterwards," read 1/ZG 76's combat report, "the Ju 52 formations arrived with the bulk of the paratroops and air-borne infantry." Then they came in droves. As one transport squadron after another flew in, the aircraft soon blocked the asphalt runways. None the less, in the course of the afternoon the whole of Infantry Regiment 324 managed to get down.

By the evening Oslo was in German hands, "according to plan"—the first capital city ever to have fallen to airborne troops. Two days later the chief of X Air Corps, Lieutenant-General Geisler, gave First-Lieutenant Hansen a warm handshake.

"But for your squadron," he said, "things might have turned out very differently!"

At the same time as the Oslo transports received the order to turn back, another formation further west plunged into a cloud-bank over the North Sea. It was the twelve Ju 52s of 7 Squadron/KG zbV 1, headed for Stavanger.

At their head flew the squadron commander, Captain Günther Capito, and on board was 3 Company/Parachute Regiment 1, under First-Lieutenant Freiherr von Brandis, due to be dropped on Stavanger-Sola airfield.

Though the air-crews had all been trained in blind-flying, they had previously never done this in formation, or indeed over the sea. So now the situation was "dicey". If two machines collided, it would be the end for all on board, for there was not a life-belt amongst them.

"The whole squadron was swallowed up in the clouds," Capito reported later. "Despite the closest formation, the nearest plane was like a phantom."

The decision whether to go on or turn back was now his alone. It was a hard one to make, but he decided to proceed. He could only hope that over the Norwegian coast the weather would clear. An approach through the mountains in the present visibility would be suicidal. But luck was with them. "After half an hour it grew steadily lighter, and suddenly the clouds parted. We were through. 3,000 feet below us the sea glittered in the sun, while some sixty miles off, ahead and to starboard, the Norwegian coast could be seen quite clearly."

Then Capito glanced back to take stock of his formation. One after the other Ju 52s came popping out of the dark cloud-bank at all sorts of different spots. It took half an hour before they had all collected. There were only eleven of them: the twelfth never appeared. Later it was ascertained that the pilot had not kept to his course, and had landed in Denmark. At least no aircraft was written off, as in the case of Oslo, where two had collided and crashed into the sea.

Now close above the wave-tops the eleven planes stole further north. The bad-weather front had cost much time. At 09.20 they reached the latitude of Stavanger, turned sharply right and made landfall.

Everything now happened in swift succession. Surprise must not be lost. Only thirty feet above the ground the squadron droned up a side valley, turned sharp north, leapt over a chain of hills—and there ahead was the target airfield. The paratroops had long since got ready. The broad hatches of the 52s were opened, and the men waited for the signal hooters to sound.

Captain Capito pulled his command aircraft up to 400 feet and at once throttled back. This was the pre-ordained altitude for the drop. "Our speed had to be low," he reported, "to keep the paratroops close together. And to fly at only 400 feet above an enemy with his finger on the trigger is not exactly good life insurance."

The hooters went off and the men jumped out. Within seconds they were all gone—twelve from each machine. Their weapon-containers were thrown after them, then at full throttle the aircraft dropped down to the deck again to get below the flak's angle of fire, and so away. They had completed their mission.

Over a hundred parachutists went swaying down, but before First-Lieutenant Brandis could collect them together, they were met by a hail of machine-gun fire. Then suddenly two Me 110s screamed over the airfield firing their guns in counter-attack. They belonged to First-Lieutenant Gordon Gollob's 3 Squadron/ZG 76—and were the only two to have reached Stavanger through the bad weather. Two others were missing, and the rest had been forced to turn back.

The main Norwegian resistance came from two well-protected emplacements on the airfield boundary. The parachutists hurled hand-grenades

25. In the occupation of Denmark and Norway paratroops were used for the capture of bridges and airfields in the enemy's rear.

26. The subjugation of Norway was a risky operation only made possible by the mass deployment of 500 transport aircraft. The picture shows Ju 52/3Ms after landing at Oslo-Fornebu.

27. The British Fleet off Norway was attacked by KG 26 and KG 30 with varying success. The picture shows the crew of a Ju 88.

28. Arado 196 floatplanes capture the damaged British minelaying submarine *Seal* in the Kattegatt.

through the embrasures, and after half an hour the airfield was in their hands. It remained to clear the runway of wire obstacles, then Stavanger-Sola was also ready for the first transport squadrons to land.

The German command had hoped that the Norwegians, like the Danes, would offer no resistance to the landings. The operational orders of X Air Corps included the words: "Efforts will be made to give the operation the appearance of a peaceable occupation."

Accordingly the bomber force allocated to "*Weserübung*"—comprising in any case only ten *Gruppen* of bombers and one of dive-bombers[1]—was either held in reserve or else restricted to "demonstration" flights. One *Gruppe* of KG 4, for example, was ordered at 06.30 to drop leaflets over Copenhagen. Another, III/KG 4, was to make a show of strength by flying in squadrons over Kristiansand, Egersund, Stavanger and Bergen, to coincide with the German landings by sea and air.

At the same time He 111 bombers of III/KG 26 flew in over Oslo Fiord, where, however, they were attacked by Captain Dahl's Gladiators. This, and the burning hulk of the *Blücher* in the Dröbak Narrows, removed any doubt that the Norwegians intended resistance by every means they had.

Thereupon Captain Hozzel's dive-bomber *Gruppe*, I/StG 1, went off from Kiel-Holtenau at 10.59 with twenty-two Ju 87s to attack the rock fortresses of Oskarsborg and Akershus. They reported seeing their bombs strike their targets.

Other squadrons of KG 4 and KG 26, with *Kampfgruppe* 100, bombed Oslo-Kjeller airfield, flak positions on Holmenkollen, and coastal batteries on the islands in Oslo Fiord. Under the pressure of these bombardments most of the Norwegian strong-points were captured by the German airborne troops by the evening of April 8th. But during the morning of that day a quite different target had manifested itself. At 10.30 reconnaissance planes reported numerous British battleships and cruisers off Bergen. It was the Home Fleet under Admiral Forbes.

It was an appearance which X Air Corps had anticipated, and for which it had kept its "naval" bombers in reserve. Towards noon forty-one He 111s of the "Lion" *Geschwader*, KG 26, and forty-seven Ju 88s, of the "Eagle" *Geschwader*, KG 30, took off. For over three hours the British fleet was attacked almost without let-up. The battleship *Rodney* was hit by a 1,000-lb. bomb, which failed to penetrate her armoured girdle; the cruisers *Devonshire*, *Southampton* and *Glasgow* were damaged, and the destroyer *Gurkha* was sunk west of Stavanger.

During the weeks that followed—that is, for the duration of the whole Norwegian campaign—British warships and transports were subjected again and again to bombing by the Luftwaffe. This rose to a crescendo during the Allied counter-landings in central Norway. Between April 14th and 19th two British divisions, plus Polish and French troops, were put ashore at Namsos and Andalsnes, north and south of Trondheim.

Once more an operation by paratroops was called for. In the evening of April 14th, 1 Company/FJR 1, under Lieutenant Herbert Schmidt, was dropped at Dombas in the Gudbrandsdal to prevent the Norwegians who had withdrawn from Oslo linking up with the British units landed at Andalsnes. Bad weather, however, made it impossible to supply the company from the air, and after ten days' stout resistance its men were taken prisoner.

[1] For Order of Battle during "Operation *Wesermünde*", see Appendix 4.

But the Luftwaffe continued its attacks on the British expeditionary force, on its supply ports, and as always on the fleet. Its sovereignty over the Norwegian zone could not be contested by the British air squadrons, some of which were operating at extreme range from bases in northern Scotland, others from aircraft carriers. After only two weeks, the Allied expeditionary force was forced to re-embark at the same ports at which it had landed, and for this swift German success the Luftwaffe was largely responsible.

In the Kattegat and Skagerrak—the two arms of the sea dividing Denmark from Norway and Sweden—things did not go so well, and the Germans suffered considerable loss. Twelve British submarines had been lying in wait since April 8th. German troop transports bound for southern Norway had no means of circumventing this invisible enemy. They just had to run the gauntlet.

The first two transports were claimed on the day of the submarines' arrival. On the 9th the cruiser *Karlsruhe* had to be abandoned after being torpedoed by the submarine *Truant*. On the 11th another torpedo from the *Spearfish* severed the rudder and propellors of the cruiser *Lützow* as she returned from Oslo. Numerous further transports were either damaged or sunk.

Towards the end of the month larger British submarines began laying mines in the Kattegat. Things reached the stage where counter-measures were vital if supplies and reinforcements for Norway were to be maintained.

To undertake them Küstenfliegergruppe 706, under Major Lessing, was transferred to Aalborg. Equipped with Heinkel He 115 and Arado Ar 196 seaplanes, its crews had for weeks been busy carrying out their prescribed, monotonous and exhausting duties: Reconnoitre the sea—escort ships—search for submarines in square X. . . .

But on May 5, 1940 their world brightened. It was a Sunday. Two Arados took off in the dark for an early reconnaissance. Their commanders, Lieu-tenants Günther Mehrens and Karl Schmidt, wanted to be over their allotted sea area before dawn. At night the submarines surfaced, so the best chance of sighting them was at first light.

At about 02.30 Mehrens' Arado was flying slowly over the Kattegat, altitude 150 feet, and the pilot was steering north, not far from Swedish terri-torial waters. Suddenly Mehrens spotted a shadowy silhouette ahead and to starboard. The Arado banked towards it and went down. Yes, certainly it was a conning tower! It slanted obliquely: the bows were in the air, and the stern was awash. Yet the submarine was moving—eastwards, towards Sweden.

Mehrens fired a burst of 20-mm cannon ahead of the conning tower, then picking up the signal lamp, he flashed the letter "K"—international code for "Heave to immediately!"—followed in morse by "What ship?" On the bridge of the submarine—it was in fact the *Seal*—Lieutenant-Commander Rupert P. Lonsdale ordered Petty-Officer Waddington to flash an incomprehensible answer. He wanted to gain time.

The *Seal*, an exceptionally large vessel of 1,520 tons, had been laying mines in the Kattegat when she grazed one herself, and the explosion sent her to the bottom. After several anxious hours the crew had managed to re-surface her. But she was badly holed and could only move very slowly. The captain had decided that the only chance was to make for the nearby Swedish territorial waters.

Mehrens saw through the bluff. The vessel could only be British. Telling his pilot to climb to 3,000 feet, he reported his find on the radio. Then he dived on the target, released one 100-lb bomb and pulled up again. Within a few seconds a fountain of water gushed from the sea some thirty yards away from the submarine. He repeated the attack, but the second bomb also missed. Then he hammered the conning tower and water-line with his guns. Aboard the submarine Lonsdale himself jumped to the twin Lewis-guns and returned the fire.

Then another bomb fell beside the vessel. Lieutenant Schmidt's Arado had appeared on the scene and taken over the attack. The fourth and last bomb finally scored a near-miss. The *Seal* rocked drunkenly, then suddenly signalled "S O S". The moment of decision had arrived. In the engine room the water had risen so high that the one remaining diesel ceased to function. The submarine wallowed motionless.

Lonsdale was responsible for the lives of sixty men, and the *Seal* was a dead duck, which unless he surrendered would inevitably be sunk. A white table-cloth was brought up to the bridge, and he waved it over his head.

Schmidt hardly believed his eyes. Two Arados had captured an out-size submarine? Such a thing had never happened before! But what now if it started up again and suddenly submerged? Not a soul would believe the fantastic story. He needed proof. What better proof than the captain himself?

At that he went down on the water and called across:

"Who is the captain? Dive in, swim over and come aboard!"

Lonsdale took off his shoes, leapt from the bridge and swam over in a crawl. Schmidt stood on a float and helped the Englishman out of the water. Then he pushed him into the observer's seat and climbed in behind him. Lonsdale protested about Swedish territorial waters, but the German shook his head energetically.

The Arado took off again and set course direct to Aalborg. Certainly it was not every day that one returned from a reconnaissance flight with a British submarine commander on board. Meanwhile Mehrens had looked around till he found the fishing steamer *Franken*, which was on submarine patrol under Lieutenant Lang. Guided by the Arado to the *Seal*, Lang took off its crew and even succeeded in towing it to Frederikshavn.

Later, at 05.00 at Küstenfliegergruppe 706's base at Aalborg, a man in still dripping trousers acknowledged the birthday salutations of German air force officers. His identification papers had given it away. Lieutenant-Commander Lonsdale had just become thirty-five years old. It was a birthday he was not likely to forget.

The Battle of the North Sea—Summary and Conclusions

1. The air battle in the West began with both sides exercising the utmost restraint. During the autumn and winter of 1939 neither the Luftwaffe nor the Royal Air Force were allowed to drop bombs on enemy territory. The Germans hoped this would encourage the British to make peace, while their opponents judged their forces inadequate to start a serious offensive. Thus the only permissible targets were enemy warships.

2. The widely held belief that bombers and dive-bombers could drive the enemy's naval forces from the seas was not, at the war's outset, fulfilled. Bad weather, and lack of experience in nautical flying, spotting, recognition and attack, were the contributory causes. Achievements were greatly over-estimated.

3. The first major air battle of the war—over Heligoland Bight on December 18, 1939—showed that unescorted bombers were no match for an enemy's fighter force. This applied to both sides, and led to bomber operations subsequently being conducted only at night, despite the greatly reduced chance of hitting the target. The destruction of many non-military installations later in the war can be attributed to this fact.

4. The invasion of Norway on April 9, 1940, was a very hazardous enterprise for the German high command. Success or failure depended on whether Navy and Luftwaffe could take the crucial ports and airfields by surprise. Some 500 transport aircraft did in fact achieve the first air-lift in history, and for the first time soldiers were dropped from the sky. The secret of the German paratroop weapon was thereby exposed.

3

ASSAULT ON THE WEST

1. Coup de Main at Eben Emael

The take-off signal flashed in the darkness and the sound of aero-engines rose to a roar as the first three Ju 52s began to move across the airfield. They did so more sluggishly than usual, for each dragged a heavy burden—a second aircraft without engines: a glider!

As the tow-rope grew taut the latter jerked forward and jolted faster and faster down the runway. Then, as the towing craft left the ground, the glider pilot drew the stick carefully towards him, and the rumbling of his under-carriage grew suddenly silent. Seconds later the glider was sweeping noiselessly over hedges and fences and gaining height behind its Ju 52. The difficult towed take-off had been accomplished.

The time was 04.30 on May 10, 1940. From Cologne's two airfields, Ostheim on the right bank of the Rhine, Butzweilerhof on the left, sections of three Ju 52s were taking off at thirty second intervals, each towing a glider. Becoming airborne, they steered for a point above the green belt to the south of the city, there to thread themselves to a string of lights that stretched towards Aachen. Within a few minutes forty-one Ju 52s and forty-one gliders were on their way.

The die had been cast for one of the most audacious enterprises in the annals of war: the assault on the Belgian frontier fortress of Eben Emael, and the three bridges to the north-west leading over the deep Albert Canal—the keypoints of the Belgian defence system to the east.

In each of the forty-one gliders a team of parachutists sat astride the central beam. According to their appointed task their number varied between eight and twelve, equipped with weapons and explosives. Every soldier knew exactly what his job was once the target was reached. They had been re-hearsing the operation, initially with boxes of sand and models, since November 1939.

They belonged to "Assault Detachment Koch". Ever since this unit had reached its training base at Hildesheim, it had been hermetically sealed off from the outside world. No leave or exeats had been granted, their mail was strictly censored, speech with members of other units forbidden.

Each soldier had signed a declaration: "I am aware that I shall risk sentence of death should I, by intent or carelessness, make known to another person by spoken word, text or illustration anything concerning the base at which I am serving."

Two men were, in fact, sentenced to death for quite trifling lapses, and only reprieved after the operation had succeeded. Obviously its success, and thereby the lives of the paratroops, depended on the adversary having no inkling of its imminence. Secrecy was carried so far that while the men knew the details of each other's roles by heart, they only discovered each other's names when all was over.

Theory was succeeded by practical exercises by day, by night, and in every kind of weather. Around Christmas time the operation was rehearsed against the Czech fortified emplacements in the Altvater district of the Sudetenland.

"We developed a healthy respect for what lay ahead of us," reported First-Lieutenant Rudolf Witzig, leader of the parachute sapper platoon which was due to take on the Eben Emael fortifications single-handed. "But after a while our confidence reached the stage where we, the attackers, believed our position outside on the breastworks safer than that of the defenders inside."

Outside on the breastworks . . . but now did they propose to get that far?

The construction of the fortress, like that of the Albert Canal itself, dated from the early 'thirties. Forming the northern bastion of the Lüttich (Liège) defences, it was situated just three miles south of Maastricht, in a salient hard by the Belgian-Dutch frontier. In that position it dominated the Canal, the strategic importance of which was plain: any aggressor advancing along the line Aachen-Maastricht-Brussels would have to cross it. The defence had made preparations so that all its bridges could be blown at a moment's notice.

The fortifications themselves were embedded in a hilly plateau, and extended for 900 yards north and south, 700 yards east and west. The individual emplacements were scattered, seemingly at random, over a five-cornered area (see plate following page 96). In fact, with their artillery casemates, armoured rotating cupolas carrying 75-mm and 120-mm guns, plus anti-aircraft, anti-tank and heavy machine-gun positions, they constituted a shrewdly planned defence system. The different sectors of the complex were connected by underground tunnels totalling nearly three miles in length.

The fortress seemed all but impregnable. On its long north-eastern flank was an almost sheer drop of 120 feet down to the Canal. The same applied to the north-west, with a similar drop to a canal cut. To the south it was protected artificially—by wide anti-tank ditches and a twenty-foot-high wall. On all sides it was additionally protected by concrete pillboxes let into the sides of the walls or cuttings, which bristled with searchlights, 60-mm anti-tank guns and heavy machine-guns. Any enemy attempt to get into the place seemed doomed to failure.

The Belgians had foreseen every possibility but one: that the enemy might drop out of the sky right amongst the casemates and gun turrets. Now this enemy was already on his way. By 04.35 all the forty-one Ju 52s were airborne. Despite the darkness and the heavily laden gliders behind them there had not been a single hitch.

Captain Koch had divided his assault force into four detachments, as follows:

1. "Granite" under First-Lieutenant Witzig, eighty-five men with small arms and two and a half tons of explosives embarked in eleven gliders. Target: Eben Emael fortifications. Mission: to put outer elements out of action and hold till relieved by Army Sapper Battalion 51.
2. "Concrete" under Lieutenant Schacht. Ninety-six men and command staff embarked in eleven gliders. Target: high concrete bridge over Albert Canal at Vroenhoven. Mission: to prevent bridge being blown, form and secure bridgeheads pending arrival of army troops.
3. "Steel" under First-Lieutenant Altmann. Ninety-two men embarked in nine gliders. Target: steel bridge of Veldwezelt, $3\frac{3}{4}$ miles NW of Eben Emael. Mission: as for "Concrete".
4. "Iron" under Lieutenant Schächter. Ninety men embarked in ten gliders. Target: bridge at Kanne. Mission: again as for "Concrete".

Rendezvous was duly made between the two groups of aircraft, and all set course for the west, following the line of beacons. The first was a fire kindled at a crossroads near Efferen, the second a searchlight three miles further on at Frechen. As the aircraft approached one beacon, the next, and often the next but one, became visible ahead. Navigation, despite the dark night, was therefore no problem at least as far as the pre-ordained unhitching point at Aachen. Yet for one aircraft—the one towing the last glider of the "Granite" detachment—things went wrong while still south of Cologne.

Just ahead and to starboard its pilot suddenly noticed the blue exhaust flames of another machine on a collision course. There was only one thing to do: push his Ju 52 into a dive. But he had, of course, a glider in tow! The latter's pilot, Corporal Pilz, tried frantically to equalise the strain, but within seconds his cockpit was lashed as with a whip as the towing cable parted. As Pilz pulled out of the dive the sound of their mother aircraft died rapidly away and suddenly all was strangely silent.

The seven occupants then glided back to Cologne—one of them the very man who was supposed to lead the assault on the Eben Emael fortress, First-Lieutenant Witzig. Pilz just managed to clear the Rhine, then set the glider softly down in a meadow. What now?

Climbing out, Witzig at once ordered his men to convert the meadow into an airstrip by clearing all fences and other obstacles. "I will try to get hold of another towing plane," he said.

Running to the nearest road he stopped a car and within twenty minutes was once again at Cologne-Ostheim airfield. But not a single Ju 52 was left. He had to get on the 'phone and ask for one from Gütersloh. It would take time. Looking at his watch he saw it was 05.05. In twenty minutes his detachment was due to land on the fortress plateau.

Meanwhile the Ju 52 squadrons, with their gliders behind them, droned westwards, climbing steadily. Every detail of their flight had been worked out in advance. The line of beacons to the German frontier at Aachen was forty-five miles long. By then the aircraft were scheduled to reach a height of 8,500 feet: a flight of thirty-one minutes, assuming the wind had been correctly estimated.

Squatting in their gliders, the men of detachment "Granite" had no idea that their leader had already dropped out of the procession. For the moment it was not all that important. Each section had its own special job to do, and each glider pilot knew at exactly which point of the elongated plateau he had to land: behind which emplacement, beside which gun turret, within a margin of ten to twenty yards.

It would moreover have been bad planning if the loss of individual gliders had not been provided for. As it was, each section leader's orders included directions as to what additional tasks his team would have to perform in the event of neighbouring sections failing to land.

Nor was Witzig's glider the only one to drop out. Some twenty minutes later that carrying No. 2 Section had just passed the beacon at Luchenberg when the Ju 52 in front waggled its wings. The glider pilot, Corporal Brendenbeck, thought he was "seeing things", especially when the plane also blinked its position lights. It was the signal to unhitch! Seconds later the glider had done so—all thanks to a stupid misunderstanding. It was only half way to its target, and with an altitude of less than 5,000 feet there was no longer a hope of reaching the frontier.

The glider put down in a field near Düren. Springing out, its men requisitioned cars and in the first light of day sped towards the frontier, which the Army at this time was due to cross.

That left "Granite" with only nine gliders still flying. Sooner than expected the searchlight marking the end of the line of beacons came into view ahead. Situated on the Vetschauer Berg north-west of Aachen-Laurensberg, it also marked the point at which the gliders were to unhitch. After that they would reach the Maastricht salient in a glide, their approach unbetrayed by the noise of the towing aircraft's engines.

But in fact they were ten minutes too early. The following wind had proved stronger than the met. men had predicted, and for this reason they had also not reached the pre-ordained height of 8,500 feet, which would enable them to fly direct to their target at a gliding angle of one in twelve. Now they were some 1,500 feet too low. Lieutenant Schacht, leader of "Concrete" detachment, wrote in his operations report: "For some undisclosed reason the towing squadron brought us further on over Dutch territory. Only when we were some way between the frontier and Maastricht did we unhitch."

Obviously the idea was to bring the gliders up to something like the decreed altitude. But if this move contributed to the security of the force in one way, it certainly hazarded it in another. For now the droning of the Junkers engines alerted the Dutch and Belgian defence.

The time was shortly after 05.00 hours—nearly half an hour still before Hitler's main offensive against the West was due to open. Though eight to ten minutes ahead of time, owing to the wind, the gliders needed, in fact, another twelve to fourteen to bring them over the target. At five minutes before zero hour these silent birds of prey were to swoop down amongst the pillboxes of the Canal bridges and the fortress . . . before any other shot was fired. But now the element of surprise seemed to have been lost.

At last the gliders were set free, and the noise of their mother aircraft died away in the distance. But the Dutch flak was now on its toes, and opened fire on the gliders before they reached Maastricht. The little red balls came up like toys, amongst which the pilots dodged about in avoiding action, happy that they had sufficient height to do so. None was hit, but the long and carefully guarded secret of their existence was now irrevocably exposed.

As long ago as 1932 the Rhön-Rossitten-Gesellschaft had constructed a wide wing-span glider designed for making meteorological measurements at high altitude. The following year, taken over by the newly established German Institute for Gliding Research (DFS) at Darmstadt-Griesheim, this flying observatory—known as "Obs"—was used for the first gliding courses under Peter Riedel, Will Hubert, and Heini Dittmar. It was tested for the first time in tow by Hanna Reitsch, later to become one of the world's best known women pilots, behind a Ju 52.

Ernst Udet soon got wind of the project and went to inspect the "Obs" at Darmstadt. He at once recognised a possible military application. Could not large gliders like this be used for bringing up supplies to the front line, or in support of a unit that had become surrounded? Perhaps it could even operate as a kind of modern Trojan horse by landing soldiers unnoticed behind the enemy's back.

Udet, in 1933, was still a civilian, and not yet a member of the new camouflaged Luftwaffe. 'But he informed his comrade of World War I, Ritter von Greim, about the "Obs", and shortly afterwards the Institute received a contract to build a military version. The prototype, under the designation DFS 230, duly emerged under the direction of engineer Hans Jacobs. The "assault glider" of World War II fame was thus already born.

Series production started in 1937 at the Gothaer vehicle factory. Its wings were high-set and braced, its box-shaped fuselage was of steel covered with canvas, and its undercarriage jettisonable: the landing was made on a stout central skid. This was another mark of Udet's influence: as early as the twenties he had made some venturesome landings on Alpine glaciers with a ski-undercarriage.

The unladen weight of the assault glider was only 16 cwt, and nearly 18 cwt could be loaded—equivalent of ten men plus their weapons.

By autumn 1938 Major-General Student's top-secret airborne force included a small glider-assault commando under Lieutenant Kiess. Tests had shown that such a method of surprise attack on a well-defended point had a better chance of success than parachute troops. In the latter case not only was surprise betrayed by the noise of the transport aircraft's engines, but even if the troops jumped from the minimum height of three hundred feet they still swayed defencelessly in the air for fifteen seconds. Further, even the minimum time of seven seconds to get clear of the aircraft spread them out on the ground over a distance of about 300 yards. Precious minutes were then lost freeing themselves of their parachutes, reassembling, and finding their weapon containers.

With gliders, on the other hand, surprise was complete thanks to their uncannily silent approach. Well-trained pilots could put them down within twenty yards of any point. The men were out in no time through the broad hatch at the side, complete with weapons, and formed a compact combat group from the start. The only restrictions were that the landing had to await first light, and the area had to be known in advance.

It was this dictate of time that nearly caused the whole Albert Canal and Eben Emael operations to miscarry. For the Army supreme commander proposed to launch the opening attack of the western campaign at 03.00 hours, in darkness. Against this Koch argued that his detachment must make its own assault at least simultaneously with the main one, and preferably a few minutes earlier. And before dawn this was impossible.

At that point Hitler himself intervened and fixed zero hour at "sunrise minus 30 minutes". Numerous test flights had shown that to be the earliest moment at which the glider pilots would have enough visibility.

So it was that the whole German Army had to take its time from a handful of "adventurers" who had the presumption to suppose that they could subdue one of the world's most impregnable fortresses from the air.

At 03.10 hours on May 10th the field telephone jangled at the command post of Major Jottrand, who was in charge of the Eben Emael fortifications. The 7th Belgian Infantry Division, holding the Albert Canal sector, imposed an increased state of alert. Jottrand ordered his 1,200-strong garrison to action stations. Sourly, for the umpteenth time, men stared out from the gun turrets into the night, watching once again for the German advance.

For two hours all remained still. But then, as the new day dawned, there came from the direction of Maastricht in Holland the sound of concentrated anti-aircraft fire. On Position No. 29, on the south-east boundary of the fortress, the Belgian bombardiers raised their own anti-aircraft weapons. Were the German bombers on the way? Was the fortress their objective? Listen as they might, the men could hear no sound of engines.

Suddenly from the east great silent phantoms were swooping down. Low already, they seemed to be about to land: three, six, nine of them. Lowering the barrels of their guns, the Belgians let fly. But next moment one of the "great bats" was immediately over them—no, right amongst them!

Corporal Lange set his glider down right on the enemy position, severing a machine-gun with one wing and dragging it along. With a tearing crunch the glider came to rest. As the door flew open, Sergeant Haug, in command of Section 5, loosed off a burst from his machine-pistol, and hand-grenades pelted into the position. The Belgians held up their hands.

Three men of Haug's section scampered across the intervening hundred yards towards Position 23, an armoured gun turret. Within one minute all the remaining nine gliders had landed at their appointed spots in the face of machine-gun fire from every quarter, and the men had sprung out to fulfil their appointed duties.

Section 4's glider struck the ground hard about 100 yards from Position 19, an anti-tank and machine-gun emplacement with embrasures facing north and south. Noting that the latter were closed, Sergeant Wenzel ran directly up to them and flung a 2-lb. charge through the periscope aperture in the turret. The Belgian machine-guns chattered blindly into the void. Thereupon Wenzel's men fixed their secret weapon, a 100-lb. hollow charge, on the observation turret and ignited it. But the armour was too thick for the charge to penetrate: the turret merely became seamed with small cracks, as in dry earth. Finally they blew an entry through the embrasures, finding all weapons destroyed and the gunners dead.

Eighty yards farther to the north Sections 6 and 7 under Corporals Harlos and Heinemann had been "sold a dummy". Positions 15 and 16—especially strong ones according to the air pictures—just did not exist. Their "15-foot

9. DFS 230 gliders in tow. The western campaign opened at dawn on May 10, 1940, with bold airborne operation by "Assault Battalion Koch" to capture the Albert Canal bridges f Veldwezelt, Vroenhoven and Kanne (the last blown up by the enemy) and the fortress f Eben Emael.

30. *(left)* Positions of the strategic objectives. **31.** *(below)* The German target map of Eben Emael, showing detailed tactical objectives. Nos. 9, 12, 18, 26 are casemates, each with three 75-mm guns; Nos. 23. 24, 31 are retractable rotating armoured cupolas each containing two 75-mm and two 120-mm guns; Nos. 15 and 16 turned out to be dummies; Nos. 13 and 19 are machine-gun bunkers; Nos. 3, 4, 6, 17, 23, 30 and 35 are anti-tank, searchlight and machine-gun emplacements in walls overloking canal and ditch; No. 29 is Flak position; Nos. 2 and 25 are billets.

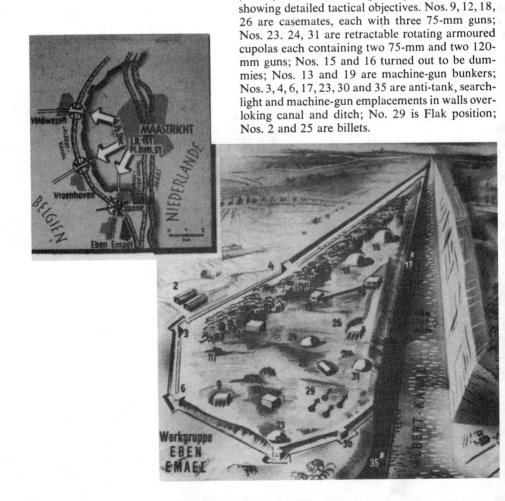

32. Engineer paratroops of "Assault Detachment Granite" after putting the fortress of Eben Emael out of action.

33. Two of the gliders which landed on the fortress plateau close beside the concrete bunkers and armoured cupolas.

34. The entrance bunker pock-marked by near-misses from *Stukas*. Engineer paratroops had already crippled the extensive fortress by destruction of its exterior positions. **35.** Part of the 120-foot wall rising from the Albert Canal with one of the built-in emplacement.

armoured cupolas" were made of tin. These sections would have been much more useful further south. There all hell had broken loose at Position 25, which was merely an old tool shed used as quarters. The Belgians within it rose to the occasion better than those behind armour, spraying the Germans all round with machine-gun fire. One casualty was Corporal Unger, leader of Section 8, which had already blown up the twin-gun cupola of Position 31.

Sections 1 and 3, under N.C.O.s Niedermeier and Arent, put out of action the six guns of artillery casements 12 and 18. Within ten minutes of "Granite" detachment's landing ten positions had been destroyed or badly crippled. But though the fortress had lost most of its artillery, it had not yet fallen. The pillboxes set deep in the boundary walls and cuttings could not be got at from above. Observing correctly that there were only some seventy Germans on the whole plateau, the Belgian commander, Major Jottrand, ordered adjoining artillery batteries to open fire on his own fort.

As a result the Germans had themselves to seek cover in the positions they had already subdued. Going over to defence, they had to hold on till the German Army arrived. At 08.30 there was an unexpected occurrence when an additional glider swooped down and landed hard by Position 19, in which Sergeant Wenzel had set up the detachment command post. Out sprang First-Lieutenant Witzig. The replacement Ju 52 he had ordered had succeeded in towing his glider off the meadow near Cologne, and now he could belatedly take charge.

There was still plenty to do. Recouping their supplies of explosives from containers now dropped by Heinkel 111s, the men turned again to the gun positions which had not previously been fully dealt with. 2-lb. charges now tore the barrels apart. Sappers penetrated deep inside the positions and blew up the connecting tunnels. Others tried to reach the vital Position 17, set in the 120-foot wall commanding the canal, by suspending charges on cords.

Meanwhile hours passed, as the detachment waited in vain for the Army relief force, Engineer Battalion 51. Witzig was in radio contact both with its leader, Lieutenant-Colonel Mikosch, and with his own chief, Captain Koch at the Vroenhoven bridgehead. Mikosch could only make slow progress. The enemy had successfully blown the Maastricht bridges and indeed the one over the Albert Canal at Kanne—the direct connection between Maastricht and Eben Emael. It had collapsed at the very moment "Iron" detachment's gliders approached to land.

On the other hand the landings at Vroenhoven and Veldwezelt had succeeded, and both bridges were intact in the hands of the "Concrete" and "Steel" detachments. Throughout the day all three bridgeheads were under heavy Belgian fire. But they held—not least thanks to the covering fire provided by the 88-mm batteries of Flak Battalion "Aldinger" and constant attacks by the old Henschel Hs 123s of II/LG 2 and Ju 87s of StG 2.

In the course of the afternoon these three detachments were at last relieved by forward elements of the German Army. Only "Granite" at Eben Emael had still to hang on right through the night. By 07.00 the following morning an assault party of the engineer battalion had fought its way through and was greeted with loud rejoicing. At noon the remaining fortified positions were assaulted, then at 13.15 the notes of a trumpet rose above the din. It came from Position 3 at the entrance gate to the west. An officer with a flag of truce appeared, intimating that the commander, Major Jottrand, now wished to surrender.

Eben Emael had fallen. 1,200 Belgian soldiers emerged into the light of day from the underground passages and gave themselves up. In the surface positions they had lost twenty men. The casualties of "Granite" detachment numbered six dead and twenty wounded.

One story remains to be told. The Ju 52s, having shed the gliders of "Assault Detachment Koch", returned to Germany and dropped their towing cables at a prearranged collection point. Then they turned once more westwards to carry out their second mission. Passing high over the battlefield of Eben Emael they flew on deep into Belgium. Then, twenty-five miles west of the Albert Canal they descended. Their doors opened and 200 white mushrooms went sailing down from the sky. As soon as they reached the ground, the sound of battle could be heard. For better or worse the Belgians had turned to confront the new enemy in their rear.

But for once the Germans did not attack. On reaching them the Belgians discovered the reason: the "paratroops" lay still entangled in their 'chutes. They were not men at all, but straw dummies in German uniform armed with self-igniting charges of explosive to imitate the sound of firing. As a decoy raid, it certainly contributed to the enemy's confusion.

2. The Truth about Rotterdam

At 15.00 hours on May 14, 1940, a heavy German air raid hit the Dutch city port of Rotterdam. Fifty-seven He 111s dropped high explosive bombs on a carefully defined triangle of ground to the north of the defended bridges over the river Maas. The resulting fires devastated a great part of the inner city, and 900 people were killed. As a result Germany was reviled before the whole world.

Although historical research has since concluded differently, many publications even today name Rotterdam as the first victim of the terror raids of World War II.

What happened really? How did the tragedy of Rotterdam occur? Only by studying the details of why the raid took place can one pass objective judgment.

"Air raid alarm red! The sirens howled in city and harbour. Through the misty dawn came the deep droning of many aircraft."

So reported a young Dutch officer stationed with his men on the boundary of Rotterdam airport. His report went on: "Round Waalhaven airfield the Queen's Grenadiers crouched lower in their trenches and dugouts. They had been manning their machine-guns and mortars since 03.00, and were tired and shivering."

A moment later the storm broke. The air was split by the piercing whistle of countless bombs. They thudded into the trenches and flak posts, smashed into the huge hangars in which, despite the alarm, a considerable station commander was letting his reserves "sleep on"!

The results were catastrophic. The hangars immediately caught fire and collapsed, burying a great number of the men beneath the ruins. At the vital airfield of Waalhaven the backbone of the defence was already

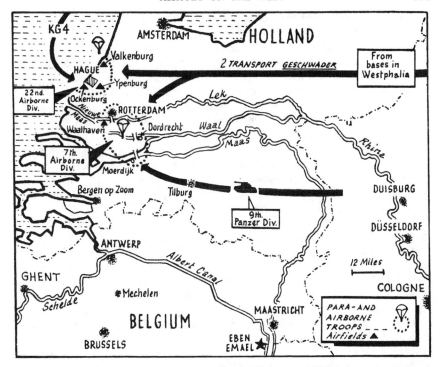

Assault on the "Fortress of Holland", May 10, 1940. After initial bombing raids by KG 4 on the Dutch airfields, two *Geschwader* of transports were used to drop paratroops or land other airborne troops between Moerdijk and Rotterdam, and at The Hague.

broken. This very precise bombing was done by the twenty-eight He 111s of II/KG 4, and was the prelude to the German air landings in the "Fortress of Holland" far behind the front. KG 4 had taken off from its bases of Delmenhorst, Fassberg and Gütersloh soon after 05.00, and was due to cross the Dutch frontier at 05.35. But before attacking, its commander, Colonel Martin Fiebig, took his *Geschwader* on a wide detour over the North Sea. He wanted to make his approach to the target airfields—Amsterdam-Schipol, Ypenburg near the Hague, and Rotterdam-Waalhaven—all of them near the coast—from the sea, i.e. from the direction of England.

But surprise was not achieved. The Dutch had been expecting the Germans to attack since May 2nd, and as the bombers crossed the coast they were greeted by fierce anti-aircraft fire. Dutch fighters bore down upon them, and the leader's own aircraft was shot down. Colonel Fiebig escaped by parachute and was taken prisoner. But the rest of his bombers went on to deliver the first attack on the airfields.

At Waalhaven the sound of bursting bombs and gunfire had hardly subsided when once again the menacing sound of aero-engines was heard approaching. This time it was from the east, and the planes were not bombers but triple-engined transports. The next few seconds were described by the young officer of the Queen's Grenadiers: "As if by magic white dots suddenly appeared over the airfield and its surrounds like puffs of cotton wool. First there were twenty, then fifty, then over a hundred of them! And still they came popping out of the planes and began their low oscillating descent. . . . A hoarse command, then every machine-gun opened up . . . at the parachutes, at the planes. With so many targets, the men just did not know where to aim. . . ."

It was III Battalion of Paratroop Regiment 1 under Captain Karl-Lothar Schulz. The battalion was under the direct command of Lieutenant-General Student's 7 Air Corps, and had been given the following orders:

"After bomber preparation, III/FJR 1 will take Waalhaven airfield by the short method (i.e., by parachuting directly on the objective) and will secure it for succeeding landings by airborne troops."

Punctually to the minute Captain Zeidler's transport *Gruppe*, the "special purpose" III/KG zbV1, reached the southern outskirts of Rotterdam, guided to the airfield by clouds of smoke from the burning hangars. The parachutists jumped and for fifteen to twenty seconds hung helplessly in the air. The Dutch fired frantically but in mounting confusion.

The worst loss suffered by the paratroops was due to an error on their own side. One Ju 52 dropped its men right over the flaming furnaces of the hangars, their silk parachutes catching fire long before they reached the ground. Most of them, however, landed close to the edge of the airfield on both sides, and went straight into the attack. That compelled the Dutch, as planned, to fire outwards. For now, to complete their confusion, there followed the third blow: a transport squadron came down to land.

They were met by light flak, and petrol streamed from their pierced tanks. One Ju 52 had two engines on fire. But they landed. Before they came to rest the doors were thrown open and out poured a cascade of field grey: two platoons of 9 Company, Infantry Regiment 16—the advance party of the air-landing force.

Now the Dutch were held from both sides in a pincers grip. Within a quarter of an hour the still numerically superior defenders were overpowered in their trenches and disarmed. Meanwhile more and more Ju 52s were coming in, narrowly missing the burning wrecks of previous aircraft. In a few minutes the whole of III Battalion had landed.

"Things went just as we had expected," wrote its commander, Lieutenant-Colonel Dietrich von Choltitz. "The sound of conflict was deafening: the howling of aero-engines and ammunition exploding in the hangars was joined by the crash of mortar fire and the rattle of machine-guns plugging the planes. Speed was the thing!"

The Dutch officer of the Queen's Grenadiers said of the astonishing swiftness of the *coup*: "The airfield had now come under fire from our heavy mortars and artillery to the north of Rotterdam. Under cover of this we hoped to withdraw the remnants of the regiment and re-form on the road. But at that moment the Germans began firing off green Very lights—our own cease-fire signal for the heavy guns! For us it was the end. Our last resistance was broken. The survivors of the brave Queen's Grenadiers put up their hands and were taken prisoner. More and more aircraft were coming in to land. Waalhaven belonged to the enemy."

But the capture of this single airfield was just the beginning. The ultimate objective of the airborne landing was the important bridges over the Maas in the middle of the city. They were to be taken by surprise and secured at both ends.

Waalhaven lies to the city's south-west. To reach the bridges III/IR 16 would have to fight their way through a maze of streets. Would the bridges not be blown long before they got there? This problem had also been provided for. During the previous evening IR 16's 11 Company under First-Lieutenant Schrader had been moved up to Bad Zwischenbahn near Oldenburg. In the middle of the night they embarked in waiting seaplanes, together with a detachment of sappers from 2/Pi 22; Then they took off from the Zwischenahner Sea, which is not a sea but an almost circular inland lake, and headed west.

The twelve obsolescent He 59 biplanes, with their great floats and box-like fuselages, were laden to the limit of their lifting power. Still in use for sea reconnaissance and rescue, they were much too slow for active operations. None the less, at 07.00 hours on May 10th, the twelve old Heinkel 59s, following the course of the New Maas, came droning in to the heart of Rotterdam—six from the east, six from the west. Flying right down on the water, they alighted close to, and on both sides of, the great Willems bridge. Then, bow-waves foaming from their floats, they trundled over to the north bank.

Sappers threw out pneumatic rafts, and jumping aboard them the soldiers paddled rapidly to land. Crawling up the walls, they crossed the Oosterkade and occupied the Leeuwen and Jan Kuiten bridges between the old harbour basins. Then, fixing the machine-guns in position, they ran across the long Willems bridge, securing this and the adjacent railway viaduct. Within a few minutes infantrymen and sappers had formed small bridgeheads on both banks of the Maas.

At once the Dutch began to counter-attack. Rotterdam was strongly garrisoned. The Germans, seeking cover behind bridge piers and walls, and entrenching themselves in corner houses, fought off the initial assaults. But they only numbered 120 men, and how long they could hold out against the superior weight of the enemy was questionable.

Suddenly a train of trams rumbled into Koningshaven, at the southern end of the bridges, with a great clanging of bells. They contained German paratroops. It was 11 Company, FJR 1, under First-Lieutenant Horst Kerfin. Unlike their comrades, this task force of fifty men had been dropped on the stadium just south of the loop in the river. Taking over the train of trams and requisitioning cars, they had then raced through the district of Feijenoord to the bridges.

Sappers and infantrymen breathed again: their first reinforcements had arrived. Kerfin's trams even managed to cross the Maas to the northern bridgehead. One hour later it would no longer have been possible. By then the Dutch had the Willems bridge under such heavy fire from their positions on the banks and in a high building that all further passage was impossible.

Meanwhile III/IR 16 from Waalhaven airfield was fighting its way through the streets with heavy losses. Though it managed to take the small bridges linking Koningshaven with the Maas island, no movement over the main river via the Willems bridge could take place for five days and four nights. On its north bank the German defenders had diminished to sixty men fighting for their lives in the face of repeated attack.

Such was the military situation that one must take into account before passing judgment on the Rotterdam air raid that followed. But before going on let us consider how the risky airborne operation against the "Fortress of Holland" ever came to take place.

As early as October 27, 1939, the commander of 7 Air Division, Major-General (as he then was) Kurt Student, had been summoned to a secret conference at the Reich Chancellery in Berlin. Besides Hitler and Student, the only other man present was the supreme commander of the armed forces, General Wilhelm Keitel.

Hitler said that he had deliberately not used the paratroops in Poland in order not to expose the secret of this new weapon unnecessarily. Now, however, with the western offensive ahead, he had "after long consideration as to how and where the airborne force could achieve the greatest surprise", formulated the following plans:

7 Air Division (four battalions) and 22 Infantry Division (airborne) would capture the region of Ghent in eastern Flanders from the air, and occupy its fortifications (the Belgian "National Redoubt") pending the arrival of German Army formations.

A smaller assault force would land by glider and subdue the strategic fortress of Eben Emael and the bridges over the Albert Canal.

Despite the sceptical attitude of the Army towards such foolhardy projects, both operations were worked out in detail. Of the two, that against Eben Emael was considered far more difficult, though for that very reason it could in the event be carried out according to plan: Student was able to keep the preparations under such a veil of secrecy that the project was never featured in the written operations plans for the offensive in the west.

It was these same top-secret plans—code-name *"GKdos Chefsache"*—which, because of a flying incident involving two Luftwaffe officers, now fell into Belgian hands.

On January 10, 1940, Major Reinberger, *"Fliegerführer* 220's" liaison officer at *Luftflotte* 2 in Münster, had to attend a conference at Cologne to discuss how the forces for the proposed air landings would eventually be relieved. To get him there the station commander of Münster-Loddenheide, Major Erich Hönmanns, offered to fly him in a communications plane. Though Reinberger was not entirely happy about making the flight in foggy weather, he eventually accepted. He took with him a yellow brief-case containing secret documents relative to the conference. Amongst these was the fourth version of *Luftflotte* 2's linked-in plans for the western campaign.

After taking off from Loddenheide Hönmanns steered south-west. Then, from one minute to the next, visibility deteriorated. Without noticing that he did so, Hönmanns crossed the Rhine, then with increasing agitation looked for a landmark. A stiff easterly wind was blowing the Me 108 "Typhoon" before it. Finally the pilot saw below him the dark band of a river. But it could not be the Rhine: it was much too narrow. The wings began to ice up, then suddenly the engine failed. The only option was to go down and make a forced landing.

Narrowly missing a couple of trees, the Me 108 bumped across a field and came abruptly to rest in a hedge. With skinned legs Reinberger climbed out of the wreckage and asked: "Where are we?"

The farmer to whom the question was addressed did not understand German but eventually answered in French that they were near Malines in Belgium. Reinberger turned pale.

"I must burn my papers at once!" he gasped. "Have you got matches?"

But Hönmanns did not have any either. Both majors were non-smokers. The Belgian farmer brought out his lighter. Reinberger stooped under the hedge away from the wind, pulled out his documents and tried to ignite them. But just as he succeeded, gendarmes arrived on bicycles and trod out the flames.

Half an hour later, during their first interrogation at a farmhouse, Reinberger made another desperate attempt to save his bacon. Sweeping the papers from the table, he shot them into the near-by stove. But a Belgian captain thrust in his hand and pulled them out again.

So it was that the German plan of operations, charred at the edges but in the main perfectly legible, fell into the hands of the western powers—a sensational event.

Opinion in the Allied camp, however, was divided as to whether the documents were genuine, or whether the whole thing was an elaborate "plant" by German counter-intelligence. As a result hardly any military conclusions were drawn from this windfall of information.

On the German side heads rolled. Hitler raged and Goering fumed. General Felmy, chief of *Luftflotte* 2, was dismissed from his post, as were his chief of staff, Colonel Kammhuber, and the commander of IV Air Corps, Lieutenant-Colonel Genth of the general staff.

The plan of operations had to be fundamentally revised. Henceforth General Manstein's "Sickle Plan" was in force, with its emphasis on an armoured break-through in the Ardennes. Now Holland, too, was included in the programme. The air landings in the "National Redoubt" near Ghent and—a further plan of Hitler's—on the fortified line of the Maas between Namur and Dinant had to be abandoned. For now the Belgians had been able to read all about them!

Only the Eben Emael project—which thanks to its double veil of secrecy had never featured on the operations plan—could still remain in force. On January 15, 1940, five days after the loss of the vital documents, General Student received from Goering his new orders.

According to the "Sickle Plan" the German army, in the course of its main thrust into northern France, must be secured against any threat to its northern flank. Artillery General von Küchler was consequently instructed to occupy Holland as swiftly as possible with the 18th Army.

Unfortunately the country was a defender's paradise owing to its numerous watercourses. Any attack from the east could be halted by flooding the land along the north-south canal. From the south the only way into the "Dutch Fortress" was via the bridges over the broad arms of the Maas and Rhine deltas at Moerdijk, Dordrecht and Rotterdam. If they could be captured before they were blown, and then held in the midst of the enemy for three, four or even five days, pending the arrival of 9th *Panzer* Division—then Holland would be defeated.

The assignment was given to General Student's reinforced 7 Air Division. On 10th May 1940 it was carried out as follows:

Moerdijk: After a precision attack by dive-bombers on bridge emplacements and flak positions, II Battalion/FJR 1, under Captain Prager was dropped at the north and south ends of the bridges simultaneously. After a short, sharp conflict the 1,300-yard-long road viaduct and the 1,400-yard-long railway viaduct over the Diep fell undamaged into German hands.

Dordrecht: Owing to the closely built-up nature of the area, here only one company, 3/FJR 1, could be dropped to storm the bridges over the Old Maas. Its leader, First-Lieutenant von Brandis, was killed, and the Dutch retook the railway bridge with a counter-attack. For three days strong elements of FJR 1 under Colonel Bräuer, and I Battalion/IR 16 (landed at Waalhaven) became locked in bitter fighting for the town.

Rotterdam: As we have seen, Waalhaven airfield was captured. III Battalion /IR 16, under Lieutenant-Colonel von Choltitz and the sixty men of the north-bank bridgehead continued to hold the Maas bridges against repeated Dutch attacks.

So far the airborne operations against the "Dutch Fortress" had justified the boldness of the idea. True, the slender German forces were everywhere engaged in bitter defensive fighting, but the bridges had been saved. All that was required now was the advance of the 9th *Panzer* Division to the north.

Student, moreover, had a separate force supposed to be operating further north under the orders of the 22nd Infantry Division's commander, Lieutenant-General Graf Sponeck. This was to be landed at the three airfields near the Hague—Valkenburg, Ypenburg and Ockenburg—with instructions to penetrate the Dutch capital and seize the royal palace, government buildings and the ministry of war.

Thanks to their previous use in Denmark and Norway, the Dutch were aware of the German airborne tactics, and had strongly fortified their airfields. They had also strewn them with obstacles. Because of the country's flatness, they were even hard to find. Many of the advance wave of paratroops were consequently dropped in the wrong place, with the result that the transport squadrons, following close behind, were subjected on landing to the full brunt of the defensive fire.

Valkenburg, west of Leyden, was supposed to be taken by two platoons of paratroops of 6/FJR 2 followed by III Battalion/IR 47, under Colonel Buhse. Leaping from their still-moving planes the latter went into the attack. It was a forlorn hope. Their planes had sunk into the soft turf of the airfield up to their axles, and could not take off again. As the Dutch fired on them, they went up in smoke. The result was that when the next transport *Gruppe* arrived with II Battalion, there was no space left on which to land, and the aircraft had to turn back.

At Ypenburg, north of Delft, the flak was so fierce that out of the first thirteen Ju 52s with 6 Company/IR 65, on board, no fewer than eleven came down in flames. With visibility blocked by smoke and fire, they went charging into the hidden obstacles and iron spikes and were broken to pieces. The surviving soldiers only managed to hold out for a short time against the weight of enemy fire.

Amongst the later formations due to land at Ypenburg was 3 Squadron of the "special purpose" KG zbV9, which had left Lippspringe at 06.06. Beside the pilot of the second machine, Sergeant Aloys Mayer, sat Major-General Graf Sponeck himself. It was at once clear that no landing was possible, so they flew on to Ockenburg. But there the same picture was unfolded: the airfield was strewn with the wrecks of aircraft. The divisional commander's plane was itself shaken by flak hits. Everywhere aircraft were wandering about in the air looking for a place to land. Many of them did so on the Rotterdam-Hague Autobahn. Others tried the coastal dunes, and sank deep into the soft sand.

Finally Mayer put his Ju 52 down in a field and came to a halt near a copse. There the general collected together a small combat force. During the evening he managed to get through faintly on his portable radio set to H.Q. *Luftflotte* 2. Kesselring ordered him to give up the attack on The Hague, and instead to advance on the northern sector of Rotterdam.

Two days later, during the night of May 12th/13th, the motley collection of warriors got there. It was scarcely a thousand strong, and in the meantime had been engaged in a running battle with powerful elements of three Dutch divisions. Sponeck went to ground in the suburb of Overschie. His force was far too feeble for an attack on the city itself.

That was the situation when, early on May 13th, the advance party of Lieutenant-General Hubicki's 9th *Panzer* Division rolled across the Moerdijk bridge to the cheers of the investing paratroops. Dordrecht was at last subdued, and in the evening the first tanks reached the southern end of the Maas bridges in Rotterdam.

III/IR 16 still held the crossing against all odds. The Willems bridge was now under heavy artillery fire. The Dutch even tried to reach it with gunboats, but failed. German losses had been heavy, and Lieutenant-Colonel von Choltitz was ordered to withdraw his sixty-man bridgehead of mixed infantrymen, sappers and paratroops under First-Lieutenant Kerfin from the northern bank. But he failed utterly to reach them, for now not even a mouse could cross the bridge alive, either by day or night.

At 16.00 hours on May 13th two civilians began waving great white flags at the southern end of the Willems bridge. As the firing ceased, they advanced hesitantly. One was the vicar of Noorder Eiland—the island in the Maas occupied by the Germans—the other a merchant. Von Choltitz bade them take themselves to the Dutch city commandant and emphasised that only by capitulating could Rotterdam be saved from devastation. In the evening the emissaries returned, trembling with fear. Their own countrymen had informed them that their closely populated island would be flattened by artillery that very night. If, Colonel Scharroo had said, the German commander had any proposals to make, he should send officers. He did not treat with civilians.

Destiny then took its course. Undoubtedly the Rotterdam garrison could effectively bar any further German advance to the north. From the strictly military point of view there was no reason why it should yield.

Understandably the German high command could equally press for a swift conclusion of the operation. It wanted Holland "cleaned up" as soon as possible in order to free forces for the main thrust through Belgium into northern France. Furthermore the 18th Army, as it attacked Holland on May 13th, feared that British landings were imminent. Thus at 18.45 General von Küchler gave the order "to break the resistance at Rotterdam by every means".

The tank attack across the Willems bridge was fixed for 15.30 hours on May 14th, and would be preceded by artillery fire and a pinpoint bombing raid on a limited area at the northern end to paralyse the enemy's power of defence.

Meanwhile, the supreme command of the forces at Rotterdam had passed from Lieutenant-General Student to the general commanding XXXIX *Panzer* Corps, Rudolf Schmidt. The latter was instructed by the 18th Army commander, von Küchler, "to use all means to prevent unnecessary bloodshed amongst the Dutch population". Accordingly, in the evening of May 13th,

Schmidt drew up a new demand for Dutch capitulation, and had it translated. Unless resistance was terminated without delay, he wrote to the city commandant, he would have to use all means to break it.

"That," he added, "could result in the complete destruction of the city. I beg you, as a man with a sense of responsibility, to take the necessary steps to prevent this."

The fateful May 14, 1940, dawned. From now on every hour, every minute, counted. At 10.40 the German emissaries, Captain Hoerst and First-Lieutenant Dr. Plutzar as interpreter, crossed the Willems bridge with the letter. First they were taken to a command post, where they had to wait. Then, blindfolded, they were driven through the city by zigzag routes and finally fetched up in an underground vault.

"We had a long and anguishing wait," said Dr. Plutzar, "well aware that precious time was ticking away."

At last, at 12.40, Colonel Scharroo received them. They at once informed him that only immediate capitulation could save the city from heavy air bombardment.

But Scharroo felt he could not make the decision alone. He would have to get in touch with his supreme commander at The Hague. He told the Germans he would send over an emissary at 14.00 hours.

As soon as General Schmidt heard of this offer—the last chance—he sent a signal by radio to *Luftflotte* 2: "Attack postponed owing to parley."

At 13.50 the Dutch emissary duly crossed the bridge. He was Captain Bakker, the commandant's adjutant. On the Maas island he was met by Lieutenant-Colonel von Choltitz. A despatch-rider went off to the Corps HQ of Major-General Schmidt, just a few hundred yards to the south. Besides him, Lieutenant-General Student of the Air-Landing Corps and Lieutenant General Hubicki of 9th *Panzer* Division were also waiting there to hear the city commandant's answer to the urgent capitulation demand of the morning. Did the Dutch realise the seriousness of the situation?

Choltitz, waiting with Bakker on the bridge for the few minutes till Corps was advised, seized the opportunity once more to emphasize the deadly danger with which Rotterdam was threatened. But the Dutch officer looked about him sceptically. There was not a shot to be heard. After days of fighting there seemed to be a cease-fire suddenly. As for the German tanks, allegedly all ready to swarm over the bridges into the centre of the city, there was not a sign of them. Perhaps they did not exist? Perhaps the Germans had hurled their imprecations "to save Rotterdam" just to hide their own weakness.

In dismay Choltitz, and soon afterwards the German generals, were forced to recognise the fact that the Dutch commandant, Colonel Scharroo, saw no immediate necessity to surrender. He still held the major part of the city, with his forces outnumbering the invaders even south of the Maas, while the remnants of the German 22 (Airborne) Division still holding out under Graf Sponeck in the northern outskirts with a few hundred men were no longer capable of launching any attack. Why then should he capitulate? In any case the Dutch supreme commander, General Winkelmann, had ordered him to answer the German demand evasively.

Captain Bakker had accordingly brought a letter for General Schmidt in which the Rotterdam commandant professed to have found an error of form

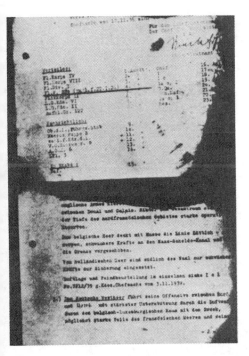
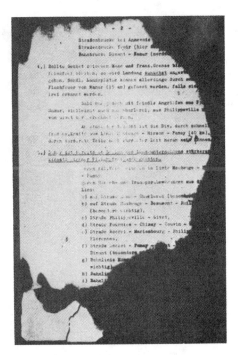

36. and **37.** Two pages of the document containing the German plan of attack on the West, which fell into Belgian hands after a forced landing by two Luftwaffe officers who failed in their attempts to burn it.

38. During the airborne operation against the "Fortress of Holland" paratroops, assisted only by close-support aircraft (as here), held the bridges at Moerdijk for three days until relieved by advancing Army units.

39. A picture, taken from 9,000 feet, after the conclusion of local hostilities, of the gutted centre of Rotterdam. Below can be seen the loop of the Maas and the previously contested bridges.

40. Rotterdam-Waalhaven airfield. In the morning of May 10, 1940, after German bombers had destroyed the hangars (top right), paratroops were dropped to clear the defences, and immediately afterwards Ju 52/3M transports landed infantry. On the following days the airfield was attacked by British bombers, till finally its surface was studded with craters.

in the German communication of the morning. It went on: "Before such a proposal can be seriously considered, it must carry your rank, name and signature. (Signed) P. Scharroo, Colonel commanding Rotterdam troops."

As General Schmidt glanced through this letter it was just 14.15. The Dutch emissary had no power of negotiation concerning the surrender. He was solely authorised to receive the German conditions.

But it was only at 14.15, too, that the Airborne Corps' signals section at Waalhaven succeeded, on the frequently interrupted wavelength, in getting through to 2 Air Division with the vital message: "Attack postponed owing to parley." At that very minute KG 54 under Colonel Lackner was over the German-Dutch frontier on its way to Rotterdam. Three quarters of an hour earlier its hundred He 111s had taken off from Delmenhorst, Hoya/Weser and Quakenbruch in order to be punctually over the target at the appointed zero-hour of 15.00.

The previous evening a liaison officer of the *Geschwader* had flown to meet General Student in Rotterdam, and taken back with him exact details of the operation, above all a map on which the enemy resistance zones had been marked. They were indicated by a triangle at the northern end of the Maas bridges. Only within this triangle was KG 54 permitted to drop its bombs.

Now, on his approach, Colonel Lackner in the leading aircraft had this map spread on his knees. Copies had also been given to his *Gruppen* and squadron commanders. The attack was confined to a strictly military target. The powerful Dutch defence force to the north of the two bridges was to be immobilised by a short, sharp blow from the air, to enable the German troops to cross. Every bomber crew had further been instructed that on the north bank was also a small bridgehead of sixty Germans, whose lives must be safeguarded.

But there was one thing the crews did not know: that at this very moment surrender negotiations were coming to a head, and that pending their outcome the German army commander had cancelled the attack. Lackner only knew that such a possibility was on the cards.

"Just before take-off," he reported, "we received information from operations headquarters on the telephone that General Student had radioed that the Dutch had been called upon to surrender Rotterdam. On our approach we were to watch out for red Very lights on the Maas island. Should they appear we had orders to attack not Rotterdam, but the alternative target of two English divisions at Antwerp."

The question was: would they recognise the lights amongst all the haze and dust raised by five days of fighting?

Meanwhile, General Schmidt was writing out in his own hand, point by point, the conditions of surrender that an out-matched opponent could honourably accept. He concluded with the words: "I am compelled to negotiate swiftly, and must therefore insist that your decision is in my hands within three hours, namely at 18.00 hours. Rotterdam South, 14.5.1940, 14.55 hours, (Signed) Schmidt."

Captain Bakker took the letter from him and returned at once to the city. Von Choltitz escorted him to the Willems bridge, and he hastened over it. Now it was exactly 15.00 hours—the time originally appointed for the air raid. "The tension was appalling," wrote Choltitz. "Would Rotterdam surrender in time?"

At that moment there came from the south the sound of many aero-engines. The bombers were on their way! Soldiers on the island loaded the Very pistols.

"Those of us on the spot," continued Choltitz, "could only hope that the necessary orders had been given, that the communications had not broken down, and that the high command knew what was happening."

But now the high command had no more control over the course of events. For half an hour, since it eventually got Schmidt's signal, *Luftflotte* 2 had been doing its best to contact KG 54 on the radio and recall it. The command directly responsible for it—the "Air Corps for Special Purposes"—had also put out urgent recall messages. As soon as its chief of staff, Colonel Bassenge, received the vital signal in Bremen, he dashed into the signals office in person and rushed out the agreed code-word for the alternative target.

Unfortunately only the *Geschwader's* own operations room was keyed to the same frequency as the aircraft in the air, and before the orders had been received and handed on much time was lost. At Munster *Luftflotte* 2's operations officer, Lieutenant-Colonel Rieckhoff, leapt into a Messerschmitt 109 and raced to Rotterdam. He hoped literally to divert the attack in person.

Even this brave endeavour came too late. The *Geschwader* was already lined up on its target. The radio operators had already withdrawn their trailing aerials, thereby drastically affecting reception. All attention was now directed to the attack.

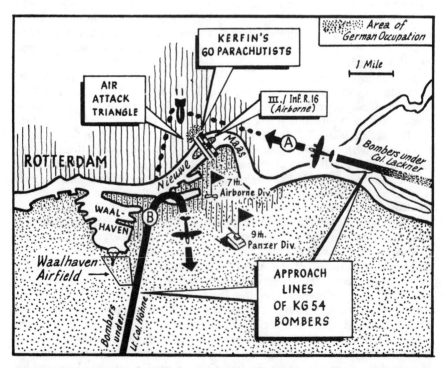

Rotterdam at 15.00 hours on May 14, 1940. The map shows KG 54's two attacking formations, "A" and "B". "A" drops its bombs in the target area, "B" recognises the red Very signals and turns away. The area of German occupation is shaded.

There remained just one slender chance: the red Very lights.

Shortly before it reached the target the *Geschwader*, according to plan, divided into two columns. The left one, under I *Gruppe's* commander, Lieutenant-Colonel Otto Höhne, turned to approach the triangle from the south-west, while Lackner himself went straight on.

"Though there were no clouds in the sky," he reported, "it was unusually misty. Visibility was so bad that I took my column down to 2,300 feet to be sure of hitting the required target and not the Lieutenant [Kerfin] and his sixty men, or the bridges themselves."

At 15.05 he crossed the Maas and reached the city's edge. The altitude was ideal for medium flak, and it duly came up. With the target ahead, no evasive action was possible. All eyes were fastened on the course of the river. In the middle of Rotterdam the New Maas makes a loop to the north, and just west of its vertex are the twin bridges. Even in the prevailing mist and smoke their straight lines were still discernible, as were the outlines of the Maas island.

Yet despite their concentrated attention, neither pilots nor observers spotted any of the red light signals. All they saw were the little red balls of the Dutch flak which came dancing up in strings to meet them. Rotterdam's fate was just a few seconds away—seconds during which Choltitz's men on the island fired Very lights by the dozen.

"My God! there's going to be a catastrophe," cried Schmidt. With Student he stood at a point where Stieltjes Straat forms a circus, watching the bombers as they passed slowly overhead, palpably seeking their target. Both generals seized Very pistols and fired vertically into the air. And still the men above saw nothing. All ground signals were swallowed up in the haze and drifting smoke from burning houses and the oily black clouds rising up from the passenger steamer *Straatendam*, set on fire by artillery.

Then it was too late. The starboard column of KG 54 droned over the target and the 100- and 500-lb. bombs went whistling down. They struck precisely in the triangular zone, in the heart of the Old City. After that it was the turn of the port column, with Lieutenant-Colonel Höhne and the staff section at its head.

"Never again," he reported after the war, "did I fly an operation accompanied by such dramatic circumstances. Both my observer, prone in front of me manning the bomb sight, and the radio-operator seated behind knew the signal I would give in the event of the bombing being cancelled at the last moment."

From the south-westerly direction of his approach the target was easy to recognise. On the inter-com. the observer counted out his measurements. Höhne concentrated solely on the island, scanning it for the possible "barrage of red Very lights". But he, too, saw nothing. Finally his observer called out: "I must let go the bombs now or they'll fall away from the target."

Höhne gave the word, then immediately caught his breath. Faintly, and just for a second or two, he had glimpsed "not a barrage but just two paltry little Very lights ascending". Turning round, he shouted to the radio-operator the code-word to turn back.

For his own machine it was too late. The automatic release had already functioned, and the bombs went down. The same thing happened aboard the section's other two planes close behind. But for 1 Squadron the short space interval sufficed. Before the bombardiers could set their levers the radio-operators gave the stop signal. They hesitated, turned questioningly around, then gazed down again on the city.

Everywhere they saw the flash of explosions. Clouds of debris spread over the houses, and columns of smoke rose upwards. Had the command section ahead not dropped its bombs? Why suddenly should they not do so? No, the orders were clear. The aircraft turned away. Höhne led his *Gruppe* to the south-west and its remaining bombs fell on the British.

So it was, that out of KG 54's hundred He 111s, only fifty-seven dropped their bomb-load over Rotterdam, the remaining 43 having been arrested from doing so at literally the last second. Subsequent enquiries elicited that, apart from Lieutenant-Colonel Höhne, not one man had spotted any of the Very lights that in fact had been sent up from the Maas island in an unbroken stream.

Altogether 158 500-lb and 1,150 100-lb bombs were dropped on the city— i.e., a total of ninety-seven tons. In accordance with the military nature of the mission, it was all high-explosive.

Yet the fact remains that the heart of Rotterdam was destroyed by fire. How could it have happened? High-explosive bombs—especially of the small size here used—were capable of destroying houses, tearing up streets, blowing off roofs and knocking down walls; and there is no question that the buildings hit were severely damaged. Such bombing can also start fires. With Rotterdam an international trading centre for oil and margarine products, they were likely to spread quickly. Fanned by the wind blowing towards the city, they ignited the old timbered houses. But could not the fire brigades have controlled them first?

The day after the raid a detachment of a German fire police regiment drove into Rotterdam with up-to-date fire engines. There was little left to save; the fire's fury had spent itself. The regiment's commander, Colonel Hans Rumpf, examined the causes of the catastrophe. His report brings to light one quite new detail:

"This world-wide trading city of almost a million inhabitants still retained, in the face of every modern development, the long out-moded principle of a citizen fire brigade. The backbone of this brigade consisted of a two-wheeled hand-operated contraption not unlike that invented by the painter Jan van der Heyden in 1672. Otherwise there were a small number of powered engines which, though without crews, could in case of need be driven to an incident, and a few pressure pumps mounted on tugboats. That was all."

Rumpf came to the conclusion that in an air raid such an out-dated fire-fighting organisation could not have helped at all. To which the Dutch would answer that it was perfectly adequate to cope with ordinary fires, and that they had never reckoned with the possibility of a heavy air raid on the centre of their city. Why should they? Was it not contrary to military law that a civil population should be attacked?

No law governing the air war of World War II, however, existed—an omission that was bitterly brought home to the statesmen concerned. The nearest approach to one was Article 25 of the Hague Convention of 1907 concerning surface warfare, which ran: "It is prohibited to attack or fire upon cities, villages, dwellings or buildings that have no means of defending themselves."

Inasmuch as Rotterdam was defended by every means, it was not covered by this Article. The German call to surrender—on pain of a heavy attack from the air—was, moreover, in accordance with Article 26, which prescribed that before fire is opened "the defenders shall be informed".

Finally, the suspicion has been voiced that Hitler or Goering deliberately ordered the raid in order to impress on all their enemies the terror of the German war machine. Such a view is disproved by sober documentary evidence. This shows that the sole objective of the raid was the tactical one of capturing the key point needed for the country's occupation and of rescuing German soldiers, some of them hard-pressed, in the north and south of the city.

The real tragedy was that the raid took place while Rotterdam's surrender was being negotiated. The fact that, despite every endeavour, fewer than half the bombers were successfully recalled at the very last second, was on the German side a matter of deep and sincere regret.

At 17.00, scarcely two hours after the raid, the city commandant, Colonel Scharroo, came over the Willems bridge to the island in person and asked to capitulate. He was a broken man. General Schmidt did his best to convince the Dutchman of his genuine regret that the air raid had after all taken place. An hour later the surrender was completed.

Survivors of the German airborne force, who for five days and four nights had held their position on the north bank, emerged from houses, cellars, and ditches. Lieutenant-Colonel von Choltitz reports:

"A young paratrooper grasped the flag which he and his comrades had displayed on the foremost house to identify themselves to the bombers. He came up like a lost soul, the other warriors of the bridgehead behind him. Many were missing, and the survivors were dirty and worn, some without weapons other than hand grenades in their pockets. Together we took over the burning city. . . ."

Then the tanks clattered northwards through the streets to relieve the remnants of 22 Airborne Division. Here and there infantry fire still flickered. The Dutch were ordered to report with their weapons at certain collection points. Suddenly coming upon one such "armed group of the enemy", a roving detachment of SS of the "Adolf Hitler Bodyguards" opened fire. At the first crackle of machine-guns General Student leapt to the window of the garrison headquarters to stop them—and promptly collapsed streaming blood from a bullet in the head. Three hours after the cease-fire that marked the hard-won success of the Airborne Corps, its leader was severely wounded by a stray bullet!

At 20.30, almost simultaneously with the fall of Rotterdam, the Dutch supreme commander, General Winkelmann, offered on the radio the capitulation of all his armed forces. The whole campaign was thus over in five days —much more swiftly than the German high command had expected. To this success the airborne forces had decisively contributed.

It had, however, been bought at heavy cost. Apart from the loss of lives, the most bitter pill was that the bulk of the great transport force had been squandered for good. Of the 430 Ju 52s engaged in the operation, two thirds either never returned from Holland or were so badly damaged as to be write-offs. The "special purpose" KG zbV 2, during the landing attempts in The

Hague area, lost ninety per cent of its aircraft. The Dutch airfields were littered with broken and burnt-out wrecks.

But there was something even worse. For the most part these aircraft had been drawn from the Luftwaffe training schools, and the men who flew them were the instructors who should have trained a new generation of airmen. In the words of the then general staff colonel Bassenge: "Theirs was a capital loss which caused a marked reduction in the rate of recruitment to the bomber units. The consequences of that did not fail to register later."

3. Break-through at Sedan

Nine bombers went hedge-hopping across-country, wing-tip to wing-tip in squadron formation. From the fields below the early morning mist rose up, impairing visibility. As the planes skipped over woods and hills and dipped into the valleys, their pilots had to keep their eyes glued to the landscape. They were flying west.

Viewed from the beam the bombers had the long, slim silhouette of the "Flying Pencil", or Dornier Do 17Z. At first light they had taken off from Aschaffenburg for their targets, which lay in France. They comprised 4 Squadron of Lieutenant-Colonel Paul Weitkus's II/KG 2, and the date was May 11, 1940, the second day of the German western offensive. On this day the whole *Geschwader* had been briefed for attacks on Allied airfields.

The squadron commander, First-Lieutenant Reimers, called on the radio: "Watch out! Maginot Line."

This was why they were hedge-hopping. They were to flash over the great fortified front before the anti-aircraft defences could be alerted. Surprise was duly achieved, and by the time a few machine-guns rattled out the Dorniers had vanished over the next chain of hills. Then, crossing the Maas (or Meuse), they reached the Aisne, and followed its course westwards. Their target was the small airfield of Vaux near Sissonne-La Malmaison. It was one of at least a dozen which lay in a semi-circle round Rheims and were being used by the British Advanced Air Striking Force.

This morning it was a hive of activity as the bombers of 114 Squadron, R.A.F., got ready for their first operation. Fuelled and bombed-up, they awaited the signal for take-off. The squadron was equipped with Bristol Blenheims, the most modern medium bomber that the Allies could at this time deploy. This and other squadrons had moved to forward bases to initiate the air war against Germany. But they were prevented from doing so.

Since the German offensive had opened the previous day, Air Marshal Sir Arthur Barratt, commander of the British air forces in France, had been snowed under with calls for help from the front. Now, for better or worse, he had to throw in his bombers wherever the German armour had opened a breach. Today it was Liège, Maastricht and the Albert Canal; tomorrow it would be Dinant, Charleville and Sedan.

114 Squadron were still waiting to go when unidentified aircraft suddenly appeared overhead at church-tower height. There was no warning, no alarm. No one considered it could be the enemy—till the bombs came raining down amongst the lined-up Blenheims. Too late, the Englishmen recognised the crosses beneath the wings.

Reimers, an experienced blind-flying instructor, had brought his squadron straight to the airfield. Now the Do 17s flew just high enough to avoid being hit by their own bomb splinters. That the Blenheims happened to be lined up as if on parade was a coincidence that no one had reckoned with. The German bombers could scarcely miss. Their 100-lb. bombs fell in regular lines right amongst them. Seconds later they went up in smoke and flame, the glare punctuated by brilliant flashes. The Dorniers made a circuit and attacked again.

Aboard one of the last of them the radio-operator, Flight-Sergeant Werner Borner, had with him as always his 8-mm ciné camera. With no enemy fighters on the scene, he took the opportunity to film his squadron's attack. His pilot, First-Lieutenant Bornschein, even made an extra circuit "for the news-reel". Altogether thirty British aircraft were counted on fire.

"No. 114 Squadron was virtually destroyed on its airfield," states the official history of the Royal Air Force. Added to other disasters, it "ended the life of the A.A.S.F. Blenheims as a useful force before it had begun".

A few days later Lieutenant-General Bruno Loerzer projected Sergeant Borner's film strip at the Führer's headquarters, as visual evidence of the precision and destruction his bombers had achieved in attacks on enemy airfields.

During the first days of the western campaign there was hardly one of these airfields—in Holland, Belgium or northern France—that escaped German bombing. Just as previously in Poland, the primary objective of the Luftwaffe was to win sovereignty in the air. That entailed not only a strong force of fighters. If bombers could succeed in knocking out the enemy's bases of operation, he would no longer be able to put a combative force into the air.

The total strength in first-line aircraft available, on May 10, 1940, to Generals Kesselring and Sperrle, commanding *Luftflotten* 2 and 3, was as follows:

1,120 bombers (Do 17, He 111, Ju 88)
324 dive-bombers (Ju 87)
42 "battle planes" (Hs 123)
1,016 short-range fighters (Me 109)
248 long-range fighters (Me 110)

plus reconnaissance and transport planes.

They were divided up amongst six Air Corps. Of these I and IV (under Generals Ulrich Grauert and Alfred Keller) had Belgium and Holland as their zone of operations. II and V (under Lieutenant-Generals Bruno Loerzer and Robert Ritter von Greim) operated in front of the southern flank of the front facing north-east France, and deployed the lion's share of the fourteen bomber *Geschwader*. Further, there was the "special purpose" Air Corps 2, responsible for the air landings in Holland, and finally VIII Air Corps under Lieutenant-General Wolfram Freiherr von Richthofen.

As in Poland, Richthofen was in charge of the main close-support force consisting of two complete *Stuka Geschwader*, plus "battle planes" and fighters. After first being engaged against the fortified front on either side of Liège and deep into Belgium, this Corps later moved to support the Sedan break-through and the advance of the armoured divisions to the Channel coast and Dunkirk.

Dunkirk! There, for the first time, the Germans were to discover that they were not invincible. But at the moment no one dreamed that the name of this little Flemish port would later be synonymous with the Luftwaffe's first appreciable reverse. Whatever the allowance for reserves and aircraft temporarily unserviceable the Germans could at any time put into the air some 1,000 bombers and dive-bombers, and as many fighters. And despite all the courage of their airmen, the Allies could do nothing to stop them.

Whit-Sunday, May 12th—the third day of the German offensive—was one of the most memorable in the war history of fighter *Geschwader* JG 27. At that moment it was a composite formation comprising the three *Gruppen* I/JG 27, I/JG 1 and I/JG 21, with its operations focused on the Maastricht-Liège break-through. After the initial fighting its commander, Lieutenant-Colonel Max Ibel, still had at his disposal eighty-five operational Me 109Es. The ground crews had worked through the night patching, repairing and exchanging parts, to make them so. Their bases were Mönchengladbach and Gymnich near Cologne.

At dawn two squadrons of I/JG 1 took off under Captain Joachim Schlichting to provide fighter cover at the bridges over the Maas and the Albert Canal for the advance of the 6th Army, with orders to attack any hostile aircraft that appeared. No doubt the British were perfectly aware of the air operation that had captured these bridges on May 10th, and of their importance for the German advance. Consequently it was expected that their aircraft would appear again in all-out attempt to destroy them.

At 06.00 First-Lieutenant Walter Adolph, leading 2 Squadron, observed some dark dots in the lightening sky to the east. Three, six, nine of them. They grew larger: too large to be fighters.

"Enemy formation over Maastricht," he called on the radio. "I'm attacking!"

Simultaneously he half-rolled and was gone, followed by his No. 2. The dots had now become twin-engined bombers, coming rapidly nearer. Red white and blue roundels . . . English . . . type Bristol Blenheim. A hundred yards astern of the last of them Adolph went down, then coming up again approached obliquely from below. The bombers stuck rigidly to their course. Hadn't they noticed anything?

In his reflector sight the Blenheim appeared as big as a haystack. He glanced momentarily to the left, saw Sergeant Blazytko closing with the next bomber, and pressed the button. Cannon and machine-guns went off together at a range of eighty yards, and little flashes dotted the target's fuselage and wings. Adolph threw his plane in a turn to avoid colliding, and looking back saw the Blenheim's port engine on fire. Suddenly the whole wing broke off. The rest of the plane seemed to stop. Then, rearing up, it went down to destruction.

Adolph at once went after another Blenheim, and within five minutes had shot down three. Three more were claimed by First-Lieutenant Braune, Lieutenant Örtel and Sergeant Blazytko. As if that were not enough, the remaining three were spotted during their escape by JG 27's 3 Squadron over Liège. After their attack First-Lieutenant Homuth and Lieutenant Borchert saw two of them crash to the ground in flames.

Still the British persisted. Their next squadrons attacked with Hurricane fighters patrolling the area. Five Battles with volunteer crews made a suicidal attempt to bomb the Albert Canal bridges at low altitude. All were shot down by flak[1].

In the course of the morning every squadron of JG 27 was thrown into the battle, often with only a forty-five minute pause between missions. As soon as they landed, the pilots ran off to be briefed for the next, while the ground crews refuelled, rearmed, and carried out minor repairs to their aircraft. All the same, the number of serviceable machines constantly dwindled.

At 11.00 the *Geschwader's* operations staff officer, Captain Adolf Galland, threw aside his papers and maps and went off on a mission with Lieutenant Gustav Rödel. West of Liège they spotted eight Hurricanes thousands of feet below, and the pair of them dived down to attack. They were Belgians, equipped with an early pattern of this British fighter. "I almost felt sorry for them," wrote Galland.

He fired prematurely, as if to give his opponent some warning, some chance to get away. The Belgian peeled off in alarm—straight into Rödel's line of fire. Then Galland attacked again, and the Hurricane disintegrated.

That was how the man who was to become one of the world's most successful fighter pilots, Adolf Galland, achieved his first victory. "I just had luck—it was child's-play." He went on to shoot down two more, and Rödel one.

By the afternoon no more Allied squadrons appeared in the sky—neither bombers nor fighters. JG 27 had cleared the air of them. It took over escort duty to the dive-bombers of StGs 2 and 77 while these attacked the enemy's armoured columns. When the last Me 109 landed it was nearly dark.

The *Geschwader's* effort for the day was 340 sorties, and each of its aircraft had made at least four or five. At a cost of four of its own planes its confirmed score against the enemy was twenty-eight. Similar reports came in from other sectors of the front.

At R.A.F. headquarters in Chauny-sur-Oise the reports from its own squadrons were like blows from a sledge-hammer. In the first three days of the German offensive the British air forces on the Continent had lost half of their 200 bombers. On Whit Sunday evening an urgent telegram arrived from the Chief of the Air Staff in London: "We cannot continue indefinitely at this rate. . . . If we expend all our efforts in the early stages of the battle we shall not be able to operate effectively when the really critical phase comes. . . ."

That phase was soon reached. On May 13th Air Marshal Barratt granted his hard-hit squadrons a day of rest. But while the French general staff concentrated all its attention on the German armoured thrust at Liège—convinced that there lay the focal point of the offensive—the entire bomber and dive-bomber forces of II and VIII Air Corps struck at quite a different spot: Sedan.

The main German thrust was indeed along a route where the French least expected it: via Luxembourg and south-east Belgium through the wooded hills and along the minor roads of the Ardennes. It was made by General von Kleist's Armoured Group consisting of XIX and XXXI Army Corps under Guderian and Reinhardt. By Whit Sunday evening, May 12th, the spearhead had already reached the Meuse in the sector Charleville-Sedan.

---

[1] For this mission the R.A.F.'s first two posthumous Victoria Crosses of the war were awarded.—*Translator's Note.*

This river, with its numerous pillboxes and artillery and field positions, represented the northern extension of the Maginot Line, and thus formed a strongly defended obstacle to the armoured forces' advance. The Luftwaffe was accordingly required to smash the resistance. By continuous attack it was to hold down the enemy long enough for German sappers to safeguard the crossing. The detailed operations plan, and its time-table, had already been worked out during long discussions between Generals Loerzer and Guderian. But suddenly the whole plan had to be changed.

On May 12th von Kleist bade Guderian report to him, and the latter flew over in a Fieseler Storch. The attack across the Meuse was fixed for next day at 16.00 hours. But when he arrived Guderian could hardly believe his ears. First, explained von Kleist, the Luftwaffe would launch a single concentrated attack on the enemy positions. After that it would be up to the *Panzer* divisions. That, at least, was what he had arranged with the chief of *Luftflotte* 3, General Sperrle.

Guderian put his objections. He pointed to his own arrangements, made down to the last detail with II Air Corps; to the whole month-long Army-Air Force discussions on the matter. Surely, he said, it had been decided that the best results would be achieved, not by a single, all-out attack, but by a continuing series of attacks by smaller formations?

Von Kleist said he was sorry, but the decision had come from a higher level. Guderian flew back pessimistically.

Next afternoon his *Panzer* divisions, 1, 2 and 10, stood ready to launch their assault on a narrow front at Sedan. Guderian, from an advanced observation post, waited in suspense for the Luftwaffe bombardment. Much, if not all, would depend on its success.

Punctually at 16.00 hours there came the drone of engines: the first *Stukas*. The enemy let off a fierce anti-aircraft barrage as the Ju 87s dived down on their target on the west bank of the Meuse. Their bombs crashed into the artillery positions. A concrete emplacement burst asunder from a direct hit by a thousand-pounder. Debris soared into the air, and the anti-aircraft fire was appreciably reduced.

Then suddenly the aircraft had vanished. Guderian puckered his brows. What was that about a single "all-out attack"? This one had been delivered by at most a single *Gruppe*!

But immediately afterwards there followed another, this time by horizontally bombing Do 17s of KG 2. In rows their bombs fell on the river-side positions. A short pause, then another attack.

"I was completely bewildered," wrote Guderian, "that each was delivered by just a few squadrons under fighter protection . . . in exactly the way I had discussed and agreed with Loerzer. Had General von Kleist changed his mind? The Luftwaffe was operating just in the way I thought most favourable for my own assault. I was delighted."

By the evening the 1st Rifle Regiment was over the Meuse. The Sedan crossing had been won. Three miles further west, near Donchery, elements of 2 *Panzer* Division, with pontoons and pneumatic rafts, were forcing other crossings. Continuous air attacks held down the enemy artillery fire and prevented the arrival of reinforcements.

II Air Corps' effort was 310 bomber and 200 dive-bomber sorties. To help it, VIII Air Corps to the north sent in its StG 77 under "*Stuka* father"

Colonel Günter Schwarzkopff, who had won fame in Poland. That evening Guderian telephoned Loerzer and offered hearty thanks for the vital assistance of his air force.

"By the way," he asked, "how was it that, despite everything, the air attacks went off just as you and I had planned them?"

Loerzer hesitated a moment, then answered with a chuckle: "The orders from *Luftflotte* 3, mucking everything up, came—shall we say—too late. They would only have confused my units, so I delayed sending them on. . . ."

May 14th drew to a close. On this day the Allied air forces, at the urgent request of the French high command, had thrown everything they had into the Sedan funnel. For the first time in the western campaign hundreds of German and Allied fighters and bombers had come into mutual conflict. The battle in the air lasted from late morning till the evening. II Air Corps' war diary named it "the day of the fighters".

Amongst the German fighter units, I *Gruppe* of the élite JG 53 was probably the most successful. Under Captain Jan von Janson it scored thirty-nine victories, five of them at the hands of First-Lieutenant Hans-Karl Meyer, three by Lieutenant Hans Ohly. II *Gruppe* under Captain von Maltzahn fought off the French Morane fighters, then dived on the Allied bombers. At the top of III *Gruppe's* score sheet appeared a name soon to become known to every German child: Captain Werner Mölders.

After downing a Hurricane, Mölders had a tenth victory stripe painted on his Messerschmitt's tail. By June 5th there were twenty-five of them, putting him ahead of every other German fighter pilot to date. Then in a wild scrimmage with nine Dewoitine fighters of the *Groupe de Chasse* II/7, Mölders was shot down by the youthful Second-Lieutenant Pommier-Layrargues and became (for the time being) a prisoner of war of the French. Altogether, during the French campaign, JG 3 under Major Hans-Jürgen von Cramon-Taubadel claimed a total of 179 enemy planes destroyed in the air.

Not far behind JG 53 on May 14th was the "Richthofen" *Geschwader*, JG 2, under Lieutenant-Colonel Harry von Bülow. When all the reports had been added up at the end of the day, it was found that the German fighter effort had totalled 814 sorties, and the wrecks of eighty-nine Allied fighters and bombers lay strewn about the Sedan sector.

It had also been a great day for the German flak. Flak Regiment 102 under Lieutenant-Colonel Walter von Hippel had moved forward with Guderian's armoured spearhead, and on May 13th its 88-mm guns, once more in a ground role, had been used with their flat trajectory to wipe out pillboxes and nests of machine-guns. Amongst the first elements to cross the Meuse, they had then taken up positions close to the pontoon bridges erected during the night. There they remained all next day under suicidal attack from the French Amiot, Bloch and Potez bombers, and the British Battles and Blenheims. The regiment's war diary records 112 enemy aircraft destroyed, most of them at low altitude.

By the evening of May 14th—"the Day of Sedan"—the desperate attempt of the Allied air forces to stop the German break-through had collapsed. The French bomber force no longer existed, and sixty per cent of the British bombers failed to return. The official history, *Royal Air Force 1939–1945*, states: "No higher rate of loss in an operation of comparable size has ever been experienced by the R.A.F."

Early in the morning of May 15th, Winston Churchill, who had just become Prime Minister, was called from his bed to take a telephone call from the French premier, Reynaud. "We are beaten," said the latter, speaking under stress. "We have lost the battle."

"Surely," answered Churchill incredulously, "it can't have happened so soon?"

But it had. A week later Guderian's *Panzers* had reached the Channel coast.

Role of the Luftwaffe in the western campaign. In carrying out the "Sickle" Plan the German army leaders, by concentrating strength on the left instead of the right, did the opposite of what their opponents expected. Within eleven days von Kleist's armoured group pushed right through to the Channel coast. Bombers and dive-bombers not only hammered the necessary breaches in the Franco-Belgian fortified line, but repulsed the Allied armoured assaults on the "Sickle's" undefended flank. Dunkirk alone could not be sealed off from the air. For that the Luftwaffe's strength was inadequate, and the British fighter bases were too near.

On the morning of May 22nd Lieutenant-Colonel Hans Seidemann, chief of staff of VIII Air Corps, flew in his Fieseler Storch to Cambrai, where the two most forward *Gruppen* of the direct-support force were now based. They comprised II/LG 2 under Captain Otto Weiss—now as ever the only unit of its kind in the Luftwaffe, still equipped with its ancient Henschel Hs 123 "battlers"—and a fighter *Gruppe*, I/JG 21, under Captain Werner Ultsch.

The fighters were there for the Henschel pilots' "personal protection", because the slow and antiquated biplanes attracted enemy fighters like magnets.

Seidemann, Weiss and Ultsch stood on the airfield discussing the next operations. The position was uncomfortable: the armour was far ahead, and the infantry had not yet arrived. Only twenty miles to the north-west, in Arras, were the British. The Allied armies in the north now saw their chance of making a break-through to the south. There, at Amiens, air reconnaissance had reported further strong concentrations of Allied armour, which was now in a position to take the German *Panzer* divisions in the rear. Clearly the success of the "Sickle Plan" hung in the balance.

"We propose to launch the *Stukas* against the enemy armour at Amiens," said Seidemann. "Perhaps you too, Weiss, will have to attack their tanks."

At that moment they all looked up on hearing the sound of an approaching aircraft. It was a Heinkel 46, an Army reconnaissance plane. Its starboard wing drooped badly, and its tail unit had been shot up. Was it trying to land? No: the observer leant out and dropped a smoke signal with a pencilled message: "Some forty enemy tanks and 150 lorries full of infantry advancing on Cambrai from north."

Seidemann could not believe it. "It must be one of our own units," he said.

But supposing it was not? In that case, the airfield stood in immediate danger of being overrun. And not his own units alone. Through Cambrai ran the main supply route for the far advanced *Panzer* Corps. And apart from some airfield flak Cambrai had no defending ground forces.

Weiss shouted an order and ran to his plane. Four Henschels of the staff flight trundled over the ground and took off on an armed reconnaissance. After only two minutes in the air they saw the tanks ahead of them. No shadow of doubt: they were French, less than four miles from Cambrai!

"Already south of the Canal de la Sensée the tanks, in formations of four to six, were sweeping on to the attack," Captain Weiss reported later. "North of the canal a long column of lorries followed hard on their heels."

The staff flight at once attacked with bombs and guns. But a mere four aircraft were powerless. Turning away, Weiss chased back in the direction of the airfield, briefing the rest of his pilots by radio. Then the whole *Gruppe* took off, and the fighters too. Going down squadron by squadron, the old "battle planes" planted their 100-lb. bombs right in the path of the tanks. With luck, the effect would be at least to tear off the caterpillar tracks. Meanwhile the fighters went for the lorries with their 20-mm cannon, and soon half of them were in flames. The infantry swarmed out and awaited the outcome of this unusual trial at arms. Who would win: aircraft or tanks?

Five or six of the latter were on fire, and another dozen or so immobilised. But the rest were still pushing on to Cambrai, and it seemed there was nothing to stop them. Suddenly, at a mere 150 yards' range, there was the crash of heavy guns. Two batteries of I/*Flakregiment* 33 had taken up positions on the edge of the town and bided their time. Within a few minutes they accounted for five Hotchkis tanks. The remainder turned and retreated.

By the afternoon the threat to Cambrai was averted. The attempt of other enemy formations to break through at Arras was thwarted by *Stukas*.

Between them the old Henschels, some fighters and Luftwaffe flak guns had dealt with a very dangerous flank attack from the north. From now on the German armoured column could proceed with its thrust to the English Channel, confident that the Luftwaffe could secure its long open flanks till the infantry caught up with it. Had the Luftwaffe not prepared the way, the armour would not have got so far in the first place.

Both tasks typified this phase of the war. Within two or three days the Allied armies realised they had only one escape route: Dunkirk.

4. The Miracle of Dunkirk

On May 24th von Kleist's Armoured Group advancing on Dunkirk from the south and west reported, for the first time, "enemy air superiority". In the evening of the 26th Guderian's XIX Army Corps' war diary contained the passage: "Very heavy activity by enemy fighters. Own fighter cover completely lacking. Luftwaffe operations against enemy sea transport remain ineffective."

What had happened? The fighting in northern France, as it approached Dunkirk, was reaching its crucial phase. The Luftwaffe was having to operate at an ever-increasing distance from most of its bases. The *Stukas* of VIII Air Corps were now based on airfields east of St. Quentin, but even from there the Channel coast—Boulogne, Calais, Dunkirk—represented the limit of their range. Richthofen had to bring his units further forward. On May 24th it was decided to move at least one fighter *Gruppe*, I/JG 27, to St. Omer, just vacated by the British, where it would be close behind the front. The staff flight duly came in to land, led by the *Geschwader* commander, Lieutenant-Colonel Ibel. He reported: "Suddenly I noticed that the airfield was being contested by German and English batteries, which were engaged in a shooting match across it from either side. . . ."

With their last drops of fuel the *Gruppe* managed to land farther south, at St. Pol. Even a few squadrons of StG 2, despite the dangerous open flank to the south left by the armour's advance, were moved up into the freshly won territory. But then there was trouble about supplying them: the vehicle columns were held up, and the air transport planes could not carry enough fuel, bombs and ammunition. To bring up the twin-engined bombers so close behind the front was quite out of the question.

That was the general picture of the outset of the Dunkirk battle. Two weeks of gruelling operations had sapped much of the Luftwaffe's strength. Many of the bomber *Gruppen* could only put some fifteen aircraft out of thirty into the air. But they went in, raining down bombs on the quays and sheds of Dunkirk harbour. Around noon on the 26th the great oil tanks on the western edge of the town went up in flames. In a precision raid *Stukas* destroyed the lock gates leading to the inner harbour. Bombs tore up the tracks of the marshalling yard; ships were set on fire; a freighter sank slowly to the bed of the battered harbour basin.

For the British these were days of hell. Having resolved to evacuate their army from the Continent, there was now no other port besides Dunkirk from which they could do so. For this purpose they put in everything they had—even their home-based fighters, hitherto held carefully in reserve, including the Spitfire Mark IIA, whose performance matched that of the Me 109E. These fighters now had one considerable advantage: Dunkirk and the whole battle zone lay well within operating range of their bases.

On May 23rd Goering's special train, which he used as a mobile head-quarters, stood at Polch in the Eifel district. As the latest reports came in, it became clear that the Allies in Flanders were caught in a giant trap. The spearhead of the German armour, at Gravelines, was thirty miles nearer to Dunkirk than were the British, still fighting round Lille and Arras. In a few days that way to the sea would also be closed.

And the Luftwaffe? Was it to play no part in the final victory? Goering was determined to make sure that it did: "My Führer, leave the destruction of the enemy surrounded at Dunkirk to me and my Luftwaffe!" A character-istically bombastic gesture.

Hitler was only too ready to comply with the suggestion. He wanted to save the armour for the continuance of the campaign against France. On May 24th the order to halt was given, and for two and a half days the *Panzers* became immobilised within reach of Dunkirk, on the line Gravelines-St. Omer-Béthune, in order to give Goering free play for his air assault.

General Jodl, chief of the army operations staff, was convinced that he had bitten off more than he could chew.

Even Kesselring, commander of *Luftflotte* 2, raised objections: "The job is completely beyond the strength of my depleted forces," he said.

But Goering had the last word: "My Luftwaffe will do it alone!"

StG 2 was flying along the coast, with the staff section at its head. The *Geschwader* commander, Major Oskar Dinort, peered downwards. Though the sun was shining, the land lay veiled in mist. The French coast was only a hazy outline. To the left lay Calais, itself unmistakable owing to the brown-black smoke mushrooming up from the fires that engulfed it. Amongst its streets and houses the 10th *Panzer* Division was fighting against the Allies resisting from the citadel and harbour, and supported by naval guns. Guderian's XIX Army Corps had asked for *Stukas* to silence the troublesome destroyers. That was Dinort's present job, and that of the two *Gruppen* under Captains Hitschold and Brückers, on this May 25th.

Though the continuous operations of the previous fortnight had welded them into an experienced and confident team, Dinort felt the stimulation and excitement of undertaking something new. For this was the first time they had been sent to attack ships: those tiny little targets that were both mobile and dangerous. What was the procedure? How did one attack? Only a few of the pilots of StG 2 had ever acquired the "knack".

Their commander screwed up his eyes, for the diffused light was blinding. The sea stretched beneath him like an endless pane of frosted glass. But suddenly upon it were a few specks of dust. They were ships. A whole lot of them, but how small! Were they supposed to hit them?

"Attack by *Gruppen*," ordered Dinort. "Choose your own targets."

At that the other two members of his section, First-Lieutenants Ulitz and Lau, turned into echelon-to-starboard behind their leader, throttled back and began to lose height. A dive on such small targets must be started as low as possible—certainly not from 12,000 feet.

Dinort's Ju 87 rolled over and peeled off, aiming for one of the larger ships. But the target wandered out of his bomb-sight and disappeared below his engine cowling. His reaction was to begin a "staircase" attack. That meant diving till you lost sight of the target, pulling out, re-sighting and diving again—perhaps several times.

At last he began the "business" dive, and by now the target was no longer a "speck of dust" but the long, slim hull of a destroyer, growing in his bomb-sight with each split-second. But suddenly it turned to port, and all Dinort could see was the foaming froth left by the propellers. He tried to follow, but the ship tightened its turn to 180 degrees—a full half-circle that the aircraft could not match. There was only one thing to do : pull out and start again.

The other forty-odd *Stukas* had much the same experience. Most of their bombs cascaded into the sea, causing impressive but useless fountains of water. The only hits scored were on a guard-boat and a transport. Two were claimed on the bows of the latter, but with unobserved result.

One after the other the squadrons pulled out and started to re-form at sea-level to head back south. This was their moment of greatest vulnerability, with speed so reduced that the machines seemed to hang in the air, and the pilot fully occupied with reseating the diving brakes, reopening the radiator shutter, readjusting the bomb-release switches and changing the airscrew and elevator trim. At the same time the pilots had to keep their eyes on their leader to make sure they all emerged from the enemy flak zone in the same direction, and further had to keep in tight formation to augment their power of defence against attack from astern.

The enemy knew that while the *Stukas* were thus preoccupied was the best moment to make a surprise attack. And now it came.

"English fighters behind us!"

The warning in his ear-phones made Dinort put his machine in a turn. High above were a number of flashing, circling dots. That meant their own fighters were dog-fighting with the enemy. But a few Spitfires had managed to break away in quest of a richer quarry : the *Stukas*.

Dinort at once throttled back and stall-turned to starboard. With no hope of getting clear away from an opponent twice as fast as himself, it was an alternative defensive measure that paid off. The Spitfire, grooved to its course, could not follow the movement because of its speed. The Ju 87 slipped out of its reflector-sight, and the eight guns fired into an empty void.

The dive-bomber's manoeuvre was very similar to that executed shortly before by the British destroyers when attacked by the Ju 87s. The same rules applied : evade, counter-turn, give no time to aim!

Seconds later the Spitfire swept over the Ju 87 from the beam and soared into the sky, where it was promptly attacked by a waiting Me 109. "We got rid of that one," called Dinort, relieved.

The above was a typical episode of the time. The previous day, May 24th, a number of *Stukas* had failed to return from their missions on the Channel coast, having been jumped by home-based Spitfires. The latter were now operating closer to their bases than were most of the German formations, which could not be brought forward nearly as quickly as the Army advanced. For Dinort's *Gruppen* of StG 2, still based at Guise, east of St. Quentin, Calais represented almost the limit of their range.

May 25th was one day after Hitler had halted the armour and left "the destruction of the foe" to the Luftwaffe. Yet on this day Richthofen's close-support Air Corps made no attacks at Dunkirk whatever. KG 77 and StG 1 were engaged against French armour heavily assaulting the over-extended German southern flank at Amiens, Graf Schönborn's StG 77 against enemy artillery firing on the supply-depot airfield of St. Quentin. With such threats to both sides of the German wedge Dunkirk itself had to wait.

But on the morning of the 25th Boulogne fell to the 2nd *Panzer* Division after two British Guards battalions had embarked and got away under a hail of fire from tanks right in the harbour area. Loaded with troops, the French destroyer *Chacal* was sunk by *Stukas* just off the pier.

For the next day, the 26th, Generals Guderian and Richthofen together arranged a concentrated *Stuka* attack on the citadel and harbour of Calais. There the British force was not to be evacuated: Churchill had ordered it to resist to the bitter end. At 08.40 the first *Geschwader*, StG 77, flew over the St. Pol airfields to collect its escort.

"We were waiting ready strapped in our cockpits as the bomb-laden *Stukas* crossed over," reported First-Lieutenant Graf von Kageneck, of I/JG 1. After yesterday's unpleasant experience with the Spitfires, Corps H.Q. was determined to run no risks. The *Stukas* were to be escorted by all three *Gruppen* of the composite JG 27.

"We were soon in the air and, after one circuit to get into combat forma-tion, quickly caught the *Stukas* up," continued Kageneck. "Then, gently weaving in close formation on either side of them, we approached the target. Even without a compass one could not have missed it, owing to the column of thick black smoke that showed the way."

Suddenly the British fighters were on the scene. But spotting the Messer-schmitts close above the dive-bomber formation, they checked.

"Our fingers itched," Kageneck went on, "but we had to stick to our charges. Perhaps they were decoys, and if we engaged them others might pounce on the *Stukas*."

Then, evidently thinking they saw a gap in the German defence, the British went down. At once the Messerschmitts climbed, turned and swung down after them. One of the Spitfires burst into flames, and nose-dived trailing a plume of smoke. A parachute opened in its wake, and the German squadron commander confirmed the victory on the radio.

Meanwhile the *Stukas* were over Calais, and dived in close clusters on the bitterly defended citadel. Their bombs left such a pall of smoke and dust over citadel and harbour that when StG 2 arrived to conduct the second wave of the attack, they could hardly see their targets. None the less they added their bombs to the seething cauldron.

Altogether the onslaught lasted for over an hour, from about 9 a.m. till 10; and the hammering of artillery continued even longer. Towards noon the 10th *Panzer* Division again assaulted the Allied positions, and at 16.45 the defenders of Calais capitulated. 20,000 men, including 3–4,000 British, were taken prisoner. In England their surrender was not yet known: supplies continued to be dropped on the burning town even the following day.

Calais had fallen to closely concerted operations by Luftwaffe and Army. Surely Dunkirk—the last escape harbour left to the British Expeditionary

Force still fighting in Flanders—could fall in the same way? After all, the German spearhead was only twelve miles away.

But there the German armour was stationary, and had been for two days already. They were being saved for another occasion. The Luftwaffe would deal with Dunkirk alone.

Yet on May 26th, too, town and harbour were attacked only by small forces from I and IV Air Corps. The three *Stuka Geschwader* of VIII Air Corps, as well as its other bombers, its Henschels and its fighters, were indeed heavily engaged: at Calais, Lille and Amiens. But not at Dunkirk.

The day before—i.e., the first day of the armour's immobilisation—VIII Air Corps' commander, Richthofen, had flown in his Fieseler Storch to von Kleist's command post to discuss further concerted measures. As it happened, the 4th Army commander, von Kluge, as well as his corps generals— Guderian and Reinhardt—were also present. Guderian's reaction to the order to halt when success was almost in his grasp has been recorded: "We were speechless."

Von Kluge now turned on the air commander. "Well, Richthofen," he said sarcastically, "I suppose you have taken Dunkirk from the air?"

"No, *Herr Generaloberst*, I have not yet even attacked it. My *Stukas* are too far back, the approach flights too long. Consequently I can use them twice a day at most, and am unable to focus them at one point of effort."

"Then what about the other air corps?"

"They lie still further back, most of them in the Reich and in Holland. Even for Heinkel 111s and Junkers 88s that is still a long way to fly."

Kluge shook his head. "And *we* are not even allowed to cross the Aa Canal for fear of getting in the Luftwaffe's way! As a result the whole of the armour is paralysed. All we can achieve now is a series of pin-pricks."

Reinhardt dutifully supported his chief: "Undoubtedly the enemy will utilise the land routes to Dunkirk that remain to him in order to escape our clutches and embark the mass of his army. Only a heavy assault by us can prevent him."

Now was the time to do it. But the 4th Army was still tied by the continued order to halt. All the arguments of von Brauchitsch, the Army's supreme commander, and his chief of general staff, Halder, had failed to prevail with Hitler.

Even that go-ahead general, Richthofen, did not rate the chances of his *Stukas* very highly in the circumstances. Hardly had he got back to his own headquarters situated in a children's convalescent home at Proisy, than he had a call put through direct to the Luftwaffe chief of general staff, Jeschonnek.

"Unless the *Panzers* can get moving again at once, the English will give us the slip. No one can seriously believe that we alone can stop them from the air."

"You're wrong," Jeschonnek replied drily to his friend. "The Iron One believes it."

He was referring to Goering. Then he added something rather remarkable: "What's more, the Führer wishes to spare the British a too crushing defeat."

Richthofen could hardly believe his ears. "Yet we are to go at them hammer-and-tongs all the same?"

41. Dunkirk. The overladen French destroyer *Bourrasque* sinks off Nieuport on May 30, 1940, after heavy air attack. Effective Luftwaffe interference with the evacuation was limited by the weather of 2½ days.

42. Two Me 110s of the "Shark" *Gruppe*, II/ZG 76, in low-level flight above the hard-hit city of Dunkirk.

43. The Ju 88 "wonder" bomber was first used in dive-bombing attacks against British warships, with greatly over-publicized results. To hit fast and maneuverable seaborne targets from the air required much practice and experience. This picture is a photo-montage, but approximates to reality.

"Quite so. With all the forces at your command."

It didn't seem to make sense, this story of consideration for the British! How could there be any if the Luftwaffe was to plaster them with everything they had? And there was Goering, despite all the scepticism of his generals, expecting to nail up a famous victory inside two days.

Now, as Calais capitulated in the afternoon of May 26th, events crowded on each others' heels:

1. In certain sectors of the Flanders front the British vacated their positions and openly began their retreat to the Channel coast.
2. Hitler and Rundstedt rescinded the halt command and permitted the armoured divisions, after a pause of two and a half days, to move forward again the following morning.
3. The Luftwaffe at last nominated Dunkirk as its main target, and for the first time ordered both *Luftflotten* to operate at maximum strength against the town and harbour.
4. At 18.57 hours the British Admiralty ordered "Operation Dynamo"— the rescue of the British Army from the continent—to be started.

A huge fleet, with a preponderance of tiny vessels, started moving across the Channel. It included destroyers and torpedo boats, trawlers, tug-towed barges, plus an uncounted number of private yachts and motor boats.

Their outlook was gloomy. Vice-Admiral Sir Bertram Ramsay, who controlled the operation from Dover, reckoned with a space of two days before the Germans made Dunkirk untenable. In that time he hoped, with his "fleet of midges", at best to pluck 45,000 men from the witches' cauldron.

As May 27th, the first day of the evacuation, dawned, it looked as if all British hopes were to be dashed. The German air attacks exceeded the worst expectations. Already by first light single *Gruppen* of KG 1 and 4 were overhead, the bombs from their Heinkels illuminating the surroundings as they exploded. But it was only the prelude. The stream of bombers never let up. KG 54's raid kindled new fires amongst the docks, and beside the long eastern mole the 8,000-ton French freighter *Aden* broke apart. Till 07.11 the raids were conducted by bombers of *Luftflotte* 2, based in western Germany and Holland.

Then came the *Stukas*. By now the sea area off Dunkirk was swarming with vessels of every kind. Picking out the larger ones, the pilots peeled off and only pressed the bomb release after diving to 1,500 feet. The 500- and 1,000-lb. delayed action missiles went whistling down. Though there were again many misses, thanks to the ships' agility, hits were also plentiful. Amongst those sunk was the French troop transport *Côte d'Azur*.

Town and harbour were given no breathing space, attacked now by Dorniers of KG 2 and 3. These had flown all the way from the Rhine-Main region, and were helped to their target by the black smoke mushrooming up from the burning oil tanks. Beneath all the smoke and dust from the fires and collapsing buildings the town itself was hardly recognisable as more bombs fell into the inferno.

At noon the British troops began evacuating the town and harbour area. Admiral Ramsay was informed that it was no longer possible to embark from the bomb-torn quays. It would have to be done from the open beaches between Dunkirk and La Panne, where there were no piers or loading facilities, and the process would be much slower.

By the end of the first day of "Dynamo" only 7,669 had been saved out of a total of over 300,000. The difficulties were immense, and there were complaints about inadequate British air cover. Admiral Ramsay reported: "Full air protection was expected, but instead, for hours on end the ships off-shore were subjected to a murderous hail of bombs and machine-gun bullets."

Nearly every British soldier who got safely back to England after passing through the ordeal asked the same question: "Where were our fighters?"

It was an injustice to the R.A.F. testified to by German bomber pilots over Dunkirk—from bitter experience.

A dozen Do 17s of III/KG 3 had just bombed oil storage tanks west of the harbour when they were jumped by a squadron of Spitfires. No German fighters were on the scene. Though the radio-operators fired desperately with their MG 15s, the speed of the attack and the superior armament of the Spitfires were such as to leave no doubt about the outcome. Half of the Dorniers either crashed in flames or were forced to make emergency landings.

III/KG 2 had a similar experience, as reported by Major Werner Kreipe: "The enemy fighters pounced on our tightly knit formation with the fury of maniacs."

With the Dorniers flying almost wing-tip to wing-tip the screen of mutually defensive fire produced by their gunners helped. Even so the radio crackled with anguished calls from the rear machines: "Badly shot up . . . must break formation . . . am trying forced landing."

II Air Corps' war diary described the 27th May as "a bad day": "With sixty-four aircrew missing, seven wounded, and twenty-three aircraft gone, today's losses exceed the combined total of the last ten days."

With the other air corps it was a similar story. If the 200 Spitfires and Hurricanes had not saved the troops from bombardment, they had certainly taken their toll of the enemy. Could the Luftwaffe keep up the pressure? Could its attacks, during the following days, be either so prolonged or effective?

On May 28th the weather worsened from hour to hour. Though individual bomber *Gruppen* attacked Ostend and Nieuport, hardly any bombs dropped on Dunkirk. Low clouds, fusing with all the smoke and dust, blotted out the whole area.

Admiral Ramsay and his team breathed again. It was now found that the harbour, after all, could once more be used. Above all, ships could tie up against the long eastern mole—a much more expeditious method of embarkation than ferrying the troops from the beaches. On this day another 17,804 men got away to England.

May 29th was heralded by pouring rain. Richthofen wrote in his diary: "All levels of the higher command were clamouring today for VIII Air Corps to go again for the ships and boats, on which the English divisions were getting away with their bare skins. We had, however, a ceiling of just 300 feet, and as general in command I expressed the view that the enemy's concentrated flak was causing greater loss to our side than we were to his."

Thirty-six hours elapsed, and virtually no bombs had fallen on Dunkirk. The stream of ships, coming and going, constantly increased. But at noon the clouds broke up, and from 14.00 hours onwards the weather was again favourable for air operations. The Luftwaffe lost no time in catching up. Three *Geschwader* of *Stukas* dived in series on the evacuation fleet. Once more the whole embarkation was shredded with bombs. One ship after another caught fire, and again the harbour was declared "blocked and unserviceable".

And at 15.32 the formations of *Luftflotte* 2 appeared again, amongst them KG 30 from Holland and LG 1 from Düsseldorf—both equipped with the dive-bombing Ju 88 (the Luftwaffe's so-called "wonder bomber").

The afternoon's score against the British Navy was three destroyers sunk, and seven damaged. This was considered by the Admiralty an excessive loss, and the modern destroyers were withdrawn. More important for the evacuation was the loss to *Stukas*, one after the other, of five large passenger ships, with all their carrying capacity: the *Queen of the Channel*, the *Lorina*, the *Fenella*, the *King Orry* and the *Normannia*. After a few hours of Luftwaffe assault "Operation Dynamo" had become direly threatened. But despite everything, on May 29th another 47,310 Allied soldiers were brought back home.

On May 30th the weather was again in league with the British. Fog and rain prevented the Luftwaffe from operating. Even the German Army made little impression on the bitterly defended bridgehead, and now had to pay for its two and a half day halt. Six days previously the armour, advancing in the enemy's rear, had only encountered slight opposition, and could have closed the trap. Now it was too late. On this day 58,823 troops, including 14,874 French, were embarked.

The 31st began with fog, but this cleared by the afternoon, permitting at least a few bomber formations to operate. But the *Stukas* were grounded the whole day, and the evacuation figure increased to 68,014.

The next day, June 1st, was clear and sunny, and once more the Luftwaffe threw in all its serviceable aircraft. Though many squadrons of Spitfires and Hurricanes were put up against them, most of them tangled with the Me 109s of Colonel Osterkamp's JG 51 and the Me 110s of Lieutenant-Colonel Huth's ZG 26. Thus the *Stukas* were able once again to dive on the evacuation fleet. Four destroyers loaded with troops were sunk at sea, plus ten other ships. Many others were hit.

Although another 64,429 soldiers got away this day, the air raids were such that Admiral Ramsay had to decide that evacuation could only be continued at night. When, therefore, the German reconnaissance planes appeared next morning, they reported the ships had vanished. Accordingly the bombers were switched to land targets, and from now on the main operations zone of the Luftwaffe was again further south. On the following day, in fact, a heavy raid was mounted on Paris.

Thus, while "Operation Dynamo" went on for nine whole days, the Luftwaffe only succeeded in seriously interfering with it for two-and-a-half— namely on May 27th, the afternoon of May 29th, and on June 1st. When the last soldiers went aboard at dawn on June 4th they brought the total number of evacuated to 338,226. For the continuation of the war it represented a decisive success that no one had reckoned with. When Dunkirk at last fell, General Halder, the Army's chief of general staff, noted in his diary: "Town and coast in our hands. French and English gone!"

In fact, some 35–40,000 French troops remained behind, and were taken prisoner. It was their stout resistance which had enabled "Dynamo" to last so long, and so many of their comrades—the British almost to a man—to be evacuated.

As German infantrymen combed the wreckage that littered the beaches, an exhausted airman stumbled forward, waving. He was First-Lieutenant von Oelhaven, squadron commander of 6/LG 1, whose Ju 88 had been shot down by Spitfires. As a prisoner-of-war he had been led over a pier composed of lorries to be taken aboard a British vessel. Seizing his opportunity, however, he had leapt into the water and hidden between the lorries under the planking.

For thirty-six hours he stuck it out, with the tide ebbing and flowing over him, till finally his countrymen appeared. For this German airman, at least, Dunkirk was a victory.

5. Channel Merry-Go-Round

The second phase of the western campaign, which began on June 5th, 1940, and ended less than three weeks later with an armistice between France, Germany and Italy, saw the Luftwaffe, on the model of the Polish campaign, mainly occupied in giving close support to the rapidly advancing army. Its next opponent would be Britain. Or would that country prefer to be "reasonable" and come to terms before the struggle re-opened and the island bore the whole brunt of the enemy's might?

On July 10th south-east England and the Straits of Dover lay covered beneath broken cloud, height about 6,000 feet, with short, sharp showers beating down. A low-pressure front was approaching from the North Atlantic, and over the rest of England it was raining cats and dogs. The weather was typical of this very wet July.

The German fighter pilots, whose units had gradually re-grouped on airfields behind the Channel coast, slapped their arms about to keep warm. Mud stuck to their flying boots, and the runways had become swamps. How were they supposed to force the British fighters into battle under such conditions? Or was there to be no battle after all?

No one seemed to know. Since the end of the French campaign most of them had been cooling their heels, while the Luftwaffe waited and watched. The authorities hoped that Britain would take steps to end the war. For bombers and fighters alike it was a time of rest.

But there were exceptions. Today reconnaissance reported at noon a large British coastal convoy off Folkestone headed for Dover. At the command post of the "Channel zone bomber-commander", Colonel Johannes Fink—it consisted of a converted omnibus stationed on Cap Gris Nez just behind the memorial to the British landing in 1914—the telephone rang. A *Gruppe* of Do 17s was duly alerted, plus another of Me 109s to act as escort, and a third of Me 110s.

Fink's mandate was "To close the Channel to enemy shipping". It looked as if the convoy was in for a hard time.

At 13.30 British Summer Time, several radar stations plotted on their screens a suspicious aircraft formation assembling over the Calais area. They were right, for at this moment—14.30 continental time—II/KG 2 under Major Adolf Fuchs, from Arras, was making rendezvous with III/JG 51 under Captain Hannes Trautloft, which had just taken off from St. Omer.

One fighter squadron took over close escort of the Dorniers, while Traut-loft went up with the other two to between 3,000 and 6,000 feet to be in a favourable position to attack any enemy fighters that assailed the bombers. The stepped-up formations then made a bee-line towards the English coast—some twenty Do 17s and twenty Me 109s. Within a few minutes they sighted the convoy.

Approaching from another direction were the thirty Me 110Cs of ZG 26 under Lieutenant-Colonel Huth, making a total of seventy German aircraft. Would the British accept the challenge?

Routine air cover for a British convoy consisted of just one flight of fighters—in this case represented by six Hurricanes of 32 Squadron from Biggin Hill. According to British sources these six had the additional dis-advantage, just before the crucial attack, of becoming split up in a rain cloud. When the first section of three eventually emerged, they were startled at the sight of "waves of enemy bombers approaching from France". Unde-terred, "the Hurricanes pounced on them—three versus a hundred", as one British report read.

In the official history of the Royal Air Force it is stated regarding these air battles of July 1940: "Over and over again a mere handful of Spitfires and Hurricanes found themselves fighting desperately with formations of a hundred or more German aircraft."

Against such evidence stands the fact that during this period the only fighter unit facing England across the Straits of Dover was JG 51, under the command of Colonel Theo Osterkamp. Thanks to the bad weather and the air battles in which they were engaged, the aircraft serviceability of his three *Gruppen*—under Captains Brustellin, Matthes and Trautloft—declined to such a degree that he had to be reinforced on July 12th by a fourth one (III/JG 3 under Captain Kienitz) to retain his operational strength of sixty/seventy Me 109s. Such a modest force had furthermore to operate with considerable discretion if its strength was not to be dissipated before the real assault on Britain began. It was not until the last week of July that JG 26 (of which Captain Galland led a *Gruppe*) and JG 52 began to take part in the Channel battle.

But back to July 10th—the date on which the Battle of Britain is regarded as having begun. The Dorniers of III/KG 2 were approaching the convoy when Captain Trautloft suddenly sighted the patrolling Hurricanes flying high above: first three, then all six of them. For the moment the latter made no attempt to interfere, but held their altitude waiting for a chance to elude the twenty German fighters and attack the bombers below them. In this way they were more of a nuisance than if they had rushed blindly to their own destruction.

Trautloft was compelled to remain constantly on watch. To engage them or just to chase them off would take his force miles away from the Dorniers, which he was committed to protect and bring safely back home. That might be exactly the Hurricanes' intention: to entice the Me 109s away by offering the hope of an easy victory so that other fighters could attack the bombers without hindrance.

Within a few minutes the Dorniers had penetrated the ships' flak zone, unloaded their bombs over the convoy, and dived to sea level for the return journey. But in these few minutes the whole situation changed.

Warned in good time by the radar plots, the R.A.F.'s 11 Group threw into the battle four further squadrons of fighters: No. 56 from Manston, No. 111 from Croydon, No. 64 from Kenley and No. 74 from Hornchurch. The first two were equipped with Hurricanes, the second two with Spitfires.

"Suddenly the sky was full of British fighters," wrote Trautloft that evening in his diary. "Today we were going to be in for a tough time."

The odds were now thirty-two British fighters against twenty German, and there would be no more question of the former holding back. Strictly the Me 110 *Gruppe* should be added to the German total, but as soon as the Spitfires and Hurricanes swept on to the scene from all sides, all thirty of them went into a defensive circle. With their single backward-firing 7.9-mm machine-guns, fired by the observers, they had little protection against attack from astern by faster fighters.

Accordingly they now all went round and round like circus horses in the ring, each protecting the rear of the one in front with its forward armament of four machine-guns and two 20-mm cannon. But that was all they did protect. As long-range fighters they were supposed to protect the bombers. Now, however, they just maintained their magic circle and made no contribution to the outcome.

Consequently Trautloft's *Gruppe* bore the brunt of the battle, which promptly resolved itself into a series of individual dog-fights. The radios became alive with excited exclamations.

A number of Hurricanes suddenly swept from 15,000 feet in a breathtaking dive. Had they "had it", or were they just trying to get away? Or was their objective the bombers headed homewards just above the sea?

Hard on the heels of one of them was First-Lieutenant Walter Oesau, leader of 7 Squadron and to date one of Germany's most successful fighter pilots. The British pilot had little chance of escape, for in a steep dive the Me 109 was considerably faster. Oesau had already shot down two of his opponents into the sea, and was on the point of scoring a "hat trick" when the Hurricane ended its dive by crashing full tilt into a German twin-engined plane. There was an almighty flash as they both exploded, then the wreckage spun burning into the water. Was it a Do 17 or a Me 110? Oesau could no longer recognise the wreckage as he pulled out over it and climbed up to rejoin his comrades.

In the heat of battle Trautloft himself saw several aircraft dive, trailing thick smoke, without being able to tell whether they were friend or foe. But once, on the radio, there came the familiar voice of his No. 2 Flight-Sergeant Dau, calling urgently: "I am hit—must force-land."

Trautloft promptly detailed an escort to protect his tail so that he would reach the French coast unmolested—if he could get that far.

Dau, after shooting down a Spitfire, had seen a Hurricane turn in towards him. It then came straight at him, head-on and at the same height. Neither of them budged an inch, both fired their guns at the same instant, then missed a collision by a hair's breath. But while the German's fire was too low, that of the British pilot (A. G. Page of 56 Squadron) connected. Dau felt his aircraft shaken by violent thuds. It had been hit in the engine and radiator, and he saw a piece of one wing come off. At once his engine started to seize up, emitting a white plume of steaming glycol.

"The coolant temperature rose quickly to 120 degrees," he reported. "The whole cockpit stank of burnt insulation. But I managed to stretch my glide to the coast, then made a belly-landing close to Boulogne. As I jumped out the machine was on fire, and within seconds ammunition and fuel went up with a bang."

Another of Trautloft's Me 109s made a similar belly-landing near Calais, its pilot, Sergeant Küll, likewise escaping with only a shaking-up. Those were the only aircraft that III/JG 51 lost, with all their pilots safe. Against this they claimed six of the enemy destroyed.

So it went on from day to day, with a fraction of the Luftwaffe waging a kind of free-lance war against England with a very limited mandate. With the small forces at his disposal—KG 2's bombers, two *Stuka Gruppen* and his fighters of JG 51—Colonel Fink was only permitted to attack shipping in the Channel.

Towards the end of July Colonel Osterkamp paraded all his JG 51 *Gruppen* on a series of high-altitude sweeps over south-east England. But Air Marshal Sir Hugh Dowding, chief of British Fighter Command, saw no reason to accept the challenge. After the heavy losses incurred in the French campaign and at Dunkirk, he was grateful for every day and week of grace to repair his force's striking power. For one thing was certain: the Germans would come, and the later they launched their attack, the better. That would be the time to send up his squadrons against them; not now, in answer to mere pin-pricks.

"Why doesn't he let us have a go?" murmured his pilots, to whom these sweeps were a provocation. But Dowding was adamant. The German radio interception service reported that British squadrons were being repeatedly instructed by ground control to refuse battle whenever an enemy formation was identified as fighters only. "Bandits at 15,000 feet over North Foreland flying up Thames estuary," they would be warned. Then: "Return to base—do not engage."

At first Dowding even refused to provide fighter cover for the coastal convoys, their protection in his view being a matter for the Navy. On July 4th, however, Atlantic convoy OA 178 had been dive-bombed off Portland by two *Gruppen* of StG 2, and with only the ships' guns to defend it had suffered the loss of four vessels totalling 15,856 tons, including the 5,582-ton auxiliary flak ship *Foyle Bank*, with nine other vessels totalling 40,236 tons damaged, some of them badly. Thereupon Churchill issued direct orders that in future all convoys were to be given a standing patrol of six fighters. These were reinforced as soon as a German formation was reported approaching.

The periphery combats that ensued have been called by historians the "contact phase" of the Battle of Britain, with the conflict proper still ahead. With nine-tenths of the Luftwaffe resting on the ground, the few aircrews operating constantly asked themselves what the object of their exercise was. Were they supposed to knock out England by themselves?

Why did the Luftwaffe not strike in full force while Britain lay paralysed after Dunkirk, and why was it virtually still grounded even three weeks later when France had been prostrated? The answer, in retrospect, has been that after the wear and tear of the "blitz" campaign against the West, its units were in urgent need of rest. They had to recoup their strength and move forward to new bases. Supply lines had to be organised and a whole lot of new machinery set in motion before the Luftwaffe could launch a heavy assault on Britain with any prospect of success.

Some of the formation leaders, both bomber and fighter, hardly agreed: "We sat about with little to do, and failed to understand why we could not get cracking."

The real reasons for the delay—which presented Britain with a sorely needed breathing space of two months in which to build up her defence—lie much deeper.

The Luftwaffe had never been properly equipped for such a conflict, simply because—by the expressed wish of the "Führer and Supreme Commander"—it was never supposed to take place. "A war against England is quite out of the question!" Hitler had assured Goering in the summer of 1938. Duly convinced, Goering had called his air chiefs to a decisive conference at his country estate of Karinhall: State Secretary Erhard Milch, Chief of the General Staff Hans Jeschonnek, and the head of the Technical Office, Ernst Udet.

At this conference the Battle of Britain was lost, just because the German participants believed it would never happen. For it was decided that all factories capable of constructing bombers would in future produce exclusively, because of its dive-potential, the Junkers Ju 88. Why was this decision so significant?

Although the performance of this new aircraft promised to surpass that of the existing Do 17 and He 111 types, it still remained a medium bomber of strictly limited range. With only two engines it could not hope to be anything else. As such it would serve for a campaign against Poland or Czechoslovakia, or even against France or other adjacent countries with which there might be war. Against the island of Britain, however, it was inadequate.

The Luftwaffe's first chief of general staff, Lieutenant-General Walther Wever, had foreseen the likely developments more clearly, and already in late 1934 had, in addition to the medium bomber, called for a four-engined "heavy bomber for distant missions". He was indeed thinking of Russia, but it was true that Britain, too, could only be effectively combated by such "strategic bomber formations", whose radius of action would extend far out over the Atlantic and thus also enable Britain's seaborne supply arteries to be attacked from the air.

As a result of Wever's pressure both Dornier and Junkers were given development contracts, and by early 1936 five prototypes each of the four-engined Do 19 and Ju 89 were flying.

"The general staff," it was declared at the time, "has great hopes for this development." True, their 600-h.p. engines rendered such large aircraft somewhat underpowered. Time, however, would remedy that. Meanwhile the four-engined bomber seemed an excellent bet.

Then came misfortune. On June 3, 1936, Wever crashed to his death over Dresden, and with him the long-range bomber was buried too. Before the year was out the general staff suddenly began referring to it as a "wash-out":

"The aircraft industry was manifestly not in a position to get heavy aircraft sufficiently quickly on to the production line so as to deliver them to the air force in the necessary time and with the necessary performance."

Nor was any other aircraft industry in the world. Even the "Flying

Fortresses", which made their appearance over Germany in 1943, had been in process of development in Britain and America ever since 1935. But in Germany everything had to go faster. Its leaders wanted an air force quickly and by magic—bombers galore, one *Geschwader* after another—so that they would have something with which to trump the cards of the outside world. It could be done only with light or medium bombers. Only they could come off the assembly lines quickly and in large numbers. Anyway, did they not prove their worth in Poland, Norway, Holland, Belgium and France?

But now, in the summer of 1940, the Luftwaffe stood on the threshold of quite a different campaign. And suddenly the gap in its equipment was revealed.

Udet, who had been the prime champion of the little *Stuka* in opposition to the heavy horizontal bomber, confessed that he had never really thought that the war with England (which he described as "a bloody mess") would actually happen.

From technical decision to soaring production was but a step. In the mid-thirties aircraft hangars shot up in Germany like mushrooms after warm rain. The firms of Dornier, Heinkel, Junkers, Messerschmitt, Focke-Wulf and many others became locked in competition.

"The Luftwaffe requires . . . the Luftwaffe has ordered . . . the Luftwaffe will pay"—such was the prevailing atmosphere. New designs for aircraft, ever faster and racier, flowed from the drawing-boards. Where engine development failed to keep pace, better stream-lining had to be substituted. International speed records were sought after, to prove the performance of the product.

Let us go back in time for a moment to Sunday, March 19, 1939, to the Junkers airfield at Dessau. Test pilot Ernst Seibert and aircraft engineer Kurt Heintz stood waiting in front of their "record kite", the Ju 88 V5 (fifth prototype). Excitement and activity were alike intense.

In expert international circles much had been rumoured about the new "fast bomber" that Junkers was to produce. In view of the fact that the Luftwaffe at this time wished to appear stronger than it really was, and the bomber bluff had already achieved an astonishing political success, the Reich air ministry in Berlin had a great interest in confirming these rumours by means of a record flight under international auspices. A previous attempt some months earlier had failed dismally. Bad weather had intervened, the port engine failed, and the pilot, Limberger, was compelled to make a forced landing at a civil airport. As he made his approach a commercial plane landed across him, and when he finally put the Ju 88 down only half the runway was left. Its high landing speed carried it slap into a hangar, and both the pilot and his passenger were killed.

Now, on March 19th, the attempt of Seibert and Heintz was preceded by a weather reconnaissance, the findings of which were radioed back to Dessau. Finally came the words: "Everything O.K. Strongly advise take-off." Shortly afterwards the Ju 88 crossed the starting point. Tensely, pilot and engineer watched the instruments, adjusting their course closely to the map so as not to waste a mile. "In this weather you ought to reach the *Zugspitze* in an hour," chief test-pilot Zimmermann had told them as they left.

They made it in fifty-six minutes, and the *Fédération Aéronautique Internationale* officially confirmed a new record for an aircraft with a two-ton pay load at 517.004 km/h. (about 323 m.p.h.) for the 1,000 kilometres. Three months later the same machine broke the 2,000-kilometre record for Germany.

Records are fine, if viewed realistically—but for a bomber that could outpace enemy fighters . . . the Luftwaffe's general staff had already given up this as a dream in 1937. Instead of being unarmed, the Ju 88—like the Do 17—was first equipped with a single rearward-firing MG 15, then more machine-guns. And instead of the intended crew of three, four men had to be packed into the confined space of the cabin. And finally, in accordance with the Luftwaffe's new doctrine, the machine must be able to act as a dive-bomber.

Thus the whole construction had to be strengthened—at the sacrifice of speed. The machine that was now put into series production had little in common with Seibert's record-breaking Ju 88 V5 but the name.

Even so the authorities had exaggerated expectations of it. Udet was full of optimism. In an interview with Professor Heinkel, who was just then developing the four-engined He 177, he said: "We don't need this expensive heavy bomber any more. It eats up far too much material. Our twin-engined dive-bombers will fly far enough and hit much more accurately. And we can build two or three of them for one of the four-engined types. The thing is to be able to build the number of bombers the Führer wants!"

The expected range of the Ju 88 bordered on the miraculous—an expectation doomed to swift disappointment. At a conference held after the summer manoeuvres of *Luftflotte* 2 the qualities of the Ju 88, then being tested at Rechlin, were recited: "It has a cruising speed of 270 m.p.h., a penetration of 1,100 miles, and can achieve ninety per cent hits in a fifty-yard circle."

These fantastic figures caused incredulous whispering amongst the Do 17 and He 111 commanders who were present. Whereat Jeschonnek, chief of the general staff, emphasising every word with a thump of his knuckles, cried out: "These qualities have been amply demonstrated at Rechlin! You can absolutely depend on them!" Perhaps as absolutely as on Hitler's word that a war with Britain could be ruled out.

It may sound strange, but there is no getting away from the fact: the Luftwaffe was not equipped for a war against that country. It possessed no bombers with which it could hope to win one. Its existing bombers were slow, vulnerable and too light. The heavy bomber was missing.

But what of its fighters? Did the Luftwaffe not have the fastest in the world?

On Whit Monday, June 6, 1938, at 10 a.m., a red Siebel communications plane made a circuit over the Heinkel works at Warnemünde on the Baltic and came in to land.

The pilot was Lieutenant-General Ernst Udet. His plane was well known throughout the Luftwaffe. Once more he had quit his Berlin desk with its "frightful pile of papers". As the man responsible for the whole of the Luftwaffe's technical development he felt he could discharge his duties best by personally testing each new type of aircraft, and his Sunday visits to the factories were an established part of his routine. But this time he was just inquisitive.

44. *(left)* The He 100, in which test pilot Dieterly set a world speed record in 1939. **45.** *(above)* Flight Captain Wendel (with Professor Messerschmitt in a Me 209, in which he shattered Dieterle's previous record with a speed of 775 km/h (about 469 m.p.h.).

46. In the air battles over the English Channel the British Spitfire showed itself a match for the Me 109 (here in pursuit).

47. The instrument panel of a Me 109.

48. As from autumn 1940, Germany's only single-engined fighter was also obliged to carry bombs.

"How's your new kite doing?" he at once asked Professor Heinkel.

"In a few days it's going to bag a record," the industrialist answered coolly.

It was a barbed remark. The "new kite" was the Heinkel He 100, a single-seater fighter that Heinkel had developed out of spite to demonstrate that he could build a fighter that was better and faster than the Me 109.

Over two years previously the Technical Office of the Reich Air Ministry had, after many comparison trials of the Me 109 (officially the Bf 109) with its rival, the He 112, chosen the former as the Luftwaffe's standard fighter, despite Heinkel's fighter possessing a smaller turning circle and better ground-handling characteristics. One reason may have been the fact that the He 112 was marginally slower.

Both machines were planned to defeat opponents, not by superior manoeuvrability as formerly, but by sheer speed—a development that veteran fighter pilots of World War I at first viewed with little enthusiasm. The prototypes had the same engine, and there was little to choose between their performances. The Messerschmitt had the slimmer fuselage, was light and structurally fairly simple; the robuster, but aerodynamically excellent Heinkel had a rather heavy and complex structure.

The choice of the Me 109 rested largely on its remarkable aerobatic qualities, which appealed to Udet especially. The Messerschmitt firm's chief test pilot, Dr. Hermann Wurster, demonstrated it in a continuous series of spirals without a hint of flat-spin, and pulled it out safely over the ground after diving vertically from 23,000 feet. It was spin-proof and dependable to dive, very manoeuvrable and light on the controls. Furthermore it could be built at a cost of less man-hours and material—a crucial consideration for Udet in his quest for high production figures.

Heinkel, however, did not give up. It was always his ambition to build the fastest aircraft, and as for the authorities, he intended to "show them".

Now, on Whit Monday, June 6, 1938, his hour had come. Udet examined the new He 100 V2 critically. The lines were still smoother than those of the He 112. It was moreover powered by a Daimler-Benz DB 601 engine of 1,100 h.p. Two and a half years earlier the output of the top German engine was still a mere 600 h.p., and the first German fighter monoplane prototypes had been obliged to use British Rolls-Royce Kestrel engines. The new engine, which was also being installed in the Me 109, was thus an important advance.

But the most remarkable item was that the usual radiator scoop had completely disappeared from below the fuselage. Without the wind resistance caused by this projection, Heinkel designers reckoned the machine would gain up to 50 m.p.h. in speed, and had, accordingly, replaced it with an evaporative cooling system in the wings.

His inspection over, Udet, who had already flown the first prototype, the He 100 V1, at Rechlin, turned to Heinkel and, with a wink, said: "Do you think *I* might fly it?"

The people around them held their breath, but Heinkel saw his chance. For weeks he had been getting the He 100 ready for a bid on the 100-km. closed-circuit speed record. If, instead of young Captain Herting, an unknown test pilot, Udet himself was at the controls, it could hardly fail to make such impact on the Technical Office that the Heinkel fighter would come under serious consideration! Of course Udet could fly it, if he would like to. The record attempt had been scheduled for that day, as Udet well knew, and the weather was getting better and better every moment. The sworn witnesses and time-keepers of the international federation were duly summoned.

The current landplane record, won for Germany in November 1937 by Hermann Wurster, stood at 610.95 km/h. (about 380 m.p.h.). It had, of course, been achieved by an Me 109, powered by the same DB 601 engine as the He 100. The 100-kilometre record was still held by the Italian Niclot, in a twin-engined Breda, Ba 88 at 554 km/h. (about 346 m.p.h.), and it was this that Heinkel now proposed to attack.

At four o'clock Udet taxied off, waving his hand in scant acknowledgement, as usual, of last-minute hints and tips. The starting line was on the beach at Bad Müritz, the turning point at Wustrow airfield, fifty kilometres distant, and soon he was on course. The machine handled splendidly, beautifully light on the controls, and giving little indication of its actual speed. Soon he saw black puffs of smoke in the sky ahead. They were blanks being fired by the Wustrow flak to mark the turning point. Udet banked steeply round it, and less than ten minutes after starting he was back, and came in to land.

The time-keepers calculated feverishly: 634.32 km/h., or 394 m.p.h. The old 100-kilometre record had been exceeded by nearly fifty m.p.h. Heinkel was particularly pleased that, with the same engine, his plane had shown itself faster than the Me 109. What would Udet have to say about that?

Udet said nothing, and looked non-committal.

Heinkel persisted. "Now I shall attack the *absolute* world record!"

"Hm," grunted Udet.

He was in an uncomfortable position. As head of the Technical Office he knew that Messerschmitt had the same intention, but could not disclose this fact. The Luftwaffe had decided on the Me 109 as its principal single-engined fighter, and nothing would now alter this decision. Accordingly this fighter must establish itself in the public eye as the best and fastest in the world. And here was Heinkel cutting across with his He 100 and his un-compromising ambition to build the fastest fighter himself!

Udet's sporting spirit made him let things take their course, despite his feeling that the Luftwaffe could not afford such competition between two of the largest aircraft constructors. So it came about that, at considerable expense, and completely independently of each other, the two firms were striving for the same goal: the absolute world record.

Since 1934 this had been held by the Italian Francesco Agellos, who had flown the Macchi C 72 racing seaplane at the fantastic speed of 709.209 km/h. (about 440 m.p.h.). But instead of the 600 h.p. with which German designers then had to be content, this had coupled engines developing over 3,000 h.p. It was, of course, specially built for the purpose, and while its floats offered considerable drag it was not confined to the limits of an airfield for landing and take-off. The records put up by Messerschmitt and Heinkel were achieved by normal landplanes with production engines, and were due largely to their aero-dynamic qualities.

There was, however, a limit to what sheer stream-lining could achieve, and to gain the extra speed needed to beat Agellos' record required engines of greater power. For this purpose Daimler-Benz delivered to both firms a specially boosted DB 601 R engine which, instead of the normal production output of 1,100 h.p., could over a short period develop 1,600–1,800 h.p., the engine revolutions being increased by the injection of a methyl alcohol. Admittedly, after an hour's running the engine would be finished, but that was a good deal longer than was needed.

Heinkel's engine duly arrived at his Rostock-Marienehe works in August 1938, and promptly excited the interest of the fitters. No one was allowed too near it. With its short endurance no test runs could be made. The He 100 V3 airframe had to undergo its trials with an ordinary production engine. But by the beginning of September all was at last ready. The weather was favourable, the witnesses and time-keepers of the *Fédération Aéronautique Internationale* in position on the three-kilometre course, which had to be flown twice in each direction. Heinkel's chief test pilot, Flight Captain Gerhard Nitschke, squeezed into the narrow cockpit. Though he had only just recovered from the crash in which another test flight had ended, he beamed with confidence. The airfield was declared free for take-off, and the plane soared upwards. A few minutes later there was a tragic ending.

What happened put Heinkel back six months in his attempt to gain the world speed record. Nitschke failed to retract the undercarriage: only one leg went up—the other stuck immovably down. In the circumstances any attempt on the record had obviously to be abandoned.

But worse was in store. When Nitschke finally got ready to land, the retracted leg refused to go down again. The whole thing was an incomprehensible misfortune, especially in the case of an airframe that had been double-checked to the last screw for its special mission. Quite clearly it was impossible to land such a fast plane on a single wheel. Its pilot flew low over the airfield several times to show the watchers the position he was in, but they already knew it too well. Heinkel himself tried to indicate to Nitschke that he should think of his own safety.

In the end the latter put the aircraft into a steep climb, slid back the cockpit canopy and jumped. Though he brushed the tail, his parachute opened. The aircraft, with its finely-tuned engine, and the months of devoted labour, were all dashed to pieces in a field.

The destruction of the He 100 V3, brought about by the incidental failure of one of its components, had the effect of spotlighting the efforts of the rival firm. It was now Professor Willy Messerschmitt's chance to get the record. But he, too, encountered difficulties.

For his own record attempt he had constructed a basically new aircraft: the Me 209. Its airframe was smaller, more compact and less angular than the standard Me 109. Its scarcely projecting cockpit canopy was situated extremely far aft on the fuselage. The chief problem was the cooling system, the normal air-intake being unacceptable because of its high drag. An attempt to reliquefy steam in the wings in a similar fashion to that employed by the He 100 met difficulty in returning the result to the engine circulation system. Finally Messerschmitt decided to let the steam escape and supply the engine with a constant flow of coolant. That meant carrying 450 litres for a mere half-hour flight.

The Me 209 VI, piloted by Dr. Wurster, was eventually flown on August 1, 1938, shortly before the He 100 crashed at Warnemünde. Messerschmitt was completing two further prototypes at Augsburg, and these were to fly in the following February and May respectively.

Suddenly, in early 1939, Heinkel was again in the ascendant. Several more prototypes of the He 100 had meanwhile been delivered to the Luftwaffe test centre at Rechlin, which meant that it could easily be put into series production. First, however, the He 100 V8 was to make a new attempt on the absolute world air speed record.

By March 1939 the time for this attempt had come. The airframe had been tested in flight, once more powered by a special DB 601 engine, highly boosted. This time the 23-year-old test pilot Hans Dieterle was at the controls, and Heinkel had mapped out a new measured course near his Berlin-Oranienburg works, where the weather was more reliable than on the stormy Baltic coast.

At 17.23 on March 30th Dieterle took off for the crucial flight, this time with no trouble from the undercarriage. Four times he tore along the course, circling wide round the turning points so as not to exceed the prescribed altitude. Within thirteen minutes of take-off he had landed again. Climbing out, he made a few joyful somersaults, convinced that he had got the record.

There followed a long and anxious period of waiting, while the time-keepers calculated, checked and re-calculated. It was the middle of the night before the result was announced: 746.606 km/h., or 464 m.p.h. After five years the Italian record of 709 km/h. had been convincingly broken, and for the first time the fastest man in the world was a German.

Naturally it was a propaganda success, if a misleading one. It was officially put out next day from Berlin that "a Heinkel He 112 U fighter" had gained the absolute speed record. The impression that the German Luftwaffe was now equipped with a new series-production fighter was later strengthened when the Reich Air Ministry borrowed the dozen He 100 D-1s built by Heinkel on his own responsibility, had them painted with spurious squadron markings, and invited the Press to photograph them as the "He 113". It did not alter the fact that for the Battle of Britain this type was non-available, inasmuch as the winning of the record made no difference to the Technical Office's decision. Consequently, to boost the prestige of its choice, the German air ministry was most anxious that Heinkel's record should be topped by Messerschmitt.

Only five days later, on April 4, 1939, the Augsburg team was almost ready when disaster struck: test pilot Fritz Wendel had to make a forced landing during preparations for the record attempt and the Me 209 V2 broke up. Patiently the Messerschmitt firm brought out once more the Me 209 V1. The Daimler-Benz "boffins" managed to raise the output of its DB 601 ARJ even more: to 2,300 h.p. for short bursts. Even to approximate this on the short trial stretch would be enough.

Days went by waiting for favourable weather. Several times the attempt was cancelled at the last moment. Finally, on April 26th, it was made. Flying the machine to its limit, Wendel managed to surpass the Heinkel's speed by just eight and a half kilometres per hour—or one fifth of a second for the three-kilometre course—establishing a new record of 755.138 km/h. or 469.22 m.p.h.

Propaganda could now boast that inside four weeks the world record, for years considered unassailable, had twice been beaten by two quite different German aircraft. And the old trick was used to alarm the world by announcing officially that the new record had been gained by an "Me 109R"—an aircraft that in reality did not exist. By pretending that a special version of the standard fighter had performed the feat, the impression was given that the service version could not be much slower. It would mean that the Messerschmitt was some 100 m.p.h. faster than any other fighter in the world, and thus virtually unassailable!

In fact, of course, the Me 209 was a *tour de force*: its top speed could be reached for a few seconds only, its supply of coolant lasted for only half an hour, and the life of the engine was scarcely more than sixty minutes.

Even so, for Heinkel and his colleagues the loss of the record was a bitter pill. But obstinate as ever, he still did not give up. He was convinced that if the tests were held in Bavaria, at an altitude 1,500 feet higher, with consequently less air resistance, his machine would prove the faster. But the Luftwaffe opposed him. As soon as word of Heinkel's fresh preparations reached Berlin, the Technical Office's chief engineer, Lucht, sent a cold rebuff: "We are not interested in any repetition of a record attempt. . . . The world record is already in Germany's possession, and to raise it fractionally is not worth the expense. I request you to refrain from any efforts in this direction."

Udet, who saw him in person, made no bones about it: "For God's sake, Heinkel, the Me 109 is and will be our standard fighter. It just won't look good if another fighter proves faster!"

So the whole German production of fighters was geared to just one type. Without doubt the Me 109 was an outstanding plane, and unity of production would be an advantage to all who flew and serviced it. But how would it be if the war lasted a long time? The Technical Office was well aware that the He 100's cruising speed was a good thirty m.p.h. faster than that of the Me 109, and that its undercarriage was a good deal stronger and offered far superior ground handling. But it dismissed these advantages with the words: "We are not worried about fighters."

In October 1939 Heinkel received a surprise. A Soviet delegation of officers and engineers announced its intention to come and examine the He 100 with a view to purchase! On checking with Berlin, he was assured that the visit was in order. The Reich air ministry approved its sale to Germany's new friends in the east.

The Russians were delighted with the Heinkel's attributes, and promptly purchased all six surviving prototypes, while three pre-production He 100Ds together with a manufacturing licence, plus twelve He 112Bs, were bought by the Imperial Army Air Force of Japan, and reached the Far East in the face of all blockade.

But meanwhile what no one had envisaged had become a fact: the war with England. And the fastest German fighter had been sold to Russia!

"No matter," argued the Luftwaffe's Technical Office. "We shall still win the war with the Me 109."

As far as the Polish, Norwegian and western campaigns were concerned, that was true. But now the war was against the British, who had Spitfires, and for the first time the German fighter plane was matched by an equal opponent. The Spitfire was just as good in the climb, even more manoeuvrable, and only slightly slower in the dive. Over the English Channel the Messerschmitt fighters received their first real baptism of fire.

By July 16, 1940, Captain Trautloft's III/JG 51, after its daily mauling by British fighters, had been reduced to fifteen serviceable Me 109s, out of an establishment of forty. Few had been shot down, but many had been hit or else had broken undercarriages or engine trouble. The operational wear and tear of the Me 109 was heavy.

Three days later, over Dover, Trautloft's fighters pounced out of the sun on a British squadron as it was climbing up in tight formation. Trautloft counted twelve Boulton Paul Defiants—a newly operational two-seater whose four machine-guns, instead of firing forward from the wings, were mounted in a rotating turret behind the pilot's cockpit. Compared with the Spitfire, which at first was only committed in small numbers, the Defiant was not a very difficult opponent for the Me 109, and after the first surprise attack five of the ponderous machines crashed into the sea in flames. Altogether the Germans claimed eleven of them destroyed. According to British sources six were a total loss. In any case it was a crushing blow to 141 Squadron, which had to be withdrawn from the Channel area.

Though all the German pilots again returned safely, many of their planes were once more badly damaged, and the following day the number of serviceable machines was reduced to eleven—an all-time low.

It was at this time that the Luftwaffe's supreme commander—who had been promoted to *Reichsmarschall*—called all the commanders of *Luftflotten* 2 and 3 to a pre-Battle of Britain conference. Goering was in an arrogant mood: "Fighting alone all these weeks on the Channel front," he declared, "*Jagdgeschwader* 51 has already shot down 150 of the enemy's aircraft—quite enough seriously to have weakened him! Think now of all the bombers we can parade in the English sky . . . the few English fighters just won't be able to contend!"

Blinded by the Luftwaffe's earlier successes, the *Reichsmarschall* badly underestimated his opponent. The struggle was to be a hard one, much longer than even the pessimists feared—and finally unsuccessful.

Assault on the West—Summary and Conclusions

1. The first few days of the campaign in the west served to show that fortifications of traditional type could no longer stand up to combined air and ground attack. After "softening up" by the Luftwaffe, they were taken by armour and infantry. Even the strongly defended line of the Meuse was forced more swiftly than anticipated.

2. Bold enterprises—such as the landing of airborne sappers on the strategic fortress of Eben Emael and at the Albert Canal bridges—achieved a temporary paralysis of the enemy, but required a swift advance by the Army as reinforcement. The lightly armed airborne units were themselves too weak to follow up their initial success.

3. The same applied to the paratroop drops and airborne landings in Holland, where full surprise was not achieved owing to the existence of this force having been revealed by its use in Norway. The defence was able to prepare against this new method of assault, and this led to the failure of the landings round The Hague. The loss of several hundred transport machines, drawn largely from the Luftwaffe's training schools, had a damaging effect on the future flow of trained personnel.

4. In France the Luftwaffe not only prepared the way for the rapid advance of the armoured corps, but safeguarded its long, exposed flanks. Though inexperienced in combating tanks, close-support and dive-bombing formations succeeded several times in thwarting armoured attacks against these flanks.

5. *The Luftwaffe's mission at Dunkirk—to prevent the evacuation by sea of British and French troops—proved too much for it. The necessary conditions for success—good weather, advanced airfields, training in pin-point bombing—were all lacking. During the nine days the evacuation lasted, on only two and a half days could the Luftwaffe operate in strength. Bombers and dive-bombers for the first time suffered heavy loss at the hands of British fighters now taking off from their bases relatively near home.*

6. *Though the remainder of the French campaign presented the Luftwaffe with no great problems, it needed to rest and recoup when it was over. Insufficient force was available for an immediate attack on England. Above all, the necessary ground organisation had to be built up in northern France. The Royal Air Force utilised the interval to strengthen its defences. Both sides were getting ready for the coming conflict.*

4

THE BATTLE OF BRITAIN

1. The Day of the Eagle

It was Monday, August 12, 1940. Low over the Straits of Dover a mixed formation of German fighters was flying westwards. Since yesterday the weather had improved, and visibility was good.

Captain Walter Rubensdörffer glanced at the English coastline rising steeply out of the water. About half-way over the Channel he spoke into the microphone:

"Calling 3 Squadron. Proceed on special mission. Good hunting. Over."

The squadron's commander, First-Lieutenant Otto Hintze, replied "Message understood" and signed off. With his eight Me 109s he maintained course for Dover, while Rubensdörffer and the twelve Me 110s of 1 and 2 Squadrons peeled off to port and flew south-west, parallel with the English coast.

Single-and twin-engined fighters—but not fighters only. Beneath their fuselages they carried 500- and 1,000-lb. bombs.

Rubensdörffer's Me 110s and 109s belonged to "Experimental *Gruppe* 210"— the only one of its kind in the Luftwaffe. For a month, under the direction of the Channel zone bomber commander, Colonel Fink, it had been attacking British shipping. In this period it had proved what the Luftwaffe chiefs hoped: that fighters too could carry bombs to a target—and attack and hit it.

Only yesterday the unit had been sent out against the British coastal convoy "Booty". Towards 13.00 hours twenty-four Messerschmitts had dived down and been greeted by its anti-aircraft fire. The ships' crews, thinking they were only fighters, were not unduly alarmed. But the planes, coming in low, had dropped bombs. There were direct hits on decks and superstructures, and two large ships had been severely damaged.

After breaking away they were pursued by Spitfires of 74 Squadron, which identified their enemy as "forty Me 110s". Rubensdörffer at once formed a defensive circle with the 110s, while his 109s joined battle with the "Spits". For now, no longer encumbered by their heavy bomb load, they were true fighters again.

All the "Experimental Unit's" aircraft were equipped with the same armament of fixed machine-guns and cannon as normal fighters. Thus they

144

were in a much better position to defend themselves than were the heavy bombers whose armament often numbered only three guns. The general theory was that these fighter-bombers, if attacked by the enemy, could form their own fighter defence.

Today, for the first time, the unit's target was not shipping or harbour installations. It was the top-secret "radio" aerials sticking up at many points along the English coast. These could be seen quite clearly by telescope across the Channel.

By systematic listening-in on the enemy's radio channels it had become known to the Germans that the British fighters were remotely controlled over the V.H.F. by ground stations. It was further known that these stations obtained their information about approaching German air formations by means of a new radio-location system, the visible "feelers" of which were these same antennae aerials on the coast.

For General Wolfgang Martini, chief of the Luftwaffe's signal communications system, this discovery had come as a shock. He had assumed that his own side was far ahead in this field.

In summer 1940 Germany possessed two types of radar:

1. The *"Freya."* This was a mobile equipment which, sending out impulses on a 240-cm wave-length, served for plotting air and sea targets from the coast. One such installation was at Wissant, west of Calais. This located British coastal convoys, which were then attacked by Colonel Fink's aircraft and by armed speed-boats.

2. The *"Würzburg".* This was only just coming into series production, and was first used by Flak regiments in the Ruhr. Using an ultra-short wave-length of 53-cm. its impulses could be sharply concentrated, and sometimes the results were startling. It could read the location, course and altitude of an aircraft with such accuracy that in the previous May a flak battery at Essen-Frintrop had shot down a British bomber which, flying above dense cloud, had felt itself quite safe.

From the technical angle, therefore, the discoveries made about the British by Martini's radar and intercept men—who had been rushed to the French coast as soon as it was occupied—were nothing new. The wavelength used was no less than 1,200 cm. and British sources have confirmed that, in particular, forecasts of the size of approaching formations were at the outset sometimes up to 300 per cent inaccurate.

It was not the enemy's technical, but his evident organisational lead that troubled Martini. The discovery that the whole length of the east and south coasts of Britain were already covered by a protective chain of listening and transmitting posts was a blow indeed. Reports from them would be evaluated in central operations rooms, and the resulting air picture used to guide the British fighter squadrons to their targets.

On the German side such an organisation did not exist. Though the "DeTe apparatus" (such was the cover name[1]) was there, its likely influence on the course of the war was not considered vitally important.

Now the German command had to think again. If, through the eyes of his

---

[1] DeTe = "Decimeter Telegraphy". English equivalent: R.D.F. = "Radio Direction Finding". The term "Radar", so familiar today, and the German term *"Funkmess"*, only came into use half-way through the war.

radar, the enemy could follow the raiding formations as they approached, or even while they formed up over France, the element of surprise—almost essential for an aggressor—would be entirely lost. The Luftwaffe would, in fact, join battle with the Royal Air Force at a serious tactical disadvantage—unless the locating stations on the coast could first be destroyed.

On August 3, 1940, the teleprinters at the headquarters of *Luftflotten* 2 and 3 tapped out a directive from General Jeschonnek, the Luftwaffe's chief of general staff: "Known English DeTe stations are to be attacked by special forces of the first wave to put them out of action."

With the *first* wave! It meant that the attack on the coastal radar installations would also be the signal for the Battle of Britain to begin!

Captain Rubensdörffer looked at his watch. By German time it was a few minutes to eleven. With his twelve Me 110s he turned north-west towards the enemy coast. The squadrons split up to make for their individual targets.

1 Squadron, led by First-Lieutenant Martin Lutz, sighted the mast of Pevensey radar station, near Eastbourne. The six aircraft climbed slowly, weighed down by their two 1,000-lb bombs. Though they were fighters, they carried twice the bomb load of a Ju 87 dive-bomber.

At last they were high enough. Flicking over, they glided down on to their target. Then, waiting till the lattice-work of the first of the four antenna aerials completely filled his reflector sight, Lutz let go his bombs.

Like a sudden squall of wind the six Messerschmitts swept over the radar station and were gone, leaving eight 1,000-lb. bombs to explode on the target. One was a direct hit on an elongated building, a second slashed the main power cable, and the transmitters broke down. Pevensey was off the air.

Five minutes flying time to the east, 2 Squadron, under First-Lieutenant Rössiger, went for a similar station at Rye, near Hastings. Their leader reported ten hits on the installations with 1,000-lb. and 500-lb. bombs. British sources confirm that all the buildings were destroyed, with the important exceptions of the transmitting and receiving blocks and the watch room.

Meanwhile First-Lieutenant Hintze, with 3 Squadron, attacked the aerial layout at Dover. Three bombs burst close by them; shrapnel hurtled into the struts, and two aerial masts tottered—but remained standing.

Everywhere it was the same story. As the attackers turned away, their efforts were marked by fountains of flying earth and black smoke, but always the aerials still sticking out above. It had been just the same in Poland during the attacks on the radio transmitting stations. No matter how accurately one aimed, the aerial masts never fell down.

Three hours later the station at Rye, with emergency equipment, was again functioning. In the course of the afternoon other stations followed suit. All broken links in the British radar chain had been repaired—with one exception:

From 11.30 onwards three *Gruppen* of KG 51 and KG 54, totalling sixty-three Ju 88 bombers, had been attacking the harbour works at Portsmouth. But one *Gruppe* of fifteen machines peeled off over the Isle of Wight and dived down on the radar station at Ventnor. Its equipment was so badly damaged that the station became a write-off. Eleven days uninterrupted labour were necessary before a new station could be constructed on the island and the gap in the chain closed.

The English masked the fact that Ventnor was out of action (and deceived the Germans) by sending out impulses from another transmitter. Though these produced no echo, the enemy, hearing them, could only suppose that the station had been repaired.

Disappointment spread. Apparently the "eyes" of the British early-warning system could only be "blinded" for a maximum of two hours. Simultaneously on August 12th, however, there began the assault on the British forward fighter bases in Kent. This at least offered better prospects of success.

At 09.30 the Dornier Do 17s of Major Outzmann's I/KG 2 launched an attack under strong fighter protection against the coastal airfield of Lympne. A hail of 100-lb. bombs ploughed up the runway and struck the hangars.

Then, just after mid-day, twenty-two *Stukas* dive-bombed a convoy in the Thames estuary north of Margate. They belonged to IV/LG 1 under Captain von Brauchitsch, a son of the Field-Marshal, the German Army's C.-in-C. They reported direct hits on two lesser tramp steamers.

Shortly afterwards, at 13.30, the most forward fighter base of all, Manston, received its first heavy attack. Once again, this was at the hands of Captain Rubensdörffer's "Experimental *Gruppe* 210". Their morning attack now paid off: the radar stations were still out of action. Only at the last moment did Manston get warning of the enemy's approach.

Below on the airfield the pilots of 65 Squadron ran for their Spitfires. The twelve of them taxied furiously to the runway, and the first section just succeeded in getting airborne. Then the Messerschmitts were directly overhead.

"The fighters were all lined up," First-Lieutenant Lutz reported. "Our bombs fell right amongst them."

One pilot striving to get off the ground was Flight-Lieutenant Quill. Since 1936 he had been a Spitfire test pilot with the Vickers company, but had recently asked to join an operational squadron, where he was now a flight commander. Suddenly the sound of his engine was drowned by hollow thuds. Instinctively he ducked, then turning his head saw an aircraft hangar fly into the air behind him.

As he tore down the runway, bombs struck the ground to left and right of him. A Spitfire disappeared in a cloud of smoke—and as suddenly emerged undamaged. At last the rumbling of his undercarriage ceased: Quill was airborne. It seemed a miracle that he had made it out of such an inferno.

Other solitary Spitfires also emerged, climbing steeply out of the cloud of black smoke that had enveloped Manston. From the air it looked as if the airfield was a write-off. The German aircrews reported: "Direct hits by twelve SC 500 (1,000-lb. land mines) and four Flam C 250 (500-lb. incendiary bombs) on hangars and billets. Four SC 500 amongst fighters taking off. Result: four Hurricanes [*sic*] and five other aircraft destroyed on ground...."

According to British reports most of 65 Squadron's Spitfires emerged unscathed from the attack. Manston, however, was badly hit. Ground control directed the fighters to land at airfields farther inland.

Next on the list of Fighter Command's coastal bases for attack was Hawkinge, then Lympne again. Both suffered similar heavy damage to Manston. Work teams toiled the whole night filling up the bomb craters and getting the runways serviceable again.

The British were now aware that the period of coastal skirmishing had ended, and that the time for the knock-out blow was at hand. August 12th was just the prelude. Though on this day some 300 bombers and dive-bombers, with strong fighter escort, were launched by *Luftflotten* 2 and 3, this force represented less than a third of their total strength.

The real attack had been fixed by Goering under the code signal "*Adlertag* August 13th", for the following morning. The leading formations of both air forces were to make landfall over the English coast at 07.30 hours.

To open the first strategic air operation in history—as the Battle of Britain was to become—nearly two thousand German warplanes stood ready. Whether a major power, with a population resolved to resist, could be subdued by air power alone remained to be seen. That, however, was the Luftwaffe's precise objective. It was an ambitious one, and the prelude to the battle had already been dramatic enough.

On June 30, 1940, just a week after the conclusion of the French campaign, Goering had issued his "General Directions for the Operation of the Luftwaffe against England." "Acting in concert, the *Luftflotten* are to operate all out. Their formations, once lined up, are to be launched against defined groups of targets."

The primary target was the Royal Air Force, its ground organisation and the industry that fed it. On the other hand Admiral Raeder demanded that the Royal Navy, supply convoys and the harbours at which they docked, should also be attacked from the air. Goering was confident that the Luftwaffe could fulfil both tasks simultaneously. But the Luftwaffe's general staff had the last word. "Until such time as the enemy's air force has been destroyed, the ruling principle of Luftwaffe commanders shall be to assault his formations at every available opportunity by day and night, in the air and on the ground—without regard to any other commitments."

The goal was clear. A detailed plan, however, was still lacking. So on July 11, 1940, new instructions from Goering included the first positive measure. Convoys in the Channel were from now on permissible targets. To attack them would expose the British fighters to the onslaught of German fighter formations. But this project had failed. Though British fighters protected the convoys from bomber assault, they were under strict orders to avoid combat with their opposite numbers.

But the chief reason for the delay in the air attack on Britain was political. The German leaders imagined, after the unexpectedly swift subjugation of France, that their country had demonstrated sufficient proof of its military invincibility to persuade the island of Britain, now all alone, to come to terms.

On July 19th the victory in the west had already been celebrated at the *Reichstag* in Berlin, where all the service leaders had attended. Practically everyone was promoted. Goering gleamed and glittered in his *Reichsmarshall's* fantastic white uniform, and the Luftwaffe itself got two field-marshals: Kesselring and Sperrle.

[Kesselring wrote after the war: "I am today perfectly convinced that none of us would have been made field-marshals after the western campaign had Hitler not thought that peace was now probable."]

In his *Reichstag* speech Hitler directed "yet another appeal to English good sense." Today there can be no doubt that a settlement with Britain would have been a great boon to his further projects. He declared: "I can

German air concentrations for the Battle of Britain. On August 13, 1940 (the "Day of the Eagle"), three German air forces with a total of 949 bombers and 336 dive-bombers stood ready for attack (for detailed order of battle see Appendix 5). The map shows the distribution of the *Geschwader* and individually operating *Gruppen* along a line of assault bases stretching from Norway to western France. Close to the Channel coast (because of their short range), stood 734 single-engined fighters, and behind them 268 twin-engined fighters. The limited range of the Me 109 fighters restricted daylight operations by the bombers to the south-eastern region of England, for unescorted their losses would have been too high. Against them the British could muster over 700 fighters for the defence of their homeland. In addition the Royal Air Force at this time possessed 471 bombers, which, however, were only used at night for small nuisance raids on Germany.

see no compulsive reason for continuing the struggle. I am sorry for the sacrifices that it will demand. . . ." He added: "If we do pursue the struggle it will end with the complete destruction of one of the two combatants. Mr. Churchill may believe that it will be Germany. I know that it will be England."

Three days later the British foreign minister, Lord Halifax, made his reply on the radio. Hitler, he said, had not uttered a single word to suggest that peace should rest on justice. His only arguments were threats. Great Britain was ruled by a spirit of inexorable resolve. She would not give up the fight.

It was the final blow to the German illusions that the British might still come to terms. The Luftwaffe must now give serious consideration as to how its war against the island kingdom was to be waged. For a plan of operations was still lacking.

On July 21st Goering summoned the chiefs of the *Luftflotten* and charged them to work out their ideas. Kesselring and Sperrle told the various Air Corps under them to do the same. Staff officers everywhere began zealously to forge their plans. All were agreed that the subjugation of the Royal Air Force must be the first and foremost aim. About how this was to be accomplished there were, however, differences of opinion.

Cutting across these deliberations came a rapid series of resolutions from the Führer.

On July 16th, three days before his *Reichstag* speech, he had issued his Directive No. 16, ordering "a landing operation against England to be prepared and, if necessary, carried out" ("Operation Sealion").

On July 31st, however, he disclosed at a conference at Obersalzberg with the Army C.-in-C., von Brauchitsch, and his chief of general staff, Halder, that he wanted to attack Russia—"the sooner the better, and preferably this year. With Russia defeated, Britain's last hope will be gone." Goering too, and the Luftwaffe's chief of general staff, Jeschonnek, learned about Hitler's *volte-face*.

Despite this, the next day the Führer issued his Directive No. 17, permitting unrestricted air and sea operations against England as from August 5th. Hitler wished to study the effects of the air raids, and then—"in eight to ten days"—decide whether the landing should be carried out in mid-September (the earliest the Navy would agree to) or not.

There was thus a parting of the ways. Officially Britain remained the next opponent, but in fact the thoughts of the supreme German leadership were turned to the east. Hitler, it is true, did not exclude the possibility that Britain might first succumb, but there is no evidence that he was convinced of this.

On August 2nd Goering issued his final orders for "*Adlertag*"—"the Day of the Eagle". First target for the joint operations of *Luftflotten* 2 and 3 was to be the British fighter arm: the Spitfires and Hurricanes in the air, their airfields, coastal radar stations, and the whole ground organisation in southern England.

On the second day the attacks were to be extended to airfields in outer London, and to be continued at full strength on the third. In this way it was hoped with a few hard blows so to reduce the Royal Air Force that air sovereignty—the pre-condition for subsequent operations—would be won.

Everything was decided except the date. To carry out the programme according to plan the Luftwaffe needed favourable weather on three consecutive days. The met. men ventured to predict such conditions at the beginning of August. But the *Luftflotten* needed about six days to prepare for their great blow. Then, when they were ready, the weather suddenly deteriorated again. "*Adlertag*" had to be postponed, both on the 10th and the 11th. At last a high pressure zone over the Azores promised a few fine days.

Goering forthwith fixed zero hour for 07.30 on the 13th. In the event the two previous days also turned out fine, and were utilised. Convoys, harbours, radar stations and the three airfields mentioned above were heavily bombarded.

Then during the night of the 12th the high pressure zone over the Azores dispersed, and "*Adlertag*" dawned with grey overcast skies, fog on most of the airfields and a thick blanket of cloud over the Channel. Goering had no choice but to cancel zero hour once again and postpone the great attack till the afternoon.

However, before the order had got through from the *Luftflotten* down to the *Geschwader*, a number of formations had already taken off. Instead of the carefully prepared concerted blow, the great "*Adler*" attack splintered off into a few individual actions, themselves hindered by bad weather.

The commander of KG 2, Colonel Johannes Fink, peered curiously through the windscreen of his Do 17. It was 07.30 on "*Adlertag*", and time for the great attack to begin. But Fink shook his head irritably. He had reached the point of rendezvous with the fighter escort, but saw ahead of him only a few Me 110s. Their antics were very odd. First they would fly up to him, then put down their noses in a dive. Finally, climbing up again, they would repeat the performance. What the hell were they up to?

Fink did not ponder long, but set course for England. Behind him followed II and III *Gruppen* under Lieutenant-Colonel Weitkus and Major Fuchs. Their target: the airfield of Eastchurch on the south bank of the Thames estuary.

Tightly together the Do 17s dropped down through the cloud bank and flew just below at scarcely 1,500 feet over English soil. No fighters to be seen: neither German nor British. The fifty-five German bombers were lucky: British radar had designated them as "only a few aircraft", and the Hornchurch controller had accordingly put up just one Spitfire squadron, No. 74, to track them down.

Fink's formation had meanwhile reached Eastchurch. Roaring over the airfield by squadrons, they bombed the runway, aircraft, hangars and storage depots. Later the English counted more than fifty bomb craters. Five Blenheim bombers were destroyed on the ground.

Only when the formation had turned for home did the Spitfires jump on them from all sides. Fink scanned the heavens, but with German fighters conspicuous by their absence, the bombers would have to fend for themselves. Without cloud cover there would have been a massacre. As it was, most of the Dorniers managed to gain its protection from the resolute attacks of the British fighters.

None the less KG 2 on this sortie lost four of its best crews. As soon as he was back Fink went storming to the telephone and furiously demanded an explanation as to why the fighters had left him in the lurch.

To his amazement he learnt that he had opened the great "*Adler*" attack of the Luftwaffe on Great Britain single-handed. Goering's cancellation order had not reached the *Geschwader* in time, and the aerobatics of the Me 110s had been designed to signal the bombers to return. But the message had failed to register.

Zero hour was now 14.00, even though the weather had become even worse.

First off was a long-range fighter *Gruppe* of twenty-three Me 110s— V(Z)/LG 1 from Caen. Its leader, Captain Liensberger, was only briefed to make landfall near Portland. After that he was left to his own initiative.

Despite the fact that the radar station of Ventnor had been put out of action the day before, the formation was reported the moment it crossed the French coast at Cherbourg. Other stations had picked it up. Even its strength was correctly estimated as "twenty plus". Only one piece of information was lacking: the type of aircraft.

The C.-in-C. Fighter Command, Air Marshal Dowding, had given orders for his fighters, where possible, to avoid combat with German fighters, and to concentrate on the greater danger represented by the German bombers. Had the British ground control officers known that the approaching force consisted merely of twin-engined fighters, they would therefore have taken no defensive action.

As it was they "scrambled" three Spitfire and Hurricane squadrons based at Exeter, Warmwell and Tangmere, and directed them to meet the enemy over the English coast.

This was just what the Germans wanted them to do. The Me 110s were to draw the British fighter squadrons into combat. When bomber formations then followed after a well-judged time-interval, these squadrons would have reached the end of their fuel, and would be helpless. Then, after they had landed to re-arm and re-fuel, was just the right moment to bomb them and their bases. So, at least, was the plan.

The German leaders were conscious that the British fighters enjoyed many tactical advantages. Fighting over their own country, pre-interception time was short, and therefore combat endurance so much the longer. They possessed a superior aircraft location system and superior ground control. And they could take advantage of the weather. To equalise these advantages, if only in part, the Germans would have to exercise tactical shrewdness. The Me 110 operation over Portland was an example of this. But it turned out to be a costly one.

Liensberger had just reached the English coast when one of his rearmost planes gave the alarm: "Spitfires astern!"

The warning put the German crews suddenly and sharply on their toes. They knew that their relatively ponderous twin-engined Me 110s were no match for the Spitfire in flying. On the other hand their armament—two forward-firing cannon and four machine-guns—if all used at once was very potent.

Consequently Liensberger promptly ordered his planes to form a defensive circle. Each could then give rear cover to the one in front.

He himself was the first to start the turn, but before he was around the British fighters, using their superior altitude, had borne down upon the rear of the procession.

One Me 110 banked off to starboard and got clear, the Spitfire's fire-burst hitting emptiness on its port beam. A second attempted avoiding action in a dive but lacked momentum: its opponent went down after him, eight machine-guns firing out of the wings.

At last the defensive circle was closed, with better chance of self-protection. But two machines had been lost already, and the British did not let go. Guns streaming fire, they dived on the circle and broke through it, presenting themselves as targets for only a split second to the horizontally-flying Messerschmitts.

All the same they were not unscathed. Two—three—British fighters broke away, trailing black smoke. But they were over their own ground, and if necessary could make forced landings. And if they had to bale out, they would not be taken prisoner.

For the Messerschmitts it was another story. Between them and France stretched 100 miles of water—a hazardous journey to make with only one engine or a shot-up tail unit, with a drooping wing and a steady loss of height. When Liensberger's *Gruppe* finally got back, five of his machines and their crews were missing, and others riddled with bullets. Apart from the tactical disadvantage the odds had been great: twenty-three versus fifty.

The epilogue came two days later. On August 15th Kesselring and Sperrle were summoned to Karinhall to receive the wrath of their chief at the lack of progress in the battle.

"... And then there was this business of the Me 110 *Gruppe* sent off alone," said Goering. "How often have I given orders, verbally and in writing, that such units are only to be sent over when range dictates the necessity!"

By this he meant that if the target was too distant for the single-engined Me 109s to escort the bombers all the way, then the long-range Me 110s were to cover the last part of the flight.

No one was happy about this idea. The campaign in the west, and still more the July battles over the Channel, had already demonstrated that the twin-engined Me 110s were no match for the enemy's much lighter and more manoeuvrable fighters. Though Goering prized them as his *élite* fighters, his "Ironsides", they in fact needed fighter escort themselves. Liensberger and his men had had none.

"The necessity for distinct orders," said the C.-in-C. angrily, "is either not appreciated or they are not given. We do not possess all that many 110s. We must use them economically."

His rebuke was not unjustified, for the whole tactical purpose of Liensberger's operation had miscarried. After his *Gruppe* had drawn the British fighters into combat, the bombers, instead of taking advantage of the resultant gap in the enemy defences, had only arrived three hours later. By this time their opponents had been able to land, re-fuel and re-arm at leisure. The whole force was thus ready for them. The German leadership was bad indeed!

So it was 17.00 hours before the *Stukas* of Major Graf Schönborn's StG 77 crossed the Channel. There were fifty-two Ju 87s escorted by Me 109s of Lieutenant-Colonel Ibel's JG 27. Targets were airfields in the Portland area. But they failed to find them. There was dense cloud at 3,000 feet. Dive-bombing was virtually ruled out.

"The attack was a flop," wrote General von Richthofen in his diary.

"Thanks to fog our formations returned without releasing their bombs. The weather forecast had been false, and the attack ordered from 'on high'. It just couldn't be done. Thank goodness the English fighters came too late!"

British ground control did in fact guide seventy fighters towards the German force from different directions. And while the Messerschmitts became locked in dogfights with the Hurricanes, the fifteen Spitfires of 609 Squadron dived steeply on the *Stukas* and shot five of them down. The slow Ju 87s just could not cope with such an attack. It was the second bitter lesson of "*Adlertag*"—the day that had been designed to demonstrate the superiority of the German Luftwaffe over its British opponents. August 13th seemed indeed to be an unlucky day.

The second wave, LG 1 under Colonel Bülowius, likewise encountered resolute and well-directed fighter opposition. But this wave consisted of swift, twin-engined Ju 88s, which made skilful defensive use of cloud cover. However, even they failed in the main to find the airfields that were their targets.

As an alternative, I *Gruppe* under Captain Kern attacked the harbour installation of Southampton. Only six Ju 88s managed to reach the important fighter base of Middle Wallop. This was a sector station controlling four squadrons of fighters. Six bombers could hardly affect it seriously. They reported hits "on groups of tents and sheds along the edge" Middle Wallop could breathe again.

The less important airfield of Andover, six miles away, fared worse. This was attacked by a dozen bombers. But the damage done was misdirected, for Andover was not a fighter base. Still, in view of the bad weather, the German crews were glad to find any target at all.

At the same time, further east, another airfield in Kent was being bombarded by aircraft of II Air Corps. Its chief, General Loerzer, sent in his own two dive-bomber *Gruppen*, plus another borrowed from VIII Air Corps.

Here, with only the Straits of Dover in between, the danger was less. Fighters of JG 26, with the Olympic gold medallist Major Gotthardt Handrick at their head, cleared the area of opposition after repulsing a few minor British attacks.

As a result eighty-six Ju 87s reached their target unmolested. At 18.15 they appeared over Detling, near Maidstone, and left it in ruins. The runway was studded with bomb craters, the hangars were aflame, and a cloud of black smoke spread and rose to the heavens. A direct hit destroyed the operations room, and the station commander himself became a casualty. Of the many aircraft on the ground the assailants estimated they left twenty either totally destroyed or burning.

There was only one snag: Detling, once again, was not one of Fighter Command's bases. It belonged to Coastal Command, the function of whose aircraft was sea patrol and reconnaissance.

The second target, Rochford on the north bank of the Thames estuary, was indeed a fighter airfield, but this was veiled by low clouds and the *Stukas* directed against it failed to find their target. They took their bombs back home with them.

In the evening the balance sheet of "*Adlertag*" was drawn up. Despite the bad weather and the delayed start, 484 bombers and dive-bombers and some

1,000 fighters of both kinds had crossed the English coast. Nine enemy air-fields were reported to have been attacked, "five of them to such good pur-pose that they could be considered to have been put out of action"

Field-Marshals Kesselring and Sperrle professed themselves satisfied with this success, even though it had cost them thirty-four of their own aircraft. To be sure, the "great blow" was still to come. The two Luftwaffe chiefs must now wait again for favourable weather to mark the day when their whole strength would be thrown into battle at once.

On the other side of the English Channel the results of August 13th were likewise judged to have been a success. The English had some reason to exult. Although three airfields—Eastchurch in the morning, and Andover and Detling in the afternoon—had "taken a pasting", none of them was a fighter base. The ground organisation of Fighter Command, on the serviceability of which depended the fate of the entire country, had not been affected.

It almost seemed as though the Germans were ignorant about which the fighter bases were, and this despite more than a year's collection and study of all available intelligence by Lieutenant-Colonel Josef Schmidt of the Luft-waffe's general staff. Target data, copies of British aerial photo-maps and an airfield atlas of Great Britain had been circulated to all commands down to *Geschwader* and *Gruppen*. The astonishingly frequent radio orders issued to aircraft in the air had been written down word for word and even "fixes" taken. Cover names, such as "Charlie Three" for Manston, had long since been decoded. So surely it must be known where the British fighters and their ground organisation could best be hit. For to destroy the enemy's fighter arm was, it may be repeated, the first and crucial task.

Instead the Luftwaffe had attacked quite irrelevant airfields. And in spite of it the German command nourished the dangerous illusion that the enemy had already been hit in his vitals.

All "*Adlertag*" had accomplished was to give Fighter Command a breath-ing space. Compared with the effective attacks of the day before on the genuine fighter airfields of Lympne, Manston and Hawkinge, those of August 13th were almost futile. Only thirteen Spitfires and Hurricanes had been shot down. Such a loss could be replaced. If there was nothing worse to come, Britain had nothing to fear.

2. Black Thursday

The weather on August 14th, when once again the enemy's fighter arm and organisation were the set targets, was so bad that no operations could be attempted by any force of *Geschwader*, or even *Gruppe*, strength. Only the nearest fighter base, Manston, received another visit by sixteen Me 110s of "Experimental *Gruppe* 210". Dropping their bombs after darting down through cloud, they again achieved surprise, and again four hangars were set ablaze. Otherwise nuisance raids by single bombers were made on southern England—just enough to keep the defences from relaxing.

The following morning, Thursday the 15th, looked like being much the same, with little prospect of any major operation. Otherwise the chiefs of the *Luftflotten* and air corps would hardly have been called in the morning to another conference with the C.-in-C. at Karinhall. But in the early afternoon the weather improved. Grey skies suddenly became blue, and the clouds parted.

At II Air Corps command post south of Calais the chief of staff, Colonel Paul Deichmann, who had remained behind, blinked incredulously at the sun. Then he hastened back to the operations room. Shortly afterwards the initial orders to his flying units had been issued. Now as before the basic precepts of "*Adlertag*" were still in force.

Next Deichmann drove to the advanced H.Q. of *Luftflotte* 2, situated at Cape Blanc Nez in an underground bunker beneath Hill 104, known as Kesselring's "sacred mountain". Kesselring and his chief of staff being away in attendance on Goering, he found only the operations staff officer, Lieutenant-Colonel Rieckhoff. The latter had just received an order from Berlin that owing to the bad weather no attacks were to be mounted.

"Too late!" said Deichmann cheerfully. "They are already off!"

Both officers left the bunker and climbed to the observation stand. Overhead droned formations of *Stukas*, course north-west. Alarmed, Rieckhoff wanted to seize the telephone and ask the top command staff in Germany whether he should recall them. Deichmann made him hold his hand till the planes reached the English coast and they saw the anti-aircraft fire going up from Dover. In resignation Rieckhoff then reported to Berlin: "The attack proceeds!"

It was noon, and II Air Corps' two *Stuka Gruppen*—Captain Keil's II/StG 1 and Captain von Brauchitsch's IV (St)/LG 1—were on their way to England. Collecting their fighter escort over Calais they once more assaulted Lympne and Hawkinge. Lympne was so badly hit that it was out of action for two days.

No one was to know that this attack was destined to spark off one of the most bitter combat days of the whole Battle of Britain: a day that, after previous disappointments, was scarcely to be anticipated; a large-scale operation that only took place because of a sudden improvement in the weather.

The usually accepted number of aircraft launched this day by the Luftwaffe against England was 1,786. But according to the Luftwaffe's "Department 8" (research) the force comprised 801 bombers and dive-bombers, 1,149 fighters of both kinds, plus another 169 planes of *Luftflotte* 5 in Norway. An outing by over 2,000 aircraft in a single afternoon!

After the initial *Stuka* attack just across the Straits of Dover, the scene changed to the north. Towards 13.30 hours the two bomber *Geschwader* of *Luftflotte* 5—KG 26 from Stavanger in Norway and KG 30 from Aalborg in Denmark—after a diagonal crossing of the North Sea were heading for the mouths of the Tyne and Humber rivers on the east coast. This enterprising operation had only been authorised the night before.

The flying distance from base to target and back was 800–950 miles. Twenty per cent had to be added to the flying time for take-off and landing, navigational errors and attack. This was equivalent to a total distance of over 1,100 miles.

Appropriate fighter escort was thus out of the question: the Me 109s would have run out of fuel before even reaching the English coast. The bombers—our old nautical friends, the Heinkel 111s of the "Lion" *Geschwader*, and their team mates the Ju 88s of the "Eagle"—thus had to fly almost alone.

To combat this risk it was hoped that the heavy attacks in the south would so pin down Fighter Command's resources there that fighter opposition to a sudden flank attack in the north-east would be minimal.

49. The H-16 version of the He 111, one of the Luftwaffe's standard bombers.

50. A view of the ground organization needed to prepare a machine such as the He 111 for an operation: 1. Met officer; 2. Master armourer; 3. and 4. Bomb loaders; 5. Flight mechanic; 6. and 7. Miscellaneous ground staff; 8. Five-man aircrew; In the center, a 2,000-lb. bomb.

51. An He 111 attacks. A standard Luftwaffe bomber throughout the war, this twin-engined aircraft possessed neither the range nor the bomb-load for a strategic offensive comparable to that carried out against Germany by the four-engined bomber fleets of the Allies.

52. The He 111 with open bomb bays.

53. An He 111 with a fender against balloon cables (in experimental use by KG 54).

But Air Marshal Dowding had made provision. While concentrating most of his squadrons in 11 Group at the battle's focal point in south-east England, he had left some in 12 and 13 Groups which covered the rest of England northwards to the Scottish border. So far these squadrons had held only a watching brief from afar. But now their hour had come.

At 13.45 hours the first attacking wave comprising sixty-three He 111s of I and III/KG 26 were still twenty-five miles away from the English coast northeast of Newcastle. They were flying at 14,000 feet, 600 feet above a cloud layer of some 6/10ths density. Suddenly there was a jumble of cries on the radio sets:

"Spitfire to port!"

"Fighters attacking out of the sun!"

"Am being shot up!"

At this critical moment the bomber formation was being escorted by twenty-one Me 110s of I/ZG 76, based at Stavanger-Forus. This was the same *Gruppe* which on December 18, 1939, had claimed the top score of Wellingtons in the Battle of Heligoland Bight and later, in the Norwegian campaign, had been the first to land on the still defended airfields of Oslo-Fornebu and Stavanger-Sola.

But now they had an almost insoluble problem. High above the bombers flew the staff flight, with the C.O., Captain Restemeyer, at their head. Today, instead of his normal radio operator, he had on board the commander of X Air Corps' radio intercept company, Captain Hartwich. Listening instruments had been built in all round him. From this flying radio intercept station he proposed to discover what British defensive moves were brewing and indicate to his own formation how to anticipate them by changes of course or altitude, or other tactical measures. It showed that X Air Corps, at least, reckoned with strong fighter opposition.

But Hartwich's observations were cut short. One of the first Spitfires to attack dived out of the sun upon "Dora", the commander's own Me 110. Before Restemeyer could turn to give battle, his plane was shredded with bullets. Then there was a shattering blow which virtually tore the machine apart. The auxiliary fuel tank must have been hit.

This plump appendage, carried beneath the fuselage and nick-named "Dachshund", held 220 gallons of petrol. Though after crossing the North Sea it was empty, the pilot had failed, owing to a fault in the construction, to jettison it, and it was full of explosive gas. The same fault had already cost the lives of many crews during the long-distance missions between Trondheim and Narvik in Norway. And now it spelt the doom of Captains Restemeyer and Hartwich. The *Gruppe* commander's plane went spinning down into the sea in flames.

The victory had been scored by 72 Squadron from Acklington. Its leader, Flight-Lieutenant Graham, now for the first time spotted the German bomber formation some 3,000 feet below him, and could hardly believe his eyes.

"There's more than a hundred of them!"

In their excitement the Englishmen had counted thirty-five Messerschmitts alone, although in fact there were only twenty-one.[1] But their excitement was

---

[1] The official work, *Royal Air Force 1939–45*, gives the total count by British fighters as "about a hundred He 111s and seventy Me 110s". In fact there were sixty-three He 111s and twenty-one Me 110s.

understandable, for the British radar observers had at first reported the strength of the German force as only "about twenty". Later they raised their estimate to "thirty plus", and gave a more southerly approach course.

Even today it is believed by the R.A.F. that on this occasion its radar system, still in its infancy, was at fault. In fact its plotting was perfectly accurate, inasmuch as the formation first reported was not KG 26 at all, but about twenty seaplanes. These had been sent out by X Air Corps to make a mock attack in the region of the Firth of Forth, in order to confuse the British defence and decoy it in the wrong direction.

KG 26's targets—the British bomber bases of Dishforth and Linton-upon-Ouse—lay much further south. But the German bombers made a serious navigational error: they made landfall seventy-five miles too far north, thus almost coinciding with the point of the mock attack.

"Thanks to this error," reported Captain Arno Kleyenstüber, staff officer at X Air Corps H.Q., "the mock attack achieved the opposite of what we intended. The British fighter defence force was not only alerted in good time, but made contact with the genuine attacking force."

For a quarter of an hour the Germans were attacked from all sides by the Spitfires of 72 Squadron, then by those of 79. Corp. Richter, flying as rearguard to the Messerschmitts, received a head wound and lost consciousness. His aircraft went down in a steep dive.

His radio operator, Warrant-Officer Geishecker, thinking it was the end, baled out. But Richter, regaining consciousness below cloud, pulled out and managed, despite his wound, to fly back across the North Sea and make a forced landing near Esbjerg. Geishecker was not seen again.

Meanwhile, First-Lieutenant Uellenbeck banked with the remaining five machines of 2 Squadron, and offered battle. He himself hit a Spitfire which dived down through cloud, trailing smoke.

But the enemy were too numerous, and he ordered his planes into a defensive circle as a last resort. He was, however, attacked himself from behind, and only some good aiming by his No. 2, Flight-Sergeant Schumacher, drove the Spitfire off. Lieutenant Woltersdorf hit two others.

Further ahead, 3 Squadron, under First-Lieutenant Gollob, succeeded in retaining contact with the bombers in spite of being violently attacked themselves. But after a few minutes only four of Gollob's Messerschmitts remained. The pilot of one of the missing ones, Flight-Sergeant Linke, told later how he had crept up on a Spitfire which had just set a Heinkel on fire.

"I got to within fifty yards' range," ran his combat report, "and did some good deflection shooting. The Spitfire reared up, then spiralled vertically down."

Seconds later he was attacked himself by two of the enemy. His plane was hit in the wing, and his port engine began to smoke and seized up.

"I pushed the stick and dived vertically through the clouds with the two Englishmen on my tail. After 2–3,000 feet I pulled out below the upper layer, having meanwhile varied my course. Going down through the lower layer I saw two Spitfires hit the water. Time about 13.58."

After that Linke managed to re-cross the North Sea with his one engine and land two hours later at Jever. Thanks to the testimony of Gollob and another pilot of his squadron, Linke was finally credited with having destroyed two Spitfires.

The end-result of this battle between I/ZG 76 and their numerically superior enemy was the loss of six Me 110s. They themselves claimed eleven Spitfires. Although even the Heinkel crews confirmed this claim in writing, it was obviously too high. It can be excused owing to the clouds, which veiled the final outcome of many engagements from sight. If two badly shot-up Messerschmitts managed to get home right across the North Sea, obviously most of the Spitfires in like case succeeded in reaching their own, much nearer, bases.

All the same, this particular battle was by no means just a "pheasant shoot", as it has hitherto been painted by British historians. According to them not one Spitfire was either lost or damaged.[1]

Meanwhile KG 26 flew down the coast searching for the targets they had missed by approaching too far north. Harassed again by British fighters, their bombs fell widely scattered over the coast and on harbour installations between Newcastle and Sunderland. The "Lion" *Geschwader* never found their original targets—the two bomber bases.

The three Ju 88 *Gruppen* of KG 30 operated more successfully without any fighter escort. Making landfall at Flamborough Head, and using cloud cover to good effect, they flew straight to their target and dived down on Driffield, a bomber base of No. 4 Group.

Four hangars and a number of other buildings were destroyed, and a dozen Whitley bombers went up in flames. Though British fighters shot down six Ju 88s out of a total of fifty, they were unable to prevent the attack.

So ended the flank attack from Scandinavia—the first and last that *Luftflotte* 5 launched in strength.

The next blow fell again in the south-east, immediately after the "Lion" and "Eagle" *Geschwader* had departed from the north-east. On the British radar screen new enemy formations could be seen assembling over Belgium and northern France. Reports to the fighter operations rooms followed in swift succession:

"Sixty plus over Ostend."

"120-plus direction Calais."

Between 14.50 and 15.06 all three Do 17 *Gruppen* of KG 3 took off from Antwerp-Deurne and St. Trond in Belgium for an attack on British airfields and aircraft factories south of the Thames. The *Geschwader* commander, Colonel von Chamier-Glisczinski, flew with the staff section at the head of Captain Pilger's II *Gruppe*, whose target was Rochester, on direct course to London.

But first the Dorniers had to rendezvous on the French coast to meet their fighter escort. For owing to the limited range of the Me 109s, the fighter *Geschwader* were concentrated near to the coast in the Pas de Calais. Over the Channel the escort then caught up, most of the fighters flying thousands of feet above their charges.

There they could manoeuvre in freedom, utilising the flying attributes and superior speed of their aircraft to the full. The tactical advantage of higher altitude would enable them to dive down on any opponents attacking the bombers below. For, as Adolf Galland, Germany's most famous surviving fighter pilot, has said: "We had no illusions about the Royal Air Force. We knew it was an opponent we had to take very seriously."

[1] This is a mystery considering that at least two Spitfires were seen to plunge into the sea.

On the afternoon of August 15th Galland himself, with his III/JG 26, had been detailed to conduct a fighter sweep over south-east England in support of the bombers. Up till now his personal score of victories stood at three, while his *Gruppe*, in the course of four operations, had collected a total of eighteen.

Besides JG 26 under Major Handrick, *Gruppen* of JG 51 (Major Mölders), 52 (Major Trübenbach) and 54 (Major Mettig) were airborne over the Straits. Whether in support of or in direct escort to the bombers, they crossed the English coast simultaneously at many points.

With radar plots appearing at so many places, the picture on the operations tables became very confused. Though eleven British fighter squadrons totalling some 130 Spitfires and Hurricanes were "scrambled", the controllers directed them all over the skies. And being in units of only squadron strength they everywhere encountered superior forces of Me 109s.

For instance 17 Squadron's Hurricanes, on patrol over the Thames estuary, had hurriedly and urgently to be recalled to their own base of Martlesham Heath, north of Harwich. Long before they got there the pilots saw columns of black smoke rising from their hard-hit airfield. And when they did arrive the Germans had gone.

Again this had been the work of "Experimental *Gruppe* 210". Unseen and unopposed the Me 110s had pushed right on to Martlesham and dropped their bombs. The runway was left studded with craters, two hangars were on fire, and workshops, stores and communications destroyed. From the air the base looked like a smoking heap of ruins, and even though such a view always does look worse than it is, days of uninterrupted labour were needed to restore Martlesham to a state of emergency serviceability.

Meanwhile KG 3 was pushing westwards over Kent, strongly guarded by fighters and thus unmolested. Captain Rathmann's III *Gruppe* delivered a fresh attack on the Coastal Command airfield of Eastchurch.

Shortly afterwards it was the turn of Rochester. Thirty Do 17s of II/KG 3, plus the *Geschwader's* staff section under Colonel von Chamier, thundered over the airfield. Though it was not a Fighter Command station, the attack was a bull's-eye. Not only did bombs fall in rows diagonally across the runway, on hangars and amongst the parked aircraft, but showers of 100-lb. fragmentation bombs crashed into the aircraft factories on the northern boundary. To finish off, the last Dorniers planted incendiary and delayed-action bombs.

"Aero-engine works repeatedly hit . . . copious flame and smoke. . . ." ran the *Gruppe's* report.

For once the report was modest. The factory concerned was the Short works, one of the most modern Britain possessed, and extensively improved only the year before. In it the first four-engined bomber, the Stirling, was under construction—an aircraft destined in the future to open Britain's strategic air attack on Germany. The main recipient of II/KG 3's accurate bombing was the store of "finished products", which was burnt out, with the result that production of this heavy aircraft was delayed for months.

All the same, it was not Britain's bombers but her fighters that were on Germany's priority list. Only by reducing them to impotence could the Luftwaffe win the battle.

Now, after the departure of KG 3, they were given a rest. For nearly two hours not a single German formation was plotted—another proof of the meagre co-operation between *Luftflotten* 2 and 3. Hitherto it was Kesselring who had been active. Now it was Sperrle's turn, 125 miles farther west. Had this attack followed immediately after the first, the enemy defence would have been hard put to cope with it. As it was, its squadrons had been given time to refuel and re-arm. As their operations tables reflected the armada building up across the Channel, the chiefs of 10 Group and 11 Group —Air Vice-Marshals Brand and Park—could prepare their counter-measures at leisure. An hour previously the "state of readiness" board in Park's underground operations room at Uxbridge had shown many squadrons "non-available" owing to previous combat. Now the "immediate readiness" panel had lighted up against nearly all of them. Thus, against Sperrle's formations the defence was finally able to put up the record total so far, of fourteen squadrons, comprising 170 fighters.

The German attacking force consisted of Ju 88s of LG 1, which took off from Orleans at 16.45; and of Ju 87s of I/StG 1 and II/StG 2 under Captains Hozzel and Eneccerus, which took off a quarter of an hour later from Lannion in Brittany. Escort was supplied by Me 110s of ZG 2 under Lieutenant-Colonel Vollbracht, and Me 109s of JG 27 and JG 53 under Lieutenant-Colonel Ibel and Major von Cramon-Taubadel. Altogether well over 200 aircraft were plotted advancing in columns towards the south of England.

Before they got there the British fighters attacked. Captain Jochen Helbig, squadron commander of 4/LG 1, had just spotted the coast ahead when his rearmost Ju 88 crews reported almost in one breath: "Fighter attack from astern!"

They were Spitfires. All guns firing, they dived right through the German formation. Masters of speed, they would then pull out, climb again and renew the attack.

Helbig looked around for his own fighters, but thousands of feet higher these were themselves locked in combat. With no help from that quarter they just had to carry on, tightening the formation to give the rear-gunners mutual covering fire.

But the Spits came at them again, clawing at the rearmost bombers from either side. The Ju 88s had no further choice but to break formation and bank.

The Englishmen promptly concentrated their attacks on single aircraft. It was an unequal combat. The "wonder bomber", once considered fast enough to elude enemy fighters by sheer speed, was in fact about 100 m.p.h. slower than the Spitfire. And against the latter's eight machine-guns firing from the wings, the Ju 88 could only defend itself with a single backward-firing one.

None the less this gun saved Captain Helbig and his crew. The radio-operator, Flight-Sergeant Schlund, who manned it, calmly reported each new attack as it developed: "Spitfire astern and to starboard—400 yards ... 300 ... 250. ..."

In the face of death this man had iron nerves. He held his fire, giving his opponent the impression that he could safely approach to point-blank range before letting go at the persistently straight-flying bomber. Then at last Schlund's machine-gun opened up, anticipating his enemy by just one decisive second.

It was the moment Helbig had waited for. Simultaneously he flung his plane to starboard, forcing it into a tight turn. The Spitfire had too much momentum to follow. Narrowly missing the 88 it shot past into the void, collecting some hits from the machine-gun as it went. Then, smoking, it disappeared from sight.

That was how one particular Ju 88 lived to fight another day. Later the same machine was to win fame by clocking up over a thousand flying hours during operations in the Mediterranean: a tribute to its durability. Helbig said of it: "The 88 was a winner . . . in the right hands a top-notch plane."

But today he lost practically his whole squadron. Apart from his own, only one other machine returned. The other five were shot down by the swarm of British fighters. The *Gruppe* to which the squadron belonged numbered at the start fifteen. Of these only three reached their target: the naval air base of Worthy Down, north-east of Southampton. Most of the others were forced to jettison their bombs.

August 15th underlined once more the dependence of bombers on fighter protection. The demand for really close escort became ever more insistent. Without it the bombers were not only vulnerable, but could not do their job.

It is true that I/LG 1, starting somewhat earlier under Captain Kern, were more fortunate. Twelve Ju 88s appeared over Middle Wallop so unexpectedly that they all but wiped out two British squadrons on the ground. The last Spitfires of 609 Squadron, among them Squadron-Leader Darley[1], took off with bombs exploding behind them in the hangars. It was the third attack on this sector station in three days, yet I/LG 1 erroneously reported on their return that they had attacked Andover. It seemed the Germans were still unaware that Middle Wallop was a far more important target.

The consequences of another target error were nearly disastrous. The operations of August 15th were not yet ended, and hardly were the Germans clear of the south coast when fresh formations were plotted over the Straits of Dover. This time there was no pause, and after their violent combats in the south a number of 11 Group's squadrons were forced to land. A large-scale attack by *Luftflotte* 2 would thus have encountered only a weak fighter opposition. In the event hardly a hundred aircraft were on their way to Kent from the east: just two *Gruppen* of bombers and a few dozen fighters.

At 19.35 Rubensdörffer's ever-active "Experimental G*ruppe* 210" crossed the English coast at Dungeness. Their fighter escort from JG 52 were close behind, but not in sight. Despite this the fifteen Me 110s and eight Me 109s, all of them weighed down with bombs, continued on their course. For the first time the important 11 Group sector station of Kenley, to the south of London, was billed for attack. The second bomber force—a *Gruppe* of Dornier 17s—had been given the adjacent station of Biggin Hill as target.

The bombing was accurate—but not on Kenley and Biggin Hill.

Having failed to make contact with the escort Rubensdörffer decided to perplex the enemy by flying a wide loop and attacking Kenley from the north. Unexpectedly the unit found itself over the southern suburbs of London, and promptly turned south to make its approach.

Sooner than expected the airfield lay ahead and the Me 110s went down to attack. Suddenly Hurricanes appeared above—but failed to get close because in a dive the heavy Messerschmitts were faster. Their bombs slammed into hangars, and at least forty training planes were destroyed. Others struck

---

[1] His Spitfire, credited with six victories, still survives in the Imperial War Museum.—*Translator's Note.*

two camouflaged aircraft and aero-engine works. Still others severely damaged a factory producing aircraft radio sets. None of this, however, took place at Kenley, but at the London airfield of Croydon. Rubensdörffer had made a navigational error!

By Hitler's express orders England's capital was not to be attacked—yet. On all German operations maps the whole area of Greater London was marked as a prohibited zone. When Goering heard of the attack on Croydon he furiously demanded a court martial. But who was left to take the blame?

Directly after the bombing, 111 Squadron's Hurricanes were on the Germans' tails. As the last Me 110 climbed up into his reflector sight Squadron-Leader Thompson had only to press the firing button. Whole chunks of wing were torn off, also bits of the port engine. The German pilot went down again and landed, the crew being taken prisoner.

The other Me 110s spiralled upwards in a defensive circle, awaiting a favourable moment to get away. For a moment the Hurricanes hesitated, for suddenly Me 109s were on the scene, presumably a fighter escort. In reality they were the "Experimental *Gruppe's*" 3 Squadron, which as usual attacked last. After hitting the target their pilots had instantly to switch from bombing to fighting, for now the Hurricanes were after them, this time two squadrons of them: 111 from Croydon and 32 from Biggin Hill.

Outnumbered, First-Lieutenant Hintze likewise ordered his Me 109s into a defensive circle, and tried to join up with that of the Me 110s. Meanwhile Rubensdörffer saw his chance of breaking away. Later the unit's combat report read: "The four other aircraft of the staff flight followed him in a shallow dive for home. They disappeared into the mist and were not seen again."

Captain Walter Rubensdörffer, "Experimental *Gruppe* 210's" commander, and his companions failed to return. The Kenley controller diverted a homeward-bound Spitfire squadron, No. 66, and effected an interception still over English soil. The battle was soon over.

On this "Black Thursday" the unit lost altogether six Me 110s and one Me 109. It showed that even fighter-bombers could not risk operating without a proper fighter escort.

Instead of Kenley it had been Croydon, and instead of Biggin Hill it had been West Malling, nearer the coast, that had been attacked. Both airfields suffered severe damage. As British fighters harried the last returning formations, August 15th finally came to an end. It was the third day of the Battle of Britain, considered by many people to have been its hottest.

What was the balance of success and loss? On the British side the fighter claims were feverishly calculated, and finally an astonishing figure was published: 182 German aircraft definitely destroyed, and another fifty-three probably.

Against this German war records show a loss of fifty-five, mostly bombers and Me 110s—but even this weighed heavily enough.

On their side the Germans similarly claimed an exaggerated score of British fighters: 111 certainly shot down, with fourteen "questionably". The official Fighter Command count was only thirty-four.

The last figure is of course deceptive. A fighter plane was only deemed to be "lost" if it crashed vertically to the ground or fell in the sea. If a pilot managed to effect a forced landing, and important parts were still usable, the machine ranked as "repairable" and did not appear on the losses list. It could be claimed, however, with some justification, inasmuch as for some time ahead it was no longer on the strength as a fighting weapon. It might be days or weeks before it became so again.

Damaged planes, added to the complete losses, certainly contributed to Air Marshal Dowding's anxiety during these August weeks. Though the aircraft industry had for months been working at full capacity, the loss of fighter aircraft was more than could be replaced.

One of Winston Churchill's first actions after becoming Prime Minister had been (on May 14th) to appoint the press baron, Lord Beaverbrook, as Minister of Aircraft Production. By cutting much red tape, and adopting the same methods as he had used in the construction of his newspaper empire, Beaverbrook effected a sharp uprise in aircraft production. Ignoring the opposition of many air marshals, he insisted on absolute priority for the output of fighters. "No other man in England could have done it," wrote Dowding after the war. In June the output reached 440 to 490 fighters a month, and continued on almost the same scale even under Luftwaffe attack.

The German fighter production figures were not comparable. Deliveries by the Messerschmitt firm of the Me 109—at that time Germany's only single-engined fighter—in June numbered 164, in July 220, in August 173, and in September 218.

So much for the supposed crushing numerical superiority of the Luftwaffe! During the decisive months it received less than half the new fighters that the Royal Air Force did. How then was the aim of "eliminating the enemy's fighter arm" to be achieved?

None the less, in the days that followed, it almost looked as though it might be. On August 16th, West Malling, attacked by mistake the evening before, was heavily bombarded and went out of action for four days. In the afternoon a Ju 87 *Gruppe* of StG 2 and a Ju 88 *Gruppe* of KG 51 devastated the important sector station of Tangmere on the south coast. Fourteen British aircraft were destroyed or severely damaged, amongst them seven Hurricanes and six Blenheim bombers.

Churchill, who seemed unconvinced by the high score of victories claimed by Fighter Command, sent a warning letter to the Chief of the Air Staff:

"While our eyes are concentrated on the results of the air fighting over this country, we must not overlook the serious losses. . . . Seven heavy bombers [lost] last night and also twenty-one aircraft now destroyed on the ground—the bulk at Tangmere—total twenty-eight. These twenty-eight, added to the twenty-two fighters, makes our loss fifty on the day, and very much alters the picture presented by the German loss of seventy-five. . . ."

The British fighter claims of seventy-five victories were moreover inaccurate. The Germans in fact lost thirty-eight machines.

But again the weather was in league with the British. In *Luftflotte* 2's operations zone such salient fighter bases as Debden, Duxford, North Weald and Hornchurch escaped the fate of Tangmere just because the attacking forces—II/KG 76, II/KG 1, III/KG 53 and I/KG 2—were unable to find them through the clouds.

On August 18th—a Sunday—the battle was resumed. Lieutenant-General Fröhlich's KG 76 made combined high-level and low-level attacks on the sector stations of Kenley and Biggin Hill. Besides the usual pock-marked runways and burning hangars that marked their passage, for the first time the Kenley operations room was put out of action.

This was a blow at the very nerve centre of the fighter defence. On the German side it was assumed that such key installations were lodged in reinforced underground cells. No one dreamed that they were located, virtually unprotected, on the airfields. Thus they were not systematically sought out. The success at Kenley was just a fluke.

But August 18th also rang the death-knell of the *Stuka*. On this afternoon VIII Air Corps sent out four Ju 87 *Gruppen* against the airfields of Gosport, Thorney Island and Ford, and the radar station of Poling on the south coast. They were caught by Spitfires of 152 Squadron and Hurricanes of 43 Squadron before they could reform for the return flight. The British fighters gave no quarter. "One *Stuka Gruppe*," wrote Richthofen in his diary, "was decimated."

The main victim was I/StG 77. Of its twenty-eight aircraft twelve failed to return, and six others were so shot up that they only just reached French soil. Amongst the missing was the *Gruppe's* commander, Captain Meisel. Adding the casualties of the other *Gruppen*, thirty Ju 87s were either lost or severely damaged. The price was too high. The *Stuka* had to be withdrawn.

Next day, punctually at noon, the generals commanding the Air Corps and the leaders of the *Geschwader* operating against England were once more summoned to Karinhall. Goering made no bones about his displeasure at the course of the battle so far—a battle which should have been decided in three days. Mistakes, he said, had been made, and they had led to quite unnecessary losses. Operations had to be much better prepared.

"We've got to preserve our fighting strength," the supreme commander declared. "Our formations must be safeguarded."

At this the bomber chiefs clamoured for a fighter-escort system that really worked. One fighter force should fly ahead and clear the field. Still others should fly above, beside and below the bombers. And yet another force should dive down with the Ju 88 units as they bombed, to protect them as they broke away.

The fighter leaders listened and frowned. Where were so many fighters to come from? The muster of first-line aircraft was sinking, and production was not keeping up. If they were to fulfil so many requirements they would need five Me 109s to every bomber. What would be left for "free hunting"— the one chance of shooting their opponents down?

In the end the main objective, "so to weaken the enemy's fighter arm that our bombers can proceed unhindered," was reiterated and accepted. But the method remained unsolved. General von Richthofen summed up the conference in his diary: "The campaign against England is to proceed energetically but differently." But how?

3. Offensive Against the Fighters

One of the first moves of the Luftwaffe command concerned its fighter leaders. The more elderly *Geschwader* commanders were relieved of their posts at almost one swoop, and replaced by younger men who had been commanding *Gruppen* and become prominent by their high score of victories. *Geschwader* commanders should, according to Goering, personally lead their formations into battle and thus set "a shining example".

The value of this measure was disputed. A *Geschwader* still mustered some sixty to eighty fighters, and to use such a large formation as a fully effective unit required not only the example of a prize marksman but experienced leadership on the ground.

However, the young men soon proved themselves worthy of the responsibility suddenly thrust upon them. Their example became contagious, and the great competition began as to which *Geschwader* would become the top-scorer. Major Mölders took over JG 51 from Major-General Osterkamp, Major Galland JG 26 from Colonel Handrick, Captain Lützow JG 3 from Lt.-Colonel Vick, Major Trübenback JG 52 from Lt.-Colonel van Merhart and Captain Trautloft JG 54 from Major Mettig. All these changes of command took place just as the main offensive against the British fighter arm opened at the end of August. Others followed: Lieutenant-Colonel von Bülow gave up JG 2 in favour of Major Schellmann, and Major von Cramon-Taubadel handed over JG 53 to his most successful *Gruppen* commander, Major von Maltzahn.

Each day saw the campaign against Fighter Command and its ground organisation wax hotter. On the morning of August 31st one German fighter squadron after another dived on the Dover balloon barrage, causing fifty or more of them to sag burning and smoking to the ground. Visible from afar in both England and France, they were the starting signal for one of the Battle of Britain's most crucial days—the culmination of the week-long bombing attacks on the inner fighter bases of 11 Group.

This Group with its twenty-two squadrons was responsible for the defence both of south-east England and of "the greatest target in the world", London. Its inner bases ringed the capital in a protective screen—Kenley, Redhill, Biggin Hill, West Malling and Gravesend to the south-east; Hornchurch, Rochford, North Weald and Debden to the east and north-east; Northolt to the west (see map on page 149).

The normal attacking force comprised only a single bomber *Gruppe* with an average of fifteen to twenty aircraft. But now these were protected by whole *Geschwader* of fighters, which outnumbered the bombers by about three to one. The latter reached their target in a compact unit. And each *Gruppe* came more than once in the day.

The first airfield to be attacked in the morning was Debden, 11 Group's most northerly sector station. Then the bombs once more ploughed up the runway at Eastchurch. Detling, already severely hit several times before, was now subjected to a fighter attack by I/JG 52 under Captain Eschwege, whose Me 109s swept low over the airfield firing cannon and machine-guns.

But the most effective attacks were reserved for the afternoon. Colonel Fink's KG 2 made its approach in two columns, the starboard one headed for Hornchurch—a sector station holding four squadrons with a total establishment of some seventy Spitfires. Three of them were already airborne and engaged somewhere in combat, but the fourth, No. 54, was still waiting in reserve on the ground when suddenly the excited voice of the airfield control officer reached them on the loud-speaker: "Scramble! Scramble! Get off the ground!"

It was a case of Fighter Command's complicated reporting and control system having strangled itself with too many strings. With radar stations transmitting whole constellations of plots from the coast, and visual sightings streaming in from the Royal Observer Corps stations studded all over the country, it could happen that operations rooms became saturated before all the information could be evaluated and appropriate action taken by the different sectors concerned. So it was that from time to time single German formations came in undetected.

This time KG 2's Dornier *Gruppe* was already lined up for its attack before Hornchurch air-raid alarm sounded. Then some of the Spitfires' engines failed to start. Most pilots, however, managed to scramble off the ground seconds before the bombs fell. But Flight-Lieutenant (now Air Commodore) Al Deere's section was too late.

Like hunted rabbits the three Spitfires raced over the airfield at different angles, getting in each other's way. Deere swore as he throttled back to avoid ramming a comrade steering a collision course. At that moment the Dorniers thundered overhead and rows of bombs came hurtling down amongst the scampering fighters. What then happened made eye-witnesses hold their breath.

Despite all the explosions around him Al Deere pulled off the ground. He was airborne! But he was only a few feet up when the blast of a new explosion first flung him upwards, then sucked him down. In the course of it the Spitfire was thrown into a half-roll, but somehow went on flying upside down only a few feet above the ground. Clods of torn-up earth thudded against the wind-screen, blocking all vision from the inverted pilot. With a shrill shriek like that of a circular saw the plane then scraped along the ground for a hundred yards, first with its tail, then—according to eye-witnesses—with the whole length of its fuselage. With a final spasm it whirled round and lay still —and not on fire! But the pilot had presumably perished.

Not far away the second Spitfire had crashed to the ground with its wings broken off. Its occupant, Pilot-Officer Edsell, came off with a pair of sprained ankles. Lifting himself out of his cockpit he crawled over to the wreck that had been his section leader's plane, and could hardly believe his eyes. Deere was neither dead nor badly wounded! His main trouble was that he could not get out—till with their combined strength they forced open the sliding canopy. Dazed, but only slightly hurt, the two of them staggered towards the brown smoke that covered their dispersal hut and the other buildings.

Even the third Spitfire pilot, Sergeant Davies, whose plane had been catapulted into a field far outside the airfield, returned from the wreck on foot—and unscathed.

The tenacity with which these three British fighter pilots not only withstood the sudden shock, but the very next day climbed into reserve aircraft to continue the battle, was characteristic of the way Fighter Command in the end surmounted the onslaught of the German Luftwaffe. The important thing was that the pilots survived. With mounting production their aircraft could be replaced.

Biggin Hill fared still worse than Hornchurch. This station lay on the direct route to London, and had been raided three times only the day before, even though fighter squadrons were airborne for its protection on each occasion. The worst damage had been meted out by eight Do 17s of III/KG 76 which specialised in low attack. Misleading the defence by flying up the Thames, they suddenly turned and assaulted the airfield from the north. 1,000-lb. bombs burst in hangars, workshops and billets. A direct hit on a shelter killed or wounded over sixty R.A.F. personnel. Gas, water and electricity were cut off at one blow, leaving Biggin Hill bereft of communications.

Today the assailant was the port column of KG 2. Many buildings, so far spared, collapsed under the weight of bombs and fires broke out. But worst of all, the operations building was hit—the nerve centre from which the three Biggin Hill fighter squadrons were controlled by radio. Crowded in one small room were the controlling officers and girls of the Women's Auxiliary Air Force who manned the telephones and manipulated the symbols representing friendly and hostile aircraft on the situation map-table.

The heavy droning of approaching German bombers drowned all other noises. Then came the whistling of falling bombs, followed by explosions drawing rapidly nearer. Seconds later there was an ear-splitting crash. The whole building shook and the walls seemed to be collapsing. All the lights went out and smoke poured through the doors. The dazed officers and girls groped their way out into the open. The bomb had exploded in the signals officer's room a few yards away.

Once more the telephone and teleprinter lines, laboriously patched up since the last attack, were out of action. When the station commander of the adjacent Kenley sector rang up to enquire how Biggin Hill had fared, he failed to get an answer. He tried again via an R.A.F. centre in Bromley, but from there, too, all lines were dead. Finally he despatched a courier by road to investigate and find out the frequencies of the now leaderless Biggin squadrons so that they could be controlled from Kenley.

"The airfield was like a slaughter-house," he reported.

The operations room had to be moved to the neighbouring village shop—from which just one of the three squadrons could be controlled with emergency equipment.

While the bombs were falling on their base the Spitfires of 72 Squadron and the Hurricanes of 79 Squadron were on patrol further south. Both were new to Biggin Hill, having been posted from the "peaceful north". 72 had in fact only arrived that very morning to replace a battleworn squadron.

The number of battle-weary squadrons, many of whose pilots were either lost or near the end of their nervous tether, was constantly increasing. By the end of August few of the original units with which Air Vice-Marshal Park had confronted the Luftwaffe on "*Adlertag*", less than three weeks before, were left in the battle zone round London. They had been replaced by fresh squadrons from the north.

That they could be replaced showed that Fighter Command's policy of leaving more than twenty squadrons for the defence of the north—only attacked by day on one occasion, August 15th—had fully proved its worth. Now the battle-weary squadrons were sent up there to rest, train their new pilots, and be brought up to strength.

The wear and tear of battle also made itself felt amongst the German fighter units, which were flying up to five sorties a day. With penetrations now far beyond the English coast, they were operating at the limit of their

54. Jeschonnek (chief of air staff), General Loerzer and supreme commander
Goering at II Air Corps H.Q. near Calais.

German and British personalities of the Battle of Britain

55. Air Marshal Dowding, chief of
British Fighter Command.

56. Field-Marshal Kesselring,
chief of *Luftflotte 2*.

57. Major-General Osterkamp, fighter commander in *Luftflotte 2*.

58. Air Vice-Marshal Park, commander of 11 Group.

59. Lt.-Colonel Mölders, commander of JG 51.

60. Group Captain "Sailor" Malan, river fighter ace of Mölders.

range, and as they returned there was the choking suspense as to whether their last drops of fuel would get them home.

"There were only a few of us," First-Lieutenant von Hahn of I/JG 3 has reported, "who had not yet had to ditch in the Channel with a shot up aircraft or stationary airscrew."

Lieutenant Hellmuth Ostermann of III/JG 54 wrote: "Utter exhaustion from the English operations had set in. For the first time one heard pilots talk of the prospects of a posting to a quieter sector."

Ostermann was one of the young airmen who had learnt some hard lessons in conflict with the British fighters. Day after day at the turn of the month, his unit had either provided escort for the bombers or had flown fighter sweeps from the Channel as far as London.

"Once more I lost contact with my squadron," he wrote. "The whole *Gruppe* had split up into dog-fights and one saw hardly a pair of planes together. The Spitfires showed themselves wonderfully manoeuvrable. Their aerobatics display—looping and rolling, opening fire in a climbing roll—filled us with amazement. There was a lot of shooting, but not many hits. In contrast to my combats in France I was now quite calm. I did no shooting but kept trying to get into position, meanwhile keeping a sharp watch on my tail. . . ."

Several attempts miscarried: before he got into range to fire the Spitfire would bank away. At last he spotted a comrade below him with a Spitfire after him.

"I at once flung my machine around and went down after it. Now I was about 200 yards behind the Tommy. Steady does it—wait. The range was much too far. I crept slowly nearer till I was only a hundred yards away, and the Spit's wings filled my reflector sight. Suddenly the Tommy opened fire and the Me in front of him went into a dive. I too had pressed the firing button after previously aiming carefully. I was only in a gentle turn as I did so. The Spit at once caught fire and with a long grey plume of smoke dived down vertically into the sea."

It was Ostermann's first victory—the first of the 102 he achieved up to 1942, when he lost his life in Russia.

During this period, from his HQ at Wissant on the French coast, Lieutenant-General Theo Osterkamp was doing everything that his designation "Fighter Commander 1 and 2" could suggest.

Since the last daylight attack on August 26th by *Luftflotte* 3 to the southwest, when forty-eight He 111s plus the staff squadron had been sent in against Portsmouth harbour under strong escort, the fighters had been regrouped. From now on its three fighter *Geschwader*, instead of flying all the way from Cherbourg to the English coast, were also packed into the Calais area with only the Straits of Dover in between.

This move echoed the precept of the General Officer Commanding II Air Corps, Bruno Loerzer, that the Luftwaffe could not afford a dispersal of its fighter strength. With the heart of the battle in south-east England, on the outskirts of London, the escort of the bombers operating there must, he said, be doubled and trebled. As a result Field-Marshal Sperrle's *Luftflotte* 3 was from now on confined to night bombing. If the bombing became much less effective, at least the assailants would need no fighter protection.

Thus the fighter effort put up on August 31st was no less than 1,301 sorties by Me 109s and Me 110s—in support of the above-mentioned attacks by a mere 150 bombers on Hornchurch, Biggin Hill and other airfields.

Against this British Fighter Command put up 978 sorties, and only in a few instances did the Spitfires and Hurricanes succeed in getting at the bombers and driving them away from their targets. With the German fighter screen present everywhere, the British fighters were forced into combat with their opposite numbers only. Thirty-nine of them were destroyed— the R.A.F.'s official figure. The Luftwaffe's loss of aircraft was thirty-two. The battle had reached its zenith.

At this point Air Marshal Dowding of Fighter Command must have been sorely tempted to counter the German air superiority in the outer-London area by sending the idle squadrons of central and northern England to support the heavily engaged ones of 11 Group. But he did not do so. He believed that the time was still not ripe to commit his final reserves.

The losses had already become very severe. The official R.A.F. figures for the month of August were 390 Spitfires and Hurricanes destroyed, and another 197 badly damaged. Comparable figures for the Me 109, drawn up by the office of the Luftwaffe's quartermaster-general, show for the same period a total loss of 231 and eighty damaged. These figures include not only the losses over England but those over the occupied countries and Germany itself.

Thus on the average two British fighters were being lost for every German one.[1] Both sides, it is true, believed that their own successes and the enemy's losses were much greater than in fact they were. Even so there were some notes of scepticism. Speaking for the Luftwaffe on September 1st at a high command conference on the course of the air battle to date, Major Freiherr von Falkenstein of the general staff said: "In the battle for air superiority the R.A.F. since August 8th has lost 1,115 fighters and ninety-two bombers, the Luftwaffe 252 fighters and 215 bombers. However, a large number of British aircraft claimed by us as destroyed can in fact be made serviceable again very quickly."

Nevertheless the inference drawn by the Luftwaffe general staff goes right to the point. Falkenstein proceeded: "The British fighter arm has been severely hit. If, during September, we seize every opportunity of favourable weather to keep up the pressure one can assume that the enemy's fighter defence will be so weakened that our air assault on his production centres and harbour installations can be greatly stepped up."

At the moment the barrier to the realisation of such aims was still holding. But it looked as though it must soon yield. The assault on London's protective screen of airfields continued. The clash of fighters in the air surrounding the capital went on from day to day.

At the beginning of September, wrote Air Marshal Dowding, the rate of loss was so heavy that fresh squadrons became worn out before convalescing squadrons were ready again to take their place. There were just not enough fighter pilots available to replace the losses in the fighting units.

It was in fact not the mounting loss of aircraft but the toll of experienced pilots that caused the gravest British anxiety, even though pilots who managed to bale out of their machines were available to fight again—unlike their German counterparts who baled out over hostile territory.

[1] This, of course, includes a high proportion lost on the ground.

Churchill has recorded that during the fortnight from August 24th till September 6th—i.e., the period of the main German offensive against the British fighter bases—103 pilots were killed and 128 severely wounded, while the corresponding loss of aircraft was double this: 466 Spitfires and Hurricanes destroyed or seriously damaged.

"Out of a total fighter strength of about a thousand," he wrote, "nearly a quarter had been lost."

Fighter Command tried to meet the gathering crisis with tactical measures. Two squadrons were to attack at a time with at least twenty aircraft. In emergency Air Vice-Marshal Park was authorised to call for reinforcements from the adjacent Groups. In the end the front-line squadrons in 11 Group were given nearly all the trained pilots in the country, leaving at most five per unit with the "convalescing" squadrons. Even the Navy and Bomber and Coastal Commands gave up pilots to the hard-pressed fighter arm.

At the beginning of September reports from the German formations indicated that for the first time the violence of the British fighter defence was slackening. That of II/KG 1 ("Hindenburg"), which on 1st September attacked the Tilbury docks on the Thames, read for instance: "Slight enemy fighter resistance easily countered by own escort."

The eighteen Heinkel 111s were in fact covered by no fewer than three fighter *Geschwader*: JGs 52, 53 and 54. On September 2nd Major Walter Grabmann, commander of ZG 76, reported to his chief, General Osterkamp, after successfully escorting KG 3 to Eastchurch: "There's not much doing over there any more." Even the twin-engined Me 110 could once more maintain its place in the English sky!

The struggle had been hard, but now it seemed that the Luftwaffe's crucial task—the subjugation of the British fighter arm—was all but fulfilled.

4. London Becomes the Target

At this fateful moment—on September 7th to be exact—the Luftwaffe was ordered from the highest quarter to make a drastic change in the nature of its operations. From now on the target was to be London!

This alteration in tactical policy is viewed by the British, from Churchill downwards, as a fundamental German mistake that saved the defences from destruction. The fighter bases at last had a breathing space and could now recover from the serious damage they had received.

The reasons for the new policy were two: one of them purely military, the other political.

On September 3rd Goering met his two *Luftflotten* chiefs, Field Marshals Kesselring and Sperrle, at The Hague. He pressed the view that current tactical policy should now be abandoned in favour of a large-scale assault on the most important target—the English capital. The only question was: could such an attack be launched without undue risk to the bomber force? Had the British fighters become sufficiently weakened? Kesselring said Yes, Sperrle said No.

Sperrle wanted the offensive against the fighter bases to continue. Kesselring put the view that they were expendable: if too badly damaged the fighter squadrons could withdraw to other bases behind London, and these, being beyond German fighter range, would thus be safe from bombers. He was indeed astonished that the British had not long since made this move to save them further losses. Their reasons must have been psychological, such as "holding the front line" and "setting an example to the people". But it was quite on the cards that they would withdraw to these more safely placed airfields now.

"We have no chance," he said, "of destroying the English fighters on the ground. We must force their last reserves of Spitfires and Hurricanes into combat in the air."

This would only be accomplished by changing the target. Even before *"Adlertag"* the importance of London had been judged by II Air Corps to be so paramount that the English would hazard the last of their squadrons in its defence.

During the whole of August, however, Hitler for political reasons had forbidden any attack on the capital. Unfortunately, owing to a regrettable lapse in navigation on the part of a few bomber crews, it had happened. On the night of August 24th/25th some isolated bombs, destined for the aircraft works at Rochester and oil tanks on the Thames, had descended over the London area, and this had sparked off a whole chain reaction.

The operations staff officer of KG 1, Major Josef Knobel, recalls vividly the teleprinter signal from Goering that early in the morning reached each unit which had operated during the night: "It is to be reported forthwith which crews dropped bombs in the London prohibited zone. The Supreme Commander reserves to himself the personal punishment of the commanders concerned by remustering them to the infantry."

The forbidden had happened. Churchill demanded from a reluctant Bomber Command, who saw no military advantage to be gained by it, an immediate reprisal raid on Berlin. The following night, accordingly, eighty-one British twin-engined bombers made the 600-mile each-way flight to the German capital. Of these twenty-nine claimed to have reached it, though according to German observations less than ten bombers, hindered as they were by heavy cloud, managed to drop their bombs at random in the target area. Military damage was nil.

It was the first of four British raids within ten days. The fact that German bombs, contrary to existing orders again fell on London, no doubt made the British leaders all the more determined to strike at Berlin.

For Hitler it was too much. He abandoned his restraint. With angry disillusionment he proclaimed: "Since they attack our cities we shall wipe out theirs."

On September 5th, from 9 p.m. till the following morning, sixty-eight bombers representing picked squadrons of KGs 2, 3, 26 and 53, delivered the first planned air raid on London's docks. Sixty tons of bombs were dropped, and the last formation reported five large conflagrations and four smaller fires.

On the afternoon of September 7th Goering stood with Kesselring and Loerzer on the coast at Cape Blanc Nez and watched his bombers and fighters droning overhead. He had, as he told radio news correspondents, "taken over personal command of the Luftwaffe in its war against England".

This time it was no fewer than 625 bombers which, in the late afternoon and through the night, headed for London. The daylight formations were protected by 648 single- and twin-engined fighters. They flew in several waves and in tight formations stepped up between 14,000 and 20,000 feet.[1]

The British fighter squadrons, lined up on their airfields in expectation of new German attacks, failed to bar the way. The approach was made from a surprise direction.

During this first big raid of the series the Luftwaffe for the first time dropped 3,600-lb bombs—over a hundred of them—on the London docks. When *Luftflotte* 3's formations arrived after nightfall they were guided to their target by the fires already raging.

So began the Battle of London: the battle designed to force the final British fighter reserves into combat before the onset of bad autumnal weather prejudiced the full impact of operations.

A week later KG 3 was flying at 12,000 feet, just over the clouds, course westerly towards London. Target: once more the docks situated on the great U-shaped loop of the Thames to the east of the city. Normally an unmistakable target, particularly on a fine day with good visibility. But the further the formation penetrated the denser the cloud became. Only occasionally did the curtain draw aside to afford a glimpse of land far below.

Horst Zander, radio operator of a Do 17, studied the air space astern and on each flank. To port and starboard flew his comrades of 6 Squadron, beyond them the other squadrons of II/KG 3. In front and behind, and somewhat higher, were other *Gruppen*—the whole *Geschwader* comprising fifty Dorniers in tight formation. And not KG 3 alone: from other directions other *Geschwader* were converging on the same target: London. And high above the bombers weaved the fighters.

Only one thing was missing, thought Zander: the "Tommies". He looked at his watch: 13.00 hours—on Sunday, September 15th. And at that moment the battle started.

For an hour already the English had been following by radar what was brewing on the far side of the Channel: first the forming-up of the bomber units over northern France, then their rendezvous with the fighters, and finally their combined approach.

Air Vice-Marshal Park, A.O.C. 11 Group, had had plenty of time to bring his twenty-four fighter squadrons to readiness. In the past few days German bombers had often reached London unmolested owing to some misunderstanding by the defence. But this time the English were determined to catch and hit them over Kent. Their fighters took off none too soon.

KG 3's first collision with the enemy took place somewhere over Canterbury. Suddenly on the inter-com. Horst Zander heard the voice of his Dornier's observer and commander, First-Lieutenant Laube: "Enemy fighters ahead!"

They were Spitfires of 72 and 92 Squadrons. To give his units more punch, Park was now sending them off in pairs.

The British squadron commanders, without waiting to get into a favourable position above the *Geschwader*, drove straight into it at the same level and from ahead . . . two dozen Spitfires on a broad front, pumping fire from every gun. Within a few seconds the Englishmen, flashing closely above or below their opponents, had swept through the whole German formation.

[1] For operations plan and order of battle of this first major air attack on London see Appendix 6.

"Machine-gun fire crackled on every side," Zander later reported, "and twice there was a hell of a thump quite close beside us. Two British fighters must have collided with two of our Dorniers. The aircraft went spinning down in flames, and below us several parachutes opened. We looked at each other and gave the thumbs-up. This time we had come out of the mêlée unscathed."

Closing the gaps that this first attack had created, KG 3's bombers drew still more tightly together and flew calmly on towards London.

Five minutes later Air Vice-Marshal Park ordered into the air his last six squadrons, hitherto held in reserve. To reinforce them five others were sent south by 12 Group to the north of the battle area. In one tight formation these squadrons flew straight into the attack over London itself. Returning bomber crews reported resignedly: "Over the target we were met by enemy fighter formations of up to eighty aircraft. . . ."

Yesterday it had been quite different. Then the bombers had only had to contend with isolated Spitfire and Hurricane attacks, and London's protection had depended almost entirely on its concentrated and accurate anti-aircraft fire. The conclusion that the British fighter defence had at last been knocked out on the ground seemed to be justified.

Imagine then the disillusionment when on this September 15th hundreds of fighters once more pounced on the German bombers . . . when at the climax of the fight, just after 13.30, some 300 Spitfires and Hurricanes were in the air simultaneously. The skies over the whole of south-east England, from the Channel coast to London, were aflame with battle, and not a single German bomber formation reached its target unmolested.

At this very hour Air Vice-Marshal Park, in his underground operations room at Uxbridge, had an important visitor, Winston Churchill. The Prime Minister had come over from his near-by country house at Chequers to witness the conduct of the battle at its nerve centre.

From his "theatre seat" in the gallery he followed in silence the tense scene being enacted on the floor below. The map-table showed the constantly changing situation. As aircraft position reports came in, girls of the Women's Auxiliary Air Force briskly changed the position of the coloured symbols on the map-table. They showed the German aggressors drawing ever closer to London.

On the wall opposite, a large illuminated board indicated the "state" of each fighter squadron: whether it was still at standby or had already taken off; whether it was engaged with the enemy or had disengaged to land and re-equip with fuel and ammunition.

It was not long before the whole lot were airborne and locked in manifold combat. Yet still further formations of German bombers were pressing on towards the capital. The critical moment had arrived. If the Germans could now throw in a completely fresh wave, there would be no opposition left to meet it.

Churchill, who had not yet said a word, now turned to Park. "What other reserves have we?" he asked. And Park replied: "There are none."

In the event 148 German bombers reached the target area on this Sunday afternoon; but the second wave failed to exploit the vacuum. It arrived two hours later—because before that the German fighters, already fully committed in the first wave, were unable to provide a fresh escort. By then, of course, the British fighters were ready again.

This day's bombing, moreover, achieved nothing like the concentrated effect of the first big daylight raid on the 7th. With dense cloud preventing any accuracy of aim, the bombs fell scattered all over London. And on their return journey the bombers went on being harried by English fighters till far beyond the coast.

It was while turning round over London, after dropping its bombs, that First Lieutenant Laube's Do 17 became involved in further combat.

"Our *Gruppe*," reported Zander, "had become split up. Every crew sought its own safety in a powered gliding race down over the sea and for home."

Suddenly his Dornier was struck hard. There was a blinding flash and black smoke poured through the cabin, directly followed by an icy gale streaming back from the shattered perspex.

"The cabin was full of blood. Our pilot was hit. In the inter-com. I heard him say feebly: "Heinz Laube, you have to fly us home!' Meanwhile we had reached the North Sea, and so had peace in which to change over. The flight mechanic put a first-aid dressing on the badly wounded pilot, and after we had disobeyed orders by requesting a bearing from Antwerp-Deurne, our observer, with his B-2 pilot's licence, took over the shot-up machine. Twenty minutes later, the aircraft bucking like a horse, he managed to land us safely."

Such, or similar, was the return of too many of the raiding force: some with dead engines or shot-away undercarriages, others with wings and fuselages riddled with holes, many with dead or wounded comrades.

September 15th had taught the German Luftwaffe two bitter lessons:

1. So far from being knocked out, the British fighter defence appeared to be stronger than ever before.
2. The close escort of the bomber formations by their own fighters had turned out to be only partially successful. Tied to their slow charges, the Messerschmitts had been unable to exploit their flying attributes and so were in a poor position to repel the Spitfires and Hurricanes.

In the words once more of Hellmuth Ostermann of III/JG 54:

"We clung to the bomber formation in pairs—and it was a damned awkward feeling. From below we looked up at the bright blue bellies of the Tommy planes. Mostly they waited there till our bombers made their turn. Then they would swoop down, pull briefly out, fire their guns and at once dive on down. All we could do was to shoot off short nuisance bursts while at the same time watching out that there was no one nibbling at our tails. Often we pulled madly on the stick till the ailerons shook, but were then unable to turn round quickly enough and could only watch as the Tommies knocked hell out of one of the bombers. . . ."

The Luftwaffe was caught up in a vicious circle. While its first and foremost objective was still to knock out the enemy's fighter arm, the British avoided combat with the Me 109 formations that were free and unshackled, and concentrated on attacking the bombers. The latter, slow and vulnerable as they were, thus had to be protected against these attacks by twice or three times as many fighters. But then the very closeness of their escort rendered these in their turn too slow and ponderous to achieve any appreciable success. And no one could see any way out of the impasse.

After the violent combats to which both the attacking German waves were subjected between 12.50 and 16.00 hours, the English claimed a bag of 185 aircraft destroyed. Churchill called September 15th the greatest and most decisive day of the air battle, and ever since it has been celebrated in the United Kingdom as "Battle of Britain Day".

On the German side, however, the battle was regarded as far from lost, even if the heavy casualties again made a change of tactics imperative. The actual number of aircraft that failed to return on that day was fifty-six, including twenty-four Do 17s and ten He 111s. The damage to several dozen others was such as to require extensive overhaul. By the final count one quarter of the entire operating bomber force had been put out of action. Such a loss was far too high. If things went on like this, the Luftwaffe would bleed to death over England.

On September 16th the *Luftflotten* and Air Corps chiefs were once more summoned to their supreme commander. Goering was red in the face with vexation. Instead of calling for remedies, he wanted culprits. One idea had become fixed in his mind: "The fighters have let us down!"

Lieutenant-General Osterkamp, their commander in the west, rose to their defence. Was it their fault, he demanded, if they were forced to adopt a method of escort that made them useless? Could they be blamed if the resulting losses could only be replaced up to less than fifty per cent? Then, controlling himself, he gave his expert evidence: "The English have adopted new tactics. They are now using powerful fighter formations to attack in force. From our radio-intercept service we know that their orders are strictly to attack our bombers. Yesterday these new tactics took us by surprise."

"That's just what we want!" Goering blustered. "If they come at us in droves, we can shoot them down in droves!"

In the face of such arguments no fruitful discussion was possible. The Luftwaffe's supreme commander had lost touch, to a disturbing degree, with operational problems. He dwelt in a world of illusions. And the men who had waged their bitter struggle tirelessly in the English skies—these men were now heaped with reproaches.

What, then, should happen now? Once again it was the proposals of the lower echelons of command that came nearest to hitting the nail on the head:

1. In favourable weather daylight raids should be continued, but in smaller formations up to *Gruppen* strength and with strong fighter protection.

2. Nuisance raids on London and important industrial targets should be made in all weathers by single bombers or fighter-bombers in order to give the enemy no rest.

3. The main weight of the air offensive should now be launched after dark.

So began the Battle of Britain's last phase, which in effect continued during the whole autumn and winter and into the spring of 1941. There

61. A British fighter attack on a German bomber near the chalk cliffs of the English coast. The Hurricane has lost its port wing, and the pilot has bailed out.

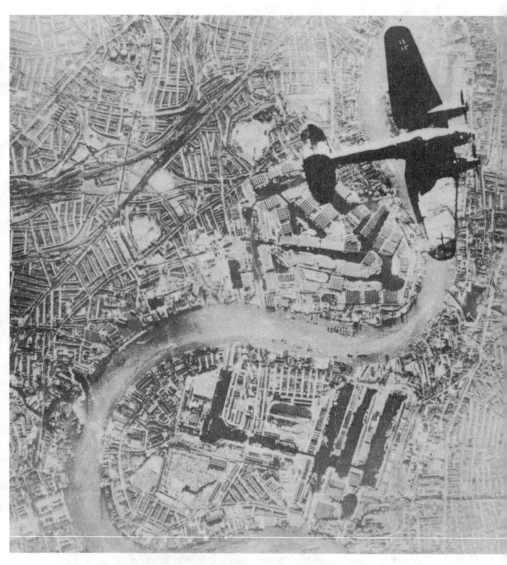

62. A Heinkel over the London docks.

began too the long dispute between the Luftwaffe's supreme command in Berlin and its leaders in the West about where and against which targets the main effort should be made in order to achieve the maximum success with minimum loss.

"The *Reichsmarschall*," reports Colonel Koller, then on the staff of *Luftflotte* 3, "never forgave us for not having conquered England."

Soon even the most optimistic had to concede that with the ever-worsening weather, and despite isolated successes, there was no longer any chance of the Luftwaffe striking a knock-out blow. Already the bombers, from their bases in Belgium and northern France, were having to plough through numerous cloud banks in pursuit of their mission. Many of the original crews, trained in blind-flying, were now either dead or prisoners-of-war, and the young airmen who had replaced them lacked experience.

Now the sacrifice of hundreds of Ju 52 transporters during the daring airborne assaults on Norway and Holland was sorely felt. Many of them had come from the Luftwaffe's blind-flying schools, together with the instructional staffs, and most had not returned. Replacing them took a long time, and the training of new recruits consequently suffered. At the time when Germany was everywhere victorious it had not seemed to matter greatly. But now it was a bitter pill to swallow.

Flying through cloud usually disrupted the formations, and valuable time was wasted in getting them together again. If on the other hand they flew round the cloud they would reach the rendezvous with the fighters too late. Alternatively they would emerge as a miles-long straggling procession virtually impossible to protect against enemy fighter attack.

With England's weather largely determined over the Atlantic, the forecasts of German meteorologists were often unreliable. Over London individual cloud banks would coalesce into one dense curtain with startling rapidity, thus making bomb-aiming impossible, or separating the bombers from their escort. The fighters, unable to fly blind and not, as their opponents were, controlled from the ground, would then have to return, for a straight flight to London and back was about the limit of their range.

On one of the last days of September such a situation led to catastrophe. En route to London a great cloud bank built up behind the bombers. In such a case standing orders were to abandon the operation and turn back. But on this occasion the commander, a young man fresh from home, saw no particular danger and went on, planning to skirt the cloud bank by a wide margin on the return.

Aware that such a detour would be beyond the Me 109s' range, he called up the escort commander and released him. But the latter, not wanting to deliver the bombers to the mercy of the Spitfires, still kept his fighter *Gruppe* in support. Once again Lieutenant Ostermann was one of the participants, and reported: "After being airborne for exactly ninety minutes we were briefly engaged by the enemy. My red warning light was already beginning to flicker, but below through a cloud gap I saw the English coast. After fighting off the enemy we pushed down through the clouds, leaving the bombers above them. Presumably we were over Dover. In this familiar region we could get home in minimum time."

It was a false assumption that cost them dear. The bombers' detour had brought the fighters far to the west.

"The squadrons had broken up and the separated planes clung to the cloud ceiling trying to save their fuel. Hanging over the water with just a few drops left was a most uncomfortable feeling, and each minute seemed like an hour. Still no land was in sight, and I realised we had crossed the coast far to the west of Dover, where the Channel is very wide. One after another the planes had to go down and ditch, leaving behind a trail of foam, a yellow Mae West and a green oil stain. At any moment I would have to do the same. . . . Then, far ahead I saw something shining. Was it land or just a patch of light? It was the coast indeed, and someone joked over the R/T: 'Norway ahead!' It released the tensions and warmed our hearts."

They had been in the air two hours—an exceptionally long time for an Me 109 even at economical cruising speed. Seven of them had been forced to ditch, another five to make belly landings with stationary airscrews on the beach near Abbeville. The enemy had scored a big success without raising a finger.

The end of the month brought new bad weather fronts moving in from the Atlantic, accompanied by north-westerly gales, lowering skies and showers of rain. The daylight bombing raids virtually petered out. But still the Luftwaffe had one surprise in store.

Already on September 20th a formation of twenty-two Messerschmitt 109s had made a sortie to London without, for once, having to escort bombers. They were, in fact, themselves protected by numerous other fighters. Between Calais and the English coast they climbed right up to 25,000 feet, then swooped swiftly down on the capital.

The British ground controllers recalled the fighter squadrons put up to meet the raid. Unless they carried bombs enemy aircraft were of no interest.

So it was that the Messerschmitts reached London unmolested. Diving down to 12,000 feet and pulling out, they had already turned for home before twenty-two 500-lb. bombs exploded in the City of London and on rail termini west of the great bend in the Thames.

Listening in on the British radio frequencies, the German intercept service reported a great confusion of orders and counter-orders. The fighters had dropped bombs!

Hardly had the Messerschmitts returned when Kesselring, exploiting the initial success, ordered a second fighter-bomber attack. Both times it was by II/LG 2, which under Major Spielvogel and then Captain Otto Weiss had, during the Polish and French campaigns, still been equipped with ancient Henschel 123 biplanes. Since then its pilots, after a training course on the Me 109E, had been equipped with the fighter-bomber version.

This would carry below its fuselage a bomb of up to 1,000 lb. By doing so, of course, the machine ceased to be a fighter. Its flight became ponderous, its speed and rate of climb reduced. Yet because of the success of the first surprise attacks the German command clung to the idea. To the dismay of the fighter pilots it was ordered that, in addition to II/LG 2 and "Experimental Unit 210", no less than a third of all the available Me 109s were to be modified to carry bombs!

It now only took Messerschmitts to force the enemy into combat and he soon adjusted himself to the new form of attack. Even the Hurricanes could make rings around the heavily laden fighter-bombers, and again heavy losses were sustained.

"We fighter pilots," wrote one of them after the war, "viewed this violation of our precious planes with disgust. We were reduced to the role of stopgaps and scapegoats."

Under the official name of "light bombers"—but dubbed "light Kesselrings" in service jargon—the fighter-bombers continued their attacks, with varying success, right through October. At last, fighter chief Osterkamp in exasperation told Jeschonnek, chief of the Luftwaffe general staff, that it would not take long, "thanks to these senseless operations", for the whole of the fighter arm to be grounded. His protests helped. In November there were only a few attacks, and at the beginning of December they were halted altogether.

But from now on criticism of the high command was never stilled. The crisis of the Battle of Britain produced a crisis of confidence in the Luftwaffe itself. And this less than three months since the battle had opened with such high hopes and promises.

Night bombing with high-frequency aids. By means of concentrated radio beams Bomber Group 100 and III/KG 28 were brought exactly over their target, while the other transmitting stations signalled the moment for "bombs away". Known as the "X"-process, it was not effectively jammed until 1941.

Meanwhile, London was attacked night after night by forces of bombers ranging in number from a hundred to 300 at a time. The darkness protected them and bestowed on them a kind of "air sovereignty" that they never achieved by day. However, the will to resist of the populace was greatly underestimated. London was as far from capitulating as were the German cities years later beneath the great assault of Allied bombers.

In mid-November the Luftwaffe made a last change of objective. Important industrial towns and ports were made the main targets, with the aim of destroying the enemy's economic potential, his sources of supply and power. But while the bombers could not miss the great city of London, mainly thanks to the shining ribbon of the Thames, the problem of finding other targets was more acute.

In the evening of November 14th two squadrons of *Kampf gruppe* 100 took off from Vannes on night operations. Their He 111H-3s were equipped with "X apparatus", a radio direction-beam invention developed by the high-frequency expert Dr. Plendl in Rechlin as far back as 1934.

From a so-called "*Knickebein*" transmitter on the French coast this beam was directed exactly on their target—Coventry—and the bombers simply steered along it, the pilot adjusting his course according to signals received on a radio set. Dots or dashes in his earphones indicated that he was straying, a continuous buzzing tone that he was on course.

On a second receiver the aircraft's radio-operator awaited the "advance signal" produced by a second beam laid across the first. When this sounded, it indicated that the aircraft was about twelve miles from the target. The operator would then press a key on a clock, causing a pointer to start running.

The next six miles served to measure the true speed of the aircraft in relation to the ground. At the end of it a third beam transmitted both a visual and an oral signal—the "main signal". The clock key was pressed again, stopping the first pointer and setting a second one in motion.

From then on the pilot had to adhere rigidly to his speed, height and course. Everything else followed automatically: as soon as the second pointer reached the first an electric contact was made and the bombs were released. At this moment the aircraft was over the centre of Coventry. The first fires began to flicker below, thus marking the target so that the following units could not miss it.

On this night every bomber formation that *Luftflotten* 2 and 3 could muster was thrown against Coventry—"an important centre of the enemy armament industry," as the orders for the operation put it. 449 bombers dropped some 500 tons of high explosive and thirty tons of incendiary bombs on the hard-hit city.

"The usual cheers that greeted a direct hit stuck in our throats," wrote one of the German bomber pilots. "The crew just gazed down on the sea of flames in silence. Was this really a military target?"

Coventry became a monument to the terror of war by bombing, the peak of which had still to be reached.

Similar radio-beam processes had been used by the Germans since the night raids started, and they did not of course remain concealed from British Intelligence. Hearing about them for the first time on September 26th, Churchill ordered immediate counter-measures. To General Ismay he wrote that if the facts of the matter were as indicated, they represented a deadly danger.

The facts were confirmed. Only in spring 1941 did the British succeed in jamming the "X" system effectively. By "bending" the beam, they could, for instance, set the bombers on a false course. Thereupon the Germans went over to the "Y" system. All the same this high-frequency weapon was not as decisive now as it became later in the war when the British "Pathfinder" units followed the pattern set by *Kampfgruppe* 100 in 1940.

In early November the condemned *Stukas* were resurrected to attack British shipping once more in the Channel. Twenty Ju 87s of III/StG 1 under Captain Helmut Mahlke were protected by no fewer than two whole fighter *Geschwader*. On November 1st, 8th and 11th, diving in succession, they achieved manifold strikes on three large convoys in the outer Thames estuary. Three days later the *Gruppe* lost a quarter of its aircraft to attacks by Spitfires owing to the fact that its escort was not on the spot.

After that, air attacks on British shipping were virtually ended by autumnal and winter storms. Only IX Air Corps, formed on 16th October out of 9 Air

Division, with the "General Wever" KG 4 as its nucleus, went on sowing mines in any weather in harbour approaches and along the convoys' coastal routes.

Even the assault on the island of Britain slowly died away. The German bomber units, hardly able to take off from their drenched and soaking airfields, were reaching the point of exhaustion. The following statistics tell the story:

In August 4,779 sorties were flown by German aircraft, dropping a total of 4,636 tons of high-explosive and incendiary bombs. In September, during day and night attacks on London, the figure was 7,260 sorties, 6,616 tons of high explosives and 428 tons of incendiaries, but in addition 669 mines in river mouths and harbours.

The zenith was reached in October, during the period of the daylight fighter-bomber attacks on London and the numerous night attacks on industrial cities. For that month the figures were 9,911 sorties, 8,790 tons of high-explosives, and 323 tons of incendiaries, but again 610 mines in coastal waters.

From November onwards the offensive diminished, with large-scale raids restricted as a rule to moonlight periods. Though Goering once more nominated London as his main objective, most of them were directed against such industrial cities as Coventry, Liverpool and Manchester, and the harbours of Plymouth, Southampton and Liverpool-Birkenhead. The month's tally was 6,205 tons of high-explosives, 305 tons of incendiaries and 1,215 mines. After that the decline accelerated: in December it was 3,844 sorties, 4,323 tons of bombs; in January 1941, 2,465 sorties and 2,424 tons; in February, a mere 1,401 sorties and 1,127 tons.

It is true that activity against England was revived in the spring, but this was largely a feint. The about-face of the German armed forces and their coming advance in the east were to be masked as long as possible. Consequently those *Geschwader* that in April and May were still in the west redoubled their efforts. The number of sorties rose again to 4,364 in March and in April to 5,448. It was in fact during this period that London received its worst raids of the war: on the night of April 16th/17th by 681 bombers, on 19th/20th by 712. Even during the first ten days of May there were fresh large-scale attacks on Liverpool-Birkenhead, Glasgow-Clydeside and again London. "The widespread impression that England is on the brink of invasion must be reinforced," ran a directive from the armed forces high command.

The fact of the matter is that "Operation Sealion", the proposed German landing in England, had been postponed indefinitely. Air sovereignty over the English south-east coast, one of the pre-conditions for venturing upon such an undertaking, had never been achieved—let alone in the three days that Goering had estimated, or even in the four weeks up to September 15th, which Hitler had nominated as the moment for the start of the invasion.

The Luftwaffe, to be sure, by its frequent changes of objective, had scarcely pursued the main one: to prepare the way for the landing of the German army. Its aim was much more ambitious: to prove for the first time the dictum of the Italian theorist Douhet that future wars could be won by strategic air attack alone. Goering would not admit that the German Luftwaffe lacked the power to do so.

Hitler had, in fact, cancelled "Operation Sealion" as early as October 12th.

Its declared postponement till the spring of 1941 because of the weather was just a blind "to exert political and military pressure on England".

For a long time Hitler had become obsessed with the idea that he had first "to lay Russia low in one swift campaign". Then, with her rear secure, Germany could launch her whole strength against the West. Priority of armament production would be given to Air Force and Navy, and sooner or later Britain, too, would be conquered.

On May 21st Field-Marshal Sperrle, chief of *Luftflotte* 3, became sole air commander in the west. Of the forty-four bomber *Gruppen*, which for ten months had been operating against Britain, only four were left. The rest, apart from some held in the Balkans, were taken home to rest and refit before turning east.

The Russian campaign was only supposed to interrupt the air battle against Britain for the time being. But for Germany it was the beginning of war on many fronts.

The Battle of Britain—Summary and Conclusions

1. The attempt during the summer and autumn of 1940 to bring Britain to her knees solely by attack from the air was unsuccessful. At the root of this failure, so pregnant with military consequence, was Hitler's conviction, as late as 1938, that there would be no war with Britain. When it came the Luftwaffe was thus not equipped for it. Above all it lacked a heavy four-engined bomber, the development of which had been halted in 1936 in favour of the dive-bomber. The Do 17, He 111 and Ju 88 were by comparison too light and vulnerable, their defensive armament too meagre, their range too limited, and their bomb-load inadequate.

2. The German fighter force at the start of the battle disposed of only some 700 first-line Me 109s. Their numbers were thus inadequate for the double role of engaging the British fighters in open combat and providing close escort for the bombers. With London the limit of German fighter range the daylight operating zone of the bombers was likewise restricted to south-east England, for without fighter escort they were far too vulnerable. The heavy Me 110 fighter was almost useless for the purpose; a twin-engined aircraft, it was no match for the British fighters. No long-range single-engined fighter was available.

3. The defence was forewarned of each attack by an unbroken chain of radar stations, which made surprise almost impossible. This and astute ground control saved the British fighter arm from being knocked out and German air sovereignty being won.

4. Contrary to German belief, and despite heavy losses, the number of British first-line fighters (also about 700) hardly sank during the battle. Production during the decisive months was more than double that of Germany's.

5. Though the Luftwaffe's chances of successful strikes against targets of potential military significance were much greater in daylight, these raids had to be abandoned in the autumn owing to bad weather and insupportable losses.

6. Goering and his top command changed from one objective to another. This split the available forces instead of concentrating them long enough at one point of effort.

7. The effect of the bombing raids, particularly at night, was usually greatly overestimated. Even the heaviest, such as those on London and Coventry, failed to break the will to resist of the hard-hit populace. They had, in fact just the opposite effect—as was shown again years later during the much heavier British raids on Germany.

8. *Germany possessed neither enough U-boats nor bombers of adequate range to strike a decisive blow against Britain's vital supply arteries by means of attacks on convoys and harbours, as outlined in "Führer-directive No. 9" of November 29, 1939.*

9. *Hitler's decision to attack Russia was taken as early as July 1940—i.e.,* before *the Battle of Britain began. From this moment on, the struggle in the west no longer had priority in the plans of the German command. Despite the bitterness of its operations against Britain, the supply of equipment to the Luft-waffe was not the most salient task. When the battle was finally broken off in spring 1941, the main strength of the Luftwaffe, like that of the Army was transferred to the east.*

5

MEDITERRANEAN THEATRE 1941

1. The Blood-bath of Crete

The plan of campaign for spring, 1941, had been fixed in autumn, 1940. As soon as weather conditions permitted, in May, the offensive against the Soviet Union was to be launched.

But Hitler underestimated the ambition of his Italian brother-in-arms, Mussolini. German measures in the Balkans—especially the dispatch of a "military mission" to Rumania to guard that country against Russian enterprises and at the same time provide a spring-board for a German advance to the east—had severely vexed the Italian leader.

"Hitler keeps confronting me with accomplished facts!" he burst out to his foreign minister, Count Ciano. "This time I shall pay him back in his own coin: when I have marched against Greece he will only learn about it from the newspapers!"

He began his venture on October 28, 1940, and just one day later the British occupied Crete—the key position in the eastern Mediterranean. For Hitler it was bad news. On November 20th he wrote to Mussolini and "with the warm heart of a friend" loaded him with reproaches. British bases in Greece would represent a threat to his southern flank. Above all he feared for the Rumanian oil fields of Ploesti, so indispensable for Germany, and now within range of British bombers. He hardly dared, he added, to think about the consequences.

He would, he complained, have asked the Duce "not to take this action without a previous, lightning occupation of Crete, and to this end I wanted to bring you practical proposals—namely, to employ a German paratroop division, and an airborne division."

Thus the possibility of capturing Crete from the air was already under consideration in November 1940. Six months later the thought was put into action. For the Italian offensive was halted almost as soon as it began. In March 1941 British army and air force units gained a foothold on the Greek mainland, but on April 6th Germany attacked Jugoslavia and Greece, and within a few weeks had overrun both countries. By the beginning of May German troops had everywhere reached the Aegean and Mediterranean coasts.

Only Crete still lay ahead, walling in the lesser Greek islands and barring the way to the outer Mediterranean. To this island bastion, 150 miles long and about twenty broad, the British had withdrawn from the mainland. They were resolved to hold on to it.

Let us turn back to April 15th, when the Balkan campaign was at its height. As twice before, in Poland and in France, the *Stukas* and other close-support formations of VIII Air Corps under General Freiherr von Richthofen were hammering breaches in the enemy's defence lines.

On this particular day the chief of *Luftflotte* 4, Air General Alexander Löhr, responsible for operations in the south-east, had an audience with his supreme commander. Goering had set up his headquarters at Semmering in Austria, and listened attentively as Löhr put forward the suggestion of concluding the Balkan campaign with a large-scale operation against Crete by the parachute and airborne units of XI Air Corps.

Five days later, on April 20th, Lieutenant-General Kurt Student, the creator of the airborne forces, himself went to see Goering and filled in the details of the plan. For Student, badly wounded at Rotterdam, had after his convalescence at once taken over the newly formed XI Air Corps, which embraced the whole airborne organisation, including the transport units.

Goering's reaction was to send Student, with the Luftwaffe's chief of general staff, Jeschonnek, to the Führer's HQ at Mönichkirchen. That was on April 21st, the day on which the Greeks capitulated to Field-Marshal List's 12th Army. Hitler merely drew attention to the fact that he himself had considered an airborne landing on Crete the previous autumn.

Since then the situation had changed for the worse, and time was now pressing. Apart from the fact that the Balkan campaign had itself postponed the attack on Russia by four weeks—from May to June—every incidental theatre of war had the effect of dissipating German military strength. Not only had the Germans been obliged to go to the help of the Italians in North Africa, but they had also sent X Air Corps to Sicily to support them against the British Mediterranean fleet and Malta.

However, despite the fact that the chief of the armed forces, Field-Marshal Keitel, and his staff recommended that the paratroops would be better occupied in the conquest of Malta—a British base which they considered more important and dangerous—Hitler still gave priority to Crete. He viewed its subjugation as the "crowning glory" of the Balkan campaign. It would be a spring-board against North Africa, the Suez Canal and the whole of the eastern Mediterranean, all of which the Luftwaffe would be able to control. He made just two conditions:

1. The forces of XI Air Corps—one paratroop and one airborne division—must suffice for the operation.
2. Despite the short time in which to prepare, the operation must be launched by the middle of May.

General Student wasted little time considering the matter. He was convinced that his formations could achieve their objective; and Hitler thought so too. After four days Mussolini also agreed, and finally on April 25th Hitler issued his Directive No. 28 for "Operation Mercury"—the capture of Crete.

At their home bases in Germany the paratroop regiments were suddenly

alerted. They had just twenty days to get ready for the biggest airborne operation in history. Would they make it?

Difficulties mounted, first in the matter of transport. Major-General Eugen
Meindl's Assault Regiment had 220 lorries too few, so the majority had to
go by train. After several days they reached Arad and Craiova in Rumania,
from where they journeyed another 1,000 miles by road to their base of operations near Athens. For three whole days the "Flying Dutchman"—the cover
name for XI Air Corps' column of 4,000 vehicles—was brought to a standstill
in the Macedonian mountains. The reason was that 2 *Panzer* Division, returning from Greece, had priority at the narrow passes of Verria and Kosani.
For Hitler had expressly ordered that troop concentrations for "Operation
Barbarossa" (against Russia) were not to be delayed by the transports for
"Mercury" proceeding in the other direction.

The inadequate road system also brought 22 (Airborne) Division—which,
with the paratroop force, had a year earlier been committed against Holland
—to a halt in Rumania. The Army declared itself in no position to help the
division get south. In its place the supreme command put Lieutenant-
General Ringel's 5 Mountain Division, already in Greece, under Student's
command. Although this was an *élite* force, which had just broken through
the Metaxas Line, it had hardly been trained for an air landing in the midst
of enemy defences.

On May 14th the last of the paratroops finally reached their appointed base
near Athens. These were 1 and 2 Companies of the Assault Regiment, which
in the course of organising rail transit for the rest of it, had been temporarily
forgotten about. They themselves had had to push all the way from Hildesheim in north Germany by road.

The aircraft units likewise had a struggle to get ready in time for the event.
For "Operation Mercury" the air commander, Major-General Gerhard, had
ten "*Kampfgruppen* zbV", comprising some 500 Ju 52s, at his disposal. But
most of them had during the Balkan campaign been daily engaged in lifting
ammunition and supplies, and now both airframes and engines urgently
required overhaul.

On May 1st the whole fleet flew off to the north. Dozens of maintenance
centres—from Brunswick, Fürstenwalde and Cottbus in Germany to Prague
and Brno in Czechoslovakia and Aspern and Zwölfaxing in Austria—
dropped all other work to devote themselves to the "good old aunts" of the
Luftwaffe, the Ju 52s. By the 15th 493 of them, completely overhauled and
many with new engines, had re-landed at bases in the Athens area. It was a
masterpiece of organisation and technical achievement.

A second problem, however, was the airfields. The few that had metalled
runways, like Eleusis near Athens, were already occupied by the bomber units
of VIII Air Corps. There remained only small and neglected fields of sand.

"They are nothing but deserts!" the commander of KG zbV 2, Colonel
Rüdiger von Heyking, bitterly reported. "Heavy-laden aircraft will sink up
to their axles."

Heyking had the misfortune to be based with his 150-odd Ju 52s of *Gruppen*
60, 101 and 102, at Topolia, on an airfield which an over-enthusiastic Army
officer had had ploughed up after its occupation "to make it more level".
The consequence was that every take-off and landing produced a quite fright-

63. A Ju 52/3M set on fire by anti-aircraft guns near Heraklion during the costly airborne assault on Crete.

64. Paratroops assembling for attack during the assault on Crete.

65. Some of the 493 Ju 52/3M transports which left Greece for Crete early on May 20, 1941, over the Aegean.

66. Ju 52/3M after a crash landing. Many were lost owing both to enemy fire and unfamiliarity with the ground.

67. The first assault troops were landed by glider at Canea and Maleme. This glider has broken up on hitting a hillside.

ful cloud of dust, which rose to 3,000 feet and blotted out the sun. In the course of a rehearsal, von Heyking worked out that after a squadron take-off it took seventeen minutes before one could again see one's own hand and a second squadron could follow.

Conditions were hardly better at the neighbouring airfield of Tanagra, where zbV *Gruppen* 40 and 105 and I *Gruppe* of Air-Landing *Geschwader* 1, under Colonel Buchholz, were based. The remaining four transport *Gruppen* lay at Dadion, Megara and Corinth—their airfields likewise of sand.

But the worst bottle-neck was fuel. To transport the chief combatants to Crete would require three successive flights by the 493 aircraft, and that meant some 650,000 gallons of petrol. Brought by tanker to Piraeus, the port of Athens, it then had to be transferred to forty-five gallon barrels, and finally transported by lorries to the remote airfields. For nothing like a regular ground organisation existed on them.

By May 17th not a single barrel had arrived—because the tanker, on its way from Italy, was blocked in the Corinth Canal. On April 26th parachuted sappers and two battalions of infantry had captured the bridge over this canal intact. But then a British anti-aircraft shell happened to strike the demolition charge after it had been removed, and the resulting explosion flung the bridge to the canal bottom, thus blocking the tanker's passage. XI Air Corps' quarter-master, Lieutenant-Colonel Seibt, had divers flown out from Kiel, and finally on May 17th the waterway was cleared. Next day at Piraeus, the time-consuming process of transferring the fuel into barrels began in feverish haste.

Thus the attack, already postponed till May 18th, was delayed another two days. Even at midnight on the 19th/20th, five hours before take-off, a few Ju 52 squadrons were still unfuelled, and the paratroops—who should have been sleeping—had themselves to lend a hand to roll the barrels to the planes. The tanks of each one had then to be filled painstakingly by hand-pump.

During the night water waggons sprayed the airfields in a vain attempt to lay the dust. The wind direction changed to 180 degrees, and in the darkness the aircraft had to be regrouped at the opposite ends. Finally, at 04.30, the first heavily laden machines rolled over the sand and disappeared into the darkness. With the airfields choking in dust, it took over an hour for the *Gruppen* to assemble overhead and fly off southwards.

The first attacking wave—1 Battalion of the Assault Regiment—was carried in 53 gliders, as at Eben Emael and the Albert Canal. All the rest, some 5,000 men, had to jump—from 400 feet—right amongst the alerted enemy. They could expect no reinforcements until the afternoon. As for the plane crews, they would not know till they got back whether they would find enough fuel at their airfields to transport the second wave.

May 20 1941, 07.05 hours. The bombardment had been in progress for an hour. Squadron after squadron of the Luftwaffe had been going down on a single point of western Crete: the village of Malemes, with its small coastal airfield and Hill 107, which commanded the approaches.

First it was bombers: Do 17s of KG 2 and He 111s of II/KG 26. *Stukas* of StG 2 followed with howling dive-bomber attacks. Then fighters of JG 77 and ZG 26 came streaking low over the hills and down along the beach, shooting up the known anti-aircraft and infantry positions.

The men entrenched against them were New Zealanders of 5 Brigade's 22nd

Battalion, with other battalions close behind the village—altogether 11,859 men under Brigadier Puttick. They knew just what their enemy was up to. An airborne landing had been expected, with Malemes as one of the three target areas. Never before had British Intelligence been so well informed about a German military plan. Surprise was out of the question.

As the air bombardment ended there was a sudden silence, broken only by

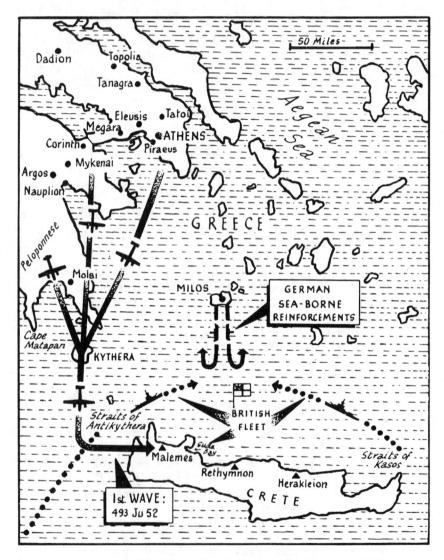

The assault on Crete, as at 07.15 hours on May 20, 1941. The first wave of 493 transport planes is shown reaching Crete from the west, after taking off from sand-and-dust airfields in Greece. At night the sea to the north of the island was controlled by units of the British Mediterranean Fleet, which prevented German sea-borne reinforcements getting through. The fate of the enterprise was thus wholly dependent on the establishment of an air-lift, itself only possible if the German parachutists succeeded in gaining possession of one of the island's three airfields: Malemes, Rethymnon or Herakleion.

a relatively peaceful sound of soughing and crackling, like trees being felled. Great fat birds dropped from the sky, gliding in almost noiselessly, then splintering on hitting the ground. They came dipping into the Tavronitis valley behind Hill 107. One banked steeply down, nearly hit an enemy position, struck the ground with a crack, bounced and went jolting over the rocky terrain. The ten men inside were thrown forward by the impact. Then, after a final thud that tore open the side of the fuselage, the glider lay still in a cloud of dust, and the occupants rushed for cover to a near-by patch of stunted bush.

That was how, at 07.15, Major Walter Koch landed beside Hill 107 with the battalion staff of 1 Airborne Assault Regiment. Other gliders sailed over their heads, most of them too high. Since unhitching over the sea seven minutes earlier, their pilots had been obliged to steer into the rising sun. Wrapped in early mist, the island dissolved before their eyes and visibility was impaired still more by the smoke of the immediately preceding bombardment. Suddenly they saw Malemes airfield already below them, with their objective, the dry river bed, just beyond. They were 300 or even 600 feet too high, and had to drop steeply down, banking to avoid being carried too far south. Some turned earlier, some later, with the result that they landed far apart instead of together, and many were dashed to pieces on the rocky ground.

Major Koch looked around him in surprise. The terrain was far more hilly than he had supposed—a feature indeterminable from the aerial photographs. The gliders vanished over the summits and landed in a whole series of depressions. Individual sections of troops were thus out of visual touch with each other. To present an effective fighting force they had to unite, but were held down by the enemy's well-directed fire. Each section was thrown on its own resources.

Nevertheless a handful of men, with the battalion staff, stormed the New Zealanders' tented camp on either side of Hill 107. It was studded with bomb craters made by the *Stukas*. According to the German operations plan the enemy was to be "surprised in his tents and prevented from interfering with the airborne landing". But there was no surprise: the camp had been evacuated. They moved on to the Hill, the ultimate target. From there the Germans, instead of the New Zealanders, would command the airfield.

Seconds later they were met by a concentration of fire from close at hand. Major Koch was shot in the head. Officers and men fell, killed or badly wounded. The survivors clawed into the ground, unable to advance another step. The whole terrace-like slope was sown with well-camouflaged defence posts, not a hint of which had been revealed by air reconnaissance.

The Assault Regiment's 3 Company was more successful. Its gliders landed right on the stony, dried-up river bed, and within seconds the anti-aircraft positions on either side of its mouth were under fire from many directions. The company commander, First-Lieutenant von Plessen, stormed the western position with one party, while another went for the guns to the east. The surviving New Zealanders put up their hands.

Immediately afterwards dozens of Ju 52 transporters came droning over the coast. At hardly 400 feet, and with engines throttled back, they were as easy to hit as hay-stacks. But the guns were silent, and after the air crews had returned to their Greek bases there was rejoicing at the small losses the first invasion wave had suffered. They owed a debt to the assault units, who had captured the guns so swiftly.

Meanwhile 3 Company had proceeded to the airfield itself. Here the enemy again put up stiff resistance, and the Germans were forced to take cover. Von Plessen tried to make contact with Major Koch, but was halted by a burst of machine-gun fire.

But all the time paratroops were dropping from the transport machines. In a few minutes hundreds of them had reached the ground to the west and east of Malemes. They comprised the rest of Major-General Meindl's Assault Regiment, whose 3 and 4 Companies had landed fifteen minutes ahead in the gliders. Their objective was the airfield, for until one of Crete's three airfields was in German hands, the transports would be unable to land reinforcements—reinforcements that the paratroops would be urgently needing at latest by the second day of the battle.

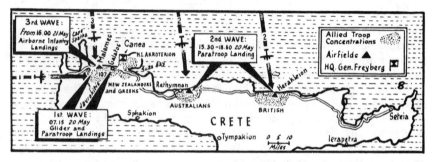

The blood-bath of Crete. Troop-carrying gliders and parachutists forming the first and second assault waves had to land amongst opponents who were forewarned and ready, and the losses were heavy. The decisive battle took place on Hill 107. During the afternoon of the second day transport planes bringing mountain infantry succeeded for the first time in landing on Malemes airfield in the teeth of enemy artillery fire.

All this was known to the defenders. Major-General Sir Bernard Frey-berg, New Zealand's gallant veteran soldier, who since the withdrawal from Greece had been the Allied commander in Crete, had a force of some 42,000 men—British, Greeks, Australians and New Zealanders—for the most part in the fortified hill positions adjoining the airfields of Malemes, Rethymnon and Herakleion. At Malemes, especially, the New Zealanders had been practising defence against airborne landings for weeks. For since the paratroop *coup* at Corinth on April 26th, and the feverish preparations on the Greek airfields—reported in detail to British Intelligence—there was no longer any doubt at General Wavell's Headquarters at Cairo that Crete was the next target for German airborne attack.

Though the heavy bomber and dive-bomber raids of the last few days—and above all the bombardment that immediately preceeded the landings—had caused losses and pinned the defenders down, most of the positions had escaped simply because they remained quite undetected from the air. The strength of the New Zealanders was virtually unimpaired, as the German paratroops were to discover to their cost.

At 07.20 III Battalion, under Major Scherber, was dropped east of Malemes. From there, after assembling, they were to advance against the village and airfield. Their fifty-three transporters, however, steered somewhat further inland so that the men, whose point of landing was the beach, would not be blown out to sea on their parachutes. As a result their descent was made over hilly terrain, supposedly free of the enemy. But it turned out that these hills too were dotted with gun-posts.

The consequences were frightful. Many of the parachutists were mortally hit while still swinging helplessly in the air. Others were left hanging in trees or were injured on striking rocks. The survivors, pinned down by the furious curtain of fire, were unable to reach their weapon containers, parachuted separately. Most of these fell into enemy hands.

Within an hour all III Battalion's officers were either dead or badly wounded. Only individual sections, led mainly by N.C.O.s, managed to hold out in favourable terrain. The whole day long they crouched in scorching heat, wearing the same heavy battle-dress they had used amongst the snow and ice of Narvik. Without water, and with only a few rounds of ammunition apiece, they hung on, hopefully awaiting the night.

When it came, the residue of 9 Company fought their way westwards right through the enemy lines till they reached the Tavronitis valley. Other groups held out for two and three days, until at last they were relieved.

"The bulk of III Battalion," read the Assault Regiment's operations report, "was wiped out after brave resistance. Out of 600 paratroops nearly 400, including their commander, Major Scherber, were killed."

The envelopment of Malemes from the east had failed. Its vital airfield could now only be taken by an attack from the west. There, west of the Tavronitis, II and IV Battalions were dropped, together with the regimental staff. They had more luck, because here the enemy's prepared positions were not occupied. Perhaps the unexpected arrival of the gliders had discouraged the New Zealanders from doing so.

At 07.30 hours nine further gliders sailed down to the bed of the valley and landed close to the only bridge by which the east-west coast road spanned the Tavronitis. Although most of them cracked up on impact, their occupants leapt out and rushed the bridge. Machine-guns hammered forth from the adjacent slopes and the detachment's leader, Major Braun, fell dead. But others reached their objective, and tearing out the demolition charges, secured the crossing.

From now on Major-General Meindl was in a position to direct his forces as they closed up from the west. Captain Walter Gericke, with a hastily gathered task force, advanced against the airfield. But under the searing machine-gun fire from Hill 107, progress was only possible in short rushes.

Somewhere on the slopes of the Hill Major Koch's force, which had landed first by glider, must lie entrenched. But where? To make contact General Meindl raised himself from cover and held aloft a signal flag. He hoped for an answer from the tented camp, where he supposed Koch to be. But it was the enemy that answered: Meindl's hand was hit by a New Zealand sharpshooter, and immediately afterwards he collapsed wounded from a burst of machine-gun fire. Nevertheless, he still kept command, and while Gericke's force attacked the crucial airfield frontally, he instructed Major Stentzler, with elements of II Battalion, to do so from the south.

Yard by yard, and with heavy losses, the Germans won ground. But on the airfield's western boundary, with their target in full view, they could go no further. The enemy was too strong.

Apart from "Force West" at Malemes, the invasion's first wave early on May 20th also included "Force Centre", whose objective was the Cretan administrative capital, Canea. This was to be led by Lieutenant-General Wilhelm Süssmann, commander of 7 Air Division. But the general never arrived in Crete. Twenty minutes after taking off from Eleusis, near Athens, the five towed gliders containing the divisional staff were overtaken by a Heinkel 111. The bomber passed so close to the general's glider that the towing cable parted from the force of its slip-stream. The lightly-built craft, which since the Corinth operation had stood unprotected from the torrid heat, reared upwards and its over-strained wings came off. The fuselage spiralled down and crashed to pieces on the rocky island of Aegina, not far from Athens. So perished the divisional leader and several staff officers before the Cretan operation had even started.

As at Malemes, the first two companies to land at Canea did so by glider, with the mission of capturing the known anti-aircraft positions. But 2 Company, under Captain Gustav Altmann, was met by heavy fire of every calibre even on the approach to its objective, the peninsula of Akroterion. Three or four gliders crashed and the rest landed far apart. So dispersed, the company failed to carry out its mission.

Five other gliders carrying 1 Company, under First-Lieutenant Alfred Genz, reached the ground close to a battery south of Canea. After some bitter close combat the fifty paratroops overcame 180 British and rushed the guns. But they failed to take the Allied command radio station, only a few hundred yards farther on.

Yet another three gliders, under First-Lieutenant Rudolf Toschka, landed in the middle of Canea, and fought their way to the anti-aircraft position there. Then they went to ground, keeping in touch by means of a portable radio with Paratroop Regiment 3, dropped some two miles west of them, and hoping hourly for relief. In answer to their appeals the regiment's I Battalion, under Captain Friedrich-August von der Heydte, managed to get to within 1,000 yards of their surrounded colleagues, then had to withdraw in the face of overwhelming fire-power. From their commanding position at Galatos New Zealanders bloodily repulsed all German attacks directed towards the capital, and British tanks came up in support. Soon I Battalion was fighting for its life.

Major Derpa's II Battalion was likewise repulsed with heavy loss, while the companies of III Battalion under Major Heilmann were broken up almost to the point of extinction. The situation compelled the regimental commander, Colonel Richard Heidrich, to radio Genz's little force in Canea: "Try to get through to us under cover of darkness."

There was no longer any question of taking the capital or the neighbouring Suda Bay.

At Athens the staff of XI Air Corps waited in vain for information, and was quite ignorant about the failures both at Malemes and Canea. General Student could only suppose that "Operation Mercury" had fulfilled expectations. The sole reports to hand were those of the returning transport units,

and these sounded favourable: "Paratroops dropped according to plan."
Only seven of the 493 Ju 52s carrying the first wave of invasion troops had failed to return. Many of the rest, however, had been compelled to circle their home airfields for up to two hours before they could get down. They had to do so individually through the impenetrable clouds of dust, and the whole thing became a shambles. Planes repeatedly collided on the ground, blocking the way for others. The dust took a greater toll than all the anti-aircraft guns of Crete.

Corps HQ repeated the call-signs of the regiment in Crete again and again, without response. At noon, nevertheless, an airfield servicing team set off for Malemes, where Major Snowatzki was to take over the organisation. As his Ju 52 circled around, the major spotted a swastika flag on the western perimeter, marking the furthest advance of the German forces. He thought, however, that it indicated Malemes had been taken, and ordered his pilot to land. As the machine came in, it became the target for concentrated enemy fire. Its pilot immediately gave full throttle, veered off and managed to get clear. With his aircraft riddled by shots he then flew Snowatzki back to Athens, where for the first time General Student learnt something of the true situation.

At almost the same moment a feeble radio message came through from "Force Central" to the effect that the attack on Canea had been repulsed with heavy loss. But it was 16.15 before the regimental staff at Malemes reported. There the 200- and 80-watt transmitters, brought over by glider, had been destroyed by the crash landings in the Tavronitis river bed. Laboriously the signals officer, First-Lieutenant Göttsche, had created a new one out of undamaged parts.

XI Air Corps' satisfaction at being at last in radio contact with Malemes was soon dissipated by the news that it brought. The first message informed HQ that General Meindl was badly wounded, and the second one read: "Waves of enemy armour from Malemes attacking over airfield and river bed." It seemed the crisis had reached its height. But worse was to come.

According to the plan of operations Rethymnon and Herakleion were to be taken in the afternoon of May 20th by the second invasion wave consisting of Parachute Regiments 1 and 2 under Colonels Alfred Sturm and Bruno Brauer. But now Student delayed their start. After such unfavourable reports from the first wave in the west of the island, it seemed better to throw in reinforcements there. But it was too late. Such a sudden change of objective was bound to have catastrophic consequences.

At the Greek bases there was enough confusion already. The second wave was due to take off at 13.00, but most of the transport units were still not ready. The impenetrable dust, the searing heat, the manifold damage and the laborious refuelling from barrels, had all been very time-consuming. Colonel von Heyking, commander of the transport *Geschwader* at Topolia, saw disaster looming, and tried to get the start delayed by two hours. But he failed to get through: the telephone lines were out of order. The over-taxed staff at Corps HQ had the same idea, but was simply unable to pass the new take-off times to all the affected units.

So it happened that bombers, *Stukas* and long-range fighters set about the bombardment of Rethymnon and Herakleion at the original zero hour before many of the transport units had even taken off from their Greek airfields.

Moreover the latter failed to follow in ordered sequence. Squadrons and even sections flew singly, bringing in the paratroops piecemeal and without cohesion. The intention of dropping them *en masse* directly after the bombardment was thus thwarted.

"Once more we found ourselves flying south over the sea," reported Major Reinhard Wenning, commander of zbV *Gruppe* 105, one of the few transport units that had left at the original time. "According to plan we should have been meeting preceding planes as they returned. But there was no sign of them."

Reaching Herakleion, Wenning's transport *Gruppe* flew parallel with the coast, and the "dropping" officer put out his yellow flag, the signal to jump, and down went the paratroops. Wenning continued: "Our battalion was supposed to act as a reserve behind other units already dropped. But on the ground we could see no trace of these. All alone, our men encountered savage enemy fire."

Only on its return flight did his *Gruppe* meet other Ju 52 formations, and the last of them arrived no less than three-and-a-half hours after the first. The second "wave" had broken up into a series of ripples. As a result, the paratroops suffered heavy losses. Just west of Herakleion airfield British tanks advanced firing at the Germans as they floated down. Within twenty minutes three whole companies of II Battalion/FJR 1, under Captain Dunz, were wiped out. Neither Herakleion nor Retimo was captured, and their two airfields remained in British hands.

But though the Allied C.-in-C., General Freyberg, had some cause to rejoice, his report betrayed anxiety: "Today has been a hard one. We have been hard pressed. So far, I believe, we hold aerodromes at Rethymnon, Herakleion, and Malemes, and the two harbours. The margin by which we hold them is a bare one, and it would be wrong of me to paint an optimistic picture. . . ."[1]

Freyberg's pessimism was soon to be justified.

In the evening the German paratroops, despite all their losses, won their first, and decisive, success. Two detachments of the Assault Regiment—one led by First-Lieutenant Horst Trebes, the other by the regimental physician, *Oberstabsartzt* Dr. Heinrich Neumann—resumed the assault on the dominant Hill 107 at Malemes, and fought their way with pistols and hand-grenades to its summit.

"Fortunately for us," Dr. Neumann reported, "the New Zealanders did not counter-attack. We were so short of ammunition that, had they done so, we should have had to fight them off with stones and sheath-knives."

General Freyberg in fact missed his chance that night of turning the tables at Malemes. Next morning it was too late, for by then VIII Air Corps' *Stukas* and fighters, in full command of the air over Crete, were pinning down the New Zealand troops in low-level attacks. The vital Hill 107 remained in German hands.

That morning, May 21st, a section of Ju 52s came in west of Malemes to make a landing. On board was "Special Detail Captain Kleye", with fresh ammunition for the Assault Regiment, whose original supply was fully spent. With the airfield swept by enemy artillery fire, the aircraft had to land on the beach. At the controls of the leading plane sat Sergeant Grünert. He looked down: the beach was studded with rocks. Then, spotting a gap,

[1] W. S. Churchill, *The Second World War* (Cassell, 1948–52), Vol. III, p. 229.

68. Lieutenant-General Kurt Student, commander of XI Air Corps (parachute).

69. Among the paratroops dropped over Crete was the former world boxing title-holder Max Schmeling.

70. A photograph of Maleme airfield taken during the airborne landing under enemy fire.

71. Maloi airfield in the Peloponnese, showing *Stukas* being prepared for an attack on the British Fleet off Crete.

72. The British cruiser *Gloucester* under air bombardment. Soon afterwards she was hit, and sank in the afternoon of May 22, 1941.

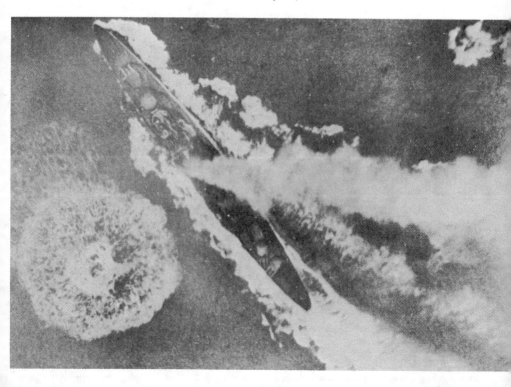

he dropped his plane into it, put down hard, and with the sand helping to brake, came to rest just short of the rocks. The ammunition, without which the assault on Malemes was doomed to failure, had been saved.

General Student was now resolved to pit all remaining reinforcements against Malemes. This same day the landing of the Mountain Division must begin—cost what it might.

At about 16.00 the first transport squadrons started to land under fire on the narrow runway. Shells from the enemy artillery burst amongst the aircraft. One Ju 52 immediately went up in flames, others sagged with broken undercarriages. But more and more came swooping down, landed, and discharged their troops. By the evening Buchholz's transport *Geschwader* had brought in the whole of Mountain Regiment 100, under Colonel Utz— shells providing their baptism of fire even as they landed.

"Malemes was like the gate of hell," reported the divisional commander, Lieutenant-General Ringel. Of every three transporters the enemy succeeded in hitting one, either setting it on fire, or shearing off a wing. Major Snowatzki had the wrecks cleared from the single runway by means of a captured British tank. Soon the sides of the airfield had become a giant aircraft cemetery, containing the remains of eighty Ju 52s.

What had once been considered impossible had come to pass; the airborne landings had turned the scale. Crete was not yet conquered, but the dice were now loaded in favour of the Germans.

2. Dive-Bombers versus the British Fleet

The sun rose blood-red over the Aegean Sea, and May 22nd promised to be hot. On the Peloponnesian airfields of Argos, Mycenae and Molae hundreds of engines roared into life as Ju 87s, Me 109s and Me 110s lined up for the take-off. Seldom had German airmen waited to do so with such impatience.

The war diary of Richthofen's VIII Air Corps explains the tension: "Since 05.00 hours today reports have multiplied of British cruisers and destroyers in the sea areas north and west of Crete."

On the previous day German reconnaissance aircraft had kept the movements of the British Mediterranean fleet under observation, and established that Admiral Sir Andrew Cunningham's force was cruising out of sight to the west of Crete. In view of German air superiority, he could not risk participating in the island struggle with his naval guns. As for the German bomber units, their support of the hard-pressed paratroops was for the moment the more important task. Only single *Stuka Gruppen* attacked the fleet, sinking one destroyer.

But during the night of May 21st/22nd the whole situation changed. Admiral Cunningham now sent two powerful battle groups, each of seven cruisers and destroyers, to take up positions off the north coast of the island. Lying in wait there, they thwarted every German attempt to bring in heavy weapons by sea (see map on page 188).

On one matter the British and German supreme commands were in agreement: both rejected the idea that the strongly defended island bastion could be taken by airborne troops alone. If the paratroops, etc., were not to find themselves in a hopeless situation, they must be reinforced from the sea by the second, or at latest the third day of the campaign. But the German transport fleet consisted only of small coasters and powered sailing-ships or caiques—all that was available in the Greek harbours.

On the night of the 21st/22nd the 1st Caique Squadron under Naval Lieutenant Oesterlin neared its destination, a landing-place west of Malemes. It had in fact started the previous day, only to be recalled half-way, then finally sent out again. This coming and going took the twenty-odd heavily laden little ships six hours to accomplish—a delay that was to cost them dear. For now they were delivered straight into the hands of the British.

Just before midnight the British cruisers and destroyers all at once opened fire. Two of the caiques immediately burst into flames, and a small steamer, carrying ammunition for the paratroops, blew up with a blinding flash. The rest sought safety in flight.

The one-sided battle lasted two-and-a-half hours. Rear-Admiral Glennie then broke off the pursuit and led his "Force D" south-west through the Straits of Antikythera. His flagship *Dido*, and the other two cruisers, *Orion* and *Ajax*, had spent a good two-thirds of their flak ammunition, and Glennie reckoned that he was in no position to withstand the *Stuka* attack that was sure to come early in the morning. In any case the German transport fleet seemed to have been completely annihilated. The British estimated that some 4,000 German soldiers had gone down with their ships.

But at first light ten scattered caiques found themselves once more off the island of Melos. The rest had been sunk, and all over the sea shipwrecked soldiers were clinging to pieces of flotsam. After a rescue operation that lasted the whole day, only 297 men were finally missing. But the British fleet had achieved its objective of preventing sea-borne reinforcements reaching Crete.

Such was the position early on May 22nd, when the Luftwaffe was again able to join battle. Lieutenant-Colonel Dinort, commander of the "Immelmann" *Geschwader*, StG 2, briefed his crews from his field caravan at Molai airfield. Reconnaissance patrols, he said, had reported ship after ship. They could not fail to find the British fleet.

At 05.30 Hitschold's and Sigel's *Gruppen* took off, formed up over the airfield and headed south-east. By this time "Force D" had departed, and been replaced by the cruisers *Gloucester* and *Fiji* and the destroyers *Greyhound* and *Griffin*, which lay twenty-five miles off the Cretan north coast. They were the first ships to feel the impact of the *Stukas*.

From 12,000 feet the Ju 87s dived down into the concentrated naval ack-ack fire. Using full speed and maximum rudder, the warships zig-zagged violently to avoid the bombs. All about them the sea boiled with mast-high columns of water. Often the bursts were so near that the cruisers steamed right beneath the cascades.

Light 100-lb. bombs struck the superstructure of the *Gloucester*, but though the fragmentation was considerable, they failed to penetrate. The *Fiji* was also only slightly damaged. All the heavy bombs missed their targets, if often by only a few yards. After an attack lasting one-and-a-half hours the *Stukas* were compelled to return to base to re-fuel and bomb-up again.

The British used the breathing space to join up with their main fleet, cruising some thirty miles west of Crete. Altogether the combined "Forces

A, B and D" represented an imposing array of two battleships (*Warspite* and *Valiant*), five cruisers and a dozen destroyers. Its commander, Rear-Admiral Rawlings, reckoned that the anti-aircraft guns of nineteen warships would be enough to scare the *Stukas* away, or at least to prevent any accuracy of aim. But the Luftwaffe was aware that, apart from the main fleet, there was another British flotilla considerably nearer: "Force C", under Rear-Admiral King. As ordered, its four cruisers and three destroyers had from first light on May 22nd been cruising to the north of Crete. Such a daylight penetration of the lion's den suited the Luftwaffe.

Twenty-five miles south of Melos Rear-Admiral King's force encountered the second German caique squadron, which had sailed at dawn for Crete. The latter was compelled to turn back, and a second massacre was only avoided by a hair's breadth. At literally the last minute rescue came from the skies in the shape of a *Gruppe* of Ju 88s.

Captain Cuno Hoffmann and his I/LG 1 had taken off from Eleusis near Athens at 08.30, and a few minutes later they were presented with a fascinating picture. Lieutenant Gerd Stamp, one of the Ju 88 pilots, saw far below him the German "midget fleet" sailing off northwards, with the British cruisers and destroyers steaming after them only a few miles away to the south.

Between the latter and their apparently certain prey, however, an Italian torpedo-boat, the *Sagittario*, had placed itself. Zig-zagging at full speed, the little vessel was laying a smoke-screen to hide its charges, meanwhile drawing the fire of the cruisers *Perth* and *Naiad*. It was high time for I/LG 1 to intervene! Captain Hoffmann gave the order, and the first Ju 88s dived obliquely into the inferno of flak. Their bombs produced two water-spouts beside the *Naiad's* gunwales, and the cruiser stopped.

Though the German convoy lay close ahead, the British admiral, fearing to risk his own ships by any further move to the north, decided to turn back. But the Luftwaffe would not let him alone. As the flotilla sped south-west, bombs rained down upon it for three-and-a-half hours, I/LG 1's Ju 88s and KG 2's Do 17s taking turns to attack. Effective near-misses put two of the *Naiad's* gun turrets out of action and tore her side open, water flooding several compartments. But the bulkheads held, and the *Naiad* steamed on at half speed.

A direct hit on the bridge structure of the ack-ack cruiser *Carlisle* killed Captain Hampton, but the vessel continued on her course, and the cruisers *Calcutta* and *Perth* successfully evaded every bomb the Germans dropped. Meanwhile Rear-Admiral King grew anxious at the expenditure of anti-aircraft ammunition, much of which had been used up during the four-hour attack of the previous day, when the destroyer *Juno* had sunk two minutes after a direct hit from a heavy bomb. Though Admiral Cunningham sent him a radio signal to stick things out on behalf of the army in Crete, he felt himself in no position to turn round and re-enter the lion's den. In fact he had himself to ask for succour, signalling Rear-Admiral Rawlings to bring the main fleet to rendezvous with him in the Straits of Antikythera to help protect his crippled cruisers.

Soon after noon the two groups made visual contact. Ten minutes later the battleship *Warspite*, Rawlings' flagship, received a direct hit, and was further damaged by a flight of Me 109 fighter-bombers of III/JG 77 under First-Lieutenant Wolf-Dietrich Huy. These attacked from directly ahead, and wrecked the warship's starboard 4-inch and 6-inch batteries. All the same, the fleet came off relatively lightly, even if the supply of anti-aircraft ammunition became hourly more critical.

The Luftwaffe, however, had not finished. VIII Air Corps' war diary records: "The *Stukas* had meanwhile been brought to readiness again for an attack on the enemy fleet in the Straits of Antikythera. Aided by Me 109s with bombs or without, by Me 110s and bombers, they were to pursue a ceaseless attack."

On May 22nd Richthofen had at his disposal the following units:

KG 2, with three *Gruppen* of Do 17s under Colonel Rieckhoff, based at Tatoi. Two Ju 88 *Gruppen* (I and II/LG 1 under Captains Hoffmann and Kollewe), plus one *Gruppe* of He 111s (II/KG 26)—based at Eleusis. Dinort's StG 2, with two *Gruppen* of Ju 87s at Mycene and Molai, and the third under Captain Brücker on the island of Scarpathos, between Crete and Rhodes. ZG 26, with two *Gruppen* of Me 110s under Captain von Rettberg at Argos. JG 77, with three *Gruppen* of Me 109s under Major Woldenga (including I/LG 2 under Captain Ihlefeld), also based at Molai in the Peloponnesus.

While the air-sea battle of May 22nd was at its height, few of these units were launched as such. As soon as their aircraft had landed to refuel and bomb-up, they took off again in pairs or sections to resume the assault. It remained to be seen whether a powerful naval force, without fighter escort, could assert itself against an opponent who ruled the skies.

Towards 13.00 hours—half an hour after the *Warspite* had been hit—the destroyer *Greyhound* was sent to the bottom by two *Stuka* bombs. She owed her doom to having been despatched alone to sink one of the caiques that had been sighted off the island of Antikythera.

As a result, Rear-Admiral King ordered the destroyers *Kandahar* and *Kingston* to the spot to pick up survivors, with the cruisers *Gloucester* and *Fiji* as anti-aircraft cover. Both of them had been in the thick of things since dawn, and had now virtually no ammunition left. On learning of this, the admiral recalled them. But by then it was too late.

Snatching their chance, a number of Ju 87 and Ju 88 sections bore down upon the isolated cruisers, and the *Gloucester* was immediately hit. Fires broke out between the funnels and spread rapidly to the whole deck. Unable to proceed, and belching smoke, the cruiser circled slowly around till at 16.00 hours an internal explosion finally sank her.

Again Rear-Admiral King faced a difficult decision, and in the end he left the *Gloucester's* crew to their fate. The report of the engagement stated that to have despatched the battle fleet in support of the *Gloucester* would simply have meant hazarding more ships. Before the next day dawned the Germans saved more than 500 British sailors, partly by means of air-sea rescue aircraft.

As a second potential target the *Fiji*, with her destroyers, was forced to make a getaway. Proceeding on an individual course to Alexandria, she never joined the main fleet again. For suddenly, at 17.45 hours, she was spotted by a single Me 109 of I/LG 2, carrying a single 500-lb bomb. The pilot, with his plane at the limit of its endurance, was about to return to base when he sighted the cruiser through a thin veil of cloud.

Twenty times this day the *Fiji* had withstood all the attacks of bombers and dive-bombers, and now she met her fate at the hands of a lone fighter-bomber. Like lightning it came down and planted its bomb close up against the ship. The bomb exploded like a mine under water and tore the ship's side out. At once the vessel hove to with a heavy list. The Me 109 pilot summoned a colleague by radio, and when the second attack took place half an hour later, the cruiser could defend herself with only feeble fire. This time the bomb scored a direct hit in the forward boiler room—the *coup de grace*. At 19.15 the *Fiji* capsized.

At dusk five modern destroyers began a fresh patrol of Crete's north coast. The British C.-in-C. had ordered them out of Malta in support. The *Kelly* and *Kashmir* shelled Malemes airfield and set fire to two caiques. But at dawn next day the Luftwaffe made a final effort. The two destroyers were harried by twenty-four Ju 87s of I/StG 2 under Captain Hitschold, and both were sunk by direct hits.

At 07.00 on May 23rd the battered Mediterranean Fleet returned to Alexandria. The first air-sea battle of Crete was over.

"The result," wrote Richthofen in his diary, "was abundantly clear. I was convinced we had scored a great and decisive victory. Six cruisers and three destroyers had certainly been sunk, with many additional hits even on the battleships. We had at last demonstrated that a fleet at sea within range of the Luftwaffe was vulnerable—provided the weather permitted flying."

The actual losses suffered by the Mediterranean Fleet between May 21st and dawn on the 23rd were two cruisers and four destroyers sunk, plus two battleships and three other cruisers damaged—not counting the scars caused by numerous near-misses.[1] Admiral Cunningham signalled London. He was afraid, he said, that in the coastal area they had to admit defeat and accept the fact that losses were too great to justify them in trying to prevent seaborne attacks on Crete.

Nevertheless the Chiefs of Staff in London required the fleet to risk everything, even by daylight, to prevent seaborne reinforcements and supplies reaching Crete. But Cunningham stuck to his guns: he could not, he said, retain sea control in the Eastern Mediterranean if the blows his fleet had received were repeated. He added that their light craft, officers, men, and machinery alike were nearing exhaustion.

Meanwhile the Ju 52 transport formations of XI Air Corps had succeeded in ferrying to Crete the augmented 5 Mountain Division under Lieutenant-General Ringel. British troop reinforcements, brought by warships and transports in darkness, encountered heavy air attacks at Suda Bay and in the Canea area.

On May 27th the German Navy for the first time succeeded in landing a couple of tanks on the island, after towing them adventurously across the Aegean in an open barge. About the same time General Freyberg reported: "The limit of endurance has been reached by the troops under my command here at Suda Bay. . . . Our position here is hopeless." His force could no longer stand up against "the concentrated bombing that we have been faced with during the last seven days".[2]

Though Churchill telegraphed once more: "Victory in Crete essential at this turning-point in the war," General Wavell answered the same day, May 27th:

---

[1] Warship casualties during the Cretan battle are detailed in Appendix 7.
[2] W. S. Churchill, *The Second World War*, Vol. III, pp. 235–6.

"Fear we must recognise that Crete is no longer tenable. . . ."

During the following night the evacuation of the British troops began. It was completed by June 1st.

So it was that victory in Crete was won by the German paratroops, together with the air-lifted Mountain Division, and supported by the ceaseless onslaught of VIII Air Corps' bombers and fighters. The ten-day struggle had cost the Germans dear, the paratroops alone losing 5,140 dead, wounded and missing out of a force of some 13,000 men.

The greatest loss had been incurred during the initial jump right amongst the alerted enemy, and the paratroops' victory was a Pyrrhic one. For the rest of the war they were virtually confined to a ground role.

During the evacuation of Crete the British Mediterranean Fleet was once more subjected to heavy air bombardment. The *Stukas* of StG 2 were now operating from Scarpanto, thus dominating the Straits of Kasos to the east of Crete. A number of cruisers and destroyers laden with troops were either sunk or severely damaged.

Already on May 26th Admiral Cunningham had suffered a new blow, when his only aircraft carrier, the *Formidable*, was subjected to heavy air attack. Late in the morning II/StG 2, which had been sent to support Rommel in North Africa, and while on the look-out for troop transports, happened upon the British battle fleet, hitherto completely unreported. The *Formidable* at once turned into the wind and sent off her fighters. But the *Stuka* commander, Major Walter Enneccerus, dived straight down to attack, followed by the squadrons of First-Lieutenants Jakob, Hamester and Eyer.

The aircraft carrier's flight deck was struck at the point of gun turret No. 10, and other bombs tore open her starboard side between bulkheads 17 and 24. She then limped back to Alexandria.

It was an echo of what had happened four and a half months previously, when the same *Stuka Gruppe* had handed out similar punishment to the *Formidable's* sister ship, the *Illustrious*, west of Malta.

II/StG 2 under Major Enneccerus, and I/StG 1 under Captain Werner Hozzel, had only just arrived at Trapani in Sicily on January 10, 1941, when they received information that a British supply convoy, with a large escort of warships, was headed westwards for Malta. Staking all, the *Stukas* swept down from 12,000 to 2,000 feet into the concentrated fire of the ships and planted six bombs on the *Illustrious*. Though she did not sink, she had afterwards to be repaired in the United States—a job requiring several months.

On the following day, January 11th, II/StG 2, guided by a "pathfinder" He 111, gave chase to the British fleet as it steamed back eastwards. At extreme range, nearly 300 miles east of Sicily, the *Stukas* attacked out of the sun and sank the cruiser *Southampton* with a direct hit in the engine-room.

This represented the first operation by X Air Corps, which in fulfilment of an agreement between Hitler and Mussolini had been posted to Sicily to bolster up the reeling Italian forces. Air General Hans Ferdinand Geisler and his staff accordingly took over the Hotel Domenico in Taormina. Their air force was given the following comprehensive duties:

Bar the narrows between Sicily and Tunis to British shipping. Mount an air offensive against Malta. Provide air support for the Italians in North

Africa, and subsequently secure the transport of the German *Afrika Korps* to Tripoli. Assault all reinforcements for Wavell's army going via the Suez Canal.

Though the last assignment seemed the most important—i.e., to hamper the British offensive in Cyrenaica—it was also the most difficult. As a base of operations against the Suez Canal the island of Rhodes was the obvious choice. Unfortunately, however, it was without stocks of fuel, and to supply it was a difficult problem. Benghazi had plenty, but within a few days it would be occupied by the British.

There, however, II/KG 26 under Major Bertram von Comiso was hastily sent from Sicily. Of its fourteen He 111s three were lost by a collision on landing, and a further three were billed for a reconnaissance role over the canal. Thus the *Gruppe's* effective strength was reduced to eight.

During the afternoon of January 17th the expected report arrived: a convoy stood off Suez, about to enter the canal from the south. Accordingly at half-hour intervals, and in darkness, the bombers took off on their mission. The two quartets of He 111s were briefed to scour the canal from opposite directions, one on the right bank, the other on the left.

From Benghazi to Suez is 700 miles, which meant that the target area was almost out of range. Only at the most economical cruising speed and airscrew trimming had the He 111s a hope of fulfilling their mission and returning to base. In view of these difficulties X Air Corps' chief of staff, Major Martin Harlinghausen, decided to lead the attack in person. Though the Corps meteorologist, Dr. Hermann, forecast an adverse wind of forty m.p.h. for the return flight, it was hoped to counter this handicap by flying at the most favourable altitude, 12,000 feet.

After a four-hour flight the He 111 carrying Major Harlinghausen, and piloted by Captain Robert Kowalewski, reached Suez and turned north. They flew along the canal, rounded Bitter Lake and continued. But not a ship did they find. The convoy seemed to have been swallowed up.

The other aircraft were sent against alternative targets, but Harlinghausen was loath to give up. On reaching Port Said, he considered returning, but instead turned and repeated the search, this time southwards. Again nothing was seen, and a stick of bombs was dropped on the Ismailia ferry. Once more they came to Bitter Lake, and suddenly there were the ships, widely dispersed and at anchor for the night.

The He 111 tried to bomb a steamship, but missed. The whole operation had failed.

The return flight straight across the desert was hair-raising. At 12,000 feet the Heinkel had unexpectedly to battle against a storm of at least 75 m.p.h. But on board the plane its strength was not realised, for it was now pitch dark, and there were no landmarks by which the ground speed could be measured. Harlinghausen calculated that they would be back in four and a half hours, but at the end of them there was no welcoming beacon. Five hours passed, then five and a half—still nothing. Finally, with his last drops of fuel, Kowalewski had to make a belly-landing in the desert. The ground was indeed so level that he could have landed normally on his undercarriage.

After a brief discussion the four airmen set fire to the wreck, and set off north-west on foot. Benghazi could not be far off, they thought. In fact, it was 175 miles.

Next morning the burning wreck was spotted, but the crew had disappeared. Only four days later were they found by a searching aircraft, which landed beside the exhausted men. Their rescuer was none other than First-Lieutenant Kaupisch, whose He 111 had been the only one to get safely back to Benghazi. Becoming aware of the high-altitude wind force, he had clung low down to the coast. All the others had made emergency landings in the desert, and three of the crews became British prisoners-of-war.

Mediterranean Theatre 1941—Summary and Conclusions

1. *With the failure of the Italian offensive against Greece, the British held a strong position in south-east Europe which implied a threat to the vital Rumanian oilfields and the southern flank of the German armies about to assault Russia. Though the Balkan campaign succeeded in averting the danger, it also delayed "Operation Barbarossa" for a whole, and perhaps decisive, month.*

2. *The conquest of Crete, envisaged as the "crowning glory" of the Balkan campaign, was only achieved at the cost of crippling losses amongst the paratroops dropped on the island. Although during the future course of the war this arm was augmented to several divisions, it was never used again for a major air-drop.*

3. *The greatest loss was incurred by the troops dropped right amongst the alerted enemy. On reaching the ground, they were mostly unable to reach their weapon containers, and were consequently wiped out. Greater success was achieved by the units which landed in territory uncontrolled by the enemy. These were able to unite and attack in force.*

4. *Air transport was greatly handicapped by the storms of dust stirred up on the Greek airfields. They prevented the second wave of paratroops being launched together as a combined force. H.Q. XI Air Corps remained in complete ignorance of the critical situation in which the first wave of paratroops found themselves till the afternoon of the day the operation started. A last-minute attempt to divert the second wave to reinforce the first wave's sector was doomed to failure.*

5. *Crete was only conquered because a final effort succeeded in capturing Malemes airfield. Though it was still under enemy fire, transports bringing troops of the Mountain Division managed to land on it during the afternoon of the second day. These vital reinforcements enabled the assault on the island to proceed.*

6. *The British Mediterranean Fleet's control of the sea and VIII Air Corps' supremacy in the air led to the first major air-sea conflict in war history. It lasted several days, and ended with a clear victory for the Luftwaffe. After suffering severe loss the British fleet was compelled to withdraw, and the fate of Crete was sealed.*

6

NIGHT DEFENCE OF THE REICH

1. The "Kammhuber Line"

With the opening of the German western offensive on May 10, 1940, British Bomber Command began its nocturnal air raids on German cities. They forced the Luftwaffe in all haste to look to the defence of the homeland —something that hitherto had been virtually neglected.

The operational baptism of the German night-fighter arm coincided with the Battle of Britain. With that in full swing, aircrew who became remustered to this new, purely defensive role, regarded their posting as a punishment. It passed their comprehension that with their country everywhere on the offensive and seemingly headed for victory, anyone should bother about an unrealistic matter of defence. Much later, when the British and then the American bomber streams became a flood, they understood.

The development of the German night-fighter arm was, and had to be, rapid. It had a long way to go from the first fumbling attempts to turn day-fighters into night-fighters. In turn searchlight belts gave way to the "Kammhuber Line" (as it was called by friend and foe), and radar-operated ground-control zones to unfettered night pursuit. From a couple of below-establishment *Gruppen* the force grew to six *Geschwader* numbering some 700 specially equipped aircraft, plus six searchlight regiments and a chain of about 1,500 radar stations stretching to Sicily and Africa. But there were many growing pains. . . .

The day of July 20, 1940, gave way to a clear moonlit night, with hardly a cloud in the sky. The countryside and towns of the lower Rhine, the Ruhr and Westphalia lay as if beneath a spotlight deliberately switched on to help the British bombers approaching from the west.

Such visibility should also, in theory, have helped the German night-fighters. But in fact, as usual, they saw nothing. It was the same old story which had been going on for weeks: the alert would be sounded, the fighters would take off towards the threatened area, then invariably fail to make contact with the enemy.

Towards midnight one more Me 110 of Germany's first night-fighter *Gruppe* took off from Gütersloh. Its pilot, First-Lieutenant Werner Streib, climbed swiftly to 12,000 feet and flew to the zone of operations. Once more the unnerving search began. Hour after hour Streib and his radio-operator, Corporal Lingen, stared into the night. Ignoring the icy blast that resulted, Streib opened the cockpit window to improve his vision. Both men waited, keyed up, for the moment that had hitherto always eluded them.

At this early stage night-fighter crews operated with no help from radar or ground control in making contact with the enemy. With the meagre vision of the human eye it was pure luck if a bomber were spotted at all, and unless the fighter reacted at once, the next second the enemy would be lost again in the darkness. The technique of night interception was still in its infancy, and many viewed it as a still-born child. With such a slender chance of success most pilots would have preferred to remain day-fighters.

But at 02.00 on July 20, 1940, Streib was given his chance. About 300 yards in front and to starboard, and somewhat lower, he suddenly saw the shadowy outline of another aircraft. Straining his eyes, Lingen then saw it too, but burst out: "It's one of our 110s!"

That made Streib doubtful too. To make sure, he crept nearer, remembering that the night-fighters' one interception so far had resulted in the destruction of one Me 110 by another. The tragic death of their comrades had embittered the crews still more.

As the pursuing plane drew nearer, it was seen that the other had two engines, and its silhouette bore a marked resemblance to that of an Me 110. Telling himself to keep calm, Streib crept in close beside it, the other crew remaining in blissful ignorance. Finally they were flying almost wing-tip to wing-tip. Then, as a gun turret glinted in the moonlight and a six-foot R.A.F. roundel loomed up on the fuselage, there could be no doubt.

"I never saw any enemy plane so close and clear," reported Streib. "Not wishing to be shot point-blank by its rear gunner, I darted away in a ninety degree turn to starboard."

It was a Whitley, with twin tail-fins just like the Me 110's. Without letting his opponent for a second out of sight Streib turned tightly and came in again from beam astern, The British crew, who no doubt at first had likewise taken the Me 110 for one of their own planes, were now alerted. At 250 yards the rear gunner opened fire.

Waiting till he could aim in peace, Streib let off two short bursts of cannon and machine-gun fire then drew to the side to observe results.

"His starboard engine was burning mildly. Two dots detached themselves, and two parachutes opened out and disappeared into the night. The bomber turned on a reciprocal course and tried to get away, but the plume of smoke from its engine was still clearly visible even by night. I attacked again, aiming at the port engine and wing, without this time meeting counter-fire. Two more bursts and engine and wing immediately blazed up. Close behind, I turned sharply away. . . ."

For three minutes the Whitley held its course, slowly sinking. Then it suddenly turned over and dived to the ground, its end marked by a conflagration and the flashes of exploding bombs. On landing, Lingen told the details of the German night-fighter arm's first victory.

With that the hoodoo was overcome, together with the pilots' scepticism about whether the night interception of an enemy plane was possible. Only two days later Streib scored a second success, and was soon followed by First-Lieutenant Ehle and Sergeant Gildner—Streib and Ehle being squadron commanders in NJG 1's first *Gruppe* under Captain Radusch. The squadrons led a nomadic life, being sent from one station to another. No one took them very seriously. With virtually the entire Luftwaffe geared to offensive action, and victory almost in sight, their defensive ploy was regarded as a redundant fifth wheel of the war chariot. Usually called to the area where British bombs had fallen the night before, they set about their mission lacking experience, ground organisation and as yet any method of vectoring them on to the enemy.

Though the approach and direction of the raiders were detected and nightly reported by the flak observation centres, the actual target areas—usually one of the Ruhr cities—were taboo. Here reigned the flak, whose "magic fireworks" no one was prepared to sacrifice in favour of the doubtful protection of night-fighters. Undaunted, the airmen stuck to the bomber approach lines, and in August Streib raised his score to four. A third squadron was formed and its commander, First-Lieutenant Griese, achieved his first victory in September. Meanwhile the *Gruppe* had moved to Vechta in Oldenburg to be earlier on the job.

In the end the night-fighter team made a sufficient break-through to win general recognition. During the first night of October 1940 Streib managed to set three Wellington bombers on fire inside forty minutes, and two more were shot down by Griese and Sergeant Kollak. Unfortunately a Ju 88, which had strayed into the path of the returning bombers, was also sent to the ground in flames. Such errors of identification were only too frequent.

After this unprecedented success Streib was invested with the Knight's Cross, promoted to Captain and given the command of his pioneer *Gruppe*, I/NJG 1. Its hard-won victories at last drew the attention of the general staff to the need for technical support. It was high time, even though the nightly raids of the R.A.F. were so far but a foretaste of those that in the coming years were to set Germany aflame.

The charge that the Luftwaffe authorities had given no thought to the protection of their homeland by night is without foundation. For their very belief in the superiority of their own air force in daylight led them to conclude that the enemy's bombers would be compelled to operate in darkness.

The result was that even before war's outbreak the *Lehrgeschwader* at Greifswald had a Me 109 squadron practising night defence with the aid of searchlights. The idea was that an illuminated aircraft could be attacked, as in daylight, by visual means. Though good visibility and cloudless skies were the pre-requisite of success, the system was continued after the war started on the grounds that the British bombers also needed such conditions to find their targets.

In 1939 a number of pilots were selected from various *Geschwader* to form the first "night-fighter squadron", 10/JG 26, under First-Lieutenant Johannes Steinhoff and equipped with Me 109s. As already mentioned, this scored its first success in the Battle of Heligoland Bight when it shot down three Wellingtons—albeit in daylight.

In February 1940 a *Gruppe*—IV/JG 2 under Major Blumensaat—

comprising several such squadrons was formed at Jever. After many fruitless operations it scored its first and only success in the spring, when Flight-Sergeant Förster spotted and shot down a British bomber in full moonlight. The trouble was that the Me 109, designed for day-fighting, could not be flown blind,[1] and was therefore hardly suitable for night operations. Many were lost taking off or landing in the dark, and often the fighter was itself illuminated by searchlights and the pilot blinded for minutes on end.

The two-seater Me 110, on the other hand, presented many advantages. Above all, with a radio-operator to take over the navigation, it could be flown blind. The idea of using it as a night-fighter first came from Captain Wolfgang Falck, commander of I/ZG 1. In April 1940 this *Gruppe*, after taking part in the occupation of Denmark, was based at Aalborg, where it was nightly attacked by British bombers. Vexed at his inability to retaliate, Falck, noting that the raids were always shortly before daybreak, conceived the notion of pursuing the bombers on their homeward course.

From then onwards his best crews, trained in blind-flying, were put at nightly readiness: the C.O. himself, Streib, Ehle, Lutz, Victor Mölders (a brother of the famous ace) and Thier. To achieve his ends, Falck also sought the help of the "*Freya*" radar installation on the coast, under Signals Lieutenant Bode, to put his dawn fighters on the path of the withdrawing raiders. But though the "*Freya*" could report direction and distance, it could not give the altitude, and though a number of bombers were sighted, they invariably vanished into the dark sea-mist. They once opened fire on a Hampden, only to see it dissolve like a spectre in the half-light.

In May 1940 I/ZG I was brought to the western front, where its commander's report on his dawn enterprises determined its future role. On June 26th, a few days after the cease-fire in France, Falck was summoned to Wassenaar, near The Hague, where at a hotel occupied by General Christiansen he was introduced to the top brass of the Luftwaffe: Goering, Loerzer and many other general officers.

In a long monologue Goering described the night defence against British bomber raids as the Luftwaffe's "Achilles' heel". No doubt he had in mind his own prestige, having pledged himself to "eat his hat" if enemy bombers ever appeared over Berlin. Finally the supreme commander turned to the bewildered Captain Falck and with a grandiloquent air named him the commander of the first German night-fighter *Geschwader*.

Such dramatics, however, could not alone conjure up a virtually new weapon in the middle of a war. When, scarcely four weeks later, the first night-fighter division was brought into being, all that its new commander— Colonel Josef Kammhuber, just returned from a prisoner-of-war camp in France—at first had to rely on was Falck's *Geschwader*, itself greatly under-strength, with just two *Gruppen*: Captain Radusch's I/NJG 1, formed out of two squadrons of the former I/ZG 1, and Major Blumensaat's III/NJG 1, formed from IV/JG 2 and only just finished converting from Me 109s to Me 110s.

In addition three Ju 88 and Do 17 squadrons had been brought together to form a so-called "long-range" night-fighter *Gruppe* under Captain Heyse. Kammhuber, a great organiser—between 1956 and 1962 as its Inspector he

---

[1] i.e. flying without visual landmarks or horizon by which a pilot could establish his geographical position or the position of his aircraft relative to the ground.

shared in the creation of the new Luftwaffe of the German Federal Republic
—named this *Gruppe* I/NJG 2, hoping that a second *Geschwader* would one
day exist.[1] However, the problem of effecting interceptions, above all on a
dark night, remained to be solved.

Kammhuber, promoted on October 16, 1940, to Major-General, with the
title "General of Night-Fighters", planned two quite different roles for his force:

1. Defensive, in a restricted zone of the German western frontier.
2. Long-range "intruder" operations against the British bombers'
   home bases.

At first he devoted himself to the former. If his fighters could not find the
enemy, he argued, the latter had to be made visible—i.e., by means of searchlights, as for the flak. To prevent mutual interference, the fighter zone would
have to lie out of the flak zone, but both would use searchlights—hundreds
and thousands of them.

The first searchlight regiment to act in close co-operation with I/NJG 1's
night-fighters was that of First-Lieutenant Fichter. He set up his searchlights and sound-locators in an oblique line west of Münster, that being the
region over which the bombers usually approached. The British reaction
was to try to avoid the illuminated zone by by-passing it at both ends.
Kammhuber replied by extending his searchlights both north and south, till
soon the whole Ruhr was protected by a belt twenty to twenty-five miles in
length.

Individual fighters were allotted their own sectors within this belt, where
they patrolled, prior to the main searchlights being switched on, around a
single marker beam. As soon as a bomber was plotted, a few searchlights
at the western periphery would switch on and try to follow it. Usually,
however, the British, crossing the illuminated zone at full boost, would be
out of it and back in protective darkness before the fighters could get on their
tails. Even if a bomber, handed on from one searchlight to another, was
illuminated for minutes on end, the fighter had no easy task. For nearly
always the latter was on an opposite course, and had to turn to make an
approach from the rear. That meant dodging the searchlights to avoid being
illuminated, and consequently blinded, himself.

It was a matter of practice, and only experienced pilots scored. It is a
fact that two thirds of the night victories won in 1940/41 fell to the long-range
intruders over England. Many young pilots, depressed by their constant
failure, lost all confidence.

"I request to be re-mustered to day-fighting, *Herr Major*."

"Why?"

"I just can't see at night."

Falck, as *Kommodore* of NJG 1, had often heard the same story. But
today it was none other than First-Lieutenant Lent speaking; the same Lent
who a year ago with three victories had been the champion of Heligoland
Bight, and later survived his contribution to the capture of Fornebu in
Norway. But now?

"Have another go, Lent," said his commanding officer. "We'll talk about
it again in a month."

Lent went on trying, and suddenly his luck turned—till in the end, with 102

[1] The progressive build-up of the German night-fighter arm is detailed in Appendix 9.

night victories, he became second only to Major Schnaufer before being killed in an accident in October 1944.

By mid-1941 the increasing success of the night-fighter arm became public knowledge. At 02.40 on June 3rd, Sergeant Kalinowski and his radio-operator, Sergeant Zwickl, obtained the first victory over Berlin—a Short Stirling. And on the 28th First-Lieutenant Eckardt, adjutant of II/NJG 1, then at Stade, shot down four British bombers, one after the other, with the help of searchlights over Hamburg. For by the end of 1941 General Kamm-huber had extended his belt of searchlights from the North Sea coast right down to Metz in France, and was prepared to stretch it even further.

But the days of illuminated interceptions were numbered. In spring 1942 Hitler himself demolished the whole laboriously erected defence line with the order: "All searchlights, including those of the apprentice and experimental regiments, will forthwith be handed over to the Flak."

It meant that the Führer had yielded to the pressure of his Gauleiters, who had been clamouring for all searchlights to be positioned directly in their threatened cities, instead of acting as a defensive barrier on the western frontier of the Reich. With that the night-fighter arm had, it would appear, to start off again from "scratch".

In fact, the darkness of night had become less impenetrable than it was at the war's outset.

In early summer 1940 Udet, as chief of Luftwaffe supply, had already, at Berlin-Schönefeld, demonstrated a fighter-control unit improvised from two "*Würzburg* A" sets. The new "*Würzburg*" could accurately measure not only the direction and range but also the altitude of an aircraft. Now it plotted two aircraft, one flown by Udet as the "fighter", the other by Falck as the "bomber".

Down on the ground Certified Engineer Pederzani, who was in charge of the "*Würzburg's*" development, traced the data supplied by each set on a map, and radioed to Udet the interception course. The general carried out the directions, and did nothing else. Yet nearly every attempt ended in an interception.

"It works!" cried Udet happily, after he and Falck had landed. "You night-fighter boys have quite a future!"

From now on success or failure no longer depended solely on the airborne crew. It was shared by a new colleague, the ground control officer, who followed every movement of their plane on his screen. With his second "eye" he tracked the enemy bomber as it entered the fighter's zone. Luftwaffe men dubbed it the "*Himmelbett*" process—and the name stuck.

In summer 1941 General Kammhuber supplemented his searchlight belt with a whole string of "*Himmelbett*" zones, whose radius was adjusted to the range of the "*Würzburgs*". That of the early ones was about twenty-two miles, but in 1942 the "Giant *Würzburg*"—so called on account of its great twenty-three foot reflector—came into service, with a range of up to forty-five miles. A "*Himmelbett*" station comprised the following apparatus:

A "*Freya*" set, range up to 100 miles, to supply early warnings.
A "*Würzburg*" for plotting the bomber.
A "*Würzburg*" for guiding the fighter.

73. The He 219, though specially designed for night-fighting, only came into service late in the war. Most night-fighter units continued right up to the end to use the old Me 110, especially equipped for the purpose.

74. Another night-fighter, an Me 110 or NJG 1, with Flight-Sergeant Goldner and his radio operator.

75   76   77

Night-fighter personalities.   **75.** General Kammhuber, creator of the night-fighter arm.   **76.** Colonel Streib, commander of NJG 1.   **77.** Major Prince Sayn-Wittgenstein, killed after achieving eighty-three victories.   **78.** Lieutenant-Colonel Lent, top-scoring night-fighter pilot after Major Schnaufer.   **79.** First-Lieutenant Becker, exponent of night-fighter technique, at a briefing with Captain Ruppel at Leeuwarden.

78   79

A "*Seeburg*" evaluation table, with a glass plate on which green and red dots were projected to represent the respective courses of the two aircraft.

Despite this outlay of technical apparatus and personnel, only a single fighter could be controlled in one zone.

"Vector 260, bandits flying on reciprocal, angels twelve, range twenty miles," would be the R.A.F. equivalent of what First-Lieutenant Werner Schulze quietly said into the microphone.

He was the controller at station "Tiger", situated on the northern Dutch coast near Leeuwarden, and he was addressing First-Lieutenant Ludwig Becker, squadron commander of 6/NJG 2. The latter and his radio-operator, Sergeant Staub, were night-fighter veterans. As early as October 16th, 1940, when no one yet believed in the possibilities of ground control, and helped only by a "*Freya*" with "AN" direction-finding, they had located a bomber and scored the Luftwaffe's first victory in a dark sky.

"In thirty seconds *Rolf* 180," the controller's voice went on. It was code for a 180-degree turn to starboard, *Rolf* meaning right, *Lisa* left. "Now!"

The green and red dots on the glass slid closely past each other. Becker put his Ju 88 in a tight right-hand turn, thereby placing himself on the bomber's tail—if the data from the ground were accurate. His eyes tried to pierce the darkness. If only the machine had its own airborne radar set! Then, scarcely a hundred yards ahead, little exhaust flames betrayed the enemy's presence.

"Tally-ho!" called Becker on the radio. "I'm attacking." And seconds later his cannon and machine-guns hammered out.

2. Night Intruders over England

Gilze-Rijen, between Tilburg and Breda in Holland, was a hive of activity. Here I/NJG 2, Germany's only long-distance night-fighter *Gruppe*, commanded by Captain Hülshoff, was based. It was late in the evening of June 25, 1941 and half a dozen crews were preparing for action.

The unit's command post was in constant telephone contact with Captain Kuhlmann's radio-intercept service. This had specially trained operators listening in to the enemy bombers on sets adjusted to the same wave-lengths. Suddenly one of them came to life with a manifold whistling and chirping, indicating that the radio-operators of a bomber unit over in England had switched on their sets to check them. And that could only mean that their aircraft were about to take off. Kuhlmann promptly handed on the news to the night-fighters. His information read:

"About sixteen bombers will take off from Hemswell, and about twenty-four from Waddington."

Both these airfields belonged to No. 5 Group, under Air Vice-Marshal Harris. It was known that the aircraft operating from them were chiefly twin-engined Hampdens.

"About fourteen Wellingtons are about to leave Newmarket," Kuhlmann further reported. This formation belonged to No. 3 Group, under Air Vice-Marshal Baldwin.

Thus, even before the bombers started, the German night-fighters were aware of their preparations. Captain Hülshoff proceeded to keep his first wave of fighters, already airborne, informed about the situation on the enemy bases. It might be that they could reach the spot and cause havoc just as the bombers took off. A second wave would be sent to attack them over the North Sea on their usual line of approach.

The third wave, however, was despatched hours later in pursuit of the bombers as they returned, and once again to attack them as they landed, seemingly secure, at their own airfields. For the Germans that was the sting: they had mostly to operate in the lion's den, over England. Often they themselves were hunted down by British night-fighters that had been put on their trail.

None the less, Kammhuber hoped for decisive results. With the locations of the enemy bases known, it was just a question of getting his own fighters on the spot at the operative moment: either as the bombers took off, or better still when the airfield lighting had to be switched on to receive them back. As the Blenheims, Whitleys or Wellingtons queued up to land, the Do 17s and Ju 88s would join the circle.

First-Lieutenant Jung, squadron commander of 2/NJG 2, did it again and again. Turning in just after his opponent, he would shoot him down on his landing approach. And that was not all. Other fighters, manned by pilots like First-Lieutenant Semrau, Lieutenants Hahn, Böhme and Völker, and Flight-Sergeants Beier, Herrmann and Köster, dived upon the illuminated airfields showering 100-lb. fragmentation bombs amongst the taxiing bombers. Though the confusion caused was usually greater than the actual damage, the best aspect of the whole thing was that the British anti-aircraft guns were forced to remain silent for fear of hitting their own aircraft.

Captain Hülshoff had divided up British Bomber Command's territory into three zones of operations: East Anglia, Lincolnshire and Yorkshire. Soon his aircrews were familiar with every airfield of all three. Though the *Gruppe* seldom had more than twenty aircraft serviceable at one time, it was able to keep up a nightly visitation.

Amongst those who set off on the evening of June 25, 1941 was First-Lieutenant Paul Bohn of 2 Squadron. In the previous fortnight he had scored three victories over England, and as his Ju 88 headed north-west into the darkness he was full of confidence.

The night-fighter version of the Ju 88 differed from the bomber version in having a solid instead of a glazed nose, plus heavy forward fire-power consisting of three 20-mm cannon and three MG 17, situated in nose and ventral gondola. Instead of four, the crew numbered three: the pilot, flight-engineer and radio-operator, represented this evening by Bohn and N.C.O.s Walter Lindner and Hans Engmann.

After a bare hour's flight ground flashes showed the British anti-aircraft guns in action, and searchlights probed the sky. Neither worried the crew. On the contrary, by indicating that they were over the coast, they served as a welcome navigation landmark for calculating their onward course.

Presently, on course 320 degrees, Bohn suddenly saw a shadow only a few hundred yards distant on his port bow, approaching at unusual speed and crossing his line of flight. Within seconds he identified it as a Whitley, and turned in the same direction. The Whitley shot past, but thanks to his good night-vision Bohn managed to keep it in sight, slowly crept up behind it until he was within eighty yards, then fired his cannon and machine-guns. The shells glimmered along the fuselage as they struck and the Whitley at once caught fire. It was not mortally hit, however, and could still make an emergency landing, so Bohn repeated his attack from the other side, this time aiming at the starboard wing. Once again the shots went home.

At the same moment the cockpit of the Ju 88 splintered, hit by the quadruple machine-guns of the British rear-gunner, who had taken up the defence of his own aircraft seconds before its demise. For directly afterwards the starboard wing of the Whitley broke off, and it crashed to the ground like a glowing torch.

"Got him!" cried Engmann, the radio-operator, just before he himself was catapulted out of his seat and through the cockpit. For the Ju 88 too was now diving headlong to earth, its guns still firing futilely into the night.

First to come to his senses was Lindner, who at once grasped the mortal danger they were in. Bohn lay unconscious over the control column, his weight pushing it right forward. With a supreme effort, Lindner pulled the lifeless body to the side, seized the stick and carried out the movements which, from his seat beside him, he had so often watched the pilot make: the movements necessary to pull the machine out of a dive. Like a bucking horse the Ju 88 righted itself—in dense fog 3,000 feet above the sea.

"This recruit is incapable of independent initiative," had been the psychologist's report on Lindner, when he had applied to become a pilot. Now, by his prompt and effective action at a moment of great emergency, he not only belied the report but saved his own and Engmann's lives. But First-Lieutenant Bohn was beyond help: he had been killed by a hit in the head.

At 12,000 feet Engmann reported by radio what had happened. "We shall try to land at base," he added.

At Gilze-Rijen Captain Hülshoff ordered a vertical searchlight to be switched on as a beacon. Its beam, however, was hidden by banks of mist, and when Lindner tried to bring the plane down through them he lost his bearings. Three times he crossed what he thought was the Dutch coast, turned back and tried again. Meanwhile Engmann repeatedly called the ground station without getting any answer.

In the end the two N.C.O.s had no idea where they were, and their only resort was to bale out. However, it seemed somehow wrong to leave their dead squadron commander all alone in the doomed aircraft, so together they lowered him through the bottom hatch. Lindner pulled his rip-cord, and the mortal remains of "Sepp" Bohn went floating down through the night, to be found and buried by French farmers a few days later.

Lindner and Engmann successfully landed by parachute near Charleville, but their Ju 88 went on flying, with set controls, over half Europe. It even crossed the Alps and reached Northern Italy, where, at the end of its fuel, it finally crashed.

As the months went by the battle in the night skies over England became a harder one. Even so, intruder operations against the night-bomber bases seemed to provide the best, perhaps the only, method of inflicting any serious damage on R.A.F. Bomber Command.

"If I want to smoke out a wasps' nest," said Kammhuber, "I don't go for the individual insects buzzing about, but the entrance hole when they are all inside."

The general did everything he could to increase the striking power of his long-range weapon. After much pressing, Goering even promised on December 10, 1940, to enlarge it from a single *Gruppe* to three whole *Geschwader*, but his chief of staff, Jeschonnek, commented sarcastically: "At this rate the night-fighters will absorb the whole of the Luftwaffe."

And Jeschonnek stuck to his guns. Kammhuber was unable to get more than twenty to thirty first-line machines—which, with the British bomber menace constantly mounting, was hopelessly insufficient. The fact is that the Luftwaffe, planned since birth for offensive action, had hitherto never developed an aircraft suitable for night-fighting. It is therefore hardly surprising that in competition for a share of the Ju 88's production, the defensive version came off badly.

Worse, however, was to follow. On October 12, 1941, another night-fighter "ace", twenty-two-year-old Lieutenant Hans Hahn, failed to return from a night mission over England. And the very next day, when the spirits of I/NJG 2 were consequently low, General Kammhuber was obliged to inform its commander that intruder operations were forthwith to be abolished by direct order of the Führer. It was a matter of pure propaganda. The German people, so argued Hitler, wanted to see the "terror bombers" brought down beside their own shattered dwellings. Far-away victories over England did nothing to improve their morale. In any case the *Gruppe* was needed in the Mediterranean, and was to be posted to Sicily.

All objections failed to prevail. Far from Kammhuber being able to sharpen his promising weapon, it was struck right out of his hand. A study of the war-time German Luftwaffe includes the following paragraph: "Stepping up its night offensive against Germany forced the R.A.F. to adopt a technically complicated take-off and landing system that was highly vulnerable to intruder operations. The German Luftwaffe's failure to exploit this opportunity must be reckoned as one of its biggest mistakes."

The R.A.F. agrees. According to the official Air Ministry publication, *The Rise and Fall of the German Air Force*, the fact that from 1941 till 1945 the R.A.F. was able to operate undisturbed from its home bases contributed decisively to Germany's final downfall.

Kammhuber's only alternative was to direct his energies to an enlargement of the night-fighter zones along the western frontier of the Reich. For this Hitler himself, in a speech at Führer HQ on July 21, 1941, had given the green light. The night-fighter "division" was on August 1st elevated to the level of a "corps", with Kammhuber as G.O.C. holding special powers. Only in such a position was he able, in mid-hostilities, to forge a new instrument of war, with all the accompanying radio and radar techniques that enabled it to function.

He accordingly set up his headquarters at Zeist near Utrecht, right in the path of the British bombers' main approach lines. From here his "*Himmelbett*" zones stretched out over Holland to north and west, with one overlapping the next, and each with a control radius of some fifty miles. He also staggered them in depth to provide continuity of defence. But the big weakness remained: only one night-fighter could be operated at one time in one particular zone.

Fortunately, in the winter of 1941/42, the British bombers, not yet having mastered the technique of formation flying in darkness, still came in separately and wide apart, and the German night-fighters could cope. The control stations *Jaguar, Delphin, Löwe, Tiger, Salzhering* and *Eisbär* in the north, and *Zander, Seeadler, Gorilla, Biber, Rotkehlchen* and *Schmetterling* in the south, became household names in the Luftwaffe because of their mounting successes.

More often, however, the ground controller brought the two dots together on his radar screen without the pilot making visual contact. Sometimes the bomber's altitude was inaccurately given, sometimes the contacting distance was too great for the pilot's eyes to pierce the intervening darkness. Before the controller could effect a second interception the bomber had usually left the zone and was out of plotting range. Since the fighter could not be taken over by the adjacent zone, it then had to turn back empty-handed.

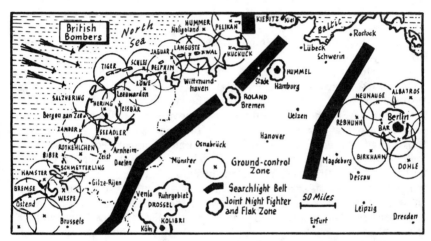

German air defence v. night bombers. The so-called "Kammhuber Line" embraced two different methods of defence: 1. A searchlight belt, approximately 35 km (22 miles) deep, for illuminated interceptions; 2. A closely integrated series of circular zones in which individual night-fighters were guided to their targets in darkness by ground controllers. Amongst the latter, *Tiger* station (on the Dutch island of Terschelling) alone participated in 150 victories.

This weakness could have been avoided by means of airborne radar to enable the fighter to bridge the last hundred or thousand yards of darkness, and on August 9, 1941, this was carried for the first time. The crew consisted of First-Lieutenant Ludwig Becker and Sergeant Josef Staub. Their Me 110 took off from Leeuwarden in Holland with a curious wire proboscis sticking out from its nose: the dipole aerial of the first German airborne radar apparatus, called "*Lichtenstein* B/C".

Becker's vision in the early days of night-fighting had been amongst the worst, but being young and ambitious he had stuck it out. His engineering studies at Technical High School had convinced him, early on, that the only prospect of lasting success for night-fighters lay in radar-directed control. As a "guinea pig" of Hermann Diehl, proponent of the "*Freya*", he had been the first to make a successful interception under such control—back in October 1940. So now he was the first to try out an aircraft equipped with its own "eyes".

The "*Lichtenstein*" apparatus, whose main feature was a cathode-ray tube such as is found today in every television set, was a new toy for the radio-operator. Sergeant Staub had practically worn it out by his efforts, when suddenly the path of an aircraft was illuminated on the screen—presumably that of the bomber towards which the Me 110 had just turned as directed by the controller, Lieutenant Jauck.

"Courier picked up by *Lichtenstein*, range 2,000 yards," Staub reported.

From now on the pilot had to rely entirely on his radio operator for information as to direction and range. It meant that the "romantic" age of flying was past: the crew had become a mutually-dependent team of instrument-watchers.

Suddenly the bomber became aware that it was being followed, and started twisting about. With the "*Lichtenstein*" antennae limited to a forward probing area of about twenty-five degrees, the result was that it twice vanished from the screen. Becker's reaction was to turn in the direction in which it had "disappeared", and both times he was lucky enough to get a new contact. Suddenly they were right behind it, and with a long burst of fire shot it down.

This victory on August 9th, 1941, finally proved that night-fighters could be scientific weapons, capable of tracking down their target themselves through that last wedge of night. But the fact of the matter was that the German radar development was sufficiently far advanced to have given them this crucial weapon a whole year sooner. As early as July 1939 the firm of Telefunken had produced such an instrument, and demonstrated it to the Luftwaffe's Technical Office in a Ju 52—only to have it promptly rejected. Without any contract the firm's engineers, on their own initiative, turned their little magic box into a radar-actuated altimeter—still without any interest being shown. Only in the spring of 1940, when the need for an airborne radar apparatus became apparent, were the old plans pulled from their pigeon hole. It was then only necessary to stand the idea on its head: instead of being directed downwards, the radar beam would look forwards. From then on everything went swimmingly—till the problem of the antennae arose.

"Because of the supposed wind resistance and loss of speed we didn't at first dare to construct a proper external antenna array," says Muth, the engineer in charge. To the Luftwaffe such a thing was anathema; so months went by in fruitless attempts to house the aerial in the cockpit, only to find that the beam developed was far too weak. The high-frequency expert Dr. Wilhelm Runge, one of Germany's radar pioneers, took Professor Willy Messerschmitt on one side:

"I ask you," he said, "surely the essentials of a night-fighter consist of an eye and a gun? If it can't see, it might just as well stay on the ground. *Ergo*, you must find a place for the eye!"

In the end, however, it was the mounting clamour of the night-fighters themselves that finally broke down the resistance. Exercising his Führer-endowed powers, Kammhuber categorically demanded that airborne radar sets be made available—with, of course, external antennae. A whole year had been wasted: his men could have had them in the autumn of 1940.

With the help of the "*Lichtensteins*" successful interceptions greatly increased. Top scorer for a long time was Captain Streib, Commander of I/NJG 1, now at Venlo. At Leeuwarden the palm was held by First-Lieutenant "Bubi" Lent—the same pilot who, despairing of his night vision, had asked to be remustered to day-fighting. Also in his squadron, 6/NJG 1, was Flight-

Sergeant Paul Gildner, who after twelve victories became the first N.C.O. to receive the Knight's Cross for night-fighting.

New names came into prominence. One was that of First-Lieutenant Egmont, Prince of Lippe-Weissenfeld, who started a night-fighter commando at Bergen aan Zee. By autumn 1941 he, Lieutenant Fellerer and N.C.O.s Rasper and Röll had brought down twenty-five British bombers. Once Lippe, during a risky training operation, managed to shear off one of his Me 110's wings, and with his radio-operator, Corporal Rennette, crashed far out at sea. After a lucky rescue, they received a teleprint from General Kammhuber: "Who gave you permission to go swimming?"

On November 1, 1941, Helmut Lent formed a new night-fighter *Gruppe*, II/NJG 2, in which First Lieutenant Schoenert—a former civil air captain and test pilot at the Weser factory in Bremen—Prince Lippe and Becker became his squadron commanders. As always, Becker remained the expert in technique. For hours each day he would instruct his junior crews in the modes of attack he had himself successfully used.

One of his methods was to approach from below and attack in a climb, so that the whole length of the bomber passed through the field of fire. Becker had brought this method to such a fine art that in his last thirty-two successful sorties he had not once been subjected to counter-fire. But from the one after that, with forty-four victories to his credit, he and Staub failed to return. This, however, was a daylight sortie: their first against American Flying Fortresses over Heligoland Bight.

Kammhuber meanwhile added link after link to his chain of defence. His ultimate objective was to man a front stretching from southern Norway to the Mediterranean, and cover the whole of Germany. As the organisation grew each zone contained more stations, each division more zones. Divisional operations rooms—at Döberitz near Berlin, Stade, Arheim-Deelen, Metz and Schleissheim near Munich—came to be housed in bomb-proof shelters, dubbed "martial opera houses" by Galland, and "Kammhuber's cinemas" by the troops.

Yet however far the net was extended, the same principle still obtained: that of a single night-fighter tied to the narrow confines of a particular zone. A system for continued pursuit beyond its boundaries did not exist.

So long as the bombers still came in individually, things went well enough. What, however, if they came in compact masses, crossing only a few of the "*Himmelbett*" zones?

The question had to await an answer. For while in the west the night-fighters went about their business of defending the Reich, and Kammhuber was still constructing his protective screen, all eyes became fastened on the east. There, at 03.15 on June 22nd, 1941 "Operation Barbarossa"—the offensive against Soviet Russia—had started on its fateful course.

Night Defence of the Reich—Summary and Conclusions

1. At the outset the British night-bombers and the German night-fighters, to carry out their conflicting missions, both required the same weather conditions: clear moonlight nights, with a minimum of cloud. To improve the optical vision of the night-fighter crews, searchlight belts were set up as a logical step. With the rapid development of radar, however, it was recognised that very soon both bombers and fighters would be able to find their targets in full darkness. Any jump ahead in the high-frequency field could be of decisive advantage to the side that made it.

2. Particularly promising in 1941 was the use of long-range fighters on "intruder" operations over the bombers' bases in England. The force available— a single Gruppe—*was however inadequate for the task. Its withdrawal to the Mediterranean theatre indicates how light-heartedly the German high command viewed the problems of home defence.*

3. The "Kammhuber Line", built up with such energy, proved that a system of night-fighters tied to individual zones could be successful so long as the enemy bombers came in singly on a broad front. The system, no matter how it was extended over the ground, could not however effectively counter the thousand-bomber raids which began at the end of May 1942.

7

OPERATION BARBAROSSA

1. Target: The Red Air Force

When, in autumn 1940, the Luftwaffe chiefs were told of Hitler's resolve to invade Russia, their reaction was one of pained surprise mingled with presentiment of disasters.

"Impossible!" said Air General Alfred Keller, scheduled to conduct the assault of *Luftflotte* 1 against Leningrad. "We've got a treaty with the Russians!"

"Don't worry your head about politics," Goering rejoined. "Leave that to the Führer."

In fact, Goering had himself tried several times to deflect Hitler from his purpose—in vain. The multi-front war that started with "Operation Barbarossa" was something with which the Luftwaffe, in the warning words of its Quartermaster-General, General von Seidel, could not possibly cope. Whatever triumphs might attend the Germans in their march eastwards, from June 22, 1941, onwards their military machine was ultimately doomed.

The altimeter of the He 111 wavered, then continued its ascent. As the machine climbed from 15,000 to 17,000 feet its crew donned their oxygen masks. And still the pilot held the control column pulled towards him. His orders were to cross the frontier at maximum height—the frontier of Soviet Russia.

Soon the hands of his watch pointed to 03.00 hours, and the date was Sunday June 22, 1941. Down below, the countryside seemed wrapped in slumber. It would not remain so for long. In just fifteen minutes it would awaken to an almighty crash of gunfire, indicating that Germany and Russia were at war—at 03.15, and not a second earlier. That was why the bombers, already on their way, flew at maximum height over a sparsely inhabited region of marsh and forest. No suspicion was to be aroused of the impending start of hostilities.

Only twenty to thirty crews had been picked for the difficult mission, from KGs 2, 3 and 53. All were experienced men, with many hours of blind-flying behind them. Arriving undetected at exactly 03.15, they were to "blitz" the fighter bases behind the Russian central front—just three bombers to an airfield.

As they approached their targets it was still dark, with the new day only starting to glimmer in the east. But down they swept, and screaming over the airfields scattered hundreds of small fragmentation bombs amongst the peacefully lined-up fighters and personnel tents.

Clearly no knock-out blow could be struck by such methods. The object was to spread confusion and delay the enemy's take-off long enough to bridge the period between the opening of the Army's onslaught and the earliest moment the Luftwaffe could strike in force.

The timing of the onslaught had been a subject of protracted and heated dispute between the general staffs of the two services. The Army wanted to invade at crack of dawn to achieve maximum tactical surprise, but at the same time wanted the Soviet air force to be stopped from intervening. That could only be achieved if it was first destroyed on the ground. Surprise, from all points of view, was the dominant factor.

Field-Marshal Kesselring, C.-in-C. of *Luftflotte* 2 based on the central sector of the eastern front, saw the problem as follows:

"My *Geschwader*, to get into formation and attack in force, need daylight. If the Army persists in marching in darkness, it will be a whole hour before we can be over the enemy's airfields, and by then the birds will have flown."

To which Field-Marshal Fedor von Bock, supreme commander of Army Group Centre, rejoined: "The enemy will be put on his guard the moment your aircraft are heard crossing the frontier. From then on the whole element of surprise will be lost."

A year before, at the opening of the western campaign, the Army had had to bow to the Luftwaffe's wishes. The glider operation against Eben Emael on the Albert Canal could only be launched at first light, and the ground troops had had to wait. But now too much was at stake. This time it was the Luftwaffe which had to be accommodating. II Air Corps' commander, General Bruno Loerzer, accordingly put in the compromise proposal of sending across just a few picked crews, at maximum altitude and so undetected, to be ready to attack at zero hour, 03.15.

In the event surprise was fully achieved. On the heels of the little advance guard the big formations were over the frontier at first light. Not a single enemy fighter was seen. The Soviet air force, numerically twice the size of the German one, remained seemingly paralysed on the ground.

It has since become known, from Soviet records, that at 01.30 hours Stalin endeavoured to warn his military authorities, and the commanders of the Red Army on the western front, that a German attack was imminent. The Moscow instructions read: "Before dawn on June 22nd all aircraft are to be dispersed on their airfields and carefully camouflaged. All units will come to immediate readiness. . . ."

But Stalin's directive was delayed somewhere along the Russian communication channels, and its receipt was overtaken by events. To most of the Russian flying regiments the German *coup* came like a nightmare bolt from the blue.

"It was early on Sunday morning, and many of the men were out on a leave pass," said Colonel Vanyushkin, commander of the 23rd Air Division, and later taken prisoner. "Our airfields lay far too close to the frontier, and their positions were perfectly well known to the Germans. Furthermore, many regiments were just re-equipping with new types of aircraft, even on operational airfields. With proverbial Russian negligence both old and new types stood all about in uncamouflaged rows. . . ."

As dawn broke the *Stukas* screamed down on the easy targets, while horizontal bombers dealt with the more distant bases, and short- and long-range fighters, coming in low, added their contribution.

The huge front, stretching from the North Cape to the Black Sea, was covered by four German *Luftflotten*. At the outbreak of the eastern hostilities they together mustered 1,945 aircraft, of which, however, a bare two-thirds, namely 1,280 machines, were serviceable. These comprised some 510 bombers, 290 dive-bombers, 440 single-engined and forty twin-engined fighters, plus about 120 long-range reconnaissance planes[1]. As already mentioned, the numerical strength of the Soviet air force was estimated as at least double the above figure.

The tasks of the German Luftwaffe had the same order of priority as against Poland in 1939 and against the western Allies in 1940: first to gain control of the air, and after that to support the Army. Would the time-worn "blitzkrieg" recipe still succeed when applied to the vast hinterland of Russia? At the start the answer seemed to be Yes—for the effect of the surprise attack on the Soviet airfields was devastating. Without any fighter opposition the 4-lb. fragmentation bombs were showered amongst the rows of Russian aircraft, and any left became simply target practice for the fighters.

"We hardly believed our eyes," reported Captain Hans von Hahn, commander of V Air Corps' I/JG 3, operating in the Lvov area. "Row after row of reconnaissance planes, bombers and fighters stood lined up as if on parade. We were astonished at the number of airfields and aircraft the Russians had ranged against us."

Russian planes went up in flames by the hundred. In II Air Corps' sector, at Bug near Brest-Litovsk, a single Soviet fighter squadron, attempting to "scramble", was bombed while still in motion on the ground. Later the airfield boundary was found littered with burnt-out wrecks.

Despite all its advantages, however, the Luftwaffe did not emerge from its eastern baptism without losses. Some of them were due to the Russian flak—others to its own bombs.

To blame were the SD 2 fragmentation bombs, called "Devil's eggs", which after being on the secret list were now dropped in large numbers for the first time. Only four pounds in weight, and round, they were equipped with little retarding wings and originally designed for use by ground-attack planes against personnel. Adjusted to explode either on impact or above ground, the result was a blast of fifty small and 250 even smaller shrapnel particles over a radius of up to forty feet. Against parked aircraft only a direct hit was effective, but this had the force of a medium anti-aircraft shell. On this occasion a large number of direct hits were scored.

But the "Devil's eggs" were unreliable. Often they stuck in the bomb magazines constructed specially for them, and with fuses live went off at the

[1] For the Luftwaffe's strength and order of battle at the outset of hostilities see Appendix 10.

slightest shock, tearing a hole in the bomber comparable to that of a direct hit by an anti-aircraft shell.

They were equally abominated by the fighters. All the Me 109s of JG 27 had been fitted with bomb-grills beneath the fuselage to carry ninety-six of them. The air pressure of flight often caused the first row to remain hung up without the pilot knowing it. Then, as he throttled back to land at his own base, they would tumble out one after the other—or wait till he was taxiing and explode just behind his machine. Some would lie in wait on the runways and give the armourers the constant and dangerous job of looking for and fielding them.

General Marquardt, chief engineer in charge of bomb development at the Luftwaffe's Technical Office, gave this opinion: "Despite their success in the first days of the Russian campaign, the life of the SD 2 was fleeting. The Soviet flak, very effective against low-level attack, soon forced our aircraft to fly higher, and without jettisonable containers these bombs could no longer be used."

For a time another fragmentation bomb, the 20-lb. SD 10, had also to be withdrawn from service, although this could be dropped from high-altitude bombers in bundles of four. On June 22nd, with no Soviet fighters and no tell-tale flak bursts in the sky, the crews of other aircraft were amazed to see several Ju 88s and Do 17s suddenly fold up in the air and crash to the ground in flames. It was always on the return flight, and sometimes not till they landed.

The reason was not far to seek. Isolated SD 10s, instead of becoming released, stuck with live fuses in the bomb racks, when again the slightest shock would send them off. In nearly all cases, that meant the total loss of the aircraft.

Kesselring at once banned all horizontal bombers from carrying them. Only Ju 87s and Hs 123s were still allowed to do so, for in their case the bombs were suspended beneath the wings, and the crews could make sure that they had really fallen.

To return to the offensive against Russia: the Luftwaffe's formations had hardly returned from delivering their first blow at dawn on June 22nd when they were bombed up again and sent on a second mission. This time they did meet opposition from Soviet fighters. Hundreds might have been destroyed on the ground, but it seemed there were still more of them.

The first heroic exploit of the "Great War for the Fatherland", as the Russians termed it, was performed by Sub-Lieutenant D. V. Kokorev of the 124th Fighter Regiment. His guns having failed in a dog-fight with a Me 110, he pulled his Rata fighter sharply around and rammed his opponent. Both aircraft crashed to the ground.

At the outset the German fighters encountered unexpected difficulties in dealing with their foes. For though the Russian I-153 and I-15 biplanes, their small and stubby Curtisses and I-16 Ratas, with their fat radial engines, were all much slower than the Messerschmitts, they were also much more manoeuvrable. In the words of Lieutenant Schiess, of JG 53's staff flight: "They would let us get almost into an aiming position, then bring their machines around a full 180 degrees, till both aircraft were firing at each other from head-on."

JG 53's *Kommodore*, Major von Maltzahn, became mad with frustration because again and again his opponent could turn out of his line of fire at the last moment and he himself kept grossly over-shooting. A similar error of calculation cost JG 27 its *Kommodore*, Major Wolfgang Schellmann, on its very first mission—a fighter sweep over Grodno. With a Rata well lined up, the major let off all his guns and the Russian plane disintegrated. In this case, however, his overtaking speed brought him so close that his own machine was struck by exploding particles. Though managing to bale out, he was posted as missing.

But the hour of the German fighters struck the same morning, when Russian bombers raided the German airfields. No one knew where they had come from: whether it was from far away, from the airfields already blitzed, or from others so far undetected. In any case, they were there: ten, twenty, thirty of them, in compact formations. And they attacked.

It happened just after the *Gruppen* of Major Graf Schönborn's *Stuka-geschwader 77* had re-landed after their first operation against fortified lines on the River Bug. There were five explosions then five black mushrooms of smoke on the opposite boundary. Only then were the bombers sighted: six twin-engined machines turning away in a wide curve.

At this moment two or three little dots were seen approaching the bombers at full speed: German fighters. They treated the *Stuka* crews on the ground to a breath-taking spectacle. 6/StG 77's squadron commander, Captain Herbert Pabst, reported:

"As the first one fired, thin threads of smoke seemed to join it to the bomber. Turning ponderously to the side, the big bird flashed silver, then plunged vertically downwards with its engines screaming. As it crashed, a huge sheet of flame shot upwards. The second bomber became a glare of red, exploded as it dived, and only the bits came floating down like great autumnal leaves. The third turned over backwards on fire. A similar fate befell the rest, the last falling in a village and burning for an hour. Six columns of smoke rose from the horizon. All six had been shot down!"

This was but one example. For the same thing happened along the whole front. The Russians bombers came in, held to their course, and made no attempt to evade either flak or fighters. Their losses were frightful. When ten had already been shot down, another fifteen would appear on the scene.

"They went on coming the whole afternoon," Pabst continued. "From our airfield alone we saw twenty-one crash, and not one get away."

The outcome of this hot and bloody June 22, 1941, was the biggest victory ever scored in a single day by one air force against another. No less than 1,811 Soviet aircraft were destroyed, against a German loss of thirty-five. 322 fell to fighters and flak, 1,489 were wiped out on the ground.

To the Luftwaffe's supreme commander, Hermann Goering, the claims seemed so incredible that he had them secretly checked. For days on end officers from his command staff picked their way about the airfields over-run by the German advance, counting the burnt-out wrecks of Russian planes. The result was even more astonishing: their tally exceeded 2,000.

Post-war Soviet publications have confirmed the success. The *History of the Great Patriotic War of the Soviet Union*, published by the Moscow Ministry of Defence, contains the following paragraph: "A decisive contri-bution to the success of the enemy ground troops was made by the German air force. . . . During the first days of the war enemy bomber formations launched massive attacks on sixty-six airfields of the frontier region, above all on those where new types of Soviet fighters were based. The result of these raids and of the violent air-to-air battles was a loss to us, as at noon on June 22nd, of some 1,200 aircraft, including more than 800 destroyed on the ground."

1,200 already by noon—and the battle continued till the evening. The Soviet report continues: "In the sector of Army Group West alone the enemy succeeded in destroying 528 machines on the ground and 210 in the air."

The sector referred to was that covered by Kesselring's *Luftflotte* 2, comprising Air Corps II and VIII under Loerzer and von Richthofen. According to German claims, too, this is where the greatest success was registered. Kesselring had already completed his first priority task—to gain control of the air—by the evening of the first day. From the second day onwards all Luftwaffe units became engaged in supporting the advance of the Army.

Behind the push of Colonel-General Guderian's *Panzer* Group 2 the fortress of Brest-Litovsk, manned by a commissar school of the Red Army, held out for a week and blocked the only supply route to the German front. Even the bombs of the *Stukas* made little impression on the citadel's three-foot thick walls. Accordingly on June 28th, between 17.40 and 18.00, seven Ju 88s of KG 3 attacked it with 3,500-lb. "block-busters". Two of them scored direct hits, and the citadel fell next morning.

As the Army pushed swiftly onward, the Luftwaffe's close-support units accompanied it, with the *Stukas* smoothing the way for the armour wherever resistance was encountered. General von Richthofen, who had done so much to perfect the "blitzkrieg" technique, now brought his VIII Air Corps in support of Colonel-General Hoth's *Panzer* Group 3, while to the south General Loerzer, putting the *Stukas* and short and long-range fighters of II Air Corps under the command of Colonel Fiebig, contributed a similar force to help the armour of Guderian.

The Soviet air force, however, was not yet knocked out. On June 30th hundreds of bombers carrying the red star again appeared over the front. Wave after wave of them came surging against the spearheads of the German armour—which, having by-passed Minsk on both sides, were developing a pincers movement for the first encirclement battle of that summer.

The Russians had not, however, reckoned with JG 51 or its capable commander, Colonel Werner Mölders. His *Geschwader* came down right over Guderian's vanguard, and the Soviet bombers, operating without fighter escort and, as usual, by squadrons, were shot down piecemeal. By the evening the fighters had accounted for 114 of them, which made JG 51 the first *Geschwader* to achieve 1,000 victories since the war began in 1939. Mölders himself shot down five, bringing his personal score to eighty-two, and five each were also despatched by Captain Joppien and Lieutenant Bär.

150 miles to the north-west, near Dünaburg, Major Trautloft's JG 54 (known as the "Greenheart" *Geschwader*) became similarly engaged. Here the Russian bombers' target was the Düna bridges, which *Panzer* Group 4 would have to cross to advance to the north-east. In this zone a long and bitter combat ended with the destruction of sixty-five Soviet machines.

Trautloft's *Geschwader*, operating with General Foerster's I Air Corps, supported the advance of Army Group North right to the gates of Leningrad, and on August 1st First-Lieutenant Scholz brought its score too up to 1,000 (623 at the expense of the Russians). JG 53 reached the same incredible figure one day earlier; while Major von Lützow's JG 3, operating with V Air Corps under Ritter von Greim, equalised on August 15th with three victories by Flight-Sergeant Steckmann.

The competition between the different fighter *Geschwader* continued week after week and month after month. But though the enormous losses suffered by the Russian air force showed that its aircraft were virtually defenceless against German fighters, it would not admit defeat. By August, or at latest September, its initial establishment of fighters, bombers and ground-attack aircraft had, according to German calculations, been completely wiped out. Yet fresh planes kept on being thrown into the battle. The Russian sources of supply seemed to be inexhaustible.

Today we know the reason. Their official war history states: "In the second half of 1941 the mass production of improved aircraft types was quadrupled. In comparison with the first half of the year, the production of LaGG-3 fighters rose from 322 to 2,141 (a more than six-fold increase), that of the Yak-1 fighter from 335 to 1,019, and that of the armour-plated ground-attack plane, the Il-2, from 249 to 1,293. 1,867 bombers were produced at three times the pre-war rate, and the industry's total production of all types in 1941 reached 15,735 aircraft. . . ."

All within a few months—and with virtually no interference from the German bomber fleets! All these were able to achieve were a few pin-pricks.

Here lay the crucial mistake of the Luftwaffe's general staff. As we have seen, General Wever in 1935 had called for a four-engined "Ural" bomber, but it was never built. None the less, at the outset of this far-ranging campaign, there was still the possibility of putting the existing bomber units under a unified command for strategic purposes. Then they could have been used as a striking force against the key centres of military supply, even if it meant operating at extreme range, and even if the targets were "only" factories making tanks or aircraft.

For bombers are basically a strategic weapon. If their effort is dispersed, their effect is dissipated. And this is just what was happening in the Russian campaign. Instead of being under a single command, the *Geschwader* were divided up amongst the Air Corps, which in turn were appointed to different Army Groups. Separate *Geschwader* were sent here and there on a multitude of individual missions, most of them dictated by the immediate needs of the Army. In effect they were given a close-support role which was not their own.

The result was that in a week of operations against tanks, at great cost to themselves, the bombers would succeed in destroying perhaps one day's output of T 34s by the Gorki factory. Though this might suit the immediate tactical aims of the Army, the bombers' own strategic potential was completely wasted.

During the night of July 21st/22nd Major-General M. S. Gromadin, in command of Moscow's defence zone, sounded the capital's first major air raid alarm. From their advanced bases round Minsk, Orsha, Vitebsk and Chatalovska, the German bombers were launching their attacks. Though the sound of the nearby encirclement battle of Smolensk penetrated to their air-fields, to Moscow the crews had a flight of 280–380 miles.

At his staff conference on July 8th Hitler had declared his "lasting resolve" to "raze Moscow and Leningrad to the ground by means of the Luftwaffe". When, a week later, nothing had happened, he said to Goering sarcastically: "Do you believe that in your Luftwaffe there is a single *Geschwader* with the pluck to fly to Moscow?" Thus the air attack on the Russian capital was triggered off as a matter of Luftwaffe prestige: a burdensome duty, carried out as a "by-product" at the expense of more important tasks.

In reality Moscow was not just the political capital, the seat of government and party. It was also the military and economic heart of the country, and above all, the communications centre and pivot of military transport. With all that, Moscow should have been the Luftwaffe's top-priority strategic target.

In the event, the initial attack on July 22nd was conducted by a scant and laboriously assembled force totalling 127 aircraft. It comprised Ju 88s from KGs 3 and 54, He 111s from KGs 53 and 55, supplemented from the west by KG 28 with its two pathfinder *Gruppen*, *Kampfgruppe* 100 and III/KG 26. Any further aircraft contribution for the task ahead was resisted by the Air Corps commanders of the eastern front, and in this they were supported by the Army chiefs. Everyone judged his own sector of operations to be the most important.

Twenty miles from Moscow the bombers encountered the first searchlights, and some *Gruppen* flew on unmolested almost to the Kremlin. But then, suddenly, the whole city turned into a roaring volcano as uncounted regiments of heavy and light flak opened up. Over 300 searchlights dazzled the bomber crews to the extent that they could hardly see their objectives. Moscow's defence against air raids almost matched that of London at the time of the "blitz".

During this raid the Germans dropped 104 tons of high explosive and 46,000 incendiary bombs without achieving any concentration. The Kremlin did not go up in smoke even though II/KG 55, whose target it was, was sure hundreds of incendiaries had hit it. Its roofs—so explained a former German air attaché to Moscow, next day—had so many layers of seventeenth-century tiles that no doubt the puny incendiary bombs had failed to penetrate.

On the following night Moscow was raided again by 115 bombers, and on the third night by a hundred. After that the number declined rapidly to fifty, thirty and a mere fifteen. Fifty-nine of the seventy-six raids on Moscow in the year 1941 were carried out by a force ranging from three to ten.

The air offensive against the heart of the enemy's war effort thus petered out almost as soon as it had begun. People then asked: was not the Luftwaffe far more effective on the battlefield, as flying artillery? In mid-September 1941 Hitler, inspired by the staggering losses the Russians had once more suffered after being encircled east of Kiev, prophesied: "Our enemy has already been beaten to his knees, and will never rise again!"

To which Stalin countered: "Comrades! Our strength is immense. Soon our bumptious enemy will be forced to recognise it!"

On September 22nd Major Trautloft, *Kommodore* of JG 54, based at Siverskaya, made an excursion to the Leningrad front. He wanted for once to examine the city closely through a telescope from the ground. For a fortnight his Messerschmitts had been circling over it, usually at high altitude because of the flak, which was worse than anything they had experienced over

80. *Stukas* have destroyed a river bridge near Vyazma and bombarded the concentration of Russian vehicles about to cross. By thus segregating the battlefields the Luftwaffe prepared the way for the German encirclement movements of summer 1941.

81. An He 111 making a low-level attack on a Russian oil conduit already burning.

82. A formation of StG 2.

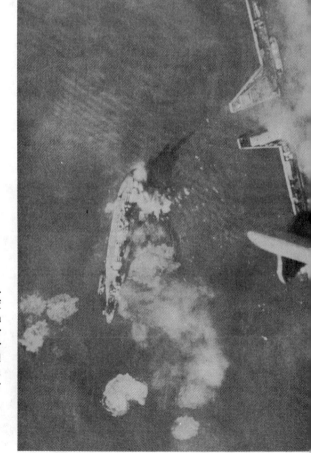

83. Attacks by StG 2 on the Russian Baltic Fleet on the Bay of Kronstadt at Leningrad went on for a whole week. On September 23, 1941, the battleship *October Revolution* was severely damaged and the battleship *Marat* sunk. This picture shows the former vessel under attack.

London. The air was alive with metal, especially over the Bay of Kronstadt, where the Red Fleet lay at anchor. The Messerschmitts, as escort to bombers raiding the city, had tangled daily with Russian Curtisses and Ratas.

Through the artillery spotter's telescope Leningrad's church towers, palaces and high blocks of flats seemed almost near enough to touch. But the city was on fire from one end to the other. High above the German outpost a force of *Stukas* dived down on the Russian warships for the third time that day. Fascinated, Trautloft watched as the twenty to thirty machines turned almost together and went down to face the flak.

At that moment a voice shouted: "Take cover, *Herr Major*, we are under attack!"

Six Curtisses closed in on the German post, their guns producing a shower of splinters. Finding himself for once in the position of a front-line infantryman, the fighter commander reacted in precisely the same way: "Where the hell," he demanded from the artillery officer lying beside him, "are our fighters?"

It was the more humiliating inasmuch as, thousands of feet above, his Messerschmitts could be seen glinting in the sun. The Army officer said with a grin: "You should know, *Herr Major*, that all available machines have been ordered by Corps to confine themselves to escorting the *Stukas!*"

Henceforth Trautloft knew what it was like to be attacked by enemy planes while watching one's own air force apparently engaged on a pleasure flight. How could the infantryman know what its orders were?

The attack by Oskar Dinort's StG 2 "Immelmann" *Geschwader* on the Red Fleet and the Kronstadt roadstead went on for a week. Since the days of Calais, ships had become an accustomed target, particularly in the Cretan battle against the British Mediterranean Fleet. Now it was the Baltic Fleet, which in Kronstadt and Leningrad comprised two battleships, two cruisers, thirteen destroyers, forty-two submarines and more than 200 auxiliary vessels—a numerically overwhelming force which threatened alike the flow of iron ore from Sweden and seaborne supplies to Finland and the Baltic ports serving the northern sector of the front.

On September 23rd I and III/StG 2 took off at 08.45 from Tyrkovo and within an hour were over their target. To protect their ships the Russians were reported to have assembled 600 heavy flak guns, so the *Stukas* approached at over 15,000 feet. Then, regardless of the inferno, they tipped over and dived down in compact groups. As they did so the battleships *October Revolution* and *Marat* loomed ever larger in their bomb sights till finally, at 4,000 feet, the bombs were released. Then, all too slowly and ponderously, the Ju 87s pulled out and climbed obliquely away.

They left the sea a boiling cauldron, and at this very moment the scene was photographed by Corporal Bayer, gunner to the *Geschwader's* technical officer, First-Lieutenant Lau. His picture showed strikes on the *Marat*, more beside her gunwales, and fires spreading on her decks. After another direct hit the 23,600-ton battleship, with her twelve 30.5-cm and sixteen 12-cm guns, broke in two and sank. This final and decisive blow was achieved by First-Lieutenant Hans-Ulrich Rudel, who in years to come was awarded the highest decorations for his work against tanks and other ground targets.

The *Stukas* reappeared that afternoon, and again every day from the 25th till the 28th. On one of them the *Kommodore*, Lieutenant Colonel Dinort, saw a Ju 87 dive vertically emitting an ever-increasing plume of black smoke, and later found it was III *Gruppe's* commander, Captain Steen. After a direct hit from a flak shell he was presumably unable to pull out, and the plane crashed straight against the side of the heavy cruiser *Kirov* in a sheet of flame.

The massive fire-power of the Russian flak, as well as their fighters, took further toll of the slow and long-obsolescent dive-bombers. But they were all the Luftwaffe had for the purpose. At each crisis on the battlefront the Army went on clamouring for air support. Hardly had the blow to the Red Fleet at Kronstadt been dealt, and the siege ring round Leningrad closed, than VIII Air Corps (to which StG 2 belonged) was recalled from the northern and posted to the central front.

There, 600 miles to the south, the encirclement battle of Kiev was raging— a battle which Hitler had forced his generals to fight against their will and which delayed the Central Army Group's advance on Moscow by a vital two months. Here, besides participating in the ground conflict, the Luftwaffe performed the further important task of blockading the battlefield. For four whole weeks its aircraft daily and systematically attacked all rail communications from east and north-east: stations, bridges, defiles, trains and locomotives. All reinforcements for Budyonny's armies were blocked, all lines of retreat disrupted.

Yet despite this immediate and local success, the Russian railway system as a whole came off virtually unscathed. To knock out marshalling yards and major junctions "for the duration" needed block-buster bombs dropped in shoals. These the Luftwaffe did not possess, nor the aircraft to carry them *en masse*. The pin-pricks it achieved were carried out by single aircraft or minute formations, whose tactics were to fly along a railway till they found a train, then shoot up some trucks, and if possible the engine. Or they would block a stretch of line with bombs. For how long?

The Russians became astonishingly skilful at repair and improvisation. Frequently stretches of track, seemingly badly hit in the evening, were in use again by the following night. To quote their official war history: "Between June and December 1941 the enemy made 5,939 air attacks on railways adjacent to the front. The average period of disruption to traffic was only five hours and forty-eight minutes."

The successful blockade of the Kiev battle sector was the Luftwaffe's last major effort before the onset of the Russian winter. Only days later it would have been impossible, for then its aircraft were bogged down in mud, many of them unable to take off or land. Supplies failed to arrive, and the shortage of spare parts, especially of replacement engines, became rapidly more acute as production lagged behind consumption.

In these autumn weeks the number of serviceable aircraft consequently declined alarmingly, some bomber and fighter *Gruppen* being reduced to a mere three or four. During the whole of October Kesselring's *Luftflotte* 2 succeeded in mounting just one strategic raid, against an aircraft factory at Voronesh—and that was carried out by a single long-range reconnaissance plane!

Fresh difficulties were encountered as the season of rain and mud gave way to that of ice, snow and arctic cold. Numerous Luftwaffe units had to be withdrawn from the front and sent home to recuperate. When in November the German Army laboriously mounted its last offensive against Moscow, long-range reconnaissance reported large-scale transport movements converging on the city from the east, especially from Gorki and Yaroslavl. But this time the Luftwaffe was incapable of doing anything about it.

In a post-war letter Kesselring had to admit that the long-term significance of these transport movements should have been appreciated but that at the time no one did so. They went on completely unmolested by the Luftwaffe.

So it was that on December 5th the Russians were able to start their counter-offensive in front of Moscow and Kalinin with fresh divisions from Siberia. The German front had to yield and the key objective, Moscow, was never reached. The bitter winter conflict had begun.

2. The Death of Udet

At a decisive moment of the war the Luftwaffe had shown that it was too weak to carry out its tasks. How did it come about? What was the reason for the lag in production? Why was it that, two years after the opening of hostilities, the operational units were still equipped with the same obsolescent types of aircraft? Above all, why had the need for a four-engined "strategic" bomber not been satisfied?

Colonel Wilhelm Wimmer, the first chief of the Technical Office, and Udet's predecessor, recalls two revealing episodes from the spring of 1935. The first occurred during a visit by Goering to the Junkers works at Dessau. Suddenly the one-time fighter pilot stood gaping at the giant wooden mock-up of a Ju 89 four-engined bomber, which Junkers was then under contract to produce. "What on earth's that?" he asked.

Wimmer explained, referring to all the general staff's discussions about a "Ural" bomber—concerning which Goering had of course been informed. But the Luftwaffe chief decided not to remember. "Any such major project as that can only be decided upon by me personally!" he said, and swept out.

The second episode was when the Reich war minister von Blomberg visited the Dornier works at Friederichshaven on Lake Constance, where the Do 19 four-engined bomber was being developed as the Ju 89's rival. After listening to Wimmer with interest, he asked: "When do you think the aircraft can be operational?"

"In about four or five years."

"Yes," said von Blomberg, blinking at the sky, "I suppose that's just about the size of it."

Right from the beginning the development of a long-range bomber rested on the supposition that one day the Luftwaffe would be at war with Soviet Russia: itself no very astute prophecy to anyone who had read Hitler's *Mein Kampf.* To reach that huge country's production centres in the Urals meant flying thousands of miles, which only a four-engined machine could accomplish. And in fact the "Ural" bomber—to use the name coined by General Wever—continued to be developed in the face of Goering's express disapproval. As we have seen, the first prototypes of both factories were, when they took the air in 1936, very promising if underpowered.

However, with Wever's fatal crash in June that year, there was no protagonist left for them—least of all Udet, Wimmer's successor at the Technical Office. As champion of the dive-bomber Udet was supported by Jeschonnek, then Lieutenant-Colonel commanding the *Lehrgeschwader.* Trials had convinced the latter that the horizontal bomber had little future: either the sighting instruments failed to work or the airmen failed to operate them properly. In any case most of the bombs missed their target by a wide margin.

State Secretary Erhard Milch, who had industrial training, feared that a four-engined bomber would absorb too much of the short supply of metals and other raw materials, and in this he was supported by the new Luftwaffe chief of general staff, Albert Kesselring.[1] Could the general aim not be achieved more quickly and more cheaply by three times the number of twin-engined machines? Within six months—i.e. in autumn 1936—Milch, Kesselring and Udet between them arranged that the further development of the four-engined bomber should be halted. This happened just as the American air force was trying out its own first four-engined bomber, the Boeing B-17, convinced that that was where the future lay.

Even in Germany opposition to the decision was not wanting. The Inspector of Bombers, General Kurt Pflugbeil, pleaded in vain, while in spring 1937 Major Paul Deichmann, chief of operations at general staff H.Q., sought a personal interview with the supreme commander. Goering received him at Karinhall, and Deichmann reiterated the arguments on behalf of the long-range bomber: the greatly extended range, the double or triple bomb-load, the superior armament, speed and altitude.

"*Herr Generaloberst*," said Deichmann, "we have to see in this thing the weapon of the future."

To which Milch (also present) responded with the categorical statement: "The policy has been decided in favour of the Ju 88. Any question of developing and constructing a four-engined bomber therefore does not arise."

Deichmann made one more attempt: "I ask *Herr Generaloberst* not to reach a conclusion before the long-range bomber has been further tested."

But Goering had succumbed to the fascination of numbers, as promised by Milch and Udet. On April 29th, 1937, he gave his official seal to the order halting all further development of the Do 19 and Ju 89, saying: "The Führer will never ask me how big our bombers are, but how many we have." And Milch personally ensured that Dornier's and Junkers' prototypes were consigned to the scrap-heap.

In autumn 1937 Jeschonnek took over from Deichmann, and soon afterwards the young colonel found himself chief of general staff. With that the die was cast in favour of dive-bombing—not only by the robust single-engined Ju 87 or *Stuka*, but by twin-engined bombers as well. Any that could not do so were before long to be scrapped. Why have—the argument ran—a large and expensive fleet of horizontal bombers when an enemy's military targets can be hit with pin-point precision by a few dive-bombers? It seemed to be the ideal way out of the raw materials' impasse, and to offer the only possibility within a few years of creating a Luftwaffe that would frighten the world.

Ernst Udet, the *Stukas'* pioneer and protagonist, stood at the height of his power. As chief of the Technical Office, he virtually directed what was then the biggest armaments concern on earth. But was this good-natured, artistic soul, who loved a life that was free—this "flying clown", as many a general staff officer disparagingly dubbed him—the right man coolly to com-

---

[1] For Kesselring's attitude to the question of a German four-engined bomber, see Appendix 11.

mand such an industrial effort with the necessary application and ruthlessness?

He himself had resisted the appointment, saying to Goering: "I understand nothing about it." To which Goering replied: "Do you think *I* understand all the things I've got to deal with? But they get done all the same. You, too, will have qualified specialists who will do the work for you."

At their head was Chief Engineer Lucht, on whose counsel and verdicts Udet was now forced to rely. He also formed personal friendships with the leaders of the aircraft industry, particularly with the gifted creator of the Me 109, Professor Willy Messerschmitt, while constantly behind him stood State Secretary Milch, who knew all about his failings. "He behaved like a father," Udet's staff chief Ploch recorded.

One big responsibility was shed by Udet when the enterprising chairman of the Junkers board of directors, Dr. Heinrich Koppenberg, became personally charged by Goering with the job of creating "a mighty fleet of Ju 88 bombers". Koppenberg could get on with it! Indeed, the latter himself complained about the 25,000-odd decreed modifications that retarded the machine's development. It was still undergoing trials when war broke out. By then there was little left of any qualities stamping it as a "wonder bomber".

Strangely enough, despite the banning of the "Ural bomber", from 1937 on there still was a four-engined aircraft under construction: the He 177, originally designed for long-range marine reconnaissance. Udet showed virtually no interest in it. Unless it could dive like lighter bombers, he offered no hope of it ever being produced for the service. And the idea of such a heavy machine being used as a dive-bomber was ridiculous.

The He 177 incorporated a principle taken over by Heinkel from his designer Siegfried Günther, who had used it seemingly successfully for the prototype of the earlier He 119: namely that of two engines, either in tandem or side by side, driving a single airscrew. In appearance it thus resembled a conventional twin-engined aircraft, an aerodynamic feature which would reduce wind resistance and so, it was hoped, increase speed.

In September, 1939, the event that was supposedly not on the cards happened: the war with Britain. Suddenly a long-range bomber was required, and the He 177 became burningly topical. In November it was flown for the first time by engineer Carl Francke (who later "sank" the *Ark Royal*) at the Rechlin test centre. He had to land again almost at once or the plane would have gone up in smoke: the oil temperature of the dual engines had soared above the red danger mark.

It was a clear warning, insufficiently heeded in the scrimmage to get the plane operational. Heinkel was given a contract to produce 120 of them monthly, as from the summer of 1940. But it was soon revoked. In February 1940 Goering, worried by the raw-material shortage, ordained a policy of maximum economy. All long-term projects and developments were to be cancelled, and the available materials devoted to supplying the front with proven aircraft types "in the greatest possible number at the greatest possible speed". Thousands of engineers and technicians found themselves redundant and were conscripted to the forces. Any aircraft not ready for operations in 1940 need not be built, for by the following year at the latest the war would be won. After the western campaign Udet himself, now raised to the rank of Air General and appointed chief of air supply, declared to his colleagues: "The war is over! To hell with all our aircraft projects—they'll no longer be needed!"

Disenchantment followed swiftly, as the Battle of Britain exposed the Luftwaffe's weaknesses. Once more production of the He 177 was ordered, and one mishap followed another. Its trials disclosed unaccountable vibrations. Wings cracked and the dual-engine assemblies, though each

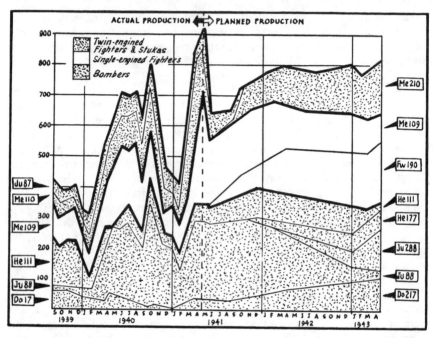

Udet's "temperature chart" of aircraft production. The arrogant assumption of the German leaders from time to time that the war was as good as won found eloquent expression in the ups and downs of the aircraft production graph. After each successful campaign it dropped. Low points can thus be seen in February 1940 and February 1941, when the monthly output sank respectively to 300 and 400 bombers, dive-bombers, single- and twin-engined fighters. The above diagram, copied from Programme No. 20c of the Luftwaffe's Technical Office dated May 19, 1941, shows the actual production up to April 1941, and from May 1941 the production that was planned for the crucial types of aircraft. The fresh decline in the summer of 1941, coinciding as it did with the start of the Russian campaign, led to Quartermaster-General Udet's downfall. Since neither the new Me 210 nor He 177 series were delivered in time to fill the gaps, the factories had again to produce the old obsolescent types of aircraft.

comprising two long-proven Daimler-Benz DB 601s, turned out anything but reliable. They were mounted very close in, and in the same narrow space was housed the hydraulic retraction system, so that leaking oil ignited on the hot exhausts. Again and again the machine crashed in flames, and the He 177 became known as the "Flying Firework".

All this could have been avoided by mounting four separate engines, but both the general staff and the Technical Office persisted in their demand for a dive-potential, and if the thirty-one-ton bomber was to dive at all, it could only do so with a dual-engine assembly.

"It is quite idiotic to expect a four-engined aircraft to dive," Goering complained to the industrialists on September 13th, 1942, two years too late, as he bemoaned the lack of a long-range bomber. "When I think about that, gentlemen, I could cry!" Had he really forgotten that five years previously he himself had ordered the "Ural bomber" to be scrapped?

After spring 1941 Ernest Udet became a mere shadow of his former self. Though he drove himself to the limit, as chief of supply he became the scapegoat for every failure, and the weight of responsibility broke him. Not only the He 177, but also the Me 210—designed as a successor both to the Me 110 and the Ju 87 *Stuka*—failed to overcome its teething troubles. Tight turns were apt to end in a flat spin, and even experienced test pilots crashed with it. But despite the danger of putting it into operations with the faults uncured, series production started.

Udet was specially upset to have these difficulties with his old friend Messerschmitt. "All these unnecessary vexations and intolerable wastes of time," he wrote to him on July 25th, 1941, "compel me to impose a higher standard of supervision over your new design." But he never brought himself to send the letter. He was a sick man, suffering from haemorrhages and unbearable headaches, which the opening of the Russian campaign did nothing to allay. He foresaw that the time was not far distant when he could no longer keep the front adequately equipped with aircraft.

On June 20th, 1941, Goering gave Field-Marshal Milch full powers to see that production "over the whole field of air armament is quadrupled in the shortest time". It meant that Milch would now be meddling in Udet's department while the latter still had the appointment. It was hardly a set-up that could be expected to work.

On August 9th, Udet flew to Goering in East Prussia with his new aircraft programme—the sixteenth since the outbreak of war. When Milch heard about it, he angrily telephoned to demand Udet's immediate return. Udet complained to Goering, who sent Milch an equally angry telegram. But at the same time he recommended Udet to take a long period of sick leave. On the 25th the latter, near to breakdown, went off for a cure at Bühlerhöhe. Two days later he received from Goering a cordial telegram, which he took as proof of confidence. He was not to know that it had been forged by friends to cheer him up, and that Goering himself knew nothing about it.

On September 3rd Milch began "new-brooming" Udet's department. He accused the engineers with sabotaging his orders, and within six days sacked the head of the planning division, Engineer General Tschersich. When on the 26th Udet returned, he was unable to prevent his long-standing chief of staff, Major-General Ploch, suffering a like fate. By October the department had been given a completely new chain of command, and Udet could hardly restrain himself.

On Saturday, November 15th, Ploch paid him a visit and told him about the shooting of Jews in the east. Udet's cup was full. At nine o'clock in the morning of the 17th State Secretary Körner and Udet's adjutant, Colonel Max Pendele, were called by Frau Inge Bleyle to his home in Berlin's Heerstrasse. Udet was dead. Before shooting himself he had written a sentence in red on the headboard of his bed: "*Reichsmarschall*, why have you deserted me?"

Pendele wiped it off—and later regretted it. Körner telephoned General Kastner, head of Luftwaffe personnel, who in turn apprised Goering. "We must feign an accident," was the latter's careful reaction. And the official press release stated: "While testing a new weapon Colonel-General Ernst Udet was severely wounded, and has since died."

Goering afterwards showed his real feelings by attempting to have Udet posthumously court-martialed. Four high-ranking judges were ordered to examine the reasons that had led him to suicide. After collecting evidence at the Technical Office for months on end, they finally delivered their report in autumn 1942, with the urgent recommendation that no proceedings be taken. Otherwise too much would come to light.

"I can only be glad," said the Luftwaffe's supreme commander, "that Udet dealt personally with his own case. Otherwise I should have been obliged to proceed against him myself." And as he spoke, tears of self-righteousness filled his eyes.

Operation Barbarossa—Summary and Conclusions

1. In the summer and autumn of 1941 two-thirds of the Luftwaffe was engaged against Russia, the remaining third being divided between the Mediterranean and the Channel front against England. Great as the eastern successes were, the wastage of material outpaced the rate of replacement, and both fighter and bomber strength declined alarmingly. The military objective of "crushing Russia in one short campaign" had not been attained before the mud and the frost of winter intervened.

2. Changes of organisation necessary to adapt the Luftwaffe to a multifront war and the vast area of eastern operations were not carried out. Proposals to form all bomber units into a single strategic command, while leaving the task of army support to a number of tactical groups equipped with reconnaissance and ground-attack planes, plus flak, were ignored.

3. The Air Corps consequently found themselves acting mainly as mere auxiliaries to the Army's ground operations, and virtually no strategic air offensive was mounted. Though one reason for this was the lack of a suitable long-range bomber, even the medium-bomber units, instead of operating as a combined force against such important strategic targets as tank and aircraft factories, were scattered all over the front.

4. Thus the Soviet aircraft industry suffered no damage, and its output greatly increased. Losses, however severe, were constantly replaced. The same applied to the production of tanks—for instance in Gorki, where the output went on virtually uninterrupted thanks to the Luftwaffe being mainly engaged in direct support of the Army.

5. The need to operate on three fronts taxed the Luftwaffe beyond its resources. The development and production crisis, which in November 1941 led to the suicide of Udet, reflected the lack of foresight of Germany's military planners, who had gambled on the war by then being long since won. Failure to develop new types of aircraft meant that the old types had to continue being produced. Soon these were no longer a match for the aircraft and weapons of their opponents, particularly in the west.

8

MEDITERRANEAN THEATRE 1942

1. Target : Malta

During January 1942 a sirocco, with incessant rain, blew in from the sea on to the slopes of Mount Etna and down over the Sicilian plains. For the Luftwaffe's bomber and fighter *Gruppen* which a few weeks before had returned to the Sicilian airfields at Catania and Gerbini, Trapani, Comiso and Gela, it was hardly a promising start to the new year.

Field-Marshal Kesselring, who, on November 28, 1941, had been withdrawn with his staff from the central sector of the Russian front and designated "Commander-in-Chief South", had ordered large-scale air operations against Malta. But though squadrons were already raiding the island, the attack in force was delayed by the weather.

February came and the rain clouds suddenly gave way to spring sunshine; the bombers flew southwards over a deep blue sea flecked with white foam crests. As the weeks went by the raids grew more numerous, and the British Mediterranean fortress grew accustomed to a round-the-clock alert. But frequent though they now were, the raids were still being mounted only by small formations.

Major Gilchrist, then Intelligence Officer of the British 231 Infantry Brigade, has given the following description: "At first the bombing was cautious. Three Ju 88s would come over three or four times a day, escorted by a large number of fighters. After a time . . . the raids increased to about eight a day, and often five Ju 88s were used. . . . The targets were airfields and dispersal units and occasionally the dockyards."[1]

That the Germans still came in sections of only three to five was no longer due to the weather, but to Kesselring's deliberate tactics of giving the enemy no rest. Whatever advantage this might have had, however, was dissipated by the fact that the defence could concentrate its fire *seriatim*, especially against individual Ju 88 dive-bombers. Losses were severe, and the aircraft that returned without being hit were few.

"I was flying close to the left of our squadron commander," reported Lieutenant Gerhard Stamp, pilot of a Ju 88. "Looking about, one could see

[1] R. T. Gilchrist, *Malta Strikes Back* (Gale & Polden, 1946), pp. 4 & 5.

our Me 109 escort. It seemed nothing much could really go wrong, especially on such a fine day."

Stamp belonged to 2 squadron of *Lehrgeschwader* 1, commanded by Captain Lüden and based at Catania. They had been briefed to dive-bomb the airfield of Luca and destroy the Blenheim and Wellington bombers based there. The Messerschmitt escort was provided by II/JG 53 under Captain "Earl" Wilcke.

From the south coast of Sicily to Malta is only fifty miles, scarcely more than a quarter of an hour's flight. As the rocky island loomed out of the water, it was not long before Valetta, the capital, with its great harbour and naval base distributed over three deep inlets, came into view. As the bombers approached they were greeted by heavy flak. The shells exploded close below them, and Stamp's machine was tossed in the air. "Let's hope the next salvo isn't a hundred feet higher!" commented Goerke, his flight mechanic.

By the spring of 1941 Malta's flak had already won a "good reputation" amongst the German bomber crews. Then the aircraft concerned had been mostly *Stukas*, and it was apparent that the British guns were centrally controlled. As hundreds of them went off at once, the manoeuvrable little Ju 87s just had time to alter height and direction before, fifty seconds later, multitudinous explosion puffs appeared exactly along their previous course. Nor was the fire at one altitude only. As the bombers went down, salvos would go off at 9,000, 6,000 and 4,500 feet, and finally all the light flak on land and on the ships in harbour would join in.

"Their flak was certainly not to be trifled with," was the verdict of Captain Helmut Mahlke, commander of III/StG 1. On February 26, 1941, a direct hit had torn an enormous hole in his starboard wing, and only a combination of luck and skill had got him back.

Since then the British flak had not rested on its laurels, and was now better still. As Stamp went down through the barrage, he thought only of getting below it. Following his C.O., he pulled out the diving brakes and, peeling off after him, aimed for Luca's crossed runways. As he descended they were reduced in his bomb-sight to one, at the end of it six bombers clustered together. The observer called out the descending altitude, then struck Stamp on his knee to indicate the last moment to bomb. A pressure on the red button atop the control column, and the bombs fell away. The Ju 88 pulled out automatically.

The C.O.'s plane ahead flew as if in a drunken frenzy, popping to left and right, and up and down, as it carried out the motions of the "flak waltz". Seconds later Stamp got ready to do the same. Right ahead was a black wall streaked with flashes and no choice but to fly through it. Thuds and bangs followed, like a multiple box on the ears.

"Undercarriage is down!" called Goerke. But it was only the flap, the legs remained up; otherwise the loss of speed would have been fatal. If the engines survive, thought Stamp, we'll be through. But at that moment Noschinski, the radio-operator, called: "Three Hurricanes attacking from starboard astern."

The fighters had been waiting on the edge of the flak zone. At full boost Stamp went low down over the sea, and Noschinski behind him gave a breathless running commentary as he watched the Hurricanes in their turn attacked by Me 109s and two of them shot down. When Stamp came in to land at Catania, half an hour later, he found the pressure pipe had been shot away

Luftwaffe assault on Malta, spring 1942.   **84, 85, 86.** *(left)* Major von Maltzahn of the fighter escort, JG 53, at his Sicilian base of Comiso. *(right)* Captain Helbig, commander of I/LG 1, whose Ju 88s later sank three British destroyers between Crete and Libya. *(below)* A Ju 88 over the Mediterranean.

87. A Me 109 of JG 27 in
desert camouflage.

Campaign in Africa

88. JG 27's legendary "ace,"
Captain Marseille. (His unit
supported Rommel all the way
to El Alamein.)

and the undercarriage could not be lowered, even with the hand pump. With a belly-landing imperative, he flew low over the hangars firing off Very lights. The airfield was promptly cleared, and ambulances and fire-engines got under way.

"After tightening our seat-belts I began the approach run," said Stamp. "With the flaps also out of action my speed was too great and I had to open the throttle and make another circuit. At the second attempt there was a tearing jolt, and I shouted to release the roof, but bouncing up, the machine again became airborne. There was little runway left. Then there was another jolt, dirt sprayed over the cockpit, and we went skidding and ploughing straight at a great concrete wall. I applied the brakes—as if that could help! Finally the plane lurched to the right and stopped ten feet away from it."

It was a hair's-breadth escape. Stamp reported to his *Gruppenkommandeur*, Captain Joschen Helbig. The latter screwed up his eyes, and said: "You don't seem to have been very popular in Malta. Perhaps you'd better take over the ops officer's job and at the end of the season get yourself a new toboggan."

The Luftwaffe's second assault on Malta—beginning in December 1941 and reaching its height in April 1942—was preceded by a bitter lesson in command of the sea. Whoever possessed Malta held the key strategic position in the central Mediterranean. For the British it represented an "unsinkable aircraft carrier". As a naval and air force base it not only protected their own shipping route from Gibraltar to Alexandria and the Suez Canal at its most dangerous point; it also threatened the Axis supply route from Italy and Sicily to North Africa, obliging the Italians to make a wide detour.

In theory it might equally be supposed that a base so near to an enemy country, in the Italians' "own" *mare nostrum*, was untenable. Italian bombers had attacked it in the summer of 1940, violently at first but soon with diminishing strength. As for the Luftwaffe's first offensive against the island—by General Geisler's X Air Corps in spring 1941—this had only the limited objective of holding down Malta while Rommel's *Afrika Korps* was being ferried across to Tripoli. In this it was successful, but the proposal of Vice-Admiral Weichold, Germany's naval chief in Italy, to occupy the battered island at once, fell on deaf ears. Malta could breathe again.

From April 6, 1941, the Luftwaffe was mainly engaged in the Balkan campaign, and two weeks later Hitler decided in favour of the risky airborne landing on Crete, despite the efforts of his general staff to persuade him that Malta, though only one twenty-sixth the size, was strategically the more important target. Then came the Russian campaign. X Air Corps had meanwhile left Sicily for operations in the eastern Mediterranean and Aegean.

Thus in the summer months of 1941 Malta had the chance to recuperate. Of three large supply convoys totalling thirty-nine transports that reached the island that year only one ship was lost. They brought weapons, ammunition, fuel and victuals. Air Vice-Marshal H. P. Lloyd, who took over command of the R.A.F. units in May, is said to have remarked: "You wouldn't have known there was a war on."

But the R.A.F. did not forget that there was: it harried the enemy with bombers and torpedo planes. Nor did the Navy. In addition to the 10th Submarine Flotilla, "Force K", comprising cruisers and destroyers, took up station there in the autumn. Malta had resharpened her sword, as the German-Italian supply convoys discovered. The sword smote from the air, on the sea, and beneath it.

On September 18th the British submarine *Upholder* torpedoed the Italian troop transports *Neptunia* and *Oceania*, both high-speed steamers of 20,000 tons laden with troops and equipment for Africa, and 5,000 men were lost. Off Benghazi bombs from three Malta-based Blenheims also sank the *Oriani*. Shipping losses of nine per cent in August rose to thirty-seven per cent by September, thus seriously affecting both the capacity and morale of the Italian transport fleet.

In November catastrophe reached its zenith. On the 9th "Force K", consisting of two British cruisers and two destroyers under Captain W. G. Agnew, detected an Italian convoy steaming by moonlight and sank the lot— five freighters and two tankers totalling 39,787 tons.

Rommel's forces in Africa suffered accordingly. He received neither munitions nor fuel by sea, and air deliveries alone were inadequate to keep his *Afrika Korps* on the march. It remained stuck on the Egyptian frontier, and the British 8th Army was able to prepare its own autumn offensive in peace. On November 18th it strode out into the desert, and by the year's end Rommel had been thrown back to Marsa el Brega, the place he had started from in the spring.

The total losses to the supply fleet in November were twelve fully-laden ships totalling 54,990 tons—or forty-four per cent of the transports that set sail. Admiral Weichold actually forwarded to Berlin the figure of seventy-seven per cent and Grand Admiral Raeder sounded the alarm at the Führer's headquarters. The alternatives were seldom clearer: either Malta must again be subdued or the *Afrika Korps* was lost. So the Luftwaffe had to return to Sicily.

Hitler recalled Kesselring from his winter H.Q. in front of Moscow, and in December General Loerzer and the staff of II Air Corps followed him to Messina. With the original *Geschwader* decimated in Russia, the Corps had to be reorganised. Fitting it out for sub-tropical warfare consumed further time. Five bomber *Gruppen*, all equipped with the Ju 88 A–4, finally arrived one after the other in Sicily, plus one Ju 87 and one Me 110 *Gruppe*. Fighter protection fell to the lot of the top-scoring JG 53, with four *Gruppen* of Me 109Fs. Altogether they represented a force of 325 aircraft. But of these only 229 were serviceable.

The units had hardly arrived before they were thrown into the battle. Single aircraft or formations of up to squadron strength patrolled the sea lanes or escorted the transports as they ran the gauntlet to North Africa, and after the long months of quietness bombs fell again on Malta. But while things became tougher for the British the Germans, though their operations were so far small in scale, were also finding them disproportionately costly.

The experience of the night-fighter *Gruppe*, I/NJG 2, was typical. Two months previously it had been carrying out "intruder" operations against British bomber bases in England—till Hitler personally cancelled this form of warfare. Though now based at Catania under Captain Jung, it had frequently to detach squadrons to North Africa and Crete, so that in Sicily itself there were seldom more than ten aircraft available at any one time. None the less, they flew day and night, and one crew after another failed to return.

On December 3rd Lieutenant von Keudell sighted a rubber dinghy in the Tyrrhenian Sea, and promptly summoned a rescue craft. By doing so he saved the life of the German air attaché in Rome, Major General Ritter von Pohl, who had come to grief while flying to join Kesselring for an initial conference on operations. Eight weeks later Keudell himself was missing after a mission against Malta.

Shortly after Christmas Lieutenant Babineck, youngest pilot of the *Gruppe*, was claimed by light flak over Valetta, after he had said over the radio: "Am diving through 10/10 cloud at 1,500 feet." Lieutenant Schleif, on a night intruder operation over Malta, shot down a Blenheim bomber in flames just as it was landing. Attempting to repeat his success on January 18th, his guns failed, and on the following night, over Luca, the flak got him at 600 feet, and his Ju 88 went down like a flaming torch. Lieutenant Haas never returned from his night pursuit of a British bomber. Lieutenant Laufs failed to find his airfield, obscured by darkness and clouds, and crashed into the slopes of Mount Etna. The adjutant, First-Lieutenant Schulz, was last seen diving into the sea just off the coast, and Corporal Teuber hurtled from 4,000 feet to destruction on Benghazi airfield after engine failure.

So it went on, day after day, week after week. To Colonel Deichmann, II Air Corps' chief of staff, the losses—especially those of the bombers over Malta—seemed almost incomprehensible. Perhaps the targets were too dispersed, with each having to be dive-bombed separately. For pin-point bombing was still the gospel according to Jeschonnek, Luftwaffe chief of general staff. It was an obsession both with him and the other Luftwaffe leaders. And over Malta it was finally exposed as a false conception.

Under Kesselring's direction Deichmann worked out a plan of his own. According to this, apart from identified anti-aircraft batteries and a few special targets, the whole tactic of dispersed dive-bombing was abandoned. In future the bombers would act as a united force, with the following programme:

1. Hit the British fighters on the ground by a surprise attack on their base, Ta Kali.
2. Attack the bomber and torpedo-plane bases of Luca, Hal Far and Calafrana.
3. Attack the docks and harbour installations of Valetta naval base.

After strong discussion this plan was approved at the beginning of March, 1942, and preparations were started. Then there was a hitch: matrixes used for multiplying copies of the orders, instead of being burnt, were found by a security officer in the act of being carted off by a dealer in a sack of waste paper. Who could be sure that the British had not already got wind of the coming operation? So the attack was delayed to see whether they changed their dispositions. But no; aerial photography showed the Spitfires and Hurricanes still concentrated at Ta Kali—that being the necessary pre-condition for surprise to succeed.

By March 20th the Germans were ready. As darkness fell the British fighters landed from the day's concluding sorties. Suddenly German bombers were again reported approaching over the sea. The Englishmen listened: it was not the usual high-pitched whine of just a few Ju 88s. It was the deeper, throbbing tone of a large formation.

As the first wave arrived, closely followed by the second, bombs rained down

—more and more of them, all on the same target, Ta Kali. Workshops and other buildings went up in flames. For this twilight assault II Air Corps had called upon every crew with night-flying experience, and the force amounted to about sixty bombers, with an escort of Me 110s and other night-fighters.

But there was another thing. Stereo photographs had revealed a ramp on the airfield's boundary, leading downward. Beside it was a huge heap of earth and rock. It presumably meant that the British had blasted out an underground hangar!

To cope with such an inaccessible target a number of Ju 88s had been fitted with 2,000-lb. armour-piercing rocket bombs. In this case the planes had once more to dive, for with a high starting velocity the rockets could penetrate such rocky ground up to forty-five feet. Meanwhile other machines attacked the ramp itself with incendiary bombs, in the hope that the burning oil would set on fire the fighters supposedly parked inside.

To this day the Germans do not know whether this attack with special weapons was successful, or indeed whether the underground hangar ever existed. The British still remain remarkably reticent about the matter. It is only on record that when the bombers attacked again next morning, they encountered no fighter opposition. With *Kampfgruppen* 606 and 806 from Catania, I/KG 54 from Gerbini, two *Gruppen* of KG 77 from Comiso, plus the fighters of JG 53 and II/JG 3 ("Udet") and the Me 110s of III/ZG 26, over 200 German aircraft were over Malta within a short period. Again Ta Kali was the target, as if no other existed on the island. It was the first example of "carpet bombing" in the whole war, and by the evening the British fighter base looked as if it had been subjected to a volcanic eruption.

On March 22nd it was the turn of the other airfields, in accordance with "phase two". But on the fourth day the "Deichmann Plan" was interrupted by the British attempt to bring a new supply convoy through to the hard-pressed island. With the Germans again in control of the air, it was a desperate attempt, and the convoy—four transports carrying munitions, fuel and victuals—had been constantly shadowed since leaving Alexandria four days earlier.

On the 22nd the Italian fleet tried to attack it, but was driven off by the strong British escort of four cruisers and sixteen destroyers. The Italian intervention meant, however, that instead of the convoy reaching Malta that night, it would only do so the next morning.

It thus fell victim to the Luftwaffe. Twenty miles off the island the transport *Clan Campbell* was sunk by a direct hit. The naval supply ship *Breconshire* was towed in a crippled condition to Marsa Scirocco bay, where further attacks finished her off. The remaining two transports foundered three days later, in Valetta harbour. Before then, during the rare pauses between raids, the British managed to rescue 5,000 tons of their valuable cargo. It represented, however, a bare fifth of what the four transports were carrying, and hard times for Malta lay ahead.

The third phase of the bombardment began at the end of the month with Valetta's harbour and docks as main target. In April the attack intensified, and Britain's destroyers and submarines were forced to depart, as the last of her bombers had done already. The mortal danger confronting the sea lanes to North Africa had been successfully combated. As his supply transports steamed into Tripoli and Benghazi unmolested, Rommel could breathe again.

In mid-April his enemy played another card. The American aircraft-carrier *Wasp* left Gibraltar and penetrated the Mediterranean to longitude five degrees east. Forty-seven brand new Spitfires took off from her deck and reached Malta with the last of their fuel. But though the *Wasp* remained out of range of the German Sicilian-based bombers, II Air Corps was kept fully informed of the enemy project by Captain Kuhlmann's radio monitoring service. Even the Spitfires' landing times could be calculated.

Twenty minutes after they had done so, and before they could be serviced, the bombs hailed down once more on Hal Far and Ta Kali airfields, after which only twenty-seven Spitfires remained serviceable. In the next few days even these were reduced by combat with JG 53's Messerschmitts.

By the end of the month the Germans hardly knew where to drop their bombs. So far as could be judged from the air, every military target had been either destroyed or badly damaged. In an order of the day II Air Corps summarised its successes: "During the period March 20th till April 28, 1942, the naval and air bases of Malta were put completely out of action. . . . In the course of 5,807 sorties by bombers, 5,667 by fighters, and 345 by recon-naissance aircraft, 6,557,231 kilograms of bombs were dropped. . . ."

It was, in fact, almost as much as had been dropped on the whole of Britain during the zenith of that battle in September, 1940.

Malta's airfields had been reduced to deserts, the quays and dockyards to wreckage and the warships themselves had been driven out. Only the crown-ing achievement remained: the occupation of the island prepared under the code-name "Operation Hercules".

Grand-Admiral Raeder had been pressing for this for a long time. Field-Marshal Kesselring also tried to get Hitler to sanction the plan. But the latter prevaricated, saying merely, "I shall do it one day!"

Meanwhile Mussolini and his chief of staff, Marshal Count Cavallero, de-clared that they would not advance another step in North Africa till Malta had fallen. Rommel even offered to lead the landing himself. But Hitler wanted to leave the conduct of the operation to the Italians. However, on April 29th at the Führer's Obersalzberg H.Q. near Berchtesgaden, Mussolini stated: "To concert the plans for such a landing we need another three months."

In three months a lot could happen.

In the evening of May 10th four British destroyers left Alexandria, set course north-north-west, and steamed at high speed into the darkness. At their head was the *Jervis*, carrying the flotilla commander, Captain A. L. Poland, followed by the *Jackal*, *Kipling* and *Lively*.

Their course was designed to bring them by next morning midway between Crete and North Africa, in the hope that they could then proceed west, far enough away from the dozen or so German air bases to north and south to remain undetected by reconnaissance aircraft. It was a slim chance, but much depended on it.

The purpose of the mission was to intercept an Italian convoy of three transports and three destroyers currently on its way from Taranto to Benghazi. For with Malta no longer in action as a naval and air base, the German-Italian supply fleet had recovered from its catastrophic losses inflicted the previous autumn and once more sailed virtually unmolested.

Its safety was further ensured by the fact that the R.A.F.'s new base between Derna and Benghazi had promptly been lost again when Rommel's bold counter-offensive against the British 8th Army at the end of January won back Cyrenaica as far as the Gazala Line. Since then the R.A.F.'s only hope of attacking the convoys was by means of long and dangerous flights past the German fighter bases in Cyrenaica. When Beaufort torpedo-planes and Blenheim bombers had attempted such an attack on a convoy eighty-five miles south-east of Malta, six of them had been shot down by its Me 110 escort supplied by Captain Christl's III/ZG 26.

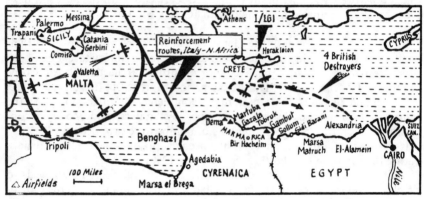

Malta and the African campaign. The strategic position of Malta, in mid-Mediterranean, can be seen at a glance. Though this British island fortress was, in April 1942, all but reduced by aircraft of the 2nd Air Corps based in Sicily, the German-Italian landing never took place, and Malta recovered its strength. The attacks, however, permitted Rommel sometimes to get his promised reinforcements, and to open his final offensive from his position at Gazala, which in the end led him to El Alamein. The attack to the west by four British destroyers ended in a hail of bombs from Ju 88s based on Crete.

So now the British Navy was to have a go. But the chances of four destroyers, coming all the way from Alexandria, achieving anything like the naval successes of November 1941, were rated at ten to one against. Captain Poland's orders were to attack only if he succeeded in intercepting the convoy off Benghazi at dawn on May 12th—and then only if he had remained undetected the whole of the previous day. For the heavy loss of British naval ships in recent weeks had shown that the Luftwaffe in the Mediterranean was making its presence felt.

On the 11th everything at first went well. Round noon the British destroyers stood between Crete and Tobruk. It was the critical moment, with the Mediterranean at this point only about 200 miles broad and under constant German reconnaissance—the British called it "Bomb Alley". Soon after noon the *Jervis* radar picked up a single aircraft, and the British officers held their breath. Had the flotilla been discovered and its position reported? Its fate hung by a thread, and a few minutes later the thread snapped. Circling well out of range the reconnaissance plane radioed: "Four destroyers, square xx, course 290, distance twenty-five miles."

On the bridge of the *Jervis* Captain Poland gave the order to turn back and head for Alexandria. His own orders—to break off the operation as soon as he was sighted—left him no alternative. But the danger was not averted.

Alerted in Athens, X Air Corps sent out the élite *Lehrgeschwader* I/LG 1 from Herakleion in Crete, followed by II/LG 1 from Eleusis in Greece.

At Herakleion the *Gruppenkommandeur*, Captain Jochen Helbig, quickly briefed his pilots. Since the Cretan air-sea battle of a year ago they had become specialists in this type of work. All knew that destroyers, with their high speed and manoeuvrability, were their most difficult opponents—likely to recede from the bomb-sight at the moment of bomb release. "It's like trying to catch a fish with your hands", as one pilot said. "It needs practice, patience, and very swift reactions."

He might have added "courage": the courage needed to dive from 12,000 feet into a wall of fire that increased each second in intensity. Helbig now ordered his men to dive down to 2,500 feet and use their accumulated speed to pull out low over the sea and so evade the worst of the flak.

The *Gruppe* had fourteen Ju 88 A-4s serviceable. As they flew south from Crete Helbig led them in a wide curve to approach the enemy ships from the south-west—a piece of deception that nearly succeeded. For the *Jervis* had just been in radio contact with two Beaufighters on their way from Africa to act as escort, and next moment they seemed to appear in the heavens. But then the seamen started: there were too many of them . . . they could only be German!

The attack began a few minutes after 15.30, Helbig leading off against the command destroyer. The sea boiled as the 500-lb. bombs exploded amongst the frantically writhing vessels. But there seemed to be no hits. No one observed the direct hit on the *Lively*, or the near miss that tore her whole side open. Within three minutes she sank, but by then the bomber crews were headed back to Crete, dispirited at their apparent lack of success. On arrival Helbig ordered the machines to be refuelled and bombed up again, and said to the crews: "We attack again this evening out of the setting sun. This time we shall dive to 1,500 feet."

At 17.00 II/LG 1 under Captain Kollewe attacked from Greece—in vain: all its bombs missed. And when Helbig made his second attack about two hours later, he this time had only seven aircraft. But they were flown by the best of his crews. There was no wind and the Mediterranean was smooth as a pond.

Taking advantage of the sinking sun he dived obliquely from astern, on the same course as the ships. This tactic enabled him to follow each evasive movement as it was made. Down came the bombs from 1,500 feet—and they struck home. Four hits were counted on one destroyer.

Following crews also hit the bull's-eye—First Lieutenants Iro Ilk, Brenner, Backhaus and Leupert. Helbig reported: "The first destroyer broke apart and sank quickly. Another was on fire, with her afterdeck under water."

That was the last the bombers saw as they flew off. In fact, the *Kipling* sank within a few minutes, followed by the burning *Jackal* next morning after a vain attempt to take her in tow. Of the four destroyers that had left Alexandria only Captain Poland's flagship, the *Jervis*, returned, with 630 survivors from the others on board.

For his *Gruppe's* success Captain Helbig was decorated with the Oak Leaves of the Knight's Cross with Swords. Kesselring sent him a case of champagne, and the German Navy a British life-belt fished from the sea in the battle area. Even the British press wrote with respect of the "Helbig Flyers".

None the less, the British had the last word. In June a convoy of eleven transports, with an unusually strong protective force, once more left Alexandria for Malta. Before it did so, however, Herakleion was visited at night by a British sabotage team, which stole up to the *Gruppe's* Ju 88s and planted mines on the starboard wing roots. Awakened by the explosions, the "Helbig Flyers" suddenly found they had no more aircraft. A reserve *Gruppe* promptly gave up its own to them.

The British were clearly resolved to leave no stone unturned in the attempt to get a convoy through to Malta. For the exhausted and starving island it was a matter of life and death.

2. Rommel versus "Hercules"

In May Malta received a new Governor—Lord Gort, the man who in 1940 had extricated the British Expeditionary Force from its desperate situation and enabled it to be evacuated at Dunkirk. When he reached the island on May 7th, 1942, the main bomber offensive from Sicily had just ended. But if the 30,000-man garrison could breathe again, its situation was anything but rosy.

"Our diet," wrote Air Vice-Marshal Lloyd, R.A.F. commander on Malta, "was a slice and a half of very poor bread with jam for breakfast, bully beef for lunch with one slice of bread, and . . . the same fare for dinner. . . . Even the drinking water, lighting and heating were rationed. All the things which had been taken for granted closed down. . . . Malta was faced with the unpleasant fact of being starved and forced into surrender from lack of equipment."[1]

A new ray of hope dawned for the garrison when, on May 9th, sixty-four Spitfires, taking off from the aircraft carriers *Wasp* and *Eagle* at about the longitude of Algiers, nearly all managed to land on the island (three fell short). This time there was no repetition of the catastrophe of April 20th when twenty out of forty-seven were immediately put out of action by an air-raid. Within seconds they were thrust into splinter-proof shelters already stocked with fuel, ammunition and equipment. After five minutes the first of them was ready to take off again.

The Germans did raid the airfields, but too late. They also missed an important target in Valetta harbour, where on May 10th the fast minelayer *Welshman* docked, bringing above all anti-aircraft ammunition. Thanks to fog, the assailants had to bomb blind, and within seven hours the vital cargo had been unloaded.

Thus the defence of Malta was strengthened at the very moment when the German air bombardment had apparently made the island ripe for assault, and just as Kesselring's *Luftflotte* 2 had (on May 10th) signalled the Führer's headquarters in East Prussia: "Enemy naval and air bases at Malta eliminated."

It took but a few days to prove the contrary. In the renewed raids during May 10–12th the Italians and Germans lost more bombers than during the whole five weeks of the main offensive with its 11,500 sorties. "In the last few days we and the Germans have lost many feathers over Malta," the Italian foreign minister, Count Ciano, noted in his diary, and the British view May 10th as the turning point of the whole battle.

On its side the Luftwaffe, having just concluded its offensive, was redistributed amongst other theatres, and could no longer attack in strength. With

[1] *Royal Air Force, 1939–45*, Vol. II, p. 203.

the new summer offensive in Russia needing every available machine, KG 77 was sent there on Hitler's personal orders. I/KG 54 was posted to Greece, while II/StG 3, II/ZG 26 and I/NJG's night-fighters were all sent to support Rommel in Africa. The same applied to the fighters: II/JG 3 and I/JG 53 went to Russia, III/JG 53 to Africa—just at the time when squadron after squadron of new Spitfires were flying into Malta. By the end of May Loerzer's II Air Corps, which in April had all but beaten Malta to its knees, was scattered to the winds.

Once more the German high command repeated its crucial mistake of embarking on a new enterprise before the current one had been concluded, thus dissipating its own strength. While Kesselring wanted to capture Malta by combined air and sea landings directly after the bomber offensive ("It would have been easy," he wrote in his memoirs) the Italians disagreed. They considered the preparations were being over-hastened, and the forces inadequate. As we have seen, Mussolini had asked for a delay of three months, and though Hitler no doubt could have insisted on an earlier date, he viewed the Italians' competence to conduct the operation successfully with deep misgiving, and gave way.

The consequence was that events in the Mediterranean theatre failed to mature as had been hoped. In both the German and Italian camps everyone had been agreed that Malta must be eliminated before any new offensive in Africa began. But now the commander of the *Afrika Korps*, Colonel-General Erwin Rommel, pointed to feverish offensive preparations opposite him on the Gazala front by the British 8th Army under General Ritchie. By starting an offensive themselves the British saw their chance of rescuing Malta. For the Luftwaffe was not strong enough to support both fronts simultaneously.

For Rommel it was a dilemma. If he waited for the fall of Malta, he himself would be overrun in the desert. On the other hand, if he anticipated the British attack, Malta would remain a threat to his rear and the supply crisis of the previous autumn might be repeated. Nevertheless the "Desert Fox" soon made up his mind. He clamoured to attack, and get in ahead of Ritchie. With the ample supply deliveries of the last few months he felt strong enough to do so. Ammunition and fuel should last four weeks, and by then he expected to be in Tobruk. After that he reckoned to halt on the Egyptian frontier, to allow Malta at last to be taken.

Thus Rommel had not expressed himself against "Operation Hercules", but in favour—*ultimately*. But now he had his way. On April 30th at Obersalzberg, Hitler and Mussolini issued the new order of priority: first, in June, Tobruk, second in July, Malta. It was a compromise about which no one was happy.

On May 26th, in the burning noonday sun, Rommel launched his attack. After twenty days of bitter fighting the battle went in his favour, and on June 21st exactly on time Tobruk fell. On the same day Mussolini wrote Hitler a letter, full of foreboding, reminding him not to forget Malta. But the Führer did not wish to be reminded. His interest in "Operation Hercules" had long since evaporated.

Yet for this very operation General Kurt Student and his XI Air Corps had been preparing the airborne landing for months. The mistakes of the operation against Crete would not be repeated. "We knew much more about the enemy's dispositions. Excellent aerial photographs had revealed every detail of his fortifications, coastal and flak batteries, and field positions. We even knew the calibre of the coastal guns, and how many degrees they could be turned inland."

The Italian leader of the operation, Marshal Count Cavallero, had at his disposal 30,000 men for the air landings alone—equivalent to the whole British garrison. Besides XI Air Corps, they included the Italian paratroop division "Folgore"—which, trained by Major-General Bernhard Ramcke, had impressed Kesselring enormously—and the Italian airborne division "Superba". For the seaborne landing no fewer than six Italian divisions, totalling 70,000 men, were ready. "It was an impressive force," said Student, "five times as strong as we had against Crete."

Major-General Conrad, now as for Crete responsible for XI Corps' transport, was again allocated ten *Gruppen* totalling some 500 Ju 52s. In view of the short distance separating Malta from Sicily, they could be expected to make four round trips the first day. He was moreover much better supplied with gliders than for Crete: besides 300 DFS 230s, each carrying ten men, there were 200 new-type Gotha Go 242s, with a capacity of twenty-five men. Some 200 glider pilots had been trained in landing with crane-parachutes. Conrad writes: "I suggested that all B-2 aircraft (single-engined training planes) should be assembled to tow the DFS 230s. As soon as the last bomb fell the latter should make pin-point landings with their crane 'chutes beside flak positions, known command posts and the mysterious caves. Immediately afterwards six transport *Gruppen* would drop their paratroops over their allotted targets, and the four carrying airborne troops would land them on the first airfield to be captured."

At the beginning of June, in the midst of these preparations, Student was suddenly ordered to the Führer's H.Q. at Rastenburg in East Prussia. Hitler listened as he made his report, interjected questions, and even admitted that a bridge-head on Malta could be successfully won.

"But what then?" he asked impatiently. "I guarantee what will happen. The Gibraltar squadron will leave port at once, and the British fleet will come steaming from Alexandria. Then you will see what the Italians will do. At the first radio reports they will go running back into their Sicilian harbours—warships, transports and all. And you and your paratroops will be left sitting on the island alone!"

Student was dumbfounded. To think that for months he had been preparing an operation that Hitler never intended to sanction! He began to object, but the Führer cut him short with the words: "I forbid you to return to Italy! You will stay in Berlin."

Significantly enough, this interview took place at the very time when the success of Rommel's campaign in Marmarica hung in the balance. When, two weeks later, Tobruk and all its booty fell into his hands, and he asked to be given *carte blanche* to pursue his battered foe to the banks of the Nile, Hitler and the high command did not dream of halting his victorious march in favour of Malta.

But the Italians did. Full of anxiety, they thought about the supply lines and the catastrophe of the previous year. They pointed to the mutually agreed order of priority: first Tobruk, then Malta, and only then Egypt. Mussolini wrote his letter of June 21st referred to above. In his reply, two days later, Hitler never so much as mentioned Malta. Instead he harped on the "historic hour", on the "unique opportunity to pursue the British 8th Army to complete destruction" and of wresting Egypt from British hands. He concluded his letter: "On us leaders the goddess of battle smiles but once. He who fails to grasp her favours at such a moment will never be able to entice her back."

As he read these lines Mussolini's eyes shone—according to General von Rintelen, the military attaché who brought the letter to him. "He looked at me proudly, and was all for an immediate assault on Egypt and the occupation of Cairo and Alexandria. Mussolini's trust in Hitler's strategy was at this time boundless. Cavallero with his counter-arguments could make no impression. The Malta operation was postponed until September, which meant that it was finally abandoned."

The Führer's treatment of Kesselring was hardly so tactful. When the latter called it "madness" for Rommel to dash onward with his own forces exhausted and the enemy's Egyptian airfields fully intact, Hitler sent the Commander-in-Chief South a signal, peremptorily ordering him to refrain from opposing Rommel's operational ideas and to give him maximum support.

Rommel hoped to reach the Nile in ten days, and within eight days Cairo was only 125 miles distant. By then he had reached a village that no one had previously heard of: El Alamein. There his offensive collapsed—the offensive that had begun so hopefully on the Gazala front over 450 miles to the west on May 26th.

On June 3rd, the battle in Marmarica had swayed to and fro. Since the second day of the offensive Rommel and his armour operated behind the enemy front, having outflanked it through the desert while the Italians made a mock frontal attack. But the Gazala front was not easy to break even from the rear, consisting as it did of a forty-mile-long minefield protected at all points by prickly desert forts. Till the last of them fell, Rommel had no freedom of action—and the last, Bir Hacheim, was bitterly defended by the 1st Free French Brigade under General Koenig. It held out for nine days, effectually preventing Rommel's further advance.

The *Stukas* were summoned, and on June 3rd StG 3 under Lieutenant Colonel Walter Sigel made the first concentrated attack. From the air the fort, with its two-mile diameter, resembled any other part of the desert. It seemed incredible that the French had dug themselves in there, and that they could not be ejected.

The bombs rained down, but mostly buried themselves in the sand. Only direct hits had any effect, and the ground troops were unable to exploit the enemy's confusion. They were too widely distributed to take such a stronghold.

Shortly after noon the second wave of *Stukas* took off from Derna, protected by Me 109s of I/JG 27. At 12.22 the Ju 87s were attacked by a Curtiss squadron, and immediately afterwards by No. 5 (South African) Squadron. Then suddenly a pair of Messerschmitts was on the scene. The leading plane was famous throughout the *Afrika Korps*, with a huge yellow "14" painted on its fuselage; the second machine was flown by Sergeant Rainer Poettgen.

The British turned defensively, but the yellow "14", briefly throttling back, attacked the first of them. A short burst, and the latter flicked over on fire. A minute later the second suffered a like fate; then the third, fourth, fifth and sixth. Said Poettgen afterwards:

"I had my work cut out counting his victories, noting the times and position, and simultaneously protecting his tail." About his companion he observed: "His judgement of deflection was incredible. Each time he fired I saw his shells strike first the enemy plane's nose, then travel along to the cockpit. No ammunition was wasted."

Few pilots have been really adept at deflection shooting. In this manner to shoot down six opponents in twelve minutes was the work of a genius. Yellow "14" was piloted by First-Lieutenant Marseille, top fighter "ace" of the Luftwaffe.

3. Rise and Fall of a Fighter Ace

Hans-Joachim Marseille, born on December 13, 1919 and a true Berliner, had reached North Africa in spring 1941 as an officer cadet with I/JG 27 under Captain Eduard Neumann. His first experience on foreign soil won him a reputation for nonchalant charm.

On the flight from Tripoli to the future base of operations at Gazala his Me 109 developed engine trouble and he had to make a forced landing in the desert, 500 miles short of his destination. His squadron circled round till satisfied that he had got down all right, then resumed its flight to the east.

Left to his own devices, Marseille first hitch-hiked for half a day on an Italian lorry, then, finding that too slow, tried his luck at an airstrip. In vain. No one knew when or whether an aircraft on its way to Benghazi or Derna would stop there. Finally he made his way to the general in charge of a supply depot on the main route to the front, and managed to convince him that as a "flight commander" it was essential that he should be available for operations next day. Could he please be given a fast car?

The young man's zeal and cheek appealed to the general and he put at his disposal his own Opel Admiral, complete with chauffeur. "You can pay me back by getting fifty victories, Marseille!" were his parting words.

"Leave it to me, *Herr General*," Marseille replied.

After driving right through the night he drew up proudly next day on Gazala airfield in the general's car. His squadron commander, First-Lieutenant Gerhard Homuth, was taken aback: the rest of them, after an intermediate landing to spend the night at Benghazi, had themselves only arrived two hours earlier. Marseille had covered the 500 miles "on foot" almost as quickly as they had in Me 109s.

Another typical incident had occurred en route. The Opel had to stop for petrol and Marseille took the opportunity to draw some pay. But when the field cashier was about to stamp his pay-book, he protested: "Not there, please! That space must be saved." It was the page reserved for decorations, and the Iron Cross 1st Class had already been recorded.

"Do you expect to get *more* than the EK I?" asked the cashier.

"Of course." So the cashier, leaving an exaggerated amount of space, said with a grin: "Now you've got room for the Oak Leaves, Swords and all!"

At twenty-one Marseille called himself the "oldest officer cadet in the Luftwaffe". He could have been a lieutenant long since but for the critical reports in his personal file. Such phrases as "bravado and playing pranks while under training" and "offences against flying regulations" made a poor impression on operational commanders, who themselves added to his file the curious reproof of "flying obscenity". His bad reputation clung to him, evoking mistrust from each new C.O., and continuing even after he had proved his worth by his first success against British fighters over the English Channel.

Now, in Africa, he wanted to prove that he was a good fighter pilot. Over Tobruk he scored the first victory of his squadron, 3/JG 27, in this new theatre—a Hurricane. But though this ranked as a good beginning he was over-impatient, chancing his arm by diving impetuously straight into the British formations, and frequently returning to base with his aircraft riddled by enemy fire.

Again and again his luck held. Once bullets ripped his leather helmet a second after he had leaned forward. After another dog-fight over Tobruk he had to make a forced landing in no-man's-land, but made his way back to the German lines. Then, with his engine shot up and his vision totally obscured by oil spurting on his windscreen, he crash-landed at his own base. It was too much for his *Gruppenkommandeur*, who hauled him up on the mat.

"You are only alive," said Neumann, "because you have more luck than sense. But don't imagine that it will continue indefinitely. One can over-strain one's luck like one can an aeroplane."

Captain Neumann was well aware of the young man's tremendous potential and fighting spirit, but also of his lack of polish and discipline. He recognised that it was his task not to discourage but to educate him—to add discretion to valour. "You have the makings of a top-notch pilot," he added. "But to become one you need time, maturity and experience—certainly more time than you have left if you go on as you have been doing."

Marseille got the message, and promised to behave better and work on himself. Only he was loath to give up his mode of attack. Instead of confining himself to attack from astern, as he had been taught in training school, he felt a pilot should have sufficient command of his machine to be able to aim his guns from any position—i.e., not only while flying straight and level, but in a turn, a climb or even a roll.

Few pilots were any good at this: in such positions most of them missed their opponents hopelessly. He himself, however, had a feel for time and distance which, after much practice, enabled him to judge exactly the right deflection. Often, while 3 Squadron was on the way back from an operation, he would request permission to break away and make dummy attacks on his comrades, meanwhile practising aiming from every angle.

It took him the whole summer of 1941 before he had perfected his skill. But then on September 24th he reaped his reward when for the first time he shot down five of the enemy in a single day: in the morning a Martin Maryland; in the afternoon—in the course of a furious turning tournament, lasting half an hour, between Halfaya Pass and Sidi Barani—four Hurricanes. Again and again he and his flight would tear into a British formation and break it up. He gained his twenty-third victory when, after detaching an enemy fighter from a defensive circle, he chased and destroyed it over Sidi Barani.

Then came the rains, flooding the German fighter bases, and after that the British autumn offensive of 1941, which pushed Rommel back to his starting point. Marseille, however, went on flying, and in February 1942, after forty-eight victories, was awarded the Knight's Cross. In April he was promoted to

First-Lieutenant, and early in June given the command of 3 Squadron. Simultaneously Captain Homuth took over I *Gruppe*, and Major Neumann the *Geschwader*. JG 27 was now at full strength in support of Rommel's vital offensive.

As Marseille's star continued in the ascendant, his aircraft, the yellow "14" became as legendary a cynosure amongst the German and Italian forces as Rommel's tank. On 3rd June, as we have seen, he shot down six Curtiss Tomahawks of the South African squadron in twelve minutes, thereby permitting StG 3's Ju 87s to pursue their attack on Bir Hacheim. But though their bombs hit the target, this southern buttress of the British Gazala line with its cunning layout of pillboxes, field and anti-tank and anti-aircraft positions totalling 1,200 units, still did not fall. Rommel, whose whole further advance was thereby threatened, called daily on the "*Fliegerführer Afrika*", Lieutenant General Hoffmann von Waldau, for the *Stuka* attacks to be stepped up.

But the enemy knew equally what was at stake. Air Vice-Marshal Coningham pitted the fighters, fighter-bombers and bombers of the Desert Air Force repeatedly against the German assailants and their bases. Sigel's StG 3 suffered severely, losing fourteen Ju 87s in a week. And the worst of it was that their own attacks were wasted owing to the failure of the troops to follow up in strength. Despite all the promptings of his commanders, Rommel declined adequately to reinforce the besieging forces, and General von Waldau angrily reported to Kesselring that thanks to the lack of co-ordination the *Stuka* raids were virtually pointless and unnecessarily costly.

Kesselring flew forthwith to see Rommel and complained. Thereupon Rommel committed Colonel Wolz's Flak Regiment 135, which had just been engaged in parrying savage British armoured attacks on the German east

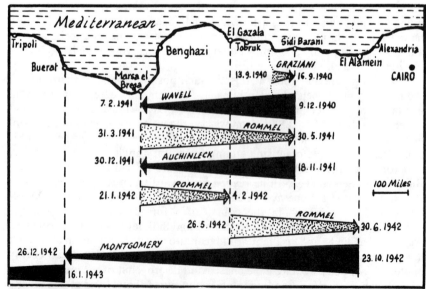

The "*pendulum*" war in North Africa. For two long years the struggle oscillated to and fro between the Germans and Italians to the west and the British to the east. In autumn, 1942, Montgomery opened the third British offensive which sealed the fate of Rommel and the *Afrika Korps* in Africa.

flank. When even that failed to help, he was obliged to withdraw combat groups from the main push to the north and pit them too against "this confounded hole in the desert".

At last the ground attack made headway, and on June 9th a whole fortnight since the start of the German-Italian offensive, the *Stukas* hammered Bir Hacheim again. A battery position one and a half miles north of the fortress was badly hit, and that evening von Waldau reported to Rommel: "We have now flown 1,030 sorties against Bir Hacheim in support of your Army." But next day three more assaults by all available bomber units were ordered. To reinforce them Kesselring sent over LG 1's Ju 88 *Gruppen* from Greece and Crete.

The first attack had to be broken off because the pilots were unable to differentiate between friend and foe owing to smoke and dust. But at midday and in the afternoon the other two waves went in, with 124 Ju 87s in the first and seventy-six Ju 88s in the second. 140 tons of bombs fell on the brave Frenchmen's positions, and this time the bombing was accurate. Before the dust and sand had cleared, the infantry and sapper units launched their assault.

As protection for the bombers 168 Messerschmitts were airborne, and for the first time in Africa encountered Spitfires. Marseille once more accounted for four of the enemy, bringing his personal score to eighty-one. During the night General Koenig and a part of his garrison broke out from the fortress and fought their way through to the British lines. And next morning, June 11th, Bir Hacheim put out the white flag.

Rommel had at last secured his rear. In the next three days he pushed north behind the British Gazala front, and on the 14th General Ritchie had to pull back his divisions. The Marmarican battle was decided. Part of the Commonwealth troops withdrew to Tobruk; the bulk, by-passing Bir Hacheim, swiftly retreated farther east. Apparently disregarding Tobruk, still uncaptured on his left flank, Rommel took up the pursuit of the battered enemy towards the Egyptian frontier.

Meanwhile Marseille and his squadron 3/JG 27 kept up their own type of pressure. Decorated by Kesselring with the "Oak Leaves" the week before, he was in action every day, and always in the same machine, the yellow " 14". Jokingly he promised to pay his ground crew N.C.O.s fifty lire for every victory, provided they had his plane in tip-top condition every morning; but his armourer, Schulte, replied good-naturedly: "Forget about it, *Herr Oberleutnant*, or you'll be a poor man!"

He now flew with dream-like precision, his machine seeming to respond automatically and immediately to his every whim, while he himself concentrated solely on his opponents. Few of them, once engaged, now got away. In the air battles above the retreating British Army near El Adem, Marseille again shot down four planes on June 15th alone. It brought his personal score to ninety-one and the *Geschwader* started a sweep-stake on when he would reach his century.

"Jochen, when are your 'Swords' due?" a companion asked one evening, as they sat with the *Kommodore*.

"The day after tomorrow at noon," Marseille laughingly replied. From anyone else it would have seemed a disgusting "line-shoot", but "our Jochen" (as they called the slim, blond youth) had remained unspoilt by success, and was popular with all, from the *Kommodore* downwards.

Next morning 3 Squadron carried out two missions without contacting the enemy. In the afternoon there was a fighter sweep, after which they were to land at the recently recaptured airfield of Gazala. When the ground crews arrived there in the evening, they were met by Marseille's No. 2, Sergeant Poettgen, shouting joyously: "He's got four again!"

Poettgen, with the job of counting his C.O.'s victories, confirming the crashes and the times, had been teasingly dubbed by his pals "the flying computer". But in fact he had often saved Marseille's life by warning him of an enemy fighter on his tail. And Marseille had as often repaid the debt by saving his loyal No. 2 in like circumstances. Now, with his score at ninety-five and one day to go to keep his promise, the atmosphere in JG 27 became electric.

On the 17th the whole *Geschwader* was sent off on another fighter sweep, hoping to intercept the British low flyers who had been making life uncomfortable for the German Army vanguard, particularly 21 *Panzer* Division. They had even hit Gazala airfield, writing off seven of JG 27's Me 109s.

At 12.35 Marseille and his flight returned, and sweeping low over their home base, waggled their wings three times. Then they made another circuit, and waggled them three times more. It meant, astonishingly enough, that Marseille had reached 101.

Dropping everything, everyone rushed towards the taxiing aircraft, intending to haul out the pilot and carry him shoulder high. First up on the wing was his flight mechanic, Meyer, but when he tried to undo the straps, Marseille waved him wearily aside. His face was ash-grey and seemingly petrified, and when he climbed slowly out, his brow was covered with sweat. Suddenly all realised that he was on the point of collapse. The accumulated strain of flying and fighting and killing without let-up, had brought him abruptly to the end of his tether.

At last he took a cigarette, still with shaking hands, and reverted to something like the gay young fighter pilot they all knew. But when he reported to his *Kommodore*, Major Neumann said to him: "You are going on leave at once!"

Marseille tried to protest. Now, just before Tobruk, in the midst of the offensive, when every man was wanted? But Neumann stuck to his guns: "You are off! What's more, you've been summoned to the Führer's headquarters to collect your 'Swords'."

Thanks to the field cashier at Derna, there was still room in his pay-book. He was away two months. But after only a fortnight the battle of North Africa took a decisive turn.

After the fall of the British-held fortress of El Adem on June 17, 1942, the Italian armoured "Ariete" division and the whole of the *Afrika Korps* stormed onwards to the Egyptian frontier. Rommel left Tobruk untaken in his rear. But Gambut, with its R.A.F. base, had to be captured first.

On June 18th it was overrun, the British airfield personnel getting away at the last moment. Now, with the direct air opposition removed, Rommel promptly turned about and assaulted Tobruk by its back door.

This time the assault was synchronised with the Luftwaffe's attacks. At 05.20 on June 20th StG 3's Ju 87s made their first dive-bombing raid. Bombs slashed open the barbed wire defences to the south-east, and beat a gap through the mine-fields half a mile broad. At once the German and Italian infantry stormed through it. After that came LG 1's Ju 88s, bombing the enemy artillery positions in front of the German spearhead. They were followed by Me 110s of III/ZG 26, firing their cannon against the machine-gun and anti-tanks posts.

Then it was the turn of Colonel Grandinetti's Fiat CR 42 fighter-bombers of the "Settore Est" unit. Finally, an hour and a half after the first attack, the *Stukas* came once more. So it went on, with wave after wave of aircraft "softening up" the narrow assault sector for the Axis ground troops, while smoke grenades marked both the point of furthest advance and the flanks, and direction bursts indicated the targets to be attacked from the air.

After bitter close combat the outer defences fell, and at 08.00 sappers started bridging the broad anti-tank trench. By noon the tanks had reached the Sidi Mahmud cross-roads, and Rommel was getting ready to penetrate the heart of the Tobruk stronghold.

The Luftwaffe now went for the Pilastrino and Solaro forts, the airfield, and the harbour shipping. The garrison commander, South African General Klopper, was bombed out of his headquarters and lost all communication with his troops. That evening he reported to Cairo that the position was hopeless. Next morning Rommel drove victoriously into Tobruk, and at 09.20 General Klopper capitulated. After withstanding every attack for twenty-eight weeks in 1941, Tobruk had fallen within twenty-eight hours in 1942.

Promoted to Field-Marshal, Rommel now stood at the peak of his fame. But despite nearly four weeks of continuous and bitter fighting, his forces were granted no rest. He drove them onwards to the east. He wanted to reach Cairo and attain total victory, and now seemed to be the chance.

On June 26th, when the *Afrika Korps* was at the gates of Marsa Matruch, there took place—as we have seen—the great "Malta or Cairo" controversy. At the famous "field-marshal" conference of Sidi Barani, between Rommel and Kesselring for Germany and the Italians Bastico and Cavallero, Rommel undertook to reach the Nile within ten days.

"The British are on the run," he said. "We should give them no chance to regroup. A later attack on the Nile delta will need stronger forces and mean higher casualties. Supplies are secured for the present by the rich haul in Tobruk. We must concentrate our whole strength, particularly the Luftwaffe, at one decisive point of effort. And that is here—here in Egypt."

Kesselring disagreed. In his view the supply problem was still unsolved, if the advance was to continue. "The Luftwaffe," he said, "badly needs rest. My crews are exhausted, and their planes in need of overhaul. As an airman I say it is madness to rush on against an enemy whose air bases are still intact. In view of the vital role the Luftwaffe would have to play, I must, for this reason alone, disagree with pushing on to Cairo."

Against him Rommel re-emphasised his own arguments. Bastico and Cavallero, who were nominally in command, agreed with him, supported in the background by Mussolini. The latter was already preparing to fly to Africa, consumed by the idea of entering Cairo on a white horse at the head of his troops. And so, with Kesselring ordered by Hitler to desist from interference, fate took its course.

"The general planning," wrote Major Neumann, commander of JG/27, "seems to envisage a forward push by the Army only. With our inadequate ground organisation we just can't keep up."

All the same the *Fliegerführer Afrika* threw all the units at his command into the battles for Marsa Matruch and El Alamein. LG 1 attacked British supply depots, StG 3 went for troop movements behind the front. JG 27's war diary records: "On June 26th the fighters sent forward to Sidi Barani were kept busy. But apart from a single petrol bowser the *Geschwader* had nothing on the spot. The pilots had to fly their missions on empty stomachs."

By the evening Lieutenant Korner had claimed five victories, Lieutenants Stahlschmidt and Schroer three each. Next morning the fighters were sent farther forward, to Bir El Astas, and two days later still farther, to Fuka. But by now whole *Gruppen* were grounded by fuel shortage.

Meanwhile the hitting power of the R.A.F., operating now from their well-constructed bases in Egypt, mounted daily. The farther the advance continued, the greater became the Luftwaffe's losses at the hands of low-flying enemy planes.

On June 30th the German bombers and *Stukas* at Fuka were prevented by a severe sand-storm from taking off to aid the assault on the El Alamein position. For three days Rommel strove to break through it, after which his strength was exhausted, and he was forced into a defensive posture. His final attempt to resume the offensive eight weeks later was doomed to failure. When General Montgomery opened his own offensive on October 23, 1942, the North African pendulum swung finally westwards.

On August 23rd Jochen Marseille, who at twenty-two by this time became the youngest captain in the Luftwaffe, returned to his post and again took over his old squadron, 3/JG 27. They were delighted to see him, and Corporal Neumann, who kept the records, sharpened his pencil. "I hope I shall be able to keep you busy," laughed Marseille.

For a whole week nothing happened. Then on September 1st—the day Rommel tried finally to wrest the initiative from his heavily reinforced enemy —air activity over the front suddenly resumed its old intensity. Marseille and his squadron made three sorties. At 08.28 and 08.39 he shot down two Curtisses and two Spitfires; between 10.55 and 11.05 while escorting *Stukas* at Alam El Halfa, eight Curtisses; finally, between 17.47 and 17.53 south of Imayid, another five Curtisses.

Seventeen victories in a single day were an all-time "high", making Captain Marseille unquestionably the world's most successful fighter pilot. However many claims in general were disputed after the war, it is established that the British official figure of losses sustained from August 31 till September 2, 1942, actually exceeded the German claims for these four days.

A month had began during which Marseille's fame transcended that of Rommel himself. On September 3rd he was awarded the highest decoration of all: the Diamonds of the Knight's Cross. On the 26th he was all but matched by an opponent flying a Spitfire, and only after a dog-fight lasting a quarter of an hour did he succeed in defeating him. It was his 158th victory, and his last.

On September 30th he took off at 10.47 with eight Me 109s of his squadron on a high-cover sweep in defence of *Stukas*. No contact with the enemy was made, but on the return flight his cockpit suddenly began smoking. He pulled open the ventilator, and more smoke belched through. The engine was on fire.

"Elbe 1 calling," came his voice on the radio. "Smoke building up badly in cockpit. I cannot see."

The squadron closed tightly round him while his old No. 2, Poettgen, gave him directions: "More to starboard—that's right. Now a bit of elevator—splendid."

"Can't see a thing," Marseille repeated, and Poettgen went on: "Just another three minutes to Alamein . . . just two minutes . . . just one more minute."

Finally they were over friendly territory, but Marseille called: "I've got to get out." He put the machine on its back, and the roof flew away, followed by his body. Then they all stared in horror: the parachute failed to open. The pilot fell like a stone, and at 11.36 hit the ground. Captain Ludwig Fransizket, commander of 1/JG 27, dashed off in a car and fetched the remains of his comrade from the desert.

Examination showed that the rip-cord had not been pulled. Probably Marseille was already unconscious, for a broad chest-wound showed that he had been struck by the tail unit of his diving aircraft.

Everyone found it hard to believe that at the peak of his fame the life of this beaming young airman had suddenly been quenched, not by combat with the enemy but by an accident.

Mediterranean Theatre 1942—Summary and Conclusions

1. Catastrophic losses amongst the German-Italian supply convoys to North Africa in autumn 1941 compelled the German high command once more to base an air corps in Sicily. With the opening of the second Battle of Malta in early 1942, the convoy position at once improved. The harder the island was hit, the more supplies got through to Rommel, and finally he was able to start his offensive from his position at Gazala.

2. The logical conclusion—to capture Malta by airborne and seaborne landings—was planned but never implemented. The most favourable moment, just after the heavy air bombardment of April 1942, was allowed to pass. While Hitler left the command of the operation to the Italians, he at the same time did not believe they were capable of carrying it through. Rommel finally brought the whole project of "Operation Hercules" to an end by his belief that, after the swift conquest of Tobruk, he could reach the Nile in a single thrust.

3. For this undertaking he demanded and received the support of all the available Luftwaffe forces in the Mediterranean. But Cairo was never reached; and Malta, no longer molested, soon recovered its strength, so that once again the graph of Rommel's seaborne supply losses ascended. In North Africa the game was up.

4. During the Malta air bombardment the advantages of attacking key targets such as airfields and harbour installations by means of large formations instead of serial dive-bombing (still advocated by the Luftwaffe chief of general staff, Jeschonnek) were clearly demonstrated. Malta was subjected to the first "carpet bombing"—albeit against military targets—of World War II.

9

WAR OVER THE OCEAN

1. The Battle of the Atlantic

Three He 111 bombers were flying westwards just above the surface of the North Sea, their slipstreams lashing the water and their pilots tensely concentrated on avoiding the single careless movement that would plunge them to destruction. For at flying speed water is as hard as stone.

They were flying low so as to duck beneath the British radar beams and thus achieve surprise for their attack on the convoy that had reportedly left Pentland Firth at noon, and was now steaming south along the Scottish coast. The autumn sun had set and twilight had descended. Only in the west was the sky still bright, and that meant favourable conditions: the bombers would attack from a dark horizon, and surprise should be complete.

In the leading Heinkel, as observer and commander, sat Major Martin Harlinghausen, X Air Corps' chief of staff. Beside him, as pilot, was his staff operations officer, Captain Robert Kowalewski. The three machines represented X Air Corps' staff section, an institution peculiar to the German Luftwaffe. The Corps, still under the command of Air General Hans Ferdinand Geisler, had now as formerly the task of attacking Britain's shipping. But its leaders were not "chair-borne". By leading the attack, they demanded nothing from the *Geschwader* and *Gruppen* that they were not prepared to undertake themselves.

Harlinghausen had developed a special method of attacking enemy ships, known as the "Swedish turnip" system. It was based on the old naval axiom that ships present the best target when approached directly from the beam. And the lower an aircraft's approach, the higher the target stands out of the water, and the clearer becomes its silhouette against the horizon. The last applies particularly at dusk, but also on starlit or moonlit nights.

They sighted the convoy about twenty sea-miles north-east of Kinnaird Head, and promptly set a parallel course to plan the attack.

"We'll take the fourth from the left," said Harlinghausen. It was the largest vessel and presumably, with its extensive hull and superstructure aft and amidships, a tanker. Kowalewski banked left towards the convoy. "I can't see her, Harling," he said.

"Another ten degrees to port," his chief corrected. He was lying prone and forward, his head almost against the cockpit Perspex, and so was able to concentrate exclusively on the target, while the pilot was farther back and otherwise preoccupied. After months of practice together, they had acquired instant mutual understanding and response.

"Now you are right on target," said Harlinghausen. He exuded calm, having first tried out his "Swedish turnip" system long before in the Spanish civil war. Then it had been with the old He 59, which could only be used for low-level surprise attack, else it would be spotted too soon and shot down.

The He 111 now approached the tanker at a speed of about 200 m.p.h. and an altitude of forty-five meters. To maintain this also needed practice, for at such height the barometric altimeter was so unreliable that it often showed the plane as flying deep under the water. Correct altitude was, however, a crucial factor in Harlinghausen's calculations, for in the first three seconds the bombs fell respectively five, fifteen and twenty-five metres, or forty-five in all. In this time the Heinkel covered a distance of 240 metres, so in order to hit the target that was the distance from which the bombs must be released. In three seconds their loss of momentum was minimal: they at first flew with the bomber and below it, then dropped against the target in a gentle arc.

The tanker's silhouette loomed ever larger from the sea, her crew still unaware of the impending blow. Kowalewski aimed directly for the superstructure, below which was the engine-room. With every second the Heinkel drew eighty metres nearer, and decks, bridge and masts took shape. Finally at 240 metres the release signal was given, and four 500-lb. bombs fell in close succession. For Harlinghausen had adjusted the mechanism to produce the minimum interval between them, namely about eight metres. In this way one at least was bound to strike.

Three seconds later the Heinkel thundered across the tanker, and almost simultaneously the bombs struck. But they only detonated after a delay of eight seconds, when the aircraft was safely away. The tanker exploded in a sheet of flame.

As the Heinkel made a circuit, burning oil was seen pouring from the stricken vessel. She was an 8,000 tonner, as had been determined from the convoy's radio exchanges. For the second Heinkel carried a monitoring team, tuned in to the same wavelength.

The convoy's defences were now alerted, but ignoring the tracer that laced towards him Harlinghausen attacked again, this time using his starboard bomb-rack against a freighter.

During 1940 he and his pilot succeeded three times in sinking two ships on one sortie by using alternate bomb-racks. By September this single crew had claimed no less than 100,000 tons of shipping.[1] After that the operating conditions grew more difficult. The defence was stepped up, and each month it became harder to approach the ships. Though the "Lion" *Geschwader*, KG 26, were trained in low-level attack and practised with cement bombs in the Norwegian fiords, their successes were small and their losses increased.

But in October, 1940, success returned. The few available four-engined

---

[1] During the first year of the war—i.e. from September 3, 1939 till August 30, 1940—the Luftwaffe claimed to have sunk a total of 1,376,813 tons. Figure published by the Allies after the war indicate that in fact they only lost some 440,000 tons to German air attack during this period.

Focke-Wulf FW 200s, brought together to form I/KG 40 at Bordeaux, were flying armed reconnaissance patrols far out into the Atlantic. On October 24th while so engaged, First-Lieutenant Bernhard Jope came upon the 42,348-ton liner *Empress of Britain*, now being used as a troopship, some sixty miles west of Ireland. Going down, he attacked not from the beam but from astern. Bombs exploded in the superstructure, and the liner hove to on fire. The British tried to take her in tow, but two days later she was torpedoed by Lieutenant Jenisch's *U 32*, which had been called to the scene by radio.

Let us move on to February 9, 1941. Twenty engines were being warmed up in front of the hangars of Bordeaux-Merignac airfield, but they represented only five aircraft: five four-engined Fw 200 "Condors".

It was six in the morning as Captain Fritz Fliegel, squadron commander of 2/KG 40 took off, followed by First-Lieutenants Adam, Buchholz, Jope and Schlosser. The heavy machines left the ground reluctantly, their fuselage- and wing-tanks being filled to capacity with nearly 2,000 gallons of fuel. Each carried a crew of six: first pilot and co-pilot, two radio-operators, flight mechanic and rear-gunner.

But the bomb load was a mere 2,000 lb. Though the Fw 200 was the heaviest machine the Luftwaffe had, it had never been designed as a bomber, being only a converted air-liner. Germany's real long-range bomber, the He 177, was still vainly in the testing stage. Considering their makeshift character, and how few they were, it is astonishing what the crews managed to achieve with these Condors.

Fliegel and his squadron headed south-west, their target a speck far off in the wastes of the Atlantic, somewhere between Portugal and the Azores. There the previous evening Lieutenant Nicolai Clausen of U-boat *U 37* had happened upon a British convoy out from Gibraltar and bound for England. It was a chance encounter, for the convoys habitually made a wide detour to avoid the Luftwaffe and U-boat bases on the French coast. As the *U 37* shadowed it, the sighting report was forwarded via C.-in-C. U-boats, Admiral Karl Dönitz, to KG 40 at Bordeaux. In the early hours of February 9th the *U 37* attacked, sinking the freighters *Courland* and *Estrellano*. Then, remaining in contact, Clausen kept the approaching Condors informed of the convoy's position. It was only a question of when they would get there.

They did so at noon, after over six hours' flight, finding the convoy some 400 miles south-west of Lisbon. Fliegel allocated the targets and went down to attack. The need to do so was itself indicative of the makeshift character of the machines. They were unable to bomb horizontally from high altitude, as heavy bombers should, because of the lack of a suitable bomb-sight. The so-called *"Lotfernrohr 7d"* only came into use much later. Fliegel had to bring his heavy plane down low over the sea, then turn towards the selected ship and try to approach from the beam so that the target would present as large an image as possible.

At 400 yards range, and an altitude of about 150 feet, he let go the first of his four 500-lb. bombs. At the same moment the flight-mechanic opened fire with the ventral machine-guns, spraying the deck positions to hold down the ship's anti-aircraft crews. Seconds later the Fw 200 roared over the mast-tops—surely a big enough target! First-Lieutenant Adam had his wing-tanks hit while still on the approach, and was lucky that his plane did not catch fire.

Petrol poured out in a sheet from holes the size of an orange, and he at once turned back in an attempt to reach the coast.

The other aircraft made repeated attacks. Buchholz, one of KG 40's "aces", missed his freighter by a hair's breadth, the bombs exploding hard by the gunwale. Fliegel and Schlosser twice scored hits, Jope once. Five freighters were sunk: the British *Jura, Dagmar I, Varna* and *Britannic*, and the Norwegian *Tejo*. At the end *U 37* came up again and sank a further vessel.

Thus convoy HG 53 had already lost half the sixteen ships that had set out from Gibraltar, despite the protection of nine escort vessels. Unless the remainder could take evasive action, the British Admiralty could only fear the worst. It took the extreme step of ordering the ships to disperse and make for their destination singly.

On the German side the success was greatly exaggerated. According to Secret Sitrep No. 520/21 of Luftwaffe Command Intelligence, 2/KG 40 reported six ships totalling 29,500 tons sunk, and three further ships totalling 16,000 tons damaged. Even experienced naval airmen found it difficult to estimate the size of ships from the air, especially while concentrating on attacking them. Thus Schlosser reported the 2,490-ton *Britannic* as a vessel of 6,000 tons, Fliegel the 967-ton *Tejo* as one of 3,500 tons. In fact only freighters of between 1,000 and 3,000 tons were at this time plying the Gibraltar route.

None the less, the Condors had accounted for five ships totalling 9,200 tons, and the number and size of their victims were not all that important. The paramount feature of their success was that for the first time it was based on close co-operation between the Luftwaffe and U-boat arms, even though on this occasion their official roles were reversed. Normally it was the function of aircraft to spot the convoys, and of U-boats to attack them. All the same, Dönitz took the success as a favourable sign. Perhaps now, at last, his submarines would receive better and more far-reaching information, instead of wasting so much of their energies in fruitless search.

In mid-March 1941 Dönitz received the new *"Fliegerführer Atlantik"*—none other than Lieutenant-Colonel Martin Harlinghausen—at Lorient, and said to him: "Imagine our situation as a land problem, with the enemy convoy at Hamburg, and my nearest U-boats at Oslo, Paris, Vienna and Prague —each with a maximum circle of vision of twenty miles. How on earth can they expect to find the convoy unless directed to it by air reconnaissance?"

The problem was as old as the war, and the idea of adapting the Fw 200 for long-range reconnaissance had already been mooted in autumn 1939 by Major Petersen, navigation officer on the staff of X Air Corps.

Created by Kurt Tank, the "Condor" had first flown in July 1937, and since then had beaten several long-distance records: Berlin-New York in twenty-five hours, New York-Berlin in twenty, Berlin-Tokio in forty-six hours eighteen minutes—all of course with intermediate landings. Export orders were mounting when the war came and put an end to the trade. By that time the Luftwaffe's failure to develop a four-engined bomber-cum-reconnaissance aircraft had become public knowledge, so when X Air Corps suggested to Jeschonnek that the Fw 200 be used as a stop-gap, he agreed. Petersen, who had flown the plane as a civil air lines pilot, was himself put in charge of the first experimental squadron, and during the Norwegian campaign it did some useful reconnaissance.

For its new role Focke-Wulf reinforced the fuselage, built in auxiliary tanks and fitted bomb brackets under the wings. With that, plus the necessary re-arrangement of the interior, the military version of the Fw 200-C was ready. It did of course still betray its civil origin: it was too weak in structure, too slow and too vulnerable. Its initial armament of a single 20 mm cannon in a turret above the cockpit, plus two machine-guns in the ventral and rear-dorsal positions, could hardly be expected to offer much defence against fighter attack.

On the other hand its range was impressive—particularly at a time when the Luftwaffe was bitterly disappointed at the failure of the Ju 88 to fulfil its earlier promise. Even the "normal" version of the Fw 220-C had an operating radius of close on 1,000 miles, plus a twenty per cent reserve for navigation errors, discharging mission, etc. With auxiliary fuselage tanks this was raised to 1,100 miles, while the "long-distance" version, with fuel containers in place of bombs, could make a round trip of nearly 1,400 miles in both directions. Flights lasting fourteen to sixteen hours were by no means uncommon.

The significance of the above was seen when I/KG 40, newly formed by Lieutenant Colonel Petersen, was posted in the summer of 1940 to south-west France on the Atlantic: 1 and 2 Squadrons to Bordeaux-Merignac, 3 Squadron to Cognac. They could carry out armed reconnaissance all the way from the Bay of Biscay to the west of Ireland, then continue on to land at Stavanger-Sola, or Vaernes near Trondheim, in Norway. On the next day or the day after they would make the same flight in reverse.

Thus, for all the improvised character of the instrument, the Luftwaffe was able to supply the far-scanning eyes that the U-boats so badly needed. Speaking on December 30, 1940, to the command armed forces staff on the situation in the Atlantic, Dönitz urged: "Just let me have a minimum of twenty Fw 200s solely for reconnaissance purposes, and the U-boat successes will shoot up!" And on January 4, 1941, the German Admiralty reiterated: "To enable our naval command centres to prosecute the war in the Atlantic systematic reconnaissance is essential."

But behind the façade of sober discussion was a battle royal as to who should have the ultimate operational control of the Condor *Gruppe*: the Luftwaffe or the Navy. On January 6th Hitler himself decided the issue with the order: "I/KG 40 will be under the command of the Commander in Chief of the Navy." And he tried to appease Goering by giving him back the Navy's *Kampfgruppe* 806, so that he could add its Ju 88s to Sperrle's *Luftflotte* 3 for the bomber raids on England.

It was one of those decisions that gave little satisfaction to either side. Dönitz won control of I/KG 40, only to find that the *Gruppe* was much weaker than he had thought. For though its full establishment was twenty to twenty-five machines, the daily serviceability state was at best six to eight —another demonstration that a plane improvised from an air-liner was un-suited to the wear and tear of operations. How could such a small handful of aircraft be expected to comb the wastes of the Atlantic with anything like the thoroughness the U-boat chief required?

On January 16, 1941, Captain Verlohr, squadron commander of 1/KG 40, sighted a convoy west of Ireland, and sank two ships totalling 10,857 tons by the "Swedish turnip" method. After that he remained in contact for several hours till his fuel was only just enough to bring him home. Meanwhile he was unsuccessful either in getting a second Fw 200 to relieve him or in bringing U-boats to the scene—they were too far away. Consequently contact was lost, night fell, and next morning the convoy was no longer to be found.

The same thing happened on January 23rd, 28th and 31st. On each occasion a large convoy was sighted, and always the aircraft was forced to leave before U-boats reached the position. On the other hand the aircraft themselves sank ships every time. In fact the sinkings achieved by "armed reconnaissance" rose from fifteen vessels totalling 63,175 tons in January, to twenty-two totalling 84,515 tons in February. These are the Allied figures that became available after the war. The contemporary claims were a good deal higher.

To carry out their long-distance missions successfully, with all that that entailed, the Condor crews had to operate at the limit of their capacity. They represented the cream of the bomber training schools, where trial crews were put together and their performance judged. And they learnt much from their senior colleagues, who as former Lufthansa pilots were already expert at blind and long-distance flying. Most successful operationally were Lieutenant-Colonel Petersen—soon to command the whole KG 40 *Geschwader*—then his *Gruppen* and squadron commanders Verlohr, Daser, Buchholz, Jope and Mayr. The last two are still chief pilots with Lufthansa today.

Yet no string of individual performances could disguise the fact that the main job of providing effective reconnaissance for the U-boat arm could never be carried out so long as the number of serviceable aircraft could be counted on the fingers of one hand. In 1941 the monthly production of Focke-Wulf Condors amounted to only four or five, which represented no net increase. As the U-boats still sailed blindly through the seas, the following dialogue would take place each morning at Dönitz's war-room at Lorient between himself and his chief of operations, Commander Eberhardt Godt:

Dönitz: "Are there any reconnaissance flights today?"
Godt: "*Jawohl, Herr Admiral.*"
Dönitz: "By how many aircraft?"
Godt: "By one, *Herr Admiral.*"

The two would look at each other and smile sadly; and Dönitz, whose U-boats were the paramount source of concern to the British, would shrug his shoulders in resignation.

Even Martin Harlinghausen could do nothing to improve the situation when, in March 1941, he became first *Fliegerführer Atlantik*, with the task of concentrating all maritime aircraft under one command. With Goering and Jeschonnek contesting the naval control of I/KG 40 from the start, Hitler finally rescinded his previous order and put the Condors too under the new *Fliegerführer's* command. But though this saved appearances, the job of providing reconnaissance for the C.-in-C. U-boats remained the same, and as the months went by there was still no increase in the force.

Harlinghausen—to whom Dönitz had allocated Château Branderion, some twelve miles distant from Lorient, as staff HQ—had moreover other tasks on hand. The first was to combat the shipping lanes from the Irish Sea through the English Channel to the Tyne; the second to support Sperrle's *Luftflotte* 3 in its attacks on British harbours.

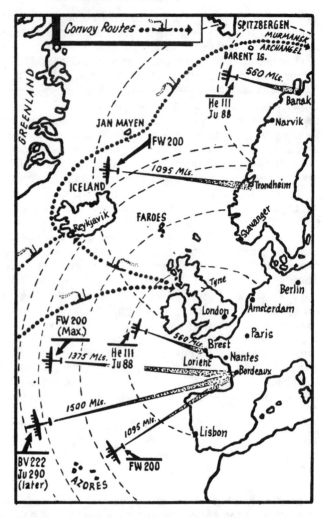

The Battle of the Atlantic. In combating the Allied supply convoys the Luftwaffe was handicapped by the restricted operating range of its aircraft. Only the Focke Wulf 200, with an endurance of sixteen hours or more, possessed an adequate radius of action, but the number available on any day was small. On the Murmansk route, where the convoys had to steam within range of Norwegian-based Heinkel 111s and Junkers 88s, their losses were heavy.

To serve this far-flung battle-line the *Fliegerführer* had the following forces at his command:

At Bordeaux: I/KG 40 (Fw 200), III/KG 40 (He 111, later Fw 200)
In Holland: II/KG 40 (Do 217)
In Brittany (Lannion): One LR reconnaissance squadron, 3 (F)/123 (Ju 88)
Three coastal *Gruppen*, two equipped with Ju 88s, the third still with He 115 seaplanes

These forces maintained daily patrols of the British shipping lanes from the Irish Sea to the Thames estuary, not only reporting convoys but attacking them. Even those "fat, tired birds", the ancient He 115s under Major Stockmann, with their two 500-lb. bombs and two forward firing fixed machine-guns, scored successes, flying from Brest to the Bristol Channel.

But the spring months of 1941 also saw a strengthening of the British defence. Not only were the convoys provided with more powerful anti-submarine escort, but the light flak defences of the mercantile ships were also greatly augmented—as the German airmen found to their cost. Low-level attack by the "Swedish turnip" method was still the order of the day, and as the planes screamed over the mast-tops they were vulnerable targets for seconds on end.

At the outset it was calculated by the *Fliegerführer Atlantik's* staff that for every aircraft lost 30,000 tons of shipping were sunk. Now the ratio abruptly changed. The aircraft, confronted with a wall of flak, could no longer get at the ships. By June the losses were so heavy that Harlinghausen had to bar the method of attack that he himself had introduced in 1939.

British counter-measures also compelled the U-boats to abandon their productive hunting grounds in the North Channel between Ireland and Scotland. Six of them were lost there between March 7th and April 5th alone, amongst them the vessels of such outstanding U-boat captains as Prien (*U 47*), Schepke (*U 100*) and Kretschmer (*U 99*), who was the only one to be rescued. Dönitz withdrew his vessels far to the west, there to conduct widespread searches of the North Atlantic, in regions mostly out of range for the Condors, whose western limit of reconnaissance was the twenty-second parallel, about 1,000 miles from their base of operations.

In mid-July, 1941, co-operation between the two arms took a new short lease of life when Dönitz sent his U-boat packs to harass the convoys leaving Gibraltar. But though the U-boat operations were thus again within the Condors' range, low-level attacks, except occasionally on isolated ships, were now out of the question, and the sighting had to be done through binoculars. None the less, they did a much better job of reconnaissance, and on a number of occasions, after the U-boats had been driven off by the escort, they led them back to the convoy's position.

In September, 1941, Dönitz brought the U-boats to the north again, and in November the Condors flew sixty-two reconnaissance missions over the North Atlantic. But though five convoys were sighted, with only one could they keep in touch for two consecutive days. The rest were lost sight of. In December there were only twenty-three missions, though on one occasion the convoy was shadowed for five whole days. "In every case," the *Fliegerführer Atlantik* war diary records, "fixes were given to bring U-boats to the scene."

After that the co-operative effort was again disrupted. The U-boats were engaged in the Mediterranean, and from January, 1942, along the Atlantic coast of America, seeking hunting grounds where the defence was still new and inexperienced. I/KG 40 was posted to Vaernes in Norway. For in 1942 the Allies began to send convoys to Russia, thereby opening up a giant new operations zone: the Arctic Ocean.

Meanwhile, on the English Channel coast, the British had since mid-1941 been waging a non-stop bomber offensive in the hope of compelling the Luftwaffe to withdraw some of its fighter units from the Russian front. But in fact the only two fighter *Geschwader* stationed on the Channel—the "Richthofen" JG 2 and the "Schlageter" JG 26—continued to oppose these raids alone. In autumn, 1941, II/JG 26 was re-equipped with the first production series of the new fighter type, the Focke-Wulf Fw 190. Acting defensively, these fighters and the Me 109s inflicted considerable losses.

The period was marked by three main episodes:

1. The vain attempt of the Luftwaffe, despite 218 sorties, to rescue the *Bismarck* from her pursuit by the British fleet (May 26–28, 1941).
2. The successful break through the Channel, aided by strong air cover, of the battleships *Scharnhorst* and *Gneisenau* and the cruiser *Prinz Eugen* (February 12, 1942).
3. The British and Canadian landing attempt at Dieppe, bloodily repulsed and with the loss of 106 British bombers and fighters (August 19, 1942).

When on May 24, 1941, *Luftflotte* 3's H.Q. in Paris was apprised of the 41,700-ton *Bismarck's* intention of docking at St. Nazaire, she had already sunk the British battle-cruiser *Hood*. The Luftwaffe was bidden to do all it could to secure her arrival at that port. It would, however, be at least two days before she could steam into range of Ju 88 and He 111 cover. Meanwhile, where was she?

On May 26th—the vital day for making contact—a low-pressure front from the north-west, with its resulting storms, made flying almost impossible. Though Harlinghausen's reconnaissance planes took off, they flew into a visionless void. At 15.45 a single Fw 200 did, however, suddenly happen upon the British battleship *Rodney*, with several destroyers. But the near-by flagship *King George V* was completely hidden by the low-scudding clouds, and unlike British long-range reconnaissance aircraft, the Condors still carried no radar aid.

According to the information given—certainly inexact in the prevailing weather conditions—the enemy's position was some 750 miles off the French coast. Yet the maximum distance the Ju 88s and He 111s could fly out to sea was 550 miles. That settled the matter, and the take-off was ordered for the following morning (27th May) at 03.00. By that time the *Bismarck's* fate had been sealed. At 21.05 the previous evening torpedoes from aircraft of the carrier *Ark Royal* had damaged her propellers and rudder, and she could no longer elude pursuit.

The last friends the battleship saw, as she fought for her life, was at 09.50 on the 27th. They were five Ju 88s of the coastal *Gruppe* 606, which had left their base hours before. In the midst of the great artillery duel they tried to intervene by diving on the nearest cruiser, but every bomb missed. When an hour later seventeen Heinkels of I/KG 28 arrived on the scene from Nantes, the *Bismarck* was already beneath the waves. Unsuccessfully they attacked the *Ark Royal*, each with two 500-lb. and eight 250-lb. bombs, all of which again missed.

After that came *Kampfgruppe* 100, II/KG 1, II/KG 54 and I/KG 77 in succession, but none of them found the enemy. For months on end these formations had been engaged in night bomber attacks on England, and suddenly to send them out over stormy seas to the limit of their range, on a job for which they had never been trained, was optimistic indeed. As for the *Geschwader* that had been so trained—KGs 26 and 30—no one thought of these until it was too late. Though the returning British fleet was again

89. *(above)* The four-engined Fw 200 Condor. A modification of a civil airliner, it saw valuable service as a long-range reconnaissance-bomber. **90.** *(below)* A Ju 88 of KG 30 pulling out after an attack on a freighter of Convoy PQ 17, bound for Russia.

91. A Heinkel 111 of the "Lion" *Geschwader,* KG 26. The first to be equipped with aerial torpedoes, this unit was the most successful on combating the Arctic convoys.

92. The He 115 floatplane of "Coastal Command," still used for torpedo attack. **93.** *(below)* Another member of "Coastal Command," the Bv 138 flying boat, used for long-range reconnaissance.

harried from the air during the whole of the following day, and hundreds of bombs were dropped, only one destroyer (the *Mashona*) was so damaged that it finally sank off the west coast of Ireland.

The German aircrews returned in chastened mood. All the 218 sorties they had flown had not helped the *Bismarck* a jot. Only next year did their fortunes change for the better: with the *Scharnhorst* and *Gneisenau* venture, Dieppe, and above all with the knock-out blow in the Arctic against Convoy PQ 17.

2. The Luftwaffe versus the Arctic Convoys

For three days, since sailing out of the Hvalfiord near Reykjavik in Iceland on June 27, 1942, PQ 17 had steamed through thick fog. Besides a tanker to supply the numerous escort vessels, and two rescue craft, it comprised thirty-six merchant ships fully laden with war equipment, raw materials and victuals for Soviet Russia.

Slowly the convoy nosed its way forward, the ships keeping close together. The fog was impenetrable: the tanker *Gray Ranger* was rammed by the freighter *Exford*, and the American *Richard Bland* ran aground on rocks. All three had to turn back, leaving thirty-three ships. In the Denmark Strait, north of Iceland, dense ice floes were encountered. But ice, cold and fog were all welcome so long as the convoy was not spotted by German long-range reconnaissance, then shadowed and finally bombed and torpedoed by the German air units based in northern Norway.

Yet the Germans were completely in the picture. I/KG 40's Condors, now based near Trondheim under their new commander, Major Ernst Henkelmann, had watched the ships collecting for weeks, and just after they set sail one of 3 Squadron's machines had roared across in the fog so low that it nearly rammed the cruiser *London*. PQ 17's departure was confirmed both by spies at Reykjavik and by the German Navy's monitoring service. From the sudden upsurge in radio traffic the latter deciphered the essential information that another large-scale Allied convoy operation was under way.

Such knowledge was, however, useless if the convoy could not now be found. Unfortunately for PQ 17, on the fourth day of its voyage the protective fog curtain cleared away. Two U-boats located it and followed in its wake. And in the afternoon the Allied seamen's worst fears were realised when an aircraft appeared. Keeping carefully out of range of the shipboard flak, it joined the procession and followed like a shadow.

By this time PQ 17 had reached the area of Jan Mayen Island, and by-passed it to the south on a north-easterly course. Here it was still out of range of German attacking aircraft based at Bardufoss, Banak and Kirkenes on the North Cape, and so long as it could maintain its course would remain so. But north of Bear Island, at latest, it would have to change course to the east, because even in summer the ice barrier prevented further passage northwards. That was the moment the Luftwaffe was waiting for.

On July 2nd four U-boats tried to attack, in vain. The strong naval escort—six destroyers, four corvettes, seven minesweepers and trawlers, two anti-aircraft vessels and two submarines—located the assailant on each occasion and drove it off. Towards 18.00 hours the first strike aircraft appeared on the scene, flying low over the water. They comprised eight He 115 seaplanes of 1 Squadron from coastal *Gruppe* 406 at Sörreisa near Tromsö, and being slow and ponderous their only hope lay in surprise.

They all attacked, each with one torpedo. But the defence was on the alert, and their approach ran into savage fire. The plane of the squadron commander, Captain Herbert Vater, was hit, and he was forced to jettison his torpedo, then alight on the water. Just before their aircraft sank he and the other two crew members managed to scramble into their rubber dinghy. Then, despite the enemy fire, First-Lieutenant Burmester alighted with his own He 115, picked them all up and managed to take off again—completely unscathed! But the torpedo attack, like that of the U-boats, miscarried thanks to the alertness of the convoy's escort.

On July 3rd the weather, from the German point of view, again took a turn for the worse, the Allied ships being protected by a low-hanging cloud bank. Despite the efforts of air reconnaissance, contact with the convoy was lost. By the next morning PQ 17 was already north of Bear Island, and so far had not lost a ship. The cloud bank lay even lower—conditions favourable to a surprise torpedo attack from the air, if the aircraft could only find their target.

It was not long before they did so. Once more they were He 115s, this time 1 Squadron of Coastal *Gruppe* 906. After a long search its leader, Captain Eberhard Peukert, located the convoy through a cloud gap at 05.00 hours on the 4th. This time the flak only opened up after the torpedoes had been launched, and one of them was right on track for the American "Liberty ship" *Christopher Newport*, of 7,191 tons. It struck in her engine room, and the muffled explosion rumbled through the convoy. The crew were transferred to one of the rescue vessels following behind, and she was finally sunk by two more torpedoes—one from the *U 457*, the other, strangely enough, from a British submarine, the *P 614*.

If PQ 17's first loss was an American vessel, the British crews caught their breath when the remaining American ships suddenly all together hauled down their flags—the maritime signal conceding defeat. However, in place of the bad-weather flags up went brand new banners carrying the Stars and Stripes—seemingly in a gesture of defiance. But.in fact, though it may have seemed a strange moment to celebrate it, the British had forgotten that it was American Independence Day.

On this July 4th the skies again cleared, but despite the good visibility there was, for the convoy, deceptive peace. It was evening before the Luftwaffe attacked again. But at latitude seventy-five degrees north "evening" meant nothing, for at this season the sun never sets, and it was light enough to attack all round the clock. At 19.30 a squadron of KG 30 from Banak made the first attack with Ju 88s. But though their bombs fell all round the ships, no hits were registered.

An hour later a larger formation appeared in the sky: the "Lion" *Geschwader's* I/KG 26 led by the senior squadron commander, Captain Bernot Eicke—the *Gruppen* commander, Lieutenant-Colonel Busch, having been posted to take up duty as *Fliegerführer Nord-West* at Stavanger. Eicke ordered his twenty-five He 111s to execute a pincers movement, and they came in low over the water from several directions. For now this standard Luftwaffe bomber could also carry a torpedo beneath its fuselage.

For this (to them) completely new type of operation the squadrons of I/KG 26 had in the spring of 1942 undergone a course at the torpedo school of Grosseto in central Italy—the Luftwaffe general staff having been impressed by the success of Italian, and still more of Japanese, torpedo planes. In Germany the development of such a weapon had virtually lapsed owing to the futile competition between Luftwaffe and Navy as to which service should control the maritime air arm. On the one hand the Navy naturally wanted to augment its forces with air torpedo units, but on the other such air units as it possessed were officially only for reconnaissance purposes. All actual striking power the Luftwaffe wished to reserve to itself. At the war's outset, however, the Luftwaffe possessed neither torpedo craft nor the crews to fly them. But the Navy had—in the shape of its He 115 "general purpose" squadrons. Armed with torpedoes, these had been attacking shipping all round Britain, despite the Luftwaffe's view that they had no right to—not, at least, under naval command.

This incredible conflict even led in the end—on November 26, 1940, to be precise—to Goering getting the Navy's air torpedo operations completely stopped, and (temporarily) even the production of the F-5 air torpedo. On November 27th the remaining stock of these—according to a report of the Quartermaster-General's office—was a mere 132, and these were being reserved for a special operation by the Luftwaffe against ships of the British Mediterranean Fleet at Gibraltar and Alexandria.

At this point Grand-Admiral Raeder, supreme commander of the Navy, had his say in a personal interview with the Führer, demanding that air torpedo attacks on British coastal shipping be continued. Hitler ordered an investigation, which showed that if air torpedoes were used in the shallow waters of Gibraltar and Alexandria, they would probably all bore into the sea bed. For launched from an altitude of a hundred feet, they would first reach a depth of a hundred feet before returning to the surface. Had Goering not considered this?

The torpedo project of the Luftwaffe supreme commander thus fizzled out, and the Navy seemed to be in the ascendant. Consequently on December 4, 1940, the chief of its operations staff, Admiral Kurt Fricke, demanded first that air torpedo attacks by his service should be energetically resumed, and second that its "general purpose" squadrons should for daylight operations be re-equipped with a suitable and more modern aircraft, namely the He 111 H-5.

But in the end it was again the Luftwaffe that prevailed. Though He 111s—and later Ju 88s and Do 217s too—were modified to carry torpedoes, it was not the Navy that got them. Though Goering was all for the Italian example being followed, many people adhered obstinately to the view expressed by Colonel Koller, chief of staff of *Luftflotte* 3: "Why drop a missile (in the shape of a torpedo) into the water in front of the ship, when as a bomb it can be dropped straight on to it?"

This view, of course, completely ignored two factors: (i) The mounting efficacy of the flak defences in preventing either low-level or dive-bombing attacks being pressed home; (ii) The far more lethal effect of a torpedo hole below water-line than of a bomb exploding amongst the superstructure, as it usually did.

Despite general staff opposition, when the torpedo weapon was finally introduced at the beginning of 1942, the service soon lost its doubts concerning its possibilities. Tactical exercises held at the torpedo school of Grosetto —officially called KSG 2 (*Kampfschulgeschwader* 2)—under the direction of that experienced nautical airman, Lieutenant Colonel Stockmann, against the target ship *Citta di Genova*, showed that losses could be minimised if surprise was achieved and the attack carried out simultaneously from different directions. Still better was a combined attack by both bombers and torpedo aircraft. But the Luftwaffe never attempted this tactically difficult manoeuvre.

Thus the attacks on PQ 17 by KG 30's Ju 88 dive-bombers and I/KG 26's He 111 torpedo craft on the evening of July 5th represented two distinct operations, an hour apart, when they might have been a single combined one. Accordingly the British defence could concentrate its full fire-power first against one, then the other.

None the less, on the second attack the convoy suffered its first hard blow. Converging from all directions, the Heinkels approached low down on the sea, and skipping the columns of water that enemy projectiles raised in their path, they pressed home their attack.

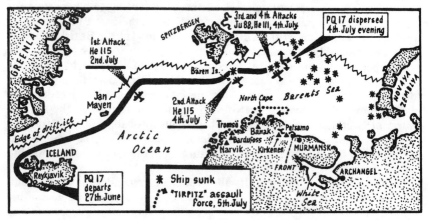

The fate of Convoy PQ 17. The map shows the route of this convoy in summer 1942 as it steamed from Iceland towards Archangel along the edge of the Arctic drift-ice. On the eighth day at sea the British Admiralty sent urgent orders for the convoy to disperse. As the ships proceeded in isolation, they fell prey to German aircraft and U-boats.

Lieutenant Konrad Hennemann had set himself to torpedo a major warship. Now, as he came in, only destroyers and other lesser vessels lay ahead. The rest were all merchantmen. He found himself wrapped in a curtain of missiles and smoke. Finally his torpedo struck the 4,941 ton freighter *Navarino* but at the same time his aircraft suffered multiple hits. It crashed into the water not far from his victim, and sank.

Also hit was the Heinkel of Lieutenant Georg Kanmayr. Dazzled by the sunlight reflected from a patch of mist, he never noticed that he was headed straight for a destroyer. The first missile smashed the cockpit canopy, wounding both Kanmayr and his observer, Sergeant Felix Schlenkermann. But they managed to ditch, and all four of the crew were rescued—by the same British destroyer that shot them down.

Captain Eicke's own torpedo struck the 7,177 ton U.S. freighter *William*

Hopper, which was abandoned and later sunk by the *U 334*. The Soviet tanker *Azerbaidzhan*, though also hit by a torpedo, could still maintain a speed of nine knots, and stayed with the convoy. When I/KG 26 had departed and the convoy Commodore, Captain Dowding, took stock, he found he had lost another two ships. Yet no one could describe such a loss as devastating. And one thing seemed quite clear: that the best defence lay in compactness. Only so could the security force hope to protect its charges from attack from the air or from under the water.

Consequently it came like a blow from a sledge-hammer when the British Admiralty in London first ordered the cruiser force to "withdraw to westward at high speed", and followed with two signals affecting the convoy itself:

9.23 p.m. "Immediate. Owing to threat of surface ships convoy is to disperse and proceed to Russian ports."

9.36 p.m. "Most immediate. My 9.23 of the 4th. Convoy is to scatter."[1]

Sauve qui peut was what, in effect, it meant. As the ships obeyed the order, their captains expected at any moment to see a squadron of German battleships and cruisers loom up on the horizon to wipe them out. But the hours passed, and nothing of the kind took place.

As a convoy PQ 17 no longer existed. It had become a scattered flock of startled, defenceless, merchant ships—sitting ducks for the prowling U-boats or German aircraft. What had happened? Had the Admiralty been at fault?

By means of their PQ convoys via the Arctic to Murmansk and Archangel, the western powers had been supplying their hard-pressed Russian allies with large quantities of war material ever since August 1941. It took the Germans a long time to recognise the danger, or do anything about it. Meanwhile new tanks and guns appeared on the eastern front in ever-increasing numbers.

Thus the first eleven PQ convoys sailed through virtually unmolested. until February 1942 when PQ 13 was attacked. By then the Germans had greatly strengthened their position in northern Norway. Hitler, who lived in constant fear that one day the Allies would re-invade that country and threaten his northern flank, had ordered powerful naval forces to the spot One after the other the battleship *Tirpitz* and the heavy cruisers *Lützow*, *Admiral Scheer* and *Admiral Hipper* had arrived at their new bases in the lonely fiords. Against the wishes of Dönitz, Hitler had further ordered a large U-boat fleet to the area.

Finally Colonel-General Hans-Jürgen Stumpff's *Luftflotte* 5, with H.Q. in Oslo, was reinforced, and bases prepared just south of the North Cape. At the climax of the anti-convoy operations, *Fliegerführer Nordost* (Colonel Alexander Holle at Kirkenes) and *Fliegerführer Lofoten* (Colonel Ernst-August Roth at Bardufoss) had the following forces at their disposal:

KG 30 (Ju 88) at Banak;
I and II/KG 26 (He 111) at Bardufoss and Banak;
I/StG 5 (Ju 87) at Kirkenes;
Coastal *Gruppen* 406 and 906 (He 115 and BV 138 recce flying boats) at

[1] S. W. Roskill, *The War at Sea 1939–1945* (H.M.S.O., 1934–57), Vol. II, p. 139.

Tromsö and Stavanger;

Two *Gruppen* of JG 5 (Me 109) distributed over various airfields;

I/KG 40 (FW 200) at Trondheim;

The long-distance reconnaissance squadrons 1(F)/22 and 1 (F)/124—equipped with Ju 88s—at Bardufoss, Banak and Kirkenes, plus the Westa 6 (weather reconnaissance squadron) at Banak.

So long as the Arctic winter continued, there was a limit to the operations the Luftwaffe could conduct in this extreme northerly theatre. Yet the high command required, unreasonably, that each Allied convoy be found, shadowed and attacked. The prologue to PQ 17 had been as follows:

On March 5, 1942, PQ 12 had been located by a reconnaissance aircraft south of Jan Mayen Island. Snow storms were raging, and it was quite impossible for an air striking force to get off. The *Tirpitz*, accompanied by three destroyers, went out, failed to find the main convoy, and only succeeded in sinking the straggling Soviet freighter *Ijora*. The British Home Fleet was at sea, and the *Tirpitz* was hard put to it to escape an attack by torpedo planes from the carrier *Victorious*.

PQ 13 (March 27th–31st) was split up by bad weather, lost two freighters to III/KG 30 under Captain Hajo Herrmann, and three more to U-boats and destroyers.

PQ 14 (April 8th–21st) tangled in fog with dense ice floes, and sixteen of its twenty-four vessels had to return damaged to Iceland. One ship was sunk by the *U 403*.

PQ 15 (April 26th–May 7th) lost three ships to torpedo aircraft. At the same time the cruiser *Edinburgh*, escorting QP 11 on the return journey from Murmansk, was, despite bad visibility, crippled by torpedoes from U-boats and destroyers, and had to be abandoned.

PQ 16 (May 25th–30th) was attacked by air formations of KG 30 and I/KG 26 amounting on the 27th to over a hundred planes. But though numerous vessels were damaged, only seven out of thirty-five—representing a tonnage of 43,205—were sunk.

Though the steadily increasing size of the convoys had been matched by an increase in the strength of the attacking forces, the loss of ships—thanks to their compact grouping and the alertness of the security screen—had so far not been intolerable, and Stalin had got most of his tanks. But the story of PQ 17, the biggest convoy yet, was—thanks to the British Admiralty—a different one.

Since its departure from Iceland on June 27th, PQ 17 was, besides its close-support force under Commander Broome, protected by a cover group of four cruisers and three destroyers under Rear-Admiral Hamilton, which cruised in the vicinity to frustrate any attack by German naval forces. Furthermore the C.-in-C. of the British Home Fleet, Admiral Sir John Tovey, was out from Scapa Flow with a long-range cover force comprising the battleships *Duke of York* and *Washington*, the aircraft carrier *Victorious*, two cruisers and fourteen destroyers. For the greatest anxiety of the Admiralty concerned the heavy German warships which, lying in wait in their Norwegian fiords, showed every sign of being about to attack the convoy themselves.

Nor was the Admiralty deceived. As soon as the German Battle Groups

I and II, under Admiral Otto Schniewind and Vice-Admiral Oskar Kummetz, got wind of PQ 17's departure, they left their moorings at Trondheim and Narvik for the north: the mighty *Tirpitz*, the *Admiral Hipper*, the *Lützow*, the *Admiral Scheer* and twelve destroyers. Their immediate destination was Altenfiord, where they were to wait air reconnaissance reports of the British fleet movements. For on the German side anxiety was also great, and Hitler had personally forbidden the ships to operate if any risk was involved. This risk was regarded as consisting mainly in the obvious presence at sea of one or more British aircraft carriers, though in addition reconnaissance had mistakenly reported two cruisers of Hamilton's force as battleships. Thus, held as on a leash, the German warships did not venture into Arctic waters. They just stayed put, waiting.

None of this, however, was known to the British. Unapprised by reconnaissance of the true position, the First Sea Lord, Admiral Sir Dudley Pound, felt himself hourly more cornered. During the evening of July 3rd and the morning of the 4th, radio reports poured in to the effect that both PQ 17 and its cover force were being shadowed by German aircraft. Consequently the Germans must have a clear picture of the situation, and know also that Admiral Tovey's Home Fleet was too far distant to prevent their warships falling on the convoy.

The decision to disperse it was triggered off by a report reaching London in the forenoon of July 4th that a Russian submarine had actually sighted the German warships headed towards the convoy. Though it was completely false, it persuaded Admiral Pound to take the very action that Admiral Tovey had, in a telephone conversation with him, termed "sheer bloody murder". All cruisers and destroyers were withdrawn, and the merchantmen were ordered to proceed, scattered and virtually unprotected.

In the event the German battle squadron did not emerge from Altenfiord until noon of the following day—only to return after a minor sortie the same evening. Scattered to the winds, PQ 17 was the right target, not for heavy warships, but for U-boats and aircraft.

The slaughter, accordingly, began on July 5th—an all-day attack by Major Erich Blödorn's KG 30, with its three *Gruppen* attacking successively under Captains Konrad Kahl, Erich Stoffregen and Hajo Herrmann. The first casualty—to a precision dive-bombing attack by Lieutenant Clausener's Ju 88—was the freighter *Peter Kerr*. There followed her to the bottom the American *Washington*, *Pan Kraft* and *Fairfield City*, the British *Bolton Castle* and the rescue vessel *Zaafaran*.

Many others were badly damaged. The *Paulus Potter*, steaming along the edge of the ice-pack close beside the *Bolton Castle*, was dive-bombed simultaneously with the latter, but whereas the *Bolton Castle* sank, the abandoned wreck of the former floated about amongst the ice-fields for a whole week till the phantom ship was finally seen and dispatched by *U 255*. And there is the strange tale of the *Washington's* survivors, who refused to leave their lifeboats when the *Olopana* steamed up to rescue them. On the 8th this freighter was herself sunk by a U-boat.

The harrying of the scattered vessels went on until July 10th, right to the entrance to the White Sea and Archangel. There some of them were found and attacked by 5 and 6/KG 30, the U.S. *Hoosier* and the Panamanian *El Capitan* being mortally hit by Captain Dohne and Lieutenant Bühler, and finally finished off by U-boats. On July 12th the C.-in-C. *Luftflotte* 5, Colonel-General Stumpff, reported to the *Reichsmarschall* "the annihilation of the major convoy PQ 17. On July 10th reconnaissance of the White Sea, the western channel of the Kola coast, and the sea area to the north, found no further merchant vessels left afloat. . . . I claim for *Luftflotte* 5 the sinking of twenty-two merchant vessels together comprising 142,216 tons."

The actual loss suffered by the convoy was in fact twenty-four ships totalling 143,977 tons, of which only eight were sunk by air attack alone, nine by U-boats, and the remaining seven "shared". The eleven surviving ships, after hiding for weeks far to the east along the coast of Novaya Zemlya, finally reached Archangel.[1]

"The tragedy," writes the British naval historian, Captain Roskill, ". . . was the consequence of trying to control the fleet from a headquarters 2,000 miles away. . . . Convoy PQ 17, with its conduct left in the hands of the men on the spot, would undoubtedly have been as successful as its predecessor."[2]

Both sides now began to get ready for the next convoy, with the Allies obliged to continue supplying help to the Russians—cost what it might—and the Germans determined to mete out the same treatment to PQ 18 as to its predecessor.

On August 1st the Luftwaffe bases on the North Cape suffered a false alarm after reconnaissance reports of a new and mammoth ship concentration in Iceland's Hvalfiord: forty-one laden freighters and three tankers, with cruisers and destroyers in attendance. Three days later came reports that the fiord was empty, with not a ship in Reykjavik roads. The convoy must consequently be under way. But where was it?

For two weeks every reconnaissance squadron of *Luftflotte* 5 was kept busy searching every corner of the Arctic Circle, utilising all the experience of Allied tactics that had been acquired. The result was completely nil. But rain clouds had obscured visibility, so when August 12th and 13th turned out fine, the search was repeated, grid-square by grid-square, no channel unexplored. The convoy appeared to have evaporated into thin air. Only on the 17th after 140 sorties lasting 1,600 hours and costing nearly a quarter of a million gallons of high octane fuel, was the two-weeks' search finally broken off.

The fact of the matter is that no convoy set out for Russia in August 1942. The convoy located off Iceland on the first of the month sailed not into the Arctic but the Atlantic, and its destination was Malta. All forces were occupied in "Operation Pedestal"—the bringing of supplies to that beleaguered island even though only four of the fourteen transport vessels got through.

PQ 18 in fact set out in September. It was first sighted on the 8th in fine

---

[1] The following is a comparative break-down of war material lost and delivered by PQ 16 and PQ 17:

		Lost	Delivered
PQ 16	Vehicles	770	2,507
	Tanks	147	321
	Aircraft	77	124
PQ 17	Vehicles	3,350	896
	Tanks	430	164
	Aircraft	210	87

[2] S. W. Roskill, *The Navy at War 1939–45* (Collins, 1960), pp. 208–9.

weather, by a triple-engined BV 138 flying boat after reaching the region of
Jan Mayen Island: thirty-nine freighters and a tanker, plus two fleet-tankers
and a rescue-ship, screened by an uncounted number of destroyers and lesser
warships.

This time the alert at the German air bases was genuine, as the reconnaissance planes held the convoy under continuous watch. But next morning
the units received a nasty shock when a further group of warships was
reported: six destroyers, a cruiser and a still bigger ship with wide-flung deck:
an aircraft carrier! It was the escort carrier *Avenger*—with a dozen fighters
and a number of anti-submarine planes on board. Hurricanes at once took
off, and the ponderous German flying boats were hard put to it to maintain
contact at maximum visual range.

For a convoy to bring its own fighter cover was something new. The
Hurricanes were, however, of the oldest type, and as Admiral Tovey remarked
to Churchill, it was ironical that transports crammed with the latest type of
Hurricanes for Russia had to be protected by their outworn predecessors.
The fighter impact on the Germans was accordingly less pronounced. Had
they been more modern fighters, both the German reconnaissance planes
and the striking force would, without fighter cover of their own, have had a
worse time of it than they did.

Late in the afternoon of September 13th the time had come. The "Lion"
Geschwader's I/KG 26 took off from Bardufoss with twenty-four He 111s.
One by one they came droning down the Malangerfiord to the point of rendezvous off the coast, then proceeded in formation, led by their new commander,
Major Werner Klümper, lately chief instructor at the Grosseto torpedo school
in Italy. They flew as low as they could to duck beneath the enemy's radar
beam. For without surprise they had little hope.

The flight continued for an hour, then two, course north-west. Cloud
ceiling was about 2,500 feet, and in a light drizzle visibility some six miles. In
the end Klümper turned to his radio-operator, but the latter shrugged his
shoulders: "No directions, *Herr Major*."

Half an hour before the formation was due to attack, the reconnaissance
plane in contact was supposed to radio the convoy's position. Clearly they
had flown past without seeing it. Since their planes had almost reached the
limit of their outward flight endurance, Klümper set a reciprocal course to
the east, and at last the convoy came into sight. As prearranged, I/KG 26
was to attack in two waves, each of fourteen torpedo craft. To give more
punch, a third wave was following up behind in the shape of a squadron of
III/KG 26 from Banak, under Captain Klaus Nocken.

To the convoy, which had just withstood without loss a dive-bombing
attack by KG 30's Ju 88s, the appearance of forty torpedo-carrying aircraft
low over the water was "like a huge flight of nightmare locusts". But it rose
to the occasion. As the first wave of Heinkels came in, shells raised tall
columns of water ahead of them—each a deadly menace in itself, and making
attack from sea-level impossible. Klümper increased the altitude to 150 feet,
and the planes twisted wildly about in evasive action. But they kept on
course.

The priority target was the aircraft carrier, but despite an intensive search
Klümper could not find it. He began to doubt whether the report of its
presence was accurate—especially as no fighters had appeared to engage

them. He was not to know that the Hurricanes were still in pursuit of the Ju 88s that had just left, or that the *Avenger* had stationed herself some distance off to be in a better tactical position.

In the event all forty Heinkels attacked the convoy's starboard column, and every ship let fly. Some aircraft were hit and had to jettison their torpedoes. But the majority pushed home their attack, releasing their missiles 1,000 yards away from the nearest vessels. Thirty of these sped simultaneously towards their targets as the aircraft squirmed away from the lethal flak.

Then down amongst the convoy hell broke loose. An explosion was heard as the first freighter was hit; then a second and a third. Sheets of flame shot skywards. And the explosions continued. The whole attack had lasted just eight minutes.

"Forty torpedo planes," writes Captain Roskill, "almost obliterated the two starboard wing columns of the convoy." He claimed that the Germans lost five aircraft.[1]

Eight ships, totalling over 45,000 tons, were indeed sunk, but Major Klümper's *Gruppe* returned without loss. It is true that all its aircraft had been hit, six of them so badly as to render them unserviceable for further operations.

The following day the weather was still more unkind to PQ 18. The sky was cloudless, without a breath of wind, and visibility extended to the horizon. There was every prospect of the torpedo planes repeating their success of the day before.

But their calculations were upset by the operations order. Goering was still smarting from the failure of the first Ju 88s to sink the aircraft carrier *Ark Royal* in the early weeks of the war, and the fact that she had recently been sunk in the Mediterranean, by a U-boat, had rubbed salt into the wound. Moreover he looked with envy at the success of Japanese naval aircraft against American aircraft carriers in the Pacific, and decided it was high time the Luftwaffe did something similar. Consequently KG 26 was now ordered to concentrate every available plane exclusively against the aircraft carrier *Avenger*. Thus they were sent to their doom.

This time Major Klümper took off with only twenty-two aircraft. The reconnaissance planes reported that the carrier was positioned ahead of the convoy. Klümper made his approach low on the water in tight formation. First smoke, then masts and funnels, and finally the ships themselves came into view. Then, with the aid of binoculars, the *Kommandeur* established that a large ship was indeed steaming ahead of the escort. It could only be the carrier. I/KG 26 split up into two formations of eleven each to make their attack from both sides.

So far so good. But just as they had abandoned their compact defensive grouping, there came a warning cry on the short-wave radio: "Watch out! Fighters ahead." And ten Hurricanes appeared. Clearly surprise had not been achieved. Warned of the Heinkels' approach, probably as a result of the radio messages passed by reconnaissance, the Hurricanes were already airborne to receive them.

"Close up in sections," Klümper ordered his now scattered aircraft, so that they would have at least some mutual protection. Then came a fresh disillusionment: their prospective target was not the aircraft carrier after all.

[1] *The Navy at War 1939–45*, p. 229.

"Break off attack," called Klümper. "Carrier north repeat north of escort. Change target accordingly."

It meant that they had to cross right over the convoy at near-zero feet, themselves a multiple target for all its hundreds of flak guns; and close past the destroyers too. As if their murderous fire were not enough, three of the Hurricanes also dived into the *mêlée*. One Heinkel crashed right amongst the ships, others had to peel off with smoking engines or badly holed fuselage or wings. It was yet another proof that, with the enemy forewarned, torpedo attacks against such strongly defended targets were suicidal. Only Major Klümper himself and one other aircraft succeeded in launching their missiles, and then only from a much too acute angle. The *Avenger* promptly turned towards them, and they passed harmlessly by.

In this vain attack I/KG 26 lost five aircraft. A further nine, though they just limped home, were so badly damaged as to be useless for further action. Thus after two missions against PQ 18 this lately so powerful unit was reduced to eight serviceable machines. Even for these the last chance to take further toll had gone. Next day the weather closed in again, and the convoy completed its voyage beneath the protection of fog or low-hanging clouds.

Altogether PQ 18 lost only thirteen ships to air and submarine attack. The remaining twenty-seven reached Archangel in good order. For the Russians their cargoes represented hundreds of modern tanks and aircraft, thousands of road vehicles, and a mass of other war and industrial materials— enough to equip a whole new army for the front.

The significance of this was not lost on the Germans. In a secret report of Luftwaffe Command Intelligence dated April 4, 1943, it was reckoned that during the year 1942 the Russian intake of supplies by the Arctic route amounted to 1.2 million tons, compared with only half a million tons via the Persian Gulf and the Far East. Besides raw materials, victuals and mineral oil, it included 1,880 aircraft, 2,350 tanks, 8,300 lorries, 6,400 other vehicles and 2,250 guns.

It was not long before the German armies on the eastern front began to feel their impact.

War Over the Ocean—Summary and Conclusions

1. From the outset of the war German air operations against the British Fleet and Allied shipping were hampered by the fact that the Luftwaffe, in the course of its hurried creation, had so far entirely neglected to train any units for this type of warfare. That task had been earmarked for stage two of its development—between 1940 and 1942. Before the latter year, so Hitler had reiterated to his Luftwaffe and Navy chiefs, no war with Britain was to be anticipated.

2. Despite the best of intentions and much liaison between the actual operations staffs of the two services, on only a few occasions did their team-work bring tactical success. The Luftwaffe could seldom furnish support on the scale the Navy required owing to the increasing demands on its resources from all other theatres of war.

3. The flying-boats and seaplanes which were first favoured for maritime warfare were, except in respect of range, much inferior to contemporary land planes with retractable undercarriages. The re-equipment of the German

"Coastal Command" with such types as the Ju 88 frequently led, however, to their use against land targets at the expense of maritime missions.

4. Successfully to combat the mobility and manoeuvrability of seaborne targets required not only training and experience, but tactical elasticity in relation to the strength of the enemy's defence. The Luftwaffe's maxim of having land-planes ready for all emergencies, including those at sea, was thus hardly likely to fill the bill. The too optimistic expectation that its aircraft might actually put the British Fleet out of action was doomed to disappointment. Only in coastal waters with mastery in the air already achieved (as in the Cretan operation) was an air offensive against the enemy fleet successful, for Germany possessed no aircraft carriers.

5. Lack of inter-service co-operation at top level was also notable in the matter of mines and torpedoes. In particular, the development of an airborne version of the latter was left to the Navy's test centre, without for a long time producing results. Torpedo planes consequently only came into general use in 1942, by which time the available types were relatively slow and ponderous.

6. The heavy losses suffered by convoy PQ 17 were largely due to a false appraisal of the situation by the British Admiralty, which gave an untimely order for it to scatter and robbed it of its main protection. The comparatively minor losses of its successor, PQ 18, can be ascribed chiefly to Goering's longing for a prestige victory against a British aircraft carrier. Further notable successes against the Arctic convoys were prevented by the weather conditions and the strength of the British naval escort.

10

DISASTER IN RUSSIA

1. The Demyansk Air-Lift

When the German offensive ground to a halt in front of Moscow in the ice and snow of December 1941, the hour of Soviet Russia had come. The belief that the Red Army was beaten, and after its frightful losses of the summer could have no more reserves to draw upon, was shown to be false. The Germans might be exhausted, but not so the Russians. Giving their enemy no breathing space, they opened their counter-offensive.

On January 9, 1942, the boundary positions between the German Army Groups North and Centre, situated on Lake Seliger and held by only two infantry divisions, were penetrated on a front of sixty miles by four Soviet Armies. The push was directed across the Valday Hills to far in the German rear. It was Stalin's reply to the German encirclement movements of the summer, and this time the target was the whole Army Group Centre.

Motley units of German troops were hastily assembled and thrown into the towns and villages in the path of the Russian advance to act as breakwaters. Velikiye Luki, Velizh and Demidov in the south, and Kholm, Staraya Russa and Demyansk in the north, became the centres of resistance. But in the second week of February the whole of General Graf Brockdorff-Ahlefeldt's X Army Corps and parts of XI Army Corps, situated in the Demyansk area south-east of Lake Ilmen, were completely cut off from their rear, and six divisions numbering some 100,000 men were surrounded. Within a few days the gap between them and the yielding German front increased to seventy-five miles.

Only one way of preventing their annihilation presented itself: an air-lift. But was it possible, by this means alone, to keep 100,000 men supplied not only with provisions and medical supplies, but also the necessary weapons, ammunition and equipment to ward off the attacks of a superior enemy—for weeks, perhaps months, in a temperature of minus forty to fifty degrees centigrade, and often in bad weather?

This was the question put on February 18th by Colonel-General Keller, commanding *Luftflotte* 1 at Ostrov, to Colonel Fritz Morzik, chief of air transport. Till now Morzik had been active with Richthofen's VIII Air Corps supporting Army Group Centre in its defensive operations. He was fully acquainted with the Ju 52 transport units, now being hastily transferred

275

to the north. He knew that their maximum strength was 220 aircraft, and that only one-third were serviceable.

"To ferry a daily quota of 300 tons to Demyansk," he answered, "I need a standing force of at least 150 serviceable machines, and we only have half that number. To double it you will have to draw on other fronts and drain the homeland of all available machines."

Keller agreed to do so.

"Secondly, to operate in winter needs more ground staff and better technical equipment. I require mobile workshops, vehicles to warm up the aero-engines, auxiliary starters, etc."

Keller said he could have the lot, if only he would get on with the job. Within twenty-four hours a crash programme had started, whereby Ju 52 formations—still under the official title of "zbV" or "special purpose" units —came flying in to their new bases at Pleskau-West and South, Korovye-Selo and Ostrov, and even Riga and Dünaburg. Morzik himself, with his operations chief, Captain Wilhelm Metscher, and the rest of the air transport staff had to make do with an H.Q. at Pleskau-South—an airfield already overcrowded by KG 4. This bomber unit, besides fulfilling its own defensive role over the whole of the operations sector, had soon itself to fly in supplies for General Scherer's troops cut off at Kholm.

As time went on, the Luftwaffe was increasingly reduced to a purely defensive weapon in aid of the encircled armies. With the *Stukas* and other ground-attack aircraft unable to cope alone, the bombers had to aid them, with the result that their own targets, far behind the front, remained unmolested. Any independent policy, any strategy of exploitation of the enemy's bottle-necks, had to go by the board in order to answer the cries for help from an army locked in a merciless winter struggle.

On February 20th the first forty Ju 52 transports landed on the hardtrodden snow of Demyansk's 800 by fifty-yard airfield. Their chief had given them just ninety minutes to discharge their cargoes before flying back again. But no organisation at first existed: everything had to be flown in—from the signals aircraft with direction-finder equipment and radio beacons, to the simplest tools. Morzik demanded the laying-out of a second landing field within the encircled area. To supply 100,000 men one airstrip was entirely inadequate. Apart from liability to enemy attack, it could be put out of action by bad weather or blocked by wrecked machines. By March the emergency strip was ready—at Pyesky, eight miles to the north of Demyansk. But only the most experienced pilots could safely use its thirty-yard wide runway, and loads were restricted to one and a half tons lest the surface of the snow gave way.

From Pleskau to Demyansk was some 150 miles, a hundred of them over hostile territory. At first Morzik sent the planes off singly at low level, but soon the Russian flak became too dangerous, and increasing numbers of fighters appeared. The transports then began to fly at 6,000 feet in tight formation, protected by fighters of Major Andres' III/JG 3 ("Udet") and I/JG 51 ("Mölders"). Usually the Russians lay in wait over Demyansk and attacked from astern as the transports went down singly to land. But as soon as German fighters appeared on the scene the enemy would disappear.

The greatest problem, however, was the Russian winter. Some of the transport *Gruppen* were thrown into the air-lift straight from flying schools in Germany. One—the zbV unit 500 under Major Beckmann—had suddenly to exchange the climate of the African desert for icy snow storms and a temperature of forty degrees below zero. For weeks on end the crews had to service their own aircraft owing to the shortage of ground personnel. Tyres would go flat because the rubber had turned brittle and cracked. Fuel tanks and even oil pipes would freeze up, with piston-scoring developing after only forty hours' flying. Hydraulic pumps broke down, instruments became completely unreliable, and radio sets failed to function. The engines themselves required constant attention.

Under such adverse conditions the serviceability state sank to twenty-five per cent of the total aircraft complement. All the more astonishing, therefore, is the fact that the air-lift succeeded. For three whole months—from February 20, till May 18, 1942, the six encircled German divisions were kept alive from the air. During this period supplies totalling 24,303 tons were delivered —a daily average of 276 tons representing enough foodstuffs, weapons and ammunition for 100,000 soldiers. In addition, the beleaguered army received over five million gallons of petrol and 15,446 replacements for the 22,093 wounded flown out. Aircraft losses were 265—less of them to the enemy than to "General Winter".

After May 18th only three transport *Gruppen* carried on the service, for by then a narrow land communication strip had been cleared of the enemy.

The air-lift to Kholm was also successful. Here 3,500 men, under the 281st Infantry Division's commander, Major General Scherer, defied attack from a pocket only one and a quarter miles in diameter, even though the Russians overran their positions on all sides of the town.

It was too small an area for an airstrip, and the Ju 52s had to land on a snow-covered meadow in no-man's-land right under the noses of the Soviet troops. Hatches were opened and the supplies dropped while the aircraft were still taxiing. Then they immediately took off again before coming under fire from the Russian artillery.

Even so, the losses suffered by Major Walter Hammer's enterprising zbV *Gruppe* 172 were too high. Subsequently supplies were either dropped by KG 4's He 111s, or landed in front of the German lines by heavy gliders of the type Go 242. In this case troop detachments would dash out under covering fire to the wrecks and rescue the vital cargoes. Though the Russians sometimes got there first, they failed to prevent enough supplies getting through to enable Scherer's force to hold out until it was liberated early in May by Grenadier Regiment 411.

The relief of Kholm saw the first engagement, under Lieutenant Colonel Dr. Bauer, of a Luftwaffe Field Battalion, consisting of volunteers from numerous Luftwaffe units. As Kholm repeatedly changed hands, the newly formed "Meindl Division"—later 21 Luftwaffe Field Division—went on fighting in this area the whole summer and autumn.

Successful as the Kholm, and still more the Demyansk, air-lifts were, they became dangerous precedents cited six months later—not at Lake Ilmen, but much further south, between the Don and the Volga. There, in the autumn of 1942, General Friedrich Paulus' 6th Army was fighting to capture Stalingrad. Seven-eighths of the giant industrial city were already in German hands when, on November 19th, the first onset of winter coincided with the launching of the expected Soviet counter-attack. Two days later the 6th Army was confronted with the alternatives of either making a fighting retreat, or allowing itself to become surrounded between the Don and the Volga.

On that day Lieutenant-General Martin Fiebig, commanding VIII Air Corps in the Stalingrad operations, telephoned the 6th Army's chief of staff, Major-General Arthur Schmidt, with Paulus himself listening in on another instrument. After referring to the pincers movement being developed by large forces of Soviet armour, Fiebig asked what the Army's plans were.

"The C.-in-C.", answered Schmidt, "proposes to defend himself at Stalingrad."

"And how do you intend to keep the Army supplied?"

"That will have to be done from the air."

The Luftwaffe general was flabbergasted. "A whole Army? But it's quite impossible! Just now our transport planes are heavily committed in North Africa. I advise you not to be so optimistic!"

Fiebig promptly reported the news to his *Luftflotte* chief, Colonel-General von Richthofen, whose telephone call in turn woke up the chief of general staff, Jeschonnek, at Goldap.

"You've got to stop it!" Richthofen shouted. "In the filthy weather we have here there's not a hope of supplying an Army of 250,000 men from the air. It's stark staring madness! . . ."

But the precedent had been established, and fate took its course.

2. The Betrayal of an Army

At 07.00 on November 22nd Lieutenant-General Fiebig was again on the telephone, repeating his warning to the 6th Army. During the night one catastrophic report had followed another. The *Stuka* and close reconnaissance airfield at Kalatsch in the great loop of the Don had been overrun. Lieutenant-Colonel Hitschbold and his men had flown off at the last moment, but their vital ground equipment was lost. Kalatsch was where the Russian pincers had closed, thereby cutting off the main supply route to Stalingrad. Three days after the offensive had opened the 6th Army was already virtually surrounded.

"I am deeply anxious," said Fiebig to Schmidt, "lest you are pinning too much faith on an air-lift. It is not practicable. Both the weather and the enemy are completely incalculable factors. . . ."

Schmidt terminated the conversation because at that moment the commander of the 4th *Panzer* Army, Colonel-General Hermann Hoth, entered the room, His army being adjacent on the south to that of Paulus, he had come to discuss the situation with him at Nizhniy-Tschirskaya. But once more a Luftwaffe general had his say, for at 08.00 the commander of 9 Flak Division, allocated to the 6th Army, came in. He was Major-General Wolfgang Pickert, who recorded the following conversation in his diary:

First Schmidt asked Pickert—a friend of his since 1925—what conclusions he drew from the threatening situation. Without hesitation Pickert replied, "I would snatch up all the forces I could and break out to the south-west."

"We cannot do that, because for one thing we don't have enough petrol."

"My Flak forces could help considerably. It is quite possible to man-handle the 160 20-mm guns across the steppe, and the ammunition can be carried."

"We have, of course, considered breaking out, but to reach the Don means thirty miles of steppe without any cover, and the ground is not yet frozen hard. The enemy will be ensconced on the western heights, and we shall have to attack him from level ground—without heavy weapons, which we shall have to abandon for lack of fuel. No, Pickert, it could only have a Napoleonic ending—quite apart from the 15,000 sick and wounded whom we should have to leave to their fate. The Army"—Schmidt concluded—"has been ordered to hold its ground at Stalingrad. Consequently we shall fortify our positions and expect supplies from the air."

Pickert, in his turn, was flabbergasted. "The whole Army? From the air—in this weather? To my mind it's quite out of the question. You must get out, I say. Get started now!"

General Paulus had listened in silence. But he was firm in his resolve. He was quite convinced that flight could only lead to disaster, and so felt obliged to array his forces in a defensive posture. That same day he flew into the pocket and set up his headquarters at Gumrak, outside the city borders. Not that Richthofen's, Fiebig's and Pickert's repeated warnings of the last twenty-four hours had not registered. Paulus demanded to be given freedom of action. His plan was to hold Stalingrad. If, however, the defence proved inadequate, or the air-lift could not fly in enough supplies, he still wished to reserve the right to try to save his army by a break-out. But to this request Hitler the same evening sent an uncompromising "No".

On the 23rd Paulus repeated his demand, urging the reasons for it. For now he himself was convinced that "punctual and adequate supplies cannot be expected". But again Hitler ordered the 6th Army to stay put on the Volga and not retreat a step. With that the Führer personally sealed that Army's fate. Was he, in fact, alone to blame?

Hitler's message to Paulus ended with the two words "AIR LIFT". Had indeed anyone, in the face of all the protestations from the Luftwaffe commanders at the front, and with the prospect of fog, ice and snow storms, dared to suggest that an air-lift was a practical proposition? What, at the highest level, had taken place since the Soviet offensive opened on the 19th?

No war diary, nor any other document, has recorded just when Goering first assured Hitler that "his" Luftwaffe could master the supply problem. It is only certain that that was what he did—and quite spontaneously, without previously consulting his advisers. Any doubt is removed by the assertions of the Luftwaffe and Army chiefs of general staff, Jeschonnek and Zeitzler. It was up to them to apprise their ultimate chiefs of the views of the front commanders. The day the 6th Army became surrounded was a Sunday, and Hitler was at Obersalzberg. In the afternoon Jeschonnek left the Hotel Geiger in Berchtesgaden and drove up to the Berghof. With Zeitzler to support him he hoped to get the Führer's ear. It proved difficult.

Later Zeitzler complained that Jeschonnek had failed to put his views convincingly. Granted, he had said that the Luftwaffe would be overtaxed by its new commitment, but not that the whole enterprise was bound to fail, let alone echoing Richthofen's words of "stark staring madness". Even so, his quiet recitation of all the difficulties for the Luftwaffe that the air-lift would entail was not without effect. General Bodenschatz, Goering's personal representative at Führer HQ, felt obliged to leave the meeting and put through an emergency telephone call to his chief at Karinhall.

At that Goering called Jeschonnek to the telephone, and expressly forbade him to "put the Führer further out of sorts". Of course the air-lift was possible.

The most reliable evidence as to how the *Reichsmarschall* ever came to give his assurance to Hitler against all informed opinion comes from his friend and World War I comrade, Colonel-General Bruno Loerzer. Goering, Loerzer reported later, often discussed the tragedy of Stalingrad with him, and repudiated the notion that he should be saddled with the blame. "Hitler took me by the sword-knot and said: 'Listen, Goering, if the Luftwaffe cannot supply the 6th Army, then the whole Army is lost.' There was thus nothing I could do but agree, otherwise I and the Luftwaffe would be blamed from the start. I could only say: 'Certainly, my Führer, we will do the job!'."

From that moment on even Jeschonnek, a dyed-in-the-wool Prussian officer, felt bound by the orders of his chief, however they might conflict with his own conviction. He ceased to oppose the air-lift, but postulated two conditions for its success:

1. That the weather conditions made flying possible.
2. That the vital take-off airfields of Tazinskaya and Morosovskaya be held at all costs against Red Army attack.

It hardly worried Hitler that neither condition could be guaranteed. That same evening he sent his order to Paulus to hold out.

Two days later, the 24th, General Zeitzler tried once more, this time alone, to make Hitler change his mind. The 6th Army, he said, had enough provisions for another few days. The Luftwaffe should muster every available aircraft and fly in fuel and ammunition only. In that way the break-out could still succeed.

Hitler sent for Goering,[1] and the *Reichsmarschall* presented himself with the words: "My Führer, I announce that the Luftwaffe will supply the 6th Army from the air."

"The Luftwaffe just can't do it," answered Zeitzler. "Are you aware, *Herr Reichsmarschall*, how many daily sorties the Army in Stalingrad will need?"

"Not personally," Goering admitted with some embarrassment, "but my staff know."

Zeitzler stuck to his guns, calculating the necessary tonnage. The Army, he said, required 700 tons every day. Even assuming that every horse in the encirclement area was slaughtered, it would still leave 500 tons. "Every day 500 tons landed from the air!" he repeated.

"I can manage that," Goering assured him. Whereat Zeitzler lost all control. "It's a lie!" he shouted.

Goering turned red, and his breath laboured. He clenched his fists as if about to fall upon the Army Chief of General Staff. Hitler's voice intervened.

[1] This scene at Führer HQ is taken from a written declaration supplied on March 11, 1955, by former Colonel-General Kurt Zeitzler (who has since died) in which he recorded his collision with Goering word for word. He, too, confirmed that the air-lift was a subject of direct agreement between Hitler and Goering, adding that Jeschonnek was under severe stricture from the latter.

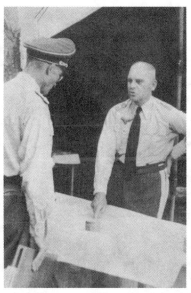

Stalingrad

94. *(left)* Colonel Kühl, C.O. of KG 55 and "Air Transport Commander 1" during the airlift. **95.** *(right)* Lieutenant-General Giebig, commander of VIII Air Corps in discussion with Colonel Stahel. His warnings about the impracticability of the air-lift were disregarded.

96. A *Stuka* attack on the city. In the winter of 1942/43 the German 6th Army was surrounded and after a bitter defence wiped out.

97. The Luftwaffe's failure to supply 250,000 men from the air alone was due primarily to the barbaric cold. The picture shows a bomb-loader working in the snow.

98. Unloading a Ju 52/3M in a Stalingrad blizzard.

He said coldly: "The *Reichsmarschall* has made his announcement, and I am obliged to believe him. The decision is up to me."

For Zeitzler that was the end of the interview. His attempt to save the 6th Army had failed thanks to Hitler's principle of never giving ground that had once been won. Whether the Luftwaffe could in fact keep 250,000 men supplied was to the Führer of secondary importance. Meanwhile, Goering's frivolous promise was a welcome pretext for his unyielding insistence that the 6th Army must stay put, albeit surrounded, at Stalingrad.

The first participant in the ensuing tragedy was the weather.

"A fine summer and autumn were behind us, and the Luftwaffe was in control of the region," reported Friedrich Wobst, veteran meteorologist of KG 55. "Hence we viewed with anxiety the inevitable season of bad weather —the Russians' best ally because it would tie the Luftwaffe's hands."

The basic weather pattern began to change on November 4th. By the 7th the cold had reached the loop of the Don, and on the 8th the thermometer at Morosovskaya, where KG 55 was stationed, suddenly fell to fifteen degrees below zero. The effect on aero-engines was immediate, with fog now and then adding to the difficulties.

This, however, was nothing compared with the situation that developed on November 17th when the cold area round Stalingrad was hit by damp warm air streaming in from Iceland. They combined to cause the worst weather possible: zero temperatures and dense fog alternating with sleet and snow. Ice on the ground inevitably meant that aircraft were swiftly iced-up and immobilised. At one blow the Luftwaffe was reduced to complete inactivity.

The Russians, well acquainted with their own weather, knew how to exploit it, and began their offensive only two days later. For weeks their preparations, observed from the air, had been reported, but nothing had been done to protect the 6th Army's extended northern flank. At the first onset the 3rd Rumanian Army's front was broken, and the whole strategic position immediately changed. And the one force that might have helped—the Luftwaffe —was grounded.

From VIII Air Corps HQ at Oblivskaya Lieutenant-General Fiebig insisted that at least some missions, by experienced crews, be flown against the enemy, and at Morosovskaya a few He 111s risked a take-off despite clouds blowing right across the ground and visibility hardly a hundred yards. Leading them was II/KG 55's commander, Major Hans-Joachim Gabriel. His machine, flown by Flight-Sergeant Lipp, raced northwards just above the steppe, and was last seen by First-Lieutenant Neumann attacking the Russian columns at zero feet, just before it was shot down by flak.

From Kalatsch, objective of the Russian break-through, Major Alfred Druschel's "battle" *Gruppe* got off, and from Karpovka near Stalingrad a few Ju 87s of StG 2. Its 1 Squadron was led, even though he was afflicted with jaundice, by the later celebrated "tank-basher" Hans-Ulrich Rudel, whose tally of missions in the east reached 2,530—greatly outnumbering that of any other pilot in the world. But on November 19th and 20th these few attacks had only pin-pricking effects on the enemy. In the evening of the 20th Colonel-General von Richthofen, C.-in-C. of *Luftflotte* 4, noted in his diary: "Once again the Russians have exploited the weather situation in masterly fashion. To save anything from the rot we *must* have good flying conditions."

But the weather remained as bad as ever. The bomber units which Richt-hofen tried to withdraw from the Caucasus front as reinforcements for the Don battle, were simply unable to get off the ground. The Russians not only closed their pincers at Kalatsch, but pushed south into the basin of the Don and its tributary, the Chir. Behind the latter lay the German air bases, above all those of Morosovskaya and Tazinskaya. If they were lost, Jeschonnek's second condition for the air-lift's success would also not be met.

The Luftwaffe became obliged to fend for itself. Colonel Reiner Stahel, commander of Flak Regiment 99, formed an emergency defence force out of anything he could lay hands on: flak batteries, maintenance parties, supply units, stragglers and men returning from leave. With this motley array he took up positions south and west of the Chir, while left and right of him, heartened by his example, Army and other Luftwaffe commanders did the same.

On November 26th such an emergency force, under another Flak officer, Lieutenant-Colonel Eduard Obergehtmann, repulsed a Soviet attack on the airfield at Oblivskaya, supported from the air by anti-tank Hs 129s and even a squadron of old Hs 123 biplanes—whose own ground-crews defended the runway and made it possible for them to land again. With VIII Air Corps HQ based at the airfield, even its staff officers joined in the fray. In the middle of it Richthofen landed and asked for Lieutenant-Colonel Lothar von Heine-mann, the chief of staff.

"He's out there manning a machine-gun, *Herr Generaloberst*," he was told by General Fiebig.

Angrily Richthofen ordered Fiebig and his staff back to Tazinskaya. They were supposed, he said, to be leading an air corps and creating an air-lift, not indulging in personal combat with the Russians. Yet if the Luftwaffe did not defend its own airfields, who would?

In the end reinforcements reached the Chir area: the first regular troop units and the first tanks. Though Colonel Stahel's emergency force still had to help man it, a defence line of sorts was with difficulty constructed by the new German chief of staff of the 3rd Rumanian Army, general staff officer Walther Wenck. It was a thin line, and it verged on the miraculous that it held. As a result the two large air-lift bases "Tazi" and "Moro"—as they were called for short—were saved. Otherwise the air-lift could never have got under way.

On November 24th *Luftflotte* 4 received from Luftwaffe high command the order to fly an initial 300 tons of supplies into the Stalingrad pocket each day: 300 cubic metres of fuel and thirty tons of weapons and ammunition. Three days later the 6th Army requested in addition flour, bread and other food supplies. Its rations were already low, for with the withdrawal into siege positions the food depots west of the Don had had to be abandoned, and the Army was now living from hand to mouth. Soon it would depend entirely on air deliveries.

Meanwhile the Ju 52 *Gruppen* were massing at Tazinskaya. Their crews included practised airmen who had flown many such hazardous missions be-fore, but also young inexperienced men—reinforcements straight from Germany. They brought with them an equally varied assortment of aircraft. Some were old and "clapped out", others so new that they had first to be run in. Amongst them were machines previously used for purely communications purposes and completely lacking in operational equipment: without fittings for radio or direction-finder sets, without winter protection, without even guns or parachutes! By the beginning of December Colonel Förster, air transport chief at Tazinskaya, had acquired eleven *Gruppen* of Ju 52s and two of Ju 86s, amounting to 320 aircraft. Yet scarcely more than one-third of them were serviceable.

Consequently on November 25th and 26th, the first two days of the air-lift, Stalingrad received only sixty-five tons of fuel and ammunition in place of the required 300. And on the third day it received virtually nothing.

"Weather atrocious," Fiebig noted in his diary. "We are trying to fly, but it's impossible. Here at 'Tazi' one snowstorm succeeds another. Situation desperate."

None the less a dozen aircraft risked a take-off. Despite the danger of icing up they flew blind the 140 miles to the Stalingrad airfield of Pitomnik, and brought twenty-four cubic metres of fuel. For a whole Army being over-run on all sides it was of course a ludicrous quota. It became only too plain that the Ju 52 transport formations alone would never be able to deliver the goods.

As a result Richthofen gave Colonel Ernst Kühl, commanding KG 55 at Morosovskaya, a dual assignment:

1. In a new capacity as transport commander he would commit his He 111s to supply-dropping at Stalingrad.
2. In his old capacity as air officer responsible for Stalingrad's defence, he would use them as air support for the Chir defence force, and pre-vent the Russians from advancing on "Tazi" and "Moro", the loss of which would sound the death-knell for the Stalingrad Army.

Kühl and his two operations staff captains, Hans Dölling and Heinz Höfe, appointed the following units for the dual role: two *Gruppen* of his own KG 55; I/KG 100 and the He 111 transport units KGs zbV 5 and 20 at Morosov-skaya-west and -south; finally KG 27 under Lieutenant-Colonel Hans-Henning von Beust at Millerovo. Together these represented a force of 190 Heinkels, all with experienced crews, to reinforce the Stalingrad supply ser-vice—as soon as the battle on their own door-step permitted. To fight the latter, Colonel Kühl was also given the "Udet" fighter *Geschwader* JG 3, plus a *Gruppe* each of *Stukas* and anti-tank planes.

On November 30th forty He 111s for the first time flew jointly with the Junkers transporters to the Stalingrad encirclement. They continued to do so day and night, singly or in sections, sometimes escorted by JG 3 fighters, but often alone despite the risk of encounter with Soviet fighters. Flying above cloud to avoid the enemy flak, they steered by the Pitomnik radio beacon, and coming down, searched the flat, snow-covered steppe for the landing field. A few parked Ju 52s would come into view, then the red landing cross, and finally the green Very lights. So guided, the Heinkels got ready to land on the hard-rolled snow.

Pitomnik had first come into service in September as an air-strip for fighters. Now the fate of a whole army depended on it. As soon as a Heinkel landed, it would be waved off the narrow runway, and men swarmed to unload the cases. Ammunition boxes were lowered from the bomb bay, and the petrol the aircraft did not itself require to get it back was siphoned from the wing tanks—to the left to supply the airfield's own fighter squadron, to the right for the tanks and army vehicles.

After a few wounded had climbed aboard, the Heinkel was ready for the return flight—unless the weather had cleared and attracted enemy fighters. In that case the pilot would wait till two other planes were ready, for a section would have enough fire-power to hold them at bay. Then it was a fifty minute flight back to "Moro" to collect more supplies, and repeat the turn-round. Such was the procedure, day and night, whenever the weather permitted.

On November 30th, thanks to the help of the He 111s, supplies delivered reached—for the first time—a hundred tons, still only a third of what Goering had promised, and only a fifth of what the Army required as a bare minimum. Next day the quota again went down owing to heavy snowfall, and on December 2nd the snow was succeeded by ice. There was a great shortage of heating equipment, and it took hours to thaw out the machines and get the engines started—hours during which the air-lift came to a standstill. Everywhere the aircraft had to be serviced in the open, with the fitters working in icy snow-storms without cover. At "Moro" an attempt to construct protective walls was brought to naught for lack of wood and metal. Fingers were frozen stiff, intricate servicing operations could not be carried out, and every engine-change became a torture. Inevitably the availability state fell to a mere twenty-five per cent.

Most of the Luftwaffe leaders had anticipated, or at least feared, such a denouement. They were still smarting from the effects of the first winter in Russia, and had expressly warned the 6th Army, when it decided to dig in at Stalingrad, not to nourish exaggerated expectations from an air-lift. Lieutenant-General Fiebig felt obliged to refer back to this warning when on December 11th, in company with VIII Air Corps' quartermaster chief, Major Kurt Stollberger, he flew into the Stalingrad pocket and received the bitter reproaches of Paulus about the complete failure of the air-lift, to date, to deliver the necessary goods. He needed, he said, a daily delivery of 600 tons, and 600 tons had been promised. Till now hardly one-sixth of that amount had been supplied.

"With that," Paulus added, "my Army can neither exist nor fight."

Fiebig could only assure him that he would do everything possible to reach the required standard. But he did not mince his words. Facing the issue, he declared categorically that the long-term provision of the 6th Army from the air still remained impossible, even if the strength of the transport force were multiplied.

All the same Paulus and his chief of staff, Schmidt, had a special request for the next few days. Colonel-General Hoth and his army were to attempt to breach the encircled area to the south-west. If this vital operation showed signs of success, the 6th Army would urgently need adequate fuel and ammunition to effect a break-out. Furthermore, its soldiers needed bread. On December 16th the last remaining rations would be handed out, and what happened after that was anyone's guess.

In response to this grave emergency the Luftwaffe's air-lift was stepped up from December 19th to 21st to an all-time high. During these three days some 450 sorties were flown, carrying over 700 tons of supplies to Pitomnik. It really looked as though the daily minimum might soon be attained. Then once more, all hopes were shattered. On the 22nd down came the fog, and during the next two days there was scarcely an improvement.

Now there was also a fresh disaster. Two armies of Russian Guards broke through the Italian 8th Army on the Don and headed south for Rostov. This threatened not only the 6th Army at Stalingrad, but the whole of the German southern front, with being cut off. But for the moment the dual Russian thrust had limited objectives: Tazinskaya and Morosovskaya. An emergency German force, consisting of elements of Signals Regiment 38 and the residue of VIII Air Corps staff under Lieutenant Colonel von Heinemann, made an attempt to hold the Russians in a gorge eight miles to the north of Tazinskaya, but failed for lack of anti-tank weapons.

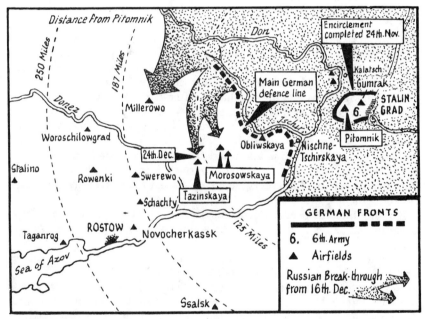

The Stalingrad air-lift. The flow of supplies for the 6th Army was greatly dependent on the distance the transport formations had to fly to reach the encircled airfield of Pitomnik. When Tazinskaya was overrun by Russian tanks on December 24, 1942, and both the Morosovskaya airfields had to be yielded on January 1, 1943, the extra distance of over 100 kilometres (62 miles) that the planes then had to fly from their new bases automatically reduced the flow.

By December 23rd it was high time for the 180 airworthy Ju 52s at Tazinskaya to make their getaway. But at this moment the supreme commander of the Luftwaffe intervened personally. He refused to allow them to go. From a distance of 1,250 miles he decided that Tazinskaya would be held until it was directly under fire. It seemed incredible. At stake was a whole transport fleet—still, for all its inadequacies, representing the one faint hope of survival for the encircled 6th Army.

At 05.20 on the 24th the first Russian tank shells fell on the northern perimeter of the airfield. One aircraft immediately went up in flames, another exploded on the runway. The rest waited with engines running. Would they now at last be allowed to go?

For an hour the *Gruppen* commanders had been clustered in the control tower's bunker, kicking their heels and awaiting the order that would spell deliverance. But Lieutenant-General Martin Fiebig could not bring himself to give it on his own responsibility. He persisted in trying to get through on the telephone to higher level, *Luftflotte* 4—despite the fact that it was known to everyone present that the exchange had been set on fire one and a half hours earlier by the Russian shelling of Tazinskaya village. Fiebig himself had seen the building burning on his way to the airfield, yet he still tried desperately to get connected to his *Luftflotte* chief, Colonel-General von Richthofen. Beside Fiebig in the shelter stood the *Luftflotte's* chief of general staff, Colonel Herhudt von Rohden, whom Richthofen, in anxious anticipation of events to come, had sent over the previous day. But von Rohden said nothing. Obviously he, too, was not prepared to counter an order from Goering.

At 05.25 a Volkswagen command car came racing over the airfield with VIII Air Corps' chief of staff, Lieutenant-Colonel Lothar von Heinemann, aboard. With Captain Jähne and First-Lieutenant Drube he had till now been manning Corps HQ in the village. After alerting the air crews, he had ordered those of the ground personnel for whom there was no room in the waiting aircraft to assemble for departure on the airfield's southern perimeter. He himself had reached the airfield just as the first Ju 52s went up in smoke. No one knew, in the shifting fog, where the shells came from, and the sounds of battle were drowned by the howl of aero-engines. Men who till now had been quietly waiting for orders, suddenly started rushing wildly about and crowding the aircraft. Panic had taken over.

Bursting into the shelter, Heinemann reported all this to Fiebig. *"Herr General,"* he panted, "you must take action! You must give permission to take off!"

"For that I need *Luftflotte* authority, cancelling existing orders," Fiebig countered. "In any case it's impossible to take off in this fog!"

Drawing himself up, Heinemann stated flatly: "Either you take that risk or every unit on the airfield will be wiped out. All the transport units for Stalingrad, *Herr General*. The last hope of the surrounded 6th Army!"

Colonel von Rohden then spoke. "I'm of the same opinion," he said.

Fiebig yielded. "Right!" he said, turning to the *Gruppen* commanders. "Permission to take off. Try to withdraw in the direction of Novocherkassk."

It was 05.30. Such a scene as was enacted in the next half hour has never been witnessed before or since. Engines roared, and with snow cascading from their wheels, the Ju 52s came rumbling through the mist from all directions. Visibility was hardly fifty yards and clouds hung almost on the ground, so low that one felt one could touch them. Most of the aircraft were heavily laden, not with the vital ground equipment to keep them serviceable on a new airfield, but still with boxes of ammunition and canisters of fuel for Stalingrad. For till the very last moment the order to proceed with the air-lift was still in force—just as if the Russians were still a hundred miles away.

As the aircraft went charging off into the unknown there was a violent explosion as two of them, taking off from completely different directions, collided in mid-airfield. Burning wreckage flew all about. Others taxied into each other, tangled their wings on take off, or smashed their tail units. Hair-breadth escapes were legion. Some, getting off the ground just in time, went screaming low over Russian tanks—this time with the mist their ally.

At 06.00 General Fiebig still stood before the control tower, with members of his staff around him, and a single serviceable Ju 52 nearby. Enemy firing had intensified, and to the left the supply depot for the 6th Army was in flames. The first Soviet tank loomed out of the mist, but went on past.

"*Herr General*," said Captain Dieter Pekrun, "it is time to go!" But Fiebig still hung about. At 06.07 Major Burgsdorf of 16 *Panzer* Division drew up and reported that the whole area was infested with enemy tanks and infantry. They should wait no longer, he said.

Fiebig, in fact, had nothing left to command. At 06.15 the last remaining Ju 52 left Tazinskaya. On board were Fiebig, Colonel Paul Overdyk, the chief signals officer, Major Kurt Stollberger, the quartermaster, and a number of other officers of the corps staff. Their lives depended on the skill of the pilot, Sergeant Ruppert. After taking off from the burning airfield he climbed high into cloud, but at 8,000 feet was still not through it. After seventy minutes the aircraft landed at Rostov-West.

From the unholy mess at Tazinskaya 108 other Ju 52s and sixteen Ju 86s came out unscathed on this Christmas Eve, and landed at various airfields. One was flown to Novocherkassk by Captain Lorenz of Signals Regiment 38, who had never been a pilot. The same evening he was handed an honorary pilot's badge by Richthofen. But some sixty aircraft—one third of the total—had been lost, and nearly all the spare parts and vital ground equipment had been left behind. All of this could have been saved if the evacuation order had come just one day in advance. What was the use of denuding Germany of the last training and communications aircraft for the Stalingrad venture, only to have them sacrificed through senseless orders?

Twenty-five miles further east, the second great air supply base, Morosovskaya, was likewise under threat, even if the Russian tanks were not yet so near. Any illusions were soon dispelled when first telephone communications with the sister airfield became disrupted, followed by reports that it was overrun. It meant that "Moro" itself was now virtually severed from the west.

Colonel Dr. Ernst Kühl, who as "Transport Leader 1" was in command of the station, took immediate action. He secured his He 111 *Gruppen* and the *Stukas* by sending them back to Novocherkassk, but remained behind with his small staff, praying that the foggy weather of the previous three days would end. If only they could fly, his bombers might still keep the Russian armour at bay.

Early on Christmas Eve the *Geschwader* meteorologist, Friedrich Wobst, roused his commanding officer and declared in high spirits: "*Herr Oberst*, we are going to have flying weather!"

Kühl glanced outdoors, saw nothing but fog, and eyed the weather man sceptically. But the latter was convinced: "Major cold front from the east. The fog will clear, and the sun will break through in two hours at most."

The operations officer, Captain Heinz Hofer, rang Novocherkassk and alerted the crews. Most of them had in any case spent the night in their machines. Within an hour the first of them landed back at "Moro", and just as the fog lifted the *Stukas* dive-bombed the spearhead of the Russian tanks. The attack caught them in steppe country without cover, and their losses were frightful. On the next day the remainder streamed back, and for the moment Morosovskaya was saved.

This success—shared by Major Dr. Kupfer's StG 2, Lieutenant-Colonel Hitschhold's anti-tank *Geschwader*, Major Wilcke's JG 3, and bombers of KGs 27, 55, and I/KG 100—demonstrated that the Luftwaffe was still capable of making its presence felt if the weather permitted, and especially if force was concentrated at the main point of effort. It was not, however, a lasting victory, for the fine Christmas weather gave way again to days of fog and icy snow-storms, and at once the Russians resumed their attack. Even though Tazinskaya was briefly recaptured by a German armoured counter-attack, both airfields had finally to be abandoned in early January 1943.

The Ju 52 transport *Gruppen* now operated from Ssalsk, the He 111s from Novocherkassk. For both the flight to Stalingrad was longer by sixty miles, which meant that the delivery rate was retarded. The events at "Tazi" and "Moro" were a bitter blow to the besieged Army, and over Christmas the air-lift had not functioned at all. Only at the New Year—on December 31st and on January 1st and 4th—did the deliveries once more exceed 200 tons. On the 2nd all flying was completely stopped by fog.

Longer flights also aided Russian counter-measures. A continuous line of flak positions was set up right along the path of the Pitomnik radio beam, compelling the aircraft to make time-consuming detours and use up fuel intended for the Stalingrad Army.

In theory the most efficient mode of operating the airlift was by a constant chain of individual aircraft continuing day and night, one after the other. In practice this was not possible because with each succeeding week the Soviet fighters became more active. Thus by day the Ju 52s could not fly singly, but had to get into formation over base and then be escorted by their own fighters. This hardly made for efficiency at Pitomnik. For hours the unloading teams had nothing to do, and then were suddenly confronted with a formation of forty or fifty aircraft at once, all hoping to be unloaded simultaneously. Needless to say they could not cope, and more time was wasted.

From the outset VIII Air Corps had requested the 6th Army to prepare other landing fields. During their visit on December 11th Fiebig and his quartermaster, Major Stollberger, had emphasized the need, pointing out particularly the airfield at Gumrak, which was in a central position adjoining Army HQ. Was the 6th Army already so weakened that it could not level out the bomb craters and smooth a runway in the snow?

It had not been done. Paulus even declined Fiebig's offer to send into the pocket an air force general to take charge of the air-lift at the receiving end —an expert who would be responsible not only for airfield construction and the unloading system, but all the other technical and tactical problems that the air-lift posed. The sole Luftwaffe general within the pocket was the commander of 9 Flak Division, Major-General Pickert. With his operations chief, Lieutenant-Colonel Heitzmann, and the C.O. of Flak Regiment 104, Colonel Rosenfeld, he had worked tirelessly to create an adequate ground organisation. Not only did they protect Pitomnik with their guns against low-level enemy attack; they had also taken over the whole flying control and supply direction. But whatever the devotion of these Flak officers, they lacked both the authority and the expertise to master the technical implications of what was, in effect, the toughest job the Luftwaffe had ever been called upon to face.

Outside the encirclement ring the 6th Army's quartermaster-general sent teams to "scrounge" what they could to supplement what the air-lift brought. And what the latter did bring was often not what the Army was most in need of. It included moist rye bread which froze solid and had to be thawed out before it could be eaten—while at Rostov huge stocks of wheaten flour and butter went untouched because of some obscure administrative order. Frozen lumps of fresh meat and vegetables containing three parts water filled precious space as if concentrated foods, as supplied to the U-boat crews and paratroops, had never been invented. In December the aircraft were even crammed with thousands of cumbersome Christmas trees and "Führer parcels"—as if the Army could live on those.

Such were the errors and inadequacies that paved the 6th Army's road to perdition—a road along which there could in any case be no return since Hitler had made his stiff-necked decision that it should stand fast at Stalingrad, and expected the Luftwaffe to make daily maintenance provision for 250,000 men in the middle of winter.

On January 9th the soldiers at Pitomnik pricked up their ears at a new sound in the air—that of a large, four-engined aircraft, a Fw 200 Condor. At 09.30 it came in to land, spraying fountains of snow as it did so. Indeed, the crew were fortunate to land on snow: it cooled the tyres, which otherwise would probably have burst from the strain imposed by the overloaded aircraft. For its cargo was four or five tons in excess of its permissible carrying capacity of nineteen tons.

A few minutes later the squadron commander, First-Lieutenant Schulte-Vogelheim, flew in, followed by five more aircraft. Their appearance stirred new hope. If the Luftwaffe could send in giant machines like these, men thought, perhaps the Army was not lost after all.

But there were only eighteen of them—drawn from KG 40 on the Atlantic coast, and thrust pell-mell into the Stalingrad supply service under the designation *Kampfgruppe* ZbV 200, with Major Hans Jurgen Willers in command. They were based at Stalino, a good 300 miles away from Pitomnik.

On January 9th the first seven Condors brought in four and a half tons of fuel, nine tons of ammunition and twenty-two and a half tons of provisions. On their return flight they took out 156 wounded. But already the second day saw the first aircraft put out of action. Schulte-Vogelheim had to turn back with engine trouble; a second plane was unable to take off for the return journey; a third landed hit by flak in engine and tail unit; a fourth with a damaged airscrew; and a fifth went missing on the return flight with twenty-one wounded aboard.

For men accustomed to the mild climate of the south-west coast of France, the sudden change to the Russian winter was a particularly hard one. At Stalino nothing had been got ready, and without hangars the Condors, trouble-prone at the best of times, had to be serviced in the open in temperatures of twenty to thirty degrees below zero. The parkas protecting the engines froze and broke like glass, and without even screens against the wind the engineer officer and his teams had to work in icy snowstorms. The single vehicle for warming up the engines had repeatedly to be used for thawing out mechanics who, spanner in hand, had literally become frozen fast to the machines.

Such were the desperate conditions under which the Luftwaffe struggled daily to achieve the impossible—only to be accused of "betraying" the 6th Army. Major Willers even tried to put Ju 290s on the Stalingrad run. These great "flying furniture vans" could carry ten tons at a time and bring out some eighty wounded on the return flight. But he only had two of them, and then only for a few days. The first, flown by Flight-Captain Hänig, made a successful round trip on January 10th. On its second it tried to take off from Pitomnik at 00.45 on the 13th with eighty wounded on board. Seconds after becoming airborne it reared up into an over-steep climb, rolled over and crashed. One N.C.O. survived. He reported that as a result of the rapid acceleration the wounded must have slid back to the stern. This made the aircraft so tail-heavy as to be uncontrollable.

The second Ju 290 was attacked over Stalingrad by LaGG–3 fighters on its very first sortie. Though its pilot, Major Wiskrandt, managed to land successfully, the machine was so badly damaged that it had to be flown back to Germany for repair.

As a last resort, an attempt was made to utilise the long-awaited four-engined bomber, the He 177. But this, too, was doomed to failure. Though a long-range bomber *Gruppe*, I/KG 50, had over forty of them undergoing winter tests at Saporoschje, it was found that only seven were immediately serviceable. Their commanding officer, Major Scheede, duly led these to Stalingrad, but was himself missing from the first flight.

As a transport plane the He 177 was in any case quite unsuitable, having little more load-capacity than the much smaller He 111. Similarly it was virtually useless for flying out wounded. After Scheede's death the He 177s, under Captain Heinrich Schlosser, flew thirteen bombing missions against the Russian encirclement at Stalingrad, and without any action attributable to the enemy seven of them crashed in flames. The "flying firework's" old fatal flaw was once more, and finally, revealed. It was clearly as useless as a fighting weapon as it was as a transporter.

But the Condors still went on supplying the Stalingrad pocket with such ammunition, fuel and provisions as they could. They continued doing so till the bitter end.

On January 10, 1943 the Russians launched their long-expected major assault. Penetrated on the south and west, the German perimeter had to be withdrawn inwards. On the morning of the 16th Pitomnik fell. Six *Stukas* and six Me 109s got off at the last moment as the airfield came under infantry fire.

The fighters, volunteers from the three *Gruppen* of JG 3 ("Udet"), had been acting as Pitomnik's base defence squadron since the beginning of December. Thanks to their tireless operations, the Russian fighters and ground-attack aircraft had been unable to prevent the arrival of supplies or the evacuation of 42,000 wounded. Led by Captain Germeroth, the squadron had during this time scored 130 victories, often with only two or

three aircraft serviceable at one time. Individually most successful was
Sergeant Kurt Ebener, with thirty-three victories against the armoured
Il-2 ground-attack planes, and the MiG-3 and LaGG-3 fighters—now
almost a match for the German Me 109s.

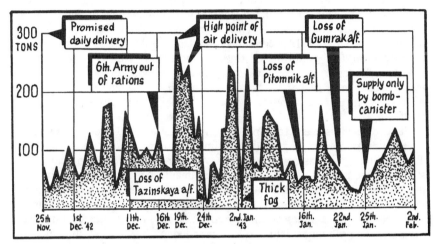

The starvation of the Army of Stalingrad. To hold out at Stalingrad the 6th Army required
a daily air delivery of 600 tons of supplies. The Luftwaffe promised 300 tons, but on the
average only managed to deliver 100. The diagram shows graphically how the flow varied
up to the capitulation of the 6th Army on February 2, 1943. Low points coincide with
impossible weather conditions or the loss of important airfields.

When, on January 16th, the six fighters eluded the Russians at Pitomnik,
they were ordered to re-land in the pocket at Gumrak. But this airfield
had not been got ready. The first plane overturned in a snow-drift, the
second charged into a bomb crater, and the third, fourth and fifth suffered
a like fate. Only the last pilot, First-Lieutenant Lukas, veered off in time
and flew west. His was the sole Me 109 to get away.

And now the transports were supposed to land at wreck-strewn Gumrak.
The same day, however, the Ju 52 *Gruppen* had to quit their own base at
Ssalsk in a hurry, for that too was being threatened by the enemy. Under
the direction of Colonel Morzik, master-planner of the Demyansk air-lift of
the previous winter, they then began to use a maize field near Sverevo,
representing the limit of their range. Within twenty-four hours Morzik
lost fifty-two of them to a Russian bombing attack—twelve being completely
burnt out and forty damaged.

Thus one blow succeeded another. On the same black January 16th
Field Marshal Erhard Milch joined Richthofen's staff train at Taganrog
with special powers from Hitler to take over and reorganise the air-lift.
But what could he do? Before he arrived the Luftwaffe had already done
everything humanly possible to save the Stalingrad Army—and failed because it was impossible from the start. Now at Pitomnik the Russians, taking
possession of the German airfield lighting and direction-finder equipment,
set up a decoy installation. A number of pilots were duly deceived and landed
right amongst the enemy.

At Gumrak itself the position steadily worsened. Its narrow runway, flanked by wreckage and bomb craters, required the utmost skill and daring at every landing. During the night of January 18th and 19th young Lieutenant Hans Gilbert managed to land his heavy Condor there in a snow-storm with visibility hardly fifty yards. Though he broke his tail-skid he successfully carried out his orders to evacuate General Hube, commander of the armoured force. On the same day Major Thiel, commander of III/KG 27 ("Boelke"), landed there in a He 111. He had been sent as VIII Air Corps' representative to report on the condition of this emergency airfield—described in the 6th Army's radio messages as "day-and-night operational". For many transporters, not prepared to risk a landing, had either turned back or merely thrown out bomb-canisters. Thiel's grim report speaks for itself:

"The airfield is easy to pin-point from 4,500–5,000 feet owing to its rolled runway, its wreckage and the numerous bomb craters and shell holes. The landing cross was covered with snow. Directly my machine came to a standstill the airfield was shot up by ten enemy fighters—which, however, did not come lower than 2,500–3,000 feet owing to the light flak that opened up on them. Simultaneously it was under artillery zone fire. I had just switched off the engines when my aircraft became an object for target practice. The whole airfield was commanded by both heavy and medium guns situated—so far as one could judge from the open firing positions— mainly to the south-west. . . .

"Technically speaking, the airfield can be used for daylight landings, but at night only by thoroughly experienced air-crews. . . . Altogether thirteen aircraft wrecks litter the field, in consequence of which the effective width of the landing area is reduced to eighty yards. Especially dangerous for night landings of heavily laden aircraft is the presence of the wreck of a Me 109 at the end of it. Immediate clearance of these obstacles has been promised by Colonel Rosenfeld. The field is also strewn with numerous bomb-canisters of provisions, none of them saved, and some already half covered with snow. . . .

"When I returned to my aircraft (after reporting to Colonel-General Paulus) I found that it had been severely damaged by artillery, and my flight mechanic had been killed. A second aircraft of my section stood off the runway in like condition. Though I had landed at 11.00, by 20.00 no unloading team had appeared, and my aircraft had neither been unloaded nor de-fuelled despite the crying need for fuel by the Stalingrad garrison. The excuse given was the artillery fire. At 15.00 Russian nuisance planes (U-2s) began to keep watch on the airfield in sections of three or four. From the outset I made it my business to look into the air control system and established that before 22.00 it was quite impossible to land a single plane. . . . If one approached, the seven lamps of the flare path would be switched on, offering a target visible for miles, whereat it would be bombed by the nuisance raiders above. The only possible measure was a short flash to enable the aircraft to position its bomb-canisters. . . ."

At 6th Army HQ, where Thiel endeavoured to discuss the manifold and insuperable difficulties besetting the air-lift, he was met only with refusals, bitterness and despair. "If your aircraft cannot land," said Paulus, "my army is doomed. Every machine that does so can save the lives of 1,000 men. An air drop is no use at all. Many of the canisters are never found because the men are too weak to look for them, and we have no fuel to collect them. I cannot even withdraw my line a few miles because the men would fall out from exhaustion. It is four days since they have had anything to eat. Heavy weapons cannot be brought back for lack of petrol, and become lost to us. The last horses have been eaten up. Can you imagine what it is like to see soldiers fall on an old carcass, beat open the head and swallow the brains raw?"

The last sentence, Thiel reported, might have been uttered by any of those present: General von Seydlitz, Major-General Schmidt, Colonel Elchlepp, Colonel Rosenfeld or First-Lieutenant Kolbenschlag. "From all sides I was heaped with reproaches."

Bitterly Paulus had continued: "What should I, as commander-in-chief of an army, say when a simple soldier comes up to me and begs: '*Herr Generaloberst*, can you spare me one piece of bread?' Why on earth did the Luftwaffe ever promise to keep us supplied? Who is the man responsible for declaring that it was possible? Had someone told me that it was not possible, I should not have held it against the Luftwaffe. I could have broken out. When I was strong enough to do so. Now it is too late."

Had the C.-in-C. forgotten that it was his own decision to defend himself at Stalingrad? Had he forgotten that every Luftwaffe forward commander, at the time he made it, had warned him not to rely on the possibility of supplying 250,000 men from the air during a Russian winter? Did he not recall that it was the glorious Führer himself who, denying Paulus's own urgent request to be given permission for a break-out, had ordered the 6th Army to stay put, and doomed it to destruction to suit his own strategic notions?

"The Führer gave me his firm assurance," said Paulus, "that he and the whole German people felt responsible for this Army, and now the annals of German arms are besmirched by this fearful tragedy, just because the Luftwaffe has let us down!"

Schmidt, his chief of staff, spoke in the same vein, concluding: "To think of this splendid army going to the dogs like this!"

"We already speak from a different world to yours," added Paulus, "for we are dead men. From now on our only existence will be in the history books. Let us try to take comfort that our sacrifice may have been of some avail."

This storm of wrath and despair had been unleashed against a mere major and *Gruppenkommandeur* of the Luftwaffe—a man who had done his duty in every respect, and with his colleagues had tried his best to accomplish an impossible task. Deeply upset, Thiel left the doomed Army's headquarters, and in his report objectively attributed the generals' outbursts to their terrible state of nervous tension. After his return from the Stalingrad pocket the transport units once more did their utmost to fly in more provisions, ammunition and fuel to the beleaguered army. Even during the final night of January 21st-22nd, twenty-one He 111s and four Ju 52s landed fully laden at Gumrak. Then this airfield, too, was overrun.

"Whatever help you bring is now too late. We are already lost," Paulus had said a few days earlier to Major Maess, commander of I/KG zbV 1. When the latter pointed out that the transport bases west of the Don were themselves under pressure by the enemy, the general answered bitterly: "Dead men are no longer interested in martial history."

After the capture of Gumrak the crews were reduced to dropping bomb-canisters only, and the flow of transport declined still further. Many of the "bombs" fell and were lost amongst the city ruins, or the men simply lacked the strength to gather them. More and more food and ammunition fell into enemy hands.

On February 2nd, a final radio message came through from XI Army Corps in the northern sector of the pocket: ". . . Have done our duty and fought to the last man. . . ." Then all contact was broken off. That evening, once more, two waves of He 111s carrying bomb-canisters flew over the city, but search as they would were unable to detect any sign of life. The battle was over.

The supreme effort that the Luftwaffe made to help is reflected by its losses. From November 24, 1942, till January 31, 1943, they lost 266 Ju 52s, 165 He 111s, forty-two Ju 86s, nine Fw 200s, seven He 177s and one Ju 290—a total of 490 machines, or five *Geschwader*. More than a whole Air Corps!

It was a shattering blow from which the Luftwaffe never recovered.

3. "Operation Citadel"

We move on five months. After the loss of the 6th Army, with its nineteen divisions, the Germans had suffered further reverses on the eastern front. All the ground, stretching to the Caucasus, won by the summer offensive of 1942 had been reconquered by the Russians in the bitter battles of the winter. So far as ice and snow had permitted, the Luftwaffe had everywhere stood by the Army in the difficult and often desperate situations that confronted it: in supplying the Khuban bridge-head, in helping it defend the Donets and Mius fronts, and in the battles for Kharkov, Kursk and Orel.

Since April the front had been stabilised. The winter fighting had left two mutually jutting salients: the German one, centred at Orel, jutting eastwards; the Russian one, jutting westwards round Kursk, adjacent to it on the north. To any general staff officer, viewing the situation on the map, it had the makings of two rival pincers movements: a German one from north and south to cut off the Kursk salient and all the Russian forces within it, and a similar Russian one at Orel.

For this double battle—the greatest of the Russian war—both sides were now energetically preparing. On it—under the code-name "Operation Citadel"—the Germans pinned their hopes of decisively defeating the now almost overwhelming Russian Army by means of an encirclement on the pattern of summer 1941. But Hitler, in the opinion of his generals, was waiting far too long before giving the word to start. The whole of June 1943 had gone by with the German assault divisions straining at the leash in vain, thus giving time for the Russians to complete their own preparations. For each side was perfectly aware of the other's intentions.

Finally, on July 1st, Hitler summoned his generals to Rastenburg and gave them a firm date: "Citadel" would start in four days' time. Experience had shown, he said, that nothing was worse for an army than to stand idly about. There was a danger, he added, that when the German divisions pushed south-west in strength, the Russians would open their own expected assault on the north of the Orel salient—in other words fall on the German rear. Should this happen, he proposed to parry the vital threat by employing every available German aircraft.

For this last effort, accordingly, the Luftwaffe concentrated as much strength as it could. Other fronts were drained and all reserves brought up from the homeland. In the end some 1,700 aircraft were made available. General Hans Seidemann, with 1,000 bombers, fighters, ground-attack and anti-tank planes, would support the thrust from the Byelgorod region, to the south, of the 4th *Panzer* Army under Colonel-General Hoth. The thrust from the north by Colonel-General Model's 9th Army would be assisted by 1 Air Division at Orel, under Major-General Paul Deichmann, with an initial establishment of 700 aircraft.

The offensive was opened on July 5th, at 03.30—and at that moment the 1,700 aircraft were to be over the front and start attacking not only the enemy airfields, but the fortifications, entrenchments and artillery positions of the deeply staggered Russian defence system.

At VIII Air Corps HQ, situated at Mikoyanovka, some twenty miles behind the Byelgorod front, feverish tension reigned. All orders had been given, and at Kharkov's five airfields, all crammed with planes, the units stood at cockpit readiness. It was ordained that the bomber *Geschwader* would take off first, form up over their bases, await their fighter escort, then set off for the front. This time such calculations were not upset by the weather: a fine clear summer day was dawning. On the other hand no one cherished any illusion of the attack being unexpected. It was hoped at most that tactical surprise would be achieved: that the Russians would be ignorant of the exact time and locality.

Suddenly, however, alarming reports reached General Seidemann from the aircraft warning service. Radio monitors had ascertained a sudden upward surge in the volume of exchanges amongst the Russian air regiments, which could only mean that a major operation was imminent. Shortly afterwards the *"Freya"* radar stations at Kharkov reported formations of several hundred aircraft approaching.

No one had reckoned with such an eventuality. The Russians were evidently aware of both the day and the hour of the German attack. They had probed one of their enemy's most closely guarded secrets, and now they were going to anticipate this attack with their own. Before a single German bomber had left the ground, they were coming with a whole army of the air to blast the densely crowded airfields of Kharkov! Catastrophe loomed. The German planes would be smashed, either motionless on the ground, or at their moment of greatest vulnerability, while trying to get off it—minutes before they delivered their own blow. During these minutes "Operation Citadel"—the last all-out effort of the German forces to turn the tables in the east—would be doomed before it started. For without maximum and continuous air support the battle could not be won.

The German fighters grasped the crisis and realised that all depended on them. The report of the approaching Soviet armada had hardly reached them at Mikoyanovka before JG 52 scrambled into the air and climbed to meet it. At the Kharkov airfields the take-off of the bombers was postponed from minute to minute. Engines turning, they waited all ready to do so as fighters of the "Udet" *Geschwader*, JG 3, taxiing through their ranks, preceded them into the air from all directions.

Seidemann, and beside him the Luftwaffe's chief of general staff, Jeschonnek, went through anxious minutes as the Russian formations passed overhead in the direction of Kharkov. Immediately afterwards the first German fighters made contact, and there developed the largest air battle of the war: two *Geschwader* of German fighters versus about 400–500 Russian bombers, fighters and ground-attack planes.

"It was a rare spectacle," wrote Seidemann. "Everywhere planes were burning and crashing. In no time at all some 120 Soviet aircraft were downed. Our own losses were so small as to represent total victory, for the consequence was complete German air control in the VIII Air Corps sector."

Thus the ranks of the Russians were already greatly thinned by the time they reached the Kharkov airfields. There they had to run the gauntlet of the powerful flak defences, with the Messerschmitts—despite the dangers from their own flak—still on their tails. As a result this admirably conceived, bold and persistent raid by the Russian air force came to naught. Its bombs fell widely scattered, and the German bomber units, threatened with extinction just previously, were still able to take off virtually unscathed, and at the appointed time.

The first few days of "Operation Citadel" were characterised by deep penetrations of the Russian defence lines on the north, and still more on the south, of their Kursk salient. As in the days of the "blitz" campaigns, and now for the last time in the war, the *Stukas* hammered breaches for the German tanks to enter. With other close-support aircraft they flew up to six missions daily.

"We were well aware how important it was for our armour that the initial air attack should be effective," reported Captain Friedrich Lang, Leader of III *Gruppe* in Lieutenant-Colonel Pressler's StG 1. Under the control of 1 Air Division at Orel, the *Geschwader* was operating against the deeply staggered Soviet defences west of Malo Archangelsk. Somewhere a gap had to be forced, through which Model's *Panzer* divisions could push and exploit their tactical superiority in a mobile battle. But the Russians defended tenaciously, and—in direct contrast with the Germans—could call upon adequate reserves.

In three days of hard fighting the southern arm of the pincers, represented by the 4th *Panzer* Army, succeeded in pushing about twenty-five miles northwards, thereby exposing its extended eastern flank. For on this flank, north of Byelgorod, stretched a belt of woodlands which General Kempf's covering divisions had not succeeded in clearing of the enemy. These woodlands thus represented a major threat to the German advance, and became the object of constant air reconnaissance.

In the early morning of July 8th, the fourth day of the offensive, the woods were being reconnoitred at low level by a section of anti-tank aircraft of the type Henschel Hs 129B-2, based at Mikoyanovka. Leading the patrol was the *Gruppenkommandeur*, Captain Bruno Meyer. Scan it as he might, the landscape seemed impenetrable. Then suddenly he saw, in the open country to the west, tanks moving—twenty, forty or more. It must be a whole brigade. And ahead of the tanks marched dense blocks of infantry, like a martial picture from the Middle Ages.

It could only be the expected Russian flank attack. Now every minute counted. Meyer started back for base, realised that would take too long, and

99. The armoured Hs 129B, with four 30-mm cannon athwart the fuselage. This was one of the German anti-tank aircraft in use towards the end of the Russian campaign.

100. The Ju 87G, with 37-mm cannon beneath the wings, another anti-tank aircraft.

101. The versatile Fw 190 in flight. As a fighter-bomber it carried jettisonable containers packed with fragmentation bombs.

102. The Fw 190 with the fragmentation bomb carrier being loaded.

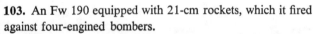

103. An Fw 190 equipped with 21-cm rockets, which it fired against four-engined bombers.

alerted his men at Mikoyanovka by radio. They belonged to IV (Anti-tank) *Gruppe* of *Schlachtgeschwader* 9 and had been posted to VIII Air Corps straight from a gun test in Germany only a few days before, just in time for "Citadel". The *Gruppe* had four squadrons, each with sixteen Hs 129 anti-tank aircraft.

Meyer ordered it to attack by squadrons, and within a quarter of an hour the first, guided by the *Kommandeur*, was making its approach. Having left the woods, the Russian tanks were advancing westwards without cover. Going right down, the Henschels attacked from astern and abeam, firing their heavy 30-mm cannon. The first tanks were hit and exploded. The aircraft made a circuit and picked out fresh targets, each firing another four or five shells.

The Russian column showed signs of confusion. This type of air attack was unknown. Previously such aircraft had mainly dropped fragmentation bombs, or made low-level machine gun attacks, when the only danger was a chance hit, say, on the caterpillar drive or through a ventilation slit. Even 20-mm cannon shells usually bounced harmlessly off the armour-plating. But now the 30-mm shells penetrated it, and within a few minutes half-a-dozen tanks lay burning on the battlefield.

Previously the Luftwaffe had fought the entire Polish and French campaigns, and also gone through the Battle of Britain with a single *Lehrgruppe*, II/LG 2, as its sole anti-tank unit. The same applied at the outset of the war with Russia. II/LG 2 still remained the only anti-tank unit, still equipped, apart from some Me 109s, with the ancient Henschel 123 biplane.

In the summer of 1941, at Vitebsk, this unit had written a page of military history which would not be credible, were it not personally confirmed by the then chief of *Luftflotte* 2, Field-Marshal Kesselring. A few Hs 123s, returning from an operation, saw below them some fifty Russian tanks engaged with German armoured vehicles. The same Bruno Meyer—then First-Lieutenant in command of a squadron—went down as if to attack them, with his squadron behind. But the trouble was that they had no more bombs, and the brace of machine-guns which fired through the airscrew arc would be useless. The only hope was to try and demoralise the enemy by diving on them, a trick which had worked before, for at full throttle the noise of the propeller resembled a barrage of artillery.

In fact the enemy did turn and run! As the Henschels came down again and again, the tank crews so lost their heads that they all drove headlong into a marsh. Unable to extricate their vehicles, they had to blow them up. After visiting the scene of this unusual battle, Kesselring testified to the fact that a single weaponless squadron had destroyed forty-seven T-34 and KV-1 tanks.

It was, of course, a fluke, and no one claimed that in the long run such light aircraft could be a match for the enemy's powerful armour. In spring 1942, II/LG 2 became merged into the first *Schlachtgeschwader*, SG 1. In the Crimean battles of 1942 one of its *Gruppen*, II/SG 1, was for the first time equipped with the new Henschel 129, whose cockpit, like that of the Russian Il-2, was heavily armour-protected. With the 20-mm MG 151 and lighter machine-guns, it also had a superior armament. Even so, any success against tanks was a matter of luck. And the number of Russian tanks constantly increased. Even *Stukas* made little impression except by direct hits, and these were rare. Against tanks, bombs were clearly an inadequate weapon, and already in 1941 the force responsible for dealing with these targets was clamouring for armour-piercing weapons. But it took a whole year for the clamour to get a hearing in the Reich.

At the Luftwaffe experimental centre at Rechlin tests were then conducted with a 30-mm MK 101 cannon fitted below the Hs 129's fuselage. It was found that the shells, with a core of tungsten, were capable of penetrating armour-plate no less than eight centimetres thick. At last an airborne "tank-basher" was on the way!

The first successes with the new weapon were scored in May, 1942, against Russian tanks which broke out during the battle of Kharkov. At that time Rechlin technical teams had equipped a few dozen Hs 129s with the 30-mm gun for action at the front. But during the German summer offensive of 1942 the "tank-bashers" were little used owing to lack of targets. With the Henschels urgently required in a more diversified role, and with a monthly production of only twenty to thirty, the consequence was that the heavy cannon were taken off again. Furthermore, when in the winter of 1942/43 Russian tanks once more penetrated the German front at many points, it was discovered that in conditions of extreme cold the anti-tank guns usually failed to work. None the less an anti-tank commando of just two squadrons, under Lieutenant-Colonel Otto Weiss, was kept as a sort of "fire-brigade" for action at vital points, and in fact often came to the rescue in the nick of time.

Early in 1943 the new weapon was at last perfected in Germany, so that by July, for the first time, there was an integrated *Gruppe*—namely Bruno Meyer's IV (Pz)/SG 9—ready to participate in what was to be history's biggest tank action to date.

From now on tank-hunting from the air gained greatly in significance. Shortly after "Operation Citadel" and the German retreat from the Orel salient, the *Stukas* also were converted to this role, changing their name from *Stukageschwader* to *Schlachtgeschwader*. First-Lieutenant Hans-Ulrich Rudel of StG 2 had already shown the way successfully with a Ju 87 carrying two 37-mm cannon, called "Flak 38", under the wings—a prototype that Junkers then produced serially as the Ju 87 G. Not that anyone could approach Rudel's success. In the last two-and-a-half years of the war he himself accounted single-handed for the almost incredible figure of 519 Russian tanks, and in January 1945 was awarded a decoration specially minted for him alone—the Golden Oak Leaves of the Knight's Cross.

By autumn 1943 the former *Kommodore* of StG 2, Colonel Dr. Ernst Kupfer, became the first *Waffengeneral der Schlachtflieger*, with five *Schlachtgeschwader* under him. They comprised fourteen *Gruppen*, equipped with Ju 87s, Hs 129s and Fw 190s. There was even an attempt to fashion a "tank-basher" out of the Luftwaffe's "all-round" aircraft, the Ju 88—carrying a 75-mm machine cannon, the "Pak 40". But though such a weapon could destroy the mightiest tank with a single shot, the aircraft became so ponderous and vulnerable that the project was rejected.

It was not long before the Russians came to recognise the "tank-bashers" as their deadliest enemy. They not only took pains to camouflage their tanks when stationary, but brought up more and more flak to protect them when in action.

As for the Luftwaffe, its expanding force of anti-tank aircraft showed that it was becoming more and more reduced to the role of a direct auxiliary to the hard-pressed eastern armies.

The new phase started, as we have seen, with the attack of Bruno Meyer's IV (Pz)/SG 9 on the Soviet armoured brigade west of Byelgorod. This was followed up by squadrons commanded by Major Matuschek, First-Lieutenants Oswald and Dornemann, and Lieutenant Orth. Soon the country was littered with knocked-out and burning tanks. Simultaneously the escorting infantry was split up by fragmentation bombs from Major Druschel's Fw 190 fighter-bomber *Gruppe*, and the rest of the tank brigade fled back to the cover of the woods.

The flank attack against the advancing 4th *Panzer* Army had thus already been repulsed by Meyer's force, acting on their own initiative, by the time the Army command, anticipating the threat to its flank owing to the sounds of battle, appealed to VIII Air Corps for this very support. But the objective of "Citadel"—the encirclement of Kursk—was not achieved, owing to the Germans' total lack of reserves. When on July 11th, only six days after the commencement of the German assault, the Russians delivered their dreaded counter-blow north and east of Orel, both Army and Luftwaffe were forced to abandon their attack in order to plug the gaps in their own front. The offensive action against the Kursk salient gave way to the battle to defend the Orel one. There, two German armies—the 9th and 2nd *Panzer*—both under the command of Colonel-General Walter Model, were threatened with encirclement. Through a wide breach in the north the Russian tanks poured irresistibly against their rear.

By July 19th a Russian armoured brigade had already blocked the Bryansk-Orel railway at Khotinez and threatened the line running south—thus imperilling the only reinforcement route for both armies. The situation was similar to that which had obtained eight months previously at Kalatsch on the Don, and which had led to the encirclement of the 6th Army at Stalingrad.

At this moment the Luftwaffe struck—with *Stukas* operating from Karachev, close to the break-through region; with bombers, fighters and anti-tank planes. Practically every battle-worthy *Gruppe* of the eastern Luftwaffe was in these last days packed into the 1 Air Division area. At last they could concentrate their effort at a single decisive spot. Nor did success elude them. Beneath the punishing blows the Russians reeled back. The whole day long the scattered tanks were harried by Lieutenant-Colonel Kupfer's Ju 87s and Captain Meyer's Hs 129s as they scattered to the north.

As a result it became possible during the following days to seal off the area of the break-through, and shortly afterwards to clear the Orel salient. Colonel-General Model sent a teleprint in which he expressed his gratitude and gave full credit to the Luftwaffe. An armoured break-through threatening two armies in the rear had, for the first time, been repulsed from the air alone.

By its vital contribution at Karachev, from July 19th to 21st, 1943, the Luftwaffe had in fact prevented a second Stalingrad on an even more terrible scale. It was its last major operation on the eastern front. From now on it was once more dispersed over the whole vast area, where its strength became steadily sapped by the calls of a new and final mission: the defence of the German homeland.

Disaster in Russia—Summary and Conclusions

1. After the failure of the 1941 "blitzkrieg" in Russia, during which the Luftwaffe operated almost exclusively in direct or indirect support of the Army, priority should have been given to strategic operations against the enemy's arms industry. The need for such operations was emphasised by mounting Russian production, especially of tanks, guns and close-support aircraft, which made themselves increasingly felt on the over-stretched German front. While from 1941 till the end of the war Germany produced 25,000 tanks, Russia during the same period produced six times that figure.

2. For attacking strategic targets in Russia the Luftwaffe felt the absence of a heavy, four-engined bomber even more acutely than it did during the Battle of Britain. Owing to its lack of dive-potential the one aircraft constructed for this purpose—the He 177—was never adequately developed. Even so, concentrated raids by available Ju 88 and He 111 formations could have had an appreciable effect, even if it meant operating at the limit of their range. A few such "strategic" operations carried out in the spring of 1943 were proof enough. But instead, the Luftwaffe was still split up into tactical units deployed directly on the front. Whatever their success in this role, all Russian loss of material was easily replaced, and from year to year the enemy grew stronger.

3. When the weakness of his forces in winter was revealed, Hitler's reaction was not to keep them mobile by withdrawing and straightening the front (as his generals advised) but to order them to stand fast and hold out. The front was thus broken up, and the Luftwaffe saddled with the new and difficult task of supplying the forces that consequently became cut off. Though this was accomplished in the case of the augmented Army Corps at Demyansk, its very success became a dangerous precedent. For when in late November 1942 the 6th Army likewise became cut off at Stalingrad, the high command believed that it too could be supplied from the air.

4. Nevertheless, Hitler's resolve that this 250,000 strong Army should stay put, and his ban on any attempt to break out, was independent of whether an adequate air-lift were possible or not. From the outset the Luftwaffe front commanders—including Richthofen who, as chief of Luftflotte 4, was the one immediately responsible—made every endeavour to discourage such a belief, yet to all arguments Hitler turned a deaf ear, and the 6th Army was consequently sacrificed. The desperate efforts of the Luftwaffe, with inadequate resources, to keep this Army alive in the face of winter conditions, and with their own bases overrun by the enemy, is one of the most tragic chapters of German military history.

5. The last major German offensive action in the east—"Operation Citadel" in July, 1943—was accompanied by the last major effort of the Luftwaffe, with 1,700 bombers, fighters and ground attack planes. But despite numerous tactical victories, such as the destruction of a whole armoured brigade from the air, the objective was never achieved owing to the overwhelming might of the enemy. The remainder of the campaign saw the Luftwaffe once again distributed over the whole front in a final attempt to give direct support to the Army. For bombers it was a desperate and futile task.

11

THE BATTLE OF GERMANY

1. The Writing in the Sky

No one who experienced them will ever forget them—those streams of Flying Fortresses.

"The '*Eisbär*' controller directed us over the Zuyder Sea, and we were the last to make contact with the enemy at 23,000 feet twelve miles west of Texel," reported Lance-Corporal Erich Handke, radio-operator of a Me 110. "Suddenly we saw the Boeing Fortress IIs ahead in a great swarm. I confess the sight put me into a bit of a flap, and the others felt the same. We seemed so puny against these four-engined giants. Then we attacked from the beam, following the pair leader, Flight-Sergeant Grimm. . . ."

There were four pairs, and they attacked in succession: eight Messerschmitt 110s against sixty Boeing B-17s—or sixteen 20-mm cannon and forty 7.9-mm machine-guns against 720 heavy 12.7-mm machine-guns. The date was February 4, 1943. Eight days previously, on January 27th, the American Flying Fortresses had mounted their first big daylight raid on Wilhelmshaven, and thereby started a new era in the air war against Germany.

Britain's R.A.F. Bomber Command, for the better safety of its aircraft, launched its raids on German cities only at night. And so far the 8th U.S. Army Air Force, which during 1942 had been assembling on English soil, had only attacked targets in France, and under strong fighter protection. But now, in full daylight, its bombers were coming to Germany, penetrating to regions as yet far beyond the reach of their fighter cover.

The British had warned their ally against such a step. They knew the strength of the German fighter defences—knowledge which they had acquired at considerable cost. But the Americans cast these warnings aside. They were confident that the fire-power of numerous B17s in tight formation was adequate protection.

January 27th seemed to have proved them right. Fifty-five Fortresses unloaded their bombs on the Wilhelmshaven harbour installations, and only encountered a few Focke-Wulf Fw 190 squadrons of JG 1 under Lieutenant-Colonel Dr. Erich Mix. On that day they were all the defence could muster for the protection of the North Sea coast, and were of course far too little to break up the American formation. But they attacked. Overtaking the bombers, they turned well ahead of them, and then raced towards them at the same height. It was a mode of attack developed, after months of combat with their new foes, by the two Channel-based fighter *Geschwader*, JG 2 ("Richthofen") and JG 26 ("Schlageter"). The classic attack from above and astern still required by ·Luftwaffe Command had proved suicidal. But from head-on the bombers were vulnerable.

With the contenders hurtling towards each other at a combined speed of some 600 m.p.h., the attack was over in seconds; and with the bomber so rapidly expanding in the fighter's reflector sight, the temptation to press the firing button prematurely was acute. Immediately after doing so the pilot had to jerk his plane up or aside to avoid a collision. Only those with the quickest reactions mastered the trick, for the slightest mistiming meant death.

On January 27th only three bombers failed to return from the attack on Wilhelmshaven, and such a slight loss seemed to confirm the American tactics. They did not hesitate to repeat such daylight attacks, which were admittedly against strictly military targets. Their next big one, on February 4th, was again directed against the North Sea coast, but this time met stronger German defence. Besides the Focke-Wulfs there were Messerschmitt 110s.

"I am in contact with fifty bandits and attacking!" called Warrant-Officer Scherer on the radio. The actual code he used was that of night-fighters, which is what these Me 110s were. Their radar antennae projected like antlers from the nose, and the crew were highly trained specialists accustomed to night interceptions of British bombers. But now it was a daylight mission against the Americans. The eight of them were led by Captain Hans-Joachim Jabs, squadron commander of II/NJG 1, based at Leeuwarden. The *Gruppenkommandeur*, Major Helmut Lent, once champion of the Battle of Heligoland Bight and by now Germany's most successful night-fighter pilot, had been forbidden to indulge in daylight operations.

Jabs was a former pilot of ZG 26, and in the summer of 1940 had tangled with Spitfires over London, when Me 110s were still being used to escort German bombers over England. After that most of the Me 110s went over to night-fighting. Now two and a half years after the Battle of Britain, daylight operations were again called for with the same old machines—against opponents now equipped with four-engined bombers.

Flying parallel with the formation, he looked for a chance to attack. Unlike British bombers the B-17s had a ventral turret carrying heavy twin machine-guns. The whole aircraft bristled with guns, leaving no blind spots. Thus the attack from below, so successful in combating Britain's night bombers, was in this case inadvisable. But suddenly Jabs detected a gap in the formation, and followed by his No. 2 darted into it. The attack came just in time to divert the enemy's fire from Scherer's plane, which had already been hit. The latter was forced to break away, with both of its crew wounded by splinters.

Meanwhile the pair consisting of Lieutenant Vollkopf and Corporal Naumann, sweeping through the swarm from head-on, succeeded jointly in hitting and detaching a bomber, which fell back with a smoking engine and its undercarriage down. Jerking his plane round, Naumann then attacked it from astern, but the American rear gunner gave as good as he got, and both the B-17 and the Me 110 dived down on fire. However, Naumann managed to pull out and make a crash-landing in shallow water on the north shore of Ameland island.

The last pair—Flight-Sergeant Grimm and Corporal Kraft, with their radio-operators Meissner and Handke—shaved past the formation's rear in a storm of firing and fell upon another lagging Boeing. Attacked in turn from the beam, from astern and above, it finally caught fire and went into a spin. It was high time, for the port engines of both the Me 110s were smoking and dead, Grimm's cockpit was splintered and Meissner wounded. As they were about to land at Leeuwarden, the starboard engine stopped too, and Grimm only got down with a belly-landing. Though Kraft landed normally, his plane was also badly shot up.

In fact, though Jabs, Grimm and Naumann each claimed the destruction of a B-17 from their first stiff daylight combat with the Fortresses, all eight of IV/NJG 1's aircraft that had been engaged emerged from it in a damaged state. Consequently for the succeeding night patrols the *Gruppe* had to draw on machines that were less operationally serviceable. Eight aircraft, with all their sensitive special equipment so essential for night-fighting in darkness, had been put out of action. And it was the same story with most of the other night-fighter *Gruppen*, now also thrown into the daylight battle.

But if machines were ultimately replaceable, men were not—and such combats always ended in the loss of highly qualified crews. These were individualistic warriors whose *métier*, after being put on the track of a mighty Lancaster bomber, was to stalk it in darkness with their own radar sets and shoot it down by surprise. Of this technique they had become masters, but in daylight it was unthinkable and their skill was wasted.

Yet they continued to be used in this way. On February 26, 1943, Captain Jabs took off with three duty flights to intercept a formation of B-24 Liberators returning from a raid on Emden. With them for the first time on a daylight operation was the squadron commander of 12/NJG 1, Captain Ludwig Becker, the night-fighter arm's leading expert in technique. What use was such technique against all the guns of daylight Liberators? His companions lost sight of him at the outset of the attack, and neither he nor his radio-operator, Staub, were seen again, though all available aircraft searched the sea until dark. Missing from his first daylight mission was the man who by his skill at night had not been hit for months, and who after forty-four victories had this very day been informed of his award of the Oak Leaves of the Knight's Cross. To the night-fighters his death brought disquiet. Was the Luftwaffe in such a bad way that specialists like Becker had to be squandered on missions completely foreign to their training?

At the beginning of April a "new" fighter *Geschwader*, JG 11 under Major Anton Mader, was formed at Jever by the splitting of JG 1. Its strength was augmented by 2 Squadron—with just nine serviceable Me 109s under Captain Janssen at Leeuwarden—from JG 27, which had just been withdrawn from Africa. Shortly afterwards JG 54 was posted to Oldenburg from the eastern front.

Everywhere fighters were in short supply: in Russia, in the Mediterranean, on the English Channel. So far the defence of the *Reich* was a long way from receiving top priority. "Produce fighters, fighters, fighters!" Udet had called shortly before his suicide, in dark foreboding of the coming battle in German skies. The programme of September, 1941, had envisaged a monthly production of only 360 of them. For a front stretching over the whole of Europe this was far too few.

Udet's successor, Milch, had doubled the figure, and for the end of 1942 even offered a monthly output of 1,000. Goering, however, merely roared with laughter and asked what on earth he proposed to do with them. Even his chief of general staff, Jeschonnek, had stated: "More than 400–500 fighters a month cannot be quartered at the front."

That was in the spring of 1942. By that autumn 500 fighters per month were being produced, and now the output was leaping from month to month: in February 1943 to 700, in March and April to over 800, in May to over 900 and in June to nearly 1,000. But the various fronts soon swallowed them up, and for the Battle of Germany, to which the writing in the sky already pointed, there were still all too few of them.

Across the Channel the U.S. 8th Air Force watched the build-up of the Reich defence with tense interest. At first the Flying Fortresses went probingly about their task, not yet knowing what opposition to expect. The resolution of the German fighters in the spring of 1943, even if they were small in numbers, indicated the need for caution. Consequently the 8th Air Force's chief, General Ira C. Eaker, produced a plan for the destruction of the German fighter arm, and its centres of production. "If," he wrote, "the growth of the German fighter strength is not arrested quickly, it may become literally impossible to carry out the destruction planned."[1]

Eaker persistently rejected the British request that the American bombers should take part in night raids on German cities. The result was a joint plan of offensive action whereby the Americans operated by day, and the British by night. The plan was carried through by its two proponents: General Eaker and Air Marshal Harris.

Sir Arthur Harris, with whose name the fate of the German cities, in the incendiary raids that followed, is indelibly associated at least in Germany, had taken over R.A.F. Bomber Command a year earlier, on February 22, 1942, to implement the directive of the War Cabinet, issued on February 14th, regarding the stepping-up of the air war against Germany.

In 1939 the British, like the Germans, had received strict orders that they were not to be the first to drop bombs on enemy soil. Even British daylight attacks on German warships off Heligoland and Wilhelmshaven ceased when, as a result of the first air battle of the war, over half the attacking Wellingtons were lost. Thus early on the R.A.F. learnt the lesson—later learnt by the Luftwaffe in the Battle of Britain—that slow and ill-defended bombers were alone no match for fighters. The only alternative was to attack in the protective darkness of night.

The relative peace that had so far characterised the war ended sharply with the opening of Germany's offensive against the West, which coincided with Churchill becoming Prime Minister. The same evening British bombers for the first time raided a German city. A few minutes after midnight on the

[1] Sir Charles Webster and Noble Frankland, *The Strategic Air Offensive Against Germany* (H.M.S.O. 1961), Vol. II, p. 20.

night of May 10/11, 1940, a few Whitleys bombed München-Gladbach, hitting the Luisenstrasse and the town centre. Four civilians, one of them an Englishwoman, were killed.

That Britain bombed German towns before her own were bombed is admitted by J. M. Spaight, late of the Air Ministry, in his work *Bombing Vindicated*, published in 1944. "There was no certainty," he wrote, "but there was a reasonable probability, that our capital and our industrial centres would not have been attacked if we had continued to refrain from attacking those of Germany. . . . It simply did not pay her, this kind of air warfare."

Spaight was right. The attempt of the Luftwaffe by its air offensive of 1940/41 to make Britain ready to sue for peace was a failure. Indeed, only military and war-industrial targets were supposed to be attacked, but owing to the imprecision of target-finding methods at that time, the civil population also suffered severely, particularly at night. On the other hand the effect of the R.A.F.'s night air-raids on Germany in 1940/41 was small. They were little more than nuisance raids, for again the technique of finding and hitting a target in darkness had hardly begun to develop. From the British point of view the results were disappointing.

But during wartime, invention thrives. The preoccupation of the Luftwaffe in the Mediterranean, and even more in Russia, gave the R.A.F. the opportunity and the time to construct a fleet of modern bombers for the battle ahead. Four-engined Stirlings, Halifaxes and Lancasters began to roll off the production lines while high frequency experts developed a navigational aid known as *Gee*, by means of which a bomber over western Germany could at any time determine its position. By early 1942 preparations had reached the stage when caution could be laid aside. This coincided with the appointment of Air Marshal Harris as chief of Bomber Command.

The new directive, which gave him the green light, expressly laid down that "the morale of the enemy civilian population and, in particular, of the industrial workers" should be the "primary object" of bombing operations. A list of priority targets was appended, with Essen at its head, followed by Duisburg, Düsseldorf and Cologne. As the whole industrial area of the Ruhr and Rhineland lay within the range of *Gee* navigation, it was hoped that the R.A.F. night bombers would be able to find their targets satisfactorily. The list further named a large number of cities outside the range of *Gee*, which were only to be attacked when conditions were especially favourable.

Appended to the name of each city was a mention of the type of industry that made it important—e.g. aircraft industry at Bremen, dockyards at Hamburg, ball-bearings at Schweinfurt. However, to emphasise that it was not these functional points, but the cities' built-up areas that were intended as the aiming points, the Chief of Air Staff, Sir Charles Portal, drew up a memorandum explaining as much. "This must be made quite clear if it is not already understood," he concluded.[1]

The tactical method of carrying out the new policy also underwent drastic change. Individual attacks by aircraft arriving over a long period—with bombs widely scattered and the effect consequently dissipated—were to be

[1] *The Strategic Air Offensive Against Germany*, Vol. I, p. 324.

succeeded by massed bombing of a circumscribed area within the shortest period possible.

All this Harris inherited. In him the planners saw the right man to translate their ideas into action. The R.A.F. had finally, in the Air Ministry phrase, "taken off the gloves". In the spring of 1942 Harris made himself felt with the following three raids on Germany:

During the night of March 28/29, 1942, 191 aircraft attacked the ancient city of Lübeck, dropping 300 tons of bombs, half of them incendiaries. In the words of *The Strategic Air Offensive Against Germany, 1939–1945*, this target was chosen because it "was largely of medieval construction so that the buildings were inflammable" and because it "was known to be only lightly defended". Afterwards it took thirty-two hours before the last fires were extinguished, and the inner city was just a smouldering heap of ruins. Over 1,000 dwellings were completely destroyed and over 4,000 partially. The raid killed 520 civilians and wounded 785. Eight British bombers were shot down by night-fighters, mostly on the return flight.

The second blow was against Rostock, the home of the Heinkel works. This time the attack was by 468 bombers over four consecutive nights, April 24th–27th. Sixty per cent of the old city was burnt out, and for the first time the term "terror raids" came to be used. It was subsequently applied to Hitler's raids of revenge on the indifferently defended cities of Exeter, Bath, Norwich and York—called by the English the "Baedeker" raids.

Finally Harris, with Churchill's express approval, collected together all the aircraft possibly available for the first 1,000-bomber raid in history: on the night of May 30, 1942, against Cologne. Wave after wave of bombers came in over a period of one and a half hours, and this time almost two-thirds of the 1,455 tons of bombs dropped were incendiaries. 1,700 conflagrations linked up into one enormous inferno. 3,300 houses were destroyed, 9,500 damaged, and 474 inhabitants killed.

This massive onslaught showed up sharply the limitations of the German night-fighters. The time was gone when the British bombers passed singly through the ground-control interception zones, manned by one fighter apiece: they now came through in hordes. Though the fighters shot down thirty-six of the Cologne raiders, thereby raising their score for the war to date to 600 victories, it was only 3.6 per cent of 1,000. Harris had reckoned with the loss of fifty aircraft, Churchill with even a hundred. From all causes the armada lost forty and another 116 suffered various degrees of damage, mostly through flak. The calculation that the effectiveness would increase, and the quota of losses sink, according to the number of bombers engaged in a single raid, had been proved correct.

The reaction of Josef Kammhuber—chief of XII Air Corps, and "General of Night-Fighters"—was to strive to improve his fighting technique. He extended his belt of "*Himmelbett*" zones to cover as much of Holland, Belgium and Germany as possible. He created more and more night-fighter *Gruppen*, and introduced new methods of ground control which permitted two, and later even three, fighters to operate simultaneously in a single zone. But the basic principle of the tied night-fighter remained the same, and Kammhuber's full programme would not only take years to complete, but would soon be rendered obsolete by events.

Meanwhile the Luftwaffe Command nourished the hope that once the

104. Three well-known fighter leaders at a map exercise in the defence of Germany. From left to right, Galland, Trautloft and Desau.

105. A shower of incendiaries being dropped by a Lancaster, Britain's most powerful four-engined bomber. German night-fighters took advantage of its inadequate defensive armament against attacks from below.

106. German fighter pilots re-live their attacks on American "Fortresses."

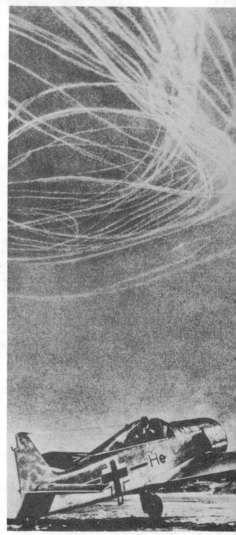

107. A grounded Fw 190 below the condensation trails of battle. This aircraft, assisted still by the Me 109, represented the Luftwaffe's main opposition to the American long-range fighter, the P-51 Mustang.

Russian campaign was won, the corner would be turned. Till this objective was achieved, the main point of effort must unquestionably remain in the east. But the time needed to achieve it had already lengthened from the expected "few months" into a whole year, and still there was no end in sight. Repeated warnings by his "General of Fighters", Adolf Galland, that the construction of a Reich defence force should not be neglected, had only irritated Goering, who answered: "All such tomfoolery will be unnecessary once I get my *Geschwader* back to the west. For me the question of defence will then be settled. But first, and as soon as possible, the Russians must be brought to their knees."

The hopes of the Luftwaffe Command were moreover encouraged by the mounting success of the existing defence. On the night of June 25, 1942, it accounted for forty-nine British bombers out of the 1,006 that raided Bremen. And on April 17th the day-fighters showed that they, too, were a force still to be reckoned with.

On the afternoon of that day twelve four-engined Lancasters, under Squadron-Leader J. D. Nettleton, flew right across France to raid the M.A.N. works at Augsburg, which produced diesel engines for U-boats. Such a precision attack was, of course, only possible in daylight. To elude the German early warning system they flew the whole distance at hedge-hopping height. None the less they were pursued by squadrons of the "Richthofen" *Geschwader*, JG 2, and overtaken south of Paris. In the ensuing combat four were shot down—one of them by Warrant-Officer Pohl, who thereby brought JG 2's wartime score to 1,000.

Nettleton continued on with the eight Lancasters he had left, and they bombed the M.A.N. factory just before light failed. It was a low-level attack, and the flak accounted for another three of the raiders. The remaining five returned to England under cover of darkness.

Bold as this venture was, the loss of seven four-engined bombers and their crews was too high a price to pay for a temporary decline in the output of diesel engines. It fortified the view of British Bomber Command that the objectives of a strategic air offensive could not be achieved in daylight. But if precision against military targets could not be obtained at night, this was hardly the main objective, which was to destroy large areas, and wipe-out whole cities. In his book, *Bomber Offensive*, Sir Arthur Harris has written:

"In no instance, except in Essen, were we aiming specifically at any one factory. . . . The destruction of factories, which was nevertheless on an enormous scale, could be regarded as a bonus. The aiming points were usually right in the centre of the town."[1]

Such were the portents under which the crucial phase of the Battle of Germany in 1943 was ushered in.

The North African sun shone glaringly on the white buildings of Casablanca. The conference was held in a luxury hotel in the villa-studded suburb of Anfa. Arched windows looked out on to the Atlantic, and through the open terrace doorways came the roar of breakers from the beach. Here, on January 21, 1943, the future fate of Germany at the hands of bombers was decided. Here the United States' President, Franklin D. Roosevelt,

[1] Sir Arthur Harris, *Bomber Offensive* (Collins 1947), p. 147.

and the British Prime Minister, Winston Churchill, put their signatures to a document drawn up by their Combined Chiefs of Staff.

Since then the Casablanca Directive, addressed to the chiefs of their bomber commands, has often been taken to mark the final sentence of death on the German cities. Any doubt that it was so is dispelled by the terms in which it opened:

"Your primary objective will be the progressive destruction and dislocation of the German military, industrial and economic system, and the undermining of the morale of the German people to a point where their capacity for armed resistance is fatally weakened."[1]

It did not, however, confine itself to a general statement of aim. It went on to list in order of priority the types of target which—so far as weather and tactical feasibility permitted—were to be attacked.

1. German submarine construction yards
2. The German aircraft industry
3. Transportation
4. Oil plants
5. Other targets in enemy war industry.

It seemed that the Americans had got their way with precision daylight attacks on industrial targets, while the British were not to be swayed from their practice of "area bombing" by night. Churchill himself writes that during the conference he had an interview with General Eaker, chief of the U.S. 8th Air Force in England, in which both reiterated their arguments. Churchill tried to convert Eaker to night bombing, but the latter stuck to his guns. In the end the British Prime Minister gave in:

"I decided to back Eaker and his theme, and I turned round completely and withdrew all my opposition to the daylight bombing by Fortresses."[2]

But what the Americans favoured hardly concerned the British. As always in the case of directives emanating from the highest level, the one from Casablanca left much room for interpretation by those who were to carry it out. And the British Bomber Command Chief, Air Marshal Harris, was resolved to pursue the tactics he had employed hitherto. Did the directive not state expressly that the nominated targets were only to be attacked when weather and tactical feasibility permitted? In that case British tactics made it unfeasible. If the Americans wanted to provoke the German fighter defences by daylight, they could. They could stick their necks out, if they refused to learn. As for the R.A.F., it would go on setting fire to the German cities at night. Had the directive not roundly declared that German morale was to be undermined?

Air Marshal Harris' interpretation of the directive can be stated in his own words: "It gave me a very wide range of choice and allowed me to attack pretty well any German industrial city of 100,000 inhabitants and above."[3]

The first blow on March 5/6, 1943, fell on Essen—the only exclusively military target the British had on their list, inasmuch as the giant complex of the

[1] *The Strategic Air Offensive Against Germany*, Vol. II, p. 12.
[2] *The Second World War*, Vol. IV, p. 545.
[3] *Bomber Offensive*, p. 144.

Krupp concern lay in the middle of the city. The attack was opened by fast, radar-guided Mosquito bombers, who put down yellow indicator-flares along the line of approach as visual guidance for the following heavy bombers. To mark the target areas "Pathfinders" dropped red and green flares for the duration of the attack.

Despite this, only 153 out of 422 twin- and four-engined bombers succeeded in unloading their bombs within three miles of the aiming point, although 367 claimed to have been over the target. Thus even with the aid of technical innovations for finding the target and marking it, the attack remained of dubious value—in so far as hitting a specific target was ever intended. The raid lasted only thirty-eight minutes, during which time 1,014 tons of bombs were dropped. The population suffered severely, especially in the residential area adjoining Krupp.

So began the R.A.F.'s "Battle of the Ruhr", which ended on the night of June 28th with a new attack by 540 aircraft on Cologne. Within a bare four months the inner cities of Essen, Duisburg and Düsseldorf were burnt out, and large areas of Wuppertal, Bochum and other towns laid in ruins.

Not satisfied with the Ruhr—where thanks to his radar-directed Pathfinders a certain concentration of bombs could always be achieved against the chosen target—Air Marshal Harris during the same period extended his raids on cities over the whole Reich: to Mannheim, Stuttgart, Nuremberg and Munich in the south; to Berlin and Stettin in the east; to Bremen, Wilhelmshaven, Hamburg and Kiel in the north.

The same four months saw the steadily increasing success of the German defence, both flak and night-fighters. The greater the distance the bombers had to fly to reach and return from their target, the greater was the chance of engaging them. From one raid alone—that of April 17th, on Pilsen in Czechoslovakia—thirty-six out of 327 bombers failed to return, and another fifty-seven were damaged. In other words 28.5 per cent had been put out of action.

Comparable losses were suffered by Bomber Command during the raids of May 27th against Essen (twenty-two aircraft destroyed and 113 damaged out of 518), of May 29th against Wuppertal-Barmen (when Me 110s of NJG 1 pursued the raiders far out to sea and out of 719 thirty-three were shot down, and sixty-six damaged mainly by flak), and of June 14th against Oberhausen (seventeen destroyed and forty-five damaged out of 203). The figures for the whole four-month period showed that of a total of 18,506 offensive sorties flown, 872 bombers had failed to return, and a further 2,126 had been damaged, some of them seriously.

But although the total loss of 872 bombers was an impressive number, it in fact represented only 4.7 per cent of the operating force. It was not enough to deter a man like Harris from the preparation of even more resounding blows.

The success of Bomber Command's offensive was, however, questionable. Although many German cities lay in ruins, had the objective been achieved? Had German industry been destroyed, or the morale of the population undermined? Nothing of the sort had taken place. After the final great bombardment of Aachen on July 13th a pause set in. It seemed that the R.A.F. was taking a breathing space before its most deadly blow of all.

2. The Battle of Hamburg

It was the evening of July 24, 1943. In 2 Air Division's huge underground operations room at Stade, on the lower Elbe, the night watch was going on duty. As the room filled up, there was a buzz of hushed voices. Dominating the scene, and almost as high and broad as the "martial opera house" itself, was a great screen of frosted glass which showed a map of Germany overlaid with a grid. On this, during enemy raids, the changing situation in the air was projected.

Behind this screen sat a score or so of Luftwaffe women auxiliaries, who, after tidying their desks and checking the projectors, waited expectantly for the first air-raid alarm. Each girl was directly connected by telephone to a radar station on the coast. As soon as one of these picked up the approaching enemy, it would make a report like this: "Eighty plus aircraft in Gustav Caesar five, course east, height 19,000." With deft hands the girl concerned would then project the information on to the indicated grid square.

In front of the screen sat long rows of ground-control officers; behind them, and higher, the commander and the liaison officers, with switchboards connecting them to the fighter units, their stations and the air-raid warning service. Still higher, in the gallery, were other projectors which showed on the screen the positions of the defending fighters.

The complex night-fighting system had once more got into gear in a crescendo of visual and vocal activity, as operational orders were given, reports transmitted, and the projected images chased each other across the screen. Some of the latter wandered about, were corrected and finally came to a standstill—"like a lot of water fleas in an aquarium," as Adolf Galland, "General of Fighters," commented sarcastically.

But this "aquarium", under Lieutenant-General Schwabedissen, was not the only one. 1 Air Division had another at Deelen near Arnhem under Lieutenant-General von Döring; 3 Air Division a third at Metz under Major-General Junck; and 4 Air Division a fourth at Döberitz near Berlin, under Major-General Huth. To deal with raids emanating from the south, the newly formed 5 Air Division under Colonel Harry von Bülow had just set up a similar organisation at Schleissheim near Munich.

But on this July 24th the inconceivable now took place. It was shortly before midnight when the first reports reached Stade, and the projections on the screen showed the enemy bomber formation flying eastwards over the North Sea, parallel with the coast. The Me 110s of NJG 3 were duly ordered off from their bases at Stade, Vechta, Wittmundhaven, Wunstorf, Lüneburg and Kastrup, and took up their positions over the sea under "*Himmelbett*" control. Meanwhile it was confirmed that the initial Pathfinders were being followed by a bomber stream of several hundred aircraft, all keeping to the north of the Elbe estuary. What was their objective? Would they turn south to Kiel or Lübeck, or proceed over the Baltic for some target as yet unknown? All now depended on closely following their course without being deceived by any feint attack.

Suddenly the Stade operations room throbbed with disquietude. For minutes the illuminations on the screen representing the enemy had stuck in the same positions. The signals officer switched in to the direct lines to the radar stations and asked what was the matter. He received the same answer from all of them: "Apparatus put out of action by jamming."

The whole thing was a mystery. Then came reports from the "*Freya*" stations, operating on the long 240-cm wave, that they too were jammed. They at least could just distinguish the bomber formation's echo from the artificial ones; but the screens of the "*Würzburgs*", operating on 53-cm, became an indecipherable jumble of echo points resembling giant insects, from which nothing could be recognised at all.

It was a portentous situation, for the control of the night-fighters entirely depended on exact information as to position and altitude being given by the "*Würzburgs*". Without it the controllers were powerless and the fighters could only fumble in the dark.

2 Air Division had to turn for help to the general air-raid warning system—to the corps of observers watching and listening throughout the land. These could only report what they saw. At Dithmarschen, not far from Meldorf, they saw yellow lights cascading from the sky; more and more of them all in the same area. Presumably they marked a turning point. The bomber stream had veered to the south-east, as fresh reports confirmed. In close order the enemy was heading parallel with the Elbe—direct to Hamburg.

The old Hanseatic city was protected by fifty-four heavy and twenty-six light flak batteries, twenty-two searchlight and three smoke-screen batteries. Hundreds of gun barrels now turned north-west. But the flak also obtained its firing data from the radar eyes of the "*Würzburgs*", and now, as the attack began a few minutes before 01.00, these eyes were completely veiled. Like the night-fighters, the flak was blind.

The commander ordered a preventive barrage. If the guns could not aim, they might at least have a discouraging effect. Soon their roar mingled with the crash of bombs. For this saturation area bombardment 791 British bombers had taken off from England: 347 Lancasters, 246 Halifaxes, 125 Stirlings—all four-engined—plus seventy-three twin-engined Wellingtons. Of these 728 reached the Hamburg area. At minute intervals they had been throwing out bundles each containing thousands of strips of silver paper. Fluttering apart, these sank slowly to earth in the form of a huge echo-reflecting cloud.

This was the secret weapon that had paralysed the German radar sets. In Britain its code-name was "Window", in Germany "*Düppel*". Cut to exactly half the wave-length of the "*Würzburgs*", they reflected the search-impulses of the German night-fighters and control sets with remarkable effect, producing millions of tiny echoes on the screen. And behind this radar smoke-screen the bombers hid.

The British had carefully guarded their secret for sixteen months, and even now the use of "Window" was a matter of controversy. It was feared its betrayal to the enemy could result in the Luftwaffe likewise using it to jam the British radar and deliver sharp vengeful ripostes. In fact, there had been the usual parallel development in Germany. As long ago as spring 1942 the German high-frequency expert, Roosenstein, had carried out experiments on the lonely Baltic coast, and likewise demonstrated that radar could be jammed by "*Düppel*". It seemed the perfect counter-weapon had been discovered.

But as soon as Goering heard about it, he imposed a strict ban on the matter being pursued any further. In no circumstances must the British get an inkling of the idea. The chief of signals, General Wolfgang Martini, had to hide the secret files deep in his safe, and even mention of the word "*Düppel*" became a punishable offence. Once more Luftwaffe Command, instead of promptly developing an antidote, simply buried its head in the sand.

In England the decision to use the stuff was finally triggered-off by a calculation of the Air Staff. This showed that in the "Battle of the Ruhr", as they called it, some 286 bombers and crews—or twenty-five per cent of Bomber Command's first-line strength—need never have been lost if "Window" had been used. It was enough to convince Churchill, who on July 15th himself gave his approval for the first mass "tinfoil" raid on Hamburg. Its effect surpassed all expectations. Of the 791 bombers that set out only twelve failed to return. A major attack seldom cost the R.A.F. so little.

But for Hamburg there began a week of horror, the worst in its 750 years of history. For "Operation Gomorrah", as the Allies called their annihilating action, was not confined to the single raid of July 24th/25th. It was followed on the 25th and 26th by two American daylight attacks on the harbour and dockyards with 235 Flying Fortresses. And on the night of the 27th 722 R.A.F. bombers resumed their work of destruction, succeeded by another 699 on the night of the 29th, with cloudless summer skies again in their favour. Only at the fourth and final blow, on the night of August 2nd, was Hamburg screened by thick clouds. Then only about half of the 740 raiders, with the ground-marking of the Pathfinders scarcely visible, claimed to have reached the target at all. But never before had Harris directed over 3,000 bombers in four nights against a single city.

The night-fighters of NJG 3 recovered quickly from their shock. Despite the continued use of "Window", and the consequent jamming of most of the radar installations, a radio "running commentary" technique was developed which enabled the bombers to be found without precise course directives. Furthermore, there were single-engined fighters over the city, and though these had to rely entirely on their "cat's eyes", the successes of the defence force again mounted. In the Hamburg raids the R.A.F. lost a total of eighty-seven bombers, and another 174 were damaged by flak.

Altogether some 9,000 tons of bombs fell on the distraught city. Hamburg was swept by a raging storm of fire, the like of which had never been experienced before, and against which all human measures were powerless. 30,482 of its inhabitants lost their lives, and 277,330 buildings—almost half the city—were reduced to ruins. The accounts of its ordeal are many, but here the question must be asked: How did the Luftwaffe react to the terrible catastrophe?

For once the shock of the Hamburg raids acted as a unifying influence on its commanders. The men around Goering, such as Jeschonnek and Milch, all began to clamour for the same thing. The whole directive must now be changed. All forces must be engaged to defend the homeland against the mass raids of the Allied bombers, by day and night.

Only Hitler remained unteachable. At a situation conference on July 25th he turned furiously on his Luftwaffe adjutant, Major Christian (who had dared to utter a different opinion) with the words: "Terror can only be broken by terror! Everything else is nonsense. The British will only be halted when their own cities are destroyed. I can only win the war by dealing out more destruction to the enemy than he does to us . . . In all epochs that has been the case, and it is just the same in the air. Otherwise our people will turn mad, and in the course of time lose all confidence in the Luftwaffe. Even now it is not fully doing its job. . . ."

Top priority must be given to raids of revenge, he said, however inadequate the force available to the man appointed for this purpose—the "*Angriffsführer England*", Colonel Dieter Peltz—might be. But no one else concurred with this policy. Amongst the Luftwaffe chiefs there was, as mentioned, an astonishing unanimity on the need to mobilise for defence. Conference followed conference—in Berlin, Potsdam-Eiche, at Goering's "Reich Hunting Lodge" of Rominten, and his command train "Robinson" at Goldap—and the decisions came one after another:—

On July 28th, after the second night raid on Hamburg, the chief of air supply, Field-Marshal Milch, was instructed by Goering that the aircraft industry would forthwith concentrate on defensive production.

On the same day Milch ordered from the electronics industry the accelerated production of an airborne radar set which would not be subject to jamming by enemy "Window". Objective: "To inflict losses on enemy night bombers in the shortest time amounting to at least twenty to twenty-five per cent."

On the 29th Colonel von Lossberg of the general staff, former bomber pilot and now a departmental chief of the Technical Office, proposed that the night-fighters should go over to "unfettered pursuit". They would be released from the confines of their "*Himmelbett*" zones, now unable to cope with concentrated bomber formations even without radar interference, and instead mix freely with the bomber streams and choose targets of opportunity. Next day this scheme was examined, and finally approved, by a commission comprising Milch, Colonel-General Weise, Generals Kammhuber and Galland, and the commander of NJG 1, Major Streib.

Finally, a new force under the name of *Jagdgeschwader* 300, formed a month previously at the suggestion of the bomber pilot, Major Hajo Herrmann, was to be increased. This force, known as the "*Wilde Sau*"— or "Wild Boars"—was equipped with single-engined fighters, with the mission to patrol directly over the threatened cities.

By August 1st these last two decisions had already become the subject of an official order by Goering which included the words: "The provision of day- and night-fighter defence will take priority over all other tasks."

Hamburg had supplied the necessary jolt. What those engaged in the defence of the Reich had so long clamoured for in vain was now being done, and the battle was not yet lost. Geared to defence the fighter arm had every prospect of making appreciable dents in the swarms of Allied bombers, both by day and by night. And in the great air battles ahead, it did so.

But revolution in favour of defence had not yet been fully accomplished before Luftwaffe Command was afflicted by a new reverse. On the night of August 17/18, 1943, British Bomber Command managed to deceive the whole German night defence in masterly fashion. The target, for the first time, was the rocket-testing centre of Peenemünde, and an assault force of 597 four-engined bombers was employed. But at the same time a mere twenty Mosquitoes made a feint attack on Berlin. By dropping a multitude of flares, they only too successfully created the impression that Berlin was the major target.

It happened to be the first night the "*Wilde Sau*" were operating in force. 148 twin-engined and fifty-five single-engined fighters searched the Berlin sky in vain—and were themselves submitted to the full force of the city's flak. The bluff was only spotted after Peenemünde had already been subjected to the first wave of bombs. Hoping to catch up, the Messerschmitts then raced northwards. At their head was II/NJG 1 under Major Walter Ehle, which from its base at St. Trond in Belgium had crossed nearly the whole of Germany.

The ensuing engagement was opened at 01.32 hours by the commander of 4 Squadron, First-Lieutenant Walter Barte. Diving on a Lancaster at 6,000 feet he fired a long burst, and as he climbed up again his radio-operator saw both wings of the enemy aircraft on fire. Three minutes later this Lancaster crashed in a sheet of flame south-west of Peenemünde.

Ehle, the commander, himself shot down two others inside three minutes, silhouetted as they were against the fires burning on the rocket-testing grounds. Barte likewise achieved a second victory, and a Lancaster with the number "17" was seen to eject three parachutes before it crashed. A young night-fighter pair, Lieutenant Musset and Corporal Hafner, alone shot down four out of a group of eight bombers before, wounded by counter-fire, they had to bale out themselves.[1] Altogether in the course of this bold and cunningly executed raid, the British lost forty aircraft, with another thirty-two damaged.

The damage to Peenemünde at first seemed greater than it was. Neither the testing blocks nor the irreplaceable construction drawings had been destroyed. At 08.00 next morning, however, the chief of Luftwaffe operations staff, Lieutenant-General Rudolf Meister, telephoned Jeschonnek to inform him that Peenemünde, which, as the birthplace of the V-weapons, was the apple of his eye, had been the target for an extremely heavy precision air attack. At this moment, Jeschonnek's secretary, Frau Lotte Kersten, and his personal adjutant, Major Werner Leuchtenberg, were waiting for him to join them at breakfast, but their chief called: "Leuchtenberg, go on over to the site. I'll follow you."

Frau Kersten waited alone for half an hour, then an hour. Usually the general was a model of punctuality. Finally she called, but getting no answer ran along to his room, hardly ten steps away. She found him stretched out on the floor, his pistol beside him. No shot had been heard.

Why had Hans Jeschonnek, chief of general staff of the Luftwaffe at the time of its lightning victories, as now at the beginning of its downfall, committed suicide? Was it the shock of the raid on Peenemünde? Leuchtenberg, called back by Frau Kersten, found a note in his chief's writing, in which he had written down his last thoughts: "I can no longer work together with the *Reichsmarschall*. Long live the Führer."

Had not Udet written something similar, just before he too took his own life in November, 1941?

Shortly afterwards Goering stamped heavily into the room, and closeted himself with the dead man for ten minutes. Then he emerged with drawn face, and finally called for Leuchtenberg.

"Tell me the whole truth," he demanded. "Why did he do it?"

Leuchtenberg looked quizzically into his supreme commander's eyes. What did Goering want to hear? Literally the whole truth? Or just some-

[1] Featured in specimen night-fighter combat report, Appendix 17.

thing that would clear himself and make it look as though the chief of general staff had been driven to suicide by awareness of his own shortcomings? Leuchtenberg decided to exploit the opportunity provided by this rare *tête-à-tête*.

"The General," he said in measured tones, "wished to shine a torch on the terrible shortcomings of Luftwaffe leadership."

Heavily Goering raised his head. The blows to his pride were raining down fast. But the more Hitler—disappointed in Goering—had turned directly to Jeschonnek in Luftwaffe matters, the more the latter had felt the sickly impact of the supreme commander's vainglory and ambition. It had started with Stalingrad, when Goering had tried to shift the blame for the failure of the air-lift—which he himself had sponsored—on to Jeschonnek's shoulders. Since then there had been many other episodes.

Jeschonnek had fallen between two stools—on one side Hitler, who believed in his talent; on the other Goering, whose orders he, as an officer, felt obliged to carry out however contrary to his own convictions. He had to endure Hitler's rage for every failure of the Luftwaffe, and Goering's sarcasm into the bargain ("You always stand in front of the Führer like a schoolboy—like a little subaltern with his hands on his trouser seams!"). Jeschonnek was the whipping boy across whose back the two "old campaigners" vented their spleen. But the back was not broad enough—it broke.

Such was the story that Major Leuchtenberg told to his supreme commander. As he listened, Goering flushed with mounting anger. But Leuchtenberg did not stop. A few weeks before he had already, at the last moment, wrenched the gun once from the hand of his chief, and now he related the latest episodes which must have acted as the final straw.

One was the recent attempt of Goering to remove Jeschonnek from his post—when the latter only heard about what was brewing from the mouth of his probable successor, Field-Marshal von Richthofen. When this move failed, owing to the opposition of Hitler, Goering embraced the general staff chief with the words: "You know, don't you, that I am your best friend?" Another occasion was when Goering, knowing that Jeschonnek had always obeyed Hitler unreservedly, for no apparent reason instructed him that the time had come when the Führer's orders should no longer be carried out one hundred per cent.

As the young officer uttered this last charge, Goering sprang to his feet. "What!" he shrieked. "You dare to say that to me?"

"You wished to hear the whole truth, *Herr Reichsmarschall*."

"You—I shall have you court-martialled!" Goering approached Leuchtenberg threateningly, then suddenly breaking down, sank to his chair and buried his face in his hands. A sob shook the massive body—an undignified performance that his closest colleagues were quite accustomed to. Since Stalingrad this theatrical man had been giving way to his grief ever more often. Not that such scenes reflected any personal purge. He just felt betrayed, deserted, deceived. Only other people were to blame—never himself.

"Very well! Now the Luftwaffe shall have a front-rank man," he promised, overcoming his moment of weakness. "Why," he wailed to Generals Meister, Martini and "Beppo" Schmid, who were waiting on the other side of the door, "why has no one ever told me the truth as this young man has done?"

As ever, he could not refrain from a dramatic speech. But within two days

Leuchtenberg had been posted to a staff job at the front, and the new chief of general staff was not Richthofen (who would have demanded full powers), but General Günther Korten, whose previous appointment was that of deputy commander of *Luftflotte* 1 on the eastern front. "For me personally a real blessing," Richthofen confided in his diary. "My appointment would soon have led to a colossal row."

Korten made no row at all. He saw his role as Goering's shadow—until July 20th, 1944, when he was mortally wounded by the bomb intended for Hitler. So in the end the control of the Luftwaffe was not altered one whit. Jeschonnek died in vain. Goering gave "haemorrhage of the stomach" as the cause of death, and falsified the date to remove any suspicion that it might be connected with the attack on Peenemünde. August 19th, and not the 18th, remains even today the official date of Jeschonnek's end.

Doubtless the general was aware of his own contribution to the decline of the Luftwaffe. "If we have not won the war by December 1942 we have no prospect of doing so," he had declared at the opening of the second summer offensive in Russia. Though much of the credit for the tactical and technical performance of the Luftwaffe during the "*blitzkriegs*" was due to him, he had persistently sponsored dive-bombing as the single recipe for success. He greatly overrated the capability of medium bombers, especially that of the Ju 88, and the build-up of a four-engined bomber fleet was correspondingly neglected. He had neither murmured against the ban on further aircraft development nor warned Hitler that the Luftwaffe was incapable of successfully waging war on a multiple front.

But the most striking evidence of Jeschonnek's failure emerges from the last months of his life. The Luftwaffe staff was fully informed about the American aircraft construction programme, and at last Jeschonnek recognised the mortal danger that such swarms of four-engined bombers represented for Germany. "A danger of such magnitude that by comparison the disaster of Stalingrad was trifling", he often declared.

His *volte-face* in favour of defence put him on the side of Generals Galland and Kammhuber who, while the Luftwaffe bled to death on the eastern and southern fronts, had for long tried to draw attention to the threat building up from the west. But even the chief of general staff failed to make any impression on Hitler. The Führer was not interested in defence: in his view victory could only be won by attack. With Jeschonnek that must have weighed heavily. Speaking confidentially on the justification of suicide, he asked, "Do you not consider that by sacrificing his own person a man can spotlight a mortal danger that otherwise would only be trifled with?"

On the morning of August 18th, 1943, Colonel-General Jeschonnek put his thoughts into action. Strangely enough he did so just as the daylight offensive of the American Flying Fortresses had brought a strong concentration of German fighters to the defence of the homeland—on the morning after the first great daylight air battle over Germany, in the course of which the limitations of the aggressors were sharply revealed.

3. The Fight by Daylight

By July 1943 the American 8th Air Force in England had already increased to fifteen bomber groups comprising over 300 B-17 Fortresses and B-24

Liberators. The only hitch was the inadequate range of their escort fighters. That of the P-47 Thunderbolt at first only extended to the coastal area of Belgium and Holland, while the twin-engined P-38 Lightning, with its double fuselage, was—like the German Me 110—no match for single-engined fighters.

On July 28th the Thunderbolts appeared for the first time with auxiliary wing-tanks, which enabled them to penetrate as far as Germany's western frontier. To be sure, it was still not far enough, but the air force commander, General Eaker, could wait no longer. It was high time he put his own plan into operation—namely, precision daylight attacks on the centres of the German aircraft industry. The fighters would protect the bombers on the outward flight up to the limit of their endurance, and meet them again on their return.

Thus, at the same time as Hamburg blazed as a result of the heavy night attacks by the R.A.F., seventy-seven Fortresses in two formations headed deep into central Germany in full daylight. Their targets were the Fieseler works at Kassel-Bettenhausen and AGO at Aschersleben, not far from Magdeburg. General Eaker aimed to strike strategically at his most dangerous adversaries, the German fighters. Both works produced the Focke-Wulf Fw 190.

German fighter *Gruppen* closed in upon the bombers long before they reached these targets. First it was the Me 109s of II/JG 11 from Jever. But the eleven Messerschmitts of 5 Squadron hung behind: each of these carried a 500-lb. bomb beneath its fuselage. Laboriously they climbed up to 25,000 feet.

Bombing bombers with fighters was new, and only practicable against tight formations. The commander of 5 Squadron, First-Lieutenant Heinz Knocke, had tried it out some weeks before with surprising success: the force of the explosion tore off a B-17's wing and the aircraft had spun into the sea. It now remained to be seen what a whole squadron could do.

The Messerschmitts ranged themselves at 3,000 feet over the bombers, matching every change of direction, then released their bombs in quick succession and went into a climbing turn to port to get clear of the explosions. The bombs had time-fuses, but success depended on correlating the positions of the opposing aircraft with the path of the bomb. That could only be estimated, and consequently many bombs were ineffective: they either exploded too far behind, or passing through the formation burst below it. Suddenly, however, there was a flash in the centre of the swarm. Sergeant Fest had scored a direct hit. It was more than that: three Fortresses seemed to stop in mid-air, then crash together. Wings went whirling through the sky, and the three planes dived earthwards trailing long plumes of smoke, followed slowly by several parachutes.

The bomb must have exploded right amongst the too closely formating aircraft, and the unexpected success brought encouragement. No longer burdened by their bombs the Messerschmitts dived down on the battered formation and tore it apart, only detaching themselves when the red lights on the instrument boards showed that their fuel was nearly exhausted.

Altogether II/JG 11 under Captain Günther Specht scored eleven victories, and from the two raids the Americans lost a total of twenty-two Fortresses, not counting another four so badly damaged that they only just reached England again.

The German claims indeed were thirty-five enemy aircraft destroyed, while the Americans believed they themselves had shot down no fewer than forty-eight Fw 190s and Me 109s. In fact, the Germans lost seven fighters.

With July 28th began "the bloody summer of 1943", as the Americans named the period during which they operated without fighter escort. On July 29th the Arado works at Warnemünde—another centre of Fw 190 production—was the target. And on the 30th, 131 four-engined bombers raided the Fieseler factory at Kassel again.

On August 1st the Americans struck in an entirely different area at an entirely different target, as their 9th Air Force, based in North Africa, opened its assault on southern Europe. One hundred and seventy-eight Liberators, crossing the Mediterranean from Benghazi, delivered a low-level attack on the Ploesti oil refineries in Rumania. But surprise was not achieved. The raiders met a lethal barrage of flak. Already decimated by this, the returning bombers were set upon and harried out to sea by such fighter forces as were available in the area: units of I/JG 4 under Captain Hans Hahn and of IV/JG 27 under First-Lieutenant Burk, plus Rumanian fighters and a few Me 110s of Captain Lutje's night-fighter *Gruppe* IV/NJG 6. Forty-eight out of the 178 Liberators were shot down and another fifty-five severely damaged. Though Ploesti was badly hit, its production soon returned to normal.

On August 13th sixty-one Liberators, again from North Africa, pushed right through to Austria and attacked the Messerschmitt works at Wiener Neustadt. This incursion met with virtually no fighter opposition. Southern Germany, with Austria, had become the object of a pincers movement—assailable both from England and North Africa. No sooner had the defence of the Reich been strengthened than it had to be split between two fronts.

None the less, its ratè of success increased. For July alone the Luftwaffe command calculated the loss to the enemy as twelve to fifteen per cent of his entire attacking force, while the 8th Air Force's own figure for the five missions it flew during that month was eighty-seven bombers lost out of 839 sorties. Even this represented over ten per cent, again not counting the heavy damage that put others out of action.

It meant, in effect, that ten missions were enough to eliminate a whole formation. Its aircraft had either been burnt out, smashed on landing or otherwise reduced to scrap. The "bloody summer" also affected the morale of the crews. In the long run such losses could not be sustained.

According to the minister of munitions and war production, Albert Speer, neither could the effects of the precision bombing of the American daylight attacks be sustained by Germany. The night bombardment of the British, despite the devastation caused, did not appreciably affect the German war potential, whereas the Americans hit the armaments industry where it hurt by going for the vital factories and exploiting the bottle-necks of production. Even if they lost many bombers on the way, the rest were enough to inflict heavy damage.

Speer expressed his concern to the Fighter General, Adolf Galland, who responded with the remedy: "Three to four times as many fighters—then the losses we inflict will be decisive."

As soon as he recognised the need, Speer exercised all his influence on behalf of the defence force—even with Hitler, whose ear he had. The chief of air supply, Erhard Milch, reached the same conclusion. After making a

108. A B-17 Fortress with open bomb doors. In their attacks on Germany these aircraft suffered severe losses until they could be protected by American long-range fighters.

109. One of the many crash-landings in England.

110. A Ju 88 night-fighter ready for take-off. In spring 1944, the German night-fighter arm reached the zenith of its success against the British Bomber Command.

tour of the fighter stations in the west he wrote Goering the following report on June 29th:

"To achieve any decisive success against American formations of between 100 and 200 four-engined bombers, the fighter forces must out-number the enemy by four to one. Successful defence against such formations, therefore, requires the commitment of 600 to 800 fighters on each occasion." Nor did he forget to praise the fighting spirit of the force already operating: "The morale of the pilots is excellent; their performance, considering their numerical weakness, cannot be stressed too much, and the leaders are well up to their task. Provided they receive new reinforcements, the prospects of the day-fighter can be viewed with complete assurance." The word "provided" was heavily underlined.

The reinforcements were in fact available, In the first eight months of 1943 the output of Me 109s and Fw 190s soared to 7,477. But the Reich defence force was not the main recipient. By Hitler's express command absolute priority was given to the eastern front and to *Luftlotte* 2 in the Mediterranean.

In Tunisia and Sicily JGs 27, 53 and 77 had been engaged in a hopeless battle against overwhelming odds. The provision of escorts for the supply ships alone taxed their resources to the full. Their losses were heavy, with hundreds destroyed on the ground by bombs. Hundreds more had to be abandoned in a damaged state because evacuation orders invariably arrived too late to save them. The wear and tear of engines surpassed the worst expectations. Meanwhile fresh reserves went on being pumped into the southern front, as into a bottomless barrel.

Thus, despite the mounting production, the number of serviceable day-fighters available for the defence of Germany rose only slowly: from 120 in March and April to 162 in early May, 255 in early June and 300 in July. By the end of August, under pressure of the American daylight offensive, the home defence force reached its all-time "high" in first-line aircraft: 405 Me 109s and Fw 190s, plus one twin-engined *Geschwader* with about eighty Me 110s and Me 410s.

Though some were newly formed units, most of them had had to be withdrawn from other fronts. From southern Italy II/JG 27 under Captain Schroer moved to Wiesbaden-Erbenheim, II/JG 51 under Captain Rammelt to Neubiberg near Munich, while a single *Gruppe* of the renowned "Greenheart" *Geschwader*, III/JG 54 under Major Reinhard Seiler, was posted from northern Russia to Oldenburg and Nordholtz on Heligoland Bight. Two complete *Geschwader* were also brought home: JG 3 ("Udet") under Lieutenant-Colonel Wilcke from the southern sector of the eastern front; JG 26 ("Schlageter") under Major Priller from the English Channel, where its experience of combat with the British and Americans was perhaps unrivalled. Both now were stationed on the lower Rhine and in Holland, right on the enemy approach routes.

Even the Me 110s, long obsolete in daylight and lately relegated to a host of inconsequential tasks, were given a new lease of life. Provided they could evade combat with enemy fighters, their firepower could still make dents in the heavy bombers. Major Karl Boehm-Tettelbach, *Kommodore* of ZG 26, distributed between Wunstorf, Quakenbrück and Hildesheim, reported the *Geschwader* ready for action.

The concentration had been effected. Each morning the pilots sat in their cockpits, ready to take off, while the German radar probed the western skies. In the underground divisional operations rooms men and women waited too. The battle could begin.

In the early morning of August 17, 1943, the German monitoring service reported unusual activity on the airfields of the U.S. 8th Air Force in England, portending a major operation. Further information received by

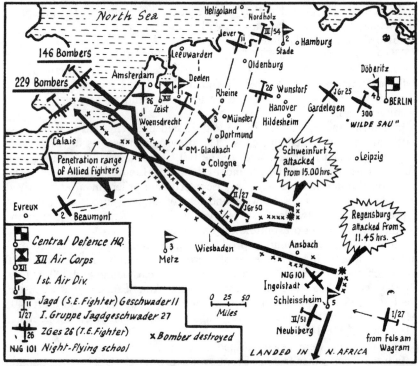

Air defence of Germany against daylight bombing. On August 17, 1943 two forces of American 4-engined bombers on their way to attack Schweinfurt and Regensburg were assailed by 300 fighters of the Reich Defence Force. A total of 60 bombers were shot down, including 10 over southern Europe (not shown). The map also indicates the command structure of the Reich defence at this time and the German air formations that took part.

1 Air Division at Deelen predicted an enemy penetration deep into central or southern Germany. As a result a number of fighter *Gruppen* on the North Sea coast received orders to move in advance to airfields west of Rheims in order to be nearer to the scene of operations. These measures soon paid off.

Shortly after 10.00 hours a formation of 146 bombers, escorted by un-counted Spitfires and Thunderbolts, crossed the Dutch coast and began to fly inland. They were shadowed at a distance by Focke-Wulf fighters of II/JG 1. These remained in contact, but did not yet attack.

Still over Holland the Americans changed course to the south, and crossed Belgium at 20,000 feet. Then, shortly before reaching the German frontier the escort had to turn back. It was the moment the Focke-Wulfs had been waiting for. Setting on the bombers from head-on and slightly above, they let fly. Then, sweeping close beneath the formation, they climbed up and turned to repeat the attack.

The first Boeings caught fire. Four dived with black smoke-plumes down into the Eifel country, the next three into the Hunsrück. And now the sky was alive with Focke-Wulfs and Messerschmitts. As soon as one *Gruppe* exhausted its ammunition, it was replaced by another.

The battle went on for a full ninety minutes without let-up. The Americans lost fourteen aircraft, leaving 132 to bomb the target—the Messerschmitt works at Regensburg-Prüfening. Meanwhile German fighter control got ready to deal out similar punishment on the return flight. Usually this was the same course in reciprocal, but this time the Americans turned south, and demonstrated their enormous radius of action by crossing Italy and the Mediterranean to land in North Africa. Even so, another ten bombers were shot down by *Luftlotte* 2 in that area, so that this formation altogether lost twenty-four B-17s, with many more damaged.

But the zenith of the August 17th battle was still to come. In the early afternoon a still larger formation, numbering 229 aircraft, crossed the mouth of the Scheldt on its way to bomb the ball-bearing works at Schweinfurt. It was given a still warmer reception than the first. This time the German fighters did not wait till the escort had turned back. While one *Gruppe* engaged the Thunderbolts, a second went for the bombers.

Amongst the first assailants was again JG 11's 5 Squadron, which had previously carried out experiments with bombs. Today its Messerschmitts had two 21-cm rockets slung under their wings. Creeping up behind, they sent these sizzling off from a range of 800 yards. The enemy formation was well staggered, and most of the rockets fell short. But two hit their targets, and these bombers literally burst asunder in the air. After this introduction the Americans did not enjoy a moment of peace during the whole remainder of their flight to Schweinfurt, or on their return. Over 300 German fighters were airborne.

From this mission thirty-six Fortresses failed to return, representing a total loss for the day of sixty, plus over a hundred damaged. Once again it had been demonstrated that relatively slow bombers in daylight were vulnerable to resolute fighter attack. It applied even to Flying Fortresses—so called because of their massive defensive armament. After this reverse they failed to appear again over the Reich for over five weeks. They avenged themselves by attacking Luftwaffe airfields in the western occupied countries under strong fighter escort.

Thus it was not until October that the U.S. 8th Air Force risked further ventures beyond the range of their own fighters, and then the lesson was rammed home even more firmly than it was in August. During one week, from October 8th to 14th in which Bremen, Marienburg, Danzig, Münster, and once again Schweinfurt, were attacked, the Americans lost 148 machines. It meant the loss, within only a few days, of nearly 1,500 airmen. Even the Americans could not replace so many. About the second Schweinfurt raid the official American historian records that the German reaction was "unprecedented in its magnitude, in the cleverness with which it was planned, and in the severity with which it was executed".

Had the German defence thereby won a conclusive victory? Perhaps—

but only if it kept pace with new developments, and realised that the Americans would now do everything they could to extend the range of their escort fighters to cover Germany itself. Once again it was Galland who pointed to this danger. To counter it—to preserve German control of the air over their own country—he called for the commitment of the world's best and fastest fighter to date. If, he argued, the enemy's fighters could not be dealt with, the bombers would fly to the targets unscathed.

But Hitler pushed his arguments unceremoniously aside, and Goering labelled them "hair-brained, flabby defeatism".

Early in 1944 the hair-brained child was born in the shape of the American long-range fighter, the P-51 Mustang. From now on the Focke-Wulfs and Messerschmitts no longer ruled the skies, and the demise of the German fighter arm began.

Yet the Luftwaffe had one more chance. The fighter that Galland had referred to was the first operational jet-engined aircraft in the world. It was only necessary that it should be launched on the right front: that of the Battle of Germany.

4. The Lost Opportunity

Shortly before 08.00 on July 18, 1942, an aircraft waited at the extreme end of the runway of Leipheim airfield, near Günzburg on the Danube. The runway was only 1,200 yards long, and every yard was needed.

Fritz Wendel, flight captain and chief test pilot with Messerschmitt, acknowledged the farewell wishes of the men on the ground with a nod of his head, and closed the roof of the cockpit. The sound of the engines rose to an ear-splitting scream.

On this machine the traditional feature of every other aircraft to date was missing: the propeller. Nor were the engines themselves of the conventional type. Instead, beneath the wings were two thickly cowled jet turbines. From their circular rear openings thundered fiery blasts that sprayed the tail unit with sand and stones.

Slowly and cautiously Wendel pushed forward the power-lever. With both feet on the brakes he held the plane for thirty to forty seconds, till the revolution counter read 7,500. 8,500 represented full power, and he could hold it no longer. He released the brakes, and the Me 262 shot forward.

With its sharp nose pointing into the air, the machine resembled a projectile. This position had the effect of blocking the pilot's forward vision. He could only keep aligned with the runway by glancing to the side. On the initial take-off of a revolutionary prototype this was a disadvantage indeed. If only, thought Wendel, it had a tricycle-undercarriage. Its undercarriage was, in fact, the only conventional thing about the plane. It accounted for its awkward stance, as a result of which the blast of the engines hit the ground and the pilot could not see. Worse, the tail unit in this position was aerodynamically "blind": it received no air-stream. There was no response from the elevator and for all its high ground-speed the machine refused to become airborne.

The spectators held their breath. Deafened by its piercing whistle, they watched as it hurtled like a racing car to the end of the runway. Surely it must have attained 110 m.p.h. long since.

That was the speed at which, so it had been calculated, the Me 262 with its five ton all-up weight, must leave the ground. During ground tests early in the morning Wendel had reached it in just over 800 yards, without, however, getting the tail unit off the ground. And the remainder of the distance was only just long enough to stop in. Each time he had come to a halt close beside the boundary fence.

"No plane can fly without a propeller," the doubting Thomases had said. It looked as though they might be proved right.

This time Wendel put fortune to the test. He had been advised as to how, in such a situation, he could still get the stubborn tail into the air. It was a most irregular and dangerous procedure, but he had to risk it. At 110 m.p.h. and full power, he suddenly trod briefly but sharply on the brakes. It worked. The plane tipped forward on its axis, and the tail came clear of the ground. Horizontal motion at once produced an air-stream, and at last pressure could be felt from the elevator. Wendel reacted swiftly. Very gently, almost automatically, he lifted the aircraft off the ground.

The first Me 262 was airborne—and how it flew! The chief test pilot, who had nursed it from the beginning, was at last rewarded for all his trouble. He pushed the stick a bit forward to gain more pace, and felt himself pressed backwards into his seat. The Messerschmitt shot like an arrow up into the sky. What was more, the higher it climbed, the faster it flew. The astounded Wendel stared at his instruments. Since he himself had raised the absolute world speed record on April 26, 1939, to 469.22 m.p.h. with the Me 209, it had only been exceeded by his colleague, Heini Dittmar, in the rocket-propelled Me 163. And with the veil of secrecy in which wartime rocket development was shrouded, the new record had never been claimed.

Now the third prototype of the Me 262, with its twin Jumo 004 jets, was soaring above the world-record mark on its very first flight. 500 m.p.h. on the clock, without a murmur! Suddenly Wendel felt really happy in this sensational aircraft. He throttled back, then re-accelerated: the engines responded splendidly. Then in a wide circuit he swept in to land, put down smoothly, and rolled to a stop. The first flight of the Me 262 V-3—the world's first jet aircraft ever to reach the stage of series production—had lasted just twelve minutes.

"She's wonderful!" beamed Wendel, as Professor Messerschmitt came up to meet him. "I've never enjoyed a first flight more."

In the afternoon he flew the machine again. If time was to be made up the real tests must begin at once. For Messerschmitt had waited a long time for the engines. The air-frame had been flown by Wendel as long ago as April 1941—powered by an old piston engine that was quite inappropriate to the new streamlined frame. But it was at least a start, and it enabled some of the flying characteristics to be gauged. Six months later the first turbo-jets arrived from B.M.W. in Berlin. They ran satisfactorily on the bench, and on March 25, 1942, were submitted to their first flying test.

For this occasion the Me 262 V-1 presented a curious spectacle. Besides the turbines under the wings, the old piston engine was still in the middle. For Wendel this was just as well, for he had hardly reached 150 feet before both the former cut out one after the other, and he only got down again by using the conventional engine's full power. The turbines had not withstood the strain: in both cases the compressor blades were broken. Such teething troubles were to be expected, but it was a long wait before fresh engines became available, and meanwhile the V-1 prototype stood like an orphan in the hangar.

Finally the Jumo 004s arrived, and as we have seen were successful. On its first jet-powered flight the Me 262 revealed a performance that its creators had hardly dared hope for. Now Wendel tested its every feature, had small modifications made, and flew again. After the tenth flight, during which the plane reached well over 500 m.p.h., he advised the factory management to get ready for series production. Such a decision could not, of course, be taken by Messerschmitt alone. Till now the contract had only been for three prototypes, nothing more. So the supply chief in Berlin—Milch—was put in the picture, and he in turn set the wheels turning at the official Rechlin test centre.

On August 17th, just one month since the Me 262's initial flight, there arrived from Rechlin an experienced test pilot in the shape of staff-engineer Beauvais, to submit the new plane to exhaustive trials. As he edged himself into the narrow cockpit, Wendel reminded him once again of the trick with the brakes to elevate the tail. He himself would take up station at the 800-yard mark to indicate when Beauvais should execute this manoeuvre. Then he watched as the machine approached. But its speed was too low—nothing like 110 m.p.h. None the less, as he came abreast, the pilot braked. The tail-wheel came up, but then fell impotently down again. Beauvais tried it a second time, then again just before the airfield perimeter.

Somehow the machine became airborne, and whizzed over the ground at perhaps three feet—but much too slowly ever to gain height. Seconds later a wing-tip touched a refuse heap, and with a loud report the Messerschmitt crashed on top of it in a cloud of dust. Miraculously the pilot climbed out of the wreckage almost unscathed.

This accident put back the Me 262's final development by months. Though a replacement air-frame was rapidly constructed, and even new engines were available, the Reich Air Ministry in Berlin had no confidence. The whole project, it was argued, was still too much in its infancy. There could be no question of sanctioning any series production. And no one pressed for this as an urgent matter. Milch merely urged intensified production of those aircraft types that had already proved their worth in the past. New projects stood in the way of such an aim being realised: they simply funnelled-off productive capacity.

By the summer of 1942 the Americans had already been in the war for nine months, and their first four-engined bombers were appearing over the continent. In 1943 they would number hundreds, in the following year thousands. As already said, Luftwaffe Command possessed exact and dependable figures of their aircraft construction programme. And at this vital moment a German fighter had been created that was 125 m.p.h. faster than any other fighter in the world—enough to alarm all Germany's enemies. It could have been operational within a year, to cope with the Allies when they opened their main air offensive. Thus it could be rationally supposed that it would be given top priority, and all scientific and material resources harnessed to the production of air-frames and turbo-jet engines. Yet no leading personality in the Luftwaffe took upon himself the responsibility of saying as much, or even seemed to be aware of the unique opportunity.

It was not until December 1942 that the Technical Office put production of the Me 262 on its programme—and then only for 1944 at a planned output of only twenty planes per month. The fastest fighter in the world became shunted onto a siding; it seemed that the Luftwaffe had no interest in it.

It was not the first time that the Luftwaffe hierarchy was so short-sighted. Nor, for all its promise, was the Me 262 the world's very first turbo-jet aircraft. The history of the development of such a plane went back to before the war. Then the breaking of the world speed record, first by the He 100, and shortly afterwards by the Me 209, clearly showed that piston-engined aircraft had just about reached the limit of their possible performance. Whatever their power output, their engines would not propel them at more than about 465 m.p.h. If the velocity of sound was ever to be reached, or even passed, a completely new method of propulsion was needed. The principle of this was already known in the mid-thirties: instead of being dragged through the air by a propeller, the plane would be driven by a constant-recoil system. Three alternatives seemed to present themselves:

1. *A turbo-jet engine* whereby inducted air was compressed, charged with fuel, and finally ignited in the combustion chamber—thrust being created by the high-speed issue of the gases through the rear nozzle.
2. *The rocket engine.* Carrying within itself the necessary oxygen and fuel, this was independent of the outside atmosphere. Though the thrust developed was considerably greater than that of a jet engine, the rocket constituent was consumed within seconds.
3. *The "ram jet" engine.* This, in principle, was the least complex, the inducted air being compressed simply by meeting a central contraction in the "stove-pipe". Though the resulting thrust was very powerful, the aircraft required an auxiliary engine as a prime-mover before high speed produced sufficient pressure. Experiments with this type of power unit were started by Dr. Eugen Sänger, then head of the aircraft test centre at Trauen on Lüneburg Heath.

The first German industrialist to give play to the new ideas was Ernst Heinkel. At the end of 1935 he had a meeting with the young Wernher von Braun, who was then still experimenting with so-called "rocket-stoves" at Kummersdorf firing range near Berlin. Braun was convinced that rockets could also be used as aircraft propellents, but as an employee of the Army's missile section he was without the wherewithal for aviation projects. Heinkel accordingly sent him the fuselage of an He 112 for bench experiments, together with a few aircraft technicians. With the arrival of test pilot Erich Warsitz from Rechlin, the hazardous enterprise could begin.

With an infernal noise, Braun's rocket motor, mounted in the He 112 fuselage, was fired off and its attendants cowered behind a concrete screen. Several times the combustion chamber exploded, and twice Heinkel had to send a replacement fuselage. There followed a whole plane, complete with its standard engine. The rocket engine was added, but Warsitz was only to ignite this after becoming airborne. However, during a preliminary run-up on the ground the whole He 112 blew up and the pilot was catapulted through the air.

Instead of giving up, Warsitz personally asked Heinkel for a new plane. With this, in the summer of 1937, the first rocket-powered flight was made. The He 112 shot heavenwards, circled the airfield and landed undamaged.

Heinkel then proceeded on his own initiative to develop the He 176, an aircraft specially designed for a rocket power-unit. It was a tiny little thing, only 4 ft. 7 in. high and 17 ft. long, with the fuselage wrapping the cockpit and engine like a garment. There was no question of the pilot sitting normally: he lay on his back as if in a deck-chair, but with a full field of view. Udet, looking at the wings, with their total area of some fifty square feet, remarked, "Just a rocket with a running board."

Meanwhile the chemical specialist, Dr. Hellmuth Walter, had been developing, at Kiel, a more regular type of rocket engine with a thrust of 1,200 lb. which was considerably more reliable than Braun's "rocket-stove". Equipped with this Walter engine, the He 176 was subjected to its first runway tests on the shore of Usedom Island in the Baltic, and in the spring of 1939 they were continued by Warsitz at Peenemünde. The danger consisted not so much in bestriding a fiery rocket, as in stopping again within the narrow confines of the airfield. "Ground loops" were regular occurrences. Eventually on June 20, 1939—a calm day with good visibility—the time had come for Warsitz to make up his mind. The machine had reacted well along the runway, and after a final moment of being airborne in the afternoon, he gave the order: "Get ready for the first flight."

His determination infected the factory engineers, despite all their warnings and forebodings. They made a final check and inserted the dangerous engine ingredients, while two fitters ran up with a sucking-pig as a gesture of good luck. Then they watched as the He 176 raced down the runway, hit a small unevenness, and inclined dangerously to the side. But Warsitz kept control, righted the spitting little monster, and finally lifted it closely above a near-by wood. On the previous runway tests he had been obliged to curb all acceleration, but now as the aircraft soared to freedom he was tightly compressed against his supports. In a few seconds he had been carried far out over the Baltic—and it was already time to turn back and re-locate the airfield. For the rocket burnt for just one minute. It cut out on his approach. Even so the plane's speed was excessive, but the wheels took the shock, and after a long run he came to a standstill. There was a deep silence, before it was broken by the cheers of the spectators.

Warsitz immediately telephoned Heinkel, who had no idea that the flight had taken place. "*Herr Doktor*," he said, "I am happy to report that your He 176 has just achieved the first unassisted rocket flight in history! As you can hear, I am still alive."

The news created a stir at the Reich Air Ministry, and the very next morning Milch, Udet and numerous engineers of the Technical Office hurried over to Peenemünde. Warsitz repeated his sixty-second ride on his fire-belching mount, acknowledged by grateful plaudits. None the less, Milch and Udet rejected the He 176. Instead of acclaiming the historic moment with triumph, their faces were angry. By developing this machine without consulting the Ministry, Heinkel had once again stuck his neck out. It was time he was cut down to size.

"That's no aeroplane!" Udet stormed, and promptly banned all further experiments with "this volcano-bottomed object". Heinkel and his colleagues—

including Warsitz, who had risked his life trying it out—were left standing speechless on the airfield.

Heinkel indeed fought the decision, and on July 3, 1939 even succeeded in arranging a demonstration flight in front of Hitler and Goering at Roggenthien near Rechlin. But again interest centred almost exclusively on the achievement of the pilot, hardly at all on the epoch-making little machine. Heinkel could keep his "rocket toy"; no contract for further development would be given. When the outbreak of war finally sealed its fate, the He 176 found its way to the aviation museum in Berlin. There, still packed in its cases, it was destroyed in a bombing raid in 1944.

Little better fortune attended Heinkel's parallel development of the turbo-jet He 178, which besides great velocity promised considerably longer flight duration. In 1936 he set up a "hush-hush" section at his Rostock works, where the young physicist Pabst von Ohain worked day and night on a turbo-jet engine. That did not suit the Reich Air Ministry either. Heinkel, Berlin thundered, was a manufacturer of aircraft. He would kindly leave the development of aero-*engines* to the firms concerned.

But the aero-engine industry had other worries. The Luftwaffe was arming at break-neck speed, and if the still appreciable lead held abroad in piston engines was to be caught up with, there was no time to start playing about with immature theories. Only late in 1939 was a development contract for a turbo-jet engine granted—to Junkers at Dessau and B.M.W. Messerschmitt was to design an air-frame for it.

Thus Heinkel, whose own initiative had put him a good step ahead, was by-passed. It did not upset him; he just carried on, determined as ever to show the "Berlin gentry" what he could do. Ohain's first turbine had been running since September 1937, and a year later he had produced a more powerful one, which in summer 1939 was fitted to the He 178. So it came about the Flight-Captain Erich Warsitz, a few weeks after flying the first rocket aircraft, also flew the world's first jet aircraft. That was on August 27, 1939, just five days before the war started. Thus in Berlin no one had time for the He 178, and it was not until the Polish campaign had been over for weeks that Heinkel succeeded in demonstrating his brain-child before Milch and Udet. Goering did not bother to attend.

After an initial false start the plane swept over their heads, deafening them with its howling turbine and thundering its message home. But the leaders of military aviation were already dazzled by the Luftwaffe's swift victory in Poland, and to short-sightedness was added arrogance. "Before that comes to anything, the war will long since have been won. . . ."

So the He 178 was also awarded no contract—just as a faulty assessment of the situation in February 1940 put a development ban "on all projects that have not reached the production stage within a year".

At the outbreak of war Germany was thus well ahead of her enemies in the field of both rocket and jet power units. Had she bothered to exploit this lead, she could later have countered the greater numerical strength of the Allied air forces with technically superior weapons. But the whole advantage was squandered.

Even so, the inventive impulse cannot be strangled, and work went on despite the ban. Messerschmitt not only constructed the air-frame of the Me 262 (for which there were still no engines) but at Augsburg took over from the D.F.S. (research institute for sail-planes) the designer Alexander Lippisch. The latter had for years been working on the idea of a tail-less delta-shaped aircraft, culminating in the DFS 194. His work at Messerschmitt's now produced the Me 163, first flown by Heini Dittmar, and which was to be powered by a Walter rocket engine. It was a short, thickset little plane, and its first objective was to attain the long-dreamed of 1,000-kilometre mark in speed.

In the spring of 1941 Dittmar put it through its trials at Peenemünde. At each flight he took aboard more fuel, and each time the aircraft became faster. From 800 km/h. it rose to 880 and then 920. On May 10th Dittmar decided to try for the crowning figure. The plane shot off into the heavens, and within a minute had reached 13,000 feet. Then, levelling out, he proceeded at full throttle till 950, 980 and finally 1,000 km/h. were indicated. Suddenly the machine vibrated, the tail unit began to flutter, and it went into a headlong dive. Dittmar quickly cut out the rocket, after which the plane recovered and he was able to pull out and glide safely to land.

The final speed was measured at 1,004 km/h.—approximately 625 m.p.h. It was the nearest approach to the sound barrier yet reached by man.

Later the Me 163 was developed as an interceptor, with flight trials undertaken by volunteers of "Test Commando 16" under Captain Wolfgang Späte, at Bad Zwischenahn near Oldenburg. In the last months of the war it was actually used operationally against Allied bombers.

Greater prospects of success, however, were offered by the Me 262 jet fighter, in which the Reich Air Ministry had so far shown so little interest. Its attitude only changed after the plane had been flown by the thirty-one-year-old fighter leader, Adolf Galland. This was on May 22, 1943, nearly a year after Wendel had first flown it and clamoured for it to be equipped with a tricycle undercarriage. Nothing, however, had been done about it: the Air Ministry did not hold with this "American invention". So Galland too had to master the trick of taking off with the dangerous conventional undercarriage. Having done so he, like all who had flown the plane before him, at once sensed its tremendous power, vibration-free speed and rate of climb. Like an arrow he shot down in a mock attack on another aircraft that happened to be passing.

He was most impressed. If only, he thought, he could equip his fighter units with such an aircraft soon enough, and in sufficient numbers, the Battle of Germany need still not be lost. But beset with questions on landing, he merely said: "It's like flying on the wings of an angel."

He did, however, at once report to Milch and Goering. The Me 262, he said, was a project of prime importance. It could turn the tables and the tide. He seemed to have convinced the two of them. Yet even now series production did not begin, for one man was against it: Hitler. He did not want a new fighter. He did not want defence: only attack. He wanted bombers, nothing else. When on November 26, 1943, after a further six months of delay, the Me 262 was demonstrated at Insterburg in his presence, he astonished Professor Willi Messerschmitt with the question:

"Can this aircraft carry bombs?"

Messerschmitt said yes—so could any aircraft in the last resort. Then he hesitated, thinking about the implications. . . . But Hitler did not let him utter another word. "So there at last is our blitz-bomber!" he cried triumphantly.

The people about him were stunned to silence. It had suddenly become one of the Führer's "irrevocable resolves", and no subsequent protests changed it. The world's first jet fighter was to be weighed down with bombs. Its superiority was gone.

A whole string of technical difficulties at once arose. Bombs would make the take-off weight too heavy for the slender legs. Undercarriage and tyres had to be reinforced. For bombing missions the range was inadequate, so auxiliary tanks had to be built in. That displaced the centre of gravity, upsetting the plane's stability. No approved method of bomb-suspension, nor even a bombsight, existed for such a plane, and with the normal fighter reflector-sight bombs could only be aimed in shallow angle of dive. For regular dive-bombing the machine was too fast safely to be held on target. An order from Führer HQ expressly forbade such dives—or indeed any speed exceeding 470 m.p.h.

The crews of Major Unrau's I/KG 51, chosen to fly the "blitz-bomber" operationally, were in despair. In horizontal bombing trials they failed to hit a thing: their bombs often landed over a mile from the target. Only after the airframe had been strengthened, and they could attack on a shallow dive, did results improve.

Meanwhile eight months had elapsed since Hitler's decision. By this time the Allied invasion had taken place, and with the break-through at Avranches the front in Normandy was fluid. Only at this point, in the early days of August, 1944, was an operational team of Me 262 jet bombers posted to Juvincourt, near Rheims, assigned to participate in the battle.

It was under the command of Major Schenck and consisted at the outset of just nine aircraft. Of these two broke up on leaving Germany owing to faulty servicing. Incompletely trained, the pilots had never previously taken off with a full gross weight, and a third machine was lost in the course of the intermediate landing at Schwäbisch-Hall. The pilot of the fourth failed to find Juvincourt, had to force land, and was likewise lost to the strength.

Out of the nine aircraft there thus remained five to oppose the Allied forces, now breaking out from their bridgehead. Though by the end of October they had been reinforced by another twenty-five, though II/KG 51 joined them with the fighter-bomber version of the Me 262, and with experience flying accidents became virtually a thing of the past—what could a mere handful of jet bombers achieve? It was much too little and far too late.

Hitler's gambit—to turn the first jet fighter into a bomber—was yet another example of his "intuition" upsetting the apple-cart.

5. Night-Fighters at their Zenith

Late in the afternoon of July 30, 1943, a blue-grey Luftwaffe staff car raced from Potsdam to Berlin. The man at the wheel, Major Hajo Herrmann, was leading a dual life. During the day he lectured the "Tactical-technical Promotion Group" under the auspices of Luftwaffe Command at Wildpark Werder; at night he scoured the skies in a Focke-Wulf 190.

Herrmann was determined to demonstrate that his ideas were right, but so far experts and superior officers alike had only greeted them with sympathetic smiles. Now, when he drove up at Staaken airfield, other pilots—

volunteers from air staffs and flying schools—were waiting. Below the fuselage of each of the aircraft was suspended an auxiliary 400-litre tank, permitting a good two and a half hours' flight. During the evening the little formation flew over to München-Gladbach. A clear, cloudless night was indicated.

Around midnight Herrmann learnt that the R.A.F. were on their way. A powerful bomber formation was reported over the Dutch coast, headed towards the Ruhr. Within minutes ten Me 109s and Fw 190s of his experimental team were in the air. They did not fly to meet the enemy—whom they would never find without ground control—but instead climbed up to the bomber's reported height over the expected target area of Duisburg-Essen. There they waited in the sky, with eyes trained to the west.

The bombers were by now passing through the "*Himmelbett*" zones of the ground-controlled twin-engined night-fighters, and what Herrmann expected came to pass. Far off a flaming torch appeared, sinking slowly earthwards. It meant that the Me 110s had shot down a bomber, and its demise marked the path of the oncoming swarm. "They're coming straight for us," he called on the radio.

Then another bomber crashed to the left: they must have turned south. Suddenly coloured lights sailed through the heavens: the marker flares of the Pathfinders. "Head for the Christmas trees," he called again.

The German fighters were treated to a fascinating firework display, seemingly quite close at hand. While countless searchlight beams probed the sky, yellow, green and red parachute flares sank slowly to the ground, followed by the flashes of the first sticks of incendiaries. As the fires spread, they supplied the final guiding light to the target. It was Cologne—farther away then Herrmann had at first supposed. At full throttle they raced towards it.

The searchlights had already illuminated several bombers, flooding them with chalk-white light and holding them for minutes on end. This was the basis of Herrmann's plan. Unamenable to radar guidance, on which the twin-engined fighters depended, he and his men had to rely on their eyesight. That could only be effective with the aid of the searchlights. It meant operating directly over the target area, right amidst the barrage of their own flak. Unlike the orderly and decorous method of night-fighting that had reigned hitherto, these fighters charged into the battle "like wild boars". Whoever coined the phrase, "Wild Boars"—or "*Wilde Sau*"—was the name they continued to bear.

Suddenly Herrmann found himself behind a brightly illuminated bomber—and approached so close that he himself was blinded by the searchlights. Round him burst the shells of the heavy flak. "It was like sitting in a cage made of fire and glowing steel," he reported. It was no new experience, for he himself was accustomed to flying bombers. Baptised by the barrage of London, he had survived the lethal concentrations of the Arctic convoys, and emerged from perhaps the heaviest flak of the war—that of Malta—suffering only from shock.

When therefore, after hearing his plan, the "Luftwaffe Commander Central", Colonel General Weise, told him, "Do not under-estimate the German flak," Herrmann knew all about it already. He arranged with Major-General Hintz, commander of 4 Flak Division in the Ruhr, that his guns would only fire up to an altitude of 20,000 feet, leaving the zone above that free for the

"*Wilde Sau*". Should a fighter's pursuit take him below the prescribed level, the pilot would proclaim his presence by means of light signals.

It sounded very complicated, even though exercises over Berlin had shown such a delimitation of zones to be possible. At any rate Hintz had agreed to try it out. Now, however, Herrmann was not over the Ruhr, but over Cologne, where 7 Flak Division knew nothing about the arrangement. Its officers had no idea that in the field of fire of their 88-mm batteries there were German fighters mixing with the British bombers. The green and red Very lights being fired off at 20,000 and 23,000 feet meant nothing to the men on the ground.

Herrmann delayed a moment, decided to disregard the danger, and ordered his men to attack. He was so close to the Lancaster that in the glare of the searchlights he could see the rear-gunner in his turret. The latter was calmly looking down at the burning city. In his experience the only danger from night-fighters was in the dark during the outward and return flights—not in the blaze of light over the target itself. But times had changed. Herrmann fired a burst from his four cannon, the Lancaster immediately caught fire, turned left, then fell like a glowing torch.

Climbing up out of the flak, Herrmann looked around. Three or four bombers were burning in the sky, and when he landed there was only one of his own planes missing. Counting up the claims he arrived at the score of twelve. This he reported to Berlin, including the remark "despite all the metal in the air!" In the circumstances he considered it pretty good as a first serious test of what the "*Wilde Sau*" could do.

The result set the wheels moving. Goering, who had sanctioned the experiment six days previously after listening to Majors Herrmann and Baumbach, got the former out of bed early next morning and summoned him to Karinhall to give a detailed report. When the thirty-year-old inventor of the tactics came away, he took with him an order to form a complete *Geschwader* of "*Wilde Sau*", under the designation "JG 300".

Without doubt another event contributed to this development. On June 24th, Josef Kammhuber, G.O.C. of XII Air Corps and "General of Night-Fighters"—fell out of grace with the Führer.

Kammhuber, as we have seen, had been systematically building up the night-fighter arm since 1940, unshaken by all reverses. One was when the searchlight weapon was struck from his hand after the Gauleiters had claimed all searchlights for their cities; another when Hitler personally put a stop to the promising Intruder operations over British bomber bases. Kammhuber persisted, till by summer, 1943, his "*Himmelbett*" zones stretched from the northern point of Jutland to the Mediterranean, and he commanded five *Geschwader* comprising some 400 twin-engined fighters, with a sixth in course of formation. But he was not satisfied. Secret reports of the Allied air-armament programme, particularly in America, made it plain that against the coming fleets of four-engined bombers the German night defence would be overwhelmed.

Dutifully Kammhuber worked out prosposals as to how the threat could be combated. He saw the solution not so much in a new tactical approach, calculated to free the night-fighters from the narrow confines of their "*Himmelbett*" zones, as in a large-scale extension of the organisations in being. Instead of six *Geschwader*, he wanted eighteen with zones of control spread over the whole of Germany. Current and costly radar set-ups would be replaced by advanced apparatus and new processes of control, plus airborne sets with much greater range. All this would mean major re-adaptations in the electrical and electronics industries, but Goering had already half approved the programme when the day came for it to be laid before Hitler.

On June 24, 1943, Kammhuber was summoned to the "*Wolfschanze*" to clarify his proposals, as he thought. But the Führer did not let him get a word in. He simply harped on the American production figures, which Kammhuber had taken as the starting point of his memorandum. There they were in black and white: the Americans were producing 5,000 military aircraft month after month.

"It's absolute nonsense!" Hitler raved. "If the figures were right, you'd be right too! In that case I should have to withdraw from the eastern front forthwith and apply all resources to air defence. But they are *not* right! I will not stand for such nonsense!"

The figures had been compiled by the Armed Forces Command Intelligence Staff (Ic), and had hitherto gone undisputed. Now the Chief of Armed Forces, Keitel, as well as Goering, listened to the Führer's outburst with red faces. But no one dared to contradict him. Kammhuber's proposals were rejected out of hand. The night-fighters were already destroying enough enemy bombers to act as a deterrent.

With that the generals were dismissed. Goering, dumb as a fish in front of Hitler, now turned on Kammhuber and heaped him with reproaches. With his "idiotic requests" he had made him, the *Reichsmarschall*, look an ass. "If you want to take over the whole Luftwaffe," he cried, "you'd better take over my appointment too!"

Shortly afterwards Kammhuber was displaced as G.O.C. XII Air Corps in favour of Major-General Josef "Beppo" Schmid, till now head of Luftwaffe Command Intelligence Staff. The former remained "General of Night-Fighters" till mid-November 1943, then lost this title too, as well as all further influence. The man who had been responsible for the whole build-up of the night-fighter arm found himself posted to Norway.

Such was the immediate background of Major Hajo Herrmann's proposal for a variant in the technique of night-flying represented by the "*Wilde Sau*". His ideas did not appear too devious at all. Only a limited number of bombers could be destroyed in the ground-control zones, and too many were coming in and devastating the cities. Over the target area they were often held by searchlights for minutes on end—probably long enough for fighter attack. No complicated system of control was necessary, and although interception was, of course, more difficult than in daylight, the fact that it still depended on the human eye meant that normal single-engined fighters could be employed.

From the outset Herrmann never claimed to have found a panacea, nor did he aim to supplant the radar-guided units. He only proposed to supplement them—and then exclusively over the target area, whose defence had so far depended solely on flak. He was not to know that the result of the July successes of his pioneers was to focus attention on them as the only current hope of turning the tide. For Herrmann had scarcely started the formation and training of the new JG 300's three *Gruppen* at Bonn-Hangelar, Rheine and Oldenburg, when the storm broke over Hamburg and the whole radar system, on which the controlled night-fighters and flak were dependent, was thrown out of its stride by the British use of "Window".

The very next day the JG 300 *Kommodore* received a telephone call from Goering. "Herrmann," said the latter in earnest tones, "Hamburg has been attacked, and it has never been so bad. The whole night-fighter force has been put out of action. You are now the only person I can rely on. You must start operations at once—even if it is only with a few machines."

On the second night of the bombardment—that of July 27th/28th—Herrmann accordingly sent in a dozen fighters over the burning city. Even twin-engined machines participated in the "*Wilde Sau*" manoeuvre, and the British losses went up. By August 1st the Luftwaffe Commander Central, Weise, had issued an order that, because of radar jamming, *all* units of the night defence force would, "like the single-engined Herrmann *Geschwader*, operate forthwith above the flak/searchlight zone of the enemy's objective." In other words, all night-fighters would adopt "*Wilde Sau*" tactics. Even Kammhuber, at this time still at the head of XII Air Corps, directed that in view of its current ineffectiveness, the "*Himmelbett*" procedure was for the present to be abandoned in favour of the new method.

Soon whole *Geschwader* of both single and twin-engined fighters were chasing through the sky on seeing fires break out in the distance, hoping to catch the raiders while these were still over their target. It was not an easy task. On the night of August 17th/18th, as we have seen, the fighters concentrated over Berlin when the real raid was on Peenemünde. On the other hand, when on August 23rd/24th Berlin was the genuine target for 727 bombers, the divisional operations rooms at Stade and Döberitz established their direction in such good time that the controllers' "running commentary" was able to name the target over an hour in advance.

Thereupon the night-fighter *Gruppen* converged on the capital from all sides, and as the R.A.F. bombers reached the Spree and set their first marker flares, hell broke loose. Berlin's huge searchlight belt, miles in diameter, turned night into day. To the accompanying roar of flak—limited by Weise's order to a firing altitude of 14,500 feet—a night battle ensued that cost the British fifty-six four-engined bombers.

A week later the same thing happened. Again the "*Wilde Sau*", on the spot in good time, engaged the raiders directly over Berlin. This time forty-seven Lancasters, Halifaxes and Stirlings were shot down. Despite the enemy's jamming devices which put the whole of the German radar and ground-control systems out of action—and despite his new H2S sets which presented to the bombers a radar impression of the territory over which they were flying—the first three major Berlin raids on the nights of August 23rd and September 1st and 4th cost British Bomber Command 123 four-engined bombers destroyed, plus another 114 damaged. Altogether this represented fourteen per cent of the total number committed. It was a higher loss than ever before, and sustained at the very moment the enemy believed the German defence to be beaten. The long overland route to the capital enabled the controllers to determine in good time that Berlin was the target, and so effect a mass interception at the focus of attack.

Luftwaffe Command reacted with guarded optimism. On August 25th

Milch stated: "We are fully confident that we are hitting the enemy, by day and by night, harder than before. It is the only way we can keep the German arms industry, and the people who man it, going. If we fail, we shall be overrun. . . ."

Even Goering termed the "night of Berlin" a decisive victory for the defence, which had raised the spirits both of the Luftwaffe and the civilian population.

In September Herrmann received instructions to raise his newly formed JG 300 to a division of three *Geschwader*, while he himself was promoted to the rank of Lieutenant-Colonel as its commander. However, each *Geschwader*—JG 300 under Lieutenant-Colonel Kurt Kettner at Bonn-Hangelar, JG 301 under Major Helmut Weinreich at Neubiberg near Munich, and JG 302 under Major Manfred Mössinger at Döberitz—only possesseed enough aircraft to equip one *Gruppe* each. The others had to share the planes of day-fighter *Gruppen*—a double strain that many aircraft failed to withstand, and which adversely affected the serviceability states of all units concerned.

With the advent of autumn weather, the number of clear and cloudless nights became progressively less. Furthermore, British Bomber Command chose to operate in bad weather, knowing that this would hinder the defence. Even so, the "*Wilde Sau*" went on taking off in conditions that previously would have been considered impossible for single-engined fighter missions. Herrmann said in retrospect: "We were obliged to continue harassing Bomber Command in the weather conditions which we had imposed on it. Had we failed to do so, the R.A.F. would have dominated Berlin from the air."

As it was, the Battle of Berlin became a life-and-death struggle which lasted from November 18, 1943, till March 24, 1944. During this period there were no fewer than sixteen major raids on the German capital in implementation of Air Marshal Harris's aim "to wreck Berlin from end to end." "If the U.S.A.A.F. will come in on it," he added, "it will cost between us 400–500 aircraft. It will cost Germany the war."[1]

Harris stated his belief that the mass committal of his best bombers, the four-engined Lancasters, against Berlin and other cities could force a German capitulation by April 1st, 1944.

Such was the massive assault against which the German night-fighters, by means of the "*Wilde Sau*" tactics, had to contend in the bitter winter months of 1943/44. Every means was exploited to improve visibility over the target, and so improve the fighters' chances of success. With the British bombers bombing now through cloud, they could no longer be individually illuminated by searchlights. But with the latter's glare shining through, reinforced by that of the burning city, a glowing curtain was formed against which the bombers, seen from above, were silhouetted like crawling insects. Herrmann even proposed that the citizens should abandon their black-out, and help the cause by shining as much light as possible through their windows and doors. After all, he argued, the British were not now bombing visually, but by their H2S sets. But this suggestion was rejected by *Reichsminister* Goebbels, the *Gauleiter* of Berlin.

A further counter-measure was as follows. Whenever the British Pathfinders dropped their "Christmas trees" to mark the target for the following

[1] *The Strategic Air Offensive Against Germany*, Vol. II, p. 192.

bombers, special German aircraft would drop their own flares to illuminate the assailants from above. The secondary effect of this, as observed by the fighters, was that the bombers no longer attacked *en masse*, but as a strung-out stream. The bombs thus fell scattered, instead of in concentrated groups.

But the successes achieved by the *"Wilde Sau"* in the course of their bad-weather operations were soon overshadowed by the losses they suffered themselves. Single-engined fighters were unable to fly "blind", and even when they were equipped with receiver sets homing them to the radio beacon of an airfield, the landing approach through cloud too often caused crashes. More and more pilots felt compelled to bale out because any landing attempt would be lethal. Sometimes they could not even find their airfield.

Success depended entirely on whether ground direction, in the face of all the enemy's radar-jamming and decoy raids, could interpret the actual target in time. That meant half-an-hour before the attack—enough to enable the *"Wilde Sau"* to concentrate. To determine the target the controllers had to rely purely on their experience, often even on their intuition. And in the prevailing weather conditions their guess was often terribly wide of the mark.

The end result was that the star of the *"Wilde Sau"* waned at almost the same rate as its comet-like ascent. On March 16, 1944, 30 Air Division was already dissolved again, leaving only a few *Gruppen* to pursue the previous operations.

At the same time, however, the twin-engined night-fighters acquired a new lease of life on becoming equipped with the *"Lichtenstein"* SN2 airborne radar sets, which were impervious to "Window". Once more the streams of enemy bombers could be assaulted in the course of their outward and homeward flights. The high-point was reached on March 30, 1944, during an attack on Nuremberg, when British Bomber Command suffered the worst losses in its war-time history—exactly two days before Air Marshal Harris claimed that Germany would be forced to capitulate as a result of his own bomber offensive.

For the time of year the weather, in the evening of March 30, 1944, was exceptionally good—clear, still, and to the west cloudless. At their bases stretching in a wide arc from northern France, across Belgium and Holland, west and north Germany, to Berlin, the night-fighter crews climbed aboard their aircraft and assumed cockpit readiness. Towards midnight the moon would be up, illuminating everything in a gentle light. Better conditions for the defence could not be wished for. If the British really came, they were in for a bad time.

At about 23.00 hours Major-General Josef Schmid, G.O.C. I Fighter Corps, gave the order to take off. Till now only small enemy formations had been operating—Mosquito attacks on night-flying airfields in Holland, and Halifaxes minelaying in the North Sea—and the defence had not been deluded by such diversions. It was waiting for the main attack, heralded by unmistakable signs of preparation across the Channel. Finally the first wave of bombers was reported heading south-east over the sea towards Belgium. Before they made landfall most of the German fighters were airborne to meet them.

The chief of 3 Fighter Division at Deelen, Major-General Walter Grabmann, had ordered his units to take up preliminary positions near radio beacon "Ida", south of Aachen. Those of Colonel Hajo Herrmann's I Fighter Division at Döberitz, and Major-General Max Ibel's 2 Division at Stade flew all the way to beacon "Otto", east of Frankfurt. Whether such measures would be successful depended much on luck; for no one in the divisional operations rooms could predict with any certainty which route the bombers would take, whether they would double back on their tracks, or what feint attacks they had in store.

Meanwhile the fighter crews listened carefully to the "running commentary" broadcast from the ground. Recognising the significance of this, the British had for a long time succeeded in jamming it. But since the strength of the transmissions had been stepped up, it had been coming through again.

"Couriers flying in on a broad front between the mouth of the Scheldt and Ostend," was the commentary now. "Many hundreds. Courier spearhead south of Brussels, course ninety degrees. Height 16,000–22,000 feet."

What were they up to? In which direction would they turn? Their present course would take them close to both "Ida" in the north and "Otto" in the south, at both of which the fighters were concentrated.

This was exactly what happened. For nearly 150 miles, till they were past Fulda, the bombers steered strictly eastwards. Why Bomber Command —master as it was of the technique of diversions and of abrupt changes of course by the main force—had this time ordered the Lancasters and Halifaxes to fly direct, remains a mystery. For the effect was to drive them straight into the night-fighters' arms.

In the last few months the British had been sending Mosquito long-range night-fighters over Germany, with the result that the Me 110s now carried a crew of three. Behind First-Lieutenant Martin Drewes tonight, as he headed across Belgium for the radio beacon "Ida", sat back-to-back his radio operator, Corporal Handke, and a gunner, Sergeant Petz, whose main job was to keep watch aft and guard the crew against being "jumped". His presence now paid off. For though no one expected any action before at least reaching the beacon, Petz suddenly sat up and called: "Hold hard! A four-engined plane just crossed over us. There it goes—off to the left."

The other two quickly swivelled their heads in that direction, but it was too late. The Messerschmitt was flying too fast, and the bomber was lost. But where there was one, there would be others. Drewes turned east and Handke switched on the radar set, the new "*Lichtenstein*" SN 2. As the two tubes lit up—the left one for indicating direction of target, the right one height —Handke in his turn started: there were plots on both, three of them quite distinct, at different bearings and distances. "We are right in the middle of the bomber stream," he called.

To approach the nearest bomber it was necessary to climb somewhat, and whether they found it or not was now up to the radio/radar-operator. He directed the pilot entirely by his set. Finally the indicated range had closed to 1,000 yards. "He must be right ahead of us," said Handke, "and a bit higher."

Suddenly Drewes recognised the four little exhaust flames, and immediately afterwards the dark outline of the bomber silhouetted by the moonlight

111. The rocket-powered Me 163, used towards the war's end as target protection against enemy bombers.

112. The He 162, the "People's Fighter." A hurried design, it made no contact with the enemy.

113. The first jet bomber, the Arado 234B, which became operational from the end of 1944.

114. The Me 262, here equipped as a night-fighter with auxiliary fuel tank and SN-2 antennae.

115. The first turbojet aircraft to fly (on August 27, 1939), the He 178.

against the sky. "Range 600 yards," Handke read out. He could do no more: the SN 2 still did not function inside 500 yards.

Slowly the fighter crept up beneath its prey—a Lancaster. Unsuspecting the latter went on flying straight and level. Drewes adjusted his speed to that of the enemy, and began to climb again. Three pairs of German eyes were riveted aloft on the great menacing shadow that hung there. They were now only fifty yards off, and the small projection representing the air-to-ground radar installation was clearly visible. Otherwise no other modifications presented themselves to their gaze. The Lancaster was still without a ventral gun position, and was thus from below still blind and vulnerable. Were the British really unaware that the majority of their losses were due to attack from that quarter?

Drewes put his eye to the reflector-sight on the cockpit roof and aimed carefully for the enemy's port inboard engine. This sight was adjusted to the two 20-mm cannon behind the cockpit which fired upwards at an angle of seventy-two degrees. It was consequently unnecessary to align the aircraft in order to bring the fixed guns in the nose to bear: the enemy aircraft could equally well be hit from below while flying parallel.

Now, as the pilot pressed the firing button and the "*schräge Musik*", or "slanting music", opened up, hits flashed from the opponent's wing. To aim for the fuselage risked detonating the bomb-load and involving the fighter as well in the ensuing explosion. As it was, the whole wing was soon ablaze, and with a sharp turn to port the German night-fighter pulled out of the danger zone. The Lancaster's death struggle lasted five minutes as it flew briefly onwards as an airborne pyre, then fell away steeply earthwards. The violent explosion of its crash indicated that all its bombs were still on board.

By now Drewes' plane was gaining altitude to the east, where other flaming torches in the sky clearly indicated the route the British bomber stream had taken.

This then was the night on which British Bomber Command sustained its heaviest losses, and German Night-Fighter Command achieved its most outstanding success, in the air battle over Germany. Certainly the weather, together with the timely concentration of the fighter force in the right positions, played a vital part. But the fact remains that this same force, six months after its technical "knock-out", in the summer of 1943, now again represented a crucial threat to the whole continuation of the enemy bomber offensive. That it could do so was thanks, in large measure, to its "*Lichtenstein*" SN 2 airborne radar—and to its "slanting music."

The first British use of "Window" during the battle of Hamburg in late July and early August 1943, besides putting out of action the flak and night-fighter control systems on the ground, likewise jammed the radar sets then carried by the aircraft themselves. All of these at that time operated on a wavelength of fifty-three centimetres. Furthermore the original "*Lichtenstein*" B/C set, with an angle of search of only twenty-four degrees, severely restricted the fighter's scope: if a bomber, once picked up, turned out of the radar beam, the chances of re-contacting it were small. Fortunately the new SN 2 happened to be already in process of development when the B/C was rendered completely useless by the jamming of its wave-length. The new sets combined the advantages of a much wider angle of search (120 degrees) and a 330-cm wave-length which would not be subject to jamming for at least some-time.

After Hamburg, production of the SN 2 was given top priority. By the beginning of October the first night-fighters were equipped with it, and within three months its use had become general. Though the forward aerial array was a good deal more cumbersome, it was a small price to pay for the advantage of no longer having to fly blind.

The operating range of the SN 2 was also considerably superior to that of its predecessor. An opponent could be picked up at a distance slightly in excess of the altitude at which the aircraft was flying: e.g. at a height of 5,500 metres (or 18,000 feet) the range would be about six kilometres (three and three-quarter miles). Thus once the fighter had been fed into the bomber stream by the "running commentary" from the ground, it could do the rest for itself.

In consequence British Bomber Command, which in November, 1943, was confident that it had won air sovereignty over Germany, was by December again suffering heavy losses. In January and February the casualty rate continued to ascend, and finally reached an all-time high in March 1944.

As for the "schräge Musik", this weapon was invented entirely in the field, and though a number of distinguished night-fighter pilots—including Helmut Lent, Heinz-Wolfgang Schnaufer, and the two flying princes, Lippe-Weissenfeld and Sayn-Wittgenstein—have since been credited with fathering the idea, the man who really did so was an N.C.O. armourer called Paul Mahle.

While passing through the weapons test centre at Tarnewitz, Mahle had noticed a Do 217 bomber equipped experimentally with obliquely-firing guns to defend it from enemy fighters. The idea germinated in his mind and left him no peace. If he could only mount cannon like this in the roof of an Me 110, it could attack the enemy four-engined bombers from below in their blind spot without any fear of meeting counter-fire. Though the approach was usually made from below already, the Me 110 could only make the ultimate attack by lining up astern and bringing its fixed, forward-firing guns to bear. By doing so it entered the field of fire of the enemy's quadruple tail guns. From below, moreover, the bomber presented a much larger target and also no armour-plating. Its broad wings carrying the heavy engines and bulky fuel tanks could be set on fire with a minimum of hits.

Improvising with such resources as he could find, Mahle set to work. He anchored two 20-mm MG FF on a platform of hardwood, and mounted the reflector sight on the roof of the cockpit. The pilots of II/NJG 5 at Parchim, to which Mahle then belonged, at first viewed the proceedings with distrust, but then agreed to try out the idea on operations. During the raid on Peenemünde, on the night of August 17/18, 1943, the first two enemy bombers were shot down by this means by Corporal Hölker of 5 Squadron/NJG 5. He was followed by Lieutenant Peter Erhardt of 6 Squadron, with four victories inside thirty minutes. On October 2nd the *Kommandeur*, Captain Manfred Meurer, wrote in his report: "To date II/NJG 5, using the experimental oblique armament, has achieved eighteen victories without loss or damage to themselves. . . ."

The news soon spread among other units. It seemed that a kind of life insurance had been invented, and Paul Mahle became a much sought-after man. He reports: "I soon had many well-known night-fighters amongst my clients, all wanting me to fit the '*schräge Musik*' to their kites."

The inspiration of an armoury flight-sergeant had led to the birth of a new and vital weapon, whose production was finally taken over under the auspices of the Reich Air Ministry itself. Mahle received a written testimonial and 500 marks as inventor's fee. By 1944 there were few night-fighters still flying without the weapon, and the tally of enemy bombers that suddenly burst into flames without their crews knowing what had hit them constantly mounted.

In January the British losses rose to 6.15 per cent of all sorties against Berlin, and to 7.2 per cent during the attacks on Stettin, Brunswick and Magdeburg. But the effectiveness of the German defence was not confined to destruction. Harassed all the way to their distant target with bombs on board, many of the bombers were forced to turn back in a damaged condition. Combat and evasive action scattered the remainder over the sky so that they no longer arrived on target as a coherent force. Much as Berlin and the other cities suffered from the bombing terror of the winter of 1943/44, they were spared the total extinction that had been the enemy's prognosis. To quote from the British official history, *The Strategic Air Offensive against Germany*:

"Bomber Command was compelled, largely by the German night-fighter force, to draw away from its primary target, Berlin, to disperse its effort and to pursue its operations by apparently less efficient means than hitherto. . . . The Battle of Berlin was more than a failure. It was a defeat."[1]

Three major air battles above all led to the turn of the tide. On the night of February 19/20, 1944, Leipzig was the target for 823 four-engined bombers. Although the R.A.F. did its best to confuse the German picture of the air situation by means of decoy courses and diversionary attacks, and although the main bomber stream was headed for Berlin and only at the last moment turned south, the night-fighters remained with it. Seventy-eight bombers failed to return to England.

Secondly, the final attack of the assault on Berlin on March 24th/25th cost Bomber Command seventy-two of its aircraft.

Lastly came the night of March 30th/31st, when the German fighters gathered in moonlight round the two radio beacons to repel the raid on Nuremberg.

Ten minutes after First-Lieutenant Martin Drewes of III/NJG 1 shot down his first Lancaster, he was put on the track of a second by radio-operator Handke's SN 2. The enemy machine was flying at 23,000 feet, and Drewes had a long climb before he was beneath it. He aimed and fired, but after the initial burst the guns jammed. Alerted, the Lancaster first banked then suddenly dived steeply away. Drewes was hard put to it to follow, but finally again got below and waited for his opponent to settle down. Then he attacked again, this time with the nose-guns. The Lancaster at once caught fire, dived and blew up while still in the air, strewing burning particles amongst the woods of the Vogelberg.

"All around the enemy were going down like swatted flies," Handke

[1] pp. 206 and 193.

said in his report. "First-Lieutenant Drewes shot down a third bomber twenty kilometres north of Bamberg, this time again with '*schräge Musik*'."

Gruppen from all parts of Germany took part in the success. First-Lieutenant Helmut Schulte, a squadron commander of II/NJG 5, flew all the way from Mecklenburg and encountered the bomber stream south of Frankfurt. His first attack accounted for one of the British Pathfinders, which exploded on the ground in a cascade of red, green and white flares. Altogether he bagged four, and another four fell to the guns of Lieutenant Dr. Wilhelm Seuss of IV/NJG 5, who had started from Erfurt.

But the greatest operational success of this night was achieved by a crew of I/NJG 6, consisting of First-Lieutenant Martin Becker and his radio-operator Johanssen and rear-gunner Welfenbach. Taking off from Mainz-Finthen at 23.45, they made contact twenty-five minutes later with a formation of Halifax bombers east of Bonn. Between 00.20 and 00.50 they shot down no less than six of them—helped as they were by the flaming wrecks which marked the route of this northerly wing of the bomber stream over Wetzlar, Giessen and Alsfeld to Fulda. At that point Becker was obliged to return to base, but taking off again he re-contacted the bombers on their return flight, and at 03.15 destroyed another of them over Luxembourg. That made his score seven in a single night.

The war diary of I Fighter Corps records that on this night it despatched 246 sorties by single- and twin-engined fighters. The single-engined "*Wilde Sau*" failed to engage the enemy owing to the fact that Nuremberg was announced too late as the target. On the other hand the twin-engined fighters claimed 101 bombers destroyed, plus six "probables". British sources stated that of 795 Halifaxes and Lancasters committed ninety-five failed to return and another seventy-one were severely damaged, twelve of these becoming write-offs on landing.

It was the biggest night air battle of World War II, and the total loss of twelve per cent of the operating force was too high even for British Command. The night air offensive was suspended, its failure being plain. But if the German night-fighters had won their greatest victory of the war, it was also their last.

6. The Last Stand

Despite the terrible destruction of German cities, despite all the hardship and death it brought to the civilian population and industrial workers—whose ordeal was now often worse than that of the soldiers at the front—it was not, as we have seen, area bombing by night that struck the vital blow at German survival.[1]

This mission was accomplished to a far greater extent by the selective and precision bombing of the American Eighth Air Force in daylight. By careful choice of target, this first blocked the bottle-necks of armaments production, and finally brought the whole German war machine to a standstill.

"It is better to cause a high degree of destruction in a few really essential

---

[1] This is not accepted in the U.K. "In the last year of the war Bomber Command played a major part in the almost complete destruction of whole vital segments of German oil production, in the virtual dislocation of her communications system and in the elimination of other important activities."—*The Strategic Air Offensive Against Germany*, Vol. III, p. 288.—*Translator's Note*.

industries or services than to cause a small degree of destruction in many industries", the American Committee of Operations Analysts had postulated as long ago as March 8, 1943. And to this policy the U.S. bombers had adhered. During the whole of 1943 the B–17 Fortresses and B–24 Liberators of General Ira C. Eaker's command in England had pitted themselves against military and war-industrial targets on the Continent.

The year had shown that heavy losses were incurred by the bombers whenever their targets lay beyond the range of their escorting fighters. And in 1943 the whole of Germany was beyond the latter's range. It had become clear that the defensive potential of the multi-gunned Fortresses had been overrated. Though both the B–17s and B–24s flew in close-packed "combat boxes", staggered vertically, the undaunted German fighters succeeded time after time in separating individual bombers from their boxes, then hunting them down after they had been deprived of the combined fire-power of their fellows.

The U.S.A.A.F. had been warned against such tactics by the R.A.F., whose argument had apparently been proved. Both the British and the Germans, early in the war, had learnt the lesson that bombers without fighter protection could only penetrate deeply over enemy country at the cost of losses which in the long run became insupportable. In 1943 the Americans had still to learn the lesson. In August and October, particularly, the two daylight raids on Schweinfurt, heart of the German ball-bearing industry, had been opposed with such fury that afterwards a long dotted line of crashed bombers marked their route.

October 14, 1943 was perhaps the blackest day in the whole history of the strategic air offensive against Germany. The *"dicker Hund"* (as the bomber stream was dubbed in German fighter parlance) was assailed almost without respite by some 300 single- and twin-engined fighters: Me 109s, Fw 190s and Me 110s. Of the 291 Fortresses that took off for Schweinfurt, 220 forced their way resolutely to the target and unloaded 478 tons of bombs. But no less than sixty never regained their English bases. Their shattered, burnt-out hulks formed a trail stretching hundreds of miles across Belgium, Luxembourg, Germany and France. Seventeen others reached England so severely damaged that they were beyond repair. Together they represented a total loss of over twenty-six per cent of the operating force, and in addition a further 121 aircraft had been less severely damaged. It was clear that no air force in the world could afford such losses and continue to operate.

Thus the lessons of the air war to date were learnt again and underlined— namely that a dedicated fighter force, acting in defence of its own country, would always retain air superiority against formations of daylight bombers, even if the latter's defensive armament (like that of the B–17s) numbered no less than thirteen extra-heavy machine guns which, multiplied many times over by the combat box, represented a veritable barrage. Without their own fighter escort, they were still not a match for enemy fighters.

Yet the American reaction to this initial failure of their daylight offensive differed from that of the British and the Germans earlier in the war. Unlike them, they did not turn to bombing under the protection of darkness. Rather, they sought the solution in a long-range fighter, capable of escorting and protecting their bomber formations right into the heart of Germany. In 1943 such a fighter was not available. Although the flying and combat capabilities of the tough single-seater P–47 Thunderbolt matched those of its Messerschmitt and Focke-Wulf opponents, its endurance was inadequate for long-range escort. In the summer and autumn of 1943, despite a 108-gallon auxiliary tank beneath the fuselage, the Thunderbolts were obliged to turn back at the German frontier and leave the bombers to their fate.

The first attempt to solve the problem was by means of the twin-fuselage P–38 Lightning, which began long-range escort duty in November 1943. In the end this fighter, with two auxiliary tanks beneath the wings, could reach Berlin. But it was a twin-engined machine, and the outcome, as already stated, was much the same as the Germans had experienced with the Me 110. Being somewhat heavier, and less manoeuvrable, the Lightnings could not hold their own with the German single-seater Me 109s and Fw 190s.

To find a fighter with all the necessary attributes, the Americans had to look further. Finally they settled on a type which, even in 1942, had still been completely out of favour: the P–51 Mustang.

The history of this fighter had been unusual. Originally ordered by the R.A.F. in 1940 from the North American Aviation factory, it had been developed and constructed for use in Britain. The first specimeris were delivered in autumn, 1941, but the R.A.F. was disappointed. It was found that the Mustang's maximum speed declined in inverse proportion to its altitude. At 15,000 feet—the height at which many of the decisive combats of the Battle of Britain had been fought—it was markedly inferior to the latest versions of Europe's best single-seater fighters, the Spitfire and the Messerschmitt. With no conventional role possible for it in Fighter Command, the R.A.F. converted it into a fighter-bomber.

The British did, however, discover where the Mustang's failing lay. Whereas the strength and aerodynamic quality of the frame left nothing to be desired, its Allison engine, developing a mere 1,150 h.p., was simply inadequate to power it. Trials were therefore carried out, both in England and America, with Merlin engines, and finally the American Packard-Merlin V–1650 was adopted. As a result the P–51's performance increased quite astonishingly. Its speed and manoeuvrability suddenly exceeded those of both the German fighter types; and moreover its endurance permitted it to fly from a base in England right over central Germany. The Mustang had become the very escort fighter for which the bombers of the Eighth A.A.F. had for so long waited in vain.

At the outset of 1944 the Americans established a new high command for the conduct of strategic air operations over Europe: H.Q. U.S. Strategic Air Forces (USSTAF), under the command of General Carl Spaatz. New commanders were also appointed to the individual Air Forces. In England Lieutenant-General James H. Doolittle took over the Eighth from General Eaker, while the Fifteenth, newly formed in Italy, came under the command of Major-General Nathan F. Twining. Together they formed the two forces between which Germany was to be crushed. For the strategic objective of the year 1944 was not in doubt: top priority was the destruction of the Luftwaffe.

"The German Air Force had on occasion taken heavy toll of the U.S. bombers", runs the official history of the United States Army Air Forces in World War II. "As German fighter strength in the west increased, it had become apparent that an all-out attack on Nazi air power would be a necessary preliminary to any successful strategic bombardment campaign and to the great invasion of Europe planned for the spring of 1944."[1]

Thus the Allies, at the turn of the year 1943–4, found themselves in a similar position to that of the Germans in the summer of 1940: no invasion could take place before air superiority had been achieved. Three and a half years previously the German Luftwaffe had failed to win the Battle of Britain, and Hitler had been forced to postpone the date of his invasion. Finally he gave up the whole idea of a landing in the hope of first subduing the Soviet giant.

The importance that the Allies, in their turn, now attached to the elimination of the Luftwaffe as a precondition of further enterprises is underlined in the New Year message sent by the U.S.A.A.F. Chief of Staff, General Arnold, to his commanders in Europe: "It is a conceded fact that OVER-LORD and ANVIL will not be possible unless the German Air Force is destroyed. Therefore, my personal message to you—this is a MUST—is to *'Destroy the Enemy Air Force wherever you find them, in the air, on the ground and in the factories'*."[2]

The objective was clear. Over 1,000 four-engined daylight bombers stood at readiness, and for the first time there were available long-range fighters capable of escorting them all the way to their targets. The only remaining requirement was a week of continuous fine weather and good target visibility. Then Operation ARGUMENT—the destruction of every German factory that produced fighters—would be launched.

The weather over Germany cleared for the first time on January 11, 1944. As the clouds parted, the countryside was illuminated by the winter sunshine. And though the improvement was only of short duration, the Eighth Air Force struck at once. Towards noon no less than 663 bombers took off and were directed in three large formations all towards the same target: the fighter production region of Brunswick-Halberstadt-Aschersleben.

This target area lay on the direct air route to Berlin, from which it was less than a hundred miles distant. As the bombers' course was frantically plotted in the German operations rooms, for a long time it seemed they were headed straight for the capital. Without more ado the fighter *Gruppen* were scrambled.

The Americans, however, had already begun to experience difficulties. Though visibility over the target was good, England had been wrapped in cloud, and the process of take-off and forming up had cost the bombers valuable time. Now, as they flew on, the weather became still worse, and General Doolittle decided to recall the second and third formations in midflight. A contributory factor in this decision was, no doubt, the violent Messerschmitt and Focke-Wulf attacks to which his force had already been subjected after only reaching the Dutch-German frontier. For at this stage the Americans did not yet possess enough long-range fighters to escort all the bombers all the way.

On turning back over western Germany the Fortresses and Liberators of the second and third waves consequently dropped their bombs on alternative targets or simply in the open country, and made off home. That left

---

[1] *The Army Air Forces in World War II*, Vol. III, p. xi.
[2] Ibid., p. 8.

only the first formation—consisting of 238 bombers out of the original 663 —to push on to the target. But on this day there was only a single fighter group—forty-nine Mustangs—to escort them there and back. The appearance of these over central Germany, hitherto far beyond the range of Allied fighters, must have come as quite as shock to the German fighter command. For the first time its Me 109s and Fw 190s, whose orders were to go strictly for the bombers, were confronted over their own country by equal, or even superior, opponents. But there were only forty-nine of them, and they could not be everywhere at once. Furthermore, their rendezvous with the bombers had been premature, and their fuel was getting low. These factors, together with skilful control of the German fighters by their ground stations, permitted the latter to pierce the screen and once again assault the bombers.

Three German fighter divisions were involved: No. 1, centred at Döberitz near Berlin and commanded by Colonel Hajo Herrmann, inventor of the "*Wilde Sau*" night-fighting tactics; No. 2, centred at Stade on the Elbe and commanded by Major-General Ibel, who had for long been *Kommodore* of JG 27; No. 3, centred at Deelen in Holland and commanded by the veteran Colonel Walter Grabmann of twin-engined fighter fame, who had once flown the unequal Me 110 against Spitfires over Britain. Together, the three of them today had 207 single- and twin-engined fighters to launch against the enemy bomber stream.

And today, once more, the bloody scenes of the summer and autumn of 1943 were re-enacted. Despite their efforts, the bombers failed to ward off the attacks. Their crews even reported a seeming improvement in German tactics, and stated that their enemy was better armed than previously. Whenever they closed into compact formation to produce an impenetrable screen of fire, the German twin-engined fighters would fire their rockets into the box from a safe distance, and score every time. If, on the other hand, the bombers loosened their formation, down came the Me 109s and Fw 190s on their now more vulnerable opponents.

174 bombers were billed to attack the AGO works in Aschersleben, one of the Fw 190 production centres; but before they reached this target thirty-four of them, or twenty per cent, had already been shot down. The total loss suffered by the Eighth Air Force, on this first 1944 attempt to knock out the centres of German fighter production, was sixty heavy bombers, plus five fighters. On their side, the Americans claimed to have shot down 152 German fighters. The actual figure—as can be read in the war diary of I Fighter Air Corps—was thirty-nine.

So far there could be no more convincing evidence of the fact that the German fighter arm, far from being knocked out, had utilised the winter respite to gather greater strength than it possessed before. Yet any thoughts of ultimate success were an illusion. The appearance of the Mustang, with its incredible radius of action, caused the men responsible for German fighter operations and fighter production—above all *General der Jagdflieger* Adolf Galland and *Reichsminister* Albert Speer—to view the future with dismay.

For there was one element in the German situation that the planners of the Allied strategic air offensive never dreamed of taking into account. This was that the German fighter arm had to contend not only with its enemies in the air, but with its own ultimate command. Even now, Hitler and Goering were not interested in fighters, but only bombers. At the hour of crucial danger to their country their minds were bent, not on its defence, but on vengeful raids on England.

As already reported, the R.A.F.'s raids of annihilation on Hamburg in July, 1943, had shaken Luftwaffe Command into a *volte-face*: in future top priority was to be given to the defence of Germany. Yet this decision was never accepted by Hitler. To his warlords Speer could only justify his mounting fighter production figures by diplomatic talk and subterfuge. Whenever Hitler took a decision, it was at the expense of the fighters. The worst was his "unalterable decision" to adapt the first jet fighter of the world, the outstanding Me 262, as a bogus "blitz" bomber. This product of the Messerschmitt factory was the very fighter that would have made all the difference to Luftwaffe Fighter Command in the decisive air battles of 1944. When it was ultimately available as such, it was in ever-decreasing numbers, and far too late.

Convincing proof of the decline in the fighter defence of Germany is seen in the aircraft availability figures for February 1944: 345 single-engined and 128 twin-engined machines. Though production had meanwhile greatly increased, these figures were virtually the same as in autumn, 1943. The explanation is that the other fronts—to the east, south and on the English Channel—had swallowed the rest.

Such were the omens for the Luftwaffe when the Americans opened their "Big Week" of systematically planned attacks on the aircraft factories, with the object of striking the final death-blow to the German fighter arm. By February it had become "a matter of such urgency that General Spaatz and General Anderson (his deputy for operations) were willing to take more than ordinary risks in order to complete the task, including the risk of exceptional losses that might result from missions staged under conditions of adverse base weather". On February 8th, Spaatz directed that "ARGUMENT must be completed by 1st March, 1944".[1]

That the German side was fully aware of the danger threatening the fighter production and assembly works is revealed by the man finally responsible for all air supply, *Generalluftzeugmeister* Field-Marshal Erhard Milch. In an interview with his departmental chiefs on February 15th, a few days before "Big Week" began, he protested strongly at the number of brand new aircraft standing on the factory airfields of Messerschmitt. "If the enemy strikes there," said Milch, "even the highest production figures will be of no avail. The machines will be destroyed before they ever reach the front!"

He promptly ordered the aircraft to be dispersed and camouflaged in the adjacent woods, and their passage through the Luftwaffe's technical trial centres to be speeded up. But before his orders could be carried out, the Eighth Air Force struck. Milch, who had left Berlin on a fresh tour of inspection to various factories, found himself trapped amidst a hail of bombs, and confronted again and again by smoking ruins.

On February 19th the USSTAF meteorologists at last predicted a continuous period of favourable weather. A wedge of high pressure, moving slowly south from the Baltic, cleared the clouds over Germany. It was the moment the bombers had awaited for months. Despite the difficulties of getting under way—England was still wrapped in a 5,000-foot thick girdle of

[1] *The Army Air Forces in World War II*, Vol. III, p. 31.

cloud—and despite the scruples of General Twining, whose Fifteenth Air Force was engaged in the struggle for the Anzio bridgehead in Italy, on February 20th General Spaatz spoke his three decisive words: "Let 'em go!"

At this moment over 700 four-engined bombers of the R.A.F. had just returned from their night attack on Leipzig, less seventy-eight Lancasters and Halifaxes which had been shot down in flames after violent combat with German night-fighters. But already the engines of nearly 1,000 other bombers were warming up on their English airfields: sixteen combat wings of Fortresses and Liberators, and in addition seventeen American fighter groups comprising Lightnings, Thunderbolts and Mustangs, plus sixteen fighter squadrons of the R.A.F., with Spitfires and Mustangs also. Finally 941 heavy bombers and over 700 fighters crossed the Channel and advanced in a mighty stream towards Germany on what was, to date, the mightiest strategic air attack in history.

The targets, once again, were the various·works of the aircraft industry in central Germany, between Brunswick and Leipzig: ATG and Erla (Leipzig); Heiterblick & Möckau, and Lutter-Miag (Brunswick), Junkers (Bernburg, Halberstadt and Aschersleben), and many others. One special formation was to diverge from the main route, cross Denmark and the Baltic, and fly as far as Tutov in Mecklenburg, and even Posen.

All the target factories were hit, and some severely damaged. The Americans, who, after their experiences on January 11th, anticipated a fresh onslaught from the German fighters, breathed a sigh of relief. This time their strong fighter escort, tangling in countless dogfights with the Messerschmitts and Focke-Wulfs, mostly prevented the latter from getting at the bombers. Although the Americans had deliberately taken a risk, and "exceptional losses" were expected, the end result was that out of the whole mighty armada only twenty-one bombers failed to return to their English bases. The American "Big Week" had started well. For the first time the German fighters had been vanquished.

The following night R.A.F. Bomber Command was again in action, with 600 aircraft operating against Stuttgart, another centre of the German aviation industry. Then, hardly had the morning of February 21st dawned, than the Americans got ready for their next blow. Again the two Lutter-Miag factories were the target, plus numerous Luftwaffe depots and airfields.

On the 22nd the assault on German fighter production was stepped up even more. For now General Twining's Fifteenth Air Force in Italy was in a position to take a hand. While his bombers attacked the Messerschmitt works at Regensburg from the south, General Doolittle's Eighth Air Force again attacked the factories in central Germany, and also Gotha and Schweinfurt.

But on this day many things went wrong. Over England the cloud curtain was so thick that a number of bombers collided before they had penetrated it. Above the clouds many combat wings failed to assemble, and others, straggling across the Channel in bad weather, likewise never managed to form up. There was nothing for it, in the case of the 2nd and 3rd Bombardment Divisions, but to call off the whole operation, and order their bombers back to base.

That left only the 1st Division to carry out the raid, and it was given a hot reception. The protracted endeavour of the Americans to form up over England had given plenty of time for German fighter control to make its defensive dispositions. In his underground operations room at Deelen in Holland, Colonel Grabmann, commanding 3 Fighter Division, tensely studied the enemy movements in the sky steadily reported by radio intercepts and radar. It was then up to him to sense the enemy's intentions and course, and so throw in his fighters with maximum effect. In the event he hit the bull's-eye. Ordering off JG 1 and JG 11 from Westphalia, he brought them against the enemy in good time and almost simultaneously. Hardly had the Fortresses crossed the German frontier than they were set upon from every side.

For the Americans it was an unexpected development. Recently the German fighters had concentrated exclusively on target defence, or at most made themselves felt during the last sixty miles of the approach. But today they attacked much further to the west, when thanks to the wretched conditions governing their departure the bombers were scattered all over the sky. Furthermore, apart from a few escorting Thunderbolts, the American fighter defence was not yet on the scene. Rendezvous with the Mustangs was due to take place only later, to repel the expected German attack in the target area. Thus the change of tactics on the part of the Germans suddenly presented the Messerschmitts once again with a golden opportunity.

The fiery trail of combat extended over hundreds of miles. From the Rhineland, over Westphalia and Hannover, and right to the Harz mountains, forty-one four-engined bombers went down in flames. Of the initial force of 430, most of them recalled, a mere ninety-nine finally reached their primary targets. Only the Ju 88 night-fighter factories in Bernburg and Aschersleben were effectively hit; the others escaped damage.

As for the operations against Gotha and Schweinfurt, they never took place, for the force intended to attack them had been recalled. That left Major-General Huth's 7 Air Division, whose mission was to sweep the skies of southern Germany, with a free hand to oppose the Fifteen Air Force's attack from the south. Though the Messerschmitt works at Regensburg were bombed, from this force too another fourteen bombers failed to return to Italy. This time the American pincers movement had malfunctioned.

Thus the success of "Big Week" and Operation ARGUMENT still hung in the balance. On February 23rd, bad weather again set in, and the Americans used the pause to rest their crews, who after three days of uninterrupted operations sorely needed it. In Berlin Field-Marshal Milch, newly returned from his tour of inspection amongst the bombs, stated his conclusions:

"The situation of our leading production centres," he said, "is highly strained, not to use a stronger word . . . The raids of the last weeks and months have been concentrated almost exclusively on our single- and twin-engined fighter output, and in the last few days have been especially intense . . . In July last year, for the first time, we achieved an output of 1,000 single- and 150–200 twin-engined fighters, the latter figure including night-fighters. By November we hoped to reach some 2,000 and 250 respectively. We were not successful because each heavy air attack reduced production. First, raids were made on the Me 109 factories in Regensburg and Wiener Neustadt . . . then came a series on the Fw 190 works.

"Now these factories have been hit again, and in addition our night-fighter plants, such as those of Lutter-Miag producing the Me 110, and the Junkers ones producing the Ju 88/Ju 188 night-fighters at Bernberg, Halberstadt and Aschersleben . . . The output of the Erla works at Leipzig should this month have been some 450 aircraft. Though they came through the raids of Saturday night, February 19th/20th, well, next day production here too was seriously compromised . . . What has happened has reduced output at Erla by some 350 machines, at Messerschmitt by another 150–200, and at Wiener Neustadt also by 200 machines less than planned for . . .

"In this month of February our output should have been 2,000 fighters, but there is now no hope of that figure being attained. We can be happy if we produce 1,000–1,200 . . . As for the March figures," Milch concluded, "I calculate that, far from reaching 2,000, they may well sink below 800."

Had Milch foreseen the battering his fighter production centres were to take in the next few days, his prognostication might have been gloomier still. But as already indicated it turned out to be over-pessimistic.

After their day of rest, on February 24th over 600 bombers, from England and Italy, again set course simultaneously for Germany. This time the pincers closed. From the south eighty-seven Fortresses attacked the Daimler-Benz aero-engine works in Styria (eastern Austria). Against the invaders Major-General Huth sent up both his fighter Geschwader—JG 3, stationed in Franken, and JG 27, based in Austria. Once again the German fighters showed that they had lost none of their hitting power. The rearmost combat box was completely annihilated, all ten of the Fortresses that comprised it falling victim to the single-engined fighters' 20-mm guns and the Me 110s' rockets. Altogether the Fifteenth Air Force lost seventeen bombers, twenty per cent of its entire force.

Yet while the battle over Austria raged, the Eighth A.A.F.'s bomber stream was heading from the west to Schweinfurt and Gotha, thereby confronting German fighter command with a difficult situation. To close the existing gap, the north German divisions were obliged to send their units south. This in turn opened up a gap in the north, thereby permitting a second assault wave of the Eighth A.A.F. to reach Tutow, Kreising and Posen in the north-east almost unmolested.

Though the Schweinfurt-Gotha wave lost forty-four bombers out of the 477 sent out, it hit the Gothaer Waggonfabrik (producers of the Me 110) and the ball-bearing works hard. Scarcely had the sun set when the attack was followed by a night raid of R.A.F. Bomber Command. For by now Sir Arthur Harris was ready to co-ordinate his Lancasters with the Americans in a day-and-night "double blow". There was no missing the target. Schweinfurt was still burning from the daylight raid twelve hours before as the 700 Lancasters rained down their bombs. But although the ball-bearing factory took another heavy battering, the overall drop in production was actually less than after the 1943 raids, owing to the fact that about a third of the plant had meanwhile been dispersed.

Was Air Marshal Harris, after all, right? He had always been highly sceptical about precision raids on key industries as a method of winning the war. As for the ball-bearing industry, he declared: "I am confident that the Germans have long ago made every possible effort to disperse so vital a production. Therefore, even if Schweinfurt is entirely destroyed, I remain confident that we shall hear no more of the disastrous effects on German war production now so confidently prophesied."[1]

Yet Harris found few people in England who shared his opinion. The

[1] Webster/Frankland: *The Strategic Air Offensive Against Germany, 1939-1945*, Vol. II, p. 65.

divergence was clearly expressed by the Chief of Air Staff, Sir Charles Portal:
"If it had been tactically possible to concentrate one quarter of our total
bombs dropped on Germany upon any one of several classes of target, e.g.,
oil, ball-bearings, aero-engines or airframe factories, and possibly many
others, the war would have by now been won . . . If we can pick a key
industry the result per ton of bombs must inevitably be vastly increased."[1]

Whatever Harris's opinion, on January 14, 1944, a combined directive of
the British and American Air Staffs ordered him "to attack Schweinfurt as his
first priority".[2] There followed the "double blow" of February 24th/25th.
And twenty-four hours later one even more devastating was struck. For
"Big Week" was not yet ended. In the battle to come both the scale and
destructiveness of the bombardment reached their zenith—as did the desperate attempts of the defence to inflict crippling losses.

On February 25th, weather favourable to the offensive extended all the way
to southern Germany. Above all, target visibility was excellent. USSTAF
accordingly decided on a knock-out blow to two main targets of ARGU-
MENT that hitherto had suffered little: the Messerschmitt works in Regensburg and Augsburg.

In his operations bunker at Schleissheim near Munich the commander
of 7 Air Division, Major-General Huth, was faced with two bomber streams
converging simultaneously from south and west on the common target of
Regensburg. He decided to pit the bulk of his fighters against the southern
force comprising 176 aircraft. From that direction no American fighter
escort had today been detected, and in the past the bombers had often flown
unprotected. He was justified in his assumption: thirty-three bombers
were shot down—again one fifth of the operating force.

The force from the west was a good deal stronger, and accordingly suffered
less. Fighters from north and central Germany tangled in mortal conflict
with the escorting Mustangs, and seldom got through to the *"dicker Hund"*
(the bombers). Of these the Eighth A.A.F. lost only thirty-one out of 738,
though the combined loss of sixty-four Fortresses and Liberators for the day
was still serious. The overall damage wrought by over 800 bombers was,
however, massive. Their bombs fell on Regensburg-Prüfening and Obertraubling, on Augsburg, Stuttgart and Furth. At the Messerschmitt works,
thanks to the excellent target visibility, hardly one stone remained on top of
another. The workshops of what had long been the world's most famous
fighter, the Me 109, were reduced to heaps of rubble. In Augsburg a night
raid by the R.A.F. completed the destruction.

With this final blow at German fighter production, "Big Week" came to
an end. The success of the enterprise was proclaimed in every Allied newspaper. At the headquarters of the Strategic Air Forces the reconnaissance
photographs showed everywhere nothing but ruins. Yet had the objective
really been attained?

In Luftwaffe Command consternation reigned; there was despair amongst
the leaders of the aviation industry. At the ministry of war production, and
the office of *Generalluftzeugmeister* Milch, conference followed conference.
Orders were issued to all concerned to take extreme measures to save the
remnants of the vital fighter production industry and get it going again.

[1] Ibid., pp. 67–8.   [2] Ibid., p. 69.

Initial reports from the individual plants encouraged little hope. At the Gotha works the destruction was such as to prevent all production for six to seven weeks. Yet at Erla in Leipzig 160 damaged aircraft, salvaged from the ruined workshops, were in most cases found, astonishingly, to be repairable. At Regensburg the Messerschmitt factory was so devastated that it was first decided not to resurrect it, but start up afresh on another site. Then it was discovered that the vital machine tools had suffered less than had been feared, many needing simply to be freed from the rubble that had fallen on them. Four months later the works had fully regained their former output. As for Messerschmitt, Augsburg, it resumed production on March 9th—i.e. only two weeks after the "double blow".

Thus the urgent measures produced astounding results. The dispersal of essential plant, already begun on the initiative of the firms themselves, was now officially ordered by Speer's ministry. A final consequence of "Big Week" was a complete re-organisation at the top, in Berlin. On March 1st, the ministry of war production was given its own "fighter staff", led by the energetic official, Saur. It meant that fighter production was removed from the competence of the Reich Air Ministry (RLM), which had always allocated over-much capacity to bombers.

Reichsminister Speer expressed his conviction that unless the armaments industry were effectively protected, particularly against the dreaded daylight precision raids of the U.S.A.A.F., it would collapse. Despite the destruction wrought by "Big Week", Saur's task was to boost fighter production to the limit. New programmes were drawn up, labour redirected from other work, material allocations raised. Finally, help was rendered by the Allied Air Staffs themselves. Temporarily convinced that German fighter production could never recover from the blows it had so recently received, they suspended further attacks upon it for some time.

An idea of the rapidity with which the industry recovered can be seen from the following production tables:

(a) *Single-engined Fighters*

Month (1944)	Me 109	Fw 190	Total
February	905 (80)[1]	209 (108)[2]	1114 (188)
March	934 (93)	373 (314)	1307 (407)
April	1011 (44)	461 (344)	1472 (388)
May	1278 (40)	482 (367)	1760 (407)
June	1603 (140)	689 (457)	2292 (597)

(b) *Twin-engined Fighters*

Month (1944)	Me 110/410	Ju 88	Do 217[3]	He 219[3]	Total
February	125	92	5	5	227
March	226	85	19	11	343
April	340	185	25	24	574
May	365	241	8	13	627
June	335	271	15	15	636

[1] Figures in brackets denote variants of the Me 109 designed for close reconnaissance.
[2] Figures in brackets denote variants of the Fw 190 used for ground attack.
[3] Night-fighter versions.

The above tables clearly indicate that the monthly output of 2,000 single-seater fighters, as required by the Luftwaffe, had already been reached by mid-1944. And in the second half of the year Saur and his team pushed production even higher. "Big Week" notwithstanding, deliveries in 1944 were the highest of any year of the war, reaching a total of 25,285 fighters. The fact that soon the German defence could no longer withstand the on-slaught of the strategic bomber offensive was thus not due to failure in the supply of fighter aircraft. It was due to something else.

The bitter contest for air sovereignty over Germany had cost the defence severe losses in aircrew. Each passing week saw the American fighter escort grow stronger. With the Mustangs, especially, outclassing their opponents in speed and manoeuvrability, even experienced German fighter pilots had to take a risk if they hoped to prevail. All too many veterans were shot down, and their replacements were of indifferent quality. With no priority claims on personnel, Luftwaffe fighter command had to take what it got; and with time pressing, adequate training had to go by the board. Thrown into battle when they were only half ready, the young recruits were obliged to take off in all kinds of weather, and to penetrate cloud often thousands of feet thick; though blind-flying was at a premium, it was something few pilots had learnt. Above the clouds the commanders strove desperately to gather their flocks into formations of adequate size and hitting power, and by the time they succeeded, the Thunderbolts and Mustangs, as like as not, already enjoyed an altitude advantage. As German losses mounted alarmingly, so did the faith in their own command of those engaged in the hopeless struggle progressively decline.

"Between January and April 1944 our daytime fighters lost over 1,000 pilots", declared the *General der Jagdflieger*, Adolf Galland, in a report to the RLM. "They included our best squadron, *Gruppe* and *Geschwader* commanders. Each incursion of the enemy is costing us some fifty aircrew. The time has come when our weapon is in sight of collapse."

The German fighter arm nevertheless made a last desperate effort to rob the Americans of air sovereignty over its own country. On March 3rd, some P-38 Lightnings appeared over the Reich capital of Berlin in brilliant sunshine. A day later a formation of the Eighth A.A.F. took off under fighter escort for the same target, but with bad ground visibility only twenty-nine Fortresses got through. On March 6th the weather finally improved, and 660 four-engined bombers took off for the capital, with the intention of forcing the German defence into combat. Confident in the ever-thickening screen of their escort, the Americans reckoned to knock out the German fighter arm in the air as well as on the ground. "It was hoped," runs the relevant passage from the history of the American air war, "that the German fighters would react quickly to any threat to Berlin and would in the ensuing air battles suffer heavy losses . . . If there was any target for which the G.A.F. would fight, surely that target was Berlin."[1]

On September 7, 1940, working on the same hypothesis, the Luftwaffe had switched its attack to London in the course of the Battle of Britain. Using the British capital as a bait, it had likewise planned to confront the careful tactics of R.A.F. Fighter Command with the challenge of a decisive

[1] *The Army Air Forces in World War II*, Vol. III, p. 48.

battle. Now, three and a half years later, the route to Berlin throbbed to the droning of bombers, while the condensation trails of fighters in endless combat streaked the sky. For the German defence had accepted the challenge. It flew to meet the massed bombers and their swarms of escort fighters with new tactics of their own, launching its attacks in formations of *Geschwader* strength, or sixty to eighty aircraft at a time.

Such a combat formation usually consisted of three *Gruppen*, of which only one was earmarked for direct attack upon the bombers. The role of the others was to engage in battle with the Mustangs and Thunderbolts. Within a few weeks the Germans had also found an antidote to the Mustang's superiority in flight by equipping at least a proportion of their Messerschmitts with a high-altitude engine, the Daimler-Benz 605 AS. So equipped, the Me 109 could again outstrip its opponents, particularly in the climb. It could also attain a higher altitude—which, in the skirmishing for position, was of paramount importance.

Three such high-altitude *Gruppen*—III/JG 1 at Paderborn, II/JG 11 at Hustedt, and I/JG 5 at Herzogenaurach in the south—were detailed, when an approaching enemy armada was reported, to wait high up in the sky. Then, swooping down on the American escort fighters, they would engage them and draw them off, thus leaving the bombers open to attack by the German heavy fighters—above all the armour-plated Fw 190, now with four cannon and two machine-guns.

The high-altitude version of the Me 109 of course carried no auxiliary fuel tank, which meant that its endurance was very limited. Further to reduce its weight, it carried no outboard guns. Yet it was worth it. One pilot reported: "We fly at 33,000, 35,000 and sometimes up to 37,000 feet, while the highest the enemy can reach is 30,000. Down swoops a flight, knocks one of them out, and before the others have seen what has happened, we are poised above them again."

The success of such tactics was, however, limited. It was not always possible to draw off enough of the American fighter escort to provide conditions in which the heavy and somewhat clumsy German single-engined fighters, or the Me 110s with their rockets, could operate. As time went on, the task became more difficult in proportion as the number of American fighters increased.

Yet on March 6th, there again developed one of the most bitterly contested air battles of the war. Against the bomber stream the Germans sent up some 200 single- and twin-engined fighters, and the conflict lasted for hours. In the end the wrecks of sixty-nine American bombers and eleven fighters dotted the countryside, but the German losses were worse: eighty fighters. Nearly half the defending force was either destroyed or so damaged that the machines had force-landed. The war of attrition had reached the mortal phase when neither courage nor skill availed further.

Two days later, on March 8th, when the Americans again sent a force of 590 bombers and 801 fighters against Berlin, the impact of the German defence was notably weaker. Though admittedly at a cost of thirty-seven bombers and seventeen fighters, the assailants attacked their targets with deadly precision—the Erkner ball-bearing factory, in particular, suffering complete destruction. A third raid on the capital, on March 22nd, by 669 bombers, was only lightly opposed. Of the twelve bombers lost, flak claimed the most, fighters none.

Over south Germany, too, the German fighter arm suffered a crippling blow. On March 16th, another bomber stream of the Eighth A.A.F. was assailed near Augsburg by forty-three Me 110s of ZG 76. As soon, however, as the first bombers went down in flames, the American escort was on the spot. Far swifter and more manoeuvrable than their opponents, they had them at their mercy. Twenty-six Me 110s were shot down, and the rest hunted back to their airfields. After this disaster III/ZG 76 was disbanded, leaving the other *Gruppen* to be re-equipped, shortly afterwards, with a new type of aircraft, the Me 410. The old Me 110—the *Zerstörer*—with which the Luftwaffe had entered the war far back in 1939, could at last no longer show itself in the German skies.

In March, April and May, 1944, the daylight offensive continued, with only occasional opposition when conditions were especially favourable for the defence. Mostly the Americans found no more German fighters in the air. The situation has been summed up by the former commander of 3 Fighter Division, Major-General Grabmann, in his contribution to a post-war study of the defence of Germany: "The Americans had reached the stage of enjoying complete air mastery over the Reich. The total number of fighters we still had left represented, at best, less than half the number of escort fighters the Americans used on a single raid. The latter thus no longer had to bother about special manoeuvres to mislead the defence. Their fighter preponderance was such that, in fine weather particularly, they could send out whole formations in advance to shatter the Germans before they were in position ..." Galland holds, too, that the transition of the U.S. fighters from strictly defensive bomber escort to offensive action against the German fighter units marked the decisive turning point.

Thus despite the output of machines, which mounted from month to month, the fighter defence of the Reich was finally a mere shadow of its former self. By May 24, 1944, its operational strength had actually declined to the following:

	Single-engined Fighters	Twin-engined Fighters
North Germany (1, 2 and 3 Divisions):	174	35
South ,, (7 Division)	72	0
Total	246	35

By this date the Americans, on their side, were in a position to put up 1,000 long-range fighters at one time to roam at will over the whole of the Reich, almost to its eastern frontier. Nothing could underline more clearly the complete air sovereignty that the Allies, after so many fierce battles, had achieved. The above-mentioned study of the wartime defence of Germany makes three points in summary of the outcome:

1. The increasing strength of the enemy was not matched by any increase in defensive operations.

2. The percentage loss to the enemy became so minimal that the defence ceased to have any deterrent effect.

3. Losses suffered by the defence in the long run passed the limit of endurance.

The fact remains that the final result was attained, not by the annihilation of the German aviation industry, but by the impact of fighter on fighter in the sky. It was only because the German fighters rose to combat the attack on the factories that the bombing achieved, albeit somewhat indirectly, its purpose of knocking out the German fighter arm.

With the German skies swept virtually clear of opposition, the Bombardment Groups of the Eighth and Fifteenth Army Air Forces could pick their targets at will—or rather, in accordance with the priorities decreed by the planners of the strategic air offensive. In April 1944 the main priority was still the aviation industry, plus airfields and communications networks. But in May there began the main assault on the ultimate sources of German war potential: oil, hydrogen and synthetic fuel. This would represent the final death-blow.

On May 12th, 935 heavy bombers, escorted by over 1,000 fighters, appeared again over Germany. At Frankfurt-am-Main they met a ruthless frontal attack by German fighters. Two, then three, American combat wings became split up, and a few bombers were shot down. But the bulk of the bombers veered further east, to hit the synthetic oil plants of Brüx, Böhlen, Leuna, Lützendorf and Zwickau. There were still 800 of them, and they hit their targets fair and square. Brüx ceased to produce entirely. At Leuna up to sixty per cent of the output was affected.

Meanwhile, since mid-April the Fifteenth A.A.F. had been launching hundreds of bombers from the south against the Rumanian oil fields and refineries of Ploesti. Within six weeks these were raided heavily no less than twenty times.

On May 28th and 29th, it was again the turn of the Eighth A.A.F. Ruhland, Magdeburg, Zeitz, and (once again) Leuna were all severely damaged. 224 Liberators hit Pölitz so hard that synthetic oil production there entirely ceased for two whole months. With a former monthly output of 47,000 tons, this represented the greatest single loss of aviation fuel. In May the total production of this sank by 60,000 to only 120,000 tons—30,000 tons less than the Luftwaffe's minimum monthly requirements. That during the summer months, at the time of the invasion, the Luftwaffe still continued to receive ample supplies, was thanks entirely to the strategic reserve amassed by the Armed Forces High Command.

By September, however, the whole supply system had broken down, and the Luftwaffe's allocation was a mere 30,000 tons—one fifth of its minimum requirements. What use was it now for the aviation industry, saved by superhuman efforts from ruin, to go on turning out thousands of aircraft each month? Factory-fresh as they were, they just became so much scrap. The Luftwaffe lacked both the fuel and pilots necessary to fly them against the enemy.

Looking back, it would now appear that if the Allies had launched their strategic offensive against oil targets earlier, they would have obtained the results they did so much the sooner, and thereby appreciably shortened the war. In this connection the statement of Albert Speer, former *Reichsminister* of Armaments and War Production, in the course of his interrogation on July 18, 1945, holds special interest. He said, *inter alia*:

"The Allied air attacks remained without decisive success until early 1944.

This failure, which is reflected in the armaments output figures for 1943 and 1944, is to be attributed principally to the tenacious efforts of the German workers and factory managers and also to the haphazard and too scattered form of attacks of the enemy who, until the attacks on the synthetic oil plants, based his raids on no clearly recognisable economic planning . . . The Americans' attacks, which followed a definite system of assault on industrial targets, were by far the most dangerous. It was in fact these attacks which caused the breakdown of the German armaments industry. The attacks on the chemical industry would have sufficed, without the impact of purely military events, to render Germany defenceless. . . ."[1]

Meanwhile the bulk of the Allied air forces were engaged in preparing the way for the invasion on June 6, 1944, and afterwards in support of the Allied armies in France. Against the overwhelming strength that these air forces could now bring to bear the Luftwaffe could do virtually nothing. What could tactics, planning, experience, courage or even self-sacrifice achieve when the total force Field-Marshal Sperrle and his *Luftflotte* 3 could put into the air was 198 bombers and 125 fighters, against an Allied force of 3,467 bombers and 5,409 fighters?

German propaganda fostered belief in a miraculous weapon that would still turn the tables. In its absence the Luftwaffe strove in vain against odds of twenty to one.

In the south the losing campaigns in Tunisia and Sicily had cost it whole *Geschwader* numbering hundreds of aircraft. In the three battles of Cassino its paratroops, now operating purely as ground troops, held out even after first the monastery, and then the town, had been reduced by American carpet-bombing to rubble. "I doubt," the Allied C.-in-C., General Alexander, telegraphed to Winston Churchill, "if there are any other troops in the world who could have stood up to it, and then gone on fighting with the ferocity they have."[2]

In the north a small Luftwaffe force—two *Gruppen* of KG 26 with torpedo-planes—still tried to combat the Arctic convoys on their way to Russia. All it achieved, thanks to the powerful defence, was the sinking of a single ship—the 7,177-ton *Henry Bacon* on February 23, 1945.

In the east the Luftwaffe managed to deliver a final surprise blow. Long-range bombers of Air General Rudolf Meister's IV Air Corps on the night of June 21/22, 1944, attacked the airfield of Poltava in the Ukraine, on which 114 Flying Fortresses had landed a few hours earlier in the first "pendulum" operation to the east of the Eighth Air Force. After marker aircraft of KG 4 had illuminated the airfield with their flares, KGs 27, 53 and 55 succeeded in destroying forty-three of the bombers, plus fifteen Mustang fighters, and damaging another twenty-six. In the words of the American work, *The Army Air Forces in World War II*, "The enemy's blow was brilliantly successful". But the formation of such a long-range bomber force came years too late, and soon, owing to the constant withdrawal of the front, the main strategic targets in Russia were out of range—quite apart from the wear and tear entailed by the increasing role of bringing relief to the hard-pressed Army.

[1] Webster/Frankland: *The Strategic Air Offensive Against Germany 1939–45*, Vol. IV, pp. 380, 383, 384.
[2] W. S. Churchill, *The Second World War*, Vol. V, p. 395.

Over Germany itself the Allies finally resumed their day and night bombardment, and in the end won full control of the air; by day thanks to hundreds of escorting long-range fighters; by night thanks to new tactics and new jamming devices which in the autumn of 1944 finally put even the night-fighters' "*Lichtenstein*" SN 2 radar sets out of action.

With the last ditch reached, an attempt was finally made to defend the Reich with the world's first jet fighter, the Me 262—despite Hitler's interdiction even to speak of it as a "fighter". An experimental unit was formed at Lechfeld, near Augsburg, under Captain Thierfelder—who crashed in flames on one of the first trial operational sorties. He was succeeded by Major Walter Nowotny, previously a distinguished fighter pilot on the eastern front. Nowotny soon recognised that much training would be necessary before he could expect to lead his team with any prospect of success. Luftwaffe Command did not listen: it demanded operations forthwith.

At the beginning of October 1944 Nowotny and his unit—now a *Gruppe*—were posted to the airfields of Achmer and Hesepe, near Osnabrück, athwart the main American bomber approach route. The daily sorties they could put up against the enemy formations and their powerful fighter escort numbered a mere three or four. Yet, in the course of a month, these few jet fighters knocked out twenty-two aircraft. But by the end of the month they themselves had been reduced from thirty to three serviceable planes—few as a result of enemy action, nearly all owing to technical ineptitude. For many pilots the only previous experience of flying such a revolutionary aircraft had consisted of a few circuits of the airfield.

After Nowotny, like his predecessor, had died in action, a new fighter *Geschwader*, JG 7 ("Hindenburg") was formed under the command of Colonel Johannes Steinhoff, with one of its *Gruppen* (No. III) inherited from Nowotny. Under the command successively of Majors Hohagen and Sinner, this was the only one which, operating under the most difficult conditions from Brandenburg-Briest, Oranienburg and Parchim, continued to make real contact with the enemy.

The main operational difficulty was the fact that, whereas the Fortresses opened their defensive fire at 800 yards, the fire of the fighters' 30-mm cannon only became effective inside a range of 250 yards. Now once more—though again too late—a new weapon became available to overcome the difficulty. This was the so-called "R 4 M" 5-cm rocket, whose trials had been conducted by "Test Commando 25" under Major Christl. With twenty-four of these all fired at once from simple wooden rails beneath the wings, the cone of fire was not unlike that of a shotgun. Moreover, they could be launched from out of range of the enemy's guns. Usually at least one rocket "connected", and that invariably spelt the destruction of the bomber.

So equipped, III/JG 7 in the last week of February 1945 alone destroyed forty-five four-engined bombers and fifteen long-range fighters, with minimum loss to themselves. But at this stage of the war the high rate of success of some forty jet fighters was but a pin-prick. The bomber streams over Germany now often numbered over 2,000 aircraft at a time. Of a total of 1,294 Me 262s built, perhaps only a quarter ever became engaged with the enemy. Many failed to survive their trials at the hands of the numerous test

116. The writing in the sky. A flight of Me 110s of II/ZG 26 about to attack a formation of invading daylight bombers, which are turning away. (The photograph was taken from the fourth German fighter.)

117. The Me 262, the world's first jet fighter was vastly superior in performance to any of its opponents. Thrown into the struggle at the eleventh hour, it was just too late to have any effect on the outcome of the war. This is one of the few genuine photographs ever taken of the Me 262 in flight.

118. An Me 262A-1 surrendered to the Americans by its pilot at the Rhein-Main airport near Frankfurt. *(Official U.S. Air Force photo)*

119. Me 262s damaged by U.S. 15th Air Force bombers at the jet assembly plant near Obertraubling aerodrome. *(Official U.S. Air Force photo)*

commandos, but most never got off the ground—even though fuel for jets was one item Germany was never short of.

Yet in the final weeks of the war one other Me 262 unit was formed. This was called the so-called *Jagdverband* (JV) 44. Though its strength in machines was no greater than a single squadron, it was led in person by no less a figure than Adolf Galland himself. So it was that Galland, who had started the war in 1939 as a squadron commander, with the rank of First-Lieutenant, ended it as a squadron commander again, though with the rank of Lieutenant-General. For on January 20, 1945, as *General der Jagdflieger*, he had fallen into disgrace.

His "squadron" comprised some of the surviving cream of the old fighter aces. All of them in the past had themselves commanded units of up to *Geschwader* strength, and most of them were highly decorated. They included Colonel Johannes Steinhoff (as second in command), Colonel Lützow, plus lieutenant-colonels, majors and captains. The existence of JV 44 represents the final chapter in the tragic decline of that once proud and titanic combat force, Luftwaffe Fighter Command.

Ever since the failure of the Battle of Britain, Goering had never ceased to vent his spleen on the German fighters. That air superiority over England had been impossible to achieve with the forces available; that in the Mediterranean theatre Luftwaffe losses had escalated from year to year against Allied air forces of ever growing strength; that finally the always inadequate resources allocated for the task had failed to protect the homeland against the strategic bomber offensive—the blame for all of these was laid by the Luftwaffe's supreme commander at the door of his fighters, whom he accused of lack of aggressiveness, and even cowardice. That the explanation might be found in the mistaken strategy and armaments policy of the high command itself did not, apparently, occur to him. In the last years of the war the paradoxical situation actually obtained, where the utterances of the chiefs of the Allied air forces betrayed more respect for the courage and fighting ability of the German fighter arm than did anything said by its own commander-in-chief.

As we have seen, defence—in Hitler's eyes—was always a matter of low priority. If Speer and Saur, in 1944, raised fighter production to an all-time high, this took place against the express intent and wish of the Führer. As disaster followed disaster on every front, so did the choleric wrath of the German dictator increasingly descend on anyone who dared gainsay him. Where the Luftwaffe was concerned, he listened only to talk of offensive action; to the need for air defence he was deaf. When, as late as August 1944, Speer and Galland personally expressed to him the crying need for German fighter strength to be concentrated in the defence of the Reich, Hitler merely threw them out, shouting that they should obey his orders. Next day he proclaimed that the whole fighter arm was disbanded, and instructed Speer to switch from fighter production to flak guns. As a practical proposition it of course made nonsense, and Speer was obliged to assemble figures and tables to prove it.

Hitler's attitude coloured that of Goering, who never rose to the defence of his Luftwaffe, but simply passed downwards the ruinous orders from above. Once in autumn, 1943, when the defence against an Allied raid had miscarried, he summoned his fighter commanders to Schleissheim near

Munich, and heaped them with reproaches. Ever since the Battle of Britain, the *Reichsmarschall* declared, far too many fighter pilots had won decorations they did not deserve.

At that General Galland wrenched his own Knight's Cross from his neck, and flung it down resoundingly on Goering's table. An icy silence ensued, but Goering took no action. He merely resumed the discussion, but with much greater sobriety and logic.

Again and again Galland sought to ward off the annihilation of his weapon by building up a strategic fighter reserve. In the face of continuous enemy raids, he strove to hold back part of the output of fighter planes for the training of new pilots. The sudden appearance of a concentrated force, 1,000 or 2,000 strong, could still, after all, result in a resounding blow being struck against the Allies.

Yet time and again Galland found himself robbed of his carefully fostered nucleus, and saw it thrown prematurely into battle. It happened, on Hitler's orders, at the end of July 1944, when a reserve of over 800 machines was squandered on the invasion front. Caught up in the turmoil of retreat, it was virtually wiped out. It happened again, though on a far greater scale, during the Ardennes offensive, after a new reserve of over 3,000 had been built up. Though its pilots had never been trained in ground attack, it was sacrificed in a brief and futile attempt to support the Army.

"At this moment," Galland confesses, "I lost all spirit for the further conduct of hostilities." Just as his fighter arm had again acquired astonishing strength, to the point when it could once more challenge Allied air control over Germany, it was given its final death-blow by the crazy orders of its own high command.

By this time Galland had already been suspended from any active role in his position as *General der Jagdflieger*, even if his official replacement by Colonel Gordon Gollob, likewise a highly-decorated officer, did not occur until January 1945. By this time, too, the situation had come to such a pass that the pilots of Luftwaffe bomber command—whose own operations, owing to the shortage of aviation fuel, had come to an end—were undergoing conversion courses on fighters. After all, as Goering stated publicly, they were bold and aggressive fellows, compared with their fighter colleagues.

The fighter arm had had enough. Just after New Year, 1945, a deputation of former *Geschwader* commanders, led by Colonel Günther Lützow, holder of the "Oak Leaves", penetrated the portals of the high command to protest against the continued defamation of their service. Hitler refused to receive them, but thanks to the good offices of Field-Marshal Ritter von Greim and the chief of air staff, General Koller, they were granted an audience with Goering.

Lützow had got ready a memorandum of demands, which he began to read. Firstly, the existing authority exercised by bomber command over fighter command must come to an end. Secondly, the Me 262 aircraft should be allocated, not to the bombers, but to the fighters. Thirdly, the commander-in-chief was asked to desist from his imputations of lack of fighting spirit, and his insults, to fighter personnel.

Goering broke in. "It is mutiny!" he cried out imperiously. "I will have you shot!"

In the end Lützow was banished to Italy, and forbidden to set foot on

German soil. Goering then went on to open proceedings against Galland, whom he believed, mistakenly, to be the wire-puller behind the scenes. As *General der Jagdflieger*, Galland had not been allowed personally to fly. But now, when Hitler heard about the row, he cut it short by yielding to the veteran pilot's wish to take the air again at the head of a combat unit of Me 262s.

Goering could not do otherwise than agree, but fired a parting shot by ordering Galland to take all the "mutineers" with him. The dismissed general was only too willing to oblige. Fighting once more side by side with such a distinguished team, he would at last be able to show what the Me 262, as a fighter, could do. And that was how *Jagdverband 44* was born.

On February 10th 1945, IV/JG 54 at Brandenburg-Briest handed over its fourth squadron to be reformed by Galland in JV 44, and soon the latter received its first jets. Colonel Steinhoff, who had formed the first Me 262 *Geschwader*, JG 7, now passed on its command to Major Weissenberg, and, as another "mutineer", joined JV 44 where he made his comrades familiar with the new machines. Finally the strangest fighter outfit of World War II flew off in close formation to the south German airfield of Lager Lechfeld and to München-Riem, whence through March and April it was engaged in repeated operations against the American fighters and bombers. In these the overriding superiority of the world's first jet fighter was proved to the hilt, as the squadron's victories mounted to dozens.[1] Yet this tiny unit in the south had no greater prospect of seriously affecting the absolute air superiority now enjoyed by the Allies than had JG 7, operating in northern and central Germany.

Attack by jets had for long been anticipated by the American command, and in mid-March 1945 its full impact was encountered. On the 18th 1,250 bombers set course for Berlin to deliver the heaviest attack on the capital of the whole war. Despite difficult weather conditions, German fighter control was successful in bringing thirty-seven Me 262s of I and II/JG 7 against the enemy. Though the bombers were escorted by no less than fourteen fighter groups of the recently so superior P-51 Mustang, the jets pierced their defensive screen without trouble. Outclassed by the easy, elegant flight of the Me 262s, the Mustangs had suddenly become ponderous and outmoded aeroplanes. The jets claimed nineteen certain victories, plus two probables, for the loss of two of their own aircraft. The American figures were twenty-four bombers and five of their fighters lost.

A single squadron (10/NJG 11) was also equipped with jets for night-fighting. During the night of March 30th/31st First-Lieutenant Welter showed the capabilities of the Me 262 in this role by shooting down four Mosquitos.

On April 4th forty-nine Me 262s of JG 7 attacked a formation of 150 bombers over Nordhausen, claiming ten certainly, and probably fifteen, though on this day the Eighth A.A.F.'s attack was in the Hamburg region. Next day Galland's JV 44, taking off with only five Me 262s, accounted without loss for two bombers out of a large, heavily escorted force.

[1] Colonel Steinhoff told me in 1953, when he was helping to found the Luftwaffe of the Federal Republic, that with an average serviceability of six aircraft JV 44 destroyed some forty-five to fifty enemy planes in the short time that it operated. He himself was terribly burned in a crash-landing on almost the last day of the war. Today as Lieutenant-General, he commands the Air Force of the Federal German Republic.—*Translator's Note.*

The terrific advantage enjoyed by jets against piston-engined fighters was probably given its best demonstration on April 7th. That day the Luftwaffe, under the operations code-name "*Wehrwolf*", directed its attack, not as usual against the bombers, but against their fighter escort. Without appreciable loss to itself, JG 7 alone claimed as many as twenty-eight of them. On the other hand 183 Me 109s and Fw 190s were hunted to death by the Mustangs. According to the war diary of I Air Corps the day saw the loss of no less than 133 of them, with seventy-seven pilots killed. Thus on this occasion the claim of the American fighter groups to have shot down over 100 German fighters, though held by their command to be an exaggerated one, was in fact perfectly correct. Unfortunately the American Army Air Forces history, though recording the loss of seven bombers, makes no mention of the Mustang losses incurred in this last great air battle of the war.

Only three days later, however, the German jets paid the penalty. Formations totalling 1,200 bombers entered the Berlin area and devastated their bases at Oranienburg, Burg, Brandenburg-Briest, Parchim and Rechlin-Larz by carpet-bombing. Though the jets knocked down ten of them, they themselves were obliged, with their airfields gone, to withdraw to others as far distant as Prague.

Apart from a few isolated actions, that marked the end of the Me 262 confrontation. No longer were a few stout-hearted German pilots, however superior their planes, in a position to challenge the Allied sovereignty of the air.

Developed already before the war, for years neglected and even banned by Germany's supreme military director, and then thrown into the struggle at the eleventh hour—Germany's jet fighter remains a tribute to German inventiveness even at a time of crisis. Its effect on the outcome of the war was, however, negligible.

By now many famous night-fighter pilots had been lost: Major Prince Sayn-Wittgenstein and Captain Manfred Meurer on January 21, 1944—the former at the hands of a Mosquito just after shooting down five British bombers. Helmut Lent, holder of the "diamonds", perished with his crew after 110 victories when an engine cut out on landing. But Germany's top-scorers of night- and day-fighting both survived: Major Heinz-Wolfgang Schnaufer, *Kommodore* of NJG 4, and Major Erich Hartmann, *Kommodore* of JG 52. The former achieved 121 victories at night; the latter, an Me 109 pilot, a world record of 352 by day.

But the German Luftwaffe was dead, its downfall inseparably linked to the military collapse on every front. Of Germany's total war production of 113,514 aircraft, no less than 40,500 were constructed in 1944—i.e. both during and after the devastating raids on the aircraft industry. During the long struggle some 150,000 Luftwaffe personnel had met their death, over 70,000 of them aircrew, and many in the final months, fighting to the bitter end.

On November 8, 1944, five Messerschmitt 262s of Nowotny's unit took off from their bases bear Osnabrück to give battle to American bombers. Day after day their airfields had been subjected to attack by United States fighter-bombers—so much so that they had only been able to take off and land under the protection of a whole *Gruppe* of Fw 190s and concentrated flak.

On this day Major Nowotny had been forbidden to take off, but when the returning bombers were reported, he ignored the order and led the last of his serviceable Me 262s into action. A few minutes later he reported a victory— his 258th of the war. But his next report on the radio boded ill: "One engine has failed. Will try a landing."

The men at Achmer operations HQ amongst them Colonel-General Keller and the fighter chief, Adolf Galland, rushed into the open. The whine of Nowotny's jet was heard approaching. Then he appeared low over the airfield, but with a whole flock of Mustang fighters on his tail. They were hunting the crippled Me 262 like a pack of hounds. For Nowotny to attempt to land now would be suicide. Instead, with one engine only, he decided to fight it out.

Climbing steeply up, he turned and came down after them just above the ground. But suddenly there was a piercing flash and an explosion. No one knew whether he had been hit or whether the wild chase had brought him into contact with the earth. In any case Walter Nowotny was dead, at the age of twenty-three.

None of the spectators said a word. However long it might still drag on, the war, they knew, was lost.

The Battle of Germany—Summary and Conclusions

1. At the outset of the Russian campaign in 1941 it was expected that the Luftwaffe's operations in the east would be of short duration, and that soon it could again be launched in force against Britain. In the event a process of wear and tear began which mounted with each succeeding year. With only a few Luftwaffe units in the west, the British, and as from 1942 the Americans, were able to prepare for the Battle of Germany without hindrance.

2. The Luftwaffe calculated that even with a small force of fighters it could repel any air attacks on the homeland by day, and that by night the bombers would fail to hit their targets. But the overwhelming strength of the Allies, with new navigational and target-finding methods, led to concentrated bombing even by night.

3. Though the German night-fighter arm achieved mounting success, this failed to keep pace with the increasing strength of the bomber formations. The "Himmelbett" procedure, by which a single night-fighter was put into contact with a bomber by means of close ground-control, functioned satisfactorily so long as the bombers arrived and departed over a broad front and strung out in time. The later tactics of compact bomber streams could only be met by means of independent fighters carrying their own radar.

4. Intruder operations over British bomber bases were only resumed for a short period and with feeble forces. The failure to prosecute this promising type of warfare contributed much to Bomber Command's effective strength.

5. The devastating night raids on Hamburg at the end of July 1943 at last jolted Luftwaffe Command into giving air priority to the home front over all others. Only Hitler still insisted that offence, not defence, was the Luftwaffe's paramount role. That led, above all, to his lamentable decision that the world's first jet fighter, the Messerschmitt 262, must be converted into a high-speed bomber.

6. The daylight attacks on Germany by the American Flying Fortresses involved them in heavy losses so long as their escort fighters could not protect them along the whole of the route. From 1944 onwards the possession of such long-range fighters—of which Germany herself had felt the need over Britain in 1940—enabled the Americans to win air control over Germany by day.

7. British Bomber Command's endeavour to decide the issue of the war by means of carpet-bombing of the German cities was unsuccessful. The morale of the inhabitants stood up to the crucial test, while the timely decentralisation of factories enabled war production to reach its highest-ever output in 1944, at the peak of the bombardment.

8. Victory for the Allies was due, much more, to the overwhelming superiority of their tactical air forces during and after the invasion, and to the strategic bombing of bottle-necks of fuel production and transportation—all of which hastened the collapse of the German armed forces. In other words it was the attacks on military targets, and not those on the civil population, which besides other factors decided the issue. That lesson should never be forgotten.

APPENDICES

APPENDIX 1

Luftwaffe Order of Battle against Poland on September 1, 1939

Under direct command of Goering
HQ Potsdam:
  8 and 10 Recce Squadrons/L 2
  Signals Unit 100
  Kampfgruppe for Special Missions
  7 Air Division (Student)—at
  Hirschberg, Silesia, with nine
  Transport Gruppen.

Luftflotte 1 (East)—Kesselring
HQ Henningsholm/Stettin:
  1 and 3 Recce Squadrons/121

  1 AIR DIVISION (Grauert),
  HQ Crössinsee, Pomerania:
    2 Recce Sqdn/121,
    KG 1, KG 26, KG 27,
    II and III/StG 2,
    IV (St)/LG 1,
    4 (St) Sqdn/186,
    I/LG 2 (fighters),
    I and II/ZG 1,
    Coastal Gruppe 506.

  EAST PRUSSIA COMMAND
  (Wimmer), HQ Königsberg:
    1 Recce Sqdn/120,
    KG 3, I/StG 1,
    I/JG 1, I/JG 21.

  "LEHR"—DIVISION (Foerster),
  HQ Jesau, E. Prussia:
    4 Recce Sqdn/121,
    LG 1, LG 2.

Luftflotte 4 (South-east)—Löhr,
HQ Reichenbach, Silesia:
  3 Recce Sqdn/123

  2 AIR DIVISION (Loerzer),
  HQ Neisse:
    2 Recce Sqdn/122,
    KG 4, KG 76, KG 77, I/ZG 76.

  FLIEGERFUHRER zbV
  (Richthofen), HQ Oppeln:
    1 Recce Sqdn/124,
    StG 77, (St) LG 2,
    II (Schlacht) Gruppe LG 2,
    I/ZG 2.

Total aircraft deployed: 648 bombers, 219 dive-bombers, thirty ground-attack planes ("Schlacht")—i.e. 897 "bomb-carriers"—plus 210 single- and twin-engined fighters, 474 reconnaissance planes, transporters, etc. Figures do not include Army aircraft and home-defence fighters.

APPENDIX 2

Luftwaffe Losses in the Polish Campaign

(Compiled on October 5, 1939 by the Quartermaster-General of Luftwaffe Command for the period September 1 to 28, 1939.)

Aircrew	Killed	189
	Missing	224
	Wounded	126
Ground Personnel	Killed	42
	Wounded	24
Flak units in Artillery role	Killed	48
	Missing	10
	Wounded	71
	Total	734

Aircraft Losses:

Reconnaissance Machines	63
Single-engined Fighters	67
Twin-engined Fighters	12
Bombers	78
Dive-bombers	31
Transports	12
Marine and Miscellaneous	22
	285

N.B. A further 279 aircraft of all types were counted as lost to strength, being over ten per cent damaged.

APPENDIX 3

Strength and Losses of the Polish Air Force in September 1939

(Quoted from figures issued by the Sikorski Institute in London, and from Adam Kurowski's *Lotnictwo Polskie 1939 Roku*, published in Warsaw 1962.)

1. *Strength*	Operational Units	Training Schools and Reserves
Fighters:		
P 11c	129	43
P 7	30	75
Light Bombers:		
P 23	118	85
Bombers:		
P 37	36	30
Reconnaissance:		
R XIII	49	95
RWD 14 "Czapla"	35	20
	397	348

2. *Losses*

Most of the training and reserve aircraft were sent up as replacements in the first few days of the campaign. Aircraft lost on operations numbered 333, including eighty-two by the Polish Bomber Brigade. 116 serviceable planes were flown over the Carpathians, mainly on September 17th, and were interned in Rumania.

APPENDIX 4

Luftwaffe Order of Battle for the Scandinavian Invasion
Bases on April 9, 1940

Bombers:
Kampfgeschwader 4	Fassberg, Lüneberg, Perleberg
Kampfgeschwader 26	Lübeck-Blankensee, Marx (Oldenburg)
Kampfgeschwader 30	Westerland (Sylt)
Kampfgruppe 100	Nordholz

Dive-bombers:
I *Gruppe/Stukageschwader* 1	Kiel-Holtenau

Fighters (twin- and single-engined):
I *Gruppe/Zerstörergeschwader* 1	Barth
I *Gruppe/Zerstörergeschwader* 76	Westerland (Sylt)
II *Gruppe/Jagdgeschwader* 77	Westerland (Sylt)

Reconnaissance:
1 *Staffel/Fernaufklärer* 122 *Gruppe*	Hamburg-Fuhlsbüttel
1 *Staffel/Fernaufklärer* 120 *Gruppe*	Lübeck-Blankensee

Coastal:
Küstenfliegergruppe 506	List (Sylt)

Paratroops:
I *Bataillon/Fallschirmjäger-Regiment* 1

Transports:
I–IV *Gruppen/Kampfgeschwader* zbV 1	Hagenow, Schleswig, Stade, Uetersen
Kampfgruppe zbV 101	Neumünster
„ „ 102	Neumünster
„ „ 103	Schleswig
„ „ 104	Stade
„ „ 105	Holtenau
„ „ 106	Uetersen
„ „ 107	Hamburg-Fuhlsbüttel
I–III *Gruppen/Kampfgeschwader* zbV 108 (seaplanes)	Nordeney

APPENDIX 5

Luftwaffe Order of Battle against Britain on "Adlertag", August 13, 1940

Luftflotte 5 (Stumpff), HQ Kristiansand:

X AIR CORPS (Geisler):
KG 26 (He 111)
KG 30 (Ju 88)
I/ZG 76 (Me 110)

Luftflotte 3 (Sperrle), HQ Paris:

VIII AIR CORPS (von Richthofen):
StG 1 (Ju 87)
StG 2 (Ju 87)
StG 77 (Ju 87)
JG 27 (Me 109)
II/LG 2 (converting to Me 109s in Germany)

V AIR CORPS (von Greim):
KG 51 (Ju 88)
KG 54 (Ju 88)
KG 55 (He 111)

IV AIR CORPS (Pflugbeil):
LG 1 (Ju 88)
KG 27 (He 111)
StG 3 (Ju 87)

Under FIGHTER COMMANDER (Junck):
JG 2 (Me 109)
JG 53 (Me 109)
ZG 2 (Me 110)

Luftflotte 2 (Kesselring), HQ Brussels:

I AIR CORPS (Grauert):
KG 1 (He 111)
KG 76 (Do 17 & Ju 88)
KG 77 (Ju 88—not initially operating)

II AIR CORPS (Loerzer):
KG 2 (Do 17)
KG 3 (Do 17)
KG 53 (He 111)
II/StG 1 (Ju 87)
IV (St)/LG 1 (Ju 87)
Experimental *Gruppe* 210 (Me 109 and Me 110)

9 AIR DIVISION (Coeler):
KG 4 (He 111 & Ju 88)
I/KG 40 (Ju 88 & Fw 200—in course of formation)
Kampfgruppe 100 (He 111—"Pathfinders")

Under FIGHTER COMMANDER 2 (Osterkamp):
JG 3 (Me 109)
JG 26 (Me 109)
JG 51 (Me 109)
JG 52 (Me 109)
JG 54 (Me 109)
ZG 26 (Me 110)
ZG 76 (Me 110)

NIGHT-FIGHTER DIVISION (Kammhuber):
NJG 1 (Me 110)

APPENDIX 6

Operational Orders of I Air Corps for the first attack on London, September 7, 1940

From G.O.C. I Air Corps   Corps HQ 6.9.40
Ia Br.B.Nr. 10285 g.Kdos. N.f.K.

1. In the evening of 7.9. *Luftflotte* 2 will conduct major strike against target Loge.*
   To this end the following units will operate in succession:
   For the Initial Attack: at 18.00 one KG of II Air Corps
   For the Main Attack: at 18.40 II Air Corps
                         at 18.45 I Air Corps, reinforced by KG 30
   *Code-name for London.

2. *Disposition of I Air Corps Units:*
   KG 30 (plus II/KG 76):   on right
   KG 1   :   central
   KG 76 (less II/KG 76) :   on left
   For target see general Appendix.

3. *Fighter Cover*
   (a) Purpose of Initial Attack is to force English fighters into the air so that they will have reached end of endurance at time of Main Attack.
   (b) Fighter escort will be provided by *Jafü* 2 in the proportion of one fighter *Geschwader* for each bomber *Geschwader*.
   (c) ZG 76 (for this operation under I Air Corps command) will as from 18.40 clear the air of enemy fighters over I Air Corps targets, thereby covering attack and retreat of bomber formations.
   (d) *Jafü* 2 guarantees two Fighter *Geschwader* to cover I and II Air Corps.

4. *Execution*
   (a) Rendezvous:
       To be made with Fighter Escort before crossing coast. Bombers will proceed in direct flight.
   (b) Courses:
       KG 30: St. Omer—just south of Cap Gris Nez—railway fork north of "Seveneae"—target.
       KG 1: St. Pol—"mouth of la Slack"—Riverhead—target.
       KH 76: Hedin—north perimeter of Boulogne—Westerham—target.
   (c) Fighter escort:
       JG 26 for KG 30
       JG 54 for KG 1
       JG 27 for KG 76
       In view of the fact that the fighters will be operating at the limit of their endurance, it is essential that direct courses be flown and the attack completed in minimum time.

(d) Flying altitudes after RV with fighters:
   KG 30: 15,000 – 17,000 ft.
   KG 1: 18,000 – 20,000 ft.
   KG 76: 15,000 – 17,000 ft.
   To stagger heights as above will provide maximum concentration of attacking force. On return flight some loss of altitude is permissible, in order to cross English coast at approximately 12,500 ft.

(e) The intention is to complete the operation by a single attack. In the event of units failing to arrive directly over target, other suitable objectives in Loge may be bombed from altitude of approach.

(f) Return flight:
   After releasing bombs formations will turn to starboard. KG 76 will do so with care after first establishing that starboard units have already attacked. Return course will then be Maidstone—Dymchurch —escort fighter bases.

(g) Bomb-loads:
   He 111 and Ju 88: No 100 lb. bombs
   20 per cent incendiaries
   30 per cent delayed-action bombs of 2–4 hours and 10–14 hours (the latter without concussion fuses)
   Do 17: 25 per cent disintegrating containers with BI EL and no SD 50. Load only to be limited by security of aircraft against enemy flak. Fuel sufficient for completion of operation and marginal safety to be carried only.

5. To achieve the necessary maximum effect it is essential that units fly as a highly concentrated force—during approach, attack and especially on return. The main objective of the operation is to prove that the Luftwaffe can achieve this.

6. I Air Corps Operational Order No. 10285/40 is hereby superseded.

By order of the G.O.C.
(signed) Grauert.

APPENDIX 7

Losses of the British Mediterranean Fleet to attack by VIII Air Corps off Crete May 21 to June 1, 1941

Date	Sunk	Severely Damaged	Slightly Damaged
21 May	Destroyer *Juno*		Cruiser *Ajax*
22 ,,	Destroyer *Greyhound*	Cruiser *Naiad*	
	Cruiser *Gloucester*	Battleship *Warspite*	A.A. Cruiser *Carlisle*
	Cruiser *Fiji*		Battleship *Valiant*
23 ,,	Destroyer *Kashmir*		
	Destroyer *Kelly*		
26 ,,			Carrier *Formidable*
			Destroyer *Nubian*
27 ,,			Battleship *Barham*
28 ,,			Cruiser *Ajax*
29 ,,	Destroyer *Imperial*	Cruiser *Orion*	Destroyer *Decoy*
	Destroyer *Hereward*		Cruiser *Dido*
30 ,,		Cruiser *Perth*	Destroyer *Kelvin*
31 ,,			Destroyer *Napier*
1 June	A.A. Cruiser *Calcutta*		

Total sunk: 3 Cruisers
               6 Destroyers

Total Damaged: 3 Battleships
                  1 Carrier
                  7 Cruisers
                  4 Destroyers

APPENDIX 8

Composition and Losses of German Forces in the Airborne Invasion of Crete, May 20 to June 2, 1941

Deployed under command of XI Air Corps:
    7 Air Division and Corps H.Q. Units: 13,000 men
    5 Mountain Division: 9,000 men

Total: 22,000 men

Killed, missing or wounded from the above and from transport aircrews:

Officers	Other Ranks	Aircraft Losses (Ju 52)
368	6,085	271

N.B. Losses amongst defending Allied troops were estimated in war diary of XI Air Corps as at least 5,000.

APPENDIX 9

Progressive Composition of the German Night-Fighter Arm

Formations	Date formed	Commanders
Geschwader 1	June 1940	Major Falck
		Lt.-Col. Streib (July 1943)
		Lt.-Col. Jabs (Feb. 1944)
I/NJG 1	June 1940	Capt. Radusch, Capt. Streib
II/NJG 1[1]	July 1940	Capt. Heyse
II/NJG 1[2] (new)	Sept. 1940	Capt. Graf Stillfried, Capt. Ehle
III/NJG 1[3]	July 1940	Capt. von Bothmer
IV/NJG 1[4]	Oct. 1942	Capt. Lent
Geschwader 2	Nov. 1941	Capt. Hülshoff
		Maj. Prince Sayn-Wittgenstein (Jan. 1944)
		Col. Radusch (Feb. 1944)
		Maj. Semrau (Nov. 1944)
		Lt. Col. Thimmig (Feb. 1945)
I/NJG 2[5]	Sept. 1940	Capt. Heyse, Capt. Hülshoff
II/NJG 2	Nov. 1941	First-Lieut. Lent
III/NJG 2[6]	March 1942	Capt. Bönsch
III/NJG 2 (new)	July 1943	Capt. Ney
Geschwader 3	March 1941	Col. Schalk
		Lt.-Col. Lent (Aug. 1943)
		Col. Radusch (Nov. 1944)
I/NJG 3	Oct. 1940	Capt. Radusch, Capt. Knoetzsch
II/NJG 3	Oct. 1941	Maj. Radusch
III/NJG 3	Nov. 1941	Capt. Nacke
IV/NJG 3	Nov. 1942	Capt. Simon
Geschwader 4	April 1941	Col. Stoltenhoff
		Lt.-Col. Thimmig (Oct. 1943)
		Major Schnaufer (Nov. 1944)
I/NJG 4	Oct. 1942	Capt. Herget
II/NJG 4	April 1942	Capt. Rossiwall
III/NJG 4	May 1942	Capt. Holler
IV/NJG 4[7]	Jan. 1943	Capt. Wohlers
Geschwader 5	Sept. 1942	Maj. Schaffer
		Lt.-Col. Radusch (Aug. 1943)

[1] Renamed I/NJG 2 in September 1940.
[2] Formed from previous 1/ZG 76.
[3] Formed from previous single-engined night-fighter *Gruppe*, IV/JG 2.
[4] Up till October 1, 1942, the previous II/NJG 2.
[5] Engaged in Intruder operations over England till the ban on October 11, 1941
[6] Renamed II/NJG 2 in October 1942.
[7] Renamed I/NJG 6 on August 1, 1943.

		Maj. Prince Lippe-Weissenfeld (March 1944)
		Lt.-Col. Borchers (March 1944)
		Maj. Schönert (March 1945)
I/NJG 5	Sept. 1942	Capt. Wandam
II/NJG 5[1]	Dec. 1942	Capt. Schönert
III/NJG 5	April 1943	Capt. Borchers
IV/NJG 5	Sept. 1943	Capt. V. Niebelschütz
V/NJG 5[2]	Aug. 1943	Capt. Peters
Geschwader 6	Sept. 1943	Maj. Schaffer
		Maj. Wohlers (Feb. 1944)
		Maj. von Reeken (Mar. 1944)
		Maj. Griese (April 1944)
		Maj. Lütje (Sept. 1944)
I/NJG 6		Maj. Wohlers
II/NJG 6	Aug. 1943	Maj. Leuchs
III/NJG 6	May 1944	Capt. Fellerer
IV/NJG	June 1943	Capt. Lütje

The above six *Geschwader*, all formed by September 1943, represented the backbone of the German night-fighter defence. Towards the end of the war they were augmented by numerous other units whose constant changes of name, etc., make them difficult to tabulate. Amongst these were the independent *Gruppen* of NJG 100 and 200, which saw service in Russia and were known as the "railway night-fighters" because their ground control operated from trains; also NJG 101 and 102 at Ingolstadt and Kitzingen, originally formed from operational squadrons of the Schleissheim training school, and from September 1944 each comprising three *Gruppen*. In September 1943 were formed the short-lived single-engined *Geschwader*, JG 300, 301 and 302, known as the "*Wilde Sau*." Finally there were NJG 10, an experimental unit for trying out new radar devices, and the two *Gruppen* of NJG 11, formed from experienced "*Wilde Sau*" pilots. Of these one squadron—10/NJG 11 under First-Lieutenant Welter—was the one and only night-fighter unit equipped with the Me 262 jet.

[1] Renamed III/NJG 6 on May 10, 1944.
[2] Renamed II/NJG 5 on May 10, 1944.

APPENDIX 10

Luftwaffe Order of Battle at Outset of Russian Campaign, June 22, 1941

(F = L.R.Recce, zbV = transport, SKG = fighter-bomber, SK = ground-attack, Ob.d.L. = Supreme Commander, Luftwaffe).

Luftflotte 4 (Löhr)
HQ Rzewszow
(with Army Group South—
Rundstedt):
    4 (F)/122 (Ju 88), KGs zbV 50 &
    54 (Ju 52), JG 52 (Me 109F).

V AIR CORPS (Greim):
    KG 51 (Ju 88) KG 54 (Ju 88),
    KG 55 (He 111), JG 3 (Me 109F),
    4 (F)/121 (Ju 88).

IV AIR CORPS (Pflugbeil):
    KG 27 (He 111), JG 77 (Me 109E),
    3 (F)/121 (Ju 88).

II FLAK CORPS (Dessloch)
(with Panzer Group 1—Kleist).

Luftflotte 2 (Kesselring),
HQ Warsaw-Bielany
(with Army Group Centre—Bock):
    Recce Gruppe (F)/122 (Ju 88),
    JG 53 (Me 109F).

II AIR CORPS (Loerzer):
    SKG 210 (Me 110), KG 3 (Ju 88),
    KG 53 (He 111 H2-6), StG 77
    (Ju 87), JG 51 (Me 109F), KG
    zbV 102 (Ju 52).

VIII AIR CORPS (Richthofen):
    KG 2 (Do 17Z), StG 1 (Ju 87),
    StG 2 (Ju 87), ZG 26 (Me 110),
    JG 27 (Me 109E), IV/KG zbV 1
    (Ju 52), 2 (F)/11 (Do 17P).

I FLAK CORPS (Axthelm),
(with *Panzer* Groups 2 and 3—
    Guderian and Hoth)

Luftflotte 1 (Keller),
HQ Norkitten/Insterburg
(with Army Group North—
Leeb):
    2 (F)/Ob.d.L. (Do 215),
    KG zbV 106 (Ju 52).

1 AIR CORPS (Foerster):
    KG 1 (Ju 88), KG 76 (Ju 88),
    KG 77 (Ju 88), JG 54 (Me
    109F), 5 (F)/122 (Ju 88).

FLIEGERFÜHRER BALTIC
    (Wild):
    Coastal Gruppe 806 (Ju 88),
    Recce Gruppe 125 (He 60, He
    114, Ar 95).

Luftflotte 5 (Stumpff),
HQ Oslo:
    KG zbV 108 (Ju 52).

FLIEGERFÜHRER KIRK-
    ENES:
    5/KG 30 (Ju 88), IV (St)/LG 1
    (Ju 87), 13/JG 77 (Me 109),
    1 (F)/120 (Ju 88).

Total Aircraft deployed: 1,945 (= 61 per cent of Luftwaffe strength).
Serviceable Aircraft: 510 bombers, 290 dive-bombers, 440 single-engined fighters, 40 twin-engined fighters, 120 reconnaissance.

APPENDIX 11

Statement Issued on March 17, 1954 by Field-Marshal Kesselring on the Subject of Luftwaffe Policy and the Question of a German Four-engined Bomber[1]

Without denying that valid arguments in favour of a German four-engined bomber existed, I feel bound to refer to the views expressed in many contemporary conversations, particularly with Jeschonnek . . . Unless one is aware of the actual situation obtaining in the nineteen-thirties, false conclusions will be reached. The situation can be summarised as follows:

1. The Luftwaffe had to be created out of nothing, for the previous decade was entirely unproductive.
2. Up till mid-1935 all practical endeavour had to be carried out in secrecy, thus retarding its efficacy.
3. To convert their designs into concrete results, both air-frame and aero-engine manufacturers needed time.
4. Both of them had much to learn by experience before they were in a position to deliver really serviceable products.
5. Development and production were handicapped by the prevailing shortage of raw materials and fuel.
6. Despite all its growing pains the aviation industry was confronted with the need for converting from relatively light to relatively heavy production (i.e. bombers).
7. Such a process was also essential to a programme of general training, especially at a time when blind-flying, bad-weather flying etc., were viewed as "mumbo-jumbo".
8. With aircraft planning (e.g. that of the "Ural bomber") years ahead of the contemporary political situation, the political programme adjusted itself to the available technical wherewithal. This sufficed for a war in Western Europe with its implicit limitations on air strategy.

The following conclusions emerge. Even if the role of the Luftwaffe had been viewed as a strategic one, and a well thought-out production programme devised to cover it, by 1939 there would still have been no strategic Luftwaffe of any real significance. Even the U.S.A., which, untroubled by war, was in a position to conduct large-scale planning, only began to deploy strategic bombers in 1943.

For this reason it was too much to expect Germany to possess a strategic air force as early as 1940 or 1941. Even if suitable aircraft had been available —itself hardly within the bounds of possibility—we should certainly not have had them, or trained crews to fly them, in the numbers necessary for a successful and decisive air operation. It is even questionable, to say the least, whether output could have kept pace with losses.

With the prevailing shortage of raw materials, the production of strategic bombers in any adequate numbers could only have been achieved at the expense of other aircraft types. One of the lessons of the second world war was the number of aircraft and quantity of munitions it takes to dislocate the economy of a nation.

[1] As Luftwaffe chief of general staff in 1936/37, Kesselring forbade further development of a four-engined bomber.

Such an objective—in the first years of the war, without the additional armaments potential of adjacent states—was for Germany unattainable. First an extension of the productive area had to be obtained.

Apart from that, many dispassionate critics were firmly convinced that the rapid successes of German arms were only achieved thanks to the direct and indirect deployment of the whole Luftwaffe in support of the ground troops. Only where the Luftwaffe had prepared the way did the Army advance. For this purpose our main requirement was a close-support force which was not, and could not be, basically under Luftwaffe operational control.

Even if absolute priority had been given to the creation of a strategic air force, with consequent disregard of a close-support force, the following types of aircraft would still have been necessary:

1. The same numbers of short- and long-range reconnaissance planes (twenty-two per cent);
2. Probably even more fighters, particularly of the long-range variety (thirty per cent);
3. Marine aircraft (eight per cent).

That would have left a maximum capacity of forty per cent for the production of long-range bombers—enough for 400–500 of them.

So far as I can assess the position regarding raw materials, fuel and productive potential both of aircraft and trained crews, I can only say that a strategic air force would have been created too late, and the Army would have suffered for want of direct and indirect air support.

How such a strategic Luftwaffe would have affected the course and outcome of the war is impossible to say. The fact remains that Germany's basic error was to open hostilities when she did. Given that, any criticism of the actual role that the Luftwaffe fulfilled can only be theoretical.

APPENDIX 12

Production of Main German Types of Aircraft, 1939–1945

From records of Dept. 6 (Quartermaster General), Luftwaffe Command.

Ar 196	435	(Seaplanes)
Ar 234	214	(Bombers)
BV 138	276	(Seaplanes)
BV 222	4	,,
Do 17	506	(Bombers)
Do 217	1,730	,,
Do 215	101	,,
Do 18	71	(Seaplanes)
Do 24	135	,,
Do 335	11	(Fighters)
Fi 156	2,549	(Communications)
Fw 190	20,001	(Fighters)
Fw 200	263	(L.R. Recce)
Fw 189	846	(Recce)
Go 244	43	(Transport)
He 111	5,656	(Bombers, Transport)
He 115	128	(Seaplanes)
He 177	1,446	(Bombers)
He 219	268	(Night-fighters)
Hs 126	510	(Recce)
Hs 129	841	(Ground-attack)
Ju 52	2,804	(Transport)
Ju 87	4,881	(Dive-bombers)
Ju 88	15,000	(Bombers, Recce, Night-fighters)
Ju 188	1,036	(Bombers)
Ju 290	41	(L.R. Recce)
Ju 352	31	(Transport)
Ju 388	103	(Bombers)
Me 109	30,480	(Fighters)
Me 110	5,762	(T.E. Fighters, Night-fighters)
Me 262	1,294	(Jet-Fighters, Fighter-Bombers)
Me 323	201	(Transport)
Me 410	1,013	(High-speed Bombers)
Ta 154	8	(Fighters)
Ta 152	67	(Fighters)
Total	98,755	

APPENDIX 13

Production According to Year and Purpose

From Sept.	1939	1940	1941	1942	1943	1944	1945	Total
Bombers	737	2,852	3,373	4,337	4,649	2,287	–	18,235
Fighters	605	2,746	3,744	5,515	10,898	25,285	4,935	53,728
Ground-attack	134	603	507	1,249	3,266	5,496	1,104	12,359
Recce	163	971	1,079	1,067	1,117	1,686	216	6,299
Seaplanes	100	269	183	238	259	141	–	1,190
Transport	145	388	502	573	1,028	443	–	3,079
Gliders	–	378	1,461	745	442	111	8	3,145
Communication	46	170	431	607	874	410	11	2,549
Training	588	1,870	1,121	1,078	2,274	3,693	318	10,942
Jet	–	–	–	–	–	1,041	947	1,988
	2,518	10,247	12,401	15,409	24,807	40,593	7,539	

Grand Total 113,514

APPENDIX 14

German Aircraft Losses on the Russian Front, June 22, 1941, to April 8, 1942

(Despite the victorious campaign in the summer and autumn of 1941, the Luftwaffe suffered severe losses in both men and material. The latter amounted to over one third of German production during the whole period.)

Period	Lost	Damaged
June 22, 1941—August 2, 1941	1,023	657
August 3, 1941—September 27, 1941	580	371
September 28, 1941—December 6, 1941	489	333
December 7, 1941—April 8, 1942	859	636
Total	2,951	1,997

APPENDIX 15

The Stalingrad Air-Lift

Extract from the report of Transport Commander 1, Colonel Ernst Kühl, who was responsible only for the He 111 formations. The Ju 52 and other formations were under the command of Transport Commander 2.

1. *Formations Deployed*

Unit	Period	He 111 mark
I/KG 55	29.11.42 – 31. 1.43	H6, H16
II/KG 55	29.11.42 – 30.12.42	H6, H11
III/KG 55	1. 1.43 – 31. 1.43	H6, H11, H 16
Command Sec./KG 55	29.11.42 – 31. 1.43	H6, H16
I/KG 100	29.11.42 – 30. 1.43	H6, H16, H 14
I/KG 27	20.11.42 – 30. 1.43	H6
II/KG 27	29.11.42 – 30. 1.43	H6
III/KG 27	18. 1.43 – 30. 1.43	H16, H6
KG zbV 5	29.11.42 – 3. 2.43	P2, P4, H3, H2, H6
KG zbV 20	3.12.42 – 13. 1.43	D, F, F2, P4, H3
Attached Squadrons 'Gaede', 'Glocke', 'Gratl'		H5, H6

2. *Operating Bases*

MOROSOVSKAYA	29.11.42 – 1. 1.43	
(KGs zbV 5 and 20	29.11.42 – 26.12.42)	
NOVOCHERKASSK		
(KGs zbV 5 and 20	29.12.42 – 13. 1.43)	
STALINO–NORTH		
(KG zbV 5	21. 1.43 – 3. 2.43)	

3. *Effort Achieved* (29.11.42 – 3. 2.43)

   (a) Total Sorties: 2,566

   (b) Effective Sorties 2,260 (or 91%)

   (c) Deliveries   Tons

	Tons
Provisions	1,541.14
Ammunition	767.50
Misc.	99.16
	2,407.80

b/forward 2,407.80 tons

Fuel cu.m.		
B 4	609.07	
'Otto'	459.35	
Diesel	42.60	
	1,111.02	= 887.00 tons

3,294.80 tons

Average load per aircraft during period mainly of landings
(29.11.42 – 16. 1.43):   1.845 tons
Average load per aircraft during period mainly of air drops
(17. 1.43 – 3. 2.43):   0.616 tons

4. *Return Flight Effort*
      Wounded: 9,208 Officers and Other Ranks
      Empty Containers: 2,369
      Sacks of Mail: 533

APPENDIX 16

German Aircrew Losses, 1939–1944

(Figures of Quartermaster-General, Luftwaffe Command)

Period	Killed and Missing		Wounded and Injured		Total
	Operational Units	Training Units	Operational Units	Training Units	
1.9.39 – 22. 6.41 (22 months)	11,584	1,951	3,559	2,439	18,533
22.6.41 – 31.12.43 (30 months)	30,843	4,186	10,827	2,698	48,554
1.1.44 – 31.12.44	17,675	3,384	6,915	1,856	29,830
Grand Totals:	60,102	9,521	21,301	5,993	96,917
Officers:	9,928	1,037	3,490	474	14,929

APPENDIX 17

Specimen Night Combat Report

(From August 18, 1943, over Peenemünde)

(a) *Standard Claim Form*

1. *Time (Date, Hour, Minute) and Location of Crash:* 18.8.43
   02.01 hrs., Peenemünde. *Height:* 6,000 feet.
2. *Names of Crew making Claim:* Lt. Musset, Cpl. Hafner.
3. *Type of Aircraft Destroyed:* 4-engined enemy bomber.
4. *Enemy Nationality:* British.
5. *Nature of Destruction:*
   (a) *Flames and black smoke:* Flames and white smoke.
   (b) *Did E/A shed pieces (name them) or blow up?—*
   (c) *Was it forced to land? (State which side of the front and whether normal or crash landing.)—*
   (d) *If landed beyond the front, was it set on fire on the ground?—*
6. *Nature of Crash (only if this could be observed):*
   (a) *Which side of the front?:—*
   (b) *Was it vertical or did it catch fire?:* Landed nearly flat in cloud of dust.
   (c) *If not observed, why not:* The wreckage was found.
7. *Fate of Enemy Aircrew (killed, baled out, etc.):* Not observed.
8. *Personal Report of Pilot is to be attached.*
9. *Witnesses:* (a) *Air:* Corporal Hafner (radio-operator, 6/NJG 1)
   (b) *Ground:—*
10. *Number of Attacks carried out on E/A:* One.
11. *Direction from which each Attack was carried out:* Left, astern and below.
12. *Range from which effective Fire was directed:* 40–50 yards.
13. *Tactical Position of Attack:* From astern.
14. *Were any Enemy Gunners deprived of Defence Potential?:* Not observed.
15. *Type of Ammunition used:* MG 17 and MG 151/20.
16. *Consumption of Ammunition:* Not ascertainable, because Me 110 crashed.
17. *Type and Number of Guns used in Destruction of E/A:* 4 MG 17, 2 MG 151/20.
18. *Type of own Machine:* Me 110 G4.
19. *Anything else of tactical or technical Interest:* Nil.
20. *Damage to own Machine caused by Enemy Action:* Nil.
21. *Other Units operating (incl. Flak):* "Wilde Sau".

(Signed) *Rupprecht*
Captain and Squadron Commander

(b) *Pilot's Personal Report*

(in respect of 4 victories claimed by Lt. Musset/Cpl. Hafner on 1.8.43 over Peenemünde).

Musset, Lieutenant
5. /NJG 1   *Geschwader* H.Q. 19.9.43

At 23.47 hours on 17.8.43 I took off for Berlin on a "*Wilde Sau*" operation. From the Berlin area I observed enemy activity to the north. I promptly flew in that direction and positioned myself at a height of 14,000 feet over the enemy's target, Peenemünde. Against the glow of the burning target I saw from above numerous enemy aircraft flying over it in close formations of seven or eight.

I went down and placed myself at 11,000 feet behind one enemy formation.

At 01.42 I attacked one of the enemy with two bursts of fire from direct astern, registering good strikes on the port inboard engine, which at once caught fire. E/A tipped over to its left and went down. Enemy counter-fire from rear-gunner was ineffective. Owing to an immediate second engagement I could only follow E/A's descent on fire as far as a layer of mist.

I make four claims, as follows:

1. Attack at 01.45 on a 4-engined E/A at 8,500 feet from astern and range 30–40 yards. E/A at once burned brightly in both wings and fuselage. I observed it till it crashed in flames at 01.47.

2. At 01.50 I was already in position to attack another E/A from slightly above, starboard astern and range 60–70 yards. Strikes were seen in starboard wing, and E/A blew up. I observed burning fragments hit the ground at 01.52.

3. At 01.57 I attacked another 4-engined E/A at 6,000 feet from 100 yards astern. Burning brightly in both wings and fuselage it went into a vertical dive. After its crash I saw the wreckage burning at 01.58. Heavy counter-fire from rear-gunner scored hits in both wings of own aircraft.

4. At 01.59 I was ready to attack again. E/A took strong evasive action by weaving. While it was in a left-hand turn, however, I got in a burst from port astern and range 40–50 yards, which set the port wing on fire. E/A plunged to the ground burning brightly, and I observed the crash at 02.01. Enemy counter-fire from rear-gunner was ineffective.

A few minutes later I attacked another E/A which took violent evasive action by weaving. On the first attack my cannon went out of action owing to burst barrels. I then made three further attacks with MG and observed good strikes on starboard wing, without, however, setting it on fire. Owing to heavy counter-fire from enemy rear-gunner I suffered hits in own port engine. At the same time I came under fire from enemy aircraft on the starboard beam, which wounded my radio-operator in the left shoulder and set my Me 110's port engine on fire. Thereupon I broke off the action, cut my port engine and flew westwards away from target area. No radio contact with the ground could be established, and ES-signals were also unavailing. As I was constantly losing height, at 6,000 feet I gave the order to bale out.

As I did so I struck the tail unit with both legs, thereby breaking my right thigh and left shin-bone. After normal landings by parachute my radio-operator and I were taken to the reserve military hospital at Güstrow.

At 02.50 the Me 110 crashed on the northern perimeter of Güstrow.

(Signed) Musset.

APPENDIX 18

Victories of German Fighter Pilots in World War II[1]

German day and night-fighter pilots were credited with the destruction on all fronts of some 70,000 enemy aircraft, of which some 45,000 were on the eastern front. 103 pilots attained a score of a hundred or more, thirteen of over 200, and two of over 300 victories. It would be wrong, however, to judge any individual's contribution solely by his number of victories, for a high score represented a combination of skill, luck and opportunity. The circumstances varied greatly according to the year, the sector of the front, experience and technical wherewithal. One has only to mention such renowned fighter pilots as Balthasar, Wick and Trautloft, whose contribution bore no relation to their personal scores, to reveal the difficulty of awarding merit.

A. Day-Fighters

1. Holders of the Oak Leaves with Swords and Diamonds, in chronological order of award, with date of death where relevant, and personal scores:

Colonel Werner Mölders, JG 51, *General der Jagdflieger*, 22.11.41; 115 (14 in Spain, 68 in West).
Lieutenant-General Adolf Galland, JG 26, *General der Jagdflieger*, JV 44; 103 in West.
Colonel Gordon Gollob, JGs 3, 7, *General der Jagdflieger*; 150 (144 in East).

Captain Hans-Joachim Marseille, JG 27, 30.9.42; 158 in West.
Colonel Hermann Graf, JGs 52, 50, 11; 211 (202 in East).
Major Walter Nowotny, JG 54, 8.11.44; 258 (255 in East).
Major Erich Hartmann, JG 52; 352 (348 in East).

2. Holders of Oak Leaves with Swords, and Pilots with over 150 victories, in alphabetical order:

Major Horst Ademeit, JG 54, 8.8.44; 166 in East.
Lieutenant-Colonel Heinz Bär, JGs 51, 77, 1, 3, 28.4.57; 220 (124 in West).
Major Gerhard Barkhorn, JGs 52, 6, 44; 301 in East.
Major Wilhelm Batz, JG 52; 237 (232 in East).
First-Lieutenant Hans Beisswenger, JG 54, 6.3.43; 152 in East.
Major Kurt Brändle, JGs 53, 3, 3.11.43; 180 (170 in East).

Captain Joachim Brendel, JG 52; 189 in East.
Lieutenant-Colonel Kurt Bühligen, JG 2; 108 in West.
Lieutenant Peter Düttmann, JG 52; 152 in East.
Major Heinrich Ehrler, JGs 5, 7, 6.4.45; 204 (199 in East).
Major Anton Hackl, JGs 77, 11, 26, 76, 300; 190 (125 in East).
First-Lieutenant Anton Hafner, JG 51, 17.10.44; 204 (184 in East).

[1] Compiled by Hans Ring from original records of German Fighter Pilots' Association.

Colonel Herbert Ihlefeld, JGs 77, 11,1,52; 130 (9 in Spain, 56 in West).

First-Lieutenant Günther Josten, JG 51; 178 in East.

Captain Joachim Kirschner, JGs 3, 27, 17.12.43; 188 (20 in West).

First-Lieutenant Otto Kittel, JG 54, 14.2.45; 267 in East.

Major Walter Krupinski, JGs 52, 11,26,44; 197 (177 in East).

Captain Emil Lang, JGs 54, 26, 3.9.44; 173 (c. 145 in East).

Captain Helmut Lipfert, JGs 52, 53; 203 in East.

Colonel Günther Lützow, JGs 3, 44, 24.4.45; 103 (85 in East).

Lieutenant-Colonel Egon Mayer, JG 2, 2.3.44; 102 in West.

Major Joachim Müncheberg, JGs 26, 51, 77, 23.3.44; 135 (102 in West).

Colonel Walter Oesau, JGs 51, 3, 2, 1, 11.5.44; 125 (8 in Spain, 44 in East).

First-Lieutenant Max-Helmuth Ostermann, JG 54, 9.8.42; 102 (93 in East).

Lieutenant-Colonel Hans Philip, JGs 54, 1, 8.10.43; 206 (28 in West).

Colonel Josef Priller, JGs 51, 26, 20.5.61; 101 in West.

Major Günther Rall, JGs 52, 11, 300; 275 (271 in East).

First-Lieutenant Ernst-Wilhelm Reinert, JGs 77, 27; 174 (103 in East).

Major Erich Rudorffer, JGs 2, 54, 7; 222 (136 in East).

Captain Günther Schack, JGs 51, 3; 174 in East.

Captain Heinz Schmidt, JG 52, 5.9.43; 173 in East.

Major Werner Schroer, JGs 27, 54, 3; 114 (102 in West).

First-Lieutenant Walter Schuck, JGs 5, 7; 206 (198 in East).

Lieutenant Leopold Steinbatz, JG 52, 15.6.42; 99 in East.

Colonel Johannes Steinhoff, JGs 52, 77, 7; 176 (149 in East).

Captain Max Stotz, JG 54, 19.8.43; 189 (173 in East).

Captain Heinrich Sturm, JG 52, 22.12.44; 158 in East.

First-Lieutenant Gerhard Thyben, JGs 3, 54; 157 (152 in East).

Major Theodor Weissenberger, JGs 7, 5, 7, 10.6.50; 208 (175 in East).

Colonel Wolf-Dietrich Wilcke, JGs 53, 3, 1, 23.3.44; 162 (25 in West).

Major Josef Wurmheller, JGs 53, 2, 22.6.44; 102 (93 in West).

B. *Night-Fighters*

1. Holders of Oak Leaves with Swords and Diamonds:

Colonel Helmut Lent, NJGs 1, 2, 3, 7.10.44; 110 (8 by day).

Major Heinz-Wolfgang Schnaufer, NJGs 1, 4, 15.7.50; 121.

2. Holders of Oak Leaves with Swords, and Pilots with over fifty victories, in alphabetical order:

Captain Ludwig Becker, NJGs 2, 1, 26.2.43; 46.

Captain Martin Becker, NJGs 3, 4, 6; 57.

Major Martin Drewes, NJG 1; 52.

First-Lieutenant Gustave Francsi, NJG 100, 6.10.61; 56.

Captain Hans-Dieter Frank, NJG 1, 27.9.43; 55

Lieutenant Rudolf Frank, NJG 3, 26.4.44; 45.

Captain August Geiger, NJG 1, 27.9.43; 53.

First-Lieutenant Paul Gildner, NJG 1, 24.2.43; 44.

Captain Hermann Greiner, NJG 1; 50.

Major Wilhelm Herget, NJGs 4, 3; 71 (14 by day).

Colonel Hajo Herrmann, JGs 300, 30, and O.C. 1 Air Division; 9.

Major Werner Hoffmann, NJGs 3, 5; 52.

Lieutenant-Colonel Hans-Joachim Jabs, NJG 1, 50 (22 by day).

Captain Reinhold Knacke, NJG 1, 3.2.43; 44.

Staff-Sergeant Reinhard Kollak, NJGs 1, 4; 49.

Captain Josef Kraft, NJGs 4, 5, 1, 6; 56.

Major Prince Lippe-Weissenfeld, NJGs 2, 1, 5, 12.3.44; 51.

Lieutenant-Colonel Herbert Lütje, NJGs 1, 6; 53.

Captain Manfred Meurer, NJGs 1, 5, 21.1.44; 65.

Colonel Günther Radusch, NJGs 1, 3, 5, 2; 64.

Captain Gerhard Raht, NJG 2; 58.

Captain Heinz Rökker, NJG 2; 64.

Major Prince Sayn-Wittgenstein, NJGs 3, 2, 21.1.44; 83.

Major Heinz-Woolfgang Schnaufer, NJGs 1, 4, 15.7.50; 121.

Major Rudolf Schönert, NJGs 1, 2, 5, 100; 64.

Colonel Werner Streib, NJG 1; 66.

Captain Heinz Strüning, NJGs 2, 1, 24.12.44; 56.

Flight-Sergeant Heinz Vinke, NJG 1, 26.2.44; 54.

First-Lieutenant Kurt Welter, JG 300, NJG 11; over 50 (fate unknown).

Major Paul Zorner, NJGs 2, 3, 5, 100; 59.

APPENDIX 19

Losses of the German Civil Population
in Air Raids, 1939–1945

The Federal Statistical Office in Wiesbaden has arrived at the following figures of people killed within the boundaries of the German Reich as they existed on December 31, 1937:

Civilian Population	410,000
Non-military Police and	
Civilians attached to Armed Forces	23,000
Foreigners and Prisoners of War	32,000
Displaced Persons	128,000
	593,000

Wounded and Injured: 486,000

For the greater German Reich existing on December 31, 1942 (but excluding Bohemia and Moravia), the number of people killed was 635,000, including 570,000 German civilians and displaced persons.

By comparison Great Britain lost approximately 65,000 civilians.

Losses suffered by the German Armed Forces amounted to 3·8 million killed.

Dwellings destroyed inside present Federal Republic:	2,340,000
,, ,, ,, ,, Soviet Occupation Zone:	430,000
,, ,, ,, Berlin:	600,000
	3,370,000

For detailed information concerning human and material losses in individual German provinces and cities, see Hans Rumpf's *Das war der Bombenkrieg* (Stalling-Verlag, Oldenburg).

BIBLIOGRAPHY

Ansel, Walter, *Hitler confronts England*, Duke University Press, Durham, 1960.

Bartz, Karl, *Als der Himmel brannte*, Sponholtz, Hanover, 1955.

Baumbach, Werner, *Zu spät?*, Pflaum, Munich, 1949.

Bekker, Cajus, *Augen durch Nacht und Nebel, Die Radar-Story*, Stalling, Oldenburg, 1964.

Bishop, Edward, *The Battle of Britain*, Allen & Unwin, London, 1960.

Böhmler, Rudolf, *Fallschirmjäger*, Podzun, Bad Nauheim, 1961.

Braddon, Russell, *Cheshire V.C.*, Evans Brothers, London, 1954.

Brickhill, Paul, *Reach for the Sky*, Collins, London, 1954.

Churchill, Sir Winston, *The Second World War* (6 vols.), Cassell, London, 1948–54.

Collier, Basil, *The Defence of the United Kingdom*, H.M. Stationery Office, London, 1957.

Conradis, Heinz, *Forschen und Fliegen, Weg und Werk von Kurt Tank*, Musterschmidt, Göttingen, 1955.

Craven, W. F. and Cate, J. L., *The Army Air Forces in World War II* (7 vols.), University of Chicago Press, 1949–55.

Duke, Neville, *Test Pilot*, Wingate, London, 1953.

Feuchter, George W., *Geschichte des Luftkriegs*, Athenäum, Bonn, 1954.

Forell, Fritz v., *Mölders und seine Männer*, Steirische Verlagsanstalt, Graz, 1941.

Frankland, Noble (*see* Webster, Charles).

Galland, Adolf, *Die Ersten und die Letzten*, Schneekluth, Darmstadt, 1953.

Gartmann, Heinz, *Traumer, Forscher, Konstrukteure*, Econ, Düsseldorf, 1958.

Girbig, Werner, *1,000 Tage über Deutschland. Die 8 amerikanische Luftflotte im 2. Weltkrieg*, Lehmanns, Munich, 1964.

Görlitz, Walter, *Paulua, Ich stehe hier auf Befehl*, Bernard & Graefe, Frankfurt, 1960.

Green, William, *Floatplanes*, Macdonald, London, 1962.

Green, William, *Famous Fighters of the Second World War* (4 vols.), Macdonald, London, 1962.

Green, William, *Flying Boats*, Macdonald, London, 1962.

Green, William, *Famous Bombers of the Second World War* (2 vols.), Macdonald, London, 1964.

Hahn, Fritz, *Deutsche Geheimwaffen 1939–45*, Hoffmann, Heidenheim, 1963.

Harris, Sir Arthur, *Bomber Offensive*, Collins, London, 1947.

Heiber, Helnut, *Hitler's Lagebesprechungen*, Deutsche Verlagsanstalt, Stuttgart, 1962.

Herhudt v. Rohden, Hans-Detleve, *Die Luftwaffe ringt um Stalingrad*, Limes, Wiesbaden, 1950.

Hubatsch, Walter, "*Weserübung*", *Die deutsche Besetzung von Dänemark und Norwegen 1940*, Musterschmidt, Göttingen, 1960.

Irving, David J., *The Destruction of Dresden*, London, 1963.

Jacobsen, H. A., *1939–1945, Der Zweite Weltkrieg in Chronik und Dokumenten*, Wehr und Wissen, Darmstadt, 1961.

Johnen, Wilhelm, *Duell unter den Sternen*, Barenfeld, Düsselfdorf, 1956.

Keiling, Wolf, *Das Deutsche Heer 1939–1945* (2 vols.), Podzun, Bad Nauheim.

Kens, Karlheinz, *Die Alliierten Luftstreitkräfte*, Moewig, Munich, 1962.

Kesselring, Albert, *Soldat bis zum letzten Tag*, Athenäum, Bonn, 1953.

Knoke, Heinz, *Die grosse Jagd, Bordbuch eines deutschen Jagdfliegers*, Bösendahl, Rinteln, 1952.

Koch, Horst-Adalbert, *Flak, Die Geschichte der deutschen Flakartillerie 1935–1945*, Podzun, Bad Nauheim, 1954.

Loewenstern, E. v., *Luftwaffe über dem Feind*, Limpert, Berlin, 1941.

Lusar, Rudolf, *Die deutschen Waffen und Geheimwaffen des 2. Weltkrieges und ihre Weiterentwicklung*, Lehmanns, Munich, 1959.

McKee, Alexander, *Entscheidung über England*, Bechtle, Munich, 1960.

Melzer, Walther, *Albert-Kanal und Eben-Emael*, Vowinckel, Heidelberg, 1957.

Middleton, Drew, *The Sky Suspended*, Secker & Warburg, London, 1960.

Murawski, Erich, *Der deutsche Wehrmachtbericht 1939–45*, Boldt, Boppard/ Rh., 1962.

Nowarra, H. J. and Kens, K. H., *Die deutschen Flugzeuge 1933–45*, Lehmanns, Munich, 1961.

Nowotny, Rudolf, *Walter Nowotny*, Druffel, Leoni, 1957.

Osterkamp, Theo, *Durch Höhen und Tiefen jagt ein Herz*, Vowinckel, Heidelberg, 1952.

Payne, L. G. S., *Air Dates*, Heinemann, London, 1957.

Pickert, Wolfgang, *Vom Kubanbrückenkopf bis Sewastopol*, Vowinckel, Heidelberg, 1955.

Playfair, I. S. O., *The Mediterranean and Middle East* (4 vols.), H.M. Stationery Office, London, 1960.

Priller, Josef, *Geschichte eines Jagdgeschwaders* (*Das JG 26 1937–45*), Vowinckel, Heidelberg, 1962.

Ramcke, Bernhard, *Vom Schiffsjungen zum Fallschirmjäger-General*, Die Wehrmacht, Berlin, 1943.

Richards, Denis, and Saunders, Hilary St. G., *Royal Air Force 1939–1945* (3 vols.), H.M. Stationery Office, London, 1953–55.

Ries, jr., Karl, *Markierung und Tarnanstriche der Luftwaffe im 2. Weltkrieg*, Hoffmann, Finthen, 1963.

Rohwer, Jürgen and Jacobsen, H. A., *Entscheidungsschlachten des Zweiten Weltkrieges*, Berhard und Graefe, Frankfurt, 1960.

Rudel, Hans-Ulrich, *Trotzdem*, Dürer, Buenos Aires, 1949.

Rumpf, Hans, *Das war der Bombenkrieg*, Stalling, Oldenburg, 1961.

Rumpf, Hans, *Der hochrote Hahn*, Mittler & Sohn, Darmstadt, 1952.

Schellmann, Holm, *Die Luftwaffe und das "Bismarck"-Unternehmen*, Mittler & Sohn, Frankfurt, 1962.

Seemen, Gerhard v., *Die Ritterkreuzträger 1939–1945*, Podzun, Bad Nauheim, 1955.

Seversky, A. P. de, *Entscheidung durch Luftmacht*, Union, Stuttgart, 1951.

Siegler, Fritz Frhr. v., *Die höheren Dientststellen der deutschen Wehrmacht 1933-1945*, Institut für Zeitgeschichte, Munich, 1953.

Sims, Edward, *American Aces of the Second World War*, Macdonald, London, 1958.

Spetzler, Eberhard, *Luftkrieg und Menschlichkeit*, Musterschmidt, Göttingen, 1956.

Spremberg, Paul, *Entwicklungsgeschichte des Straustrahltriebwerkes*, Krauss-kopf-Flugwelt, Mainz, 1963.

Taylor, John W. R., *Best Flying Stories*, Faber & Faber, London, 1961.

Thorwald, Jürgen, *Ernst Heinkel, Stürmisches Leben*, Mundus, Stuttgart, 1955.

Udet, Ernst, *Mein Fliegerleben*, Deutscher Verlag, Berlin, 1935.

Webster, Sir Charles and Frankland, Noble, *The Strategic Air Offensive against Germany 1939-1945* (4 vols.), H.M. Stationery Office, London, 1961.

Wood, Derek and Dempster, Derek, *The Narrow Margin*, Heinemann, London, 1962.

Ziegler, Mano, *Raketenjäger Me 163*, Motor Presse, Stuttgart, 1961.

Zuerl, Walter, *Das sind unsere Flieger*, Pechstein, Munich, 1941.

INDEX